FINANCIAL ACCOUNTING AND CORPORATE REPORTING

A CASEBOOK

FINANCIAL ACCOUNTING AND CORPORATE REPORTING

A CASEBOOK

KENNETH R. FERRIS
Southern Methodist University

1987

BUSINESS PUBLICATIONS, INC.
Plano, Texas   75075

© BUSINESS PUBLICATIONS, INC., 1987

ISBN 0–256–03554–**7**

Library of Congress Catalog Card No. 86–71236

Printed in the United States of America

1 2 3 4 5 6 7 8 9 0 K 4 3 2 1 0 9 8 **7**

*This book is dedicated
to my wife,
Marilyn, and my children,
Matthew Thomas
and Katherine Miller*

List of Contributors

M. Edgar Barrett, *Southern Methodist University*
Thomas Bonoma, *Harvard University*
Thomas G. Evans, *University of South Carolina*
Kenneth R. Ferris, *Southern Methodist University*
Dennis P. Frolin
Oscar Holzmann, *University of Miami*
Michael C. Knapp, *Texas Christian University*
James A. Largay III, *Lehigh University*
James M. McInnes, *Massachusetts Institute of Technology*
Kenneth A. Merchant, *Harvard University*
Joseph G. San Miguel, *Naval Postgraduate School*
Thomas I. Selling, *Dartmouth College*
John K. Shank, *Dartmouth College*
Ray G. Stephens, *Ohio State University*
Clyde P. Stickney, *Dartmouth College*
Martin E. Taylor, *University of South Carolina*
Kirk L. Tennant, *Southern Methodist University*
Michael F. van Breda, *Southern Methodist University*

PREFACE

Tell me, I'll forget;
Show me, I may remember;
Involve me, I'll understand.

An old proverb
(source unknown)

Most accounting academicians, including myself, were educated in the classic classroom style of lecture and problem review. This approach was, and still is, extremely effective given a specific set of academic objectives. Those objectives—the understanding of a preferred or generally accepted set of accounting principles and an understanding of how to apply those principles—seem to be most clearly associated with undergraduate accounting education. It is only at the advanced undergraduate level, and most obviously at the graduate level, that the focus of the educational process in accounting moves from one of conceptualization and preparation to one of analysis and utilization. When the focus of learning shifts in this way, it is no longer clear that the classic lecture/problem-solving approach is pedagogically superior.

Having taught accounting to both graduate and undergraduate students, using both the traditional and the case method, it has been my experience that the effectiveness of the pedagogical style is indeed a function of the educational objectives. I have found the lecture approach to be extremely successful with undergraduate students, particularly because of their need to avoid as much uncertainty as possible. At the advanced undergraduate level, for selected courses, and at the graduate level, in general, I have found the case method to be a superior approach. Thus, this book of cases was prepared with that particular set of students in mind.

The book contains over 50 cases written by instructors who teach, or who have taught, predominantly at the graduate level. The content covers a full array of financial accounting and corporate reporting topics, and hence, given the large number of cases and the wide topical coverage, the book may be effectively used either in a one- or two-semester (or quarter) course sequence. The case materials have been organized in a structure that parallels that of most accounting textbooks; thus, the casebook may be conveniently used in conjunction with one or more conventional financial accounting textbooks as the primary text, or together with selected readings in a contemporary topics course.

The cases included in this book have been used in classrooms at Dartmouth College, Harvard University, Lehigh University, The University of Miami, The Naval Postgraduate School, The Ohio State University, Southern Methodist University, Texas Christian University, and The University of South Carolina. The cases include current case settings, such as the 1982 bankruptcy of Penn Square Bank or the 1984 near-bankruptcy of Middle South Utilities, as well as a number of popular older cases that are still widely used—for example, the Chrysler Corporation case and the Stirling Homex Corporation case.

The case settings are for the most part real, although to achieve certain educational goals it has been necessary to construct a number of artificial case settings as well. Most of the "live" case settings have remained undisguised; however, in several instances, where confidential data was made available, company names, dates, and places have been altered. Finally, given that considerable diversity exists between instructors about the actual implementation of the case method, an attempt was made to provide flexibility in the use of the case materials. Cases were selected that varied in length, as well as in the level of analytical rigor demanded from the student. Where possible, an attempt also was made to provide two or more case studies for each individual topic. Hopefully, the availability of multiple cases of varying length and rigor will provide the user with greater flexibility in course structure and design.

Because many students will have had little or even no prior experience with the case method, an introductory piece, Questions and Answers about Case Learning, has been included in the Appendix to the book. Instructors may find this a useful departure point, as I do, for their classes.

The contributors to this casebook are, individually, noted academics with significant prior writing experience. Several have widely adopted textbooks or casebooks currently on the market. The identification and location of good case materials is difficult, and thus I am particularly indebted to the contributors to this book, without whom the project would not have been possible.

Kenneth R. Ferris

CONTENTS

PART FOUR   Equity Valuation   179

PART FIVE   Funds Flow and Financial Statement Analysis   297

PART SIX   Issues in Corporate Financial Reporting   327

PART ONE

The Fundamentals of Accounting

The Accounting System and Financial Statement Preparation

CASE 1.1

Solartronics, Inc.*

Solartronics, Inc., a small Texas-based manufacturer and distributor of solar energy panels, was in its first year of operation. The company was conceived and controlled by two retired executives. John Holden, an engineer by profession, developed the basic patent for the solar panels. He lacked adequate resources to finance the venture. Pete Blocker's chosen field of endeavor was real estate. He, too, possessed few liquid assets. However, as the result of earlier investments, he owned a small, unoccupied building that could easily be converted into a plant for the manufacture of solar panels. An independent appraisal valued the lot at $40,000 and the building at $26,000. Sorely missing the challenging life of the executive suite, the two men decided to create Solartronics, Inc., with (no par) stock issued in the amount of $100,000.

Convinced that there existed excellent market opportunities for the solar panels, Holden approached a local bank in order to obtain the necessary capital. The loan officer admitted that Solartronics appeared to be a profitable and timely venture. He claimed, however, that the bank was in no position to commit funds unless certain essential financial statements were submitted. He informed Holden that the bank's policy would require the following information to be presented:

- A statement of financial position (balance sheet) classifying Solartronic's assets and equities as they would appear in the preproduction stage.
- An income statement for the first year of normal operations.
- A projected balance sheet as it would appear at the close of the first operating year.

* This case was prepared by Charles T. Sharpless and M. Edgar Barrett. Copyright © 1977 by M. Edgar Barrett. All rights reserved to the authors.

Finding the banker's demands more than reasonable, the two executives acquiesced. Aided by some additional guidelines set forth by the bank, they identified the following categories of financial data related to transactions occurring during Solartronics' organizational stage:

1. Holden would receive 34,000 shares of common stock in exchange for rights to the patent. Blocker, on the other hand, would receive the 66,000 shares of common stock in exchange for the lot and building.
2. Incorporation fees, attorney's fees, and officers' salaries during the organizational stage would amount to $11,500.
3. Costs of purchasing specially tooled machinery, including consulting fees and overhead, were estimated at $25,000. Raw material purchases during that stage were estimated at $3,000.
4. Solartronics would borrow $50,000 from the bank. Interest, at the rate of 5 percent, would be payable annually, with the principal to be repaid in five annual installments.

Using the preceding information, Holden and Blocker derived a projected balance sheet (see Exhibit 1).

In order to comply with the remaining requirements, the executives estimated that the following transactions would occur during the first year of operations:

1. Revenue derived from the sales of finished goods during the first calendar year, $160,000. All sales during this first year of operations would be on a cash basis.
2. Supplemental purchases of supplies and raw materials estimated for that year, paid for by the close of the year, would amount to $50,000.
3. Payment of accrued interest on bank loan, $2,500. Repayment of principal on bank loan, $10,000.
4. Payroll expenses for direct labor involved in production would amount to $45,000. Selling and administrative expenses incurred during said year would amount to $10,000.
5. Projected cash outlays for the purchase of new equipment and machinery, $5,000.
6. Closing inventory of raw materials expected to amount to $10,000.
7. Accumulated depreciation was calculated as follows: machinery, with an estimated useful life of 10 years, $3,000; building, with an estimated useful life of 20 years, $1,300.
8. The following costs incurred during the developmental stage were to be charged against income earned in current year: incorporation fees, attorney's fees, and officers' salaries.
9. Solar panels were to be produced to fill firm orders paid for in cash. All solar panels produced during the operating year were to be purchased by consumers, leaving no closing inventory of finished goods.
10. The cost of the patent would be amortized over its legal life of 17 years.
11. Income taxes would be calculated at $8,340. Solartronics would pay 60 percent of its tax bill by the end of the year.
12. Dividends paid to shareholders would amount to $20,000.

EXHIBIT 1

SOLARTRONICS, INC.
Projected Preproduction Balance Sheet

Assets		Equities	
Cash	$ 10,500	Notes payable	$ 50,000
Raw material inventory. . . .	3,000		
Machinery	25,000		
Building	26,000		
Land	40,000		
Organizational costs	11,500	Common stock	100,000
Patent	34,000	Retained earnings. . . .	–0–
Total assets	$150,000		$150,000

Clearly, the above events would be interrelated and would occur throughout the year. For example, the initial cash balance provided funds for production, and, as the finished goods were sold, the funds received were used to pay for cash expenses and continuing operations.

QUESTIONS

1. Starting with the opening balance sheet shown as Exhibit 1, determine the net effect of *each* of the above summary transactions on that financial statement. For purposes of this question, you should imagine that the firm's *only* financial statement was a balance sheet.

2. Prepare the following financial statements, per the request of the loan officer: an income statement for the first year of operations and a closing balance sheet for that same year.

Smith & Son Printing, Inc.*

At the age of 40, Mr. Smith had worked 25 years for a small general-jobbing printing firm in his home town, a medium-sized community in southern Massachusetts. In 1975, he had been appointed works manager of the company and subsequently acquired considerable experience with the production technology of printing, along with experience in the methods and problems of administering a printing works. Increasingly of late, he had become involved in the marketing and sales aspects of the business, and in the coordination of sales with production. Through this exposure, he had realized that a growing part of the market for print was not being catered to by companies in the local area—namely, the demand for low-quality, low-priced materials for retail promotion, price tickets, and the like. This type of printing called for high-volume production, with relatively little concern for the quality of the actual print or absolute trueness of color. Most of the local printing firms had either developed a particular specialty or else were general jobbing printers, with an emphasis on high-quality bespoke (custom-made) products; these latter firms were not cost-competitive for high-volume, low-quality work, which was in the main placed with printing firms in Boston. However, Mr. Smith believed that a local firm could be more competitive on price in supplying local demand and could give a higher level of service at the same time.

Accordingly, Mr. Smith began to form plans to set up a company to supply the particular market demand he had identified. During 1984, he made initial contact with a number of prospective customers, as a result of which he was considerably encouraged that a satisfactory level of orders would be forthcoming and maintained. He ascertained that a suitable machine, a KORD, could be obtained secondhand in New York, and that he could acquire modest, but adequate premises, with room for subsequent expansion in a new industrial development on the outskirts of town. Finally, he put together his plans and was successful in getting the interest and support of a group of local investors for his proposal.

At the beginning of 1985, Mr. Smith left his employment with his present company to devote his full-time effort to the new venture.

ORGANIZATION AND INITIAL FINANCING OF THE COMPANY

A company was formed under the name of Smith & Son Printing, Inc. Twenty thousand shares of common stock were authorized and issued, and these were purchased

---

* This case was prepared by J. M. McInnes and Michael F. van Breda. Copyright © 1985 by J. M. McInnes and Michael F. van Breda. All rights reserved to the authors.

for $20,000 by Mr. Smith and the group of investors. A bank loan of $20,000 was also arranged with a local bank and drawn down in total. This loan was secured by a lien on the production equipment to be purchased, had a five-year term with equal annual prepayments of $4,000, carried an interest rate of 2 percent above the New York commercial rate, payable quarterly in arrears, and required the deposit by Smith & Son of 10 percent of the outstanding balance of the loan with the bank. In addition, the bank agreed to make available to Smith & Son a line of credit of up to $15,000, a limit which would be reviewed at the end of the first year of operations.

A board of directors, comprising most of the investor group, was formed, and Mr. Smith was appointed president and chief executive of the company. The board authorized Mr. Smith to make an immediate payment to himself of $4,000 from the company's funds in recognition of the work he had already put into the conception of the venture; Mr. Smith used this money to purchase his portion of the company's share capital. A further $1,000 was spent on legal fees and other costs of forming the company.

FIRST YEAR OF OPERATIONS

At the end of the first year of operations, Mr. Smith was naturally anxious to discover how well the firm had done. He collected all of the source documents relating to the company's operations—sales invoices, payroll records, material purchase invoices, and so on—and began the task of preparing the accounts.

During the year, Smith & Son had purchased premises and installed the necessary production and handling machinery, along with fixtures and fittings for a small office. At year-end, $60,000 worth of plant and equipment had been acquired; $50,000 had been paid for and $10,000 still awaited payment. It was estimated by Mr. Smith that Smith & Son would qualify for a total of $4,000 of investment tax credit with respect to the acquisition of these assets.

As the factory was acquired and fitted out for production, insurance contracts were negotiated on the assets, and the company became liable for other payments, such as property tax. During the year, various occupancy costs (insurance, property tax, etc.) in the amount of $4,000 were incurred and paid.

Smith & Son had gained immediate acceptance from a number of customers, and demand quickly exceeded production capacity. While capacity was being built up, Mr. Smith kept prices relatively low to discourage some potential customers from switching their current suppliers, and he also carefully selected customers with reputations for prompt and reliable payment. During the first year, Smith & Son had invoiced sales of $120,000, and at year-end $20,000 was still to be collected from customers. One customer had contracted, and paid in advance, for $4,000 worth of goods; at year-end, half of these goods and services had been supplied and were included in the figure of $120,000, while the other half were still to be delivered.

During the year, Smith & Son had purchased materials with an invoice amount of $60,000. At year-end, $28,000 was still owed to suppliers on these purchases. Manufacturing wages and expenses of $24,000 were incurred during the year; at year-end, $1,000 was still owed to the workers.

Selling and administrative expenses of $20,000 had been incurred, and, at year-end, $2,000 of this remained to be paid. Interest expense of $2,000 had been paid, and a further $500 was due.

Although the line of credit had been used during the year, at year-end Smith &

Son owed no money on this debt. The $4,000 due on the bank loan was scheduled for payment during the first week of January 1986, the week following the year-end cutoff. A call to the bank revealed a year-end cash balance of $8,000.

Mr. Smith now turned to examine the fixed assets to estimate the amount of depreciation expense which should be recognized to reflect the usage of these assets. He required the assistance of several employees to judge the economic, or technical, life of each asset, particularly of the production assets, and any residual value which they might have at the end of their useful lives, in order to arrive at an estimate of the appropriate depreciation expense. Eventually, $4,000 was established as a reasonable and prudent amount.

Mr. Smith then examined prepaid expenses. He determined, for example, that several of the insurance contracts for which premiums had already been paid had expired by year-end. Of the total prepaid expenses, on average three quarters of their service potential had expired.

The next task was to determine the value of the inventory on hand at year-end. Smith & Son had no cost accounting system, and so Mr. Smith had to rely on a process of deduction, which went as follows.

He first decided that depreciation should be considered as part of the value added by production, and that this expense should be charged to work-in-process rather than being charged straight to the income account.

Then he checked the physical quantities of paper, ink, and other supplies in the storeroom and matched these up with purchase invoices to establish a value for purchased materials still on hand and not yet issued into production. He calculated a purchase value of $5,000 for these inventories. Since $60,000 was the amount of total materials purchased during the year, he deduced that $55,000 worth had been issued to production.

He then had to estimate the value of work still in the factory and of jobs awaiting packing and shipping to customers. This was a very rough procedure since Smith & Son had not yet installed a job-cost system. However, rough prior estimates were made of the work and cost required for a job to assist with production scheduling and pricing. The company had about a two-week throughput time on average between initiating a job into production and shipping the completed work to a customer. Mr. Smith, therefore, assumed that factory wages and expenses for two weeks pertained to jobs in process; moreover, he prorated an amount of depreciation to work-in-process. Finally, by the same process as described previously, he valued the material content of work in the factory and in dispatch. His work sheet showed the following:

Materials in work-in-process.	$3,000
Two weeks of factory wages and expenses. . . .	2,000
Depreciation expense prorated to work-in-process	400
Ending work-in-process.	$5,400

The Board's Reaction

When Mr. Smith explained to the board the results of the first year of operations, there was a general reaction of some jubilance. Sufficient cash was available to support a dividend, and it was felt that the profitable operations justified such an action. Thus, a 10 percent dividend was declared and minuted; Mr. Smith left the meeting and made a last entry to the accounts before drawing up the final unaudited statements for the year.

At the board meeting at which the final dividend was approved, Mr. Smith subsequently presented to the directors his thoughts on expansion of the production capacity of the factory. He was of the view that business could easily justify addition of another machine. The directors gave their approval in principle to this, pending receiving and considering a fuller proposal justifying the investment.

QUESTIONS

1. Prepare a balance sheet for Smith & Son Printing, Inc. as of December 31, 1985.

2. Analyze the effect of each event described in the case on the balance sheet of the company, using the fundamental accounting equation.

3. Prepare an income statement for Smith & Son Printing, Inc. for the year ended December 31, 1985.

4. Prepare a cash flow statement for the company. Do you support the idea of a 10 percent dividend based on this information?

Photovoltaics, Inc.*

Photovoltaics, Inc. was a Texas-based manufacturer and distributor of photovoltaic solar energy units. The company was founded in 1979 by Arthur Manelas and Harry Linn. Manelas, formerly a research scientist with NASA, had been operating a small photovoltaic manufacturing company in Massachusetts when Linn, a marketing consultant to industry and himself an owner of a solar energy company in Oregon, proposed the joint venture.

The founders had planned to take advantage of a major shift in consumer attitudes from fossil fuel energy production to cleaner, cheaper energy generation using wind, water, or sun. The joint venture would merge Linn's marketing experience and access to capital with Manelas's prior manufacturing knowledge and government patent on the photovoltaic unit.

The development of photovoltaic technology had begun in 1954 when scientists at the Bell Laboratories found that crystals of silicon could turn sunlight into electricity. The scientists observed that an electric current was produced when photons, or light energy, would strike silicon atoms, thereby causing electrons to be released. The first application of this technology involved the U.S. space program; NASA used photovoltaic solar cells to power the Vanguard I satellite in 1958.

Today, photovoltaic cells are used to power buoys in shipping channels, transmitters on mountain tops, and communication equipment on offshore drilling platforms. In remote locations in Indonesia, Africa, and Australia, where electrical service neither exists nor is cost-justified, photovoltaic arrays are used to generate electricity to power such life-sustaining equipment as water pumps and medical refrigerators storing vaccines.

Compared with power generated from such traditional sources as hydroelectric, coal, or oil-fueled plants, early photovoltaic arrays were prohibitively expensive (e.g., $2,000 per peak watt). Recent technological advances, however, made the cells so efficient and economical (i.e., $1.85 per peak watt) that they were now competitive with existing alternative energy sources. Elmer B. Kaelin, president of the Potomac Edison Company, warned utility executives that the day was quickly approaching when "homeowners will have every incentive to install solar collectors and pull the plug on the electric company."

Convinced that there existed excellent market opportunities for the solar arrays,

---

* This case was prepared by Kenneth R. Ferris. Copyright © 1984 by Kenneth R. Ferris. All rights reserved to the author.

9

Linn began preparing a prospectus that could be used to help raise capital to significantly expand Manelas's current operations. The two founders had located a manufacturing facility in Lowell, Massachusetts, that would cost approximately $8 million to acquire and equip with updated production equipment. Based on his prior experience, Linn knew that prospective investors would expect to see:

- A statement of financial position (balance sheet) classifying the company's assets and equities as they would appear at the preproduction stage.
- A pro forma earnings statement for the first year of operations.
- A pro forma balance sheet as it would appear at the end of the first year of operations.
- A pro forma cash flow statement for the first year of operations.

In anticipation of preparing these reports, Linn collected the following information and arrived at the following projections:

DATA RELATED TO PREPRODUCTION TRANSACTIONS

1. Ten million shares of common stock (par value $1) were authorized for sale by the charter of incorporation. Manelas received 500,000 shares in exchange for rights to the photovoltaic patent, and Linn received an equal number of shares after capitalizing the firm with $500,000 in personal funds.
2. Incorporation and attorney's fees amounted to $27,000.
3. The $8 million purchase price of the manufacturing facility and equipment was to be allocated as follows: building—$4.5 million; land—$750,000; and equipment—$2.75 million. In addition, raw materials and partially completed solar units had been purchased on credit from Manelas's original manufacturing company at a cost of $1.3 million. A note, secured by the inventory itself and accruing interest at a rate of 10 percent per annum on the unpaid balance, was issued to Manelas.

PROJECTED DATA

4. Sales of common stock to independent investors and venture capitalists would total 2.5 million shares. A selling price of $3.25 per share was set and transaction costs of 1.5 percent of the stock proceeds were projected.
5. Revenues from the sale of solar arrays for the first year were projected to be $480,000, with one fifth of this amount estimated to be uncollected by year-end. The company had decided to follow a particularly rigid credit policy until operations were well established; hence, no provision for bad debts would be established as no uncollectible accounts were anticipated.
6. Cash purchases of raw materials were estimated at $70,000; the cost of units sold was projected at $215,000.
7. Insurance on the building, equipment, and inventory was expected to cost $2,700 per year.
8. Labor costs were estimated at $72,000; selling and administrative costs were projected at 2 percent of gross sales.
9. The useful life of the acquired assets were estimated to be:

Building: 20 years
Equipment: 10 years

Linn decided to write the patent off over its legal life of 17 years and the organizational costs (i.e., incorporation and attorney fees) over 5 years.

10. Salaries to Linn and Manelas were set at $20,000 each for the first year.

11. No principal repayments would be made on the 10 percent notes issued to Manelas during the first year of operations.

12. Income taxes would be calculated as follows:

Income Level	Tax Rate
$ 0– 25,000	15%
25,001– 50,000	18
50,001– 75,000	30
75,001–100,000	40
100,001 +	46

The company would be required to pay 80 percent of its taxes by year end.

13. Fifty percent of net income after taxes would be distributed to investors as dividends.

QUESTIONS

1. Consider the informational needs of a developing company. Design an efficient accounting system for Photovoltaics,, Inc. What accounts would be needed?

2. Prepare the four accounting statements needed for the prospectus.

3. As a prospective investor in the company, what factors would you look for in the accounting statements to help you decide whether or not to invest in the venture?

The Role of the Auditor, Professional Ethics, and Corporate Accountability

CASE 1.4

Penn Square Bank*

At 7:05 P.M. on July 5, 1982, a squad of FDIC federal examiners locked the doors of the Penn Square Bank of Oklahoma City, Oklahoma. Thus ended the legacy of a small shopping center bank that grew from total assets of $29 million in 1974, when it was acquired by the flamboyant B. P. "Beep" Jennings, to an asset structure of over $500 million at the time of its closing. The more than $1.5 billion in losses suffered by Penn Square, its affiliated banks, uninsured depositors, and the FDIC insurance fund made this bank failure the most costly in U.S. history. The deluge of lawsuits subsequent to the closing of Penn Square ensnared a wide range of parties, including the former bank's directors and officers, money brokers that funneled huge sums of depositors' funds into the bank, correspondent banks of the failed institution, and the bank's auditing firm—Peat, Marwick, Mitchell & Company.

Peat Marwick became an easy target of critics attempting to assign the burden of responsibility for the bank's collapse. The federal banking agencies, the money brokers, Penn Square's sister banks, and even the U.S. House of Representatives, which investigated the bank's failure, pointed accusatory fingers in the direction of Peat Marwick. Representative Fernand St Germain, chairman of the U.S. House Committee on Banking, Finance and Urban Affairs, was particularly critical of Peat Marwick's role in the Penn Square debacle. At one point in the hearings, a Peat Marwick partner explained that his firm's audit report was intended only for the bank's directors, and not for the general public, implying that external parties had not and should not have relied on Peat Marwick's unqualified opinion issued three

---

* This case was prepared by Michael C. Knapp. Copyright © 1985 by Michael C. Knapp. All rights reserved to the author.

months prior to the bank's demise. The partner's caveat provoked an indignant response from Rep. St Germain:

> You are not aware of the fact that the people at Penn Square dealing with brokers gave your reports . . . to people, credit unions, S&Ls around this nation who put enormous sums of money into this institution based on your audit reports, since that was all that was available. . . . Did it come as a complete and total surprise to you, like the fact that when you get to be 10 years old you find out there is no Santa Claus?[1]

Peat, Marwick, Mitchell & Company endured considerable criticism for its role in the Penn Square saga. Ultimately, this client relationship, which lasted only seven months, may prove to be not only one of the shortest for Peat Marwick but also one of the most costly.

THE HISTORY OF PENN SQUARE

Penn Square Bank was incorporated in 1960 and during its entire 22-year history was located in a small shopping center mall in an upper-middle-class neighborhood of northwest Oklahoma City. For many years, the bank primarily served the banking needs of the small businesses in the mall and residents of the surrounding community. The role of the bank changed rapidly, however, after being acquired by Jennings in 1974. Under the direction of Jennings, the bank became caught up in the oil boom and drilling fervor of the late 1970s and went on a lending spree to oil and gas speculators, a spree that resulted in the bank doubling its total assets every two years from 1976 to 1982. When closed by the FDIC, oil and gas loans accounted for over 80 percent of the bank's assets.

Penn Square's explosive growth was engineered primarily by one individual, William Patterson, who was hired by Jennings in the late 1970s as a favor to a family friend. Patterson, then in his mid-20s, was given a job as a loan officer, even though he had only limited prior lending experience. Within 18 months, the affable Patterson was placed in charge of managing the bank's oil and gas loan portfolio and had become the protégé and most trusted ally of Jennings. Patterson became known for his idiosyncracies, which included wearing a Mickey Mouse hat while doing business with prospective clients, and drinking beer from his cowboy boots at swank Oklahoma City "watering holes."

In order to finance its rapid growth, Penn Square was forced to continually expand its deposit base. The bank attracted a significant amount of deposits in a short period of time by offering interest rate premiums on large "jumbo" CDs that were 25 to 150 basis points above prevailing market rates. Even though the bank did grow at a phenomenal rate, at closing Penn Square was still only a medium-sized bank. In terms of total assets, Penn Square ranks as only the seventh largest bank ever closed by the FDIC. Thus, the Penn Square failure was not noteworthy because of its size, but rather because some of the nation's largest banks had become involved in the speculative oil and gas lending activities of Penn Square's energy division.

In the late 1970s, Patterson became so successful in attracting oil and gas ventures to Penn Square that his bank, because of its limited size, was unable to supply the

---

[1] This and all subsequent quotations are taken from Committee on Banking, Finance and Urban Affairs, House of Representatives, *Penn Square Bank Failure* (Washington D.C.: U.S. Government Printing Office, 1982).

necessary funds to many prospective customers. At that point, Patterson convinced several major metropolitan banks to help finance the largest of these oil and gas ventures. Penn Square would arrange the lending "syndicates" and perform all necessary administrative functions, such as obtaining appraisals and engineering estimates of oil reserves. In some cases, Penn Square served strictly as a middleman in the loans. Rather than assume an equity interest in these "100 percent participations," Penn Square would simply be paid a fee for its efforts by the other banks. Seattle First National Bank, Continental Illinois, and Chase Manhattan were among the metropolitan banks that loaned significant sums of money to oil and gas ventures via Penn Square. Continental Illinois alone provided over $1 billion to Penn Square customers, while Chase Manhattan provided more than $200 million.

As a result of President Carter's energy conservation policies and overproduction by OPEC countries, oil and gas prices began falling in 1980. Many, if not most, of the Penn Square–backed exploration ventures were aimed at recovering oil and gas from the deepest reservoirs, reservoirs that hadn't been tapped before because low prices made it economically infeasible. As the price of crude oil suddenly dropped several dollars per barrel, these ventures quickly became unprofitable.

By early 1980, the Office of the Comptroller of the Currency (OCC) had turned a wary eye in the direction of Penn Square. The large profits, booming loan volume, and unheard of growth rates had caused the OCC to become suspicious. An investigation by OCC federal bank examiners in that year uncovered many violations of banking laws, including insufficient liquidity, inadequate capital, and poor loan documentation. Later that year, the OCC forced the bank's directors to sign an "administrative agreement" promising to undertake remedial measures to correct these problems.

Actions taken by Penn Square in response to the OCC order included the hiring of a new president, Eldon Beller, a banker with strong credentials in the Oklahoma City business community, as well as the hiring of several other key executive officers who had prior banking experience. Additionally, loan review and documentation procedures were tightened and codified and the reserves for loan losses were increased 100 percent over the previous year.

The measures taken by Penn Square resulted in a more positive evaluation of the bank's condition by federal bank examiners in the fall of 1981. However, shortly after the examiners left the bank, the oil glut worsened, forcing increasing numbers of small exploration companies—the backbone of Penn Square's clientele—out of business. Critics allege that Penn Square, faced with the need for steady growth in order to continue attracting large investors and participant banks, returned to its former ways. In the last seven months of its existence, Penn Square loaned over $1 billion to oil and gas speculators, by direct loans or indirectly through participants, eclipsing even its own pre-1980 frantic lending pace.

By the time federal examiners returned to the bank in the spring of 1982, the condition of the bank had deteriorated alarmingly. The bank was in such poor condition that in the last few weeks before its closing the Federal Reserve was forced to extend several million dollars in emergency loans to keep it solvent. Finally, in July of 1982, the OCC concluded that the bank was beyond rescue and ordered the FDIC to take control and serve as the bank's receiver.

DISMISSAL OF ARTHUR YOUNG

The Oklahoma City office of Arthur Young & Company served as Penn Square's independent auditing firm from 1976 through 1980. Beginning with the fiscal year ended December 31, 1979, Penn Square Bank became a subsidiary of the newly formed bank holding company, First Penn Corporation; nevertheless, the de facto audit client remained Penn Square Bank. For the years ended December 31, 1976, through December 31, 1979, the bank received unqualified opinions from Arthur Young. In 1980, however, the Arthur Young auditors issued a qualified opinion, stating that they were unable to satisfy themselves "as to the adequacy of the reserve for possible loan losses" (see Exhibit 1).

During the Congressional hearings in the fall of 1982, Harold Russell, managing partner of the Oklahoma City office of Arthur Young, was asked to define the problems that his firm encountered during the 1980 audit. Russell reported that Penn Square's loan documentation practices had deteriorated between 1979 and 1980. In particular, Arthur Young found that many loans did not have current engineering reports documenting oil reserves, while others had engineering reports that did not include an opinion of the engineer or did not list the assumptions that the engineer had used in estimating the volume of the reserves. When asked if these problems had been discussed with bank management, Russell replied affirmatively and noted that Jennings was "not pleased" with the audit firm's decision to qualify its opinion. Without prior warning, Jennings informed Russell in late November 1981 that the bank had decided to employ, instead, the audit firm of Peat, Marwick, Mitchell & Company. Even though media reports implied that Arthur Young had been dismissed because of the qualified opinion, Penn Square officials repeatedly denied that such was the case.

The Congressional investigative committee was particularly interested in determining why Peat Marwick had been selected as the successor audit firm. Jim Blanton, then managing partner of the Oklahoma City office of Peat Marwick, reported that his firm was acquainted with many of the bank's officers. Under questioning by the committee, Blanton also reported that a number of Peat Marwick's Oklahoma City partners had previously obtained over $2 million in loans and a $1 million line of credit from Penn Square. These loans presented the audit firm with an independence "problem" that had to be resolved before the bank could be accepted as a client. The agreement reached between the two parties was that Penn Square would "fully participate out" the loans and the line of credit to other banks. Even though these participations were intended to be nonrecourse transactions, Blanton reported that on July 1, 1982—just four days prior to the bank's closing—Peat Marwick learned that one of the loans had been repurchased by Penn Square, an action which was "completely contrary to our prior understanding with the bank."

THE 1981 PEAT MARWICK AUDIT

In a typical audit engagement, the planning and internal control procedures are performed prior to the fiscal year-end. In 1981, however, Peat Marwick's audit of Penn Square was constrained since the client was not obtained until late in the fiscal year. Such situations often require the audit firm to make last-minute changes in the work assignments of its staff, to work additional overtime, and to delay the "sign-off" dates of specific engagements. These complications can negatively affect the quality of service provided by audit firms to their clients.

Mr. Blanton submitted to the Congressional investigative committee a detailed memorandum which discussed, among other items, his firm's 1981 audit of Penn Square. Apparently, the focal point of the 1981 audit was the bank's allowance for loan losses. Blanton noted that the allowance for loan losses at December 31, 1981, was more than twice that of December 31, 1980, and that Penn Square had written

EXHIBIT 1
Arthur Young & Company's 1980 Penn Square Audit Opinion

The Board of Directors
First Penn Corporation

We have examined the accompanying balance sheets
(company and consolidated) of First Penn
Corporation at December 31, 1980 and 1979, and the
related statements (company and consolidated) of
income, stockholders' equity, and changes in
financial position for the years then ended.
Except as stated in the following paragraph, our
examinations were made in accordance with
generally accepted auditing standards and,
accordingly, included such tests of the accounting
records and such other auditing procedures as we
considered necessary in the circumstances.

We were unable to satisfy ourselves as to the
adequacy of the reserve for possible loan losses
at December 31, 1980, due to the lack of
supporting documentation of collateral values of
certain loans.

In our opinion, except for the effects of such
adjustments, if any, on the 1980 financial
statements (company and consolidated) as might
have been determined to be necessary had we been
able to satisfy ourselves as to the adequacy of
the reserve for possible loan losses, the
statements mentioned above present fairly the
financial position (company and consolidated) of
First Penn Corporation at December 31, 1980 and
1979, and the results of operations (company and
consolidated) and the changes in financial
position (company and consolidated) for the years
then ended, in conformity with generally accepted
accounting principles applied on a consistent
basis during the period.

Arthur Young & Company
March 13, 1981

off $4.8 million in loans in 1981, compared to just slightly more than $600 thousand
in 1980.

Mr. Blanton also reported that his firm paid particular attention to the $15 million
in problem loans that had resulted in the Arthur Young qualification. By the end
of 1981, a significant portion of those loans had been repaid by the borrowers. For

those loans that were still outstanding as of December 31, 1981, Blanton reported that the documentation problems referred to by Arthur Young had been remedied to a large extent by the establishment of a credit review department and by other remedial measures undertaken by the bank. In support of this contention, Blanton noted the OCC's October 1981 examination, which commended the bank's directors for the improvement in Penn Square's administrative and operating policies.

The results of the Peat Marwick audit apparently left little doubt in the minds of the engagement team that the bank's financial statements were fairly stated. Nevertheless, the Peat, Marwick workpapers contained a lengthy memorandum written by Dean York, partner in charge of the Penn Square engagement, which outlined the sensitive nature of the audit and the reasons leading him to conclude that an unqualified opinion was justified. The structure of that opinion, shown in Exhibit 2, was somewhat unusual and apparently required the approval of several other partners including Blanton.

Even though testimony of the Peat Marwick partners provided support for the firm's acceptance of the adequacy of Penn Square's 1981 allowance for loan losses, Congressional investigators were not convinced that the balance sheet of the bank fairly presented its financial condition. For instance, Congressman Barnard noted that Penn Square had reserved a much smaller percentage of specifically identified problem loans than was normal according to statistics made available by the federal bank agencies. In rebuttal, York stated that loan review "is a highly judgmental area, and there are different rules of thumb used."

In addition to the loan loss reserves, the congressional investigators also reviewed the "management letter" which Peat Marwick provided to the Penn Square directors upon completion of the audit. That letter was critical of several facets of Penn Square's internal accounting controls, and the investigators were confused about why these problems had not been mentioned in the audit report. At one point in the hearings, Congressman Wortley asked Blanton whether the internal controls of the bank were "adequate."

Mr. Blanton: No, sir. We don't believe that they were adequate.

Congressman Wortley: Well, did you criticize them in the public statement?

Mr. Blanton: No, sir.

Congressman Wortley: You only criticized them in the management letter?

Mr. Blanton: That is correct.

Congressman Wortley: Do you think that is fair to the public? And is that a custom of the profession?

Mr. Blanton: I am not sure that I can determine what is fair or unfair to the public. I can say that it is a normal procedure to issue a management letter, and that we do not address in the financial statements or in footnotes all of the problems of a client.

Congressman Wortley: Well, do you not feel that you have a responsibility to someone other than your client, in this case Penn Square? Is the whole purpose of an audit not to make certain that things are verified and the public is adequately informed of it, and shareholders and investors and depositors?

A final facet of the independent audit that the investigative team scrutinized was communications between the Peat Marwick auditors examining Penn Square and auditors from the same firm who examined the financial statements of Chase Manhattan. The congressional committee was concerned that Chase Manhattan, as a result of those communications, had become aware of banking law violations by Penn Square

EXHIBIT 2
Peat Marwick's 1981 Penn Square Audit Opinion

The Board of Directors and Stockholders
First Penn Corporation

We have examined the consolidated and parent-only
financial statements of First Penn Corporation and
subsidiaries and the consolidated balance sheet of
Penn Square Bank, N.A., and subsidiary as listed
in the accompanying index. Our examination was
made in accordance with generally accepted
auditing standards, and accordingly included such
tests of the accounting records and such other
auditing procedures as we considered necessary in
the circumstances. The financial statements for
the year ended December 31, 1980, for First Penn
Corporation as listed in the accompanying index,
which are included for comparative purposes, were
examined by other auditors whose report, dated
March 13, 1981, was qualified because they were
unable to satisfy themselves as to the adequacy of
the allowance for possible loan losses due to the
lack of supporting documentation of collateral
values of certain loans. As described in note 4 to
the accompanying financial statements, the
subsidiary bank, during 1981, formalized its
approach to the evaluation of credit risks within
the loan portfolio and documentation of the loan
files with respect to credit and collateral
information. The consolidated balance sheet for
Penn Square Bank, N.A., and subsidiary as of
December 31, 1980, which is included for
comparative purposes, was included in the
consolidated balance sheet of First Penn
Corporation but was not presented separately and,
therefore, not covered by the aforementioned
auditors' report dated March 13, 1981.

In our opinion, the aforementioned financial
statements present fairly the consolidated and
parent-only financial position of First Penn
Corporation and subsidiaries at December 31, 1981,
the results of their operations and the changes in
their financial position for the year then ended,
and the consolidated financial position of Penn
Square Bank, N.A., and subsidiary at December 31,
1981, in conformity with generally accepted
accounting principles applied on a basis
consistent with that of the preceding year.

Peat, Marwick, Mitchell & Co.
March 19, 1982

as well as the deteriorating financial condition of the bank. Congressman Weber posed the following question: "In other words, by virtue of the fact that Peat Marwick worked as an auditor for both banks, Chase came to have earlier knowledge of this particular bank's situation?" Such knowledge could have been used by Chase to recover funds that it had made available to Penn Square. Subsequent to the hearings, Chase was sued by the FDIC for an alleged improper withdrawal of funds from Penn Square just a short time before the bank's closing.

The Peat Marwick partners denied that the communications between the Oklahoma City and New York City offices of their firm had provided Chase Manhattan with inside information concerning the condition of Penn Square. Congressman Weber pursued this issue by asking Blanton whether independent auditors are required to protect the confidentiality of sensitive information they obtain from clients.

> **Blanton:** That is correct.
>
> **Congressman Weber:** And the thing that clouds the issue here is that we may be dealing in an area of civil fraud or actual illegality, and the question is at that point, do you maintain the confidentiality of those potential violations of law from other people who may be affected by that information, I assume. Is that the way you read that question also, or that problem?
>
> [Pause.]
>
> **Congressman Weber:** Can you answer?
>
> **Blanton:** I am thinking. I really do not know the answer to that question. It obviously has been the subject of much debate among accountants.
>
> **Congressman Weber:** You are in a situation of a conflict of interest. You are representing two clients who have conflicting interests. The interest of one client is to keep the information totally confidential. The interest of the other client, of course, is to be informed.
>
> **Blanton:** I think that I can safely say that it is our firm policy that we do not ever discuss the condition of one client with another client.

PENN SQUARE—AN AUDIT FAILURE?

The evidence introduced into the Congressional testimony that was most damaging to the credibility of the Peat Marwick audit was an OCC report that labeled the firm's 1982 audit "unacceptable." That report, dated March 31, 1982, stated:

> The unqualified opinion [issued by Peat Marwick] was rendered despite the identification of excess collateral exceptions, discovery of incidences where the bank was making payments of principal and interest to the correspondent banks on certain participations without first receiving payment from the borrowers, and acceptance of a reserve for possible loan losses which was deemed inadequate by the examiners during their review of the loan portfolio.

Congressman Weber noted that the results of the spring of 1982 OCC audit— performed almost simultaneously with that of Peat Marwick—uncovered "serious problems." Unfortunately, the Peat Marwick audit team did not have access to the results of the OCC audit, nor did the independent auditors' own examination lead them to conclude that the problems were as severe as later noted in the OCC report. Given the economic constraints on an independent audit firm, Peat Marwick was forced to arrive at a decision on the Penn Square financial statements based on the evidence collected via random test checks. Such economic constraints are normally not present in audits performed by federal bank examiners.

The testimony of the Peat Marwick partners tends to indicate that the audit firm may have overrelied on the controls implemented by the bank as a result of the

1980 OCC order. Making matters worse were the favorable conditions depicted by the OCC examiners who visited the bank in the fall of 1981. In retrospect, it appears that the new controls were only temporarily effective.

At least one definitive conclusion can be drawn from analyzing the autopsy of the Peat Marwick audit: The alleged Penn Square audit failure would not have occurred had oil prices continued their upward surge. As noted by one of the congressional investigators, Penn Square was a "house of cards" built on the assumption of continually escalating oil prices. In the future, audit firms will likely look more warily upon prospective clients whose futures are more dependent on exogenous variables than on the decisions of a prudent, disciplined management team.

QUESTIONS

1. What characteristic of the Penn Square loan portfolio caused the business risk (i.e., risk of business failure) of this bank to be much higher than it would have been otherwise? How does the relative business risk of an audit client affect the degree of audit risk that an audit firm faces?

2. Does the level of professional responsibility increase when one audit firm replaces another (particularly when a qualified opinion has previously been issued)? Why? What measures *should* the auditing profession adopt to minimize "opinion shopping"?

3. Did the Penn Square loans to the Peat Marwick partners present the audit firm with an "apparent" or "de facto" independence problem? Identify the conditions under which it would not have been necessary for the loans to have been sold by Penn Square.

4. Should independent auditors report on the quality or adequacy of a client's internal controls to external report users? What is the purpose of the "management letter"?

5. One of the Peat Marwick partners implied that his firm's audit report was intended only for the benefit of the bank's board of directors. Under common law, were any other parties justified in relying on Peat Marwick's audit report? Penn Square Bank and the holding company of which it was a subsidiary were privately owned. Does this fact change your answer?

6. Would Peat Marwick have violated professional standards if its New York City office had informed Chase Manhattan that Penn Square had violated certain banking laws? What if the New York City office had informed Chase Manhattan that Penn Square was apparently on the verge of bankruptcy?

H. J. Heinz Company*

In April 1979, S. Donald Wiley, senior vice president, secretary, and general counsel for the H. J. Heinz Company, received information alleging that the Heinz U.S.A. Division (HUSA) had transferred income between fiscal years 1974 and 1975.[1] An undisclosed source claimed that HUSA incurred expenses in 1974 for advertising services not rendered and then actually received an advertising service, a cash rebate, an expense reversal, or a vendor credit from the advertising agency in 1975. The advertising agency that had been implicated by these allegations stated that both HUSA and Star-Kist Foods, a subsidiary of Heinz, had solicited such invoices.

Wiley subsequently reported this information to top management at Heinz—R. Burt Gookin, chief executive officer, Anthony J. F. O'Reilly, chief operating officer, and Frank M. Brettholle, chief financial officer. These executives called a special meeting of members of the audit committee who, in turn, hired the New York law firm of Cravath, Swaine, and Moore (Cravath) to investigate the allegations and to prepare a report for the audit committee of the company's board of directors. Cravath subsequently engaged the accounting firm of Arthur Young & Company and retained the law firm of Lowenstein, Sandler, Brochin, Kohl, Fisher & Boylan to assist with their investigation.

SCOPE OF THE INVESTIGATION

To determine the existence of income transferral or other practices violating the established policies of Heinz, the attorneys and accountants conducting the investigation examined the following areas:

1. Transactions or practices which may have significantly affected the accuracy of the accounts of the company or the security of its assets.
2. Transactions or practices which may have violated the code of ethics of the company.
3. Illegal political contributions which may have been made by or on behalf of the company.
4. Payments which may have been illegal, improper, or otherwise questionable.

---

* This case was adapted with permission from a case written by Professor Joseph G. San Miguel and Research Assistant Robert A. Maginn, Jr., Harvard Graduate School of Business, with funding from the Touche Ross Foundation. Copyright © 1982 by Joseph G. San Miguel. All rights reserved to the authors.

[1] The fiscal year of H. J. Heinz Company ends on the Wednesday closest to April 30.

5. Factors which may have contributed to the existence, continuation, or nondisclosure of any of the foregoing transactions.

In delineating the scope of the investigation, the audit committee's report noted that "the areas of advertising, market research, sales promotions, legal and consultants' fees, commissions and brokers' fees, distribution charges, license agreements, purchasing of commodities and packaging materials, inventory valuation, sales and cash" received extensive review.

THE H. J. HEINZ ORGANIZATION STRUCTURE AND PHILOSOPHY

H. J. Heinz operates under a two-tier organizational structure, which includes a world headquarters in Pittsburgh, Pennsylvania, and a group of affiliates spread across the United States and around the world. Heinz uses the term *affiliates* to refer to its divisions and subsidiaries; this appellation is adopted here.

The affiliates operate as autonomous entities manufacturing processed food products, such as ketchup, tuna, canned soup, baby food, cat food, and frozen potato products, and market their products both directly through restaurants, hotels, and grocery accounts, and indirectly through brokers, agents, and food service distributors. They primarily use the "Heinz" trademark, but also use other trademarks, such as "Star-Kist" for tuna, "9-Lives" for cat food, "Ore-Ida" for frozen potato items, and "Weight-Watchers" for weight-control programs. Each affiliate has an independent management, including a chief executive officer with the title of president or managing director. This chief executive officer serves as the only line of communication between the affiliate and world headquarters (see Exhibit 1).

In 1979, Heinz reported sales of $2.47 billion and net income of $110.4 million. The results of operations for 1979 marked the 16th consecutive year in which both the sales and earnings of the corporation had increased.

World headquarters was composed of the corporate officers on the executive committee of the board of directors, the corporate controller and his staff, and the area directors who oversee certain groups of affiliates. Collectively, these individuals function as an administrative center coordinating corporate-wide financial affairs and setting overall performance standards.

Referring to this two-tier structure in its report, the audit committee noted that "it is particularly significant that, for the most part, Affiliate Financial management was divorced from world headquarters . . . [t]he financial and accounting officers of a particular affiliate reported, and were solely responsible, to the chief executive officer of that affiliate." The investigating team claimed that this arrangement created "a communications gap."

> In its simplest form, there seemed to be a tendency to issue an order or set a standard with respect to achieving a financial result without regard to whether complete attainment was possible. The management philosophy of the company seemed to have instilled a feeling that the ones who produced merited rewards. Rather than admit that an order or goal could not be accomplished or seek mitigation, some subordinates apparently sought means, proper or improper, to provide the required result.

THE MANAGEMENT INCENTIVE PLAN

Heinz administers a management incentive program (MIP) for a select group of 225 officers and senior executives from world headquarters and its affiliates. Heinz

EXHIBIT 1
Organization Chart

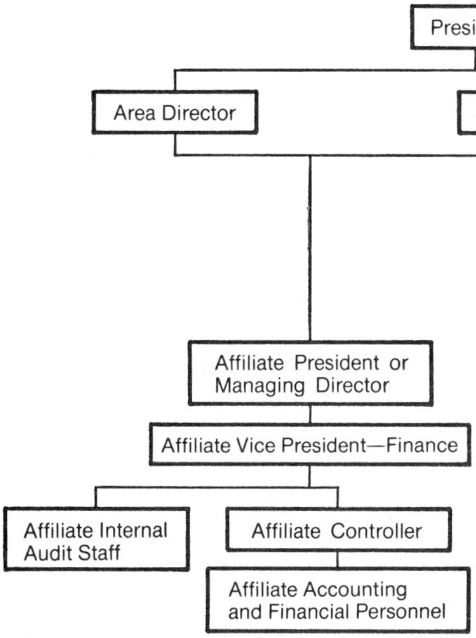

also has a long-term incentive plan based on operating results for a three-year period in which 19 senior executives participate.

The Heinz MIP emphasizes short-term (one-year) operating results and represents a substantial percentage of the participant's annual income, ranging as high as 40 percent. The award of incentive compensation is substantially based on the achievement of certain company and affiliate net profit after-tax (NPAT) goals. Two levels of NPAT goals, a fair goal and an outstanding goal, are set for each affiliate and for the company as a whole. The management development and compensation committee of the board of directors and the chief executive officer determine the NPAT goals for the company at the beginning of the fiscal year. This committee of the board consists entirely of outside directors. After the fair and outstanding NPAT goals have been set for the company, the chief executive officer, chief operating officer, senior vice president–finance, and senior vice president–corporate development establish unilaterally the NPAT goals and any additional goals, such as improved cash flow, for each affiliate. Personal goals for each plan participant are established by the participant and his or her supervisor.

The number of MIP points received by each plan participant determines his or her incentive compensation. Points are awarded to each participant for the individual's achievement of personal goals, for the company's achievement of the fair or outstanding NPAT goal, and, where applicable, for the affiliate's achievement of a fair or outstanding NPAT or other goal.

The audit committee's report noted that the "point grading between fair and outstanding was weighted to provide a greater proportional award to achieving a NPAT at or near the outstanding goal." However, bonus points for NPAT in excess of the outstanding goal, when awarded, were given at the sole discretion of the management development and compensation committee.

FINDINGS OF THE INVESTIGATION

The audit committee's independent investigation revealed that improper accounting and other practices had occurred at Heinz U.S.A., Star-Kist Foods, Ore-Ida Foods, and three undisclosed foreign affiliates. The improper practices and reporting had taken place both within the individual affiliates (the departmental level) and between the affiliate and world headquarters (the affiliate level). The audit committee's report contained the following conclusions:

> During the investigatory period, there was a conscious effort in certain of the affiliates to transfer income from one fiscal year to another for the purposes of providing affiliate managements with a financial "cushion" toward the goal for the succeeding year.
>
> However, the effect of these practices on NPAT for the company was not material in relation to the annual consolidated income statements of the company in the aggregate over the investigatory period. Such practices did, however, have a significant effect on certain quarterly consolidated income statements of the company and on certain balance sheet accounts.

The first significant income transferral practices at HUSA took place in fiscal year 1974. The audit committee's report claims that world headquarters apparently sought to have HUSA reduce its expected 1974 profits because the company was close to exceeding the profit ratio limits set by wage and price controls. (Business firms in the United States were subject to mandatory wage and price controls during the Heinz 1974 fiscal year.) However, no evidence indicated that world headquarters instructed HUSA to use improper accounting or other practices to reduce profits.

In 1974, HUSA had a bean wholesaler obtain a supply of navy beans, which HUSA had previously contracted to purchase at a price substantially below the then prevailing market price. HUSA then acquired and used beans selling at the higher market rate. Six months later, over a three-month period, HUSA received three equal checks from the bean wholesaler representing HUSA's profit from the transaction. As a result of this arrangement, HUSA improperly deferred $1.4 million of fiscal year 1974 income to fiscal year 1975. Also during fiscal year 1974, HUSA solicited and expensed $2 million of invoices for advertising services that were not rendered. An additional $332,360 of improper expenses were recognized by HUSA at the departmental level in fiscal year 1974. The investigating team found that an adjustment of $2 million reversing advertising expenses was made to HUSA's reported earnings when world headquarters calculated MIP points for HUSA in 1974.

From fiscal year 1974 through fiscal year 1979, HUSA continued to record improper invoices in one fiscal year and then recover the expense in subsequent fiscal years through cash rebates, expense reversals, vendor credits, and actual services. Various departments at HUSA separately adopted similar practices by recording some invoices in advance and deferring others. The investigating team obtained documents indicating that HUSA had "intentionally" transferred income of $1.4 million between 1975 and 1976 by writing down its sugar inventory from $0.37 to $0.25 per pound in 1975 (in 1976, the sales price of commodities containing sugar did not decline as some had anticipated). In fiscal years 1975 and 1976, HUSA inflated accruals related to its sales incentive programs and its shipping costs. In fiscal years 1977 and 1978, HUSA employees transferred sales to the subsequent year by postdating shipping documents (e.g., fiscal year 1977 shipments were improperly dated in fiscal year 1978). And in fiscal years 1977 and 1978, HUSA transferred income to the subsequent period by not recording vendor credits on a timely basis.

Ore-Ida Foods, a subsidiary of Heinz and one of the largest frozen food processors in the United States, also participated in the improper accounting practice of soliciting and expensing advertising invoices when an advertising service had not been rendered. Ore-Ida's management believed that world headquarters knew of this practice, which continued at Ore-Ida through fiscal year 1979. When world headquarters allocated MIP points for Ore-Ida in fiscal year 1975, it adjusted the reported earnings by reversing the "prebilled advertising expense" of $1.8 million. The audit committee reported no additional improper accounting or other practices at Ore-Ida.

The investigation revealed that, prior to 1971, Star-Kist Foods began obtaining and expensing advertising invoices before the related services were performed. Star-Kist followed this practice in order to accumulate an "advertising savings account," which effectively served to transfer income to subsequent periods. Star-Kist also transferred sales from one fiscal year to the next by postdating shipping documents.

Finally, the investigating team discovered that three foreign affiliates had also participated in various practices transferring income between fiscal years. Using the same methods as the domestic affiliates, the foreign affiliates delayed or accelerated advertising expenses according to the income needed to meet profit goals. The foreign affiliates also controlled their income by overstating or understating accruals and engaging in questionable treatment of their inventory, pension fund, and prepaid advertising accounts. The investigation also revealed a number of incidents in which payments amounting to $80,000 were made to government employees of a foreign country by the affiliate in that country.

MANAGEMENT AND THE INDEPENDENT AUDITORS: RESPONSIBILITY FOR FINANCIAL REPORTS

According to their view of the accounting practices used to achieve financial objectives, affiliate management often expressed the opinion that any accounting practice was acceptable if the company's independent auditors agreed, or did not object, to the practice. The investigating team found that "[t]here did not seem to be an adequate recognition that the responsibility for the accounting was the company's and not that of the independent accountants . . . [r]ather, in some cases the relationship seemed to be regarded as almost adversarial."

Legally, the board of directors is responsible for the affairs and actions of the corporation. At Heinz and at most other large corporations based in the United States, the board establishes an audit committee to oversee corporate financial reporting and internal financial control. Traditionally, the responsibility for financial statement presentation and information has rested with the company's management. The independent auditors usually ask management to sign a statement, a management representation letter, accepting ultimate responsibility for fair and accurate financial reporting. Peat, Marwick, Mitchell & Company requested such a statement from Heinz (see Exhibit 2). Generally, independent auditors will accept responsibility for financial statement misrepresentation only if they were negligent in applying those tests and procedures dictated by generally accepted auditing standards (GAAS). This position

EXHIBIT 2
H. J. Heinz Company

Responsibility for Financial Statements

The company has prepared the accompanying consolidated financial statements and related information included herein for the years ended May 3, 1978 and April 27, 1977. The opinion of Peat, Marwick, Mitchell & Company, the company's independent certified public accountants, on those financial statements is included. Management has the primary responsibility for the integrity of the financial information included in this annual report and to ascertain that the financial information accurately reflects the financial position of the company and its operating results. Such information was prepared in accordance with generally accepted accounting principles appropriate in the circumstances, based on best estimates and judgments and giving due consideration to materiality.

The internal control system maintained by the company is designed to provide reasonable assurance that assets are safeguarded from loss or unauthorized use and to produce records adequate for preparation of financial information. There are limits inherent in all systems of internal control based on the recognition that the cost of such systems should not exceed the benefits to be derived. The company believes its system provides this appropriate balance.

The internal control system is augmented by a corporate internal audit staff that has direct access to the Audit Committee of the Board of Directors and meets periodically with that committee. The company's Audit Committee is composed entirely of outside directors. The members of the Audit Committee are identified in the listing of Officers and Directors elsewhere in this annual report. The Audit Committee meets periodically with the company's independent public accountants, management, and the internal auditors to review the work of each and to satisfy itself that each is properly discharging its responsibilities. The independent certified public accountants have free access to this committee to discuss the results of their audit work and their opinions on the adequacy of internal financial controls and the quality of financial reporting.

has been criticized by some financial statement users and by certain members of the Securities and Exchange Commission (SEC) who want independent auditors to accept greater responsibility for accurate financial statement information.

Prior to 1976, the internal auditors at Heinz reported to affiliate management. After 1976, Heinz began to centralize its internal auditors into a corporate audit staff under a director of corporate audit. The audit committee's report noted that there were 13 corporate and 11 affiliate internal auditors in 1979. A survey of companies in 1976 indicated the average number of internal auditors employed by a company the size of Heinz was 41. The internal auditors at Heinz perform both financial and operational audits, concentrating almost exclusively on the major domestic affiliates.

The audit committee's report noted that the internal auditors at one affiliate participated in the improper income transferral practices. The committee recommended that all internal auditors at the affiliate level be transferred to the corporate level or at least report to the corporate level. The committee also recommended more extensive internal auditing of compnay affiliates around the world and recommended regional audit managers and an increase in the number of competent personnel necessary to carry out these recommendations.

THE BOARD OF DIRECTORS AND THE AUDIT COMMITTEE

An article appearing in the May–June 1980 edition of the *Harvard Business Review* began with this observation:

> While the responsibilities of corporate directors have significantly increased in the past decade, neither the proper role of the audit committee nor the duties and liabilities of its members have yet been defined by the Securities and Exchange Commission, the New York Stock Exchange, the American Institute of Certified Public Accountants, or the courts.
>
> As a matter of state corporation law, the board is vested with full responsibility for the direction and management of the corporation. In practice, the almost daily reports of corporate wrongdoing suggest that directors may have taken their role as overseers of management's authority too lightly.[2]

In recent years, legislation and various actions taken by segments of the business community have expanded the scope of director responsibility. In 1977, legislation of the Foreign Corrupt Practices Act (FCPA) established stricter internal control and recordkeeping requirements for public companies. Although management is principally responsible for the company's compliance with the FCPA, the American Institute of Certified Public Accountants (AICPA) and the Securities and Exchange Commission have both extended the responsibility for monitoring such compliance to the board of directors, in particular to the audit committee. Also, the listing agreement for the New York Stock Exchange (NYSE) requires domestic companies to maintain an audit committee.

The report of the audit committee at H. J. Heinz recommended that the Heinz audit committee take a more pervasive role in the affairs of the company (see Exhibit 3). The suggested role included recommending the appointment of the independent

---

[2] "The Audit Committee: A Guide for Directors," *Harvard Business Review*, May–June 1980, pp. 174–75.

EXHIBIT 3
H. J. Heinz Company

Description of Audit Committee

Basic Function

To assist the Board of Directors in discharging
its fiduciary responsibilities to the shareholders
and the investment community in the preservation
of the integrity of financial information
published by the Company. To maintain free and
open means of communication between the directors,
the independent accountants, the internal
auditors, and the financial management of the
Company. To ensure the independence of the
independent accountants.

Composition

The Audit Committee shall be appointed by the
Board of Directors and consist of at least three
persons who shall be directors, but not officers
or employees of the Company, and who shall be free
from any relationships that might in the opinion
of the Board of Directors be considered to be a
conflict of interest.

Responsibilities

1. Review the performance of the independent
accountants and the evaluation of such performance
by financial management and the internal auditors
and make recommendations to the Board of Directors
with respect to the appointment, reappointment or
termination of the independent accountants.

2. Review with the independent accountants, the
internal auditors, and financial management the
scope of the proposed audit for the current year,
the audit findings and the financial statements
and the reports of the independent accountants
with respect thereto. Ensure the independence and
objectivity of the independent accountants. Meet
with them alone at their request and periodically.

3. Review the Company's unaudited quarterly
financial statements as well as other documents
required to be filed by the Company with the
Securities and Exchange Commission.

4. Review and evaluate the Company's internal
financial and operational controls and
organization with the independent accountants, the
internal auditors and financial management and
ensure their quality and effectiveness. Ensure the
independence and objectivity of the internal audit

EXHIBIT 3 *(concluded)*

function by reviewing the nature, extent and quality of the internal audit. Meet with the internal auditors alone at their request and periodically.

5. Review the independent accountant's evaluation of the performance of financial management and the internal auditors.

6. Review the activities of the Foreign Corrupt Practices Act Compliance Committee and the development of the programs of such Committee. Review any violations or potential violations of the Foreign Corrupt Practices Act brought to the attention of the Audit Committee.

7. Review administrative budgets, actual results against these budgets, and expense accounts of the Chairman and the Chief Executive Officer.

8. Review the actions taken to ensure compliance with the Company's Code of Conduct and the results of confirmations and violations of such Code. Assist in the review and promulgation of revisions or modifications to the Code of Conduct as may be necessary.

9. Consider such other matters in relation to the financial affairs of the Company and its accounts and in relation to the internal and external audit of the Company as the Audit Committee may, in its discretion, determine to be desirable.

10. Periodically review existing corporate policy with respect to the Audit Committee and recommend any revisions or modifications to such policy as may be necessary to meet current requirements.

Meetings

The Audit Committee shall hold at least four regular meetings per year and such additional meetings as it shall deem desirable. Such meetings shall, at the discretion of the Audit committee, be attended by the independent accountants, the internal auditors, financial management, and such other persons as appropriate. Two of the regular meetings shall consist of a pre-audit meeting and a meeting prior to the issuance of the Company's annual financial Statements.

auditors and ensuring their objectivity; meeting alone with the independent auditors; setting the scope of the audit; reviewing the performance and conclusions of the independent auditors, of the internal auditors, and of the financial management of the company; observing the work of the Foreign Corrupt Practices Act Compliance Committee; overseeing the financial affairs of the company; and reevaluating periodically the role of the audit committee itself.

In its 1980 annual report, Heinz included the following note:

> The company has been advised that the United States Securities and Exchange Commission has issued a private order of investigation concerning the practices that were the subject of the Audit Committee inquiry and report, a copy of which was filed with the Securities and Exchange Commission. The company has not been informed what action, if any, the Commission may take with respect to these matters. (Note 15)

QUESTIONS

1. Explain in theory and cite examples of how the income transferral and other practices discussed in this case would cause changes in the company's income statement.

2. To what extent do you believe the Heinz organizational structure, management philosophy, or management incentive plan influenced company personnel to engage in improper accounting or financial reporting practices? What changes, if any, would you recommend to reduce the potential for repetition of these practices.

3. Consider yourself to be in a management position at a large U.S. corporation, such as Heinz; you are asked to decide what functions should be assigned to the internal audit group, what position internal audit should take within the company's organizational structure, and what questions would be raised by an increase in emphasis on operational audits assessing the efficiency and effectiveness of the company's performance in financial and nonfinancial areas. What are your decisions?

4. Using the Heinz audit committee as a guide, discuss the potential roles and responsibilities of an audit committee.

5. Would you recommend changes in the roles of Congress or the Securities and Exchange Commission in the corporate financial reporting process?

PART TWO

Revenue and Expense Recognition

Datapoint Corporation*

In 1968, the Computer Terminal Corporation was incorporated in San Antonio, Texas, and began operations as a supplier of dispersed data processing systems. In 1970, the company went public and subsequently changed its name to Datapoint Corporation in December 1972. The company reported its first year of profitable operations in 1973, with income of $2 million on sales of nearly $19 million.

During the 1970s, Datapoint achieved recognition for its innovatively small, stand-alone computers. Other product lines were also added: multicomputer networks, telephones and switching systems, and the "Integrated Electronic Office" system. So successful were the company's products that record profits were reported for a span of 39 consecutive quarters through 1981. Datapoint's income for fiscal year 1981 reached $48.8 million, delivering an earnings per share of $2.45.

Datapoint's operational success was widely recognized in financial circles, and, during the third quarter of 1981, its common stock reached a record high of $67.50 per share. Approximately 67 percent of the company's 19.5 million common shares were held by institutional investors.

MARKETING STRATEGY

In early 1980, Datapoint attempted to refocus its marketing strategy. In the past, the company had achieved its success primarily on the sale of dispersed data processing systems and networking products. Datapoint marketing executives, however, saw the future in "Integrated Electric Office" systems, and thus attempted to aggressively penetrate this market. Additional sales personnel were hired, more than doubling the existing number, and the management force was built up in anticipation of the increased sales which would result from this new marketing emphasis. To encourage competition within the salesforce, the company established rigid quarterly sales budgets and a compensation system which rewarded those who exceeded the quotas.

The economy, however, posed a challenge to this new marketing force: 1980 was an election year and Ronald Reagan was swept into office on promises of ending the U.S. recession by reducing inflation, interest rates, and, ultimately, unemployment.

"BAD NEWS"

The first hint that the new marketing strategy had been a failure was received by the market on February 2, 1982. Harold O'Kelley, president and chief executive officer, announced that company projections for the second quarter of 1982 would not be met. The stock market reacted sharply to O'Kelley's announcement and, on the following day, the company's share price dropped $8.375, from $49⅜ to $41.

---

* This case was prepared by Kenneth R. Ferris from publicly available information. Copyright © 1985 by Kenneth R. Ferris. All rights reserved to the author.

On the succeeding day, the stock price was again down, falling $4.75 to $36.25 per share.

Uncharacteristically, Mr. O'Kelley had earlier predicted that second quarter results would be above the $0.66 per share reported in the fourth quarter of 1981. "Wall Street isn't used to negative news from Datapoint. The company has had a traditional history that, if it ever surprised anybody, it was on the upside."

But the bad news was just beginning. On March 18, 1982, Datapoint officials held a news conference for some 200 market analysts and stockbrokers. The company reported that it was now unable to "predict second half results because of economic uncertainties." Harold O'Kelley announced that the company's second quarter backlog was down slightly from the first quarter, and that Datapoint had decided to remove from its backlog some previously booked orders that didn't appear firm in the face of the "economic uncertainties." On the following day on the New York Stock Exchange, Datapoint was the most actively traded stock, dropping $5.75 per share or nearly 17 percent of its value, to $28.625.

In mid-April 1982, the first of several shareholder lawsuits was filed against Datapoint alleging that the board of directors and corporate officers had sold Datapoint stock on the basis of "material, nonpublic information." The suit charged that officials of the company had sold approximately 100,000 common shares at prices between $49 and $57 from June 1981 to January 1982 while being "privy to knowledge that the company would be unable to maintain its earnings growth patterns of previous years." At the time of the suit, Datapoint shares were trading at $21 per share.

On April 30, Datapoint revealed that its string of 39 consecutive quarters of profit gains would be broken—the company disclosed that it would report a loss for the third quarter of 1982. Datapoint blamed its poor results on the weak U.S. economy, but also acknowledged that it would have to reverse "a significant amount of sales recorded in the current and prior quarters." Wall Street analysts hypothesized that the company had become a victim of its own aggressive marketing strategies—hard-driving and hard-pressed sales personnel had apparently recorded as firm sales equipment that customers either wouldn't or couldn't pay for. On the day following the announcement, Datapoint shares fell $4.875 to $16.75 per share.

In the following 10 days, three notable events occurred: (1) a Datapoint shareholder filed suit in federal court charging officers and directors of the company with fraud by allegedly making false statements about the firm to run up the price of the stock; (2) Standard & Poor's added Datapoint to its Credit Watch list of companies whose credit ratings may be subject to change; and (3) the company asked for and received the resignations of three vice presidents and two other executives, while a sixth executive was forced to resign from the board of directors. One former Datapoint vice president was quoted as saying: "Soon we'll be used as a case study of bad business judgment and overly aggressive marketing at every business school in the country."

INDEPENDENT INVESTIGATION

In the aftermath of these events, Datapoint's independent auditors, Peat, Marwick, Mitchell & Company, were retained to review the company's domestic backlog of sales and receivables. The following was revealed:

1. Datapoint recognized revenue from equipment sales at the time of shipment. Shipments were typically sent to distributors, who then resold the equipment to the final consumer. Consistent with industry practice, such shipments carried a right of return or refusal.

2. Intense corporate pressure had built up over several recent quarters to reach "unreasonable and unattainable sales goals." Hard-pressed sales representatives reportedly asked Datapoint distributors and other customers to order millions of dollars of computer equipment, months in advance, with payment not required until delivery. This allowed the representatives to record as sales such orders, even though in many cases the equipment had not even been manufactured. Also, since revenues were booked at the time of shipment, additional unsolicited shipments could be sent to distributors at the last moment in order to meet quarterly sales quotas.

3. Beginning as early as September 1980, Datapoint marketing personnel used personal funds or false expense vouchers to pay storage fees for equipment (that had been booked as sold) that distributors either couldn't sell, couldn't pay for, or had refused to accept.

4. An elaborate warehousing and brokering scheme was developed in which Datapoint sales representatives used favorable discounts and payment terms in order to help distributors sell, store, and ship equipment. At the extreme, for example, during the summer of 1981 when distributor warehouse space was unavailable, a large shipment needed to meet expected sales quotas was sent to a fictitious customer, "Joe Blow," in care of a hotel on South Padre Island, Texas. After several weeks, the "mistake" was corrected and the shipment was placed with a legitimate distributor.

5. To achieve projected quotas, sales representatives disregarded company credit policies, failing to undertake normal credit investigations prior to shipping equipment and even delivering equipment to customers judged not to be creditworthy.

6. The corporate emphasis on sales was at least in part linked to pressures to maintain the market pace of the company's common stock. Executive compensation packages were directly tied to the price of the common stock in that executive performance cash bonuses were paid on the basis of the stock price as of August 1 of each year.

EPILOGUE

Before the close of fiscal year 1982, Datapoint stock reached a low of $11 per share—a decline of over $56 per share since the previous year's high and a loss of over $800 million in shareholder wealth. During the third quarter of 1982, management reported a net loss of nearly $23 million, which was more than double the size of any quarterly gain in the corporation's history. The investigation by Peat, Marwick, Mitchell & Company revealed approximately $15 million in unjustified sales, which were subsequently reversed against third quarter results. Institutional shareholdings, which accounted for nearly 67 percent of Datapoint's stock in 1981, fell to less than 10 percent of the outstanding shares. And Datapoint, its corporate officers, and Peat, Marwick, Mitchell & Company were named as codefendants in more than a dozen shareholder lawsuits.

QUESTIONS

1. Evaluate the operating policies and revenue recognition procedures followed by Datapoint Corporation. Are they reasonable? What suggestions for improvement, if any, would you make?

2. Consider top management's role in the prevention of fraud. How could Datapoint's problems have been identified, and prevented, by top management?

3. How would you correct for the $15 million in overstated sales revenue? What adjustments would you make? (See Exhibits 1 and 2, the unaudited financial statements for the third quarter 1982.)

EXHIBIT 1

DATAPOINT CORPORATION
Consolidated Condensed Statements of Earnings
(in thousands, except share data)

	Three Months Ended April 30.		Nine Months Ended April 30.	
	1982	1981	1982	1981
Revenue:				
Sales	$ 38,822	$ 71,876	$195,458	$204,291
Lease and service	60,580	45,026	172,230	124,134
Total revenue	99,402	116,902	367,688	328,425
Cost of revenue:				
Sales	27,844	31,222	87,124	91,610
Lease and service	40,809	27,028	108,365	74,658
Total cost of revenue	68,653	58,250	195,489	166,268
Gross profit	30,749	58,652	172,199	162,157
Operating expenses:				
Engineering and product development	11,799	9,535	33,926	26,524
Marketing	49,632	25,092	124,815	67,828
General and administrative	4,462	3,742	11,847	10,400
Total operating expenses	65,893	38,369	170,588	104,752
Operating income (loss)	(35,144)	20,283	1,611	57,405
Financing income (expense), net and other	(1,875)	2,380	(1,894)	4,722
Earnings (loss) before income taxes and minority interests	(37,019)	22,663	(283)	62,127
Federal, foreign and state income taxes	(14,077)	9,733	565	26,682
Earnings (loss) before minority interests	(22,942)	12,930	(848)	35,445
Minority interests in earnings of partially owned companies	(51)	(57)	(51)	(133)
Net earnings (loss)	$(22,993)	$ 12,873	$ (899)	$ 35,312
Fully diluted:				
Earnings (loss) per share	$(1.14)	$ .63	$ (.04)	$ 1.79
Average shares	20,180,391	20,501,562	20,352,437	19,683,412

EXHIBIT 2

DATAPOINT CORPORATION
Consolidated Condensed Balance Sheets
(in thousands)

	April 30, 1982	July 31, 1981
Assets:		
Cash	$ 20,395	$ 4,754
Short-term investments	33,668	199,503
Receivables, net	121,622	110,467
Inventories:		
Finished products	58,262	20,390
Work in process	23,766	20,780
Raw materials	33,392	33,252
Total inventories	115,420	74,422
Prepaid expenses	3,700	2,049
Total current assets	294,805	391,195
Property, plant and equipment, net	75,789	55,126
Equipment leased to customers, net	78,246	69,604
Investments in partially owned companies	9,182	3,016
Excess of cost of investment over net assets acquired, net	93,004	15,749
Long-term receivables	3,952	4,584
Distributorship agreement, net	16,167	—
Other assets	3,633	2,831
Total assets	$574,778	$542,105
Liabilities, Deferred Revenue and Stockholders' Equity:		
Accounts and notes payable	$ 46,575	$ 35,671
Other current liabilities	61,578	50,971
Total current liabilities	108,153	86,642
Long-term debt, exclusive of current installments	129,686	129,603
Deferred income taxes	2,737	2,737
Deferred revenue	8,375	2,131
Minority interests	(302)	2,569
Stockholders' equity	326,129	318,423
Total liabilities, deferred revenue and stockholders' equity	$574,778	$542,105

(UNAUDITED)

The accompanying notes are an integral part of these statements.

Cajun Construction Company*

In June of 1980, the Cajun Construction Company was employed by the Port Authority of New Orleans, Louisiana, to assist in the construction of a World Trade Center complex. The company was to construct the superstructure of a multistory office building as part of the city's harbor redevelopment. The redevelopment project was associated with the 1984 World's Fair to be held in that city. The construction agreement called for work to begin not later than August of 1980, and required the company to construct the concrete frame for the building.

Under the terms of the three-year contract agreed to, the company was to receive a total of $8 million in cash payments from the Port Authority to be paid as follows: 25 percent when the work was 30 percent complete, 25 percent when the work was 60 percent complete, and the remaining 50 percent when the contracted work had been fully completed. The contract, which was of a fixed-price variety and hence did not provide for cost overrun recoupment, required that completion percentage estimates be certified by an independent engineering consultant before any cash progress payments would be made.

In preparing its bid, the company had estimated that the total cost to complete the project would be $7.2 million, assuming no cost overruns. Hence, under optimal conditions, the company anticipated a profit of approximately $800,000.

During the first year of the contract, the company incurred actual costs of $2.16 million, and on June 30, 1981, the engineering consulting firm of C. Hayes & Associates determined that the project had attained a 30 percent completion level. In the following year, the company incurred actual costs of $2.34 million. As of June 30, 1982, the firm of C. Hayes & Associates determined that the project had attained at least a 60 percent completion level. In their report to the Port Authority, however, the consulting engineers noted that the company might be facing a potential cost overrun situation. In response to this observation, the directors of the company noted that they had anticipated that a number of economies of scale would arise during the final phases of construction and thereby offset any prior cost overruns.

By May of 1983, the company had completed the remainder of the project. Actual costs incurred during the year to June 30, 1983, amounted to $2.8 million. The firm received a certification for the fully completed work.

ACCOUNTING DECISION

Prior to the issuance of the 1981 annual report, the controller's office of the company determined that the proceeds from the World Trade Center contract would be ac-

---

* This case was prepared by Kenneth R. Ferris. Copyright © 1985 by Kenneth R. Ferris. All rights reserved to the author.

counted for using the "completed contract" method. Under this approach, the recognition of income is postponed until essentially all work on the contract has been completed. This method previously had been utilized by the company to account for construction contract income, and it appeared to be a prudent alternative, given the possibility of some cost overrun during the life of the current contract.

Under the completed contract approach, revenues (and thus expenses) are recognized upon completion or substantial completion of a contract. In general, a contract is regarded as substantially complete if the remaining costs to complete the project are insignificant in amount. Funds expended under the contract are accounted for in an asset account, "construction in progress," while progress payments received during the construction phrase are accounted for in a deferred or unearned revenue account. Although income is not recognized until completion of the contract, any expected losses should be recognized immediately when identified.

The primary advantage of the completed contract method is that reported operating results are based on actual results, rather than on estimates. The principal disadvantage is that the method may produce results inconsistent with the actual performance of the firm if the contract extends over more than one reporting period.

In the process of reaching the decision to use the completed contract method, the controller's office of the Cajun Construction Company had reviewed *Accounting Research Bulletin No. 45*, "Long-Term Construction-type Contracts." This pronouncement identifies the "percentage of completion" method as the preferred method of accounting for long-term construction contract income, at least when the estimated costs to complete a contract and the extent of construction progress can be reasonably estimated. Under this method, revenues are recognized in proportion to the amount of construction actually completed in a given period. The principal advantage of this method is that performance is reported as the work is actually undertaken, rather than at some later date; thus, accounting information users are provided with up-to-date information as to the relative effectiveness and performance of the company. The primary disadvantage is that the method requires the use of estimation procedures, thereby potentially allowing estimation error to enter into the performance reporting process.

QUESTIONS

1. Assuming that the company had no other sources of revenues or expenses, determine the level of profits to be reported for the years ended June 30, 1981, 1982, and 1983, utilizing the following revenue recognition methods:

   a. Percentage of completion.
   b. Completed contract.
   c. Cash basis. (Note: Assume that the Port Authority remits cash payments on the same day as work completion certification.)

2. Which set of results (from Question 1) best reflects the economic performance of the company over the period 1981–1983? What criteria did you apply in the foregoing assessment?

3. a. Assuming that the company decided to change its method of accounting from the completed contract to the percentage of completion method on July 1, 1982, what journal entries would be required?

   b. How should the percentage of completion be determined? Explain why.

Thousand Trails, Inc.*

"Some people see us here in a pup tent ready to pull up stakes the first time that the creditors come around," observed C. James Jensen, chairman of Thousand Trails, Inc. "But for the first time in the company's history, revenues from our three profit centers—membership sales, preserve operations, and interest on membership contracts—exceeded $100 million, and the future of Thousand Trails now seems assured."

CORPORATE BACKGROUND

Founded in 1969, Thousand Trails was the pioneering firm of a new industry—the private membership campground resort industry. The Seattle, Washington–based company owns, operates, and sells memberships in a 30-resort network located in nine states throughout the United States and in British Columbia, Canada. While most of the resorts are located on the West Coast, in Washington, Oregon, and California, additional properties are owned or developed in Arizona, Nevada, Texas, Illinois, Ohio, and Virginia.

The company's unique concept originated with its founder, Milton G. Kuolt. During the early 1960s, Kuolt became impressed with the booming business in recreational land sales and membership-based tennis, golf, and country clubs. The idea of combining both trends gave rise to Thousand Trails, and, in 1971, Kuolt acquired his first wilderness area.

The oil crisis in 1973 and the recession of 1974–75 provided the company with its first real financial tests. After weathering this period of financial uncertainty, the firm then faced the 1979 crisis of scarce gasoline supplies and soaring prices, which frightened many motorists and travelers off the highways and severely reduced the profits of such traditional campground operators as Kampgrounds of America, Inc. But while the operations of traditional campground companies were significantly hampered, Thousand Trails achieved an 89 percent increase in earnings on a 49 percent increase in sales. According to Kuolt, the closeness of the company's wilderness preserves to large metropolitan areas (within 100 miles), where most of its members reside, enabled campers to make round-trips to the sites on a single tankful of gas.

Thousand Trails offers its members exclusive use of its campground facilities and amenities, which are usually comparable to those found at vacation resorts (e.g., swimming pools, tennis courts, hiking trails, athletic fields, trading posts, dances,

---

* This case was prepared by Kenneth R. Ferris and Connie J. Johnson. Copyright © 1985 by Kenneth R. Ferris. All rights reserved to the authors.

and movies). In addition, however, the company maintains one half of each site in its natural wilderness state. Thus, members are able to enjoy country club-type facilities in a wilderness setting.

One of the principal reasons for the company's continued growth has been an ever-increasing demand for outdoor recreational opportunities at a time of steadily diminishing public supply. A 1983 report prepared by the Outdoor Recreation Policy Review Group concluded that "outdoor recreation is more important than ever in American life. . . . Yet, governments at all levels have been retrenching and providing less recreation opportunities." Similarly, reports by the Recreation Vehicle Industry Association and by the A. C. Nielsen Company suggest that demand for campground facilities has never been greater, and will continue to grow. The RVIA estimates that "RV sales in 1983 were up 40 percent, making it the industry's best year since 1978." An A. C. Nielsen study reports that, as of 1983, there were 60 million campers in the United States, 40 percent of whom camp in recreational vehicles; the study also projected that the number of campers would grow by 4.4 million by the end of the decade.

MEMBERSHIP

A membership in the campground network entitles the purchaser to use of any existing or future facilities for an unlimited number of visits. A "lifetime" membership, moreover, may be passed on to heirs for up to three generations.

Memberships range in cost from $6,500 to $7,500, plus annual dues of $210. For members with recreational vehicles, which represent approximately 80 percent of the total, a regular lifetime membership sells for $6,500, plus annual dues. For those individuals not owning an RV, the company began offering in 1983 a new "vacation membership," which features company-owned RVs and trailers leased at a daily rate, for an initial membership fee of $7,500; this new membership format accounted for 30.5 percent of all memberships sold in 1983.

Memberships are typically sold on an installment basis, with terms ranging from 24 to 84 months, a stated interest rate of 15 percent, on a nonrecourse basis. During 1983, the company managed a receivable portfolio of approximately $90 million, with an average yield of 14.9 percent.

Nearly 90 percent of all new members finance their membership through the company. To finance a membership, the company requires that members have a minimum income of $15,000 annually, a job, and a down payment of $800, which can also be financed; a credit rating or bank account is not required to qualify for membership financing, and Thousand Trails sales representatives are given considerable latitude in deciding to whom the company will grant financing.

Membership in the campground network conveys no actual ownership interest in the company or any of its resorts. Further, the company does not guarantee continuity of services at any of its existing campgrounds or the development of any future campgrounds.

OPERATIONS

Thousand Trails generates revenues from three related profit centers: membership sales, preserve operations, and financial services.

In 1983, sales of memberships totaled $79.9 million, with on-site marketing and selling conducted at 21 campground locations. Potential members are identified

---

EXHIBIT 1
Computation of Return on Investment from Membership Sales—Typical Resort including 600 Campsites and Standard Amenities

Investment in property, including land cost, and purchased and developed amenities	$ 5,000,000
Potential membership sales (6,000 units)	$38,000,000
Less: Marketing cost (44%).	16,720,000
Net contribution.	$21,280,000
Return on investment	4.3:1

Source: Thousand Trails, Inc., 1983 Annual Report.

EXHIBIT 2
Projected Contribution from Preserve Operations

Potential memberships	6,000
Annual dues revenues (at $210 per member). . . .	$1,260,000
Less: Annual operating costs (including pro-rata portion of overhead)	500,000
Annual contribution per preserve	$ 760,000

Source: Thousand Trails, Inc., 1983 Annual Report.

---

through direct mail solicitations, which promise guaranteed gifts and prizes if individuals attend a one-and-one-half-hour sales presentation at one of the company's resorts. The company estimates that 10 memberships may be sold for each planned campsite without creating resort overcrowding, and each resort is projected to generate a "return on investment of 4.3 to 1" (see Exhibit 1).

According to the company's annual report, membership sales "are recorded in full upon execution of membership agreements" (i.e., three days after contract signing). All marketing costs and an allowance for uncollectible accounts are also recorded upon contract execution. Operating preserve land and development costs, including estimated costs to complete operating preserves, are charged against membership sales based on the ratio of actual memberships sold to total planned memberships.

Revenues from preserve operations consist primarily of membership dues, which are assessed at a rate (currently $210) designed to cover resort operating costs and a pro rata share of overhead costs. At a typical resort, the break-even point for preserve operations is assumed to occur when 40 percent of all potential memberships are sold (see Exhibit 2); at full membership level, the annual contribution per resort is projected to be $760,000. Additional revenues are generated from trading post sales and other on-location services.

The financial services division of Thousand Trails manages its portfolio of receivables and generates income from the interest spread between the company's borrowings under a bank line of credit and its financing of memberships. Substantially all membership contracts receivable are pledged as collateral.

EXHIBIT 3
Operating Highlights: Five-Year Summary

Selected Income Statement Data
(in thousands except per share amounts)

Year Ended December 31,	1983	1982	1981	1980	1979
Membership Sales	*$79,971*	*$56,454*	*$40,006*	*$33,950*	*$21,396*
Gross Profit on Membership Sales	*31,715*	*23,173*	*14,422*	*13,802*	*10,405*
Gross Profit on Preserve Operations	*1,995*	*1,298*	*880*	*383*	*366*
Net Earnings	*12,004*	*7,761*	*3,327*	*4,536*	*2,790*
Primary Earnings Per Share	*1.85*	*1.45*	*.71*	*1.13*	*.78*
Fully Diluted Earnings Per Share	*1.81*	*1.34*	*.68*	*.95*	*.78*

Selected Balance Sheet Data
(in thousands)

December 31,	1983	1982	1981	1980	1979
Current Assets	*$23,666*	*$15,981*	*$10,967*	*$ 7,575*	*$ 8,014*
Current Liabilities	*22,118*	*15,001*	*9,395*	*7,755*	*6,950*
Membership Contracts Receivable (Net)	*82,373*	*53,443*	*34,696*	*23,482*	*13,949*
Operating Preserves	*82,282*	*56,167*	*39,003*	*29,658*	*15,356*
Total Assets	*151,767*	*102,299*	*70,822*	*52,567*	*34,280*
Debt:					
Long-Term	*28,206*	*23,183*	*22,344*	*20,498*	*17,527*
Bank Line of Credit	*25,033*	*24,279*	*15,855*	*6,811*	*3,300*
Total Deferred Income Taxes	*29,033*	*18,505*	*11,437*	*8,458*	*4,256*
Shareholders' Equity	*60,299*	*30,194*	*17,865*	*14,110*	*7,107*

Source: Thousand Trails, Inc., 1983 Annual Report.

FUTURE PROSPECTS

As of 1983, Thousand Trails had achieved a five-year compound growth rate of 52 percent in earnings, 41 percent in sales, and 35.5 percent in its return on equity (see Exhibit 3). Whether this type of growth is sustainable has been questioned by financial analysts based on recent company filings with the Securities and Exchange Commission. In a year-end 1983 filing with the SEC, Thousand Trails reported: "The company has experienced peak membership sales at new preserves during the first year or two of operations." As of December 31, 1983, the company reported that it had 51,100 members, or approximately one third of the total planned memberships for sale based on existing, operating preserves; the average age of the preserves was 3.5 years.

Exhibits 4–9 present data from the 1983 financial statements.

QUESTIONS

1. Evaluate *(a)* the company's method of revenue recognition and *(b)* its method of accounting for land and development costs. Would you suggest any alternative method?

2. Evaluate the quality of the company's accounts receivables. Would you consider the receivables of "good quality" as collateral for lending purposes?

EXHIBIT 4

THOUSAND TRAILS, INC., AND SUBSIDIARIES
Consolidated Statements of Earnings

Year ended December 31,	1983	1982	1981
Membership Sales	$79,971,000	$56,454,000	$40,006,000
Costs Attributable to Membership Sales:			
Marketing expenses	35,209,000	24,892,000	19,831,000
Preserve land and improvement costs	13,047,000	8,389,000	5,753,000
General and administrative expenses	11,827,000	8,612,000	7,141,000
Provision for doubtful accounts	3,977,000	2,241,000	1,866,000
	64,060,000	44,134,000	34,591,000
Income From Membership Sales	15,911,000	12,320,000	5,415,000
Preserve Operations:			
Membership dues	7,355,000	4,982,000	3,304,000
Trading post and other sales	2,749,000	2,015,000	1,482,000
	10,104,000	6,997,000	4,786,000
Less —			
Cost of trading post sales	2,400,000	1,839,000	1,346,000
Maintenance and operations expense	5,709,000	3,860,000	2,560,000
General and administrative expenses	1,506,000	973,000	711,000
	9,615,000	6,672,000	4,617,000
Income From Preserve Operations	489,000	325,000	169,000
Other Income (Expense):			
Interest income	10,147,000	6,622,000	4,153,000
Interest expense	(3,957,000)	(4,203,000)	(3,213,000)
Other	42,000	35,000	(147,000)
	6,232,000	2,454,000	793,000
Earnings Before Deferred Income Taxes	22,632,000	15,099,000	6,377,000
Deferred Income Taxes	10,628,000	7,338,000	3,050,000
Net Earnings	$12,004,000	$ 7,761,000	$ 3,327,000
Net Earnings Per Share:			
Primary	$1.85	$1.45	$.71
Fully diluted	$1.81	$1.34	$.68

See notes to consolidated financial statements.

EXHIBIT 5

THOUSAND TRAILS, INC., AND SUBSIDIARIES
Consolidated Balance Sheets

Assets December 31,	1983	1982
Current Assets:		
Cash	$ 770,000	$ 703,000
Current portion of notes, contracts and accounts receivable—		
Membership contracts	20,382,000	13,568,000
Other	1,558,000	1,025,000
	21,940,000	14,593,000
Allowance for doubtful accounts	(1,111,000)	(646,000)
	20,829,000	13,947,000
Inventory and prepaid expenses	2,067,000	1,331,000
Total Current Assets	23,666,000	15,981,000
Notes, Contracts and Accounts Receivable, less current portion:		
Membership contracts	66,740,000	42,546,000
Real estate contracts	732,000	788,000
Other	218,000	179,000
	67,690,000	43,513,000
Allowance for doubtful accounts	(3,638,000)	(2,025,000)
	64,052,000	41,488,000
Operating Preserves:		
Land	17,702,000	12,347,000
Improvements	64,580,000	43,820,000
	82,282,000	56,167,000
Costs applicable membership sales	(38,466,000)	(25,427,000)
	43,816,000	30,740,000
Preserves Under Development, at cost	6,592,000	2,244,000
Investment in Real Estate, at cost	2,773,000	2,793,000
Construction and Operating Equipment, net of accumulated depreciation of $3,174,000 and $2,085,000	5,293,000	3,480,000
Other Assets, at cost	5,575,000	5,573,000
	$151,767,000	$102,299,000

Liabilities and Shareholders' Equity December 31,	1983	1982
Current Liabilities:		
Accounts payable	$ 2,415,000	$ 1,836,000
Accrued salaries	3,714,000	1,949,000
Prepaid membership dues	1,887,000	1,064,000
Other liabilities	1,180,000	1,289,000
Current portion of long-term debt	5,896,000	4,350,000
Deferred income taxes	7,026,000	4,513,000
Total Current Liabilities	22,118,000	15,001,000
Long-Term Debt, less current portion	47,343,000	43,112,000
Deferred Income Taxes	22,007,000	13,992,000
Commitments and Contingencies (Note G)		
Shareholders' Equity:		
Common stock, no par value — Authorized, 15,000,000 shares		
Issued, 6,798,097 and 5,472,826 shares	29,358,000	11,252,000
Retained earnings	30,941,000	18,942,000
	60,299,000	30,194,000
	$151,767,000	$102,299,000

See notes to consolidated financial statements.

EXHIBIT 6

THOUSAND TRAILS, INC., AND SUBSIDIARIES
Consolidated Statements of Shareholders' Equity

	Common Stock		Retained
	Shares	*Amount*	*earnings*
Balance, January 1, 1981	4,476,890	$ 6,160,000	$ 7,950,000
Debenture conversions	84,186	310,000	
Issuance of common stock	21,301	118,000	
Net earnings			3,327,000
Balance, December 31, 1981	4,582,377	6,588,000	11,277,000
Debenture conversions	76,159	286,000	
Issuance of common stock	814,290	4,378,000	
Foreign currency translation			(96,000)
Net earnings			7,761,000
Balance, December 31, 1982	5,472,826	11,252,000	18,942,000
Debenture conversions	77,803	296,000	
Issuance of common stock	1,247,468	17,810,000	
Foreign currency translation			(1,000)
Net earnings			12,004,000
Balance, December 31, 1983	6,798,097	$29,358,000	$30,945,000

See notes to consolidated financial statements.

EXHIBIT 7

THOUSAND TRAILS, INC., AND SUBSIDIARIES
Consolidated Statements of Changes in Financial Position

Year ended December 31,	1983	1982	1981
Operations:			
Cash received—			
Membership sales	$27,738,000	$22,582,000	$18,003,000
Collections on contracts receivable,			
including interest	28,619,000	19,278,000	13,258,000
Dues and preserve revenues	10,507,000	7,336,000	5,133,000
Other	211,000	133,000	(69,000)
	67,075,000	49,329,000	36,325,000
Cash expended—			
Marketing expenses	34,211,000	23,211,000	19,983,000
General and administrative expenses	11,788,000	7,739,000	7,130,000
Preserve maintenance and operations	9,001,000	6,127,000	4,571,000
Principal payments on debt related			
to preserve properties	4,337,000	3,744,000	2,032,000
Interest expense	3,957,000	4,203,000	3,213,000
	63,294,000	45,024,000	36,929,000
Cash provided by (used in) operations			
before preserve improvements	3,781,000	4,305,000	(604,000)
Cash expended for preserve improvements	(18,391,000)	(11,275,000)	(6,837,000)
Cash used in operations	(14,610,000)	(6,970,000)	(7,441,000)
Other Sources (Uses) of Cash:			
Issuance of common stock	17,756,000	4,161,000	10,000
Proceeds of borrowings collateralized			
by contracts receivable	851,000	8,646,000	9,069,000
Principal payments on notes payable			
and credit line arrangements	(1,109,000)	(735,000)	(743,000)
Acquisition of preferred stock		(3,000,000)	
Purchase of construction and operating			
equipment, net of related borrowings of			
$1,388,000, $1,072,000 and $1,588,000	(2,943,000)	(1,490,000)	(789,000)
Other, net	122,000	(81,000)	(566,000)
	14,677,000	7,501,000	6,981,000
Increase (Decrease) in Cash	67,000	531,000	(460,000)
Cash:			
Beginning of year	703,000	172,000	632,000
End of year	$ 770,000	$ 703,000	$ 172,000

See notes to consolidated financial statements.

EXHIBIT 8

THOUSAND TRAILS, INC., AND SUBSIDIARIES
Notes to Consolidated Financial Statements
Three Years Ended December 31, 1983

Note A
Significant
Accounting
Policies:

General

The Company and subsidiaries operate membership-based destination resort campgrounds (preserves) in the United States and Canada. All significant intercompany transactions and balances have been eliminated in the accompanying financial statements.

Revenue recognition

The Company sells memberships for cash or on installment contracts. Revenues are recorded in full upon execution of membership agreements. Installment sales require a down payment of at least 10 percent of the sales price. All marketing costs and an allowance for estimated contract collection losses (based on historical loss occurrence rates) are recorded currently.

Members are assessed annual dues which are used for preserve maintenance and operations, member services and allocated general and administrative expenses. The Company establishes dues at rates intended to fully provide for such expenses when active memberships sold reach approximately 40 percent of total memberships available for sale. Membership agreements provide for annual adjustment of dues to reflect increases in the Consumer Price Index.

Operating preserves

Operating preserve land and improvement costs, including estimated costs to complete preserves in accordance with the Company's development plans, are aggregated by geographical region and recorded as a cost of membership sales based upon the ratio of actual memberships sold within each region to the total memberships planned by the Company to be available for sale within the region. The maximum number of memberships which will be sold in a geographical region is determined based on members' historical use of the Company's preserves in that region. The Company currently plans to sell 10 memberships for each campsite. Preserve utilization statistics are reviewed on a regular basis, and the number of total planned memberships available for sale will be revised in the event future experience indicates the 10 to 1 ratio is no longer appropriate. As of December 31, 1983, the Company had 51,100 members, which represented approximately one-third of the total planned memberships for sale on operating preserves.

The Company generally incurs indebtedness in connection with the acquisition of preserve land and improvements. It is the Company's policy to reduce such indebtedness in a proportion at least equal to the ratio that memberships sold bears to total memberships available for sale. The Company capitalizes interest as a component of the cost of significant improvements of preserve properties.

Preserves under development

Costs related to preserves under development are classified as operating preserve land and improvements in the appropriate geographical region when development has been completed to the extent that the preserve is reflected in the Company's marketing program as available for use by members.

Investment in real estate

Land acquired in excess of that necessary for operating preserves or preserves under development is classified as investment in real estate. Real estate contiguous to operating preserves is infrequently used but is generally available for use by members until disposition or further development. Certain parcels of the real estate contiguous to operating preserves are subject to land use permits required in connection with development of the preserves. Prior to disposition or development of such parcels, the Company will be required to obtain waivers or modifications of such restrictions from local governmental authorities.

Depreciation

Depreciation is provided on the straight-line method over the assets' respective useful lives.

Foreign currency translation

The Company translates the financial statements of its Canadian subsidiary into U.S. dollars at exchange rates in effect as of the balance sheet dates. Unrealized translation gains and losses are included in retained earnings.

Earnings per share

Earnings per share of common stock are computed based on the weighted average common and equivalent shares outstanding during the year retroactively restated for the 3 for 2 stock split effected February 22, 1983. Stock options, rights and warrants to purchase stock are included in the

EXHIBIT 8 *(continued)*

computation of earnings per share when dilutive. The effect of an assumed conversion of the Company's convertible subordinated debentures is also included in the computation of fully diluted earnings per share.

Note B
Membership
Contracts
Receivable:

Membership contracts receivable bear interest at an average rate of 14.9 percent and currently are written with initial terms of 24 to 84 months with an average term of 61 months. The Company has no obligation to refund monies received or provide further services to members in the event a membership is cancelled for nonpayment of contractual obligations.

Aggregate annual principal payments on membership contracts are as follows:

Year ending December 31,	
1984	$20,382,000
1985	20,058,000
1986	18,173,000
1987	14,952,000
1988	10,036,000

Substantially all membership contracts receivable are pledged as collateral for debt.

Note C
Long-Term Debt
and Line Of Credit:

Long-term debt and line of credit consist of the following:

December 31,	1983	1982
Real estate contracts and capitalized leases, 6.5 percent to 13.25 percent (average 9.1 percent), payable in aggregate monthly installments of $491,000 and $351,000 including interest	$23,096,000	$16,810,000
Notes, 6 percent to 18 percent (average 12.6 percent), payable in aggregate monthly installments of approximately $60,000 and $131,000 including interest	1,967,000	3,137,000
Equipment and other contracts, 10 percent to 23.8 percent (average 15.7 percent), payable in aggregate monthly installments of $116,000 and $98,000 including interest	2,492,000	2,253,000
13 percent convertible subordinated debentures, due 1994, callable December 1984, interest payable quarterly	651,000	983,000
	28,206,000	23,183,000
Line of credit	25,033,000	24,279,000
	53,239,000	47,462,000
Current portion	(5,896,000)	(4,350,000)
	$47,343,000	$43,112,000

Substantially all of the Company's assets are pledged as collateral for the above debt. Aggregate annual principal payments during each of the next five years are as follows:

1984	$5,896,000
1985	7,104,000
1986	5,741,000
1987	3,583,000
1988	3,489,000

The debentures are convertible into common stock at $4.24 per share, subject to adjustment. The indenture requires semiannual sinking fund payments of $41,000. At the option of the Company, debentures converted to common stock were used to offset sinking fund requirements through December 31, 1983.

At December 31, 1983, the Company had a line of credit of $50,000,000 consisting of a $25,000,000 revolving line of credit and a $25,000,000 term

EXHIBIT 8 *(continued)*

loan. The term loan is restricted to acquisition and development of properties and bears interest at the 26-week Treasury Bill rate plus 4 percent (13.6 percent as of December 31, 1983). As of December 31, 1983, the Company had drawn $6,675,000 under the term loan agreement. The institution providing the term loan owned 22 percent of the Company's outstanding common stock as of December 31, 1983.

The revolving portion of the line of credit bears interest at the bank's prime lending rate plus 1 percent (12 percent as of December 31, 1983). At the option of the Company or the bank, the balance outstanding under this portion of the line may be converted to a term loan payable in 36 equal monthly installments. The Company is restricted from payment of cash dividends without the bank's approval. None of the amount due under the revolving line of credit is included in the current portion of long-term debt.

Note D
Deferred
Income
Taxes:

The provision for deferred income taxes consists of the following:

Year ended December 31,	1983	1982	1981
Federal	$ 9,539,000	$6,563,000	$2,640,000
Foreign and state	1,089,000	775,000	410,000
	$10,628,000	$7,338,000	$3,050,000

The tax effect of items reported in different periods for financial statement and income tax purposes is as follows:

Year ended December 31,	1983	1982	1981
Installment sales	$13,309,000	$9,200,000	$4,570,000
Capitalized interest	211,000	805,000	670,000
Amortization of site improvements	(4,033,000)	(1,642,000)	205,000
Decrease (increase) in tax basis net operating loss carryforward	977,000	(1,138,000)	(2,350,000)
Other, net	164,000	113,000	(45,000)
	$10,628,000	$7,338,000	$3,050,000

Investment tax credits are recorded as a reduction of the income tax provision in the year available.

Note E
Incentive
Stock Plans:

The Company has two stock option plans under which common stock is reserved for issuance to officers and key employees. Under the 1979 plan, options are exercisable 25 percent each year commencing one year after the date of grant, and expire after 10 years. Options granted under the 1980 plan are exercisable in full after one year and expire five years after date of grant. Options are priced at not less than market value at date of grant.

In 1980, the Company adopted a key employee incentive compensation plan and a marketing benefit plan for sales personnel, both of which were terminated in April 1982, subject to rights existing on the date of termination.

Information with respect to options and rights granted under the plans is as follows:

EXHIBIT 8 *(continued)*

| | | | Options outstanding | | | |
	Authorized	Available for grant	Shares	Price per share	Currently exercisable	Exercised
Balance at December 31, 1982	568,348	51,055	269,559	$3.47-$11.54	179,300	247,734
granted		(39,300)	39,300			
exercised			(143,534)		(143,534)	143,534
forfeited		8,570	(8,570)		(7,525)	
exercisable during year					82,433	
Balance at December 31, 1983	568,348	20,325	156,755	$3.56-$23.00	110,674	391,268

In 1982, the Company reserved 450,000 shares for issuance under a stock purchase plan for officers and key employees. The plan provides for sale of common stock to participants on a cash or installment basis at a price not less than market value. Shares purchased on installment are issued and recorded in the financial statements upon receipt of payment. Of the shares reserved for issuance under the plan, 191,250 shares were purchased by officers in 1982 at $3.83 per share and 231,500 shares were purchased by officers in 1983 at an average price of $20.86 per share. During 1983, 143,663 shares were issued under the plan.

In November 1983, the Company agreed to sell to its president and chief operating officer 50,000 shares of common stock at $23.00 per share, payable in installments. As of December 31, 1983, none of these shares had been issued.

Note F
Post-Employment
Agreements:

During 1983, the Company entered into post-employment agreements with certain key officers. The agreements provide for preretirement death benefits, post-employment consulting, retirement benefits and an agreement not to compete. Cost to the Company under these agreements was $275,000 in 1983.

Note G
Commitments
and Contingencies:

Certain of the Company's preserves have been developed, and must be operated in compliance with the provisions of applicable land use permits. Management believes the Company is in compliance with such permits and, in the future, will make applications for new permits or for modifications of existing permits as considered necessary for preserve operations or for further development.

The Company has agreed to purchase five properties for use as future preserves, subject to obtaining applicable land use permits. The aggregate purchase price of these properties is $4,100,000, which will be financed by the sellers under agreements requiring approximately 20 percent down payment with the balance payable over periods not to exceed seven years and interest rates averaging 10 percent.

Note H
Costs
and Expenses:

The Company capitalizes interest as a component of the cost of significant improvements to preserves. Total interest costs were $6,411,000 in 1983, $6,756,000 in 1982 and $5,092,000 in 1981, of which $2,454,000, $2,553,000 and $1,879,000, respectively, were capitalized.

Preserve operating costs in excess of those necessary for preserve operations and member services are incurred to provide support for the Company's marketing program. Such costs are included in marketing expenses as follows:

Year ended December 31,	
1983	$1,234,000
1982	963,000
1981	767,000

EXHIBIT 8 *(concluded)*

Note I
Quarterly
Financial
Information
(Unaudited):

The following table sets forth quarterly financial information (in thousands except per share
data).

	First quarter	Second quarter	Third quarter	Fourth quarter
1983:				
Membership sales	$8,722	$21,773	$31,317	$18,159
Gross profit	2,967	8,975	12,892	6,881
Earnings before taxes	1,698	7,012	9,729	4,193
NET EARNINGS	873	3,604	5,001	2,526
Earnings per share:				
Primary	$.14	$.59	$.75	$.36
Fully diluted	.14	.57	.73	.35
1982:				
Membership sales	$6,704	$17,697	$21,764	$10,289
Gross profit	2,029	7,781	9,559	3,804
Earnings before taxes	408	5,273	6,948	2,470
NET EARNINGS	212	2,742	3,613	1,194
Earnings per share:				
Primary	$.05	$.55	$.63	$.22
Fully diluted	.05	.52	.60	.17

EXHIBIT 9
Accountants' Report

January 27, 1984
Seattle, Washington

Board of Directors and Shareholders
Thousand Trails, Inc.
Seattle, Washington

We have examined the consolidated balance sheets of Thousand Trails, Inc. and subsidiaries as of
December 31, 1983 and 1982, and the related consolidated statements of earnings, shareholders' equity
and changes in financial position for each of the three years in the period ended December 31, 1983. Our
examinations were made in accordance with generally accepted auditing standards and, accordingly, included such tests of the accounting records and such other auditing procedures as we considered necessary
in the circumstances.

In our opinion, the consolidated financial statements referred to above present fairly the financial
position of Thousand Trails, Inc. and subsidiaries as of December 31, 1983 and 1982, and the results of
their operations and the changes in their financial position for each of the three years in the period ended
December 31, 1983, in conformity with generally accepted accounting principles applied on a consistent
basis.

Touche Ross & Co.

Touche Ross & Co.
Certified Public Accountants

Six Flags Over Texas*

In 1969, the Great Southwest Corporation reported record earnings. In his letter to the shareholders, Angus G. Wynne, chairman of the board of GSC, commented:

> For Great Southwest Corporation, 1969 was a year of merger and expansion. The company established itself as one of the most profitable real estate developers in the nation. And our merger with Macco Corporation in March provided a solid foundation for company growth and increased profits in the years ahead. We immediately ushered in this new era of growth with the acquisition of Richardson Homes Corporation, a leading mobile home manufacturer.
>
> In 1969 our net earnings soared 20 percent over 1968 to $34.4 million or $1.08 per share on revenue of $141.3 million. This compares to 1968 net earnings of $27.4 million or $.87 per share on revenue of $117.1 million.
>
> We are extremely proud of our record earnings. And we are equally proud of the high caliber of the housing, commercial/industrial, and recreation developments from which we gain our earnings.
>
> We are a people-oriented company, hence each of our projects is inspired by our basic concern for people and their environments. As a result of that philosophy and our uniquely broad corporate structure, we are able to develop all types of environments, from housing communities with acres of open space, to industrial parks filled with sculpture.
>
> Our understanding of environments and our ability to create these environments is reflected in the success of our thematic recreation parks, Six Flags Over Texas and Six Flags Over Georgia.
>
> GSC's goal is to broaden its horizons as a leading developer of environments. In 1970 and beyond, you will find GSC in any area that involves people and their environments—at home, at work, and at play.

BACKGROUND

GSC was a real estate development company headquartered in the southwest United States. The company was a 90 percent–owned subsidiary of the Penn Central Transportation Company and had recently received considerable media coverage over its proposed development of a chain of thematic amusement parks. By 1968, GSC had two such parks in operation—one located in Georgia and the other in Texas. In

_____

* This case was prepared by Kenneth R. Ferris and John K. Shank from publicly available information. Copyright © 1984 by Kenneth R. Ferris and John K. Shank. All rights reserved to the authors. The situation is taken from an earlier Harvard College case, "Great Southwest Corporation" (9-172-042), written by John K. Shank.

1969, the company changed its corporate policy regarding these parks from one of "constructing and operating" to one of "constructing, operating, *and* selling."

In December of 1968, prior to the adoption of this new policy, GSC arranged the sale of its "Six Flags Over Georgia" park to a group of investors. The selling price of the amusement park was approximately $23 million, and the sale resulted in a gain of over $4.8 million. In its 1968 annual report, GSC reported the gain as an extraordinary item.

The sale of the park was financed by a $2 million down payment and a 30-year, nonrecourse, 7 percent note for $21 million. The note was payable in annual principal installments of $700,000 beginning in March 1975. Shortly after the transaction, the group of investors contributed the amusement park to a new limited partnership in which the Great Southwest Atlanta Corporation was the general partner. GSAC, a wholly owned subsidiary of GSC, became the exclusive operator of the "Six Flags Over Georgia" park.

"SIX FLAGS OVER TEXAS"

In June of 1969, GSC arranged the sale of its second thematic park, "Six Flags Over Texas." The amusement park, which had been carried on the books of GSC at a net book value of $9.3 million, was sold for $40 million to a group of 152 investors.

The sale was financed with a $1.7 million down payment and a 35-year, 6.5 percent note for $38.3 million. The note was secured by the park itself and called for a prepayment of $3.93 million, representing interest for the first three years. Beginning in 1972, payments of approximately $2.3 million (principal and interest) per year were to be made for the next 32 years. At the time of the sale, the prime rate of interest was approximately 8 percent.

Shortly after the sale was completed, the group of investors transferred title to the park to a limited partnership in which Six Flags Over Texas, Inc., a wholly owned subsidiary of GSC, was the general partner. SFOT, Inc. thus became the sole and exclusive manager of the amusement park. Under the terms of the new limited partnership agreement, any operating losses, depreciation and amortization charges, and tax credits would accrue to the 152 limited partners.

Because of the 1969 change in corporate policy regarding amusement parks, GSC treated the gain on the sale of the Texas park as an ordinary item. In addition, to establish consistency in the application of this accounting treatment, the gain from the prior year's sale of Six Flags Over Georgia was reclassified as an ordinary sale. This change in accounting practice resulted in a qualified auditor's opinion (see financial statements, Exhibits 1–4).

SHAREHOLDER LAWSUIT

In February of 1971, a group of GSC shareholders filed a $16 million lawsuit against the company. The suit alleged that GSC "misrepresented and failed to disclose adequately the nature and quality" of its 1969 net earnings. The class action suit claimed that approximately $29 million of the 1969 earnings resulted from the sale of the "Six Flags Over Texas" amusement park, and that the transaction should not have been accounted for as a sale in that payments resulting from the transaction were not due for several years.

As a consequence of the misrepresentation, the shareholders alleged that they failed to sell some 32,000 shares of GSC common stock in 1969 when the share price was approximately $44. During February of 1971, the shares traded as low as $2.60 per share.

QUESTIONS

1. Do you agree with the accounting treatment utilized by GSC to account for the sale of the "Six Flags Over Texas" amusement park? Substantiate your position.

2. Evaluate the quality of reported earnings and assets. Prepare a list of those items that concern you.

EXHIBIT 1

GREAT SOUTHWEST CORPORATION
Consolidated Balance Sheet
As of December 31, 1969, with Comparative Figures for 1968

Assets	1969	1968
Cash	$ 8,272,349	$ 4,720,519
Receivables (substantially pledged) (notes 1, 4, 7 and 16):		
Bulk land sales	71,513,937	70,145,376
Mortgages and notes receivable ($2,470,090 due in 1970)	77,952,950	30,542,463
Real estate sales ($585,678 due in 1970)	16,089,820	10,893,779
Joint ventures and other accounts	24,335,108	7,960,795
Total receivables	189,891,815	119,542,413
Prepaid expenses	1,586,658	435,488
Inventories, at the lower of cost (principally first-in or first-out) or market	2,494,283	680,584
Property held for resale (including development and carrying costs) at cost (substantially collateralized) (note 5)	104,152,531	81,953,607
Investment in joint ventures and unconsolidated subsidiary, at equity (notes 1 and 2)	13,421,806	14,681,522
Property, plant and equipment, at cost (notes 3, 5 and 7):		
Land and land improvements	6,110,532	6,214,225
Buildings	26,306,620	23,836,007
Operating plant and equipment	5,863,851	12,361,482
Construction in progress	3,932,891	3,077,850
	42,213,894	45,489,564
Less accumulated depreciation	6,100,745	8,850,747
Net property, plant and equipment	36,113,149	36,638,817
Deferred charges and other assets (partially pledged) (note 9)	7,582,176	3,154,058
Cost of acquired subsidiaries in excess of book value of related net assets (note 1)	28,921,304	16,661,109
	$392,436,071	$278,468,117

See accompanying notes to financial statements.

EXHIBIT 1 *(concluded)*

Liabilities and Stockholders' Equity	1969	1968
Accounts payable .... $	4,679,936	$ 5,710,813
Accrued liabilities (note 9)	4,783,693	4,164,235
Federal and state income taxes (note 8):		
Current	5,937,552	2,671,104
Deferred	24,618,364	13,215,043
Due to parent company (note 11)	—	13,916,084
Bonds, mortgages and similar debt ($38,350,654 current) (note 5)	113,721,538	93,665,818
6% subordinated convertible notes (note 6)	696,000	1,686,000
Other notes payable ($41,473,949 current) (note 7)	62,954,979	25,873,932
Deferred interest ($13,108,748) and other credits	17,330,108	16,443,690
Stockholders' equity (notes 11 and 12):		
Cumulative preferred stock, $1 par value (note 10):		
Voting	23,743,449	31,895,950
Nonvoting	5,000,000	5,000,000
Preferred stock, $10 par value:		
Voting; 20,000,000 shares authorized, none issued ..	—	—
Nonvoting; 10,000,000 shares authorized, none issued	—	—
Common stock, $.10 par value. Authorized 100,000,000 shares; issued 27,993,136 (notes 5, 6 and 13)	2,799,314	1,801,053
Capital surplus (notes 11 and 13)	55,951,484	22,724,638
Retained earnings (notes 5 and 8)	70,219,654	39,699,757
Total stockholders' equity	157,713,901	101,121,398
Commitments and contingent liabilities (notes 8, 12 and 15)	$392,436,071	$278,468,117

EXHIBIT 2

·GREAT SOUTHWEST CORPORATION
Statement of Consolidated Earnings
For the Year Ended December 31, 1969,
With Comparative Figures for 1968

	1969	1968 (notes 8 and 16)
Sales	**$120,667,714**	$104,826,910
Operating revenues	**12,949,517**	23,405,206
Net earnings from joint ventures	**1,900,239**	2,381,544
Interest income	**8,088,472**	2,420,827
Other income	**632,500**	319,717
	144,238,442	133,354,204
Cost and expenses:		
Cost of sales and selling expenses	**66,162,967**	72,008,710
Operating expenses	**7,919,494**	15,078,374
General and administrative expenses	**11,113,524**	5,821,350
Depreciation (notes 3 and 18)	**1,829,749**	3,603,878
Interest and debt expense	**5,669,334**	3,880,267
	92,695,068	100,392,579
Earnings before income taxes and extraordinary item	**51,543,374**	32,961,625
Federal and state income taxes (note 8):		
Current	**5,844,400**	2,913,030
Deferred	**11,335,481**	4,486,150
	17,179,881	7,399,180
Earnings before extraordinary item	**34,363,493**	25,562,445
Extraordinary Item	**—**	1,862,500
Net earnings	**$ 34,363,493**	$ 27,424,945
Earnings per share of common stock (notes 12 and 17):		
Earnings before extraordinary item	**$1.08**	$0.81
Extraordinary item	**—**	.06
Net earnings	**$1.08**	$0.87

See accompanying notes to financial statements.

EXHIBIT 3

Notes to Financial Statements, December 31, 1969

(1) General

The consolidated financial statements are comprised of the accounts of Great Southwest Corporation and Subsidiaries, except for a mortgage finance company formed in 1968. The accounts of this subsidiary are not material and the investment in the subsidiary is carried at equity. All significant intercompany transactions have been eliminated.

On December 19, 1969 the Company purchased all of the outstanding stock of Richardson Homes Corporation for $15,378,500. The purchase price may be increased by an additional $5,000,000 contingent upon the amount of net earnings of Richardson Homes

EXHIBIT 3 *(continued)*

Corporation over a four year period commencing January 1, 1970. The Company has placed in escrow notes receivable totaling $5,021,600 at December 31, 1969 as security for this contingent payment. The excess of the purchase price over net assets of Richardson Homes Corporation, $12,247,123, has been included as "cost of acquired subsidiaries in excess of book value of related net assets" in the consolidated balance sheet.

The cost of acquired subsidiaries in excess of book value of related net assets at dates of acquisition is considered by management to have continuing value and is not being amortized.

Net assets of subsidiaries exceeded Great Southwest's investments in the subsidiaries by $50,212,439 which excess is included in the consolidated financial statements as retained earnings.

(2) Investment in joint ventures and unconsolidated subsidiary

The total assets and liabilities of various real estate joint ventures at December 31, 1969 and the Company's equity therein and in the unconsolidated subsidiary are summarized below:

Assets	Total	Company's equity
Joint ventures:		
Cash	$ 426,049	314,809
Receivables from real estate sales ($74,549 of the Company's equity due within one year)	11,758,009	9,225,373
Reserve for discounts	(226,829)	(172,475)
Real estate held for sale or investment, at cost	70,232,951	36,382,380
Land, buildings and equipment held for investment, at cost	8,482,302	316,869
Other assets	7,003,030	1,773,928
Total assets	$ 97,675,512	47,840,884

Liabilities		
Bank loans payable	$ 279,594	164,191
Other loans payable	3,147,674	3,134,111
Accounts payable and accruals	7,014,274	5,864,195
Real estate loans	33,490,047	24,698,036
Deferred income	551,765	524,451
Other liabilities	495,035	296,292
Total liabilities	44,978,389	34,681,276
Net assets and equity—joint ventures	$ 52,697,123	13,159,608
Equity in unconsolidated subsidiary		262,198
		$ 13,421,806

(3) Property, plant and equipment

Depreciation is provided on the straight-line basis over the estimated useful lives of the respective classes of property, plant and equipment as follows: buildings, 2½% to 10%; land improvements, 5% to 10%; operating equipment, 5% to 33⅓%.

(4) Receivables

Receivables from bulk land sales are comprised of the following:

EXHIBIT 3 *(continued)*

	Interest rate	Principal payments begin	Maturity	Balance
Note due in annual payments of $5,286,277 to $6,929,231	7%	1984	1988	$30,400,000
Note due in annual payments of $500,000 (principal or interest as designated by maker), principal amount $12,010,536 less reduction to recognize prior liens	7%	1970	1977	8,010,536
Land sale contract due in semi-annual payments of $478,750	9%	1971	1978	7,660,000
Land sale contract due in annual payments of $1,000,000 to $2,221,269	7½%	1971	1974	5,221,269
Other notes and contracts	5.45 to 9%	1970	1979	20,222,132
				$71,513,937

Mortgages and notes receivable are comprised of the following:

	Interest rate	Principal payments begin	Maturity	Balance
Note due in annual instalments of $700,000, secured by amusement park known as Six Flags Over Georgia	7%	1975	2004	$20,599,500
Note due in annual instalments of $1,094,331, secured by amusement park known as Six Flags Over Texas	6½%	1971	2005	38,301,585
Other notes	None to 9½%	Various	Various	19,051,865
				$77,952,950

Receivables from real estate sales are secured by second trust deeds and conditional sales contracts, and are stated net of reserve for losses from home sales of $555,848.

(5) Bonds, mortgages and similar debt
Bonds, mortgages and similar debt are summarized below:

	Total	Current instalments
$4,600,000 of 9½% General Mortgage Bonds, due in 1976, and $2,500,000 of 9½% General Mortgage Bonds due March 1, 1977, secured by certain land, property and equipment	$ 7,100,000	600,000
Mortgage loans secured by certain land and buildings, with interest at 4⅞% to 12%, payable in varying instalments to 1999	106,621,538	37,750,654
	$113,721,538	38,350,654

The Company is required to make annual payments of $600,000 through February 1, 1975 to a sinking fund for the redemption of the General Mortgage Bonds due in 1976. While conditional payments may be required upon the sale of property, no such pay-

EXHIBIT 3 *(continued)*

ments were required as a result of property sales to December 31, 1969. The bond indenture contains restrictions with respect to cash dividends and acquisition or retirement of capital stock. These restrictions were not operative at December 31, 1969.

In connection with the sale of its General Mortgage Bonds, the Company sold Warrants to purchase, at $2.20 per share, 2,102,110 shares of its common stock. These outstanding, Warrants are exercisable at any time to March 1, 1977, and were purchased by Pennsylvania Company (parent company) from the holder of the General Mortgage Bonds.

(6) Subordinated convertible notes

The Subordinated Convertible Notes may be converted on any date before June 1, 1971 into common stock of the Company at the conversion price of $1.90 per share. During 1969, notes in the amount of $990,000 were exchanged for 521,046 shares of the Company's common stock. At December 31, 1969, 366,314 shares of the Company's common stock were reserved for conversion of the notes.

(7) Other notes payable

Other notes payable are summarized as follows:

	Total	Current instalments
Long-term notes:		
Banks:		
Furniture and equipment loans with interest from 7½% to 9½%	$ 1,121,286	346,899
Advance on an $18,000,000 construction loan, payable on October 1, 1971, secured by real estate and improvements known as Six Flags Over Mid-America and a mortgage note receivable, which note is secured by Six Flags Over Texas in the amount of $38,301,585	2,048,871	—
	3,170,157	346,899
Others:		
7% notes, secured by stock of a subsidiary, payable in monthly instalments of approximately $80,000	5,786,654	951,231
7% unsecured notes, payable in quarterly instalments of approximately $63,000	1,156,765	251,127
Note payable, secured by certain mortgage notes receivable, interest 4¾% over prime rate, payable as collections are made on pledged notes	1,342,788	131,625
6% unsecured notes, payable to Penn Central Transportation Company Plan for Supplemental Pensions in equal annual instalments beginning August 1, 1970 through 1986	2,500,000	147,058
10% note payable due in 1972, secured by a pledge of a $30,400,000 bulk land sale receivable	7,500,000	—
Various other long-term notes	2,253,927	401,321
	20,540,134	1,882,362
Total long-term notes	23,710,291	2,229,261

EXHIBIT 3 *(continued)*

Short-term notes:
  Banks:

8½% to 11¼% notes payable to banks secured by certain receivables and property, due at various dates to July 1, 1970	**13,700,000**	13,700,000
Unsecured notes payable to banks, with interest from 8½% to 9½%	**10,800,000**	10,800,000
Unsecured note payable to bank, with interest at ½% over prime rate	**6,000,000**	6,000,000
Unsecured note payable to bank, with interest at 13%	**1,000,000**	1,000,000
	31,500,000	31,500,000
Others:		
Note payable, secured by certain real estate receivables, with interest at 4% above prime rate	**2,000,000**	2,000,000
8½% unsecured notes due April 1970	**1,000,000**	1,000,000
12¼% unsecured note due December 1970	**3,017,079**	3,017,079
Various other short-term notes	**1,727,609**	1,727,609
	7,744,688	7,744,688
Total short-term notes	**39,244,688**	39,244,688
	$ 62,954,979	41,473,949

(8) Federal and state income taxes

The Company is a majority-owned subsidiary of Pennsylvania Company (which, in turn, is a subsidiary of Penn Central Transportation Company) and, for Federal income tax purposes, includes its operations as a part of a consolidated return. In 1968, the Company entered into an income tax allocation agreement with Penn Central Transportation Company wherein a charge is made in lieu of Federal income taxes, equal to 95% of the tax which would be due if the Company's operations were reported in a separate return. Macco Corporation and Subsidiaries were not subject to the tax allocation agreement until March 21, 1969, the date of the merger with Great Southwest Corporation.

Subsequent to the date that the Company's annual report for the year ended December 31, 1968 was submitted to the shareholders, but prior to the date of filing the Federal income tax return for such year, management of the Company changed its election with respect to the reporting of income on certain sales of Macco Corporation and its subsidiaries. As a result of this change, income which the Company had previously intended to report on the instalment basis for tax purposes was all reported in 1968 taxable income. Accordingly, deferred taxes were decreased and net earnings for 1968 were increased by $7,436,508 ($.25 per share) over amounts previously reported.

The Federal income tax returns of certain subsidiaries for periods through September 30, 1965 are currently being examined by the Internal Revenue Service. In the opinion of management, the effect of possible deficiencies, if any, which may result from such examination will not be material.

Earnings before income taxes include substantial amounts which are taxed at capital gains rates.

(9) Deferred charge

Under the terms of a settlement agreement dated January 1, 1969 the Company paid $3,000,000 to an officer in July and August 1969. The unamortized balance at Decem-

EXHBIT 3 *(continued)*

ber 31, 1969, $2,250,000, is included in deferred charges and other assets and is being amortized over a four-year period which ends December 31, 1972. Of the amount paid, $1,500,000 will be forfeited if the officer resigns prior to January 1, 1972. As security for this obligation the officer has pledged 70,000 shares of the Company's common stock owned by him.

Settlement agreements with two other officers of the Company and one officer of a subsidiary obligate the Company to pay up to $4,000,000 in ten equal annual instalments to these persons, if they remain in the employ of the Company or subsidiary until after December 31, 1972. The liability (discounted at the rate of 8½% per annum) relating to these settlement agreements has been accrued in the accompanying balance sheet.

(10) Preferred stock

Cumulative preferred stock at December 31, 1969 is summarized as follows:

	Number of shares issued	Amount
Voting—authorized 130,000,000 shares:		
Series A 6%	3,500,000	$ 3,500,000
Series B 7%	3,650,000	3,650,000
Series C 7.6%	16,410,980	16,410,980
Series E 8.4%	182,469	182,469
Total voting	23,743,449	$ 23,743,449
Nonvoting—authorized 20,000,000 shares:		
Series A Senior 6½%—5,000,000 shares	3,000,000	$ 3,000,000
Series B Senior 7%	2,000,000	2,000,000
Total nonvoting	5,000,000	$ 5,000,000

Shares of the voting Series A, B and C Cumulative Preferred Stock are callable at any time at $1.20 per share plus accrued dividends. In the event of involuntary or voluntary liquidation, holders of such shares are entitled to $1.00 or $1.20, respectively, plus accrued dividends. The Company is obligated to make annual contributions to a sinking fund sufficient to retire 33⅓% of the maximum number of shares of Series E Cumulative Preferred Stock outstanding at $1.40 per share plus accrued dividends. During 1969, 91,551 such shares were retired. In the event of voluntary or involuntary liquidation, holders of the Series E Cumulative Preferred Stock are entitled to $1.40 per share plus accrued dividends.

The various classes of voting Preferred Stock have equal voting rights with common stock. Except as specifically set forth in the Articles of Incorporation or as provided by law, holders of nonvoting shares shall not have the right to vote.

Beginning November 1, 1971, the Company shall redeem annually at par, plus accrued dividends, 5% of the total number of shares of Series A Senior 6½% Cumulative Preferred Stock issued prior to that date (after deducting therefrom the number of shares, if any, theretofore redeemed at the option of the Company) until all such stock is retired. In addition, the Company has the option to redeem all or part of the outstanding shares beginning November 1, 1972 at prices ranging from $1.05 per share on that date to $1.00 per share on November 1, 1992. The holders of Series A Senior 6½% Cumulative Preferred Stock are entitled to $1.00 per share plus accrued dividends in the event of voluntary or involuntary liquidation.

Holders of Series B Senior 7% Cumulative Preferred Stock (nonvoting) are entitled to the same distribution in the case of involuntary liquidation as the holders of Series A Senior 6½% Cumulative Preferred Stock. The Company has the option to redeem at any time all or part of the outstanding shares of Series B 7% Senior Preferred Stock at prices ranging from $1.10 per share if prior to May 1, 1978, to $1.00 per share if after

EXHIBIT 3 *(continued)*

April 30, 1992. These prices also apply in the case of voluntary liquidation. Beginning April 30, 1972, the Company shall redeem, at par plus accrued dividends, 100,000 shares annually (after deducting therefrom the number of shares, if any, theretofore redeemed at the option of the Company).

(11) Capital stock

In April 1969, the shareholders approved a 10 for 1 stock split and authorized 10,000,000 shares of a class of nonvoting preferred stock, $10 par value per share and 20,000,000 shares of a class of voting preferred stock, $10 par value per share. Shares of $10 Voting Preferred Stock and $10 Nonvoting Preferred Stock may be issued from time to time in one or more series, each such series to have such designation and such relative rights, preferences, qualifications, limitations and restrictions as shall be fixed and determined by resolution adopted by the Board of Directors.

In December 1969, the Company issued 1,400,610 shares of common stock to Pennsylvania Company in consideration of the cancellation of debt aggregating $25,210,978. The excess of market value over the par value of common stock issued, $25,070,917, has been credited to capital surplus.

(12) Acquisition subsequent to December 31, 1969

In January 1970, the Company issued 933,333 shares of its common stock for all the capital stock of I. C. Deal Companies, Inc. The Company intends to record the transaction on a pooling of interest basis. The accounts applicable to the acquired company are not included in the accompanying financial statements because audited financial statements of I. C. Deal are not presently available.

Management of the Company believes the transaction will not have a material effect on financial position as of December 31, 1969 or results of operations for 1969 or 1968. Earnings per share amounts for 1968 and 1969 have been computed as though these shares were outstanding at the beginning of each year.

(13) Stock option plan

At December 31, 1969, 300,000 shares of the Company's common stock were reserved for issuance to key employees through a qualified stock option plan. On February 24, 1969 an option was granted to the president of the Company for 160,000 shares at $15.60 per share, an aggregate of $2,496,000, which was the market value on that date. On June 16, 1969, options were granted for 112,000 shares at $30 per share, an aggregate of $3,360,000, which was the market value on that date. On September 23, 1969, options were granted for 28,000 shares at $23.75 per share, an aggregate of $665,000, which was the market value on that date. During 1969, options became exercisable for 40,000 shares at $15.60 per share, an aggregate of $624,000; 28,000 shares at $30 per share, an aggregate of $840,000; and 7,000 shares at $23.75 per share, an aggregate of $166,250. The options are exercisable 25% each year beginning on the date granted and expire five years after the date of grant. No options were exercised during the year ended December 31, 1969.

On February 26, 1970, the Board of Directors authorized the cancellation of the $30 and $23.75 options. The Board also issued options for 140,000 shares at the market price on that day.

In 1959 the Company adopted a restricted stock option plan under which 1,000,000 shares of common stock were reserved for granting to key employees. During 1968, 170,000 shares were exercised at $1.045 per share, an aggregate of $177,650. The market values at the dates exercised were $7.50 (as to 90,000 shares) and $11.20 (as to 80,000 shares) per share, an aggregate of $1,571,000. This plan has been superseded by the qualified plan adopted in 1969.

The Company accounts for stock options at the date exercised by crediting common stock for the par value of shares issued and crediting capital surplus for the excess of the option price over the par value.

EXHIBIT 3 *(continued)*

(14) Retirement plan
The Company and certain of its subsidiaries have a trusteed pension plan covering certain employees. The Company's policy is to fund pension cost accrued. The unfunded past service cost of the plan was approximately $266,000 at January 1, 1969 and is being amortized over a thirty-year period. Retirement plan expense, including prior service cost, for 1969 was insignificant.

(15) Commitments and contingent liabilities
Annual rentals applicable to long-term leases in effect at December 31, 1969 approximate $2,000,000 through 1975 and $1,000,000 thereafter through 2031.

The Company or its subsidiaries have guaranteed certain obligations of other parties aggregating approximately $8,650,000.

(16) Sale of amusement parks
On December 31, 1968, Great Southwest Atlanta Corp., a subsidiary of the Company, sold all of the property and equipment of Six Flags Over Georgia, an amusement park, for $22,980,157 resulting in a net gain of $4,813,400. Upon completion of the sale, the purchaser, Six Flags Fund, Ltd., contributed the amusement park to a limited partnership in which Great Southwest Atlanta Corp. is the General Partner and operator. As partial consideration for the sale, Great Southwest Atlanta Corp., received a 7% mortgage note in the original amount of $21,000,000 which is secured by the amusement park. The note is payable in annual principal instalments of $700,000 beginning in March 1975 and is subject to optional prepayments without penalty.

On June 30, 1969, Great Southwest Corporation sold all of the property and equipment of Six Flags Over Texas, an amusement park, for $40,000,000 resulting in a net gain of $17,530,170. Upon completion of the sale, the purchaser, Six Flags Over Texas Fund, Ltd., contributed the amusement park to a limited partnership in which Six Flags Over Texas, Inc., a wholly-owned subsidiary of Great Southwest Corporation, is the General Partner and operator. As partial consideration for the sale, the Company received a 6½% mortgage note in the amount of $38,301,585 which is secured by the amusement park. The note is payable in annual principal instalments of $1,094,331 beginning in March 1971 and is subject to optional prepayments without penalty.

Subsequent to the sale of Six Flags Over Georgia, the Company changed its policy toward amusement parks from one of constructing and operating such parks to one of constructing, developing, selling and operating such parks. Accordingly, the sale of the amusement park known as Six Flags Over Georgia in 1968 has been reclassified from amounts previously reported to reflect the transaction as an ordinary sale rather than as an extraordinary item.

(17) Earnings per common share
Earnings per common share were computed by dividing earnings on which per share amounts are based by the weighted average number of shares of common stock and common equivalent shares outstanding during the year after giving retroactive effect to the ten-for-one stock split in April 1969. The 6% Subordinated Convertible Notes have been considered to be the equivalent of common stock from the time of their issuance and shares issuable on conversion have been added to the number of common shares outstanding. The number of common shares was also increased by the number of shares issuable on the exercise of warrants and options and reduced by the number of common shares which are assumed to have been purchased with the proceeds from the exercise of the warrants and options.

(18) Supplementary profit and loss information
Following is a summary of supplementary profit and loss information (charged directly to profit and loss as expenses) for the two years ended December 31, 1969:

EXHIBIT 3 *(concluded)*

	1969	1968
Maintenance and repairs .... $	1,045,213	$ 1,247,323
Taxes, other than on income	596,958	1,393,597
Rents	682,389	598,001
Management and service contract fee	19,350	19,800

No royalties have been paid.

In addition to depreciation shown separately in the statement of consolidated earnings, immaterial amounts were charged to clearing accounts and subsequently apportioned to land held for resale.

EXHIBIT 4
Auditor's Opinion

THE BOARD OF DIRECTORS
GREAT SOUTHWEST CORPORATION:

We have examined the consolidated balance sheet of Great Southwest Corporation and consolidated subsidiaries as of December 31, 1969 and the related statements of earnings and stockholders' equity for the year then ended. Our examination was made in accordance with generally accepted auditing standards, and accordingly included such tests of the accounting records and such other auditing procedures we considered necessary in the circumstances.

In our opinion, the accompanying consolidated balance sheet and statements of consolidated earnings and stockholders' equity present fairly the consolidated financial position of Great Southwest Corporation and consolidated subsidiaries at December 31, 1969 and the results of their operations and the changes in stockholders' equity for the year then ended, in conformity with generally accepted accounting principles which, except for the changes (which we approve) in income tax allocation (note 8), and in accounting for the sales of amusement parks (note 16), have been applied on a basis consistent with that of the preceding year after giving retroactive effect to the above-mentioned changes in accounting.

Peat, Marwick, Mitchell & Co.

March 6, 1970

Crime Control, Inc.*

> Sales and marketing prowess may well account for the rapid growth in Crime Control's customer base; however, another wholly distinct talent is responsible for the sharp rise in its operating results—namely an ability to devise creative tax and accounting strategies. (*Barron's,* November 15, 1982.)

In early 1970, James Bowman began selling and installing electronic security systems using his garage in Indianapolis, Indiana, as his office. On the other side of town, Donald Gray had begun a similar business. In 1977, the two men merged their operations and formed a Subchapter S corporation.[1] The new venture was called Crime Control, Inc.

At the time of the merger, the newly formed company had 500 customers and nearly $100,000 in receivables. Over the next five years, the company would experience tremendous growth, attracting over 12,000 customers and attaining a level of over $50 million in receivables. In January 1982, Crime Control, Inc. went public issuing 725,000 common shares at a price of $10 per share; 10 months later the stock was trading at over $20 per share.

BACKGROUND

Crime Control, Inc. designs, markets, installs, services, and monitors electronic security systems used primarily by businesses. The company pioneered the concept of providing monitoring services from a centralized location, thereby eliminating the costly use of branch offices and on-site security personnel. Upon receiving an alarm signal at one of its computerized monitoring stations, company personnel notify appropriate fire or police officials, as well as the customer (see Exhibit 1). The company's systems are used to monitor for such conditions as medical emergency, electric power interruptions, freezer temperature suitability, water pressure adequacy, and environmental temperature levels, in addition to burglary and fire.

Recent operations had demonstrated substantial opportunities for growth. Sales grew from $686,000 in 1978 to over $5.8 million in 1980, with projected sales in

---

* This case was prepared by Kenneth R. Ferris and Ann Gunn. Copyright © 1985 by Kenneth R. Ferris. All rights reserved to the authors.

[1] A "Subchapter S" corporation is a tax-option corporation which has elected, by unanimous consent of its shareholders, not to pay any corporate tax on its income and, instead, to have its shareholders pay taxes on its income even though such income may not be distributed. Subchapter S corporations are limited to 10 or fewer shareholders.

EXHIBIT 1
Alarm Monitoring Centers

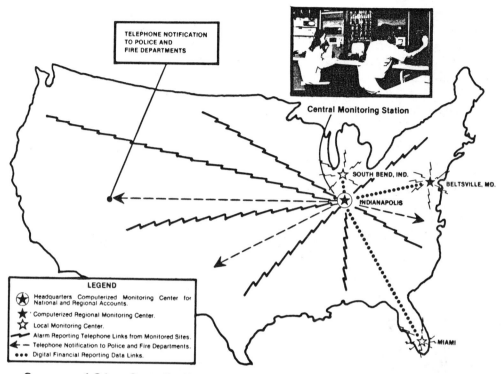

Coverage of Crime Control's Alarm Monitoring Centers. National accounts with sites in 48 states are monitored from the company's Indianapolis headquarters.

excess of $14 million for 1981. Similarly, earnings grew from $97,000 in 1978 to nearly $1.0 million in 1980, with 1981 projections of $1.4 million.

Much of the company's recent growth was attributable to the unprecedented rise in crime in the United States. From 1971 to 1980, violent crimes increased by 60 percent and property crimes by 54 percent. Another factor, however, had been the acquisition of other monitoring alarm companies, thus offering rapid entry into new geographic areas. According to the company's prospectus, "Management believes that because of the historical fragmentation of much of the protective service industry, suitable opportunities exist for making acquisitions on an economically attractive basis." During the period 1978–80, Crime Control, Inc. acquired the assets and customer lists of eight companies in the central station alarm business. The company's growth strategy also emphasized the conversion of acquired companies' subscribers to longer-term lease agreements; such conversions resulted in increased lease revenue.

LEASING AND FINANCING POLICIES

Approximately 80 percent of the company's security systems are leased to customers, which is normal practice in the industry. The remaining systems are sold outright, typically for installation in private residences or governmental agencies. Unlike most of its competitors, Crime Control normally requires customers' leasing systems to enter into a lease contract with a term of at least five years, with a bargain renewal option for at least one additional three-year period. The "bargain rate" for the renewal period is guaranteed to be at least 10 percent less than the rental rate in effect at the end of the preceding lease term. The estimated useful life of the security system is normally 10 years.

Crime Control accounts for its equipment leases as "sales-type" leases under the "capital lease" method of accounting. From the standpoint of the lessor, sales-type leases are installment sales. Under *FASB Statement No. 13*, a sales-type lease is characterized by the earning of a manufacturer's or dealer's profit (or loss). To be classified as a sales-type lease, the lease must meet several criteria at its inception: (1) collectibility of the minimum lease payments is reasonably predictable and (2) no important uncertainties exist regarding the cost to be incurred by the lessor under the terms of the lease. In addition, however, such leases must also satisfy one or more of the following criteria, which define a "capital lease":

1. The lease transfers ownership of the property to the lessee.
2. The lease contains a bargain purchase option.
3. The lease term is equal to or greater than 75 percent of the estimated economic life of the leased asset.
4. The present value of the minimum lease payments, excluding such executory costs as insurance, maintenance, and taxes, equals or exceeds 90 percent of the fair market value of the leased asset.

If the above criteria are satisfied, *FASB Statement No. 13* permits the lessor to record the lease agreement as a sale, at the present value of the future minimum lease payments.

According to the company's prospectus for its public offering:

> At the inception of each lease the Company records as income from the "lease sale" the present value of the equipment portion of the rentals during the initial term and the bargain renewal term (an aggregate of eight years). This is calculated by aggregating the present value of the 96 monthly rent installments (net of estimated cost of servicing and monitoring), each discounted at the rate implicit in the lease (which normally approximates 2 percent over the prevailing prime rate as of the inception of the lease). Once the present value is recognized as revenue, the amount recorded is unaffected by any subsequent change in the prime rate. The balance of the payments under the lease contract (net of servicing and monitoring costs) not immediately recognized is recorded as unearned interest. The portion of the payments representing income for monitoring and servicing the system is reported as revenue earned over the term of the lease contract. All direct costs of the system, including cost of goods sold and selling and installation expenses (but excluding financial costs), are expensed at the time of reporting the lease sale.

Leases that are not converted to long-term lease contracts are recorded under the operating lease method of accounting, in which rental payments are reported as income when earned and costs are expensed as incurred.

Exhibit 2 illustrates the impact (before expenses) of a sales-type lease transaction.

CUSTOMER BASE

The majority of the company's customers are small commercial enterprises, whose insurance companies typically require that they have an operating alarm system in

EXHIBIT 2
Crime Control, Inc.—Sales-type Lease

Assumptions: $600 installation fee; $60 monthly lease payment of which $10 per month is allocated to the executory costs of service and monitoring; 96-month lease term (initial 60-month term plus 36-month bargain renewal period); a residual value of the leased property of $100; implicit interest rate of 15 percent.

Balance sheet (impact at lease inception):

Cash (installation fee)			$ 600
Total minimum lease payments receivable (96 months at $60 per month)	$5,760		
Amounts allocated to service and monitoring (96 months at $10 per month)	(960)		
Minimum lease payments receivable.	4,800		
Allowance for doubtful accounts (1 percent of the total minimum lease payments receivable	(58)		
Net minimum lease payments receivable		$4,742	
Estimated residual value of lease property		100	
Unearned interest income:			
Equipment portion	(1,979)		
Residual value portion.	(70)		
		(2,049)	
Net investment in sales-type lease.			2,793
Addition to assets before expenses*.			$3,393

Income statement (impact at least inception):

Installation fee		$ 600	
Present value of $4,800 minimum lease payments		2,821	
Equipment sales-lease.			$3,421
Reduction of cost of equipment sold (present value of the $100 residual value of leased property)			30
Provision for doubtful accounts.			(58)
Income before expenses*			$3,393

* If the implicit interest rate had been 19 percent, the Addition to Assets and Income before Expenses would have been $2,862, a 16 percent reduction caused by a 4 percent increase in the implicit rate.

---

order to maintain burglary insurance coverage. Crime Control is, however, dependent on several major customers. As of November 30, 1981, the eight largest national accounts were:

Customer Name	Number of Locations	Number of States Represented
Radio Shack	1,300	47
The Wickes Corporation	255	36
Peoples Drug Store, Inc.	201	9
Church's Fried Chicken.	55	3
Eighty Four Lumber Co.	51	14
Fleenor Auto Stores, Inc.	49	3
High's Dairy, Inc.	36	3
Xerox Corporation.	22	10

For the first nine months of 1981, Radio Shack and Peoples Drug Stores, Inc. represented 32 and 13 percent, respectively, of the company's total lease sales, or an aggregate of 45 percent of total lease sales.

The financial statements shown in Exhibits 3–8 and the accompanying footnotes

EXHIBIT 3
Report of Independent Certified Public Accountants

Board of Directors and Shareholders
Crime Control, Inc.
Indianapolis, Indiana

We have examined the balance sheets of Crime Control, Inc., as of September 30, 1981 and December 31, 1980 and 1979, and the related statements of income, changes in shareholders' equity and changes in financial position for the nine month period ended September 30, 1981 and for each of the three years in the period ended December 31, 1980. Our examinations were made in accordance with generally accepted auditing standards and, accordingly, included such tests of the accounting records and such other auditing procedures as we considered necessary in the circumstances.

In our opinion, the financial statements referred to above present fairly the financial position of Crime Control, Inc., at September 30, 1981 and December 31, 1980 and 1979, and the results of its operations and changes in its financial position for the nine month period ended September 30, 1981 and for each of the three years in the period ended December 31, 1980, in conformity with generally accepted accounting principles applied on a consistent basis, after restatement for the changes, with which we concur, described in Note 2 to the financial statements.

COOPERS & LYBRAND

Indianapolis, Indiana
December 14, 1981, except as to Note 12 the date
   of which is January 25, 1982

EXHIBIT 4

CRIME CONTROL, INC.
Balance Sheets
At September 30, 1981, and December 31, 1980, and 1979

	December 31,		September 30,
	1979	1980	1981
ASSETS			
Cash and cash investments (Note 5)	$ 506,744	$ 1,045,999	$ 389,627
Net investment in sales-type leases (Notes 1, 4 and 7)	2,231,338	5,591,852	10,205,948
Accounts receivable (Note 1)	128,079	465,321	789,820
Inventory (Notes 1 and 7)	234,108	374,689	888,306
Property and equipment, net of accumulated depreciation (Notes 1, 6 and 7)	294,729	881,534	1,634,583
Purchased rights to customer lists, net of accumulated amortization (Notes 1 and 3)	238,864	1,405,727	2,423,995
Other assets	75,314	12,192	66,486
	$3,709,176	$9,777,314	$16,398,765
LIABILITIES			
Accounts payable...	$ 30,945	$ 341,972	$ 849,404
Accrued wages, taxes and other	132,422	202,263	595,717
Notes payable (Note 7)	2,491,047	6,529,007	11,587,632
Total liabilities	2,654,414	7,073,242	13,032,753
SHAREHOLDERS' EQUITY			
Common stock, no par value, 1,000 shares authorized, issued and outstanding (Note 10)	11,160	11,160	11,160
Additional paid-in capital	618,654	1,418,654	1,418,654
Retained earnings (Notes 7 and 10)	424,948	1,274,258	1,936,198
Total shareholders' equity.........................	1,054,762	2,704,072	3,366,012
	$3,709,176	$9,777,314	$16,398,765

The accompanying notes are an integral part of the financial statements.

EXHIBIT 5

CRIME CONTROL, INC.
Statements of Income
For the Nine-Month Periods Ended September 30, 1980 (unaudited), and 1981,
And for Each of the Three Years in the Period Ended December 31, 1980

	Years Ended December 31,			Nine Months Ended September 30,	
	1978	1979	1980	1980	1981
				(unaudited)	
Revenues:					
Equipment sales—lease	$485,986	$2,381,444	$4,354,852	$2,224,922	$5,640,449
Equipment sales—direct	125,581	127,835	342,449	146,096	762,106
Service and monitoring fees	58,340	217,338	594,234	223,444	1,378,199
Interest earned on leases	15,724	146,387	524,311	344,854	1,010,904
Other	—	9,742	22,270	11,076	21,319
	685,631	2,882,746	5,838,116	2,950,392	8,812,977
Expenses:					
Cost of equipment sold	143,344	374,792	878,199	590,677	1,612,086
Salaries and wages	212,503	858,722	1,219,014	693,908	2,551,203
Administrative and general	101,916	485,445	1,067,107	669,928	1,690,637
Provision for doubtful accounts	—	40,000	110,680	48,750	319,468
Taxes, other than income taxes	20,221	42,698	78,326	43,069	208,526
Interest	12,302	119,124	566,091	329,442	1,181,663
Depreciation	14,870	51,393	136,531	127,598	181,343
Amortization of purchased rights to customer lists	21,200	42,899	132,858	49,083	406,111
	526,356	2,015,073	4,188,806	2,552,455	8,151,037
Income before provision for income tax	159,275	867,673	1,649,310	397,937	661,940
Provision for income tax—deferred (Note 1)	62,000	—	—	—	. .
Net income	97,275	867,673	1,649,310	397,937	661,940
Provision for income tax—pro forma (Note 1)	—	359,000	723,000	175,000	260,000
Pro forma net income	$ 97,275	$ 508,673	$ 926,310	$ 222,937	$ 401,940
Pro forma net income per share	$ .05	$ .25	$ .46	$ .11	$ .20

The accompanying notes are an integral part of the financial statements.

appeared as part of the prospectus for the 1982 public offering of Crime Control, Inc.

QUESTIONS

1. Evaluate Crime Control's method of accounting for its security system leases. Describe the impact of this accounting policy on the financial statements. Do you agree with the company's approach?

2. Evaluate the impact of the lease accounting method on the company's cash flows. Restate the income statement for 1981 assuming that security system leases were accounted for using the "operating lease" accounting method.

EXHIBIT 6

CRIME CONTROL, INC.
Statements of Changes in Shareholders' Equity
For the Nine-Month Periods Ended September 30, 1980 (unaudited), and 1981,
And for Each of the Three Years in the Period Ended December 31, 1980

	Common Stock		Additional Paid-In Capital	Retained Earnings
	Shares Issued	Amount		
Year ended December 31, 1978:				
Shares issued (Note 1)	1,000	$11,160	$ 16,654	$ —
Net income	—	—	—	97,275
Balance at December 31, 1978	1,000	11,160	16,654	97,275
Year ended December 31, 1979:				
Deferred income taxes eliminated	—	—	62,000	—
Cash dividends paid	—	—	—	(540,000)
Contribution by shareholders	—	—	540,000	—
Net income	—	—	—	867,673
Balance at December 31, 1979	1,000	11,160	618,654	424,948
Year ended December 31, 1980:				
Cash dividends paid	—	—	—	(800,000)
Contribution by shareholders	—	—	800,000	—
Net income	—	—	—	1,649,310
Balance at December 31, 1980	1,000	11,160	1,418,654	1,274,258
Nine months ended September 30, 1981:				
Net income for the period	—	—	—	661,940
Balance at September 30, 1981 (Note 10)	1,000	$11,160	$1,418,654	$1,936,198
Nine months ended September 30, 1980 (unaudited):				
Net income for the period	—	$ —	$ —	$ 397,937
Balance at September 30, 1980 (unaudited)	1,000	$11,160	$ 618,654	$ 822,885

The accompanying notes are an integral part of the financial statements.

EXHIBIT 7

CRIME CONTROL, INC.
Statements of Changes in Financial Position
For the Nine-Month Periods Ended September 30, 1980 (unaudited), and 1981,
And for Each of the Three Years in the Period Ended December 31, 1980

	Years Ended December 31,			Nine Months Ended September 30,	
	1978	1979	1980	1980	1981
				(unaudited)	
Source of funds:					
Net income	$ 97,275	$ 867,673	$1,649,310	$ 397,937	$ 661,940
Items not requiring (providing) funds in the current period:					
Increase in sales-type leases	(373,829)	(1,897,509)	(3,471,194)	(1,797,684)	(4,933,564)
Provision for doubtful accounts	—	40,000	110,680	48,750	319,468
Depreciation and amortization	36,070	94,292	269,389	176,681	587,454
Loss (gain) on sale of equipment	—	14,150	1,605	1,873	(2,448)
Provision for federal income tax-deferred	62,000	—	—	—	—
Total used in operations	(178,484)	(881,394)	(1,440,210)	(1,172,443)	(3,367,150)
Increase in notes payable	393,197	2,097,850	4,037,960	854,697	5,058,625
Capital contributed by shareholders	27,814	540,000	800,000	—	—
Proceeds from sale of equipment	—	33,855	7,270	570	120,039
Decrease (increase) in other assets	(500)	(74,814)	63,122	56,744	(54,294)
Increase in accounts payable	19,559	11,386	311,027	137,702	507,432
Increase (decrease) in accrued liabilities	11,216	121,206	69,841	(104,250)	393,454
	272,802	1,848,089	3,849,010	(226,980)	2,658,106
Application of funds:					
Purchase of rights to customer lists	48,000	254,963	1,299,721	168,463	1,424,379
Cash dividends paid	—	540,000	800,000	—	—
Increase in accounts receivable	29,749	98,330	337,242	45,373	324,499
Purchase of equipment held for sale or lease	26,357	207,751	140,581	(61,979)	513,617
Purchase of property and equipment	69,941	339,056	732,211	129,696	1,051,983
	174,047	1,440,100	3,309,755	281,553	3,314,478
Increase (decrease) in cash and cash investments	$ 98,755	$ 407,989	$ 539,255	$ (508,533)	$ (656,372)

The accompanying notes are an integral part of the financial statements.

EXHIBIT 8

CRIME CONTROL, INC.
Notes to Financial Statements

1. Summary of Significant Accounting Policies:

Crime Control, Inc. (the Company) provides electronic alarm systems, including service and monitoring, to commercial and residential customers, all of which is considered to be one business segment. The Company was organized on December 30, 1977 and on January 1, 1978 issued shares of common stock in exchange for all of the outstanding stock of Guardian Alarm Co., Inc., and the net assets of Empire Protective Services (a sole proprietorship). Guardian Alarm Co., Inc. was liquidated into Crime Control, Inc. upon acquisition. The common stock issued by the Company in these acquisitions was ascribed an amount ($27,814) equal to the undepreciated cost incurred by the former entities for the assets acquired.

EXHIBIT 8 *(continued)*

1. Summary of Significant Accounting Policies—(Continued):

Unaudited Financial Statements

The results of operations for the nine month period ended September 30, 1980 contain, in the opinion of management, all adjustments necessary to present fairly the results of operations for the period.

Sales-Type Leases

Sales-type lease receivables include equipment sales, service and monitoring and are generally due in monthly installments over a term of five years with a bargain renewal option for an additional three years. The bargain renewal option allows the lessee the option to renew at 10% less than the rental rate in effect at the expiration of the initial lease term. The Company believes there is reasonable assurance that its customers will exercise the bargain renewal option based upon the scheduled rent reduction, an industry average customer life of 10 to 13 years, and the "penalty" the customer would incur in the form of an installation fee to change to different equipment. The leases have been accounted for as sales-type leases under the provisions of Statement of Financial Accounting Standards ("SFAS") No. 13 since the lease term exceeds 75% of the estimated economic life of the equipment (10 years).

Certain residential leases entered into in 1978 are reported as sales-type leases because the present value of the minimum lease payments exceeds 90% of the fair value of the leased assets.

Operating Leases

Rentals and monitoring fees relating to operating leases, generally related to companies acquired, are recorded as billed on a monthly basis under the provisions of SFAS No. 13.

Income Recognition

Income is recognized on equipment sales when the equipment is delivered and installed. Income from service and monitoring is recognized as income on a straight-line basis over the term of the contract. Unearned interest income on lease contract receivables is amortized to income over the lease term so as to produce a constant periodic rate of return on the net investment in the lease (see Note 4).

Inventory

The inventory of equipment held for sale or lease and related repair parts is stated at the lower of cost (first-in, first-out method) or market.

Property and Equipment

Property and equipment are stated on the basis of cost, net of accumulated depreciation computed on the straight-line method over the estimated useful lives as follows:

Vehicles..	3 years
Equipment	5-10 years
Purchased alarm systems.........................	8 years

The cost, less related accumulated depreciation, of purchased alarm systems under contracts converted to sales-type leases is charged to cost of equipment sold at the date of conversion. The cost of systems remaining under operating leases is depreciated on the straight-line method over the estimated useful life.

Purchased Rights to Customer Lists

The excess of cost of purchased alarm system companies over the fair value of the tangible assets acquired is ascribed to the unexpired portion of lease contracts and the customer lists ("customer lists").

EXHIBIT 8 *(continued)*

1. Summary of Significant Accounting Policies—(Continued):

Such costs are amortized over ninety-six months. The Company uses the sum-of-the-years-digits method during the initial two-year period, during which many of the customers are expected to be converted to long-term, sales-type leases, and the straight-line method thereafter.

Bonus Arrangements

The Company has no established bonus or incentive compensation plans. The Board of Directors may award discretionary bonuses, which for 1979 amounted to $50,000. No other bonuses have been paid or accrued.

Federal and State Income Taxes

The Company has not been subject to income taxes since the date of the election under Subchapter S of the Internal Revenue Code (January 1, 1979). Under Subchapter S the shareholders have consented to the inclusion of the effects of the Company's operations in their own federal and state income tax returns. At the date of the election the Company had a net operating loss carryover of $72,000 expiring in 1993, which could be utilized if the election is terminated (see Note 10). The provision for income taxes-pro forma assumes the Company had no Subchapter S election.

The Company accounts for all its lease contracts as operating leases for federal income tax purposes.

Pro Forma Net Income Per Share

Pro forma net income per share is computed based on the weighted average number of shares of common stock outstanding after adjustment for the stock split (see Note 10). The number of shares used was 2,000,000 for all periods.

2. Changes in Accounting:

The amortization policy used in previously issued financial statements for 1978 and 1979 differed from that described herein in that purchased rights to customer lists were previously amortized on the straight-line method and unearned income was amortized on the sum-of-the-years-digits method. The results of operations for the years 1978, 1979 and 1980 have been restated to reflect the change in order to better match the cost of purchased rights to the revenues derived on customer conversions and to recognize unearned income in accordance with the interest method prescribed by SFAS No. 13. The net effect of the changes was not material. Additionally, salary expense for 1979 was increased for a $50,000 bonus paid January 2, 1980 with a corresponding decrease in 1980 expenses.

3. Acquisitions:

In 1979 the Company acquired the assets of Centurion Alarm & Security Services Corporation (Centurion) in South Bend, Indiana for $50,000 in cash and a $432,000 note including interest at 6% (present value of $295,000 with interest imputed at 13.5%).

During 1980, the Company expanded its customer base through the acquisition of certain assets of two alarm system companies. In May 1980 certain assets (primarily a customer list plus inventory and equipment at Miami, Florida) were purchased from Farrey's Wholesale Hardware Co., Inc. (Farrey's) for cash ($71,000) and a $200,930 note including interest at 6% (present value of $127,612 with interest imputed at 21%).

In November 1980 the assets of Alarm Services Corporation, doing business as Beltway Alarm Services Co. (Beltway), an alarm system company located near Washington, D.C., were purchased for $1,300,000 cash and a $1,136,452 note including interest at 6% (present value of $704,118 with interest imputed at 18%). The note is payable in installments of $200,000 through 1986 and $136,452 in 1987; however, if the Company completes an offering of equity securities, $200,000 becomes due within 10 days of the receipt of the proceeds with the balance payable in four equal annual installments. The present value of the note has been calculated assuming a repayment schedule of $434,113 in 1982 and annual installments of $234,113 through 1985.

EXHIBIT 8 *(continued)*

3. Acquisitions—(Continued):

During 1981, the Company acquired certain assets of two additional alarm system companies, both of which had been operated as divisions of larger corporations. In March 1981, the Company purchased the customer list and some other assets of Seaboard Service Systems, Ltd. (Seaboard), a division of Peoples Drug Stores, Incorporated located near Washington, D.C. for $300,000 in cash and a $450,000 note including interest at 6% (present value of $377,792 with interest imputed at 17.5%). The note is payable in installments to October 1985; however, it becomes due within 10 days of the receipt of the proceeds of a public offering of equity or debt securities. Interest is imputed assuming the due date of the note will be accelerated by reason of such an offering.

In July 1981 the assets of the Miami Alarms Division of Wackenhut Electronic Systems Corporation (Wackenhut) were purchased for $500,000 cash, a 15%, $600,000 promissory note and a $575,000 convertible promissory note including interest at 6% (present value of $373,838 with interest imputed at 15%). If the Company successfully completes a public offering of equity securities, Wackenhut can demand payment of one-half of the principal amount of the convertible note with the balance due over seven years, or convert all or part of such note to common stock at 85% of the average market price for the five trading days preceding the date of conversion.

The purchase price of each of the above acquisitions, discounted at the prevailing interest rate at the time of acquisition to reflect the present value of the notes payable, exceeded the fair value of the tangible assets acquired as follows:

Selling Entity	Adjusted Purchase Price	Fair Value of Tangible Assets	Amount Allocated to Value of Purchased Rights to Customer List
Centurion	$ 345,000	$ 90,037	$ 254,963
Farrey's	198,612	50,380	148,232
Beltway	2,004,118	848,605	1,155,513
Seaboard	677,792	21,800	655,992
Wackenhut	1,473,838	709,625	764,213

All of the above acquisitions have been accounted for by the purchase method and, accordingly, results of operations have been included in the statements of income since the respective dates of acquisition.

If Beltway (the significant 1980 acquisition) had been acquired on January 1, 1979 and included in the Company's results of operations for 1979, the unaudited pro forma results would have been:

Revenues	$4,458,000
Pro forma net income	$ 165,000
Pro forma net income per share	$ .08

If Wackenhut (the significant 1981 acquisition) had been acquired on January 1, 1980 and had been included in the results of operations for 1980, along with the pro forma results of Beltway as if Beltway had been acquired on January 1, 1980, the unaudited pro forma results would have been:

Revenues	$8,921,000
Pro forma net income	$ 242,792
Pro forma net income per share	$ .12

If Wackenhut had been acquired on January 1, 1981 and had been included in the results of operations for the nine months ended September 30, 1981, the unaudited pro forma results would have been:

Revenues	$9,646,000
Pro forma net income	$ 320,415
Pro forma net income per share	$ .16

The effect of the Farrey's results cannot be determined because the assets acquired represented a division without separate financial statements and subsequent to the acquisition all of Farrey's financial records were destroyed in a fire in an area affected by the May 1980 riots in Miami, Florida. Based on the limited information available, management does not believe the effect of the Farrey's acquisition, if known, would be material to the Company. The results of operations of Centurion and Seaboard are not material to the Company; therefore, pro forma results have been omitted.

EXHIBIT 8 (continued)

4. Net Investment in Sales-Type Leases:

The net investment in sales-type leases consists of the following:

	December 31,		September 30,
	1979	1980	1981
Total minimum lease payments receivable	$ 4,662,074	$12,814,727	$23,148,162
Amounts allocated to service and monitoring............	(868,704)	(2,861,869)	(4,570,729)
Minimum lease payments receivable	3,793,370	9,952,858	18,577,433
Allowance for doubtful accounts	(40,000)	(130,000)	(234,000)
Net minimum lease payments receivable............	3,753,370	9,822,858	18,343,433
Estimated residual value of leased property	—	180,000	392,000
Unearned interest income...........................	(1,522,032)	(4,411,006)	(8,529,485)
	$ 2,231,338	$ 5,591,852	$10,205,948

There were no uncollectible accounts charged to the allowance in 1978 and 1979; the amounts charged-off in fiscal 1980 and the nine months ended September 30, 1981 were $20,680 and $215,468, respectively.

Interest, ranging from 12% to 22%, has been imputed on lease receivables based on an amount which normally approximates 2% in excess of the prime lending rate at the inception of the respective leases. Management believes such rate approximates the implicit interest rate based on the credit worthiness of the lessees. In each of the next five years approximately $3,700,000 of the total minimum lease payments receivable matures with the balance of $4,600,000 due after five years.

The residual value of the leased equipment for 1980 and 1981 leases is based on its estimated fair value at the end of the 8-year lease term. In prior years the Company had estimated the residual value to be insignificant.

The Company has one major customer which accounted for revenues of $2,070,000 in the nine months ended September 30, 1981 and $1,060,000 in 1980. Another customer accounted for $775,000 in revenues in 1979.

5. Cash and Cash Investments:

At December 31, 1980 cash investments represent $900,000 in a repurchase agreement earning interest at 15.5%. Cash and cash investments include non-interest bearing compensating balances held by lenders pursuant to certain loan agreements as follows (see Note 7):

Date	Amount
December 31, 1979...............................	$ 80,000
December 31, 1980...............................	$ 95,000
September 30, 1981	$315,000

6. Property and Equipment:

Property and equipment consist of the following:

	December 31,		September 30,
	1979	1980	1981
Vehicles..	$112,302	$ 294,110	$ 749,724
Central monitoring station and other equipment	240,919	527,426	672,096
Purchased alarm systems on operating leases	—	250,000	552,000
	353,221	1,071,536	1,973,820
Accumulated depreciation	58,492	190,002	339,237
	$294,729	$ 881,534	$1,634,583

EXHIBIT 8 *(continued)*

7. Notes Payable:

	December 31, 1979	December 31, 1980	September 30, 1981
Lease loans, collateralized by certain sales-type leases, payable in monthly installments of $29,760, plus interest at rates ranging from 12% to 25%, with maturities from September 1982 to December 1986	$ 966,939	$1,488,624	$ 2,383,338
Equipment loans, collateralized by equipment, payable in monthly installments of $19,516, including interest at rates ranging from 12% to 20%, with maturities from November 1981 to September 1986	224,216	282,050	497,819
Acquisition loans, payable to former owners of purchased companies:			
Centurion, payable in monthly installments of $6,000, including interest at 6% less unamortized discount (based on imputed interest rate of 13.5%) to August 1985	279,975	242,381	214,569
Farrey's, payable in annual installments of $50,233 to 1984 ($200,930 including interest at 6% less unamortized discount based on imputed rate of 21%).	—	127,612	110,925
Beltway, payable to a former officer of the Company in installments of $434,000 in 1982 and $234,000 annually through 1985 ($1,136,452 including interest at 6% less unamortized discount based on imputed interest rate of 18%). See Note 12	—	696,659	696,659
Seaboard, payable in annual installments of $90,000 to 1985 ($450,000 including interest at 6% less unamortized discount based on an imputed rate of 17.5%); becomes due within 10 days of the receipt by the Company of the proceeds of a public offering; interest imputed assuming accelerated maturity by reason of such offering	—	—	362,258
Wackenhut, 2 notes, $600,000 payable in annual installments of $85,714 plus interest at 15% to September 1988; $575,000, convertible, including interest at 6% less unamortized discount based on an imputed rate of 15%	—	—	973,837
Term loans, collateralized by substantially all assets acquired in certain acquisitions, payable in monthly installments through April 1986, with interest at prime plus 2.5% (currently 22.5%)	—	1,500,000	1,100,000
Line of credit for $6,000,000 ($3,000,000 in 1979) expiring in April 1987, collateralized by certain lease receivables and equipment, payable in monthly installments of $124,400, plus interest at rates ranging from prime plus 2.5% to prime plus 5% (average interest rate of 23.6%)(a)...	—	565,299	4,811,714
Payable to a bank, repaid January 1981 with interest at prime plus 2.5%, 100% collateralized by a repurchase agreement of the same amount......................	—	900,000	—
Other, payable from November 1981 to June 1986 with interest ranging from prime plus 2% to prime plus 2.5% (currently 22.5%)	1,019,917	726,382	436,513
	$2,491,047	$6,529,007	$11,587,632

(a) The underlying loan agreement provides for availability subject to levels of monthly lease amounts and equipment and installation costs for certain leases; each amount advanced is due in monthly payments over 60 months.

The acquisition loans are generally collateralized by the assets purchased, and substantially all the above debt is guaranteed by certain corporate officers. Certain lines of credit also require compensating balances as described in Note 5.

EXHIBIT 8 *(continued)*

7. Notes Payable—(Continued):

The principal portion of notes payable due in the next five years (based on succeeding twelve month periods after September 30, 1981) is as follows:

Due Within:	Amount
One year	$ 3,318,000
Two years	2,293,000
Three years	2,203,000
Four years	1,913,000
Five years	1,633,000
	11,360,000
After five years	228,000
	$11,588,000

Information relating to lines of credit and certain lease loans is as follows:

	December 31, 1980	September 30, 1981
Average aggregate amount outstanding during the period	$570,000	$4,750,000
Maximum amount outstanding at any month end	$840,000	$7,210,000
Weighted average interest rate during the period	19.9%	22.7%

The loan agreements restrict payments of cash dividends, issuance and retirements of capital stock, incurrence of certain indebtedness and advances to officers and stockholders without the consent of the lenders.

8. Related Party Transactions and Commitments:

The Company rents its home office building from an officer of the Company on a month-to-month basis. Related rent expense totaled $4,500 for the nine months ended September 30, 1981 and $5,000 for the year ended December 31, 1980.

The Company leases its Beltsville, Maryland office from a former officer of the Company under a 5-year lease expiring October 1985 that requires monthly payments of $5,128.

Total rent expense for all facilities was:

Date	Amount
Year ended December 31:	
1980	$ 40,421
1979	12,601
1978	6,000
Nine month period ended September 30:	
1981	127,907
1980 (unaudited)	15,521

9. Income Taxes:

The following is a reconciliation of 1978, 1979 and 1980 income taxes calculated at the United States federal statutory rate to the actual (1978) and pro forma (1979 and 1980) provisions for income taxes:

	Years Ended December 31,		
	1978	1979	1980
Provisions for taxes on income at statutory rate	$ 76,000	$399,000	$759,000
Investment tax credit	(2,000)	(21,000)	(17,000)
Benefits resulting from use of graduated tax brackets	(12,000)	(19,000)	(19,000)
	$ 62,000	$359,000	$723,000

The pro forma provisions for taxes for the nine month periods ended September 30, 1980 and 1981 were calculated based on the expected effective annual tax rate for fiscal 1980 and 1981 of 44% and 39%, respectively.

If the Company were a taxable corporation, deferred income taxes at September 30, 1981 would approximate $1,400,000 resulting from the reporting of lease income on the operating method for income tax return purposes and the capital lease method for financial reporting purposes. The reversal of the related timing differences will result in a provision for income taxes and currently payable income taxes greater than that at customary income tax rates in the absence of originating timing differences. The tax losses passed through to the shareholders for the years 1979 and 1980 (which would be available as a corporate net operating loss carryover if not for the Subchapter S election) totalled approximately $2,000,000.

EXHIBIT 8 *(concluded)*

10. Shareholders' Equity:

On December 14, 1981 the Company increased its authorized shares of common stock to 5,000,000 shares and declared a 2,000-for-1 stock split. All per share amounts have been retroactively restated to give effect to the split.

Completion of a public offering in 1982 will terminate the Company's Subchapter S election retroactively to January 1, 1982. Pursuant to the rules of the Securities and Exchange Commission all retained earnings accumulated to such date will be transferred to additional paid in capital.

On December 11, 1981 the shareholders of the Company approved an Employees' Stock Purchase Plan for which 100,000 shares have been reserved. The plan provides all full-time employees, except beneficial holders of 5% or more of the Company's stock, an opportunity to purchase common stock at 90% of fair market value. Purchases are limited to a percentage of annual compensation.

On the same date the shareholders approved an Incentive Stock Option Plan for which an additional 100,000 shares have been reserved. Options may be granted to any employee (except persons who would directly or indirectly own more than 5% of the Company's common stock, subject to certain limitations as to amount) and become exercisable proportionally over 6 years with an expiration date no later than 10 years from date of grant.

Both of the above plans are subject to administration by the Board of Directors.

11. Contingencies:

The Company has a contingent liability of $92,000 for telephone service resulting from non-payment of billed WATS services for the period from August 1980 to September 1981. A lawsuit filed by the Company against Indiana Bell Telephone Company requesting damages for misrepresentations in selling WATS service is pending. Management intends to vigorously pursue the lawsuit and is of the opinion that the contingent liability and the lawsuit may be offset.

12. Subsequent Events:

By an agreement dated as of November 25, 1981 the purchase price of the Beltway assets was adjusted to reflect the resolution of a preacquisition contingency related to the recurring monthly revenues derived from the purchased customers' contracts. The accounting entry to record the purchase has been retroactively adjusted under the provisions of SFAS No. 38 to reflect the purchase price and repayment terms as described in Notes 3 and 7.

On December 10, 1981 two letters of intent were signed by the Company and Thomson McKinnon Securities Inc. relating to offerings of equity and subordinated debt securities. The Company anticipates filing a Registration Statement on Form S-1 on or about December 16, 1981 with respect to the proposed sale by the Company of up to $10 million of Common Stock in a firm commitment underwriting. The subordinated debt offering would be a best efforts private placement of straight and convertible debt of approximately $14 million.

On December 14, 1981 the Company concluded negotiations for an addition of $3,000,000 to its primary line of credit ($6,000,000 limit at September 30, 1981) through the participation of a third bank. Also at that date the Company and shareholders were negotiating with a bank for a $3,000,000 loan to the shareholders who in turn would loan such amount to the Company. No agreement has been reached regarding such loan, which is expected to be completed by December 31, 1981.

On January 5, 1982 the Company agreed to acquire certain assets and a portion of the customer list of D. J. Enterprises, Inc. (doing business as Bur-tel II), for a maximum purchase price of $750,000. The present agreement provides for the purchase of rights to customers representing approximately $22,000 in monthly lease revenues for cash ($440,000) and a deferred payment of $110,000, including interest at 9%, due in February, 1983. The Company also agreed to purchase additional rights to customers representing approximately $8,000 in monthly lease revenues for up to an additional $200,000 during the succeeding 13 months. Management anticipates allocating the majority of the purchase price to purchased rights to customer lists. The results of operations of Bur-tel II are not material to the Company; therefore, historical and pro forma results have been omitted.

On January 19, 1982, the Company was served with notice of a complaint alleging unauthorized use of the name "Crime Control, Inc.", in the State of Maryland. The suit seeks to enjoin the Company from the use of that name in Maryland and seeks an unspecified amount of compensatory and punitive damages. Management intends to vigorously contest the suit and believes that any liability resulting therefrom will not be material to the Company's operations or financial condition as a whole.

The Oil Company of Western Australia*

In 1975, the Oil Company of Western Australia (hereafter, the Company) was formed as a joint venture between a subsidiary of Kenab, Inc., a U.S.-based company, and the Offshore Oil Company of Australia. The purpose of the joint venture was to engage in offshore oil and gas exploration in the North West Shelf, an area located off the western coast of Australia. The venture was a merger of convenience: Offshore Oil had significant quantities of property under lease in that area but lacked the necessary cash flow to support exploration activity, while Kenab lacked leases but had both sufficient cash flows and available equipment to undertake a significant exploration project.

By 1979, the Company had identified three areas of commercially justified recoverable oil reserves. At this point, the U.S. parent of the Company decided that the venture should become self-sustaining and consequently ceased funding of its operations. In an effort to generate the necessary funds for further exploration, the Company began selling "carved-out production payments."

Under these carved-out production contracts, the Company received immediate cash and in return guaranteed the purchaser the future cash flow from a specified percentage of the oil extracted from an existing producing property. For example, the Company might sell for $1 million cash the right to receive up to $1.5 million from the proceeds of, say, 10 percent of the oil produced from a specific producing property. These agreements enabled the Company to generate immediate cash flows to help fund the further development of these producing areas, without incurring the cash drain for interest and principal repayment associated with borrowed funds.

Under the terms of the contract, the Company would continue to operate the property and bear all costs of producing the oil. However, since the transaction was, in effect, a sale of oil in the ground, the liability of the Company was limited. Thus, in the event that insufficient quantities of oil were recovered from the property, thereby preventing the production contract buyer from recovering his initial investment, no liability to repay the shortfall was incurred by the Company. In general, however, the level of risk assumed by the buyer would typically be very low; and where the level of risk was high, the buyer would be compensated by an increased spread between the purchase price of the contract and the expected future cash return.

---

* This case was prepared by Kenneth R. Ferris. Copyright © 1984 by Kenneth R. Ferris. All rights reserved to the author. The situation was suggested by an earlier Harvard College case, "Ravenwood Oil Company," written by F. Robert Madera and David F. Hawkins.

FINANCIAL RESULTS

In 1980 and 1981, the Company recorded profits from carved-out production contracts sold, but not satisfied by production, of $580,000 and $6.8 million, respectively. The Company treated the revenue from these contracts as earned in the year in which the sale was consumated. In addition, the Company established a provision for the estimated future costs of production and consequently "booked" the net profit. Typically, all contracts were satisfied by production within 12 months of their sale.

In the latter half of 1981, the world supply of oil reached unprecedented heights and an oversupply situation developed, consequently driving world oil prices down. In the United States and in Australia, the profit margins and profit levels of oil and gas companies were severely strained. On the advice of its U.S. parent, the Company decided to change its method of accounting for carved-out production payments. Effective January 1, 1982, all profits on production payment contracts would be deferred until the oil had been extracted and sold. In order to make its financial statements comparable, the Company also decided to restate its 1981 financial statements utilizing the new accounting treatment. Under the old accounting treatment, the firm had reported net profits of $2.46 million and $5.015 million, respectively, in 1980 and 1981.[1]

For the year ended December 31, 1982, the Company reported a net loss of $1.375 million from normal oil and gas sales (i.e., exclusive of *any* profits from production payment contracts). Excluded from this figure was a potential profit of $1.275 million from production payment contracts sold but not satisfied in 1982.

QUESTIONS

1. Assuming that the film had *not* changed its method of accounting for carved-out production contracts, determine the net profits that would have been reported in 1982.

2. Determine the net profits to be reported in 1982 and the adjusted profit figures for 1980 and 1981 utilizing the new method of accounting for revenues from production payment contracts.

3. Which of the two methods most fairly presents the results of the Company's operations? Substantiate your position.

4. What explanation can you suggest for the adoption of the new accounting treatment?

5. Assuming that the shares of the Company were publicly traded, what impact would this change in accounting method likely have on the market price of the Company's shares?

---

[1] To be consistent with its U.S. parent, the Company reported results on a fiscal year ending December 31.

PART THREE

Asset Valuation

Marketable Securities

Leasco Corporation*

The following item concerning Leasco Corporation appeared in the December 31, 1979, issue of *Business Week:*

> *"Inappropriate" accounting?*   On October 19, Leasco bought 250,000 shares of Reliance, or 3.2 percent of the total. Leasco then disclosed in its 10-Q report filed with Securities and Exchange Commission for the third quarter that it would employ the equity method of accounting for its investment in Reliance. This means that Leasco will report as part of its earnings 3.2 percent of Reliance's net profits.
>
> Normally, a company does not use the equity method unless it has bought at least 20 percent of another company. However, the accounting principle says that what should determine the use of the method is the ability of the investor to influence operating and financial policies. "Since Reliance Group and Leasco are, in effect, being controlled by the same officer and directors, under generally accepted accounting principles an equity method of accounting is appropriate," says Leasco's 10-Q report.[1]

BACKGROUND

Leasco Corporation (Leasco) is engaged in the business of worldwide leasing of computer equipment and fee transactions involving underwriting and brokerage of such leases and computer equipment. Prior to May 14, 1979, Leasco was wholly owned by Reliance Group, Incorporated (Reliance).

Until 1968, Reliance was primarily in the business of computer leasing and computer software services and formed a subsidiary, Europa, to conduct its computer leasing business in Europe. In 1968, Reliance transferred its computer leasing business, assets

* This case was adapted with permission from a case written by Professor Joseph G. San Miguel and Research Assistant Pradip P. Shah, Harvard Graduate School of Business, with funding from the Touche Ross Foundation. Copyright © 1982 by Joseph G. San Miguel.

[1] David G. Santry, "Inside Wall Street," *Business Week,* December 31, 1979, p. 42.

and liabilities (other than those related to Europa), to a wholly owned Delaware subsidiary, Capital. After 1968, Reliance's computer leasing activities declined as a percentage of its total revenues when the company acquired Reliance Insurance Company, CTI International, Inc., and other businesses. In 1967, computer leasing activities accounted for approximately 36 percent of Reliance's revenues; this percentage dropped to 8 percent in 1974 and to about 3 percent for the year ended December 31, 1978.

In December 1978, Reliance restructured its worldwide computer leasing operations under a new subsidiary, Leasco Corporation, which would be spun off as a dividend to Reliance's common shareholders. In accordance with this plan, the board of directors of Reliance declared a dividend of up to 1 million shares of Leasco common stock, to be distributed to holders of Reliance common stock on the basis of one share of Leasco common stock for each six shares of Reliance common stock.

This stock dividend resulted in a $10 million reduction in Reliance's retained earnings. Leasco's initial capital structure comprised $10 of million of common shareholders' equity and $25 million of preferred shareholders' equity. The $10 million represented the net book value of Europa and the $25 million reflected the net book value of Capital, the former subsidiaries of Reliance. Reliance retained financial interest in Leasco through ownership of the preferred stock. Reliance also declared that it would record any excess of preferred dividends over Leasco's cumulative net income as deferred income until it was earned by Leasco.

REASONS FOR DISTRIBUTION

In the prospectus relating to the distribution of the Leasco shares, Reliance explained the reasons for spinning off the computer leasing activities. According to the prospectus, Reliance determined in 1975 that it would concentrate its business activities and resources in the areas of property and casualty, life and health, and title insurance, the leasing of cargo containers, and management services. The prospectus further stated that the operating management of the computer leasing business believed that there were many new investment opportunities for computer equipment, but, because of Reliance's business emphasis, Reliance was not willing to commit the resources necessary to exploit and expand the computer leasing business. The separation of the computer leasing business would create a new public company that would be in a position to take advantage of opportunities for new investments in computer assets; that would have separate, direct potential access to the public and private financing markets; and that would seek investments and acquisition in other businesses, including investments in securities.

The Leasco shares were distributed to Reliance common shareholders on May 14, 1979. Immediately following the distribution, Leasco directors, officers, and employees owned, directly or indirectly, 14.8 percent of Leasco's common stock. Saul P. Steinberg, founder and chief executive officer of Reliance and chairman of the board of Leasco, obtained beneficial ownership of 160,178 shares of Leasco common stock—11.73 percent of the total.

LEASCO'S OPERATIONS AND PERFORMANCE

Most of the leases written by Leasco were operating leases, although some finance leases had been written and remained in effect. Both types of leases had fixed rental rates for their stated terms, but only in the finance leases did the rental payments for the initial lease term return to Leasco its invoice cost of the leased equipment plus interest charges and related expenses. Such costs, charges, and expenses were recovered in operating leases by lease extensions or by re-leasing the equipment to several users over its useful life.

Leasco's computer equipment consisted primarily of IBM System/360 and IBM System/370 mainframes and peripherals. In 1977, IBM announced another system of computers—the System/303X and, in early 1979, IBM announced a new series of central processing units—the 4300 series. Leasco believed that IBM's new models offered successively more system for less money per unit of computing power. This reduced the resale value of previously introduced systems and the rates at which those systems could be leased. In addition, on several occasions, IBM reduced the selling price of its equipment, which also reduced the resale value and rerental rates of such equipment. As a result, Leasco was finding it extremely difficult to remarket certain of its computer mainframes and peripheral equipment.

The prospectus stated that Leasco would be unable to remarket many models of its computer equipment as they came off-lease, and it could give no assurances as to the length of the revenue-producing life of its remaining computer equipment. Leasco also stated that the amount of equipment off-lease would increase substantially. Leasco's competition included IBM itself, which leased as well as sold its computers and which dominated the industry because of its ability to change prices and introduce new models.

During the five years ended December 31, 1978, Reliance's Computer Leasing Group experienced substantial operating losses (see Exhibits 1–5 for financial statements). However, it continued to yield sizable cash flows due to the large amount of depreciation. Under the accounting method employed, computer leasing operations would not contribute to profits until all related costs had been recovered. The prospectus revealed that, based on a current five-year forecast of its computer leasing business as then conducted, Leasco did not expect to have earnings in any one of the next five years sufficient to meet the dividend requirements on its preferred stock. Indeed, Leasco expected that there would be substantial losses, which could wipe out the current book value of common shareholders' equity. However, based on the amount of noncancelable lease receivables at December 31, 1978, it expected net cash generation to continue in the future. The prospectus also disclosed that Leasco did not anticipate paying cash dividends on its common stock in the foreseeable future and that rental rates at which Leasco had been able to release its equipment had declined substantially since December 31, 1977, and were expected to continue to decline. It further stated that Leasco was dependent on IBM for maintenance of most of its equipment and, if IBM were to curtail maintenance service or greatly increase rates for maintenance of certain types of equipment which Leasco owned, it would be difficult to remarket such equipment.

No over-the-counter market existed for trading in Leasco common stock. The prospectus stated that Leasco common stock did not then, and might never, qualify for listing on a regional or national securities exchange making it difficult for a shareholder to determine accurately the value of the shares or to sell the shares.

LEASCO'S ACQUISITION OF RELIANCE STOCK

During the spring and summer following the Leasco spin-off, Saul Steinberg increased his holdings of Leasco common stock to 655,257 shares out of the 1.46 million shares outstanding. Steinberg thus acquired effective control of 50.7 percent of Leasco common stock. On October 19, 1979, Leasco bought 250,000 shares of Reliance, or 3.2 percent of the total. Leasco also announced that it was considering the acquisition of up to an additional 1 million shares of common stock of Reliance in market transactions from time to time.

Leasco then disclosed in its third quarter 10-Q report filed with the Securities and Exchange Commission that it would employ the equity method of accounting for its investment in Reliance. This meant that Leasco would report as part of its earnings 3.2 percent of Reliance's net profits. Leasco's reported profits would be increased by this accounting practice. For 1979, Reliance reported a net income of $217.2 million. Leasco's 3.2 percent share of that income of Reliance would amount to more than $2 per share. Leasco's net income from its own operations for the third quarter amounted to $226,000 against a loss of $431,000 for the corresponding period of the previous year. For the 10 months ended December 31, 1979, Leasco had a net income before equity accounting of $332,000.

After Leasco's decision to adopt the equity method in accounting for its investment in Reliance, Leasco stock price per common share jumped to $35½ from $28. Earlier in the year, Leasco stock had traded at $11¾. At the end of December 1979, it was trading at about $34. Thus, against the initial book value of $10 million, the value at market prices of Leasco common stock totaled $50 million.

METHOD OF ACCOUNTING FOR INVESTMENTS

Paragraph 1 of *Accounting Research Bulletin No. 51* states: "There is a presumption that consolidated financial statements are more meaningful than separate statements and that they are usually necessary for a fair presentation when one of the companies in the group directly or indirectly has a controlling financial interest in the other companies." The generally accepted condition for controlling financial interest is ownership of a majority (over 50 percent) of the outstanding voting stock. The power to control may also exist with a lesser percentage of ownership, for example, by contract or court decree. A corporation which is controlled directly or indirectly by another corporation is referred to as a "subsidiary."

Where investments are held in stock of companies other than subsidiaries, they are usually accounted for by one of two methods: the *cost method* or the *equity method*. Under certain circumstances, the *market value method* may provide the best presentation of investments.

Under the *cost method,* the investor records an investment in the stock of an investee at cost, and treats as income all dividends received that are distributed from net earnings of the investee after the date of acquisition by the investor. Any excess of dividends received over earnings after the date of the investment are considered a return of investment and are recorded as reductions of the cost of the investment.

Under the *equity method,* the investment is recorded at cost, and periodic adjustments are made to recognize the investor's share of the investee's earnings or losses after the acquisition date. The amount of the adjustment is included in the determination of the investor's net income. Such adjustments are similar to those made in preparing consolidated statements, including adjustments to eliminate intercompany gains and losses and to amortize, if appropriate, any difference between investor cost and underlying equity in the net assets of the investee at the date of investment. The adjustments also reflect the investor's share of changes in the investee's capital.

Dividends received by the investor are recorded as a reduction in the book value of the investment.

Under the *market value method,* the investor recognizes both dividends received and changes in market prices of the stock of the investee company as earnings or losses from an investment.

In its *Opinion No. 18,* the Accounting Principles Board discussed the various methods of accounting for investments in common stock. The board stated that, while it believed that the market value method provides the best presentation of investments in some situations, further study is necessary before the method is extended beyond the current practice of using it only in special circumstances. The board concluded that the equity method ought to be applied for investments in common stock of all unconsolidated subsidiaries and of all corporate joint ventures. The board also concluded that the equity method should be followed by an investor whose investment in voting stock gives it the ability to exercise significant influence over operating and financial policies. The board recognized that determining the ability of an investor to exercise such influence is not always clear. In order to achieve a reasonable degree of uniformity in application, it concluded that an investment (direct or indirect) of 20 percent or more of the voting stock of an investee should lead to a presumption that in the absence of evidence to the contrary an investor has the ability to exercise significant influence over an investee. Thus, an investment of less than 20 percent of the voting stock of an investee should ordinarily be accounted for at cost.

LEASCO'S METHOD OF ACCOUNTING

As mentioned earlier, Leasco announced that it would employ the equity method of accounting for its investment in 3.2 percent of Reliance common stock. Leasco's 10-Q report stated that, "Since Reliance Group and Leasco are, in effect, being controlled by the same officers and directors, under generally accepted accounting principles an equity method of accounting is appropriate." The prospectus filed in connection with the Leasco spin-off had stated, "Leasco may be deemed to be under the control of Reliance Group through certain of its directors and executive officers." The prospectus further pointed out that, though Reliance would normally exercise only 4 percent of the total voting power of all classes of Leasco stock, failure to pay full cumulative dividends equal to one and a half times the annual dividend would enable the holders of the preference stock to elect two additional members of the board of directors of Leasco.

QUESTIONS

1. Evaluate Leasco's method of accounting for its investment in Reliance. Do you agree with this approach? Justify your position. If you disagree, what alternative method would you suggest? Why?

2. Evaluate the equity market response to Leasco's decision to adopt the equity method in accounting for its investment in Reliance. Does this evidence confirm (or refute) the notion of an efficient capital market? Explain.

EXHIBIT 1
Leasco Corporation

Computer Leasing Group
(subsidiaries of Reliance Group, Incorporated)

Combined Statement of Operations

Year Ended December 31	1978	1977	1976	1975	1974
			(In thousands)		
Revenues:					
Equipment rentals	$30,588	$34,772	$40,153	$47,507	$51,261
Earned income on direct financing leases (note b)	2,218	1,131	1,416	6,334	12,101
Interest and other income (note f)	4,154	5,082	3,610	1,057	895
	36,960	40,985	45,179	54,898	64,257
Expenses:					
Depreciation—computer rental equipment (notes c and 3)	29,061	30,192	32,535	36,928	46,648
Interest (note f)	3,318	4,861	7,367	13,596	21,857
Selling, general and administrative (notes b, e and f)	4,973	6,490	6,981	7,157	16,974
Foreign currency translation and exchange (gain) loss	718	1,431	(1,309)	(3,597)	4,016
	38,070	42,974	45,574	54,084	89,495
Income (loss) before income tax (provision) benefit	(1,110)	(1,989)	(395)	814	(25,238)
Income tax (provision) benefit (note d):					
Current	(1,172)	(1,035)	(581)	(91)	2,325
Deferred	2,608	341	(349)	1,203	8,470
Investment tax credit recapture	—	—	—	—	(5,332)
	1,436	(694)	(930)	1,112	5,463
Income (loss) before extraordinary loss ...	326	(2,683)	(1,325)	1,926	(19,775)
Extraordinary loss—early extinguishment of debt (note g)	—	—	—	(4,328)	—
Net income (loss)......................................	$ 326	$(2,683)	$(1,325)	$(2,402)	$(19,775)

EXHIBIT 2
Leasco Corporation

Computer Leasing Group
(subsidiaries of Reliance Group, Incorporated)

Combined Statement of Changes in Financial Position
(in thousands)

Year Ended December 31	1978	1977	1976	1975	1974
Source of Funds:					
Income (loss) before extraordinary loss	$ 326	$(2,683)	$(1,325)	$ 1,926	$(19,775)
Depreciation—computer rental equipment	29,061	30,192	32,535	36,928	46,648
Foreign currency translation and exchange (gain) loss	718	1,431	(1,309)	(3,597)	4,016
Other	(3,331)	(257)	496	(993)	(8,344)
	26,774	28,683	30,397	34,264	22,545
Extraordinary loss	—	—	—	(4,328)	—
Funds provided from operations	26,774	28,683	30,397	29,936	22,545
Increases in notes payable	4,392	17,287	7,411	43,246	53,210
Decreases in computer rental equipment	6,982	3,404	7,832	2,025	1,439
Decrease in accounts and direct financing lease receivables	4,613	—	4,434	2,490	—
Increase in deferred income	—	3,068	—	—	382
Investments by parent	—	—	—	—	12,582
Sales of direct financing lease receivables	—	—	—	63,868	9,700
Other—net	1,852	7,173	1,613	784	5,671
	44,613	59,615	51,687	142,349	105,539
Application of Funds:					
Repayments of notes payable and limited recourse financing	23,329	40,485	35,281	134,906	67,450
Increases in amounts due from Reliance Group and affiliates	7,108	7,660	10,501	11,513	20,485
Decrease in deferred income	3,289	—	69	702	—
Increase in accounts and direct financing lease receivables	—	7,002	—	—	3,729
Increases in computer rental equipment	2,590	2,607	2,387	4,219	24,760
Dividends	—	—	—	4,002	—
	36,316	57,754	48,238	155,342	116,434
Increase (decrease) in cash	8,297	1,861	3,449	(12,993)	(10,895)
Cash, beginning of year	13,896	12,035	8,586	21,579	32,474
Cash, end of year	$22,193	$13,896	$12,035	$ 8,586	$ 21,579

See notes to combined financial statements.

EXHIBIT 3
Leasco Corporation—Pro Forma Financial Information

Computer Leasing Group
(subsidiaries of Reliance Group, Incorporated)

Pro Forma Combined Statement of Operations
(in thousands, except per share amounts)

The following table sets forth a combined historical statement of operations for the Computer Leasing Group for the year ended December 31, 1978, and as adjusted as if Leasco commenced business on January 1, 1978.

	Year Ended December 31, 1978	
	Historical	As Adjusted
Revenues:		
Equipment rentals	$30,588	$30,588
Earned income on direct financing leases	2,218	2,218
Interest and other income	4,154	2,942(A)
	36,960	35,748
Expenses:		
Depreciation—computer rental equipment	29,061	29,061
Interest	3,318	3,015(B)
Selling, general and administrative	4,973	4,920(C)
Foreign currency translation and exchange loss	718	718
	38,070	37,714
Loss before income tax (provision) benefit	(1,110)	(1,966)
Income tax (provision) benefit:		
Current	(1,172)	(1,207)
Deferred	2,608	2,608
	1,436	1,401(D)
Net income (loss)	326	(565)
Preferred stock dividend requirements	—	(2,500)
Net income (loss) applicable to common shareholders	$ 326	$(3,065)
Net loss per common share		$(1.92)
Average common shares outstanding (in thousands)		1,600

(A) Reflects the elimination of interest income of $1,523,000 on the 8% note receivable from Reliance Group; and is net of interest income of $311,000 resulting from investment of $4,145,000 additional cash.

(B) Reflects interest saved of $697,000 on the 5¾% Debentures which are not assumed by Leasco; interest saved of $312,000 on existing debt repaid; and is net of additional interest expense of $706,000 on new bank borrowings.

(C) Represents elimination of $53,000 amortization of deferred debt expense on the 5¾% Debentures.

(D) Represents adjustment of tax benefit, which is limited by the availability of taxes previously provided.

EXHIBIT 4
Leasco Corporation

Computer Leasing Group
(subsidiaries of Reliance Group, Incorporated)

Pro Forma Combined Statement of Changes in Financial Position
(in thousands)

The following table sets forth a combined historical statement of changes in financial position for the Computer Leasing Group for the year ended December 31, 1978, and as adjusted as if Leasco had commenced business on January 1, 1978.

	Year Ended December 31, 1978	
	Historical	As Adjusted
Source of Funds:		
Net income (loss)	$ 326	$ (565)
Depreciation—computer rental equipment	29,061	29,061
Foreign currency translation and exchange loss	718	718
Other	(3,331)	(3,331)
Funds provided from operations..	26,774	25,883
Increases in notes payable	4,392	4,392
Decreases in computer rental equipment	6,982	6,982
Decrease in accounts and direct financing lease receivables	4,613	4,613
Other - net..	1,852	1,852
	44,613	43,722
Application of Funds:		
Repayments of notes payable and limited recourse financing	23,329	23,329
Increases in amounts due from Reliance Group and affiliates	7,108	—(A)
Decrease in deferred income..	3,289	3,289
Increases in computer rental equipment	2,590	2,590
Preferred dividends	—	2,500
	36,316	31,708
Increase in cash	$ 8,297	$12,014

(A) Intercompany accounts assumed to be eliminated as of the beginning of the year.

EXHIBIT 5
Leasco Corporation

Computer Leasing Group
(subsidiaries of Reliance Group, Incorporated)

Pro Forma Combined Balance Sheet
(in thousands)

The following table sets forth a combined historical balance sheet
for the Computer Leasing Group.

ASSETS December 31, 1978	Historical	Adjustments	As Adjusted
Cash (including time deposits of $19,622 of which $15,048 are pledged)	$ 22,193	$ 4,145 (A) 135 (D)	$26,473
Accounts and direct financing lease receivables, less allowances of $1,665	17,557	—	17,557
Computer rental equipment—at cost, less accumulated depreciation of $241,203	30,434	—	30,434
8% notes receivable from Reliance Group, due October 31, 1990	24,800	(24,800) (C)	—
Due from Reliance Group and affiliates—net	13,511	(13,511) (C)	—
Other assets	3,857	(169) (B)	3,688
	$112,352	$(34,200)	$78,152

LIABILITIES AND SHAREHOLDERS' EQUITY

	Historical	Adjustments	As Adjusted
Notes payable	$ 8,213	$ 4,145 (A)	$12,358
Accounts payable and accrued expenses	4,233	—	4,233
Deferred income	4,297	—	4,297
Federal and foreign income taxes, principally deferred	5,944	—	5,944
	22,687	4,145	26,832
Senior subordinated debentures and notes	27,467	(11,147) (B)	16,320
Preferred stock, par value $1 per share, 1,000,000 shares authorized; issued and outstanding: 25,000 shares of Series A—at redemption value, as adjusted	—	25,000 (E)	25,000
Common stock	12	(12)	—
Common stock, par value $.10 per share, 5,000,000 shares authorized, 1,600,000 shares issued and outstanding, as adjusted	—	160	160
Additional paid-in capital	65,815	(55,975)	9,840
Retained earnings (deficit)	(3,629)	3,629	—
	62,198	(52,198) (F)	10,000
	$112,352	$(34,200)	$78,152

(A) New bank borrowing of $7,430,000 less prepayments of debt of $3,285,000.

(B) 5¾% Debentures and related deferred debt expense not assumed by Leasco.

(C) Intercompany accounts not transferred to Leasco.

(D) Net cash transferred to Leasco by Reliance Group.

(E) New Leasco preferred stock issued to a subsidiary of Reliance Group.

(F) Net effect of adjustments (B) through (E) on common equity:

(B)	$ 10,978
(C)	(38,311)
(D)	135
(E)	(25,000)
	$(52,198)

Teledyne, Inc. (A)*

Teledyne, Inc. manufactures and sells a wide variety of industrial, aviation-related, electronic, and specialty metals products. In addition, the firm wholly owns two property and casualty insurance companies (Argonaut Insurance Company and Trinity Universal Company), and has a 95 percent ownership interest in a life insurance company (Unicoa Corporation). While it is common for insurance companies to invest in equity securities, most limit their equity exposure to approximately the value of their net worth. This, however, was not true of the Teledyne insurance subsidiaries. By the end of 1976, for example, the equity exposure of Argonaut Insurance Company exceeded seven times its net worth. This case examines Teledyne's accounting for those equity investments.

During the mid-1970s, Teledyne began acquiring significant holdings in other companies through its unconsolidated insurance subsidiaries. During this period, the company invested over $400 million in such investments. Not only was the size of the investment unusual, but also its concentration. Approximately $356 million of the funds had been invested in only nine different companies (see Exhibit 1).

This unusual concentration of funds raised considerable speculation about the purpose of the investments. Many Wall Street analysts viewed the shareholdings as an extension of Teledyne's previously successful growth-by-acquisition strategy. Company officials, however, referred to the holdings as merely "passive investments."

Teledyne, Inc. was founded in 1960 and during the next decade grew from a small contracting firm with sales of $4.5 million to a major conglomerate with sales of $1.3 billion. With the exception of two years, Teledyne's earnings doubled or tripled every year from 1960 to 1970; in 1966 they quadrupled. Much of this growth was achieved through acquisitions—a total of 145. By 1970, however, Teledyne had abandoned its growth-by-acquisition strategy. During the early 1970s, Teledyne made only one minor acquisition.

FINANCIAL REPORTING ISSUES

In December 1975, the Financial Accounting Standards Board issued *FASB No. 12,* "Accounting for Certain Marketable Securities." This statement requires companies to value their intercorporate investments on a portfolio basis using the "lower of

---

* This case was prepared by Kenneth R. Ferris. Copyright © 1984 by Kenneth R. Ferris. All rights reserved to the author.

EXHIBIT 1
Partial Intercorporate Investment Portfolio (as of December 31, 1977)

Company	Approximate Number of Common Shares Owned	Shares Owned as a Percent of Common Shares Outstanding	Cost Basis (000s)	1977 Reported EPS	1977 Dividends per Share	12/31/77 Market Price per Share	12/31/77 Aggregate Market Value (000s)
Brockway Glass	1,054,400	21.7	$ 35,034	$4.07	$1.40	$29.25	$ 30,841
Colt Industries	419,125	5.3	21,949	8.10	2.56	48.00	20,118
Curtiss-Wright	2,352,700	28.5	39,117	1.91	0.60	18.75	44,113
Eltra	906,800	8.0	26,244	3.75	1.14	25.50	23,123
Walter Kidde	1,949,000	19.5	57,963	5.12	1.25	28.00	54,572
Litton Industries	8,298,733	22.2	115,551	1.40	0.00	14.50	120,332
National Can	1,226,900	18.3	17,777	1.45	0.59	15.75	19,324
Reichhold Chemicals	1,369,000	19.8	25,401	1.70	0.74	15.50	21,220
Rexnord	929,600	5.5	16,540	2.67	0.71	16.75	15,571
			$355,576				$349,214

Source: *Fortune*, January 16, 1978, p. 73.

Cost or Market" method. Valuation revisions, which may be either downward or upward to a maximum of original cost, are to be reported on the income statement for those investments classified as "current," and on the balance sheet as a contra-Owners' Equity item for those investments classified as "noncurrent."[1] In addition, for those noncurrent investments in which the investor can "exercise significant influence and control" over the investee's operating policies, *APB Opinion No. 18* (March 1971), entitled "The Equity Method of Accounting for Investments in Common Stock," requires that such investments be valued using the equity method.

According to *APB Opinion No. 18*, an investment of 20 percent or more of the voting stock of an investee is generally indicative of an ability to exercise significant influence. Under the equity method, consolidated net income includes the investor's proportionate share of the net income (or loss) reported by the investee. Further, any dividends paid by the investee to the investor are treated as an adjustment (i.e., a liquidating dividend) to the investment account.

Prior to 1977, the majority of the Teledyne investments were accounted for using the "lower of Aggregate Cost or Market" method. In 1977, however, Teledyne adopted the equity method for some of these investments. According to the company's 1977 annual report (see Exhibits 2–8 for financial statements and selected footnotes) the equity method was adopted for those investments for which the aggregate voting interest exceeded 20 percent for at least one full quarter of the year. This accounting change produced an incremental increase in 1977 earnings per share of $0.88.

QUESTIONS

1. What criteria should be used to classify intercorporate investments as either "current" or "noncurrent"? Using these criteria, classify the investments listed in Exhibit 1 and determine the income statement and balance sheet effects of your classification scheme.

2. Assuming that the 1977 accounting change was *not* undertaken, how would the investments listed in Exhibit 1 appear in Teledyne's financial statements?

3. Assuming that Teledyne desired to maximize reported net income, what classification scheme for the investments listed in Exhibit 1 would produce the highest level of reported net income? (Ignore considerations of "fair" presentation.)

---

[1] Investment companies, brokers, and dealers in securities, life and casualty insurance companies, and other industries that follow specialized accounting practices must comply with *FASB No. 12* to a limited extent. In those industries which permit unclassified balance sheets, all marketable securities are to be classified as noncurrent.

EXHIBIT 2

TELEDYNE, INC. AND SUBSIDIARIES
Consolidated Statements of Income
For the years ended December 31, 1977, and 1976

	1977	1976
Consolidated Sales	$2,209,731,000	$1,937,556,000
Consolidated Costs and Expenses:		
Cost of sales	1,624,913,000	1,437,169,000
Selling and administrative expenses	266,968,000	254,606,000
Interest expense (Notes 4 and 10)	16,990,000	18,756,000
Interest income	(10,777,000)	(9,230,000)
Provision for income taxes (Note 9)	159,800,000	123,000,000
	2,057,894,000	1,824,301,000
Income of Consolidated Companies	151,837,000	113,255,000
Equity in Net Income of Unconsolidated Subsidiaries, after allocated interest expense and income tax items (excludes equity in unrealized depreciation on marketable equity securities of $28,071,000 in 1977 and unrealized appreciation of $35,157,000 in 1976) (Notes 4 and 10)	42,245,000	23,544,000
Net Income	$ 194,082,000	$ 136,799,000
Net Income Per Share (Note 2):		
Primary	$16.23	$10.63
Fully Diluted	$15.86	$10.36

EXHIBIT 3

TELEDYNE, INC. AND SUBSIDIARIES
Consolidated Statements of Retained Earnings
For the years ended December 31, 1977, and 1976

	1977	1976
Balance, Beginning of Year, as previously reported	$ 494,345,000	$ 379,894,000
Effect on prior year of equity accounting (Note 15)	1,920,000	—
As restated	496,265,000	379,894,000
Net income	194,082,000	136,799,000
Fair value of common stock dividends (Note 6)	(20,914,000)	(17,619,000)
Cash dividends on preferred stock	(1,739,000)	(2,365,000)
Difference between cost and book value of Unicoa treasury stock	—	(444,000)
Balance, End of Year	$ 667,694,000	$ 496,265,000

The accompanying notes are an integral part of these statements.

EXHIBIT 4

TELEDYNE, INC. AND SUBSIDIARIES
Consolidated Balance Sheets
December 31, 1977, and 1976

Assets

	1977	1976
Current Assets:		
Cash	$ 44,668,000	$ 42,256,000
Marketable securities, at cost which approximates market	242,300,000	190,382,000
Receivables, less reserve of $10,820,000 in 1977 and $10,784,000 in 1976	252,445,000	211,124,000
Inventories (Note 3)	161,167,000	144,274,000
Prepaid expenses	6,006,000	6,414,000
Total current assets	706,586,000	594,450,000
Investments in Unconsolidated Subsidiaries (Note 10):		
Life insurance companies	252,080,000	236,627,000
Casualty insurance companies	180,059,000	97,894,000
	432,139,000	334,521,000
Property and Equipment, at cost (Note 4):		
Land..	16,950,000	16,808,000
Buildings...	113,120,000	109,409,000
Equipment and improvements.......................................	401,434,000	378,937,000
	531,504,000	505,154,000
Less accumulated depreciation and amortization	287,861,000	270,910,000
	243,643,000	234,244,000
Other Assets:		
Cost in excess of net assets of purchased businesses (Notes 8 and 10) ..	30,795,000	30,419,000
Other	6,977,000	13,911,000
	37,772,000	44,330,000
	$1,420,140,000	$1,207,545,000

The accompanying notes are an integral part of these balance sheets.

EXHIBIT 4 *(concluded)*

Liabilities

	1977	1976
Current Liabilities:		
Accounts payable	$ 96,733,000	$ 95,889,000
Accrued liabilities	147,702,000	132,253,000
Accrued income taxes (Note 9)	105,900,000	88,100,000
Current portion of long-term debt (Note 4)	5,192,000	4,709,000
Total current liabilities	355,527,000	320,951,000
Long-Term Debt (Note 4)	313,350,000	315,457,000
Deferred Income Taxes (Note 9)	58,000,000	65,800,000
Other Long-Term Liabilities	10,066,000	9,863,000
Commitments and Contingencies (Note 7)		
Shareholders' Equity:		
Preferred stock (liquidation preference $18,261,000 in 1977— Note 6)	516,000	516,000
Common stock (Notes 5 and 6)	32,340,000	32,340,000
Additional paid-in capital	445,885,000	432,360,000
Retained earnings (Note 4)	667,694,000	496,265,000
Equity in unrealized depreciation on marketable equity securities of unconsolidated subsidiaries (Note 10)	(5,643,000)	—
	1,140,792,000	961,481,000
Less treasury stock, at cost (Note 6)	457,595,000	466,007,000
Total shareholders' equity	683,197,000	495,474,000
	$1,420,140,000	$1,207,545,000

EXHIBIT 5

TELEDYNE, INC. AND SUBSIDIARIES
Consolidated Statements of Changes in Financial Position
For the years ended December 31, 1977, and 1976

	1977	1976
Working Capital was Provided by:		
Net income	$194,082,000	$136,799,000
Equity in net income of unconsolidated subsidiaries before allocated interest expense and income tax items (Note 10)	(31,673,000)	(10,319,000)
Depreciation and amortization of property and equipment	48,239,000	47,282,000
Other amortization and charges not affecting working capital	2,532,000	6,128,000
Change in deferred income taxes	(7,800,000)	10,200,000
Working capital provided from operations	205,380,000	190,090,000
Increase in long-term debt	7,804,000	4,512,000
Dispositions of property and equipment	2,766,000	9,043,000
Issuance of common stock for employees' stock purchase and option plans and the exercise of warrants	1,014,000	4,204,000
Conversion of 3½% subordinated debentures	—	21,381,000
Other, net	5,532,000	(4,225,000)
	222,496,000	225,005,000
Working Capital was Applied to:		
Investments in and advances to unconsolidated subsidiaries	71,588,000	9,728,000
Additions to property and equipment	60,404,000	37,255,000
Reduction in long-term debt	11,205,000	61,012,000
Dividends on preferred stock	1,739,000	2,365,000
Acquisition of treasury stock	—	166,947,000
	144,936,000	277,307,000
Increase (Decrease) in Working Capital	$ 77,560,000	$(52,302,000)
Working Capital Increase (Decrease):		
Cash	$ 2,412,000	$ 1,824,000
Marketable securities	51,918,000	20,689,000
Receivables	41,321,000	40,840,000
Inventories	16,893,000	(4,710,000)
Prepaid expenses	(408,000)	(919,000)
Accounts payable	(844,000)	(22,757,000)
Accrued liabilities	(15,449,000)	(8,613,000)
Accrued income taxes	(17,800,000)	(78,800,000)
Current portion of long-term debt	(483,000)	144,000
	$ 77,560,000	$(52,302,000)

The accompanying notes are an integral part of these statements.

EXHIBIT 6

TELEDYNE, INC. AND SUBSIDIARIES
Consolidated Statements of Capital Stock,
Additional Paid-in Capital, and Treasury Stock
For the years ended December 31, 1977, and 1976

	Preferred Stock ($1 Par Value)	Common Stock ($1 Par Value)	Additional Paid-In Capital	Treasury Stock
Balance, December 31, 1975	$516,000	$32,340,000	$407,689,000	$318,080,000
Stock issuance:				
Conversion of 3½% subordinated debentures (445,730 shares)	—	—	12,656,000	(8,725,000)
Common stock dividend (347,130 shares)	—	—	10,790,000	(6,836,000)
Stock option and purchase plans (163,720 shares)	—	—	972,000	(3,227,000)
Exercise of warrants (11,150 shares)	—	—	258,000	(227,000)
Conversion of $6 series preferred stock (273 common shares issued)	—	—	(5,000)	(5,000)
Acquisition of common (3,161,929 shares) and preferred stock (209,212 shares)	—	—	—	166,947,000
Balance, December 31, 1976	516,000	32,340,000	432,360,000	466,007,000
Stock issuance:				
Common stock dividend (342,836 shares) .	—	—	13,633,000	(7,290,000)
Stock option plan (48,172 shares—Note 5)..............	—	—	(200,000)	(1,023,000)
Exercise of warrants (4,393 shares—Note 5)	—	—	96,000	(95,000)
Conversion of $6 series preferred stock (212 common shares issued)	—	—	(4,000)	(4,000)
Balance, December 31, 1977	$516,000	$32,340,000	$445,885,000	$457,595,000

The accompanying notes are an integral part of these statements.

EXHIBIT 7
Auditor's Report

To the Shareholders and
Board of Directors, Teledyne, Inc.:

We have examined the consolidated balance sheets of Teledyne, Inc. (a Delaware corporation) and subsidiaries as of December 31, 1977 and 1976, and the related statements of income, capital stock, additional paid-in capital and treasury stock, retained earnings and changes in financial position for the years then ended. Our examinations were made in accordance with generally accepted auditing standards, and accordingly included such tests of the accounting records and such other auditing procedures as we considered necessary in the circumstances. The consolidated financial statements of Unicoa Corporation and subsidiaries were examined by other auditors whose reports thereon have been furnished to us. Our opinion expressed herein, insofar as it relates to the amounts included for Unicoa Corporation and subsidiaries, is based solely upon the reports of the other auditors. Teledyne's investment in Unicoa was 18 percent in 1977 and 19 percent in 1976 of consolidated assets and its equity in Unicoa's net income, after allocated interest expense and income tax items as described in Note 10, was 7 percent in 1977 and 12 percent in 1976 of consolidated net income.

In our opinion, based upon our examinations and the reports of other auditors referred to above, the accompanying consolidated financial statements present fairly the consolidated financial position of Teledyne, Inc. and subsidiaries as of December 31, 1977 and 1976, and the results of their operations and changes in their financial position for the years then ended, all in conformity with generally accepted accounting principles consistently applied during the periods.

ARTHUR ANDERSEN & CO.

Los Angeles, California,
January 15, 1978.

EXHIBIT 8

TELEDYNE, INC. AND SUBSIDIARIES
Notes to Consolidated Financial Statements (excerpts)

(1) Summary of Significant Accounting Policies. *Principles of Consolidation.* The consolidated financial statements of Teledyne, Inc. include the accounts of all its subsidiaries except its insurance and finance subsidiaries. The investments in unconsolidated subsidiaries, which include advances, are accounted for by the equity method. All material intercompany accounts and transactions have been eliminated. Certain amounts in the 1976 consolidated financial statements have been reclassified to conform with the 1977 presentation.

Currency Translation. All assets and liabilities of foreign subsidiaries and other foreign currency assets and liabilities are translated at current rates with the exception of inventories, property and equipment and prepaid expenses which are translated at historical rates. Net translation gains and losses are included in operations in the period in which they occur.

Inventories. Inventories are stated at the lower of cost (last-in, first-out and first-in, first-out methods) or market, less progress payments received. Costs include direct material and labor costs and applicable manufacturing and engineering overhead. Sales and related costs are recorded as products are delivered and as services are performed, including products and services under long-term contracts. Costs of products delivered and services performed under such long-term contracts are removed from inventory and charged to cost of sales at amounts approximating actual cost. Any foreseeable losses are charged to income when determined.

Depreciation and Amortization. Buildings and equipment are depreciated on straight-line and declining balance bases. Estimated useful lives are 5 to 45 years for buildings, and 3 to 20 years for machinery and equipment. Leasehold improvements and patents are amortized on a straight-line basis over the life of the lease or patent. Maintenance and repairs are charged against income as incurred and betterments and major renewals are capitalized. Cost and accumulated depreciation of property sold or retired are removed from the accounts and the resultant gain or loss is included in income.

Cost in Excess of Net Assets of Purchased Businesses. Except for an immaterial amount being amortized, cost in excess of net assets of purchased businesses relates to businesses purchased prior to October 31, 1970 and is not being amortized.

Research and Development. Company funded research and development costs are expensed as incurred. Costs related to customer funded research and development contracts are charged to income as sales are recorded.

Pension Expense. Pension expense is accrued at amounts equal to normal cost plus a portion of prior service costs.

Income Taxes. Provision for income taxes includes state, Federal and foreign income taxes. Deferred income taxes are provided for timing differences in the recognition of income and expenses, income of the domestic international sales corporation not currently taxed, and undistributed earnings of subsidiaries, except for a portion of the earnings arising from life insurance operations. Investment tax credits are amortized over the estimated lives of the related assets.

Other Investments. Investments held by Teledyne's unconsolidated subsidiaries are accounted for by the equity method in the Company's consolidated financial statements when the aggregate voting percentage has exceeded 20 percent for one full quarter. The most recent publicly available financial statements of each investee company are used in determining Teledyne's voting percentage and share of earnings.

EXHIBIT 8 *(continued)*

(10) Investments in Unconsolidated Subsidiaries. Equity in net income of unconsolidated subsidiaries, after allocated interest expense and income tax items, for the years ended December 31, 1977 and 1976, was as follows:

	1977	*1976*
Equity in net income (loss) of:		
Life insurance companies......................................	$23,401,000	$20,634,000
Casualty insurance companies	8,272,000	(10,315,000)
	31,673,000	10,319,000
Allocated interest expense	(12,964,000)	(12,504,000)
Income tax credits	28,842,000	26,571,000
Provision for deferred taxes on equity in		
net income of investments (Note 15)	(5,306,000)	(842,000)
	$42,245,000	$23,544,000

The Company's investment in life insurance companies consists primarily of a 95.3 percent ownership in Unicoa Corporation (Note 11). The Company's investment in casualty insurance companies consists primarily of the investment in domestic casualty insurance companies (Note 12), principally Argonaut Insurance Company and Trinity Universal Insurance Company; these subsidiaries are wholly-owned as to voting securities. Included in the equity in net income (loss) of the life and casualty insurance companies are amounts representing the incremental effect of accounting for certain investments by the equity method (Note 15).

The income tax credits consist of amounts ($6,612,000 in 1977 and $6,377,000 in 1976) related to the allocated interest expense and amounts ($24,253,000 in 1977 and $20,194,000 in 1976) related to losses of unconsolidated subsidiaries which are recoverable in Teledyne's consolidated tax return but which are not available to the unconsolidated subsidiaries on a separate return basis, reduced in 1977 by a provision ($2,023,000) for taxes which will become due upon distribution of the earnings of the unconsolidated subsidiaries. The effective tax rate used in computing the income tax credits related to losses of unconsolidated subsidiaries differs from the statutory U.S. Federal income tax rate of 48 percent principally because of tax exempt investment income.

Interest expense was allocated to unconsolidated subsidiaries based on the ratio of the Company's average investment in unconsolidated subsidiaries to average total capital.

The Company's equity in the net assets of its unconsolidated subsidiaries, including advances, was $217,258,000 in 1977 and $135,115,000 in 1976, including its equity of $138,036,000 and $80,687,000, respectively, in their retained earnings. In consolidation, a portion of the difference between the Company's investments in purchased subsidiaries and the book value of their assets has been allocated to bonds and stocks and amortized over the applicable maturity of the bonds or charged or credited to income upon their disposition. The Company's investment exceeded its equity in net assets by $196,798,000 in 1977 and $196,644,000 in 1976. Such excess is in addition to the excess shown in the consolidated balance sheets and is not being amortized since, in the opinion of management, there has been no diminution in its value. The Company's equity in net income (loss) of its unconsolidated subsidiaries includes losses on sales of investments of $1,402,000 in 1977 and $6,874,000 in 1976.

The Company's unconsolidated subsidiaries carry marketable equity securities, including those accounted for by the equity method in the consolidated financial statements of Teledyne, at the lower of aggregate cost or market. The Company's equity in the gross unrealized gains and the gross unrealized losses, which are not included in the determination of the results of operations, was $27,051,000 and $31,015,000, respectively, at December 31, 1977, after adjusting for the effect of the use of the equity accounting method for certain investments. The reduction to the lower of cost or market is reflected in the consolidated financial statements as a reduction in the investments in unconsolidated subsidiaries and in shareholders' equity. Changes in unrealized depreciation have no effect on net income.

EXHIBIT 8 *(continued)*

(11) Unicoa Corporation and Subsidiaries. The following condensed statements summarize the consolidated financial position and operating results of Unicoa Corporation and subsidiaries. Unicoa Corporation was 95.3 percent owned by Teledyne at December 31, 1977 and 1976.

Consolidated Balance Sheets

	December 31.	
	1977	*1976*
Assets:		
Investments:		
Bonds and notes, at amortized cost (market: 1977—$305,782,000; 1976—$238,879,000)	$306,519,000	$242,885,000
Stocks, principally at lower of aggregate cost or market (market: 1977—$238,545,000; 1976—$232,311,000)	233,092,000	214,333,000
Mortgage loans on real estate, less reserve of $6,990,000 in 1977 and $6,120,000 in 1976	109,413,000	121,077,000
Real estate, at cost less accumulated depreciation	41,698,000	46,350,000
Loans to policyholders	16,791,000	15,548,000
Invested cash	136,000	1,960,000
Total investments	707,649,000	642,153,000
Cash	3,330,000	2,756,000
Uncollected premiums	25,507,000	22,744,000
Deferred policy acquisition costs	115,032,000	110,290,000
Cost in excess of net assets of purchased businesses	25,796,000	26,234,000
Other assets	17,407,000	23,362,000
	$894,721,000	$827,539,000
Liabilities:		
Policy reserves and liabilities	$631,192,000	$595,088,000
Notes payable to banks	22,200,000	16,300,000
Mortgage loan payable	6,626,000	7,466,000
Subordinated debentures	18,340,000	18,142,000
Other liabilities	64,651,000	55,950,000
Shareholders' equity	151,712,000	134,593,000
	$894,721,000	$827,539,000

Consolidated Statements of Income

	Year Ended December 31.	
	1977	*1976*
Income:		
Premiums and other insurance income	$269,076,000	$262,667,000
Net investment income	33,419,000	34,565,000
Other income	3,701,000	5,817,000
	306,196,000	303,049,000
Expenses:		
Benefits paid or provided	148,213,000	162,661,000
Insurance expenses	134,361,000	111,777,000
Provision for income taxes	3,575,000	5,597,000
	286,149,000	280,035,000
	20,047,000	23,014,000
Loss on Sale of Investments (excludes unrealized depreciation on marketable equity securities of $12,587,000 in 1977 and unrealized appreciation of $28,935,000 in 1976)	(2,132,000)	(3,125,000)
Net Income	$ 17,915,000	$ 19,889,000

EXHIBIT 8 *(continued)*

The above statements have been prepared on the basis of generally accepted accounting principles which differ from statutory insurance accounting practices. Life insurance premiums are recognized as revenue when they become due, and revenues, benefits and expenses on accident and health insurance are recognized over the period to which the premiums relate. Deferred taxes are provided for timing differences in the recognition of income and expense.

Marketable equity securities, including those accounted for by the equity method in the consolidated financial statements of Teledyne, are carried at the lower of aggregate cost or market. Any valuation allowance necessary to reduce these securities from cost to market, if lower in the aggregate, is reflected in the consolidated financial statements as a reduction in shareholders' equity; any changes thereto have no effect on net income. The net unrealized appreciation was $5,141,000 at December 31, 1977 and $17,728,000 at December 31, 1976. Shareholders' equity has been reduced by $796,000 at December 31, 1977 representing the equity in the unrealized depreciation on marketable equity securities held by UIC Investments, Inc., a 20 percent owned unconsolidated subsidiary.

A portion of life insurance income is not subject to Federal income tax until such amount exceeds certain limitations or is distributed to shareholders as dividends. At December 31, 1977, up to $55,000,000 (at current tax rates) would be required for possible Federal income taxes which might become due, in whole or in part, in future years if any portion of $114,000,000 of the gains from operations since January 1, 1959 (which includes $3,000,000 from both 1977 and 1976) becomes includable in taxable income as a result of such limitations, including distributions in excess of $24,800,000 as dividends.

(12) Domestic Casualty Insurance Subsidiaries. The following condensed statements summarize the combined financial position and operating results of the domestic casualty insurance subsidiaries, all of which are wholly-owned by Teledyne as to voting securities.

Combined Balance Sheets

	December 31.	
	1977	*1976*
Assets:		
Investments:		
Bonds, at amortized cost (market: 1977—$394,163,000; 1976—$394,084,000)	$388,261,000	$401,955,000
Stocks, principally at lower of aggregate cost or market (market: 1977—$322,188,000; 1976—$311, 594,000)	320,152,000	293,492,000
Invested cash	168,313,000	26,636,000
Total investments	876,726,000	722,083,000
Cash	21,187,000	18,172,000
Agents' balances and uncollected premiums	45,885,000	45,011,000
Other receivables	26,305,000	32,803,000
Deferred policy acquisition costs	13,118,000	11,975,000
Property and equipment, at cost less accumulated depreciation	4,152,000	4,392,000
Cost in excess of net assets of purchased businesses	4,783,000	4,783,000
	$992,156,000	$839,219,000
Liabilities:		
Loss and claim reserves	$622,287,000	$574,152,000
Accrued loss adjustment expenses	103,506,000	97,938,000
Unearned premiums	101,571,000	90,968,000
Other liabilities	49,270,000	36,572,000
Shareholders' equity	115,522,000	39,589,000
	$992,156,000	$839,219,000

EXHIBIT 8 *(continued)*

Combined Statements of Operations

	Year Ended December 31.	
	1977	1976
Income:		
Net premiums earned	$365,927,000	$331,257,000
Net investment income	40,768,000	38,316,000
	406,695,000	369,573,000
Expenses:		
Losses and loss adjustment expenses	295,491,000	279,941,000
Underwriting expenses..	105,306,000	94,112,000
Provision for income taxes	7,256,000	2,354,000
	408,053,000	376,407,000
	(1,358,000)	(6,834,000)
Gain (Loss) on Sale of Investments (excludes unrealized depreciation on marketable equity securities of $16,620,000 in 1977 and unrealized appreciation of $16,045,000 in 1976)	630,000	(4,135,000)
Net Loss	$ (728,000)	$ (10,969,000)

The above statements have been prepared on the basis of generally accepted accounting principles which differ from statutory insurance accounting practices. The principal subsidiaries included in the combined financial statements are Argonaut Insurance Company and Trinity Universal Insurance Company. Premium income, policy acquisition costs, and policyholder dividends are recognized ratably over the period to which the premiums relate. Losses and loss adjustment expenses are provided at the estimated amounts necessary to settle incurred claims. Deferred taxes are provided for timing differences in the recognition of income and expenses to the extent such deferred taxes are determined to be recoverable. In 1976, $3,806,000 of cost in excess of net assets of purchased businesses was charged to operations since such excess represented no further value to the Company.

Marketable equity securities, including those accounted for by the equity method in the consolidated financial statements of Teledyne, are carried at the lower of aggregate cost or market. Any valuation allowance necessary to reduce these securities from cost to market, if lower in the aggregate, is reflected in the combined financial statements as a reduction in shareholders' equity; changes thereto have no effect on the results of operations. The net unrealized depreciation on marketable equity securities was $1,248,000 at December 31, 1977, and the net unrealized appreciation was $15,372,000 at December 31, 1976.

Investments in stocks includes $34,177,000 in 1977 and $40,032,000 in 1976 of investments in the common stock of unconsolidated subsidiaries accounted for by the equity method. Shareholders' equity has been reduced by $3,183,000 representing the equity in the unrealized depreciation on marketable equity securities held by UIC Investments, Inc., an 80 percent owned subsidiary accounted for by the equity method. Shareholders' equity includes $20,000,000 of certificates of contribution issued in 1975 to Teledyne in exchange for $20,000,000 of Teledyne's 10% subordinated debentures (included in bonds in the above combined balance sheets).

Taxable income of the domestic casualty insurance subsidiaries is included in the consolidated income tax return of Teledyne. Certain of the subsidiaries reimburse Teledyne for their portion of Teledyne's consolidated Federal income tax liability. No income tax credits have been included in the domestic casualty combined financial statements since the losses for tax purposes could not be carried back to recover prior years' taxes on a separate return basis.

(13) UIC Investments, Inc. The following condensed statements summarize the financial position and operating results of UIC Investments, Inc. UIC Investments, Inc. is 80 percent owned by Trinity Universal Insurance Company and 20 percent owned by a wholly-owned subsidiary of Unicoa Corporation.

EXHIBIT 8 *(continued)*

Balance Sheets

	December 31,	
Assets:	*1977*	*1976*
Investments in common stock, at the lower of aggregate cost or market (cost: 1977—$170,548,000; 1976—$97,814,000)	$166,569,000	$ 97,021,000
Short-term investments, at cost which approximates market	2,700,000	13,560,000
Cash......	92,000	210,000
Accrued investment income	356,000	418,000
	$169,717,000	$111,209,000
Liabilities:		
Notes payable to banks	$120,000,000	$ 55,000,000
Accounts payable	2,971,000	4,974,000
Accrued interest	993,000	439,000
Notes payable to affiliates	51,035,000	47,200,000
Shareholders' equity (deficit).....	(5,282,000)	3,596,000
	$169,717,000	$111,209,000

Statements of Operations

	Year Ended December 31,	
	1977	*1976*
Investment income	$ 3,762,000	$ 974,000
Interest expense	9,517,000	1,554,000
Other expenses	122,000	31,000
Gain on sale of investments	185,000	—
Net Loss	$ (5,692,000)	$ (611,000)

Short-term investments are carried at cost, which approximates market. Investments in common stocks, including those accounted for by the equity method in the consolidated financial statements of Teledyne, are carried at the lower of aggregate cost or market. Any valuation allowance necessary to reduce common stocks from cost to market, if lower in the aggregate, is reflected in the financial statements as a reduction in shareholders' equity; changes thereto have no effect on the results of operations. The net unrealized depreciation on common stocks was $3,979,000 at December 31, 1977 and $793,000 at December 31, 1976.

Taxable income of UIC Investments, Inc. is included in the consolidated tax returns of Teledyne. No income tax credits have been included in the financial statements of UIC Investments, Inc. since the losses for tax purposes could not be used on a separate return basis.

(14) Fireside Securities Corporation and Subsidiaries. The following condensed statements summarize the consolidated financial position and operating results of Fireside Securities Corporation and subsidiaries. Fireside Securities Corporation is a wholly-owned subsidiary of Argonaut Insurance Company.

Consolidated Balance Sheets

	December 31,	
	1977	*1976*
Assets:		
Cash......	$ 2,744,000	$ 1,979,000
Bonds, at amortized cost (market: 1977—$8,748,000; 1976—$18,705,000)	8,775,000	19,119,000
Loans receivable	133,117,000	117,211,000
Premises and equipment, at cost less accumulated depreciation	1,533,000	1,262,000
Other assets	839,000	1,829,000
	$147,008,000	$141,400,000
Liabilities:		
Investment certificates	$124,464,000	$116,739,000
Amounts due Teledyne, Inc.	—	5,458,000
Other liabilities	3,015,000	1,470,000
Shareholder's equity	19,529,000	17,733,000
	$147,008,000	$141,400,000

EXHIBIT 8 *(concluded)*

Consolidated Statements of Income

	Year Ended December 31,	
	1977	1976
Revenues:		
Interest on loans	$ 23,461,000	$ 20,413,000
Other income	3,914,000	3,438,000
	27,375,000	23,851,000
Expenses:		
Interest on investment certificates	8,040,000	7,752,000
General and administrative	13,287,000	11,013,000
Provision for losses on loans receivable	2,810,000	1,482,000
Provision for income taxes	1,442,000	1,408,000
	25,579,000	21,655,000
Net Income	$ 1,796,000	$ 2,196,000

The consolidated financial statements of Fireside Securities Corporation include the accounts of all its subsidiaries. Loans receivable are stated net of unearned discount. Deferred income taxes are provided for timing differences in the recognition of income and expenses.

Taxable income of Fireside Securities Corporation and its subsidiaries is included in the consolidated income tax return of Teledyne.

(15) Other Equity Investments. During 1977, the Company adopted the equity method of accounting for certain investments owned by its unconsolidated subsidiaries. The consolidated financial statements for 1976 have been restated to reflect the effects of the use of equity accounting. The incremental effect of the use of this method was to increase equity in net income of unconsolidated subsidiaries and net income by $10,436,000, or $0.88 per share ($0.86 fully diluted), in 1977 and by $1,920,000, or $0.16 per share ($0.14 fully diluted), in 1976. Investments accounted for by the equity method, and approximate voting percentages based on the most recent publicly available data, were: Brockway Glass Company, Inc. (22 percent), Curtiss-Wright Corporation (28 percent) and Litton Industries, Inc. (22 percent).

Teledyne's equity in the aggregate carrying value of these investments was $217,952,000 and $138,041,000 at December 31, 1977 and 1976, respectively. The aggregate market value of these investments, based on quoted market prices, was $203,785,000 at December 31, 1977. Teledyne's equity in the net income of these companies, after income taxes, was $12,879,000 in 1977 and $5,264,000 in 1976; these amounts include dividends received by Teledyne's unconsolidated subsidiaries. Income taxes have been provided at appropriate rates for that portion of the equity in net income received as dividends and at capital gains rates on the balance.

Teledyne's aggregate equity in the net assets of these companies exceeded the carrying value of the investments by approximately $18,000,000. Of this amount, approximately $5,000,000 has been considered to be related to cost in excess of net assets of purchased businesses reported in the financial statements of the investee companies; the remaining balance is not being amortized.

Inventories

Lakeside Enterprises*

Lakeside Enterprises is a manufacturer of parts used mainly in lawn mowers and other small machines. For many years, the company manufactured these parts in several states across the United States. Early in 1984, however, one of the company's principal customers announced its intention to buy machines completely ready for assembly from Japan. The news forced Lakeside to close its Kentucky plant and dispose of its inventories at that location.

The company's 1984 annual report, which appeared early in 1985, disclosed that the closure of the Kentucky facility had precipitated a dramatic deterioration in their business accompanied by a significant liquidation of their inventories. The notes to the financial statements made the following facts about their inventories available to shareholders.

NOTE 1—SUMMARY OF SIGNIFICANT ACCOUNTING POLICIES

Inventories are stated at the lower of cost or market value. Cost of inventories is determined by the last-in, first-out method [LIFO] which is less than current cost by $87,609 and $55,592 at December 28, 1983, and December 30, 1984, respectively.

During 1984, inventory quantities were reduced resulting in a liquidation of LIFO inventory quantities carried at lower costs prevailing in prior years as compared with the 1984 cost of production. As a result, income before taxes was increased by $62,310, equivalent to $2.10 per share after applicable income taxes, of which $26,190 before tax, equivalent to $0.88 per share after applicable income taxes, was reflected in cost of product sold and the balance was included as a reduction of the shutdown/disposal provision (see Note 6).

NOTE 6—SHUTDOWN/DISPOSAL PROVISION

In the third quarter of 1984, a provision was recorded for the closing of the Kentucky facilities which are to be sold or otherwise disposed of. The after-tax provision of $55,595 is equivalent to $2.93 per common share and covers estimated losses on the disposition of property, plant, and equipment, and inventories and employee severance and other costs. Net sales or products from these facilities included in consolidated sales totaled $92,465 in 1982, $121,012 in 1983, and $147,554 in 1984.

The note regarding quarterly results told a similar story.

NOTE 12—QUARTERLY RESULTS (UNAUDITED)

During the third and fourth quarters of 1984, inventory quantities were reduced, resulting in a liquidation of LIFO inventory quantities carried at lower costs prevailing in prior years as compared with the cost of 1983 production. As a result, income before taxes was increased by $62,310, equivalent to $2.10 per share after applicable income taxes, of which $36,120 before taxes, equivalent to $1.22 per share after applicable income taxes, was included as a reduction of the shutdown/disposal provision (see Note 6) with the balance reflected in cost of goods sold.

Examination of their situation revealed that, in 1981, they had moved from keeping their inventory on a first-in, first-out (FIFO) basis to a LIFO basis. A note to their financial statements at the time described the change.

NOTE 2—CHANGE IN INVENTORY VALUATION METHOD

In 1981, the company adopted the last-in, first-out (LIFO) method of determining costs for substantially all of its U.S. inventories. In prior years, inventory values were principally computed under the lower of cost or market, first-in, first-out (FIFO) method.

The effect of the change on the operating results for 1981 was to reduce net earnings after tax by $4,714, or 25 cents per share. The inventory balance at December 31, 1981, would have been $7,365 higher if inventory costs had continued to be determined principally under FIFO, rather than LIFO.

It was not practical to determine prior year effects of retroactive LIFO application.

The income statements for the years 1981 through 1984, along with the inventory shown in the balance sheet for each year, appear in Exhibit 1. Details of the units purchased each year appear in Exhibit 2.

QUESTIONS

1. Using the 1981 footnote, explain the change in the inventory valuation from FIFO to LIFO. What are the costs and benefits of such an accounting change?

2. Compute the LIFO reserve for each year and show how the company arrived at the effect of $62,310 for the liquidation of LIFO inventory in 1984. Assume an effective tax rate of 36 percent.

EXHIBIT 1
Lakeside Enterprises—Selected Financial Data

	1981	1982	1983	1984
Revenue	$1,058,422	$1,236,091	$1,421,526	$1,277,107
Cost of sales	797,232	958,210	1,085,134	971,550
Gross margin	261,190	277,881	336,392	305,557
Selling and administration.	192,775	207,332	209,884	212,567
Loss on write-off (net).	–0–	–0–	–0–	55,595
Income tax	24,629	25,398	45,543	33,476
Net income	43,785	45,151	80,965	3,919
Inventory (per ending balance sheet).	$ 147,304	$ 208,948	$ 232,006	$ 111,904

EXHIBIT 2
Lakeside Enterprises—Inventory Summary

	Units	Unit Cost
Opening inventory.	60,000	$2.00
Purchases in 1981	103,652	2.00
	293,920	2.10
Cost of sales	383,920	
Purchases in 1982	282,220	2.20
	153,450	2.60
Cost of sales	407,650	
Purchases in 1983	193,210	2.70
	202,250	2.90
Cost of sales	386,920	
Purchases in 1984	196,320	2.90
	82,000	3.00
Cost of sales	332,580	

Chrysler Corporation*

In February of 1971, Lynn Townsend, chairman of the board of Chrysler Corporation, made the following observations in his letter to the company's shareholders:

> Sales of Chrysler Corporation and consolidated subsidiaries throughout the world in 1970 totaled $7.0 billion, compared with $7.1 billion in 1969. Operations for the year resulted in a net loss of $7.6 million or $0.16 a share, compared with net earnings of $99.0 million or $2.09 a share in 1969.
>
> Net earnings for 1969 are restated to reflect a retroactive change in the company's method of valuing inventories, from a LIFO (last-in, first-out) to a FIFO (first-in, first-out) cost basis, as explained in the notes to financial statements. The LIFO method reduces inventory values and earnings in periods of rising costs. The rate of inflation in costs in 1970 and for the projected short-term future is so high that significant understatements of inventory values and earnings result. The use of the LIFO method in 1970 would have reduced inventory amounts at December 31, 1970, by approximately $150 million and did reduce inventory amounts reported at December 31, 1969, by approximately $110 million. Also, the use of the LIFO method in 1970 would have increased the loss for the year by approximately $20.0 million, and its use in 1969 reduced the earnings as reported for that year by $10.2 million. The other three U.S. automobile manufacturers have consistently used the FIFO method. Therefore, the reported loss for 1970 and the restated profit for 1969 are on a comparable basis as to inventory valuation with the other three companies. Prior years' earnings have been restated to make them comparable.
>
> Results of operations for the first three quarters of 1970 were previously reported on the LIFO method of valuing inventories. The restated results, on the FIFO method of valuing inventories, for the four quarters of 1970 are as follows:

	Net Earnings (Loss) (millions)	Earnings (Loss) a Share
1st quarter	$(27.4)	$(0.57)
2nd quarter.	10.1	0.21
3rd quarter	2.1	0.05
4th quarter	7.6	0.15
1970	$ (7.6)	$(0.16)

Additional information about the company's inventory accounting change, as well as the related tax effect, appeared in the footnotes to the financial statements:

_____

* This case was prepared by Kenneth R. Ferris from publicly available information. Copyright © 1984 by Kenneth R. Ferris. All rights reserved to the author. The situation is taken from an earlier Harvard College case, "Chrysler Corporation: The 1970 Accounting Change" (9–173–157).

Inventories—Accounting Change

Inventories are stated at the lower of cost or market. For the period January 1, 1957, through December 31, 1969, the last-in, first-out (LIFO) method of inventory valuation had been used for approximately 60 percent of the consolidated inventory. The cost of the remaining 40 percent of inventories was determined using the first-in, first-out (FIFO) or average cost methods. Effective January 1, 1970, the FIFO method of inventory valuation has been adopted for inventories previously valued using the LIFO method. This results in a more uniform valuation method throughout the corporation and its consolidated subsidiaries and makes the financial statements with respect to inventory valuation comparable with those of the other United States automobile manufacturers. As a result of adopting FIFO in 1970, the net loss reported is less than it would have been on a LIFO basis by approximately $20.0 million, or $0.40 a share. Inventory amounts at December 31, 1969, and 1970 are stated higher by approximately $110 million and $150 million, respectively, than they would have been had the LIFO method been continued.

The corporation has retroactively adjusted financial statements of prior years for this change. Accordingly, the 1969 financial statements have been restated resulting in an increase in Net Earnings of $10.2 million, and Net Earnings Retained for Use in the Business at December 31, 1969, and 1968 have been increased by $53.5 million and $43.3 million, respectively.

For U.S. income tax purposes the adjustment to inventory amounts will be taken into taxable income ratably over 20 years commencing January 1, 1971.

Taxes on Income

Taxes on income as shown in the consolidated statement of net earnings include the following:

	1970	1969
Currently payable:		
U.S. taxes (credit)	$(81,800,000)	$50,000,000
Other countries	44,300,000	36,300,000
Deferred taxes	16,100,000	(6,000,000)
As previously reported		80,300,000
Adjustment in deferred taxes for change in inventory valuation		11,400,000
Total taxes on income (credit)	$(21,400,000)	$91,700,000

The change in inventory valuation resulted in a reduction in income taxes allocable to the following year of approximately $56 million at December 31, 1969.

Reductions in taxes resulting from the investment credit provisions of the Internal Revenue Code are being taken into income over the estimated lives of the related assets. The amounts of such credits which were reflected in net earnings were $6,300,000 in 1970 and $5,400,000 in 1969.

Thus, the change in the method of accounting for inventories was made as of January 1, 1970, and consequently necessitated a retroactive adjustment to Chrysler's 1969 retained earnings (see financial statements in Exhibits 1–4). Further, to provide comparability, the 1969 earnings statement was restated to reflect the FIFO method.

QUESTIONS

1. Why did Chrysler change its method of accounting for inventories?

2. Compare the benefits resulting from the change with the costs of making such a change; do you feel that the accounting change was warranted?

3. Under what financial and market conditions can a firm optimally switch from LIFO to FIFO? from FIFO to LIFO?

EXHIBIT 1

CHRYSLER CORPORATION AND CONSOLIDATED SUBSIDIARIES
Consolidated Statement of Net Earnings
For Years Ended December 31, 1969, and 1970

	1970	1969*
Net sales	$6,999,675,655	$7,052,184,678
Equity in net earnings (loss) of unconsolidated subsidiaries	(6,210,013)	(6,286,309)
Other income and deductions	(19,962,022)	23,261,424
	6,973,503,620	7,069,159,793
Cost of products sold, other than items below	6,103,250,974	5,966,732,377
Depreciation of plant and equipment	176,758,139	170,305,745
Amortization of special tools	172,568,348	167,194,002
Selling and administrative expenses	386,041,866	431,706,851
Pension and retirement plans	121,406,136	114,577,630
Interest on long-term debt	46,998,713	31,702,530
Taxes on income (credit)	(21,400,000)	91,700,000
	6,985,624,176	6,973,919,135
Net earnings (loss) including minority interest	(12,120,556)	95,240,658
Minority interest in net loss of consolidated subsidiaries	4,517,536	3,730,564
Net earnings (loss)	$ (7,603,020)	$ 98,971,222
Average number of shares of common stock outstanding during the year	48,693,200	47,390,561
Net earnings (loss) a share	$(0.16)	$2.09

* Restated to reflect the change made in 1970 in accounting for inventories and to conform to 1970 classifications. The 1969 net earnings and net earnings a share, as previously reported, were $88.8 million and $1.87 respectively. See Inventories—Accounting Change note.

EXHIBIT 2

CHRYSLER CORPORATION AND CONSOLIDATED SUBSIDIARIES
Consolidated Balance Sheet
For Years Ended December 31, 1969, and 1970

	1970	1969*
Assets		
Current assets:		
Cash	$ 95,807,393	$ 78,768,440
Marketable securities—at cost and accrued interest.	60,607,134	230,562,926
Accounts receivable (less allowance for		
doubtful accounts: 1970—$15,700,000;		
1969—$13,400,000)	438,852,496	477,880,423
Refundable U.S. taxes on income	80,000,000	—
Inventories (see Inventories—Accounting		
Change note).	1,390,681,228	1,335,198,128
Prepaid insurance, taxes, and other expenses	83,299,833	80,087,753
Income taxes allocable to the following year	17,415,554	27,186,281
Total current assets	2,166,663,638	2,229,683,951
Investments and other assets:		
Investments in and advances to associated		
companies outside the United States	24,907,266	15,496,619
Investments in and advances to		
unconsolidated subsidiaries.	675,212,687	577,052,868
Income taxes allocable—noncurrent.	22,301,845	32,465,250
Other noncurrent assets.	44,971,952	55,814,937
Total investments and other assets	767,393,750	680,829,674
Property, plant, and equipment:		
Land, buildings, machinery, and equipment.	2,949,256,417	2,825,623,645
Less accumulated depreciation.	1,593,482,362	1,451,750,556
	1,355,774,055	1,373,873,089
Unamortized special tools.	447,449,636	379,153,112
Net property, plant, equipment	1,803,223,691	1,753,026,201
Cost of investments in consolidated		
subsidiaries in excess of equity.	78,491,382	78,184,245
Total assets	$4,815,772,461	$4,741,724,071

* Restated to reflect the change made in 1970 in accounting for inventories.

EXHIBIT 2 *(concluded)*

CHRYSLER CORPORATION AND CONSOLIDATED SUBSIDIARIES
Liabilities and Shareholders' Investment
For Years Ended December 31, 1969, and 1970

	1970	1969*
Liabilities		
Current liabilities:		
Accounts payable and accrued expenses.	$1,095,984,194	$1,116,607,970
Short-term debt.	374,186,273	477,442,371
Payments due within one year on long-term debt	34,572,552	39,825,038
Taxes on income	43,136,332	9,969,436
Total current liabilities	1,547,879,351	1,643,844,815
Other liabilities:		
Deferred incentive compensation.	2,726,641	7,493,823
Other employee benefit plans.	63,462,301	55,575,476
Deferred investment tax credit	21,774,580	25,598,022
Unrealized profits on sales to unconsolidated		
subsidiaries	49,280,076	47,336,034
Other noncurrent liabilities.	68,733,595	89,870,533
Total other liabilities	205,977,193	225,873,888
Long-term debt:		
Notes and debentures payable.	671,053,172	466,951,466
Convertible sinking fund debentures.	119,999,000	119,999,000
Total Long-term debt	791,052,172	586,950,466
International operations reserve	35,500,000	35,500,000
Minority interest in net assets of consolidated		
subsidiaries	79,742,516	95,149,271
Shareholders' investment:		
Represented by—		
Common stock—par value $6.25 a share:		
Authorized 80,000,000 shares; issued and		
outstanding 49,498,979 shares at		
December 31, 1970, and 47,942,136		
shares at December 31, 1969	309,368,619	299,638,350
Additional paid-in capital	484,020,938	455,739,253
Net earnings retained for use in the business	1,362,231,672	1,399,028,028
Total shareholders' investment.	2,155,621,229	2,154,405,631
Total liabilities and shareholders' investment	$4,815,772,461	$4,741,724,071

* Restated to reflect the change made in 1970 in accounting for inventories.

EXHIBIT 3

CHRYSLER CORPORATION AND CONSOLIDATED SUBSIDIARIES
Consolidated Statement of Additional Paid-in Capital
For Years Ended December 31, 1969, and 1970

	1970	1969*
Balance at beginning of year	$455,739,253	$421,184,933
Excess of market price over par value of newly issued shares of common stock sold to the thrift-stock ownership programs (1,556,843 in 1970; 927,276 in 1969)	28,281,685	33,796,320
Excess of option price over par value of shares of common stock issued under the stock option plans (none in 1970; 25,172 in 1969)	—	758,000
Balance at end of year	$484,020,938	$455,739,253

* Restated to reflect the change made in 1970 in accounting of inventories.

EXHIBIT 4

CHRYSLER CORPORATION AND CONSOLIDATED SUBSIDIARIES
Consolidated Statement of Net Earnings Retained for Use in the Business
For Years Ended December 31, 1969, and 1970

	1970	1969*
Balance at beginning of year	$1,399,028,028	$1,351,453,762
Adjustment (for the years 1957 through 1968)		43,309,750
As restated		1,394,763,512
Net loss	(7,603,020)	
Net earnings as restated		98,971,222
	1,391,425,008	1,493,734,734
Cash dividends paid ($0.60 a share in 1970 and $2.00 a share in 1969)	29,193,336	94,706,706
Balance at end of year	$1,362,231,672	$1,399,028,028

* Restated to reflect the change made in 1970 in accounting of inventories.

Fixed Assets

West Virginia Coal Company*

Near the end of 1978, Ralph and Joe Miller formed the West Virginia Coal Company. According to the charter of incorporation, the purpose of the new business was to "locate, develop, extract, and transport" coal reserves in the state of West Virginia. The company remained closely held until January 1982, at which time a small public offering of common shares was held. According to the prospectus, the funds raised through the public offering would be used to acquire coal reserves and removal and transportation equipment, and to construct miscellaneous facilities for the administration of the company's coal operations.

Approximately $3 million was raised through the offering and, during 1982, was dispersed as follows:

1. In February, the West Virginia Coal Company paid $2.2 million for a tract of land containing estimated coal reserves of 3 million tons; following extraction and reclamation, it was anticipated that the land would have a resale value of $200,000 as crop land.

2. The following equipment was purchased:

Quantity	Item	Estimated Useful Life	Price
1	Bulldozer	10 years	$ 95,000
1	Earth-mover with stripping bucket	5 years	312,000
3	Coal trucks	3 years	60,000 (each)

The scrap value of the equipment at the end of its useful life was anticipated to be nominal. Signed checks for the equipment were delivered to the vendors on April 1.

* This case was prepared by Kenneth R. Ferris. Copyright © 1984 by Kenneth R. Ferris. All rights reserved to the author.

3. Two structures were constructed on the tract of land:

	Estimated Useful Life	Cost
Administrative building	12 years	$100,000
Storage facility for equipment	12 years	50,000

It was anticipated that it would not be economically feasible to remove the two buildings from the land after the coal operations had terminated. In addition, it was uncertain whether or not the facilities might have alternative uses to subsequent landowners. Construction of the two facilities was completed in late June.

During May and June 1982, the company spent an additional $250,000 to develop the tract of land (e.g., removing trees and laying roads). Finally, during the second half of the year, extraction operations began. By the end of 1982, 600,000 tons of coal had been mined and sold to the Monongahela Power Company at an average price of $13 per delivered ton.

Operating expenses, exclusive of depreciation and depletion, and selling and administrative expenses incurred in connection with the mining operations totaled $210,000.

QUESTIONS

1. Before financial statements can be prepared for the year ended December 31, 1982, a number of accounting policy decisions must be made. Prepare a list of those policy decisions, and for each area requiring a decision, describe what approach (i.e., accounting method) you would take and explain why you chose that approach. Assume that these decisions are to be made for financial reporting purposes only, and a tax rate of 50 percent.

2. Based on the accounting policies that you selected in Question 1, prepare an income statement for 1982 and a partial balance sheet as of December 31, 1982.

3. Assume that *(a)* coal producers are eligible for a 10 percent statutory percentage depletion allowance and that *(b)* a firm may choose to deplete its natural resources on either a unit-of-production basis or the statutory percentage basis for tax purposes. Which method would the West Virginia Coal Company use to deplete its reserves? Why?

Union Carbide Corporation*

On January 24, 1980, the management of the Union Carbide Corporation announced several changes in accounting policy that would become effective as of the beginning of that year. In a statement to security analysts, Mr. Louis G. Peloubet, controller of Union Carbide, estimated the impact of these changes on earnings per share to be as follows:

Accounting Policy Change	1979 per Share Impact	Estimated 1980 per Share Impact
• Lengthening the depreciable lives of machinery and equipment	$1.28	$1.37
• Switch to flow-through method of accounting for the investment tax credit.	0.21	0.26
• Adoption of *FASB Statement No. 34* (capitalization of interest).	—	0.30
	$1.49	$1.93
• Nonrecurring addition to net earnings of previously deferred investment tax credits	—	3.22
Total increase in EPS	$1.49	$5.15

This case concerns the accounting for these changes and their impact on the reported earnings and cash flows of the Union Carbide Corporation.

INTEREST CAPITALIZATION

In 1979, the Financial Accounting Standards Board adopted *Statement No. 34,* "Capitalization of Interest Costs." This accounting standard required companies to capitalize the interest costs associated with the self-construction of assets. Prior to the adoption of this standard, companies were permitted either to expense such costs or to capitalize them into the cost basis of the asset under construction. Thus, the purpose of the statement was: to standardize accounting practice between companies; to provide consistency in economic value between purchased versus self-constructed assets (i.e., typically the cost of borrowed funds to an original asset manufacturer is added to the asset's sale price and passed onto the final consumer); to give a more accurate picture of the overall cost of a company's investment (i.e., interest costs are a legitimate

---

*This case was prepared by Kenneth R. Ferris from publicly available information. Copyright © 1984 by Kenneth R. Ferris. All rights reserved to the author.

cost of acquiring the use of a new asset and should be reflected in the total cost of that asset); and to better match the costs of acquiring an asset with the revenues that it subsequently produces.

FASB Statement No. 34 applies to all new assets that are constructed or otherwise produced for a company's own use, for example, a building, a piece of equipment, or even the development of oil and gas reserves for an energy company. The statement also requires the capitalization of interest on assets constructed for subsequent sale or lease, such as a shopping center or a commercial office building.

Under this accounting rule, if the specific cost of borrowing associated with a capital project is known, this value must be capitalized into the asset's cost basis for depreciation purposes. If, on the other hand, the company finances the construction out of internal funds or from general borrowings, the implied interest to be capitalized is determined by using the average effective interest rate on all of the firm's outstanding debt. Once the asset has been placed into service, no further capitalization is required, and previously capitalized interest costs will flow through the income statement as part of the depreciation expense on the new asset.

All companies were required to implement *FASB Statement No. 34*, effective December 15, 1979. The Union Carbide Corporation adopted this accounting procedure for the fiscal year beginning January 1, 1980.

INVESTMENT TAX CREDIT

In 1962, the U.S. government introduced the investment tax credit in an effort to stimulate capital investment. The ITC permitted a credit directly against a company's federal income tax liability in the year in which a "qualified" depreciable asset was purchased. The size of the credit was a function of the cost of the asset, its expected useful life, and an established credit percentage. Currently, the ITC is determined by the following:

Cumulative Credit Percentage	Expected Useful Life
2%	1 year
4	2
6	3
8	4
10	5 and over

Thus, the purchase of an asset having an expected useful life of three years would provide an ITC equal to 6 percent of the asset's cost; the maximum ITC percentage for assets having a useful life of five or more years is 10 percent.

The enactment of the investment tax credit raised certain accounting questions regarding the timing of the recognition of the tax benefit for income statement purposes. Two methods evolved: the flow-through and the deferral methods. Proponents of the view that the ITC was a selective reduction in taxes believed that the full amount of the credit should be recognized in the year the asset was acquired. This method became known as the "flow-through" approach since the full benefit of the credit flowed through from the firm's income tax statement to its earnings statement for financial reporting purposes. Proponents of the view that the ITC represented a reduction in the cost basis of the asset believed that the credit should be deferred, spread over the productive life of the asset, and thus amortized in a manner similar to depreciation of the asset's original cost; this method became known as the "deferral" method.

Prior to 1980, the Union Carbide Corporation had utilized the deferral method; but in 1980, the firm switched to the flow-through approach. According to company spokesman Peloubet, the Union Carbide Corporation felt that the deferral method had three major limitations: deferred earnings were being eroded by inflation, retained earnings were understated, and most companies used the flow-through method. A study by Price Waterhouse & Company found that 87 percent of the companies surveyed used the flow-through method of accounting for the ITC.

With the adoption of this method, Union Carbide claimed that earnings would better reflect the current impact of investment decisions and that the impact of the ITC on earnings would now be consistent with its impact on the company's cash flows. As a consequence of this accounting policy change, all new investment tax credits would flow directly into the current year's earnings as new equipment was put into service. In addition, however, $217 million in deferred investment tax credits accumulated on the balance sheet as of December 31, 1979, would be taken into 1980 earnings.

DEPRECIATION CHANGE

Prior to 1980, the Union Carbide Corporation calculated depreciation for financial reporting purposes using the straight-line method. In addition, the company estimated the useful lives of its assets using the U.S. Treasury Asset Depreciation Range (ADR) system. For tax purposes, Union Carbide used an accelerated depreciation method, along with the *minimum* ADR guideline lives, thereby obtaining the lowest tax liability.

In 1980, however, the company abandoned the ADR guidelines and adopted longer depreciable lives for a substantial portion (i.e., 70 percent) of its assets. While the change did not impact the depreciation on the firm's buildings and transportation equipment, it did impact machinery and equipment in the following areas:

	ADR Guideline Life	Revised Life
Machinery and equipment in:		
Chemicals and plastics.	11 years	17 years
Gases and related areas.	11	15
Metals and carbons.	10, 12, 14, 18	15 and 20
Batteries, home, and automotive.	11 and 12	13 and 15

The overall effect of this change was to increase the average life of the company's assets by 35 percent.

At a presentation to security analysts, Union Carbide controller Peloubet stated that the ADR guideline lives were unrealistically short, and thus tended to distort reported financial results. Moreover, the new depreciable lives were now comparable to those used by the company's leading competitors, Dow Chemical and E. I. du Pont de Nemours & Co.

Although the accounting change did achieve greater comparability in depreciable lives between Union Carbide and its competitors, increased comparability in depreciation method was not enhanced. Specifically, while Union Carbide retained its use of the straight-line method, Dow Chemical and Du Pont utilized accelerated depreciation methods. Exhibit 1 reveals the differential impact of these methods; and, as can be noted, even before the change in depreciable lives, Union Carbide's depreciation was significantly lower than that of its two leading competitors.

Financial statements and accompanying notes are shown in Exhibits 2–6.

QUESTIONS

1. Evaluate the accounting changes made by the Union Carbide Corporation in 1980. Do you believe that the changes improved the "quality of reported earnings"? Substantiate your views.

2. How did these accounting changes impact the cash flows of Union Carbide? How would an efficient capital market react to this information?

EXHIBIT 1
Depreciation Expense as a Percentage of
Average Gross Fixed Assets

	1977	1978
Dow Chemical	8.9%	8.9%
E. I. du Pont de Nemours & Co	8.1	8.0
Union Carbide (as reported)	5.6	5.8
Union Carbide (revised lives)	3.7	3.9

* Source: Bear Stearns & Co.

EXHIBIT 2

UNION CARBIDE CORPORATION AND SUBSIDIARIES
Consolidated Statement of Income and Retained Earnings
For Year Ended December 31
(millions of dollars, except per share figures)

	1980	1979	1978
Net sales	$9,994	$9,177	$7,870
Deductions (additions)			
Cost of sales	7,186	6,491	5,580
Research and development	166	161	156
Selling, administrative, and other expenses	1,152	1,053	943
Depreciation	326	470	417
Interest on long-term and short-term debt	153	161	159
Other income—net	(41)	42	(12)
Income before provision for income taxes	1,052	799	627
Provision for income taxes	360	251	205
Income of consolidated companies	692	548	422
Less: Minority stockholders' share of income	49	25	33
Plus: UCC share of income of companies carried at equity	30	33	5
Income before cumulative effect of change in accounting principle	673	556	394
Cumulative effect of change in accounting principle for the investment tax credit (Note 2)	217	—	—
Net income	890	556	394
Retained earnings at January 1*	3,486	3,120	2,905
	4,376	3,676	3,299
Dividends declared	206	190	181
Retained earnings at December 31	$4,170	$3,486	$3,118
Per share			
Income before cumulative effect of change in accounting principle	$10.08	$ 8.47	$ 6.09
Cumulative effect of change in accounting principle for the investment tax credit	$ 3.28	$ —	$ —
Net income†	$13.36	$ 8.47	$ 6.09
Dividends declared	$ 3.10	$ 2.90	$ 2.80
Pro forma			
Net income with 1980 change in accounting principle for the investment tax credit applied retroactively	$ 673	$ 573	$ 448
Net income per share†	$10.08	$ 8.73	$ 6.92

*After adjustment for a credit of $2.4 million in 1979 and a $0.3 million charge in 1978 for companies with which business combinations were effected on a pooling of interests basis.

†Based on 66,714,481 shares (65,673,908 shares in 1979 and 64,738,610 shares in 1978), the weighted average number of shares outstanding during the year.

The Notes to Financial Statements on pages 30 through 38 are an integral part of this statement.

EXHIBIT 3

UNION CARBIDE CORPORATION AND SUBSIDIARIES
Consolidated Balance Sheet At December 31
(millions of dollars)

	1980	1979
Assets		
Cash	$ 69	$ 116
Time deposits and short-term marketable securities	174	333
	243	449
Notes and accounts receivable	1,598	1,433
Inventories:		
Raw materials and supplies	588	499
Work in process	464	446
Finished goods	835	829
	1,887	1,774
Prepaid expenses	191	155
Total current assets	3,919	3,811
Property, plant, and equipment	9,636	8,730
Less: Accumulated depreciation	4,429	4,271
Net fixed assets	5,207	4,459
Companies carried at equity	239	213
Other investments and advances	119	107
Total investments and advances	358	320
Other assets	175	213
Total assets	$9,659	$8,803

Liabilities and stockholders' equity		
Accounts payable	$ 432	$ 528
Short-term debt	266	156
Payments due within one year on long-term debt	51	52
Accrued income and other taxes	275	239
Other accrued liabilities	771	766
Total current liabilities	1,795	1,741
Long-term debt	1,859	1,773
Deferred credits	899	953
Minority stockholders' equity in consolidated subsidiaries	330	294
UCC stockholders' equity:		
Common stock authorized—90,000,000 shares		
Common stock issued—67,453,673 shares (66,292,649 shares in 1979)	607	557
Retained earnings	4,170	3,486
	4,777	4,043
Less: Treasury stock, at cost—86,888 shares (87,090 shares in 1979)	1	1
Total UCC stockholders' equity	4,776	4,042
Total liabilities and stockholders' equity	$9,659	$8,803

The Notes to Financial Statements on pages 30 through 38 are an integral part of this statement.

EXHIBIT 4

UNION CARBIDE CORPORATION AND SUBSIDIARIES
Consolidated Statement of Changes in Financial Position
Year Ended December 31
(millions of dollars)

	1980	1979	1978
Cash and time deposits and short-term marketable securities at beginning of year	$ 449	$ 284	$ 323
Funds provided by			
Net income	890	556	394
Noncash charges (credits) to net income			
Depreciation	326	470	417
Deferred income taxes	185	94	85
Cumulative effect of change in accounting principle for the investment tax credit (Note 2)	(217)	–	–
Other noncash charges (credits)—net	27	(6)	28
Total funds from operations	1,211	1,114	924
Long-term debt			
New borrowings	164	370	40
Reductions	(73)	(80)	(44)
Increase (decrease) in short-term debt and current portion of long-term debt	109	(184)	157
Increase in common stock	50	36	19
Total funds from financing	250	142	172
European ethylene derivatives businesses sold (Note 4)			
Net fixed assets	–	–	267
Other assets—net	–	–	102
Long- and short-term debt assumed by purchaser	–	–	(218)
Net assets sold	–	–	151
Reductions of net fixed assets	55	23	24
Decrease (increase) in investments and other assets	22	7	(18)
Total funds from other sources	77	30	157
Total funds provided	1,538	1,286	1,253
Funds used for			
Dividends	206	190	181
Capital expenditures	1,129	831	688
Net fixed assets of Gulf Coast Olefins Company, an affiliate consolidated in 1978 (Note 4)	–	–	297
Increase in notes and accounts receivable	165	175	224
Increase in inventories	113	233	83
Decrease (increase) in payables and accruals	78	(291)	(221)
Other—net	53	(17)	40
Total funds used	1,744	1,121	1,292
Net increase (decrease) in funds	(206)	165	(39)
Cash and time deposits and short-term marketable securities at end of year	$ 243	$ 449	$ 284

Amounts reported for 1978 changes in asset and liability accounts are exclusive of changes in account balances resulting from the sale of consolidated European ethylene derivatives businesses.

The Notes to Financial Statements on pages 30 through 38 are an integral part of this statement.

EXHIBIT 5

Notes to Financial Statements—1980 and 1979

1. SUMMARY OF SIGNIFICANT ACCOUNTING POLICIES

Principles of consolidation—The consolidated financial statements include the assets, liabilities, revenues, and expenses of all significant subsidiaries except Ucar Capital Corporation, which is carried at equity in net assets. All significant inter-company transactions have been eliminated in consolidation. Investments in significant companies 20 to 50 percent owned are carried at equity in net assets, and Union Carbide's share of their earnings is included in income. Other investments are carried generally at cost or less.

Marketable securities—Marketable securities are carried at the lower of cost or market. Carrying value was substantially the same as market value at December 31, 1980 and 1979.

Inventories—Inventory values, which do not include depreciation, are stated at cost or market, whichever is lower. Cost is determined generally on the "last-in, first-out" (LIFO) method for U.S. companies and for certain subsidiaries operating outside the United States. Generally, the "average cost" method is used by all other subsidiaries.

Approximately 67 percent of inventory amounts before application of the LIFO method at December 31, 1980 (63 percent at December 31, 1979) have been valued on the LIFO basis. It is estimated that if these inventories had been valued at current costs, inventories would have been approximately $1,049 million and $786 million higher than reported at December 31, 1980, and December 31, 1979, respectively.

Fixed assets and depreciation—Fixed assets are carried at cost. Expenditures for replacements are capitalized and the replaced items are retired. Gains and losses from the sale of property are included in income.

Depreciation is calculated on a straight-line basis. The Corporation and its subsidiaries use other depreciation methods (generally accelerated) for tax purposes where appropriate.

Prior to 1980, depreciation was generally calculated utilizing 1962 U.S. Internal Revenue Service guideline lives. Effective January 1, 1980, Union Carbide commenced using revised estimated useful lives rather than the guideline lives to depreciate the cost of machinery and equipment. See Note 2.

Following is a summary of lives used for calculating depreciation in 1980:

Class of Property	Lives used
Land improvements	20 years
Buildings	20 to 40 years
Machinery and equipment	13 to 20 years*
Leasehold improvements	Lease period

*Prior to 1980, lives used were 10 to 18 years.

Patents, trade marks, and goodwill—Amounts paid for purchased patents and for securities of newly acquired subsidiaries in excess of the fair value of the net assets of such subsidiaries have been charged to patents, trade marks, and goodwill. The portion of such amounts determined to be attributable to patents is amortized over their remaining lives and the balance is amortized over the estimated period of benefit, but not more than 40 years.

Research and development—Research and development costs are charged to expense as incurred. Depreciation expense applicable to research and development facilities and equipment is included in Depreciation in the income statement ($7 million in 1980, $10 million in 1979 and $8 million in 1978).

Income taxes—Provision has been made for deferred income taxes where differences exist between the period in which transactions, principally relating to depreciation, affect taxable income and the period in which they enter into the determination of income in the financial statements.

Commencing January 1, 1980, investment tax credits have been included in income in the period earned (the flow-through method), rather than deferred and taken into income over the average guideline life of the assets earning the credit (the deferred method). See Note 2. Benefits from energy tax credits are included currently in net income.

Retirement program—The Corporation's contribution to the U.S. retirement program in each year is based on the recommendation of an independent actuarial firm using the entry age normal method. Accrued costs are funded for all employees age 25 and over, with unfunded prior service costs being amortized over periods up to 30 years.

Program costs of consolidated international subsidiaries are accounted for substantially on an accrual basis.

Net income per share—Net income per share is based on the weighted average number of shares of common stock outstanding in each year. There would have been no material dilutive effect on net income per share for 1980, 1979 or 1978 if convertible securities had been converted and if outstanding stock options had been exercised.

EXHIBIT 5 *(continued)*

2. ACCOUNTING CHANGES

Results for 1980 include the effects of several accounting changes adopted as of January 1, 1980. These changes, which do not affect income tax payments or cash flow, are described below.

As explained in Note 1, the flow-through method of accounting for the investment tax credit has been used rather than the deferred method. The flow-through method, which is utilized by a large majority of industry, avoids the decreasing impact of the investment tax credit that results from use of the deferred method during periods of continuing high inflation. This change in accounting principle increased 1980 net income for credits earned during the year by approximately $24 million, or $0.36 per share, which is included in the Consolidated Statement of Income and Retained Earnings as a reduction in the provision for income taxes. In addition, the cumulative effect of deferred investment tax credits for the periods through December 31, 1979, which amounted to $217 million, or $3.28 per share, has been reported as a non-recurring credit in the Consolidated Statement of Income and Retained Earnings under the caption "Cumulative effect of change in accounting principle for the investment tax credit." Pro forma net income and net income per share amounts, reflecting retroactive application of the 1980 change in method of accounting for the investment tax credit, are shown at the bottom of the income statement.

As also explained in Note 1, revised estimated useful lives have been used to depreciate the cost of machinery and equipment rather than the shorter Internal Revenue Service guideline lives adopted in 1962. The effect of this change in accounting estimate was to increase 1980 net income by approximately $94 million, or $1.41 per share.

Pursuant to Statement No. 34 of the Financial Accounting Standards Board, interest costs of $45 million in 1980 attributable to major capital projects in progress have been capitalized rather than charged to expense as incurred. The capitalized interest is being amortized over the average useful life of the assets. The effect of this change was to increase 1980 net income by approximately $24 million, or $0.36 per share.

3. UCAR CAPITAL CORPORATION

Ucar Capital Corporation (Capital), a wholly-owned finance subsidiary, purchases without recourse certain customer obligations from Union Carbide at a discount sufficient to yield earnings of not less than one and one-half times its fixed charges. In the Consolidated Statement of Income and Retained Earnings, Capital's income before income taxes, which amounted to $9 million in 1980, 1979 and 1978, is included in Other income—net as a reduction of discount expense, and the related income tax is included in Provision for income taxes.

The average effective interest rate on Capital's long-term borrowings, which consist of $100 million of 15-year notes due from 1983 to 1992 and $88 million of 5-year notes due in quarterly installments to September 1982 ($100 million in 1979), was 8.4 percent in 1980, 1979 and 1978.

Additional financial information relating to Capital is presented below:

Millions of dollars	December 31,	
	1980	1979
Total assets	$256	$252
Less: Total liabilities	204	204
Net assets	$ 52	$ 48

4. SIGNIFICANT TRANSACTIONS

In October 1978, the Corporation purchased the remaining interest in Gulf Coast Olefins Company (GCOC), whose principal asset is an olefins unit at Taft, Louisiana, thereby increasing its interest in GCOC to 100 percent. Concurrently, GCOC retired its long-term debt of $292 million with funds provided by Union Carbide.

Also in 1978, the Corporation sold its consolidated European ethylene derivatives businesses for net proceeds of $176 million plus assumption by the purchaser of $218 million in long- and short-term debt.

5. FOREIGN CURRENCY ADJUSTMENTS

In 1980, translation of balance sheet accounts carried in foreign currencies, and exchange gains and losses, resulted in a credit to Other income—net of $1 million ($37 million charge in 1979 and $51 million charge in 1978). The effect, after adjustments for taxes on exchange gains and losses, for minority interests, and for currency adjustments of companies carried at equity, was to increase net income in 1980 by $7 million ($29 million decrease in 1979 and $59 million decrease in 1978).

EXHIBIT 5 *(continued)*

6. INTERNATIONAL OPERATIONS

The following are financial summaries of consolidated international subsidiaries and international companies carried at equity:

Millions of dollars	Consolidated Subsidiaries		
	1980	1979	1978*
Net sales	$3,149	$2,782	$2,534
Net income	$ 239	$ 168	$ 106
UCC Share	$ 192	$ 146	$ 76
Total assets	$3,055	$2,690	
Less: Total liabilities	1,460	1,289	
Net assets	1,595	1,401	
UCC equity	$1,299	$1,140	

*Net sales includes $315 million representing sales of European ethylene derivatives businesses that were sold in 1978 and Net income and UCC share include a loss of $32 million for these operations. Net income and UCC share also include a gain of $25 million from the sale of these businesses. See Note 4.

Millions of dollars	Companies Carried At Equity		
	1980	1979	1978
Net sales*	$1,106	$ 920	$ 603
Net income	$ 61	$ 69	$ 15
UCC Share	$ 29	$ 32	$ 9
Total assets	$1,201	$ 964	
Less: Total liabilities	780	633	
Net assets	421	331	
UCC Equity	$ 172	$ 152	

*Exclusive of $82 million net sales to UCC and its consolidated subsidiaries in 1980 ($78 million in 1979 and in 1978).

7. SEGMENT INFORMATION

Audited industry and geographic segment data are presented in the Financial Review on page 18.

Union Carbide's businesses and products are described on pages 6 through 19.

8. INCOME TAXES

The following is an analysis of income tax expense:

Millions of dollars	1980		1979		1978	
	Current	Deferred	Current	Deferred	Current	Deferred
U.S. Federal income taxes	$ 62	$167	$ 82	$ 53	$ 87	$ 53
U.S. investment tax credit*	(44)	(9)	(40)	14	(58)	38
U.S. energy tax credit	(7)	–	(1)	–	(7)	–
U.S. state and local taxes based on income	13	–	11	–	10	–
Non-U.S. income taxes	151	27	105	27	88	(6)
	$175	$185	$157	$94	$120	$ 85
Provision for income taxes	$360		$251		$205	

*See Note 2, "Accounting Changes."

Deferred U.S. Federal income taxes include $127 million in 1980 ($59 million in 1979 and $50 million in 1978) related to depreciation timing differences. Deferred Non-U.S. income taxes include $35 million in 1980 ($31 million in 1979 and $13 million in 1978) related to such timing differences. Additionally, 1979 includes an $11 million credit related to changes in tax benefits in United Kingdom tax laws. The effects of timing differences for other items are not material.

At December 31, 1980, the Corporation had $19 million of Investment Tax Credit carryforward which has been recognized for book purposes as a reduction in the provision for deferred income taxes in current and prior years.

Portions of the income of several subsidiaries operating in Puerto Rico and outside the United States are exempt from income taxes under local tax statutes. Non-U.S. income taxes were reduced by $33 million in 1980 ($42 million in 1979 and $41 million in 1978) as a result of these exemptions, which expire principally in 1989.

The consolidated effective income tax rate was 34.2 percent in 1980, 31.4 percent in 1979 and 32.8 percent in 1978. An analysis of the difference between the provision for income taxes and the amount computed by applying the statutory Federal income tax rate to consolidated income before provision for income taxes is as follows:

EXHIBIT 5 *(continued)*

	1980		1979		1978	
	Millions of dollars	Percent of pretax income	Millions of dollars	Percent of pretax income	Millions of dollars	Percent of pretax income
Tax at statutory Federal rate	$484	46.0	$368	46.0	$301	48.0
Income taxes of subsidiaries operating in Puerto Rico and outside the United States	(55)	(5.2)	(68)	(8.5)	(57)	(9.1)
U.S. investment tax credit	(53)	(5.1)	(26)	(3.2)	(20)	(3.1)
Allowable depletion in excess of cost depletion	(17)	(1.7)	(15)	(2.0)	(15)	(2.4)
Domestic international sales corporation	(17)	(1.7)	(12)	(1.4)	(8)	(1.2)
Other, net	18	1.9	4	0.5	4	0.6
	$360	34.2	$251	31.4	$205	32.8

The following is a summary of the U.S. and Non-U.S. components of income before provision for income taxes:

Millions of dollars	1980	1979	1978
Income before provision for income taxes:			
U.S.	$ 585	$400	$346
Non-U.S. (includes Puerto Rico)	467	399	281
	$1,052	$799	$627

The Corporation provides for taxes on undistributed earnings of affiliates included in consolidated retained earnings to the extent such earnings are planned to be remitted and not reinvested indefinitely. Undistributed earnings of affiliates intended to be reinvested indefinitely amounted to $1.6 billion at December 31, 1980.

9. OTHER INCOME—NET

The following is an analysis of Other income—net:

Millions of dollars	1980	1979	1978
Investment income (principally from short-term investments)	$ 46	$ 39	$ 31
Foreign currency adjustments	1	(37)	(51)
Net discount expense on sales of customer obligations to Ucar Capital Corporation	(17)	(17)	(17)
Charges related to the sale of a mineral production payment	(9)	(12)	(12)
Sales and disposals of businesses and other assets*	(14)	(21)	54
Other	34	6	7
	$ 41	$(42)	$ 12

*Includes for 1980 a charge of $22 million ($27 million after tax, or $0.40 per share) accrued against the divestiture of a portion of the Corporation's metals business. Includes for 1979 a charge of $24 million ($13 million after tax, or $0.20 per share) resulting from withdrawal from the Corporation's imaging systems hardware business. Includes for 1978 a gain of $53 million ($25 million after tax, or $0.38 per share) from sale of the Corporation's consolidated European ethylene derivatives businesses.

10. SUPPLEMENTARY BALANCE SHEET DETAIL

Millions of dollars at December 31	1980	1979
Notes and accounts receivable		
Trade	$1,460	$1,334
Other	169	128
	1,629	1,462
Less: Allowance for doubtful accounts	31	29
	$1,598	$1,433
Fixed assets		
Land and improvements	$ 529	$ 489
Buildings	1,012	911
Machinery and equipment	7,186	6,647
Construction in progress and other	909	683
	$9,636	$8,730
Other assets		
Deferred charges	$ 61	$ 73
Long-term receivables	55	48
Patents, trade marks, and goodwill	59	92
	$ 175	$ 213
Short-term debt		
Commercial paper	$ 61	$ —
Bank loans	205	156
	$266	$ 156
Other accrued liabilities		
Accrued accounts payable	$ 371	$ 403
Payrolls	130	125
Other	270	238
	$ 771	$ 766
Deferred credits		
Income taxes*	$ 673	$ 491
Investment tax credit†	—	218
Mineral production payment	46	69
Deferred revenue from sales of certain customer obligations to Ucar Capital Corporation	124	123
Other	56	52
	$ 899	$ 953

*Deferred income taxes related to current items are included in accrued income and other taxes in the amount of $48 million in 1980 ($51 million in 1979).
†See Note 2, "Accounting Changes."

EXHIBIT 5 *(continued)*

11. LONG-TERM DEBT

Millions of dollars at December 31	1980	1979
Union Carbide Corporation		
3.50% Notes due semiannually to 1984	$ 60	$ 75
3.625% Notes due semiannually to 1990, issued at a discount (effective rate 4.50%)	25	27
4.50% Notes due semiannually to 1996	32	34
4.50% Notes due annually, 1985 to 1994	200	200
5.30% Sinking Fund Debentures, with equal annual sinking fund payments to 1997	170	177
7.50% Sinking Fund Debentures due 2006, issued at a discount (effective rate 7.55%) with annual sinking fund payments, 1987 to 2005	200	200
8.50% Sinking Fund Debentures due 2005, with annual sinking fund payments, 1986 to 2004	300	300
9.125% Notes due 1986, issued at a discount (effective rate 9.22%)	100	100
9.35% Sinking Fund Debentures due 2009, with annual sinking fund payments, 1990 to 2008	200	200
10.00% Notes due annually, 1984 to 1987	100	—
Pollution abatement facility obligations	142	137
Obligations under capital leases	11	12
Domestic subsidiary		
4.75% Guaranteed Debentures due 1982, convertible into Union Carbide Corporation common stock at $56.00 per share	39	39
International subsidiaries		
8.375% Canadian Dollar Notes due 1992	19	20
9.25% Canadian Dollar Notes due 1982	26	26
9.75% Canadian Dollar Debentures due 1986	21	22
10.75% Canadian Dollar Debentures due 1995	62	64
Other debt—various maturities and interest rates	203	192
	1,910	1,825
Less: Payments due within one year	51	52
	$1,859	$1,773

During 1980, $7 million of the 5.30% Sinking Fund Debentures were purchased by a subsidiary to apply against future sinking fund requirements. Previously, the Corporation and the subsidiary had purchased $73 million of the debentures.

Pollution abatement facility obligations represent state, commonwealth, and local governmental bond financing of pollution abatement facilities and are treated for accounting and tax purposes as debt of Union Carbide Corporation. The bonds mature at various dates from 1998 through 2009, and have an average annual effective interest rate of 6.13 percent. During 1980, $7 million of pollution abatement facility obligations were assumed by the purchaser of a Union Carbide facility. The Corporation has a contingent obligation with respect to these obligations.

International subsidiaries' debt includes $48 million ($59 million in 1979) due in U.S. dollars. At December 31, 1980, $362 million of international consolidated assets was pledged as security for $80 million of international subsidiaries' debt.

Payments due on long-term debt in the four years after 1981 are: 1982, $132 million; 1983, $68 million; 1984, $75 million; 1985, $44 million.

Various lines of credit are available to the Corporation and its subsidiaries. The principal domestic line of credit, which is subject to customary review and annual renewal, provides for borrowings of up to $800 million at the prime rate. There were no borrowings in 1980 under this arrangement. The Corporation as a matter of practice maintains its bank balances in amounts sufficient to compensate banks for credit lines and services.

12. LEASES

Leases that meet the criteria for capitalization set forth in Financial Accounting Standards Board Statement No. 13 have been classified and accounted for as capital leases. For noncapitalized leases, primarily involving distribution equipment and facilities, commitments under noncancelable leases extending for one year or more will require the following future payments:

Millions of dollars			
1981	$63	1986-1990	$98
1982	$52	1991-1995	$66
1983	$42	1996-2000	$48
1984	$31	After 2000	$19
1985	$25		

Total lease and rental payments under noncapitalized leases extending one month or more were $96 million in 1980 ($92 million in 1979 and $91 million in 1978).

13. UCC STOCKHOLDERS' EQUITY

At December 31, 1980 and 1979, there were 10,000,000 shares of preferred stock ($1 par value) authorized and unissued. Issued shares of common stock ($1 par value) at December 31, 1979 included 31,818 shares held by the Corporation as collateral under employee stock purchase contracts executed under the Corporation's previous stock option plans. The amount payable under these contracts, $1 million at December 31, 1979, has been deducted from common stock. There were no such shares held as collateral at December 31, 1980.

EXHIBIT 5 *(concluded)*

Issuances of shares of common stock were as follows:

	1980	1979	1978
Dividend Reinvestment and Stock Purchase Plan Issued at 95% of market price for dividend reinvestments	874,822	620,139	173,457
Issued at market price for optional cash payments	71,383	97,400	69,961
Purchased at market price by the Trustee under the Savings Plan for Employees	192,471	200,803	228,013
Issued under employee stock option plans	22,348	2,100	—
Issued in business combination transactions	—	207,138	—
	1,161,024	1,127,580	471,431

During 1980, the Corporation transferred 202 shares of treasury common stock, principally in business combination transactions (12,756 shares in 1979 and 60,574 shares in 1978).

Shares of common stock were reserved for issuance as follows:

At December 31	1980	1979
For sale under the Dividend Reinvestment and Stock Purchase Plan	2,592,838	539,043
For conversion of convertible debentures	689,697	683,592
For stock option plans:		
Options granted but not exercised	683,767	458,894
Available for granting future options	965,765	1,224,120
For sale to Trustee under the Savings Plan for Employees	143,551	136,022
	5,075,618	3,041,671

At December 31, 1980, Retained earnings included $15 million and $108 million, representing the Corporation's share of undistributed earnings of a nonconsolidated finance subsidiary and 20 to 50 percent owned companies, respectively, accounted for by the equity method. The corresponding amounts at December 31, 1979 were $10 million and $90 million, respectively. Dividends received by the Corporation and the Corporation's share of dividends received by consolidated subsidiaries from companies carried at equity aggregated $13 million in 1980 and $7 million in 1979.

14. RETIREMENT PROGRAM

The retirement program of Union Carbide Corporation covers substantially all U.S. employees and certain employees in other countries. Various arrangements for providing retirement benefits are maintained by consolidated international subsidiaries. Total program costs for 1980 amounted to $193 million ($173

million in 1979 and $158 million in 1978), of which $167 million ($148 million in 1979 and $134 million in 1978) related to the U.S. Retirement Program.

A comparison of accumulated plan benefits and plan net assets for the U.S. Retirement Program is presented below:

Millions of dollars at January 1	1980	1979
Actuarial present value of accumulated plan benefits		
Vested	$1,233	$1,241
Non-Vested	121	133
	$1,354	$1,374
Net Assets Available for Benefits	$1,385	$1,156

The weighted average assumed rates of return used in determining the actuarial present value of accumulated plan benefits were approximately 8 percent for 1980 and approximately 7 percent for 1979. The rates used reflect the expected (market) rates of return during the periods of benefit deferral as required by Financial Accounting Standards Board Statement No. 36. These rates are approximately equivalent to rates established by the Pension Benefit Guarantee Corporation, a non-profit Federal Government Corporation within the Department of Labor.

15. INCENTIVE PROGRAMS

In 1978, stockholders approved the five-year Union Carbide Incentive Compensation Plan. The plan, which became effective January 1, 1979, provides for granting stock option awards and annual bonus awards to key employees. Employees awarded options may also be awarded stock appreciation rights related to part or all of the optioned shares. On exercise, such rights would enable a holder to receive in cash or common stock the amount by which the market price of the common stock on the date of exercise exceeds the option price. The number of shares subject to options may not exceed 1,500,000. Option prices are 100 percent of fair market value on the date of the grant. Options, and any related stock appreciation rights, generally become exercisable two years after such date. Options may not have a duration of more than ten years. Annual bonus awards are cash bonuses which are intended to provide incentives for meritorious performance and total compensation levels comparable to those of major competitive employers.

Previously, in 1974, stockholders had approved the Union Carbide Incentive Program for key employees, which consisted of a combination cash payment and stock option plan and a separate cash awards plan. No further awards may be made under the 1974 Program. Option prices were 100 percent of fair market value on the date of the grant and options generally become exercisable five years after, and expire seven years after, the date of grant.

EXHIBIT 6
Report of Independent Certified Public Accountants

To the Stockholders and Board of Directors
of Union Carbide Corporation:

We have examined the consolidated balance sheets of Union Carbide Corporation and subsidiaries at December 31, 1980 and 1979, the consolidated statements of income and retained earnings and of changes in financial position for the years ended December 31, 1980, 1979 and 1978 (pages 27 through 38), and the Selected Financial Data for each of the five years ended December 31, 1980 (page 26). Our examinations were made in accordance with generally accepted auditing standards and, accordingly, included such tests of the accounting records and such other auditing procedures as we considered necessary in the circumstances.

In our opinion, the consolidated financial statements identified above present fairly the financial position of Union Carbide Corporation and subsidiaries at December 31, 1980 and 1979 and the results of their operations and the changes in their financial position for the years ended December 31, 1980, 1979 and 1978, in conformity with generally accepted accounting principles consistently applied during the period except for the changes, with which we concur, in the methods of accounting for the investment tax credit and capitalized interest costs as described in Note 2 to the consolidated financial statements. Also, in our opinion, the Selected Financial Data presents fairly the financial information included therein.

Main Hurdman & Cranstoun

Certified Public Accountants

280 Park Avenue
New York, N.Y.
February 18, 1981

Natural Resources

CASE 3.7

May Petroleum, Inc.*

Patrick Maher, assistant analyst, was skimming the 1980 annual report for May Petroleum, Inc. He had just been given an assignment to do the preliminary work on what would ultimately result in an in-depth study of May Petroleum.

He had started his job in the institutional research department of a large brokerage firm only two months prior, in July 1981. However, since he was located in the firm's Dallas office, which handled most of its energy-related business, many of his previous assignments had also dealt with oil firms. For this reason, he was aware of the fact that oil and gas firms used one of two methods of accounting for exploration and production expenditures. He knew that the majors, for the most part, used the successful efforts method and the independents usually used the full cost method. However, after a brief review of May's published financial statements, he concluded that this company (an independent oil firm) used the successful efforts method (see Exhibits 1–4).

MAY PETROLEUM, INC.

May Petroleum was an independent oil and gas exploration and production company headquartered in Dallas, Texas. Operating income for 1980 totaled almost $24 million. Net income after taxes was $4.5 million. Proved developed reserves as of year-end 1980 were 669,439 barrels of crude oil and 54,528 million cubic feet of natural gas (see Exhibit 4). Drilling capital for May's exploration efforts came from internal cash flow, registered partnership drilling programs, and joint ventures with other corporations.

May's primary areas of activities were in the Permian, Anadarko, East Texas, and Gulf Coast Basins (see Figure 1). All of its drilling programs participated in

---

* This case was prepared by Mary Pat Cormack and M. Edgar Barrett. Copyright © 1982 by M. Edgar Barrett. All rights reserved to the authors.

FIGURE 1
Drilling Program Areas

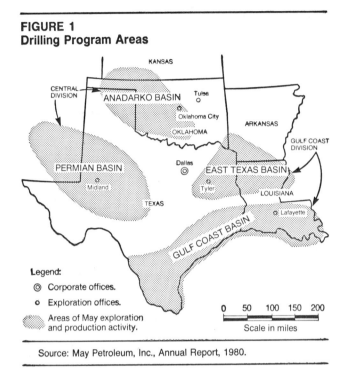

Legend:

◎ Corporate offices.

o Exploration offices.

▨ Areas of May exploration and production activity.

0   50   100   150   200

Scale in miles

Source: May Petroleum, Inc., Annual Report, 1980.

---

all the company's activities in these areas. In addition, at year-end 1980, the company held 1.3 million net acres of oil and gas leases in the western United States. These acres had recently been acquired in an attempt to balance the company's existing drilling program with exploratory prospects which had the potential of major reserve finds.

THE ASSIGNMENT AT HAND

Patrick knew that much emphasis would be placed on the company's reserve position when the final study of May was completed. However, he was intrigued by the fact that an independent firm would use the successful efforts method. He felt that, if he could convert May's income statement to the full cost method, he might be able to make some interesting comparisons to other full cost companies.

QUESTION

What change in net income for the years 1978–80 would result had May been using the full cost method?

Notes **1.** For purposes of this question, you may assume that 1978 was the first year of operations.

2. Assume that one barrel of crude oil equals 6,000 cubic feet of natural gas.

3. Make those other assumptions that you feel are warranted in order to derive the desired data. Please make note, however, of those areas which you would have treated differently if more information had been available.

EXHIBIT 1

MAY PETROLEUM, INC.
Balance Sheet—December 31, 1980

	1979	1980
ASSETS		
Current Assets:		
Cash, including time deposits of $400,000 and		
$14,500,000 respectively	$ 5,855,382	$17,294,788
Accounts receivable —		
Trade	3,353,538	4,258,808
Partnerships — estimated current portion (Note 2)	5,587,380	8,145,741
Other	37,656	254,300
Tubular goods inventory, at lower of cost or market	421,952	2,440,942
Prepaid expenses	32,864	58,695
Total current assets	15,288,772	32,453,274
Receivables from Partnerships —		
estimated noncurrent portion (Note 2)	3,185,014	5,100,726
Acreage for Sale or Transfer (Note 1)	4,428,393	6,439,370
Investment in Partnerships (Note 2)	14,418,277	27,615,578
Property and Equipment — at cost (Notes 1 and 3):		
Oil and gas properties — using the successful efforts method	10,766,500	18,499,915
Furniture, fixtures and other	673,040	1,455,973
Total	11,439,540	19,955,888
Less — Accumulated depreciation, depletion and amortization	(5,218,789)	(6,128,038)
Property and equipment, net	6,220,751	13,827,850
Other Assets	341,290	368,016
	$43,882,497	$85,804,814

LIABILITIES AND STOCKHOLDERS' EQUITY

	1979	1980
Current Liabilities:		
Short-term note payable (Note 3)	$ 48,072	$ —
Trade accounts payable	8,737,507	16,991,634
Current portion of long-term debt (Note 3)	1,981,626	616,014
Federal income taxes (Note 5)	589,857	7,590
Total current liabilities	11,357,062	17,615,238
Long-Term Debt — noncurrent portion (Note 3)	7,888,391	1,405,476
Deferred Federal Income Taxes (Note 5)	1,597,000	3,504,000
Commitments and Contingent Liabilities (Note 6)		
Stockholders' Equity (Note 4):		
Common stock, $.05 par value, 10,000,000 shares authorized,		
5,257,215 and 6,485,170 shares issued and outstanding,		
respectively	262,861	324,258
Additional paid-in capital	17,116,210	52,862,099
Retained earnings	5,660,973	10,093,743
Total stockholders' equity	23,040,044	63,280,100
	$43,882,497	$85,804,814

Source: May Petroleum, Inc., Annual Report, 1980.

EXHIBIT 2

MAY PETROLEUM, INC.
Statement of Operations
For Years Ended December 31,

	1978	1979	1980
Operating Income:			
Sales of oil and gas	$6,078,330	$11,671,606	$20,086,500
Program service fees and supervisory income	1,565,340	1,429,636	1,206,833
Sale of acreage, net	281,768	—	1,008,783
Interest income	69,148	744,877	1,446,710
Total	7,994.586	13,846,119	23,748,826
Operating Charges:			
Lease operating expenses	808,722	1,267,558	2,435,335
Depreciation, depletion and amortization	1,614,026	2,433,299	3,583,053
Exploration expenses	589,454	734,550	3,606,120
General, administrative and offering expenses, net of amounts billed to others	2,000,697	2,553,167	3,833,987
Interest expense	1,087,247	1,742,477	3,014,188
Brokerage commissions	359,163	726,742	—
(Gain) loss on sale of assets	8,710	(34,712)	(75,614)
Loss on advances to partnerships (Note 2)	—	189.047	32,618
Total	6,468,019	9,612,128	16,429,687
Income Before Federal Income Taxes and Extraordinary Item	1,526,567	4,233,991	7,319,139
Provision for Federal Income Taxes (Note 5):			
Current	121,000	482,000	248,000
Deferred	485,000	1,427,000	2,547,000
Total	606,000	1,909,000	2,795,000
Income Before Extraordinary Item	920,567	2,324,991	4,524,139
Extraordinary Item — life insurance proceeds (Note 4)	—	750,000	—
Net Income	$920,567	$3,074,991	$4,524,139
Net Income Per Share (Notes 1 and 4):			
Income before extraordinary item	$.24	$.51	$.80
Extraordinary item	—	.16	—
Total	$.24	$.67	$.80
Weighted Average Shares Outstanding (Note 1)	3,868.680	4,608,014	5,637,298

EXHIBIT 3

MAY PETROLEUM, INC.
Statement of Changes in Financial Position

	1978	1979	1980
Funds Provided:			
From operations —			
Net income before extraordinary item	$920,567	$2,324,991	**$4,524,139**
Add items not involving working capital:			
Provisions for depreciation, depletion, amortization, abandonments and dry hole costs, excluding amounts attributable to interests in partnerships . .	998,569	1,419,353	**2,406,325**
Loss on advances to partnerships	—	189,047	**32,618**
Deferred federal income taxes	485,000	1,427,000	**2,547,000**
Compensation from non-qualified stock options . . .	—	131,724	**—**
Total from operations before extraordinary item . . .	2,404,136	5,492,115	**9,510,082**
Income from extraordinary item — life insurance proceeds	—	750,000	**—**
Total from operations	2,404,136	6,242,115	**9,510,082**
Increase in long-term debt	4,504,527	12,770,490	**18,950,976**
Long-term debt acquired through exchange, repurchase and withdrawal of partnership interests	2,233,456	90,803	**272,794**
Decrease in investments in partnerships due to exchange, repurchase and withdrawal	439,121	39,709	**100,055**
Decrease in acreage for sale or transfer	2,213,995	4,952,125	**5,764,779**
Decrease in property and equipment	—	46,600	**488,339**
Issuance of common stock for —			
Cash	96,651	9,660,976	**34,975,917**
Exchanging participants' interest in properties	1,230,577	—	**—**
Total funds provided	13,122,463	33,802,818	**70,062,942**
Funds Applied:			
Increase in acreage for sale or transfer	3,267,426	7,903,163	**8,492,013**
Increase in property and equipment	4,703,373	1,149,233	**9,680,422**
Increase in non-current partnership receivables	82,947	1,531,853	**1,948,330**
Increase in investments in partnerships, net	3,162,623	7,283,426	**13,297,356**
Decrease in long-term debt	2,743,078	13,954,406	**25,706,685**
Retirement of treasury stock	—	521,875	**—**
Increase (decrease) in other assets	(99,855)	95,110	**31,810**
Total funds applied	13,859,592	·32,439,066	**59,156,616**
Increase (Decrease) in Working Capital	$(737,129)	$1,363,752	**$10,906,326**
Components Increasing (Decreasing) Working Capital:			
Cash and time deposits	$ (642,363)	$3,815,125	**$11,439,406**
Accounts receivable	1,995,431	3,476,186	**3,680,275**
Tubular goods inventory	(195,163)	121,641	**2,018,990**
Prepaid expenses	(111,838)	(7,639)	**25,831**
Short-term note payable	(1,082,526)	930,425	**48,072**
Trade accounts payable	(770,445)	(6,274,729)	**(8,254,127)**
Current portion of long-term debt	—	(222,625)	**1,365,612**
Federal income taxes	69,775	(474,632)	**582,267**
Increase (Decrease) in Working Capital	$ (737,129)	$1,363,752	**$10,906,326**

EXHIBIT 4

MAY PETROLEUM, INC.
Notes to Financial Statements

1. SUMMARY OF SIGNIFICANT ACCOUNTING POLICIES:

Principles of Consolidation — The Consolidated Balance Sheets reflect the consolidated balances of May Petroleum Inc. (the "Company") and its wholly-owned subsidiary, May Securities Corporation. All significant inter-company transactions and balances have been eliminated. The Company carries its investments in partnerships on the equity method. The Company's pro rata share of the partnerships' operations is consolidated in the accompanying Statements of Consolidated Operations and the equity in the underlying net assets (exclusive of advances) is reported as a noncurrent asset (Note 2).

Acreage for Sale or Transfer — The Company acquires non-producing acreage to be developed through its partnerships or industry partners. Consequently, such acreage is held for sale or transfer and not considered part of oil and gas properties. Cost of acreage is periodically evaluated by management and appropriate charges are made to operations.

Property and Equipment — The Company follows the successful efforts method for accounting for oil and gas exploration and development whereby costs of exploratory productive wells and all developmental costs (both tangible and intangible) are capitalized and stated at the lower of cost or estimated realizable value (determined by reference to the estimated proved oil and gas reserves). Nonproductive exploratory costs are expensed in the period incurred.

Depletion and depreciation of producing oil and gas properties are computed on a lease-by-lease basis using the units-of-production method by reference to proved reserves estimated by independent petroleum consultants. Depreciation is computed using the straight-line method over estimated useful lives of up to ten years for furniture and fixtures and four to ten years for automotive and other equipment. Amortization of leasehold improvements is computed on the straight-line basis over the life of the lease.

Upon the sale or abandonment of an entire lease or other property, the cost of the property and accumulated depletion, depreciation, and amortization are removed from the accounts and the profit or loss credited or charged to income.

Maintenance and repairs are charged to income as incurred. Major renewals and betterments are capitalized.

Program Service Fees and Supervisory Income — The Company receives program service fees for managing the operations of the partnerships. Supervisory income represents the customary monthly per-well charges to non-operators, including the partnerships, and has been accounted for as income when earned as defined in each joint operating agreement (Note 2). Monthly per-well charges to partnerships were eliminated beginning with partnerships formed in 1978. Such charges, however, continue to be made to all prior partnerships.

Sale of Acreage — The Company periodically receives proceeds from the sale of acreage. Income is recognized only to the extent it exceeds the Company's ultimate basis in the acreage sold.

General, Administrative and Offering Expenses, Net of Amounts Billed to Others — Reimbursements from joint ventures and partnerships for general and administrative expenses are treated as a reduction of general and administrative expenses in the accompanying statements. Reimbursements amounted to $1,114,473, $1,626,764 and $2,643,018 in 1978, 1979 and 1980, respectively.

Partnership Accounting Policies — The foregoing accounting policies, where applicable, are followed by the partnerships in which the Company is general partner and operator (Note 2).

Net Income Per Share — Net income per share is computed based on the weighted average common and common equivalent shares outstanding during the periods. The effect of full dilution is not material. Net income per share and weighted average shares outstanding have been restated to reflect the three-for-two stock split distributed October 21, 1980. In addition, see Note 4 for the supplemental proforma effect of the common stock sale during 1980 on net income per share.

2. INVESTMENTS IN PARTNERSHIPS:

A substantial portion of the Company's efforts and resources are directed toward the formation and management of partnerships for oil and gas exploration. The Company formed partnerships during 1978, 1979 and 1980 which had aggregate subscriptions of $8,067,500, $16,565,000 and $30,507,000, respectively.

Under the terms of the various partnership agreements, the Company, as general partner, is required to invest in the partnerships and for such investments receives a share of the partnerships' revenues and expenses as follows:

EXHIBIT 4 *(continued)*

	Combined Partnership Statements of Operations Years Ended December 31.					
	1978		1979		1980	
	Partnership Total	Company's Interest	Partnership Total	Company's Interest	Partnership Total	Company's Interest
Revenues (a)	$ 9.570.298	$4.042.973	$21.635.549	$8.856.809	$36.547.763	$14.823.920
Operating Charges:						
Lease operating	1,188,731	440,770	2,075,224	736,535	3,959,684	1,539,378
Depreciation, depletion						
and amortization	4,254,551	933,340	4,797,887	1,139,481	8,000,992	2,344,469
Exploration expenses	8,585,353	241,338	4,676,565	381,641	15,602,829	1,522,276
General, administrative, and						
program service fees (b)	1,626,499	28,805	1,861,856	167,878	2,907,875	420,192
Interest and other expenses	1,598,194	782,487	2,681,563	1,136,722	2,391,871	629,859
Total	17,253,328	2,426,740	16,093,095	3,562,257	32,863,251	6,456,174
Net Income (Loss)	$ (7,683,030)	$1,616,233	$ 5,542,454	$5,294,552	$ 3,684,512	$ 8,367,746

(a) Includes oil and gas sales and interest income.

(b) Includes program service fees and general and administrative expenses paid to the Company and organization costs.

The following are condensed combined balance sheets of the partnerships:

Assets

	December 31,	
	1979	1980
Current Assets	$10.549.811	$22.708.349
Oil and Gas Properties	51,915,120	82,197,620
Less — Accumulated depreciation,		
depletion and amortization	(13.209.688)	(17.844.175)
Net oil and gas properties	38,705,432	64,353,445
Deferred Organization Costs	109,587	132,369
Total assets	$49.364.830	$87.194.163

Liabilities and Partners' Equity

	1979	1980
Notes Payable (Note a)	$ 7,566,580	$11,087,425
Accounts Payable:		
May Petroleum Inc. (Note d)	10,291,501	14,798,192
Other	83,378	108,716
	10,374,879	14,906,908
Deferred Income	72,680	1,556,747
Unrecovered General Partner		
Acreage and Equipment		
Advances (Notes b and c)	3,361,895	5,684,634
Partners' Equity:		
General partner (Note c) —		
Equity at beginning of period	5,592,367	11,056,382
Contributions, net	169,463	2,506,816
Net income	5,294,552	8,367,746
Equity at end of period	11,056,382	21,930,944
Participants	16,932,414	32,027,505
Total partners' equity	27,988,796	53,958,449
Total liabilities and		
partners' equity	$49.364.830	$87.194.163

Notes:

(a) Substantially all the notes of the partnerships are payable out of 50% to 90% of future production to March 1990. at which time the unpaid balance is due. Substantially all the oil and gas properties are pledged as collateral.

(b) Such advances represent an investment by the Company of acreage and equipment which the partnerships record as a payable to the Company until such time as all or a portion of such acreage and equipment are determined to be chargeable to the participants as abandonment costs or to the Company as a capital contribution for acreage and equipment costs.

(c) The Company s equity reconciles to the Company's investment in partnerships as follows:

	December 31.	
	1979	1980
Equity at end of period —		
general partner	$11,056,382	$21,930,944
Unrecovered general partner acreage and equipment		
advances	3,361,895	5,684,634
Investment in partnerships	$14,418,277	$27,615,578

(d) The Company's receivables from partnerships reconcile to the accounts payable to the Company as follows:

	December 31,	
	1979	1980
Receivables from partnerships —		
Current portion	$ 5,587,380	$ 8,145,741
Noncurrent portion	3,185,014	5,100,726
	8,772,394	13,246,467
Cumulative write-offs	1,519,107	1,551,725
Accounts Payable — May Petroleum Inc.	$10,291,501	$14,798,192

(e) The above write-offs by the Company of unrecoverable receivables from the partnerships were based upon estimates of the proved oil and gas reserves of the partnerships.

EXHIBIT 4 *(continued)*

3. DEBT OBLIGATIONS:

Short-Term Debt — The short-term note payable as of December 31, 1979 was a non-interest bearing advance from a gas purchaser for $48,072 which was repaid during 1980.

Maximum short-term borrowings from banks during the years ended December 31, 1979 and 1980 were approximately $500,000 and $2,000,000, respectively, and the approximate weighted monthly average for the respective periods was $125,000 and $1,140,000. The approximate weighted monthly average interest rates were 12.7% and 16.7%, respectively.

Long-Term Debt — As of December 31, 1979 and 1980, the following long-term debt was outstanding:

	1979	1980
Financial Institutions —		
Notes payable to a domestic bank at interest rate of .5% over prime	$5,205,000	$ —
Lease inventory revolving loan agreement with a domestic bank at interest rate of .5% over prime	673,807	—
$3,000,000 lease inventory revolving loan agreements with an international bank with interest up to 1.63% over prime	1,890,000	—
Total financial institutions	7,768,807	—
Acreage purchase obligations —		
Non-interest bearing acreage purchase obligation, payable through 1983 (less unamortized discount of $229,240 and $91,744, respectively, based on imputed interest rate of 12%)	723,290	591,396
Acreage purchase obligations payable through 1983 with interest up to 8%	1,309,608	946,565
Total acreage purchase obligations	2,032,898	1,537,961
Installment Notes —		
Non-interest bearing unsecured installment notes, payable through 1984 to participants in certain Company-sponsored partnerships (Note 6) (less unamortized discount of $21,651 and $80,303, respectively, based on imputed interest rate of 12%)	68,312	326,814
Installment notes payable through 1983 at 12% interest	—	156,715
Total installment notes	68,312	483,529
Total long-term debt	9,870,017	2,021,490
Less — current portion	(1,981,626)	(616,014)
Total long-term debt — noncurrent portion	$7,888,391	$1,405,476

The aggregate annual payments on long-term debt are $616,014 for 1981, $673,186 for 1982, $647,288 for 1983 and $85,002 for 1984.

Proceeds received by the Company from the sale of 1,000,000 shares of common stock (Note 4) were used to repay approximately $23,691,000 in outstanding debt during December 1980. With the repayment of such funds, the Company reduced the borrowing bases under various fa-

cilities with its domestic bank. The lease inventory revolving loan agreements with an international bank terminated upon repayment of the facilities.

The current status of the financial institution's existing credit agreements at December 31, 1980 is as follows:

	Maximum Line	Borrowing Base	Unused Borrowing Base
Notes payable to a domestic bank, expiring 1984	$40,000,000	$5,000,000	$5,000,000
Lease inventory revolving loan, expiring 1984	8,000,000	500,000	500,000
Accounts receivable revolving loan, expiring 1981	2,000,000	500,000	500,000
	$50,000,000	$6,000,000	$6,000,000

The three revolving loan agreements discussed above require the Company not to pledge its oil and gas properties — wholly owned or owned through partnerships — or its undeveloped acreage held for sale or transfer without prior consent. The agreements also require the Company to pay a commitment fee equal to .5% of the unused borrowing base.

Acreage purchase obligations were incurred by the Company during 1979 under certain letter agreements with individuals for the purchase of lease rights in the western United States at $5.00 per net acre. The Company is required to pay $1.00 per net acre on each of the next four anniversaries of the date of the letter agreements.

4. COMMON STOCK AND STOCK OPTIONS:

Common Stock — In order to make possible a broader public market, the Board of Directors of the Company declared a three-for-two common stock split payable to all stockholders of record as of the close of business on October 3, 1980 which resulted in the issuance of 1,827,405 shares of the Company's common stock. The stock was distributed on October 21, 1980. The stock split was treated as a stock dividend and did not represent taxable income for federal income tax purposes. The financial statements have been retroactively restated for the stock split.

In September 1979 and December 1980 the Company sold 1,050,000 and 1,000,000 shares, respectively, of its common stock in public offerings for $9.33 and $36.00 a share, respectively. The net proceeds received by the Company were used substantially to reduce the Company's outstanding bank indebtedness. Assuming the shares issued by the Company during 1980 had been outstanding since January 1, 1980 and after giving effect to the reduction in interest expense which might have been realized by reducing bank indebtedness with the net proceeds on January 1, 1980, net income and net income per share of the Company would have been as follows for the year ended December 31, 1980:

Supplemental pro forma net income	$5,733,890
Supplemental pro forma net income per share	$ .87

Due to the death in March 1979 of John Edward May Chairman of the Board of the Company, the Company received $750,000 as beneficiary of a life insurance policy, and pursuant to the terms of a binding agreement, the Company purchased common stock from Mr. May's estate

EXHIBIT 4 *(continued)*

at an aggregate price of $521,875 and subsequently cancelled such shares. The proceeds from the life insurance have been reflected as an extraordinary item in the Statements of Consolidated Operations.

Stock Options — The Company has a qualified stock option plan (the "Qualified Plan") covering 562,500 shares of the Company's common stock. Under the terms of the Qualified Plan, options may be granted to the Company's employees at an exercise price at least equal to the market price of the shares on the date of grant, and options become exercisable in increments over a five-year period from date of grant. The status of the options for the period shown is as follows:

	Options Outstanding	Options Exercisable	Option Price
December 31, 1978	244,425	114,098	$3.33 to $5.33
December 31, 1979	108,540	21,045	$3.33 to $5.33
December 31, 1980	63,585	16,356	$3.33 to $5.33

No options are available for future grant due to the expiration of the Qualified Plan on May 28, 1980. All options granted prior to the expiration of the Qualified Plan continue in effect in accordance with their terms.

In June 1979, the Company adopted a non-qualified stock option plan (the "1979 Plan") covering 750,000 shares of common stock of the Company. All nonqualified stock options previously granted by the Company and still outstanding on the date the 1979 Plan was adopted were incorporated into the 1979 Plan. Certain nonqualified options granted were at exercise prices below the fair market value of the common stock at the date of grant. The status of the options for the period shown is as follows:

	Options Outstanding	Options Exercisable	Option Price
December 31, 1978	265,500	165,000	$2.67 to $ 4.59
December 31, 1979	372,450	247,725	$2.67 to $10.59
December 31, 1980	339,450	200,000	$3.33 to $29.06

5. FEDERAL INCOME TAXES:

Deferred federal income taxes result from timing differences in the recognition of income and expense for tax and financial statement purposes. The significant timing differences and the related deferred tax provisions were as follows:

	1978	1979	1980
Excess of tax depreciation, depletion, and amortization over financial	$ 97,000	$ 512,000	$ 780,000
Difference between financial and tax reporting of partnership income	837,000	1,025,000	1,246,000
Investment tax credit	(83,000)	308,000	(200,000)
Difference between financial and tax reporting of sales or exchanges of assets	(200,000)	(564,000)	(189,000)
Difference between financial and tax reporting of compensation from stock options	34,000	146,000	890,000
	$485,000	$1,427,000	$2,547,000

A reconciliation between federal income taxes computed at the statutory rate (48% during December 31, 1978, 46%

thereafter) and the provisions for federal income taxes shown in the Statements of Consolidated Operations is as follows:

	1978	1979	1980
Expected tax provisions at statutory rate	$733,000	$1,948,000	$3,366,000
Increase (decrease) in provision resulting from —			
Statutory depletion in excess of tax basis of oil and gas properties	(244,000)	(313,000)	(436,000)
Investment tax credit	(146,000)	(236,000)	(398,000)
Nondeductible offering and sales costs	283,000	412,000	158,000
Minimum tax on preference items	—	103,000	124,000
Other	(20,000)	(5,000)	(19,000)
	$606,000	$1,909,000	$2,795,000

6. COMMITMENTS AND CONTINGENT LIABILITIES:

The Company, as general partner in the partnerships, is contingently liable for up to $10,477,693 of the loans to the partnerships should partnership resources (including future production) be insufficient to meet these obligations.

The partnership agreements for each partnership formed by the Company after 1974 require the Company to offer to repurchase partnership interests from participants at amounts to be determined by appraisal in the future. The partnerships formed in 1975 through 1978 permit the participant to select either a cash repurchase alternative or an installment repurchase alternative. Starting with the partnerships formed in 1979, the participant only has a cash repurchase alternative. The aggregate amount of such repurchase offers is not currently determinable.

The Company is currently obligated to make minimum general partner capital contributions to the partnerships formed in 1975 and thereafter, as provided in the partnership agreements. The Company has currently met these obligations for minimum general partner capital contributions.

The Company has two compensation plans as additional incentives to advance the best interests of the Company for certain employees making decisions which contribute to the success of the Company. One plan provides for a cash award to be given upon the achievement of goals and objectives specified by the Company for each fiscal year. The other plan provides for an award at the sole discretion of the Board of Directors of one or more partnership units; ownership of units vests in an employee after such employee has remained with the Company until December 31st of the year following the year of the award. As of December 31, 1978, 1979 and 1980, the Company had charged to expenses $270,000, $284,000 and $368,000, respectively, for such bonuses.

7. SIGNIFICANT CUSTOMERS:

The Company's oil and gas production is sold under contracts with various purchasers. In 1978, two customers of oil and natural gas production accounted for 19% and 12% of the total oil and gas revenues. In 1979, three customers of oil and natural gas production accounted for 27%, 12% and 10% of the total oil and gas revenues. In 1980, three customers of oil and natural gas production accounted for 29%, 15% and 11% of the total oil and gas revenues.

EXHIBIT 4 *(continued)*

8. OIL AND GAS DISCLOSURES:

Costs Incurred —

The costs incurred by the Company for its own properties and by the Company through its interest in partnerships during the years ended December 31, 1978, 1979 and 1980, are set forth below:

	1978				1979		
	Company	Company Interest in Partnerships	Total		Company	Company Interest in Partnerships	Total
Property acquisition	$3,204,256	$1,672,598	$4,876,854	Property acquisition	$ 313,950	$2,451,508	$2,765,458
Exploration	27,107	591,251	618,358	Exploration	160,558	2,974,604	3,135,162
Development	459,330	2,902,628	3,361,958	Development	456,096	2,089,244	2,545,340
Total*	3,690,693	5,166,477	8,857,170	Total*	930,604	7,515,356	8,445,960
Production expenses	367,952	440,770	808,722	Production expenses	531,023	736,535	1,267,558
Total	$4,058,645	$5,607,247	$9,665,892	Total	$1,461,627	$8,251,891	$9,713,518
Depreciation, depletion and amortization	$ 619,706	$ 933,340	$1,553,046	Depreciation, depletion and amortization	$1,143,329	$1,139,481	$2,282,810

	1980		
	Company	Company Interest in Partnerships	Total
Property acquisition	$4,869,782	$4,901,046	$9,770,828
Exploration	2,951,302	6,400,312	9,351,614
Development	1,008,044	4,166,625	5,174,669
Total*	8,829,128	15,467,983	24,297,111
Production expenses	895,957	1,539,378	2,435,335
Total	$9,725,085	$17,007,361	$26,732,446
Depreciation, depletion and amortization	$ 869,229	$2,344,469	$ 3,213,698

*Includes costs on producing properties acquired through repurchase offers.

Capitalized Costs —

The capitalized costs relating to the proved and unproved properties of the Company and of the Company's interest in partnerships at December 31, 1979 and 1980, are set forth below:

	1979			1980		
	Company	Company Interest in Partnerships	Total	Company	Company Interest in Partnerships	Total
Proved Properties	$10,663,238	$ 9,801,983	$20,465,221	$17,226,315	$16,913,827	$34,140,142
Unproved Properties	103,262	4,572,492	4,675,754	1,273,600	7,841,142	9,114,742
Total	10,766,500	14,374,475	25,140,975	18,499,915	24,754,969	43,254,884
Less — Reserves for depreciation, depletion and amortization	(4,991,766)	(2,307,964)	(7,299,730)	(5,798,773)	(4,016,649)	(9,815,422)
Total Capitalized Costs, net	$ 5,774,734	$12,066,511	$17,841,245	$12,701,142	$20,738,320	$33,439,462

EXHIBIT 4 (continued)

Net Revenues —

The net revenues received by the Company and by the Company through its interest in partnerships from its oil and gas activities during the years ended December 31, 1978, 1979 and 1980, are set forth below:

	1978		
	Company	Company Interest in Partnerships	Total
Sales	$2,504,155	$3,574,175	$6,078,330
Lease operating expenses	(367.952)	(440.770)	(808.722)
Net Revenues	$2.136.203	$3.133.405	$5.269.608

	1979		
	Company	Company Interest in Partnerships	Total
Sales	$3,699,675	$7,971,931	$11,671,606
Lease operating expenses	(531.023)	(736.535)	(1.267.558)
Net Revenues	$3.168.652	$7.235.396	$10.404.048

	1980		
	Company	Company Interest in Partnerships	Total
Sales	$5,524,928	$14,561,572	$20,086,500
Lease operating expenses	(895.957)	(1.539.378)	(2,435.335)
Net Revenues	$4.628.971	$13.022.194	$17.651.165

Future Net Revenues (Unaudited) —

The estimated future net revenues from proved oil and gas reserves for the Company at December 31, 1980 (in thousands) are set forth below:

	Total Proved	Proved Developed
1981	$ 27,399	$ 27.716
1982	26.960	26.082
1983	22.872	19.679
Remainder	73.945	65.585
	$151.176	$139.062

The above table includes the Company's interest in future net revenues of the partnerships from proved reserves of $90,932 and from proved developed reserves of $82,412. The Company has no long-term supply agreements.

Present Value of Estimated Future Net Revenues From Proved Oil and Gas Reserves (Unaudited in thousands discounted at 10%) —

	1978	1979	1980
Total Company —			
Proved developed	$32.634	$54.469	$100.034
Total proved	$33.488	$56.543	$108.143
Company's Interest in Partnerships—			
Proved developed	$19.618	$36.209	$61.502
Total proved	$20.472	$38.283	$67.202

Oil and Gas Reserves (Unaudited) —

The following unaudited tables set forth the estimated quantities of proved oil and gas reserves for the Company, including its share of proved reserves (148,966 Bbls. and 16,544,704 MCF in 1978; 165,543 Bbls. and 25,912,852 MCF in 1979 and 525,625 Bbls. and 34,886,579 MCF in 1980) in properties owned through its interest in partnerships and the changes in total proved reserves during the three years ended December 31, 1978, 1979 and 1980. All such reserves are located in the United States.

	1978		1979		1980	
	Bbls.	MCF	BBls.	MCF	BBls.	MCF
Total Proved Reserves:						
Developed and Undeveloped—						
January 1	333.142	16.332.682	406.628	29.278.907	385.010	40.588.044
Revisions of previous estimates	74.024	5.872.218	(10.678)	3.353.393	51.580	945.053
Beginning of year, as revised	407.166	22.204.900	395.950	32.632.300	436.590	41.533.097
Purchases of minerals in place	22.200	1.706.000	5.163	661.083	20.268	3.465.497
New discoveries and extensions	63.000	9.034.800	55.600	13.413.330	532.292	20.851.979
Production	(85.738)	(3.666.793)	(71.703)	(6.118.669)	(97.392)	(7.158.635)
December 31	406.628	29.278.907	385.010	40.588.044	891.758	58.691.937
Proved Developed Reserves —						
January 1	330.350	15.363.775	403.813	28.310.043	379.780	38.608.048
December 31	403.813	28.310.043	379.780	38.608.048	669.439	54.528.213

EXHIBIT 4 *(concluded)*

Changes in Present Value of Estimated Future Net Revenues From Proved Oil and Gas Reserves (in thousands) (Unaudited) —

	For The Year Ended December 31,	
	1979	1980
Balance — Beginning of Year	$33,488	$56,543
Revisions of previous estimates	8,201	12,912
Increase in present value due to the passage of time	3,349	5,654
Balance — Beginning of Year, revised . . .	45,038	75,109
New discoveries and extensions, net of estimated future development costs of $484 and $865	21,175	46,383
Purchases of minerals in place	734	4,302
Production, net of production costs of $1,268 and $2,435	(10,404)	(17,651)
Balance — End of Year	$56,543	$108,143

Summary of Oil and Gas Activities on the Basis of Reserve Recognition Accounting (RRA) (in thousands) (Unaudited) (Note A) —

	For The Year Ended December 31,	
	1979	1980
Changes in present value of future net revenues of proved oil and gas reserves during the year:		
New discoveries and extensions net of estimated future development and production costs	$21,175	$46,383
Less — Applicable exploration and development costs recognized during the current year for new discoveries and extensions	(6,491)	(15,556)
Total New Discoveries	14,684	30,827
Revisions of prior year's estimates Changes in prices	6,696	12,587
Other (principally changes in quantities and rates of production)	1,505	325
Total Revisions	8,201	12,912
Increase of present value due to the passage of time	3,349	5,654
Net increase in estimated present value of future net revenues*	26,234	49,393
RRA provision for federal income taxes (Note B)	(11,809)	(22,080)
Results of oil and gas activities on the basis of RRA before general and administrative expenses, interest and other income and expense items	$14,425	$27,313

*Comparable historical oil and gas pretax income is $7,387 in 1979 and $10,863 in 1980.

Notes —

(A) Summary Policy — Under RRA, net revenues are recognized when proved oil and gas reserves are discovered from exploration and development activities. The amount of net revenues recognized is equal to the present value of estimated future revenues to be received net of exploration costs incurred and estimated lifting and development costs required to produce the reserves discovered. Future revenues are based on current prices adjusted for fixed contractual escalations and current costs in effect at the end of the year for which RRA summary information is presented. A discount factor of 10% is used in discounting future net revenues to their present value. Actual costs of acquiring unproved acreage and uncompleted exploratory wells are deferred until the properties are determined to be productive or nonproductive. At December 31, 1979 and 1980, $4,676,000 and $9,115,000, respectively, of such costs have been deferred. All costs deferred are assessed for future recoverability and any impairment is charged to expense. To the extent that costs incurred on developing proved reserves added in prior years is different than the amount originally estimated, such difference is reflected as a revision to amounts previously estimated. Costs of drilling wells to develop proved reserves added in the current year are expensed as incurred. All other exploration costs are expensed as incurred.

For purchases of minerals in place in 1979 and 1980, the excess of the purchase price over the present value of future net revenues at the date of purchase was not significant and accordingly no income is recognized on the RRA Basis.

(B) Federal Income Taxes — The Company's RRA projected federal income tax liability was determined by applying at both the beginning and end of year, the year-end statutory tax rate to the present value of future net revenues over the tax basis of oil and gas properties and any permanent differences related to statutory depletion. The increase in the projected federal income tax liability from the beginning of the year to the end of the year plus the federal income tax effect of the current year's oil and gas producing activities is the provision for federal income taxes in that year. Investment tax credit carryovers and amounts associated with estimated future development costs are reflected as a reduction in the tax liability computations.

Amerada Hess Corporation*

In December 1977, the Financial Accounting Standards Board adopted *Financial Accounting Standard No. 19*, "Financial Accounting and Reporting by Oil and Gas Producing Companies." This standard required the retroactive adoption of the "successful efforts" method of accounting. Because of governmental opposition to the method, *FASB No. 19* was subsequently amended in 1979 by *FASB No. 25*, which indefinitely suspended the required use of the successful efforts method.

In spite of the governmental opposition, most major oil- and gas-producing companies conformed to the procedures prescribed by *FASB No. 19*. This case deals with one such company.

COMPANY BACKGROUND

Amerada Hess Corporation was a fully integrated company engaged in the exploration, development, transportation, refining, and marketing of oil, natural gas, and petroleum products. The predecessor of the company, the Hess Corporation, was founded in 1920 and until 1969 was engaged primarily in refining activities. In 1969, however, the Hess Corporation successfully integrated backward into crude oil production with the acquisition of Amerada Petroleum Corporation, a leading independent crude oil producer.

As a consequence of the merger, Amerada Hess became one of the nation's major integrated oil producers. In 1978, the company ranked 18th among U.S. companies in the production of crude oil, condensate, and natural gas liquids, averaging production of 94,000 barrels per day. During 1978, the company operated approximately 15,000 oil and gas wells throughout the United States, Canada, Europe, Africa, and the Middle East. As of the end of that year, Amerada Hess owned proven reserves of approximately 280 million barrels of crude oil, condensate, and natural gas liquids in the United States alone. Worldwide, the company's reserves totaled over 929 million barrels.

Much of the company's past financial success could be attributed to its "downstream operations." Amerada Hess operated two refineries: a 700,000-barrel-a-day refinery at St. Croix, Virgin Islands, and a 30,000-barrel-a-day plant at Purvis, Mississippi. In 1979, the company began construction of a third refinery and transshipment terminal at St. Lucia, an independent Caribbean island nation.

---

* This case was prepared by Kenneth R. Ferris. Copyright © 1984 by Kenneth R. Ferris. All rights reserved to the author.

The St. Croix refinery, the largest in the world, was equipped to desulpharize "sour" (high sulphur) crude oil. This capability gave the company an advantage over many of its competitors. Sour crude was both cheaper and increasingly more abundant than "sweet" (low sulphur) crude. As a consequence, the company was able to market its products at discounted prices.

THE ACCOUNTING CONTROVERSY

Prior to 1977, a variety of methods were utilized in the oil and gas industry to account for the costs of discovering oil and gas reserves. Most of these methods could be classified under one of two broad approaches: full cost and successful efforts.

The distinction between these two approaches concerned the treatment of the costs associated with an unsuccessful, or dry, well. Under the full cost approach, the cost of an unsuccessful well is capitalized and then amortized against the oil and gas reserves produced within that same cost center. Under the successful efforts approach, these costs are also initially capitalized; however, when and if a well is found to be dry, the costs are then immediately expensed (see Exhibit 1).

In December 1977, the FASB issued *FASB No. 19,* which mandated that all oil- and gas-producing companies adhere to a particular version of the successful efforts method for purposes of reporting to shareholders. The adoption of this pronouncement was met with strong opposition from a variety of governmental agencies. The Department of Justice began an investigation of the antitrust implications of the statement. This agency argued that new and developing companies would suffer large reported losses from the immediate expensing of dry holes, while mature companies could counter such write-offs with profits from currently producing wells. The Justice Department alleged that these conditions might work to discourage competition, impair funding, and restrict entry into the industry.

The Department of Energy and the Federal Trade Commission also expressed opposition to the pronouncement. These agencies claimed that *FASB No. 19* might discourage exploration activities and thereby adversely impact the nation's energy policy.

In response to this opposition, the Securities and Exchange Commission issued *Accounting Series Release No. 253* in August 1978. *ASR No. 253* mandated that publicly held companies could utilize either the successful efforts or the full cost method. The SEC also proposed to develop a new method of accounting for oil and gas companies—reserve recognition accounting. Under this new method, costs and revenues would be recognized at the time of the discovery of oil and gas reserves, rather than at the time of sale.

In spite of this governmental opposition, many companies began conforming to *FASB No. 19* by year-end 1979.

PROPOSED ACCOUNTING CHANGE

On May 17, 1979, an article appeared in *The Wall Street Journal* concerning an anticipated change in accounting method by Amerada Hess. According to the article, the company would begin accounting for its intangible drilling, development, and leasehold costs on a successful efforts basis at the end of 1979. This change would place the company on an accounting basis consistent with *FASB No. 19* (see Exhibit 1).

Prior to the publication of *The Wall Street Journal* article, the company's common

---

EXHIBIT 1
**Excerpts—*FASB Statement No. 19* **

- This statement establishes standards of financial accounting and reporting for the oil and gas producing activities of a business enterprise. Those activities involve the acquisition of mineral interests in properties, exploration, development, and production of crude oil . . . and natural gas.
- Under the full cost concept, all costs incurred in acquiring, exploring, and developing properties within a relatively large geopolitical cost center are capitalized when incurred and are amortized as mineral reserves in the cost center are produced. . . .
- Under successful efforts costing, except for acquisition costs of properties, a direct relationship between costs incurred and specific reserves discovered is required before costs are identified as assets.
- The principal difference between full costing and successful efforts costing concerns costs that cannot be directly related to the discovery of specific oil and gas reserves. Under full costing those costs are carried forward to future periods as costs of oil and gas reserves generally; under successful efforts costing those costs are charged to expense. . . .
- Under successful efforts costing, . . . costs of acquisition and exploration activities that are known not to have resulted in the discovery of reserves are charged to expense.

---

* Financial Accounting Standards Board, "Financial Accounting and Reporting by Oil and Gas Producing Companies," December 1977. Copyright by the Financial Accounting Standards Board, High Ridge Park, Stamford, Connecticut, 06905, U.S.A. Reprinted with permission. Copies of the complete document are available from the FASB.

---

stock traded at $31 per share. Two weeks after publication, the stock was trading at $38⅛ per share. During this same period, the Dow Jones Industrial Average rose only 2 percent.

According to the *Journal,* the surge in price and volume activity of the stock could be attributed to an increase in the earnings estimate of the company by a leading oil analyst. Mr. Bruce Lazier, of Paine Webber, Mitchell Hutchins, reportedly raised his estimate of the company's 1979 earnings per share from $5.95 to $8.75 after learning of the firm's intended accounting change. "It's clear we've been substantially understating the impact of this expected change," Mr. Lazier stated. He also noted that the accounting change could add as much as $1.40 to the firm's 1979 earnings per share.

The financial information of Amerada Hess and subsidiaries is presented in Exhibits 2–7.

QUESTIONS

1. Explain the proposed change in accounting for intangible drilling, development, and leasehold costs. Is the anticipated increase in earnings per share consistent with the proposed change in accounting method?

2. Does the stock price change associated with *The Wall Street Journal* article represent an inconsistency in the theory of efficient capital markets?

3. Compare the after-tax earnings for the company under the *(a)* "successful efforts" and *(b)* "full cost" methods. For purposes of this question, assume: that 1978 was the first year of operations; a marginal tax rate of 46 percent; and 6 MCF of natural gas equals 1 BBL of crude oil. (*Note:* 6 MCF = 6,000 cubic feet.)

EXHIBIT 2

AMERADA HESS CORPORATION AND CONSOLIDATED SUBSIDIARIES
Consolidated Balance Sheet
At December 31

	1979	1978*
Assets		
Current assets		
Cash	$ 92,242,000	$ 74,265,000
Time deposits and certificates of deposit	74,860,000	112,501,000
Short-term marketable securities—at cost which approximates market	—	9,903,000
Accounts receivable		
Trade (less allowance for doubtful accounts of $2,103,000 in 1979 and $1,861,000 in 1978)	437,854,000	339,075,000
Other	123,073,000	78,571,000
Inventories	1,800,737,000	937,178,000
Prepaid expenses	71,583,000	40,870,000
Total current assets	2,600,349,000	1,592,363,000
Investments and advances		
Stock of The Louisiana Land and Exploration Company—at cost	2,262,000	2,262,000
Investments in and advances to affiliated companies—at cost plus equity in undistributed earnings	98,912,000	85,280,000
Other—at cost	1,132,000	1,257,000
Total investments and advances	102,306,000	88,799,000
Properties, plant and equipment		
Assets owned		
Exploration and production	2,069,892,000	1,662,807,000
Refining	805,988,000	765,424,000
Marketing	295,977,000	279,627,000
Transportation	321,870,000	245,964,000
Other	16,541,000	16,297,000
Assets under capital leases		
Marketing	5,392,000	5,556,000
Transportation	113,906,000	105,110,000
Total—at cost	3,629,566,000	3,080,785,000
Less reserves for depreciation, depletion, amortization and lease impairment	1,469,598,000	1,291,402,000
Properties, plant and equipment—net	2,159,968,000	1,789,383,000
Other assets		
Long-term receivables	24,535,000	15,779,000
Other	12,079,000	17,213,000
Total other assets	36,614,000	32,992,000
Total assets	$4,899,237,000	$3,503,537,000

EXHIBIT 2 *(concluded)*

	1979	1978*
Liabilities and stockholders' equity		
Current liabilities		
Notes payable.	$ 135,000,000	$ —
Accounts payable—trade.	828,954,000	800,749,000
Accrued liabilities—payrolls, interest and other.	389,791,000	155,915,000
Taxes payable.	647,075,000	245,966,000
Current maturities—long-term debt.	25,093,000	40,071,000
—capitalized lease obligations.	11,762,000	12,488,000
Total current liabilities.	2,037,675,000	1,255,189,000
Long-term debt.	829,381,000	748,935,000
Deferred liabilities and credits		
Capitalized lease obligations.	25,946,000	32,642,000
Deferred income taxes.	92,929,000	33,127,000
Other.	13,097,000	5,722,000
Total deferred liabilities and credits.	131,972,000	71,491,000
Stockholders' equity		
Preferred stock, par value $1.00		
Authorized—20,000,000 shares for issuance in series		
$3.50 cumulative convertible series		
Authorized—12,000,000 shares		
Outstanding—2,212,652 shares in 1979; 4,325,092		
shares in 1978 (aggregate involuntary liquidation		
value $221,265,000 at December 31, 1979).	2,213,000	4,325,000
Common stock, par value $1.00		
Authorized—100,000,000 shares		
Issued—36,886,780 shares in 1979; 30,176,729 shares		
in 1978.	36,887,000	30,177,000
Capital in excess of par value.	244,671,000	199,893,000
Retained earnings.	1,616,438,000	1,193,527,000
Total stockholders' equity.	1,900,209,000	1,427,922,000
Total liabilities and stockholders' equity.	$4,899,237,000	$3,503,537,000

*Restated. See Note 2.

The consolidated financial statements presented herein reflect the "successful efforts" method of accounting for oil and gas exploration and producing activities. See accompanying notes to consolidated financial statements.

EXHIBIT 3

AMERADA HESS CORPORATION AND CONSOLIDATED SUBSIDIARIES
Statement of Consolidated Income
For the Years Ended December 31

	1979	1978*
Revenues		
Sales (excluding excise taxes) and other operating revenues	$6,769,941,000	$4,701,122,000
Dividends, interest and other revenues	43,260,000	38,380,000
Total revenues	6,813,201,000	4,739,502,000
Costs and expenses		
Cost of products sold and operating expenses	4,784,967,000	3,707,686,000
Exploration expenses, including dry holes	94,932,000	70,362,000
Selling, general and administrative expenses	226,901,000	191,218,000
Interest expense	81,825,000	73,865,000
Depreciation, depletion and amortization	178,992,000	146,476,000
Lease impairment	46,548,000	73,725,000
Provision for income taxes	891,920,000	337,272,000
Total costs and expenses	6,306,085,000	4,600,604,000
Net income	$ 507,116,000	$ 138,898,000
Net income per share	$12.15	$3.36

*Restated. See Note 2.

See accompanying notes to consolidated financial statements.

EXHIBIT 4

AMERADA HESS CORPORATION AND CONSOLIDATED SUBSIDIARIES
Statement of Consolidated Retained Earnings
For the Years Ended December 31

	1979	1978*
Balance at beginning of year		
As previously reported		$1,084,980,000
Adjustment to reflect change in accounting for oil and gas exploration and producing activities (Note 2)		39,398,000
As restated	$1,193,527,000	1,124,378,000
Net income	507,116,000	138,898,000
Dividends		
Cash		
$3.50 cumulative convertible preferred stock	(11,701,000)	(19,459,000)
Common stock ($1.30 per share in 1979; $.95 per share in 1978)	(45,290,000)	(26,710,000)
Common stock—2½%	(27,214,000)	(23,580,000)
Balance at end of year	$1,616,438,000	$1,193,527,000

*Restated. See Note 2.

See accompanying notes to consolidated financial statements.

EXHIBIT 5

AMERADA HESS CORPORATION AND CONSOLIDATED SUBSIDIARIES
Statement of Changes in Consolidated Financial Position
For the Years Ended December 31

	1979	1978*
Source of working capital		
Working capital provided from operations		
Net income	$ 507,116,000	$ 138,898,000
Add: Charges not affecting working capital		
Exploratory dry hole costs	62,066,000	40,763,000
Depreciation, depletion, amortization and lease impairment	225,540,000	220,201,000
Deferred income taxes and other items	47,576,000	(13,655,000)
Working capital provided from operations	842,298,000	386,207,000
Other sources of working capital		
Long-term borrowings	436,522,000	42,698,000
Disposal of equipment	11,235,000	6,427,000
Other sources	25,881,000	8,523,000
Total other sources of working capital	473,638,000	57,648,000
Total source of working capital	1,315,936,000	443,855,000
Disposition of working capital		
Capital expenditures		
Exploration and production	516,075,000	281,558,000
Refining, marketing and transportation	142,782,000	71,310,000
Other	250,000	415,000
Total capital expenditures	659,107,000	353,283,000
Reduction in long-term debt and capitalized lease obligations	355,968,000	61,817,000
Cash dividends paid	56,991,000	46,169,000
Investments and advances	6,636,000	9,591,000
Other dispositions	11,734,000	12,428,000
Total disposition of working capital	1,090,436,000	483,288,000
Increase (decrease) in working capital	$ 225,500,000	$ (39,433,000)
Increase (decrease) in components of working capital		
Current assets		
Cash and short-term marketable securities	$ (29,567,000)	$ 74,359,000
Accounts receivable	143,281,000	50,332,000
Inventories	863,559,000	132,133,000
Prepaid expenses	30,713,000	10,524,000
Total	1,007,986,000	267,348,000
Current liabilities		
Notes payable	135,000,000	(10,000,000)
Accounts payable and accrued liabilities	262,081,000	233,319,000
Taxes payable	401,109,000	82,130,000
Current maturities—long-term debt and capitalized lease obligations	(15,704,000)	1,332,000
Total	782,486,000	306,781,000
Increase (decrease) in working capital	$ 225,500,000	$ (39,433,000)

*Restated. See Note 2.

See accompanying notes to consolidated financial statements.

EXHIBIT 6

AMERADA HESS CORPORATION AND CONSOLIDATED SUBSIDIARIES
Statement of Consolidated Changes in Capital Stock
and Capital in Excess of Par Value

	$3.50 cumulative convertible preferred stock		Common stock		Capital in excess of par value
	Number of shares issued	Amount	Number of shares issued	Amount	
Balance at December 31, 1977	5,985,830	$5,986,000	25,772,088	$ 25,772,000	$178,719,000
Conversion of $3.50 cumulative					
convertible preferred stock	(1,660,738)	(1,661,000)	3,653,581	3,654,000	(1,993,000)
Employee stock options exercised	–	–	17,045	17,000	321,000
2½% common stock dividend	–	–	734,015	734,000	22,846,000
Balance at December 31, 1978	4,325,092	4,325,000	30,176,729	30,177,000	199,893,000
Conversion of $3.50 cumulative					
convertible preferred stock	(2,112,440)	(2,112,000)	4,647,287	4,647,000	(2,535,000)
Employee stock options exercised	–	–	28,862	29,000	459,000
2½% common stock dividend	–	–	857,152	857,000	26,357,000
Exercise of warrants	–	–	217,058	217,000	8,550,000
Conversion of 6% convertible notes,					
due May 1, 1986	–	–	959,692	960,000	14,040,000
Settlement of lawsuit in connection					
with 1969 merger	–	–	–	–	(2,093,000)
Balance at December 31, 1979	2,212,652	$2,213,000	36,886,780	$ 36,887,000	$244,671,000

See accompanying notes to consolidated financial statements.

EXHIBIT 7

AMERADA HESS CORPORATION AND CONSOLIDATED SUBSIDIARIES
Notes to Consolidated Financial Statements
For the Years Ended December 31, 1979 and 1978

1. Accounting Policies

The oil and gas exploration and producing activities of Amerada Hess Corporation (the "Corporation") are accounted for under the "successful efforts" method as prescribed by Statement of Financial Accounting Standards (FAS) No. 19, Financial Accounting and Reporting by Oil and Gas Producing Companies. FAS No. 19 was adopted in 1979 and applied retroactively by restating the financial statements of prior years (see Note 2).

The Corporation's present accounting policies are described below:

Principles of Consolidation: The consolidated financial statements include the accounts of the Corporation and all significant subsidiaries.

Investments in affiliated companies owned 20% to 50% inclusive, are stated at cost of acquisition plus the Corporation's equity in undistributed net income since acquisition. The change in the equity in net income of these affiliated companies is included in other revenues in the Statement of Consolidated Income.

Inter-company items are eliminated in consolidation.

Inventories: Crude oil and refined product inventories are valued at the lower of cost or market value. Cost of such inventories is determined under the first-in, first-out method for approximately two-thirds of the inventories, and the remaining inventories are valued using the average cost method.

Inventories of materials and supplies are valued at or below cost.

Exploration and Development Costs: Costs of acquiring undeveloped oil and gas leasehold acreage, including lease bonuses, brokers' fees and other related costs, are capitalized. Provisions for impairment of undeveloped oil and gas leases are based on periodic evaluations and other factors.

Annual lease rentals and exploration expenses, including geological and geophysical expenses and exploratory dry hole costs, are charged against income as incurred.

Costs of drilling and equipping productive wells, including development dry holes, and related production facilities are capitalized.

Depreciation, Depletion and Amortization: Depreciation, depletion and amortization of oil and gas production equipment, properties and wells are determined under the unit-of-production method based on estimated recoverable oil and gas reserves. Depreciation of other plant and equipment is determined under the straight-line method using various rates based on useful lives.

The estimated costs of dismantlement, restoration and abandonment, less estimated residual salvage values, of offshore oil and gas production platforms and certain other facilities are taken into account in determining depreciation charges.

Retirement of Properties, Plant and Equipment: Costs of properties, plant and equipment retired or otherwise disposed of, less accumulated reserves, are reflected in net income.

Maintenance and Repairs: All expenditures for maintenance and repairs are charged against income. Renewals and betterments are treated as additions to properties, plant and equipment, and items replaced are treated as retirements.

Income Taxes: The investment tax credit is taken into income currently as a reduction of the provision for income taxes.

Undistributed earnings amounting to $743,829,000 of foreign subsidiaries are indefinitely reinvested in foreign operations, and therefore no provision is made for income taxes which may be payable if such undistributed earnings were remitted to the Corporation.

2. Change in Accounting for Oil and Gas Exploration and Producing Activities

In December 1979, the Corporation modified its "successful efforts" method of accounting for oil and gas exploration and producing activities to comply with the provisions of FAS No. 19. The principal changes related to the treatment of intangible drilling costs and leasehold costs. In the last quarter of 1979, FAS No. 19 was applied retroactively and, accordingly, the financial statements for prior years have been restated resulting in an increase in retained earnings at January 1, 1978 of $39,398,000. The effect on 1979 and 1978 net income was as follows:

| | Increase (decrease) | | | |
| | 1979 | | 1978 | |
	Amount	Per share	Amount	Per share
First quarter	$14,069,000	$.34	$10,931,000	$ .27
Second quarter.	14,761,000	.35	5,816,000	.14
Third quarter ...	9,135,000	.22	(13,378,000)	(.33)
Fourth quarter .	(3,158,000)	(.08)	(6,889,000)	(.17)
Total ...	$34,807,000	$.83	$ (3,520,000)	$(.09)

EXHIBIT 7 *(continued)*

3. Inventories
Inventories at December 31 were as follows:

	1979	1978
Crude oil and refined products, at lower of cost or market		
Crude oil and other charge stocks	$ 773,735,000	$424,663,000
Refined and other finished products	955,999,000	457,509,000
	1,729,734,000	882,172,000
Materials and supplies (at or below cost)	71,003,000	55,006,000
Total inventories	$1,800,737,000	$937,178,000

The inventory amounts used in the computation of cost of sales were $1,726,325,000, $880,127,000 and $741,540,000 at December 31, 1979, 1978 and 1977, respectively.

4. Stock of The Louisiana Land and Exploration Company
At December 31, 1979, the Corporation owned 2,000,000 shares of the capital stock of The Louisiana Land and Exploration Company. The market value of the 2,000,000 shares aggregated $92,500,000 ($46.25 per share) at December 31, 1979 and $43,000,000 ($21.50 per share) at December 31, 1978.

5. Short-Term Debt
Short-term notes aggregating $135,000,000 were outstanding at December 31, 1979 at a weighted average interest rate of 14.9%. The maximum amount of short-term notes outstanding at any month-end during 1979 aggregated $260,000,000. The average aggregate short-term borrowings outstanding during 1979 approximated $43,700,000 at a weighted average interest rate of 13.8%. The weighted average interest rate was determined by dividing total interest expense by the average daily outstanding short-term borrowings.

At December 31, 1979, the Corporation had available short-term bank lines of credit of approximately $435,000,000, of which $135,000,000 was utilized at the end of 1979. In accordance with various informal agreements with the banks, compensating balances are maintained at approximately 5% of the total available lines of credit plus 5% to 10% of the amounts borrowed.

There were no short-term borrowings in 1978, nor any related credit arrangements in effect.

6. Long-Term Debt
Long-term debt, less current maturities, at December 31, 1979 and 1978 consists of the following:

	1979	1978
6¾% Subordinated Debentures Due 1996 with sinking fund requirements and effective interest rate of approximately 8.4% (less unamortized discount of $9,039,000 at December 31, 1979 and $11,455,000 at December 31, 1978)	$ 74,069,000	$ 87,739,000
6¾% Debentures Due 1987 with sinking fund requirements and effective interest rate of approximately 8.4% (less unamortized discount of $1,279,000 at December 31, 1979 and $1,890,000 at December 31, 1978)	16,977,000	21,898,000
7% Marine Terminal Revenue Bonds— Series 1978 Due 2003—City of Valdez, Alaska	20,000,000	20,000,000
6% Convertible Notes, due May 1, 1986 (converted into common stock in 1979)	—	15,000,000
6% Sinking Fund Notes (due through 1986)	—	24,000,000
Notes at 5½% to 10% (weighted average rate of 9.3% in 1979 and 8.8% in 1978) payable to insurance companies (due through 1999)	541,067,000	357,498,000
Bank loans at prime rate (*) to prime rate plus ½% (due through 1987)	174,000,000	203,664,000
Other loans at rates up to 15¼% (due through 1995)	3,268,000	19,136,000
	$829,381,000	$748,935,000

*Prime rates were 15% and 15¼% at December 31, 1979 and 11¾% at December 31, 1978.

Debt discount and related finance expense are being amortized on a straight-line basis.

The aggregate long-term debt maturing during the next five years is approximately as follows: 1980—$25,093,000 (included in current liabilities); 1981—$119,088,000; 1982 —$31,054,000; 1983—$46,765,000; 1984—$56,252,000.

The Corporation's long-term debt agreements provide that minimum net current assets must be maintained and that the cumulative amount of cash dividends, stock purchases and stock redemptions after December 31, 1978 may not exceed consolidated net income, as defined, subsequent to December 31, 1978 plus $100,000,000 and a credit for certain proceeds of sales of stock. At December 31, 1979, net current assets exceeded the minimum by $312,674,000 and $550,125,000 of retained earnings was free of such restrictions.

In connection with certain debt outstanding at December 31, 1979, the Corporation maintains average cash balances with certain banks aggregating approximately $24,800,000 under informal and unrestricted arrangements.

EXHIBIT 7 *(continued)*

7. Stock Option Plan

Under the stock option plan approved by the stockholders in 1973, options have been granted to key employees to purchase common shares of the Corporation at a price of not less than 100% of fair market value at date of grant. Under the Plan, a total of 594,250* shares of common stock of the Corporation were reserved for granting to key employees. The transactions during 1978 and 1979 are summarized as follows:

	Common stock	
	Number of shares*	Option price per share*
Outstanding January 1		
1978	498,150	$13.53-$32.11
1979	325,927	$13.53-$30.12
Granted		
1978	7,175	$24.39-$29.27
1979	8,712	$25.25
Exercised		
1978	17,598	$13.53-$25.94
1979	29,221	$13.53-$24.39
Cancelled		
1978	161,800	$14.72-$32.11
1979	4,692	$16.70-$28.06
Outstanding December 31		
1978	325,927	$13.53-$30.12
1979	300,726	$13.53-$30.12
Options exercisable December 31		
1978	112,483	$13.53-$30.12
1979	152,661	$13.53-$30.12
Available for future grants December 31		
1978	219,700	
1979	215,681	

*Adjusted for 2½% stock dividends paid.

8. Incentive Compensation Award Plan

The Incentive Compensation Award Plan, adopted in 1968, provides for granting to key employees awards payable in cash and/or rights to purchase stock of the Corporation. The amount available for awards each year is limited to a maximum of 3% of the amount by which net income exceeds an amount equal to 6% of capital investment as defined by the Plan. Amounts not awarded during the year may not be carried over to subsequent years. Provisions for cash awards under the Plan were $1,000,000 in 1979 and $621,000 in 1978.

9. Stockholders' Equity

Each share of the $3.50 cumulative convertible preferred stock is entitled to one vote and to a cumulative annual dividend of $3.50, and is convertible into 2.2 shares of common stock. The vote and conversion rate are subject to adjustment in the event of stock dividends, stock splits, reclassifications and like events, except that no such adjustments will be made with respect to annual stock dividends not in excess of 2½% paid on common stock. The $3.50 cumulative convertible preferred stock is redeemable at the option of the Corporation, at a call price of $150 per share plus accrued dividends. In the event of voluntary dissolution of the Corporation, the holders of the $3.50 cumulative convertible preferred stock are entitled to $150 per share, and in the event of involuntary dissolution to $100 per share plus, in each case, accrued dividends. The aggregate involuntary liquidation value applicable to the $3.50 cumulative convertible preferred stock exceeded the aggregate par value of such shares by $219,052,000 at December 31, 1979. In the opinion of counsel for the Corporation, the excess of involuntary liquidation value of the $3.50 cumulative convertible preferred stock over the par value will not restrict retained earnings.

At December 31, 1979, the number of shares of common stock reserved for issuance was as follows:

Conversion of $3.50 cumulative convertible preferred stock	4,867,834
Stock options granted	300,726
Future grants of stock options	215,681
Total	5,384,241

10. Retirement Plans

The Corporation has non-contributory pension plans covering substantially all employees except those covered by union pension plans. Total pension expense for such plans (normal cost and amortization of unfunded past service costs) was $7,278,000 in 1979 and $6,723,000 in 1978. The Corporation's policy is to fund pension costs accrued. At December 31, 1979, based on the most recent actuarial valuations, the plans were sufficiently funded to cover all vested benefits. Unfunded past service costs approximated $5,300,000 at December 31, 1979.

EXHIBIT 7 *(continued)*

11. Provision for Income Taxes

The provision for income taxes is comprised of the following:

	1979	1978
Current		
Federal	$332,604,000	$ 54,710,000
State	32,372,000	8,138,000
Foreign	488,169,000	277,699,000
	853,145,000	340,547,000
Deferred		
Federal	(1,792,000)	(12,636,000)
Foreign	40,567,000	9,361,000
	38,775,000	(3,275,000)
Total	$891,920,000	$337,272,000

The provision for deferred income taxes represents the tax effect of transactions reported in different periods for financial and income tax reporting purposes, and resulted from the following timing differences:

	1979	1978
Depreciation	$ 19,867,000	$ 13,369,000
Intangible drilling costs	21,397,000	17,293,000
Lease impairment	(1,271,000)	(28,660,000)
Other items	(1,218,000)	(5,277,000)
	$ 38,775,000	$ (3,275,000)

The difference between the Corporation's effective income tax rate and the United States statutory rate is reconciled below:

	1979	1978
United States statutory rate	46.0%	48.0%
Income from foreign operations subject to varying income tax levies	15.7	21.9
Other items	2.1	.9
	63.8%	70.8%

The United States investment tax credit is taken into income currently as a reduction of the provision for income taxes, and amounted to $7,159,000 in 1979 and $5,967,000 in 1978.

A subsidiary of the Corporation, incorporated and operating in the U.S. Virgin Islands, has received a government subsidy amounting to 75% of the income taxes due, for a period of 16 years, commencing in 1966.

12. Net Income Per Share

Net income per share was computed on the weighted average number of shares of common stock and common stock equivalents outstanding during each year adjusted to give effect to the 2½% common stock dividend paid each year (41,763,448 shares in 1979 and 41,423,701 shares in 1978). Such fully diluted weighted average number of shares reflects the assumed conversion of all outstanding $3.50 cumulative convertible preferred stock and 6% convertible notes, and the exercise of outstanding stock options to the extent dilutive. The 6% convertible notes were converted into 959,692 shares of common stock on July 3, 1979. Interest charges (net of tax) applicable to convertible notes were eliminated in determining net income per share.

13. Supplementary Income Statement Information

The following amounts are included in costs and expenses in the Statement of Consolidated Income:

	1979	1978
Maintenance and repairs	$165,924,000	$ 94,947,000
Depreciation, depletion, amortization and impairment of properties, plant and equipment	$225,540,000	$220,201,000
Taxes, other than income taxes	$ 51,964,000	$ 43,542,000

Rents including tanker charters (exclusive of delay rentals on undeveloped oil and gas leases) are reflected in Note 15.

14. Entitlements Program

Under the Department of Energy's (DOE) Mandatory Petroleum Allocation and Price Regulations, "entitlements" are issued each month for the purpose of equalizing petroleum product costs throughout the United States.

Entitlements, which are sold to various buyers designated by the DOE, are recorded by the Corporation as a reduction of crude oil and product inventories in the month of sale and reflected as a reduction of costs of products refined or sold in the succeeding month. In 1979, approximately $199.8 million resulting from the sale of entitlements is reflected in the Statement of Consolidated Income as a reduction of cost of products sold compared with $134.2 million in 1978.

EXHIBIT 7 *(continued)*

15. Commitments and Contingent Liabilities

Leases: The Corporation and certain of its subsidiaries lease tankers, service stations, office space and other facilities and equipment for varying periods. Leases that expire generally are expected to be renewed or replaced by other leases.

In accordance with FAS No. 13, certain leases (principally tankers and service stations) have been classified as capital leases, and are included in properties, plant and equipment in the Consolidated Balance Sheet. Assets held under capital leases, less accumulated depreciation, amounted to $69,906,000 and $70,110,000 at December 31, 1979 and 1978, respectively. Future minimum rental payments applicable to capital leases and noncancelable operating leases, exclusive of minimum sublease rentals (which are immaterial), at December 31, 1979, were as follows:

	Capital leases	Operating leases
1980	$ 23,375,000	$ 70,996,000
1981	21,626,000	47,365,000
1982	17,415,000	27,840,000
1983	10,604,000	26,320,000
1984	9,344,000	23,896,000
Remaining years	23,526,000	117,165,000
Total minimum lease payments	105,890,000	$313,582,000
Deduct: Estimated executory costs	56,028,000	
Net minimum lease payments	49,862,000	
Deduct: Imputed interest	12,154,000	
Capitalized lease obligations (present value of net minimum lease payments):		
Current	11,762,000	
Long-term	25,946,000	
Total	$ 37,708,000	

Rental expense for all operating leases, other than rentals applicable to oil and gas leases, reflected in 1979 and 1978 earnings was as follows:

	1979	1978
Total rental expense	$186,528,000	$146,234,000
Less: Income from subleases	16,192,000	9,293,000
Net rental expense	$170,336,000	$136,941,000

Other: The Corporation is contingently liable for $21,500,000 as guarantor of notes of St. Croix Petrochemical Corp., a 50% owned company.

A number of lawsuits, including complaints which are class actions and allege violations of antitrust laws, are pending against the Corporation. Several of these suits seek unspecified damages and other relief. In addition, the Corporation's United States (including U.S. Virgin Islands) petroleum operations are subject to various Federal regulations pertaining to petroleum prices, crude oil and product allocations and imports, as well as continuing audits by the Department of Energy (DOE). In 1979, the Corporation received from the DOE a number of Notices of Probable Violation (NOPV's) involving substantial amounts alleging various violations of pricing and related regulations. The Corporation believes that it has properly interpreted and complied in all material respects with such regulations. It is impossible at this time for the Corporation to predict with any degree of certainty the outcome of such litigation and the issues raised in the NOPV's or which may be raised by the DOE, or their ultimate effect upon the Corporation. However, management is of the opinion, based upon information presently available to it, that it is not likely that any liability would be material in relation to the Corporation's consolidated financial position.

At December 31, 1979, the Corporation had commitments to construct or purchase facilities in the normal course of business.

There were no other commitments or contingent liabilities which, in the opinion of management, would materially affect the financial position of the Corporation.

16. Quarterly Financial Data and Business Segment Information

Quarterly financial data (unaudited) and information for 1979 and 1978 pertaining to operating revenues, net income and assets applicable to the Corporation's domestic and foreign operations are shown in the "Financial Review" section of this Annual Report.

EXHIBIT 7 *(continued)*

17. Financial and Operating Data—Oil and Gas Operations

	Total	United States	Canada	Europe	Africa and Middle East	Other Areas
			(in millions)			
Capitalized costs relating to oil and gas producing activities at December 31						
1979						
Unproved properties	$ 436.5	$ 369.1	$ 55.9	$ 2.6	$ 5.5	$3.4
Proved properties	156.5	120.8	32.3	1.4	2.0	—
Wells, equipment and related facilities	1,476.9	745.3	123.6	417.4	189.7	.9
Total costs	2,069.9	1,235.2	211.8	421.4	197.2	4.3
Less: Reserves for depreciation, depletion, amortization and lease impairment	846.5	595.0	81.5	116.7	53.3	—
Net capitalized costs	$1,223.4	$ 640.2	$130.3	$304.7	$143.9	$4.3
1978						
Unproved properties	$ 267.9	$ 224.8	$ 35.3	$ 2.4	$ 5.4	$—
Proved properties	155.4	120.5	32.2	1.4	1.3	—
Wells, equipment and related facilities	1,239.5	665.5	122.0	312.3	139.7	—
Total costs	1,662.8	1,010.8	189.5	316.1	146.4	—
Less: Reserves for depreciation, depletion, amortization and lease impairment	746.8	547.2	71.8	85.1	42.7	—
Net capitalized costs	$ 916.0	$ 463.6	$117.7	$231.0	$103.7	$—
Costs incurred in oil and gas producing activities for the years ended December 31 (whether capitalized or expensed)						
1979						
Property acquisitions	$ 205.7	$ 180.1	$ 21.1	$ .2	$ .9	$3.4
Exploration	$ 110.4	$ 70.8	$ 11.8	$ 14.6	$ 7.1	$6.1
Development	$ 232.4	$ 72.8	$ 8.2	$102.3	$ 49.1	$—
Production (lifting)	$ 173.6	$ 104.0	$ 16.1	$ 34.6	$ 18.9	$—
Depreciation, depletion, amortization, and lease impairment	$ 140.7	$ 88.1	$ 10.4	$ 31.5	$ 10.7	$—
1978						
Property acquisitions	$ 36.1	$ 27.9	$ 8.2	$ —	$ —	$—
Exploration	$ 95.2	$ 50.0	$ 22.4	$ 14.9	$ 2.9	$5.0
Development	$ 179.6	$ 62.4	$ 9.0	$ 46.3	$ 61.9	$—
Production (lifting)	$ 133.5	$ 87.5	$ 14.3	$ 20.9	$ 10.8	$—
Depreciation, depletion, amortization and lease impairment	$ 137.2	$ 104.2	$ 7.3	$ 22.7	$ 3.0	$—
*Net revenues from oil and gas production for the years ended December 31**						
1979	$1,120.1	$ 400.5	$ 74.2	$245.7	$399.7	$—
1978	$ 729.4	$ 302.6	$ 69.8	$112.6	$244.4	$—

*Net revenues consist of sales of oil and gas produced from the Corporation's net interest in proved properties, less related production (lifting) costs. Such revenues also include inter-company sales and transfers (valued at approximate market prices) of oil and gas amounting to $493.4 million in 1979 and $255.2 million in 1978. In accordance with SEC regulations, net revenues do not reflect substantial costs and charges incurred in finding and developing proved oil and gas reserves, general and administrative overhead and income taxes.

EXHIBIT 7 *(continued)*

Oil and gas reserves (unaudited): The Corporation's net oil and gas reserves have been estimated by DeGolyer and MacNaughton, independent consultants, for all geographic areas, except for the Corporation's properties in Libya. Libyan reserves have been estimated by Oasis Oil Company of Libya, Inc., the operator of the Corporation's Libyan concessions, and such estimates were investigated and determined to be reasonable and accurate by DeGolyer and MacNaughton. The estimates of the Corporation's proved developed and undeveloped reserves and proved developed reserves of crude oil and natural gas (after deducting royalties and operating interests owned by others) follow:

	Total	United States	Canada	Europe	Africa and Middle East
Net proved developed and undeveloped reserves					
Crude oil, including condensate and natural gas liquids (millions of barrels)					
At January 1, 1978	965.6	305.8	60.9	242.2	356.7
Revisions of previous estimates	6.2	5.7	(1.8)	(2.2)	4.5
Extensions, discoveries and other additions	21.4	2.4	.4	17.4	1.2
Production	(64.5)	(34.3)	(4.6)	(5.9)	(19.7)
At December 31, 1978	928.7	279.6	54.9	251.5	342.7
Revisions of previous estimates	(9.8)	16.3	—	(26.4)	.3
Extensions, discoveries and other additions	3.8	1.2	.1	2.5	—
Production	(69.7)	(33.1)	(4.7)	(10.2)	(21.7)
At December 31, 1979	853.0	264.0	50.3	217.4	321.3
Natural gas (millions of Mcf)					
At January 1, 1978	2,640.7	1,304.5	515.2	821.0	—
Revisions of previous estimates	13.9	18.6	(.2)	(4.5)	—
Improved recovery	—	—	—	—	—
Extensions, discoveries and other additions	76.3	54.6	4.1	17.6	—
Production	(215.6)	(100.1)	(29.0)	(86.5)	—
At December 31, 1978	2,515.3	1,277.6	490.1	747.6	—
Revisions of previous estimates	31.6	(8.5)	(.6)	40.7	—
Improved recovery	93.8	—	—	93.8	—
Extensions, discoveries and other additions	20.4	19.1	1.3	—	—
Production	(233.0)	(120.3)	(29.4)	(83.3)	—
At December 31, 1979	2,428.1	1,167.9	461.4	798.8	—
Net proved developed reserves					
Crude oil, including condensate and natural gas liquids (millions of barrels)					
At January 1, 1978	673.4	304.1	60.9	58.8	249.6
At December 31, 1978	676.7	277.3	54.9	77.9	266.6
At December 31, 1979	617.3	245.8	50.3	73.2	248.0
Natural gas (millions of Mcf)					
At January 1, 1978	2,441.2	1,275.0	515.2	651.0	—
At December 31, 1978	2,332.2	1,251.7	490.1	590.4	—
At December 31, 1979	2,227.6	1,138.0	461.4	628.2	—

EXHIBIT 7 *(concluded)*

DeGolyer and MacNaughton has advised the Corporation that consistent with its past practices it has included in proved reserves certain reserves for which contemplated fluid injection pressure maintenance techniques have not actually been tested in the reservoir where said reserves are located. Although the inclusion of such reserves as proved reserves may not be consistent with a literal reading of Instruction 3 of Item 2(b) of Regulation S—K and Rules 3—18(a) (2)—(4) of Regulation S—X promulgated under the Securities Exchange Act of 1934, as amended, in DeGolyer and MacNaughton's opinion such reserves qualify as proved reserves as that term has generally been understood and the inclusion of such reserves as proved reserves is consistent with DeGolyer and MacNaughton's understanding of past interpretations by the staff of the SEC of the concept of proved reserves and of the reporting practices of certain other oil companies. Such reserves may constitute a material portion of the crude oil reserves shown in the table above.

No major discovery or other favorable or adverse event has occurred since December 31, 1979 that would cause a significant change in the estimated proved reserves.

In recent years, foreign oil producing countries have made significant changes adversely affecting the operations of oil companies and their ownership of reserves. Such changes may continue in the future. The Corporation cannot predict whether such changes will occur, or their effect on the Corporation's foreign operations.

The Corporation has entered into agreements with Her Majesty's Government and the British National Oil Corporation, covering the Corporation's interest in various fields located in the United Kingdom sector of the North Sea. The agreements provide for an option to the British National Oil Corporation to purchase certain quantities, ranging from 29% to 46% of the Corporation's crude oil production from various fields at current market prices, commencing January 1, 1979.

The reserves shown in the foregoing tabulation for Europe (North Sea) include significant quantities of proved undeveloped crude oil and natural gas reserves which will require substantial future expenditures for offshore platforms, drilling and equipping wells and related facilities.

Other oil and gas data (unaudited): Information required by the Securities and Exchange Commission relating to future net revenues from estimated production of proved oil and gas reserves and oil and gas producing activities prepared on the basis of "reserve recognition accounting" is included in the 1979 Annual Report on Form 10-K (a copy of which can be obtained upon request).

18. Replacement Cost Information (Unaudited)

In compliance with regulations adopted by the Securities and Exchange Commission (SEC) in 1976, the Corporation has presented estimated replacement cost information in its 1979 Annual Report on Form 10-K. In October 1979, the SEC announced that this information will not be required for fiscal years ending on or after December 25, 1980 when FAS No. 33 is fully effective (see "Supplementary Information on Financial Impact of General Inflation" appearing in the following section of this Annual Report).

The replacement cost information requested by the SEC indicates that the current cost of replacing certain inventories and properties, plant and equipment exceeds the related historical cost amounts reported in the Corporation's financial statements. In addition, the estimated cost of sales based on current replacement cost of inventories at time of sale and depreciation based on average current replacement cost of properties, plant and equipment are higher than the related amounts reported in the Corporation's financial statements.

The replacement cost estimates included in the Corporation's Form 10-K are based on hypothetical assumptions and substantial subjective judgments which may be affected by differences inherent in estimations. The Corporation therefore makes no representations as to the validity and usefulness of the replacement cost information.

Intangible Assets

Roadway Express, Inc.*

In 1935, the U.S. government adopted legislation to regulate interstate motor carrier commerce; this legislation became known as the Motor Carrier Act of 1935. Demand for motor carrier regulation came from several sources. State governments felt that it was important to obtain control over the use of state highways and the practices of highway users. In addition, many rail and sea carriers had begun to feel the competitive impact of the motor carrier industry, and thus favored some restraint in order to maintain their ability to compete. Finally, some motor carriers themselves favored a more orderly system of competition to replace the somewhat unstable, disorganized system that evolved following World War I.

The act divided motor carriers into three classes: common carriers, contract carriers, and private carriers. With certain exceptions, the jurisdiction of the Interstate Commerce Commission (ICC) was extended to include the first two classes. The legislation provided that a "certificate of public convenience and necessity" be issued by the ICC as a condition for engaging in interstate commerce. The act, in effect, gave the ICC the authority to control entry into the industry and, consequently, its size and growth. "There was every indication that there might be an excess of motor transportation or that such an excess would develop, and that unless some measure of control was exercised, the competitive conditions resulting from this situation would imperil the stability of the motor carrier industry and its ability to serve the public."[1]

---

* This case was prepared by Kenneth R. Ferris and Ann M. Gunn. Copyright © 1985 by Kenneth R. Ferris. All rights reserved to the authors.

[1] Interstate Commerce Commission, "Historical Development of Transportation Coordination and Integration in the U.S." (Washington, D.C.: U.S. Government Printing Office, April 1950).

CERTIFICATES OF PUBLIC CONVENIENCE AND NECESSITY

The act directed the ICC to issue certificates to any common carrier who, on June 1, 1935, was operating on the given routes applied for. Thereafter, any new application would be evaluated on the merits of "whether the public convenience and necessity justified the authorization of such transportation" service. Each certificate specified the services to be rendered, the routes to be traveled, the fixed termini, if any, and the intermediate and off-route points, if any. Where there were no specified routes or fixed termini, the certificate specified the territory within which the motor carrier was authorized to operate. Applications for entry into the industry were routinely rejected, in part on the basis of protests from existing motor carriers.

Such was the case of Roadway Express, Inc. Under the "grandfather clause" of the Motor Carrier Act, Roadway had applied for certificates for those routes that it could prove it had serviced prior to 1935. After prolonged litigation, the company received a final order in 1950 granting a certificate, but service was not authorized to many of the destinations included in its original application. Anticipating such a result, Roadway had initiated an acquisition program in 1939 to expand its operating territory. The company had purchased operating rights from other carriers, or had purchased outright entire trucking companies. By 1980, Roadway had become one of the largest motor carriers of freight in the United States, operating in 40 states with a fleet of 22,293 trucks, tractors, and trailers.

MOTOR CARRIER ACT OF 1980

On July 1, 1980, the Motor Carrier Act of 1980 became federal law. The act instructed the ICC to begin granting certificates, or "operating rights," on a nonexclusive basis. The intent of the new legislation was to allow easier entry into the industry and thereby promote greater competition (see Exhibit 1). The Congressional Budget Office estimated that U.S. consumers would save between $5 billion and $8 billion a year as a result of the new regulation.

Under the new law, the ICC began granting certificates to all applicants that could satisfy their "fit, willing, and able" test. In effect, so long as a carrier could demonstrate a need for a given service and that it had the ability to provide such service, a certificate was granted. Moreover, the act provided that the ICC could issue multiple certificates for the same route and destination. In the event of a protest, the new act transferred the "burden of proof" from the applicant to those who opposed the new carrier as a market entrant.

ACCOUNTING ISSUES

Prior to the deregulation of the motor carrier industry in 1980, the restricted route certificates granted by the ICC represented a monopolistic right to the holder. In the case of initial grantees, the operating rights had no assigned value for financial statement purposes, since the rights had been granted without cost by the U.S. government. For others, however, like Roadway Express, which had purchased large quantities of the certificates from other carriers, the operating rights represented a significant intangible asset.

During the 1960s, the ICC issued very few new certificates and, as a consequence

EXHIBIT 1
The Trucking Industry since Deregulation

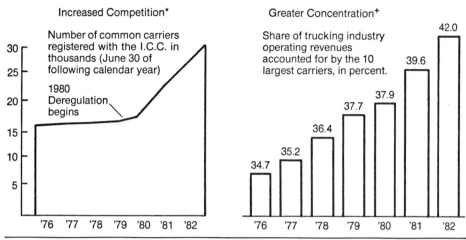

* Source: Interstate Commerce Commission.
† Source: Regulation Common Carrier Conference.

of the limited supply, drove the purchase price of such rights to unprecedented high values. By 1980, operating rights accounted for, on average, 15 percent of the equity of most motor carriers; in some cases, the rights equaled the total value of the carrier's owner's equity. So important were operating rights to industry participants that banks readily accepted these intangible assets as collateral for lending purposes.

This case concerns the accounting for operating rights following the July 1, 1980, deregulation of the trucking industry. Presented as Exhibits 2–7 are the 1979 financial statements of Roadway Express, Inc.

QUESTIONS

1. How would you account for Roadway's operating rights after July 1, 1980? Restate the 1979 financial statements to reflect this accounting.

2. Comment on the practice of lending against intangible assets, such as operating rights.

EXHIBIT 2

ROADWAY EXPRESS, INC., AND SUBSIDIARIES
Consolidated Balance Sheet
As of December 31, 1979, and December 31, 1978

ASSETS

	1979	1978
CURRENT ASSETS		
Cash	$ 11,762,669	$ 17,835,332
Marketable securities	173,190,399	186,538,300
Notes and accounts receivable—customers, interline carriers and miscellaneous (net of allowance for uncollectible accounts)	64,782,962	56,416,019
Prepaid expenses	6,774,264	5,310,097
Fuel, tires, parts and supplies	7,472,809	4,658,866
TOTAL CURRENT ASSETS	$263,983,103	$270,758,614
OTHER ASSETS—Deposits	$ 1,195,360	$ 1,238,049
CARRIER OPERATING PROPERTY—at cost		
Land	$ 21,817,587	$ 15,448,042
Structures	86,229,442	79,617,998
Revenue equipment	257,037,108	229,760,648
Other operating equipment	43,209,576	34,480,047
Leasehold improvements	665,915	929,184
Construction in progress	4,033,924	1,306,615
	$412,993,552	$361,542,534
Less allowances for depreciation	190,275,054	161,420,476
TOTAL CARRIER OPERATING PROPERTY	$222,718,498	$200,122,058
OPERATING RIGHTS	$ 26,802,090	$ 24,656,321
	$514,699,051	$496,775,042

EXHIBIT 2 *(concluded)*

LIABILITIES AND STOCKHOLDERS' EQUITY

	1979	1978
CURRENT LIABILITIES		
Accounts payable, including outstanding drafts	$ 66,403,770	$ 75,372,515
Salaries and wages	51,464,976	48,508,580
Federal income taxes..	16,688,322	24,299,097
Freight and casualty claims payable within one year	20,280,630	16,527,260
Dividend payable	3,922,157	3,067,231
TOTAL CURRENT LIABILITIES	$158,759,855	$167,774,683
OTHER LIABILITIES		
Deferred federal income taxes	$ 21,771,000	$ 18,125,000
Future equipment repairs	11,662,000	11,841,000
Freight and casualty claims payable after one year	11,568,000	7,846,000
TOTAL OTHER LIABILITIES	$ 45,001,000	$ 37,812,000
STOCKHOLDERS' EQUITY		
Common Stock—without par value:		
Authorized—25,000,000 shares		
Issued and outstanding—20,448,207 shares,		
including 800,000 shares in treasury	$ 39,898,362	$ 39,898,362
Earnings reinvested in the business.............................	293,659,834	251,289,997
	$333,558,196	$291,188,359
Less cost of Common Stock in treasury		
(800,000 shares in 1979)	22,620,000	—
TOTAL STOCKHOLDERS' EQUITY	$310,938,196	$291,188,359
	$514,699,051	$496,775,042

See notes to consolidated financial statements.

EXHIBIT 3

ROADWAY EXPRESS, INC., AND SUBSIDIARIES
Statement of Consolidated Income
Years Ended December 31, 1979, and December 31, 1978

	1979	1978
REVENUE	$1,093,661,885	$985,171,195
OPERATING EXPENSES		
Salaries, wages and benefits	$ 695,429,135	$628,218,341
Operating supplies and expenses	204,424,714	164,705,787
Operating taxes and licenses	33,770,815	33,976,133
Insurance and claims	32,729,699	28,868,906
Provision for depreciation	46,709,858	38,043,802
Net gain on disposal of carrier operating property (credit)	(2,529,826)	(3,249,055)
TOTAL OPERATING EXPENSES	$1,010,534,395	$890,563,914
CARRIER OPERATING INCOME	$ 83,127,490	$ 94,607,281
Other income—net, including interest of $14,467,197 in 1979 and $10,394,650 in 1978	14,085,697	9,809,456
INCOME BEFORE FEDERAL INCOME TAXES	$ 97,213,187	$104,416,737
Provision for federal income taxes—Note C	40,020,000	47,500,000
NET INCOME	$ 57,193,187	$ 56,916,737
NET INCOME PER SHARE	$ 2.85	$ 2.78

EXHIBIT 4

ROADWAY EXPRESS, INC., AND SUBSIDIARIES
Statement of Consolidated Earnings
Reinvested in the Business
Years Ended December 31, 1979, and December 31, 1978

	1979	1978
Balance at beginning of year	$251,289,997	$206,113,809
Add net income for year	57,193,187	56,916,737
	$308,483,184	$263,030,546
Less dividends declared (1979, $.75 per share; 1978, $.575 per share)	14,823,350	11,740,549
BALANCE AT END OF YEAR	$293,659,834	$251,289,997

See notes to consolidated financial statements.

EXHIBIT 5

ROADWAY EXPRESS, INC., AND SUBSIDIARIES
Statement of Changes in Consolidated Financial Position
Years Ended December 31, 1979, and December 31, 1978

	1979	1978
SOURCE OF FUNDS		
From operations:		
Net income	$ 57,193,187	$ 56,916,737
Charges to income not requiring funds:		
Provision for depreciation and amortization	47,470,904	38,552,797
Increase in other liabilities	7,189,000	9,980,000
TOTAL FROM OPERATIONS	$111,853,091	$105,449,534
Disposal of carrier operating property	2,942,900	3,818,408
Decrease in other assets	42,689	—
TOTAL SOURCE OF FUNDS	$114,838,680	$109,267,942
APPLICATION OF FUNDS		
Additions to carrier operating property	$ 72,249,198	$ 78,578,182
Increase in operating rights	2,906,815	397,819
Increase in other assets	—	686,489
Purchase of Common Stock for treasury	22,620,000	—
Cash dividends declared	14,823,350	11,740,549
TOTAL APPLICATION OF FUNDS	$112,599,363	$ 91,403,039
INCREASE IN WORKING CAPITAL	$ 2,239,317	$ 17,864,903
WORKING CAPITAL AT BEGINNING OF YEAR	102,983,931	85,119,028
WORKING CAPITAL AT END OF YEAR	$105,223,248	$102,983,931
INCREASE (DECREASE) IN COMPONENTS OF WORKING CAPITAL		
CURRENT ASSETS:		
Cash and marketable securities	$ (19,420,564)	$ 52,218,207
Notes and accounts receivable	8,366,943	6,828,731
Prepaid expenses and supplies	4,278,110	1,576,187
	$ (6,775,511)	$ 60,623,125
CURRENT LIABILITIES:		
Accounts payable and accrued items	$ (1,404,053)	$ 24,446,215
Federal income taxes	(7,610,775)	18,312,007
	$ (9,014,828)	$ 42,758,222
INCREASE IN WORKING CAPITAL	$ 2,239,317	$ 17,864,903

See notes to consolidated financial statements.

EXHIBIT 6

ROADWAY EXPRESS, INC., AND SUBSIDIARIES
Notes to Consolidated Financial Statements
December 31, 1979, and December 31, 1978

NOTE A—ACCOUNTING POLICIES

Principles of consolidation—The consolidated financial statements have been prepared in accordance with generally accepted accounting principles and comprise the accounts of the company and its subsidiaries, all of which are wholly owned. Intercompany transactions have been eliminated.

Marketable securities—Marketable securities, principally U. S. Government securities, are stated at cost which approximates market (see Note F).

Fuel, tires, parts and supplies—These items are used in operations and are valued at the lower of average cost or market.

Depreciation—Depreciation of carrier operating property is computed by the straight line method based on useful lives of assets— structures, 15 to 45 years; and equipment, 3 to 10 years.

Operating rights—Operating rights acquired after October 31, 1970 at a cost of $27,165,119 are amortized over 40 years.

Other liabilities—Deferred federal income taxes are explained in the third paragraph of Note C. Future equipment repairs is an accrual for estimated costs of anticipated major repairs on intercity tractors. Freight and casualty claims payable after one year represent the portion thereof not covered by insurance.

Revenue—The company recognizes revenue as earned on the date of freight delivery to consignee. Some motor carriers recognize revenue as earned on the date of freight pickup from shipper.

Net income per share—Net income per share is computed on 20,036,152 shares of common stock in 1979 and 20,448,207 shares of common stock in 1978, the average number outstanding during each year.

NOTE B—REGULATORY MATTERS

The company is a motor common carrier, subject to regulation by the Interstate Commerce Commission, and operates exclusively within the transportation industry.

Net income under Interstate Commerce Commission accounting regulations would have been greater by approximately $2,440,000 in 1979 and $3,072,000 in 1978 than herein reported. Differences are primarily in accounting for revenue, future equipment repairs and operating rights.

NOTE C—FEDERAL INCOME TAXES

Provision for federal income taxes was 41.2% of income before federal income tax in 1979 and 45.5% in 1978, differing from the statutory rates primarily because of investment tax credit, which is amortized over the lives of related assets. The tax provisions reflect such amortized investment tax credit in the amount of $3,085,000 in 1979 and $2,445,000 in 1978.

The unamortized amounts of investment tax credit, which will reduce the income tax provisions of future years, were $13,268,000 and $11,438,000 at December 31, 1979 and December 31, 1978, respectively.

The provision for federal income taxes reflects an increase in deferred federal income taxes of $1,900,000 in 1979 and $6,110,000 in 1978 arising from timing differences related primarily to investment tax credit and to depreciation, which is computed on the straight line method for book income and the declining balance method for taxable income.

NOTE D—RETIREMENT PLANS

The company contributed $35,504,000 and $27,055,000 in 1979 and 1978, respectively, to pension plans for employees subject to labor contracts, and such amounts were charged to operations. These amounts were determined in accordance with provisions of the labor contracts and the plans are not administered by the company.

Company contributions to a pension plan for employees not subject to labor contracts amounted to $4,520,000 in 1979 and $3,083,000 in 1978, as determined by actuarial calculations of normal and past service costs. Liability for vested benefits was fully funded as of January 1, 1979, the most recent valuation date. The company also

EXHIBIT 6 *(continued)*

contributed $8,615,000 in 1979 and $9,568,000 in 1978 to stock plans for the benefit of these non-union employees. All contributions were charged to operations.

NOTE E—TREASURY SHARES

The company has purchased 800,000 shares of its Common Stock from the Estate of Ruth C. Roush. Mrs. Roush was a director of the company until her death in June, 1979. The 800,000 shares were purchased at a discount of $.72½ per share from the $29 bid price for the stock on June 26, 1979, pursuant to an appraisal of the shares by an independent investment banker. The shares will be used to meet a portion of the company's future funding requirements under employee stock plans.

NOTE F—CAPITAL EXPENDITURES

The company has projected capital expenditures for carrier operating property of approximately $140,000,000 during the years 1980 and 1981. Financing will be from funds generated from operations and funds presently invested in marketable securities.

NOTE G—CONTINGENCIES

Various legal proceedings arising from the normal conduct of business, including a number of civil rights lawsuits, are pending but, in the opinion of management, the ultimate disposition of these matters will have no significant effect on the financial condition of the company.

NOTE H—SUMMARY OF QUARTERLY RESULTS OF OPERATIONS (UNAUDITED)

The following is a summary of unaudited quarterly results of operations for 1979 and 1978:

Quarter Ended	Revenue	Carrier Operating Income	Net Income	Net Income Per Share	Average Shares Outstanding
		(dollars in thousands, except per share data)			
1979					
March 24	$238,209	$ 13,691	$ 9,763	$ .48	20,448,207
June 16	231,936	11,989	8,845	.43	20,448,207
September 8	263,384	22,512	14,922	.75	19,743,445
December 31	360,133	34,935	23,663	1.19	19,648,207
1978					
March 25	198,641	13,984	8,623	.42	20,448,207
June 17	232,892	24,158	14,094	.69	20,448,207
September 9	229,545	24,406	14,369	.70	20,448,207
December 31	324,093	32,059	19,831	.97	20,448,207

The company uses a 13 four-week period calendar with twelve weeks in each of the first three quarters and sixteen weeks in the fourth quarter.

NOTE I—REPLACEMENT COST INFORMATION (UNAUDITED)

Capital investment required to replace carrier operating property in recent years has been substantially greater than the original cost of assets being replaced. Inflation affects all operating costs including, for the labor intensive trucking industry, such major expense categories as wages and fuel, but capital investment requirements are influenced by the cumulative effect of inflation over a period of years. For the company, the impact is somewhat moderated by the fact that approximately sixty percent of its investment in operating property is for tractors and trailers having relatively short lives (4 to 6 years) and obsolescence is not a significant factor. Historically, the company has been able to compensate for increased costs through efficiencies in operations and higher freight rates.

Governmental regulations and legal restrictions may affect the company's ability to compensate for future cost increases.

The company's annual report to the Securities and Exchange Commission (Form 10-K) contains information with respect to methods employed in determining replacement cost and the approximate impact it would have had on operating expenses for the year. Another aspect of inflation accounting is discussed in Note J.

NOTE J—SUPPLEMENTAL INFORMATION AND EFFECTS OF CHANGING PRICES (UNAUDITED)

Basis of Preparation of 1979 Supplemental Data
As required by Financial Accounting Standards Board (FASB) Statement No. 33, "Financial Reporting and Changing Prices," the company must provide supplemental information concerning the effects of changing prices on its

EXHIBIT 6 (continued)

financial statements. FASB objectives are to recognize the present inflationary environment and the significant effects that changing prices have on business enterprises.

Because there is presently no consensus on which aspects of inflation (if any) should be reported, the FASB has devised an experiment requiring certain large, publicly held companies to present supplemental information reflecting inflation measurements. During the experimental period the FASB decided to focus on those items most affected by changing prices, that is: (1) the effect of general inflation on properties and related depreciation expense, and (2) the effect of general inflation on monetary assets and liabilities.

The supplemental information on changing prices does not reflect a comprehensive application of inflation accounting. It describes only the inflationary effect of a rise in the general price level on the purchasing power of the dollar (called general inflation). It is important that financial statement users recognize the inherent limitations in this type of measurement. The restated amounts cannot be assumed to show actual or correct changes in values, nor do they consider operating and managerial factors that influence the value of properties and other assets.

Net Income
The accompanying supplemental financial data presents net income under two measurement methods. The company's primary financial statements are prepared based on historical costs; i.e., prices that were in effect at the time the transactions occurred. To show the effect of general inflation, historical net income is restated in dollars of the same (constant) general purchasing power, as measured by the average

level of the Consumer Price Index (CPI) for 1979. Under this measurement method, historical amounts of depreciation expense and the gain on the sale of properties are adjusted to reflect the change in the level of the CPI that has occurred since the date the related properties were acquired. The amounts of revenues and other costs and expenses already approximate average 1979 constant dollars and remain unchanged from those amounts presented in the primary financial statements.

Income Taxes
Provision for income taxes remains the same as reported in the primary financial statements. Under present tax laws, allowable deductions for depreciation do not recognize the effects of inflation. Thus, taxes are levied on the company at rates which, in real terms, exceed established statutory rates. During periods of persistent inflation and rapidly increasing prices, such a tax policy effectively results in a tax on shareholders' investment in the company.

Net Monetary Assets
When prices are increasing, the holding of net monetary assets results in a loss of general purchasing power because the amount of money received upon liquidation will be in dollars of diminished value. Net monetary assets include cash, marketable securities, receivables and fixed liabilities.

For the company the approximate change in the stated amount of net monetary assets it held during the year, shown separately in the accompanying supplemental data, has been measured by the change during 1979 in the Consumer Price Index. Funds available for distribution to shareholders are not affected.

SUPPLEMENTAL FINANCIAL DATA AND EFFECTS OF CHANGING PRICES
For the Year Ended December 31, 1979
(dollars in thousands)

Net income (based on historical costs) as reported in the statement of consolidated income..................		$ 57,193
Approximate change in historical costs due to changes in the Consumer Price Index:		
Additional provision for depreciation...........................	$15,183	
Reduction of gain on disposal of carrier operating property	1,853	17,036
Net Income restated for changes in the Consumer Price Index (in average 1979 dollars)		$ 40,157
Approximate change in the stated amount of net monetary assets held during the year due to changes in the Consumer Price Index (decrease)		$(13,303)

EXHIBIT 6 *(concluded)*

ROADWAY EXPRESS, INC., AND SUBSIDIARIES
Five-year Comparison of Selected Supplemental Financial Data and Effects of Changing Prices
For the Year Ended December 31
(in average 1979 dollars; in thousands, except per share data)

	1979	1978	1977	1976	1975
Historical cost information adjusted to reflect changes in the Consumer Price Index:					
Revenue	$1,093,662	$1,096,091	$960,648	$782,516	$679,131
Net income	40,157	*	*	*	*
Net income per share	2.00	*	*	*	*
Approximate change in the stated amount of net monetary assets held during the year due to changes in the Consumer Price Index (decrease)	(13,303)	*	*	*	*
Net assets at year end	386,123	*	*	*	*
Other information adjusted to reflect changes in the Consumer Price Index: Cash dividends declared per share	.750	.640	.569	.527	.421
Market price per share at year end	25.06	26.52	36.80	56.13	55.23
Average Consumer Price Index (1967 = 100)	217.4	195.4	181.5	170.5	161.2

*Disclosure is not required for years prior to 1979.

EXHIBIT 7
Report of Ernst & Whinney, Independent Auditors

To the Board of Directors
Roadway Express, Inc.
Akron, Ohio

We have examined the consolidated balance sheets of Roadway Express, Inc. and subsidiaries as of December 31, 1979 and 1978, and the related consolidated statements of income and earnings reinvested in the business and changes in financial position for the years then ended. Our examinations were made in accordance with generally accepted auditing standards and, accordingly, included such tests of the accounting records and such other auditing procedures as we considered necessary in the circumstances.

In our opinion, the financial statements referred to above present fairly the consolidated financial position of Roadway Express, Inc. and subsidiaries at December 31, 1979 and 1978, and the consolidated results of their operations and changes in their financial position for the years then ended, in conformity with generally accepted accounting principles applied on a consistent basis.

Ernst & Whinney

Akron, Ohio
February 18, 1980

Comserv Corporation*

In June 1983, Richard Daly, chairman of Comserv Corporation, a small computer software firm, reflected on the rationale behind his firm's decision to capitalize the costs of developing new software products:

> I believe it is very important for Comserv to be able to capitalize software development costs. We are producing assets—software that will bring in revenues in future periods— and for a fair picture of how we're doing, the costs of producing the assets must be matched against the revenues they produce. We do this by capitalizing the costs and amortizing them over a multiyear period.
>
> These software development investments are necessary for Comserv to grow, and even to survive. Forcing us to expense these costs would discourage us from investing as much as we should because our earnings would be severely penalized. I know we have some critics who are concerned about the risk of putting poor-quality assets on the balance sheet, but I think the risk is minimal because we have good controls over our development expenditures.

BACKGROUND

Comserv was founded in 1968 in Minneapolis, Minnesota, initially to provide data processing services to local businesses. In the early 1970s, the company started developing software for its clients, and by 1982 it had grown to be the largest independent supplier of software products for the manufacturing industry, with annual sales in excess of $23 million.[1] (See financial information in Exhibits 1 and 2.)

As shown in Figure 1, the bulk of Comserv's revenues was derived from a family of software products called Advanced Manufacturing, Accounting, and Production System (AMAPS). AMAPS was designed to assist manufacturers in planning, scheduling, monitoring, and controlling their operations. It was comprised of a number of modules which could be purchased separately or in combinations, and it could be adapted to meet specific customer and industry requirements.

Exhibit 3 presents an overview of the modules included in the AMAPS mainframe product (i.e., designed for large computers), most of which were fully developed by

---

* This case was prepared by Carolyn Bitetti under the direction of Kenneth Merchant as the basis for class discussion, rather than to illustrate either effective or ineffective handling of an administrative situation. Copyright © 1984 by the President and Fellows of Harvard College. Reprinted by permission of the Harvard Business School.

[1] Software refers generally to the instructions and routines used to operate and control computer hardware. Software is entered into computer memory via the terminal keyboard, disks, tapes, or other media.

EXHIBIT 1

COMSERV CORPORATION
Consolidated Statement of Operations
Years Ended December 31, 1982–1977
(in thousands, except per share information)

	1982	1981	1980	1979	1978	1977
Revenues:	$23,407	$17,667	$10,704	$6,493	$4,257	$3,084
Operating costs.	7,011	5,727	3,527	2,571	1,726	1,424
Selling expenses	8,014	5,635	3,623	1,723	1,046	693
General and administrative expenses	4,714	2,884	1,423	772	477	343
Amortization of computer software and educational courseware construction costs. . . .	1,743	720	470	314	318	199
Total costs and expenses	21,482	14,966	9,043	5,380	3,567	2,659
Operating income	1,925	2,701	1,661	1,113	690	425
Income before taxes and extraordinary item	2,067	3,628	1,441	916	538	302
Income before extraordinary item.	1,644	2,213	903	516	315	238
Net income.	1,644	2,213	903	516	315	291
Earnings per common share:						
Primary.	$ 0.49	$ 0.71	$ 0.45	$ 0.35	$ 0.23	$ 0.23
Fully diluted	$ 0.49	$ 0.71	$ 0.42	$ 0.30	$ 0.22	$ 0.23

EXHIBIT 2

COMSERV CORPORATION
Selected Consolidated Balance Sheet Data
Years Ended December 31, 1982–1977
(in thousands)

	1982	1981	1980	1979	1978	1977
Working capital	$ 9,491	$ 9,348	$ 2,327	$ 954	$ 64	$ 22
Capitalized software and coursework construction costs	15,283	7,790	4,258	2,899	2,005	1,456
Less accumulated amortization	3,937	2,194	1,473	1,075	761	443
	11,346	5,596	2,785	1,824	1,244	1,013
Total assets	51,587	25,870	11,130	6,244	3,843	2,702
Long-term debt (including current portion)	21,897	1,638	345	1,768	974	848
Redeemable preferred stock	—	—	—	200	200	—
Common stockholders' equity	$18,418	$16,721	$ 6,505	$2,074	$1,495	$1,187

1982. The AMAPS mainframe product was very successful. Datapro Research[2] rated AMAPS as the top mainframe-based manufacturing software package in both 1981 and 1982.

Training and professional support was provided to customers who purchased AMAPS. Comserv had developed a variety of educational tools, including courses, workshops, videotapes, and workbooks; some of the offerings covered topics not directly related to Comserv software and were being offered to customers who had

---

[2] A software research and publishing subsidiary of McGraw-Hill.

FIGURE 1

	1982 Revenue ($000)	Percent of Total
Software products (AMAPS).	$14,996	65%
Educational products/services. . . .	3,319	14
Professional services	2,905	12
Data processing	2,187	9
	$23,407	100%

not bought AMAPS. The professional services staff was available to assist customers in implementing AMAPS and in utilizing the system to its full potential.

Comserv's original product—processing information on Comserv computers, primarily for small businesses—had become progressively less important. As shown in Figure 1, this service generated less than 10 percent of total 1982 revenues.

Customers purchased a 99-year license to use AMAPS software, and by the end of 1982 AMAPS had been installed in approximately 300 large manufacturing companies (e.g., Bausch & Lomb, Gillette, Plough, Warner-Lambert), all of which had IBM or IBM-compatible mainframes. A typical module cost $30,000–50,000 and, if all the modules were purchased, the total price was approximately $500,000. A typical mainframe customer contract might total around $340,000, including professional services, educational services, and maintenance as follows:

	($000)
Software license	$220
Professional services. . . .	60
Educational services	40
Maintenance contract . . .	20
Total	$340

Comserv was expanding its product offerings in several directions. Some new AMAPS modules were being planned or in development, and new AMAPS versions were in various stages of development. A minicomputer version, called AMAPS 3000, was just being offered to prospective clients, primarily smaller manufacturers ($25–$75 million in sales); a version called AMAPS-G was being developed for government contractors; and a version called AMAPS-Q was being developed for use with remote terminals at manufacturing workstations.

Comserv was also expanding into international markets. Initially AMAPS was licensed to foreign subsidiaries of existing clients, but in the early 1980s offices were opened in Dublin, London, and Toronto to sell to non-U.S. corporations. International sales were expected to grow from approximately 13 percent of total revenues in 1982, possibly to 25 percent by the mid-1980s.

PERFORMANCE EVALUATION

Comserv provided annual bonuses to key employees. The bonus opportunity was approximately 30 percent of salary. Part of the bonus was based on the individual's grade level and overall company profitability. Another part was based on the accomplishment of individual performance objectives set by each employee. For a product manager, these objectives might be based on such objectives as completing projects on time and within budget.

EXHIBIT 3
AMAPS Product (Mainframes)

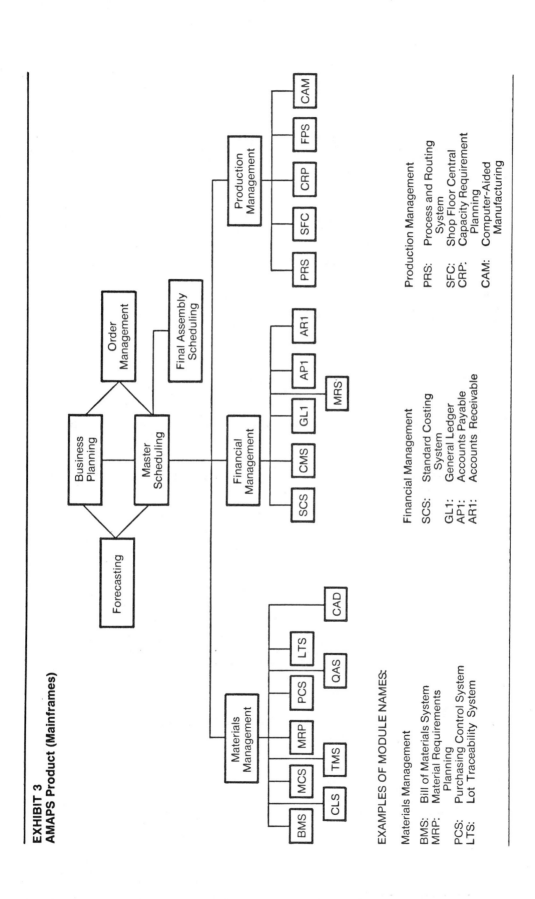

EXAMPLES OF MODULE NAMES:

Materials Management

BMS:	Bill of Materials System
MRP:	Material Requirements Planning
PCS:	Purchasing Control System
LTS:	Lot Traceability System

Financial Management

SCS:	Standard Costing System
GL1:	General Ledger
AP1:	Accounts Payable
AR1:	Accounts Receivable

Production Management

PRS:	Process and Routing System
SFC:	Shop Floor Central
CRP:	Capacity Requirement Planning
CAM:	Computer-Aided Manufacturing

Gradually, Comserv was being transformed into a produce-line organization with decision-making authority being delegated from top management to the product-line managers. The monthly financial reporting package included income statements for each product line, but this information was not yet being used to evaluate the product-line managers' performances. As the organization evolved, it was expected that greater importance would be placed on measurement of financial performance, with return on assets a key financial indicator.

THE DECISION TO CAPITALIZE SOFTWARE DEVELOPMENT COSTS

Product improvement and new product development were large expenditure areas for Comserv, and both were vital to the company's continuing success. In 1982, Comserv spent $7.5 million (approximately 33 percent of revenues) on product development.

Comserv choose to capitalize expenditures related to the construction of computer software and educational coursework. Construction costs were defined as those incurred "to enhance, improve, and adapt" existing products. This would include, for example, the costs of adding a purchasing module to AMAPS, adding an additional report to the existing material control module, or adapting AMAPS to a new type of computer. It would not include costs incurred before production was started, such as market research and product planning.

The capitalized costs were amortized over a four- to six-year period depending on the expected useful life of the product. For example, the AMAPS/mainframe software was amortized over six years, while the AMAPS/minicomputer software and the educational coursework were amortized over four years.

The rationale for capitalizing these costs was based partly on the belief that software development expenditures produce assets (software), and the costs of developing these assets should be matched against the future economic benefits that they will generate. Chairman Richard Daly explained:

> Matching expenses with revenues is a basic accounting principle, and when you violate this principle, you ought to look real hard at the reasons why. I think you'll get into trouble sooner or later. For instance, every company that expenses software construction costs is really reporting inflated margins.
>
> Take a look at the accounting definition of assets [shown in Exhibit 4]. Our software meets those criteria. We are not speculating; we are building products which we are pretty sure we will be able to sell. If we were spending money developing new modeling techniques or using a new database technology, then we'd expense it; that would be R&D. If we were going to spend $5 million building a system for the banking industry, we'd expense that, too, because we haven't demonstrated any capability in that area. But with the bulk of the products we are developing, there is no breakthrough in technology, and we have a demonstrated ability to develop marketable products.
>
> Take, for example, our purchasing module. It was built over an 18-month period, cost $735,000, and was delivered in the first quarter of 1981 to a backlog of $1.4 million within our existing account base. Cumulative revenues from that module are at least five times that now. We've got a big client base out there that's waiting for our products.
>
> Sure, there is some risk in what we do. How do you really know that the new products are going to produce revenue? We've had some minor write-offs. We developed some financial modules and then discovered that large companies don't buy financials; they have their own. So we had a small write-off, even though that work helped us develop the financial modules for our minicomputer version of AMAPS. We also had

---

EXHIBIT 4
FASB Definition of Assets

Assets

.019   Assets are probable future economic benefits obtained or controlled by a particular entity as a result of past transactions or events.

Characteristics of Assets of Business Enterprises

.20   An asset has three essential characteristics: *(a)* it embodies a probable future benefit that involves a capacity, singly or in combination with other assets, to contribute directly or indirectly to future net cash inflows; *(b)* a particular enterprise can obtain the benefit and control others' access to it; and *(c)* the transaction or other event giving rise to the enterprise's right to or control of the benefit has already occurred. Assets commonly have other features that help identify them—for example, assets may be acquired at a cost and they may be tangible, exchangeable, or legally enforceable. However, those features are not essential characteristics of assets. Their absence, by itself, is not sufficient to preclude an item's qualifying as an asset. That is, assets may be acquired without cost, they may be intangible, and although not exchangeable they may be useable by the enterprise in producing or distributing other goods or services. Similarly, although the ability of an enterprise to obtain benefit from an asset and to control others' access to it generally rests on a foundation of legal rights, legal enforceability of a claim to the benefit is not a prerequisite for a benefit to qualify as an asset if its receipt by the enterprise is otherwise probable.

Source: FASB Statement of Financial Accounting Concepts No. 3, "Elements of Financial Statements of Business Enterprises," paras. 19–20.
Copyright by Financial Accounting Standards Board, High Ridge Park, Stamford, Connecticut 06905, U.S.A. Reprinted with permission. Copies of the complete document are available from the FASB.

---

to take some write-offs on a multiplant module we were working on, some of which seemed redundant when we announced AMAPS-Q. After a lot of discussion among ourselves and with our auditors, we settled on a number—$350,000—which I feel is very conservative (i.e., on the high side). But these are very minor in comparison with the total.

Mr. Daly went on to argue that expensing software development costs would cause Comserv to reduce its development expenditures:

If you look at our history, and specifically at our software development expenditures as a percentage of revenue, you'll see that it has gone up very dramatically as we've been able to bring more money into the company and staff up. It was around 10 percent in the early years, but last year it was about 32 percent. It just wouldn't be possible to expense all that. An analyst would look at our financial statements and say: "If you had expensed all that, you'd have lost a lot of money." My reply to that is: "If we had had to expense it, we wouldn't have spent it."

Tom Johnson (controller) elaborated on the same point:

There's no question that, if Comserv were required to expense all software development, the expenditures would be discouraged. The discouragement wouldn't come from lower levels (i.e., from product proposal levels), it would come from the top. There is quite a bit of pressure to keep the levels of earnings up. We have to keep the level of investment such that we can still report adequate earnings.

PRODUCT APPROVAL PROCESS

A primary objection of those opposed to capitalization of software development expenditures was that it raised the risk of carrying assets of questionable value on the balance sheet. Mr. Daly agreed that this risk existed, but he felt that it could be limited with good management controls over development expenditures:

> As soon as you start capitalizing something (it's not only true of software), then it can be a rat hole. You know, you can put a lot of stuff on your balance sheet. For example, if revenue for the Professional Services Group is down, one could theoretically move some of their expenses into the software construction area and hide it. There's a lot of exposure there, so you have to have good control, and I think that the companies that expense [software development costs] are saying to themselves: "We can't control it."

To control expenditures for software and educational coursework development, Conserv established what was called the product approval process. This process required the review and approval of every development project at each of a series of checkpoints by a seven-member product steering committee (PSC). Included on the PSC were the vice presidents in charge of marketing, sales, product construction, product development, and business and systems planning.

The product approval process tracked each project from the early conceptual stages through the time the product was finally placed on the market. The initial idea could be described in the form of a formal product description and plan, or just in the form of a brief statement. If the PSC was willing to allow a project past the first stage, then a business plan was prepared. It included a complete description of the product, the targeted market, expected competition, projected revenues and costs for a five-year period (rough estimates), and whether or not the company had the in-house expertise to develop and support the project. Approximately 70 percent of the projects which reached the stage of being presented in a business plan obtained final approval.

If the business plan was approved, a specific review date was established, usually between 30 to 90 days in the future. At this and other review dates that would be established if the project continued to be funded, the PSC examined the progress being made, the expenditures to date, and the technical and market risk.

Comserv management felt that the product approval process provided a good, thorough review of development expenditures. The only problem was felt to be the delays sometimes imposed. Phillip Logan (vice president of product construction), commented:

> The product approval process can get in the way sometimes. Sometimes I have to put a development team on hold status while we're waiting for approvals. The earliest it turns around is a week, but it can often be about 2–3 weeks by the time the PSC reviews the business plan. The most significant delays occur when all the people aren't around, or when the PSC asks for more information.

THE CAPITALIZATION ISSUE AND THE SEC

In June 1983, the Securities and Exchange Commission issued a temporary ban (SEC File No. S7–968) against companies switching from expensing to capitalizing software development costs until the accountants were able to establish a consistent set of rules. The Financial Accounting Standards Board was waiting for recommendations from a task force formed by the AICPA[3] and ADAPSO.[4]

Richard Daly commented on what might happen if the FASB or the SEC eventually ruled against capitalization.

> If we lose this argument, I think it will be very bad for the software industry. The immediate reaction will be to reduce the size of our development expenditures.
>
> There are a few other things we could do to try to get around the problem, but none of them are what I would call satisfactory. We could try to obtain up-front payments from customers to fund a project. We're just starting to do some of this now, not for funding reasons, but to get some customer input into our development processes. We might be able to expand this procedure, but the customers have to be very cooperative. We could buy our software from outside parties because the accountants let us depreciate purchased assets. But I personally think that any company in our industry that goes out and buys a product is exposing itself to an even larger risk of write-offs because both the initial marketing and the ongoing support are very difficult. This is particularly true for companies with an integrated product line like ours. Finally, we could enter into R&D partnerships, as that keeps the investment off the balance sheet entirely. When the development is done, what is bought becomes an asset; or if you're obligated to a stream of royalty payments, it's essentially the same as amortization costs. But there are two problems. First, most of the stuff done in our industry is not R&D; and when the IRS takes a good look at it, they're going to disallow the tax benefits those R&D partnerships have generated. And second, it's very expensive financing, about three times as expensive as normal financing.

Tom Johnson (controller) reflected on the same issue:

> Richard Daly had the vision that Comserv really needed capitalization in order to operate in a realistic manner. Capitalization makes it possible for us to take a longer-range view of what we're doing. We're not making the short-sighted investment decisions that some companies which expense software development are making; those companies are looking more toward short-term results. Overall, I think capitalization would be good for most firms in our industry.
>
> This has nothing to do with liberal versus conservative accounting, as I think Comserv's accounting is generally conservative. Take the area of revenue recognition, for example. A lot of companies recognize revenue at the time they sign the contract. We wait until we ship the product and get an acknowledgment from the customer that it has been received. Some people don't consider it conservative to capitalize software development, but this is one of those cases where other qualities of accounting numbers are more important than conservatism.

QUESTIONS

1. Evaluate the accounting policy for software development costs as followed by Comserv Corporation. Do you agree with this policy?

2. Assuming that you were the president of Comserv, what accounting policy would you want to guide decisions as to whether particular software development

---

[3] American Institute of Certified Public Accountants.

[4] Association of Data Processing Service Organizations.

expenditures should be capitalized or expensed? Apply your policy to the following hypothetical projects:

Development Effort	Expected Time to Completion	Expected Cost
a. Development of a new production planning module, including demand forecasting and line-balancing algorithms.	15 months	$550,000
b. Modification of existing modules for use by customers made by Prime Computer Corporation.	9 months	$240,000
c. Development of a new family of software products for use in the travel agency industry.	3 years	$2.5 million
d. Modification of existing material-requirements-planning system to improve efficiency of processing.	2 months	$40,000

3. Would your answer to Question 2 be different if you were a president of a large diversified corporation setting accounting policy for one of your major divisions that is in the software development business?

PART FOUR

Equity Valuation

Liability Valuation

R. J. Miller, Inc.*

R. J. Miller, Inc. was a real estate development company headquartered in Charleston, West Virginia. Since its inception in 1970, the company had been involved in the development of numerous shopping centers and apartment complexes in Virginia, West Virginia, and Maryland. In 1976, the company went public with an initial offering of 2.5 million shares of common stock. The public offering was quickly sold out at $10 per share. Over the next six years, the price of the common shares would more than double.

Other than the initial public offering of stock, the company generated capital for its development projects primarily through the sale of limited partnership interests and bank borrowing. By 1979, however, interest rates had begun to climb sharply and, by 1980, the prime rate of interest (i.e., that rate charged by banks to their most preferred customers) had reached 20 percent. R. J. Miller, Inc. was not considered to be a "preferred customer," and consequently found itself facing the prospect of borrowing funds at nearly 22 percent.

To escape these high bank rates of interest, which substantially reduced profit margins, the firm decided to undertake a bond offering. On April 1, 1981, the company successfully completed the sale of 10-year 15 percent coupon rate, first mortgage bonds having a maturity value of $40 million. The bonds required semiannual interest payments and were sold to yield 16 percent. They were callable at any time after April 1, 1986, at a price of $105 per bond, and were also convertible into R. J. Miller common stock ($1 par value) at any time after April 1, 1983, at a rate of 58.82 shares of common per $1,000 bond.

Over the next two years, interest rates fell by more than 50 percent. By April of

---

* This case was prepared by Kenneth R. Ferris. Copyright © 1984 by Kenneth R. Ferris. All rights reserved to the author.

1983, the prime rate of interest had fallen to 10½ percent; the stock market, in turn, had moved into a bullish trend with the Dow Jones Industrial Average breaking the 1,200 point barrier. In response to these market trends, the price of R. J. Miller common rose to $25 per share.

QUESTIONS

Use Exhibits 1 and 2 in calculating the following:

1. Determine the amount of the proceeds from the April 1, 1981, sale of bonds (ignore transaction costs). Illustrate the December 31, 1981, balance sheet disclosures related to the debt. (Use specific dollar amounts.)

2. Determine the amount of interest expense to be deducted during the year ended December 31, 1982. (*Note:* Use the effective interest method.)

3. Assume that bonds having a maturity value of $5 million are converted into common stock on April 1, 1983. Describe the balance sheet and income statement effects of the conversion. (Use specific dollar amounts.)

4. Assume that the market yield on the outstanding bonds is 12 percent per annum and that the price per share of common is $18¾. Assume also that on April 1, 1986, the firm decides to repurchase in the open market bonds having a maturity value of $20 million. Describe the balance sheet and income statement effects of this transaction. (Use specific dollar amounts.) Do you agree with this decision?

5. Assume that the company decides to force the conversion of the remaining outstanding bonds by calling the bonds as of December 31, 1988. Assume that on that date the company's common stock was trading at $28 per share. Show the journal entries needed to record *(a)* the calling of the bonds, and *(b)* the conversion of the bonds. If you were a bondholder, what option would you take?

EXHIBIT 1
Present Value of $1 Per Period

Periods	6%	8%	12%	15%	16%
1	0.943	0.926	0.893	0.870	0.862
2	1.833	1.783	1.690	1.626	1.605
3	2.673	2.577	2.402	2.283	2.246
4	3.465	3.312	3.037	2.855	2.798
5	4.212	3.993	3.605	3.352	3.274
6	4.917	4.623	4.111	3.784	3.685
7	5.582	5.206	4.564	4.160	4.039
8	6.210	5.747	4.968	4.487	4.344
9	6.802	6.247	5.328	4.772	4.607
10	7.360	6.710	5.650	5.019	4.833
11	7.887	7.139	5.937	5.234	5.029
12	8.384	7.536	6.194	5.421	5.197
13	8.853	7.904	6.424	5.583	5.342
14	9.295	8.244	6.628	5.724	5.468
15	9.712	8.559	6.811	5.847	5.575
16	10.106	8.851	6.974	5.954	5.669
17	10.477	9.122	7.120	6.047	5.749
18	10.828	9.372	7.250	6.128	5.818
19	11.158	9.604	7.366	6.198	5.877
20	11.470	9.818	7.469	6.259	5.929

EXHIBIT 2
Present Value of $1

Periods	6%	8%	12%	15%	16%
1	0.943	0.926	0.893	0.870	0.862
2	0.890	0.857	0.797	0.756	0.743
3	0.840	0.794	0.712	0.658	0.641
4	0.792	0.735	0.636	0.572	0.552
5	0.747	0.681	0.567	0.497	0.476
6	0.705	0.630	0.507	0.432	0.410
7	0.665	0.583	0.452	0.376	0.354
8	0.627	0.540	0.404	0.327	0.305
9	0.592	0.500	0.361	0.284	0.263
10	0.558	0.463	0.322	0.247	0.227
11	0.527	0.429	0.287	0.215	0.195
12	0.497	0.397	0.257	0.187	0.168
13	0.469	0.368	0.229	0.163	0.145
14	0.442	0.340	0.205	0.141	0.125
15	0.417	0.315	0.183	0.123	0.108
16	0.394	0.292	0.163	0.107	0.093
17	0.371	0.270	0.146	0.093	0.080
18	0.350	0.250	0.130	0.081	0.069
19	0.331	0.232	0.116	0.070	0.060
20	0.312	0.215	0.104	0.061	0.051

McDonald's Corporation*

Press on. Nothing in the world can take the place of persistence. Talent will not—
nothing is more common than unsuccessful men with talent. Genius will not—unrewarded
genius is almost a proverb. Education will not—the world is full of educated derelicts.
Persistence and determination alone are omnipotent.

The credo of Ray A. Kroc, McDonald's Corporation's founder and foremost promoter,
was spinning around in Jack Greenberg's mind as he worked late in the corporate
headquarters in March 1982. As chief financial officer of McDonald's, he was analyzing
alternative strategies for financing future corporate growth. McDonald's had become
a dominant force in the fast-food restaurant business through rapid expansion and
aggressive merchandising programs. And everyone—shareholders, institutional investors, and Wall Street analysts alike—expected the aggressive thrust to continue.

THE BIRTH OF McDONALD'S

While the name of Ray Kroc is most frequently associated with the industry success
of McDonald's, he was not the originator of the fast-food restaurant concept. Two
brothers from New England, Richard and Maurice McDonald, developed the concept and established the first restaurant in California. In 1954, Kroc discovered the
McDonald brothers' restaurant, which was easily recognizable by the presence of
two golden arches, in San Bernadino, California. Kroc noted that patrons literally
"flocked" to the restaurant, often waiting in line in their automobiles just to get
into the drive-in facility.

The key to their success, thought Kroc, was that the two brothers had essentially
developed, like Henry Ford, the basics of an assembly line product: value, speed of
service, and elimination of waste. Having been in sales and marketing for over 35
years, Kroc quickly recognized the enormous potential of the concept: a food product
(the hamburger) that was cheap, nutritious, and the same every day of the year. It
could be sold for only $0.15 and still make a profit.

Kroc soon approached the McDonald brothers with a proposal to franchise the
restaurant concept. Richard and Maurice, however, were earning a substantial income
(over $75,000 a year) from the one operation and were anxious about the problems

---

* This case was prepared by Kenneth R. Ferris and Connie J. Johnson. Copyright © 1984 by Kenneth
R. Ferris. All rights reserved to the authors.

that expansion might bring. After considerable urging, the brothers finally agreed to the franchise proposal, and so the McDonald's saga began.

Lacking expertise in the areas of financing and real estate, Kroc soon hired Harry Sonneborn, a former vice president of the Tastee Freeze Company. Sonneborn convinced Kroc that expansion should take place through both company-owned and franchised restaurants; but even in the franchised operations, the company would maintain significant control by only leasing facilities to the franchisees. McDonald's would buy or lease a site, develop the property and construct the restaurant, and then release the operation to the franchisee. Under this approach, the company would earn income in a variety of ways: franchising fees, the sale of products to the franchisee, and lease income (typically 6.25 percent of a store's gross revenues).

The McDonald's expansion plan was both creative and highly profitable, but also required substantial capital investment. With only $90,000 in personal assets, Kroc was soon forced to seek outside financial assistance, and in 1961 he sold 20 percent of the company to two insurance companies for $1.5 million. This infusion of capital, however, allowed McDonald's to undertake a dramatic expansion. Within three years, the company owned 87 restaurants and had franchised 570 more. As Ray Kroc recalls:

> I wanted to go public but I couldn't because I wasn't showing a profit. I couldn't because I was pouring everything back into the business. I used to drive my accountant crazy because I would anticipate the next three months' profits and I would obligate it in the way of debt for expansion—I was going for broke.

The rest is history. In 1965, the company went public. During the first 25 years of operations, McDonald's served over 31 billion hamburgers. By 1982, the company owned or franchised more than 7,200 McDonald's restaurants throughout the United States and 30 other countries.

It was with this legacy of rapid growth and expansion that Jack Greenberg found himself faced. The corporation, moreover, had plans to open over 500 new restaurants in the next several years. He perceived a need to come up with increasingly creative methods of financing and, for this reason, decided to investigate a relatively new investment concept—zero-coupon bonds.

ZERO-COUPON BONDS

Although available in England since the early 1960s, zero-coupon bonds were first publicly offered in the United States in April 1981 by J.C. Penney's. Shortly thereafter, similar public offerings were undertaken by the Allied Corporation and by PepsiCo, Inc.; hence, the concept appeared to be gaining acceptance among major U.S. firms.

Under the terms of the bond indenture agreement, zero-coupon debentures carry no stated coupon rate. Thus, a purchaser of a zero-coupon bond receives no periodic interest payments; instead, the implied interest is retained by the company to accumulate and become payable in full at maturity. When issued, zero-coupon instruments are deeply discounted from their face value—the deep discount representing the future interest to be accumulated until maturity. In theory, the appreciation from issue price to maturity value equals the sum of the annual interest payments plus the compounding of those interest payments that would have occurred had those payments been reinvested.

The sudden appearance of this financing device in the United States appeared to be linked to the 1981 Tax Act. This law liberalized contributions to individual pension plans and provided that all wage earners could establish individual retirement accounts (IRAs). Under existing tax laws, corporate issuers of zero-coupon debentures were entitled to currently deduct the interest that accrued but that remained unpaid until maturity, whereas the bondholder (unless subject to tax-deferred status) was required to report the corresponding accretion of the original issue discount as income. Thus, prior to 1981, the market for zero-coupon instruments was somewhat limited because existing tax law required that the interest earned on such instruments be currently taxed, even though the interest had not been received in cash by the debtholder. The 1981 tax law substantially broadened the potential market by enabling a larger number of individuals to establish tax-deferred retirement accounts.

As Jack Greenberg considered these facts, he recognized that the instrument had a number of advantages as well as disadvantages. From the investor's perspective, he noted that, with a zero-coupon bond, investors could lock into a fixed yield rate on both the initial investment as well as future interest; thus, the problem of what to do with a periodic interest payment was solved. This advantage, however, might become a disadvantage relative to interest paying debt instruments in the event that market rates of interest rose above the yield rate on the zero-coupon instrument at the time of purchase. Jack recalled several of *The Wall Street Journal* articles that illustrated this point (see Exhibits 1 and 2).

From the issuing company's perspective, Jack felt that the zero-coupon instruments were particularly attractive because existing tax laws allowed the issuing firm to

---

EXHIBIT 1

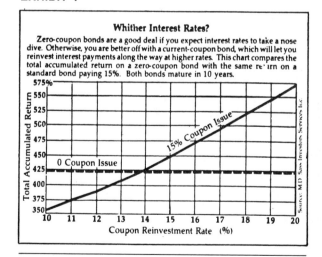

Whither Interest Rates?

Zero-coupon bonds are a good deal if you expect interest rates to take a nose dive. Otherwise, you are better off with a current-coupon bond, which will let you reinvest interest payments along the way at higher rates. This chart compares the total accumulated return on a zero-coupon bond with the same return on a standard bond paying 15%. Both bonds mature in 10 years.

Source: "New Wave of Zero-Coupon Bonds for IRAs Could Sink Investors if Interest Rates Rise," *The Wall Street Journal*, March 22, 1982.

EXHIBIT 2

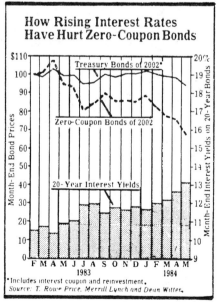

How Rising Interest Rates Have Hurt Zero-Coupon Bonds

Source: "Zero-Coupon bonds' Price Swings Jolt Investors Looking for Security," *The Wall Street Journal*, June 1, 1984.

deduct the unpaid interest currently. However, since the market value of these debt securities would almost certainly remain below their maturity value, the issuing company would essentially be precluded from early retirement of the debt by call or redemption (although retirement by open market repurchase remained an option).[1]

Overall, Jack felt that the zero-coupon instrument had more pluses than minuses, and decided to pursue the matter with the company's investment bankers.

McDONALD'S PUBLIC OFFERING

After considerable discussion with the brokerage houses of Salomon Brothers and Blyth Eastman Paine Webber, McDonald's Corporation decided to issue $150 million (maturity value) in zero-coupon notes. On August 17, 1982, an announcement of the offering appeared in the financial press (see Exhibit 3.).

The public offering was favorably received by the marketplace and, by early September, was fully sold. The offering netted the corporation $50 million, with amounts due at maturity of $40 million in 1988 and $120 million in 1994, as follows:

Price to Public per Note	Payable at Maturity per Note	Amount Sold	Yield to Maturity	Maturity Date
$500	$1,000	$20 million	12.3%	April 30, 1988
250	1,000	30 million	12.6	April 30, 1994

QUESTIONS

1. Assume that transaction and brokerage costs are nominal. How would the sale of the notes be recorded on the books of the McDonald's Corporation?

2. Prepare an amortization table (on an annual basis) for the $250 notes, utilizing the effective interest method.

3. Show the balance sheet presentation and income statement effect of the $250 notes as of December 31, 1989.

4. Assume that one half of the $250 notes are reacquired by open market repurchase on December 31, 1990, at a price of $875 per note. How would the transaction be recorded on the books of the McDonald's Corporation?

5. Assume that the remaining one half of the $250 notes are redeemed on December 31, 1992, at a premium of 5 percent above maturity value. How would the transaction be recorded on the books of the McDonald's Corporation?

---

[1] Under conventional call or redemption provisions, the issuing company may retire outstanding debt instruments before maturity by paying the debtholder the maturity value plus, in most instances, a small premium.

EXHIBIT 3

IBM: A Matter of Timing*

The tension was easily felt at 11 A.M. on Wednesday, October 3, 1979, when the top financial executives from IBM met with investment advisers from the brokerage firms of Merrill Lynch and Salomon Brothers. The purpose of their meeting was to price the largest public debt offering in U.S. corporate history.

Those attending the meeting were well aware of the numerous economic shocks that had recently hit the financial world: rapidly rising interest rates, falling stock and bond prices, gold and silver selling at record high prices, and the U.S. dollar sinking in value in foreign exchange markets. In the midst of this, the world's largest computer and business equipment company was going to the public debt market for the first time in its corporate history in an effort to borrow $1 billion. The public offering by IBM was to consist of $500 million in 7-year notes and $500 million in 25-year debentures. Because of the rapidly changing economic environment, the small group of executives and investment bankers felt a need to act quickly on the deal.

BACKGROUND

IBM had been founded in 1911 as a merger of three existing, yet previously unrelated, companies. The newly formed company was called Computing-Tabulating-Recording Company, but in 1924 adopted the corporate name of International Business Machines.

The growth of the new company was substantial and by 1955, IBM ranked 59th in *Fortune*'s roster of U.S. industrial companies. By 1978, IBM had moved up to 21st position, with sales of over $21 billion (see financial statements in Exhibit 1–3).

Growth by the company had been financed primarily with internally generated funds, largely obtained from internally developed products. In 1978, IBM's long-term debt amounted to only 2 percent of its shareholder equity of nearly $13.5 billion, and its last sale of common stock to the public had occurred over 12 years earlier in 1966.

In early 1979, however, IBM began experiencing trouble. Although the company was outdistancing its competition in both product pricing and development, the IBM share price reached new lows on heavy trading volume. Shares, selling at only 11 times reported net earnings, were being traded at values below 1969 year-end prices, in spite of the fact that earnings and dividends had increased fourfold over the decade.

_____

* This case was prepared by Kenneth R. Ferris and Connie J. Johnson. Copyright © 1984 by Kenneth R. Ferris. All rights reserved to the authors.

EXHIBIT 1

INTERNATIONAL BUSINESS MACHINES CORPORATION AND SUBSIDIARY COMPANIES
Consolidated Statement of Earnings
For the Year Ended December 31
(dollars in millions except per share amounts)

	1980		1979		1978	
Gross income:						
Sales	$10,919		$ 9,473		$8,755	
Rentals.	10,869		10,069		9,781	
Services	4,425		3,321		2,540	
		$26,213		$22,863		$21,076
Cost of sales	4,197		3,267		2,838	
Cost of rentals	3,771		3,491		3,251	
Cost of services.	2,181		1,655		1,395	
Selling, development and engineering, and general and administrative expenses.	10,324		9,205		8,151	
Interest expense	273		141		55	
		20,746		17,759		15,690
		5,467		5,104		5,386
Other income, principally interest		430		449		412
Earnings before income taxes .		5,897		5,553		5,798
Provision for U.S. federal and non-U.S. income taxes		2,335		2,542		2,687
Net earnings:		$ 3,562		$ 3,011		$ 3,111
Per share		$ 6.10		$ 5.16		$ 5.32

Average number of shares outstanding:
    1980—583,516,764
    1979—583,373,269
    1978—584,428,584

In addition to the downward market pressure on its common share price, other factors also conspired to push IBM toward its first ever public debt offering. By the fall of 1979, IBM's cash position had come under increasing pressure from a large increase in capital spending (up 24 percent from 1978). Cash was needed to support IBM's new and highly successful medium-sized computer line. During the first week following one new product announcement, IBM had booked over three years' worth of orders. In addition, the company had planned further new product announcements. Hence, the company faced considerable pressures to quickly expand production capacity on a worldwide basis.

Another contributing factor was changing consumer tastes and preferences. Equipment consumers increasingly preferred leasing new equipment, as opposed to buying. Some customers leased as a hedge against technical obsolescence, while others leased to hedge against uncertain equipment quality. As a direct consequence of the consumer shift toward leasing, IBM found itself overstocked with unwanted used equipment, which in the past had been a significant source of revenues and cash flows. With the trend toward leasing, IBM was forced to finance an increasing percentage of the computers it placed with customers. Capital tied up in leased equipment increased 55 percent in 1979 to over $4.2 billion.

EXHIBIT 2

INTERNATIONAL BUSINESS MACHINES CORPORATION AND SUBSIDIARY COMPANIES
Consolidated Statements of Financial Position at December 31
(dollars in millions)

	1980		1979	
Assets				
Current assets:				
Cash	$ 281		$ 298	
Marketable securities, at lower of cost or market	1,831		3,473	
Notes and accounts receivable—trade, less allowance:				
1980, $195; 1979, $188	4,562		4,299	
Other accounts receivable	315		372	
Inventories, at lower of average cost or market	2,293		1,842	
Prepaid expenses	643		567	
		$ 9,925		$10,851
Rental machines and parts	15,352		13,742	
Less accumulated depreciation	6,969		6,815	
		8,383		6,927
Plant and other property	11,018		9,002	
Less accumulated depreciation	4,384		3,736	
		6,634		5,266
Deferred charges and other assets		1,761		1,486
Total assets		$26,703		$24,530
Liabilities and Stockholders' Equity				
Current liabilities:				
Taxes	2,369		2,365	
Loans payable	591		933	
Accounts payable	721		682	
Compensation and benefits	1,404		1,217	
Deferred income	305		233	
Other accrued expenses and liabilities	1,136		1,015	
		$ 6,526		$ 6,445
Deferred investment tax credits		182		140
Reserves for employees' indemnities and retirement plans		1,443		1,395
Long-term debt		2,099		1,589
Stockholders' equity:				
Capital stock, par value $1.25 per share; shares authorized, 650,000,000; issued: 1980—584,262,074; 1979—583,973,258	3,992		3,974	
Retained earnings	12,491		11,012	
	16,483		14,986	
Less: Treasury stock, at cost	30		25	
Shares: 1980—455,242; 1970—378,715				
		16,453		14,961
Total liabilities and stockholders' equity		$26,703		$24,530

These factors, and others, appeared to dictate that not only was additional cash needed but that the bond market was also the best avenue to obtain those funds. With a diminished share price and a stock split as recent as April 1979, a new stock offering appeared undesirable. Short-term debt financing, on the other hand, seemed too costly and risky; the prime rate had recently been hovering around 13½ percent, but was highly volatile. Moreover, with a top investment rating (AAA) from both Moody's and Standard & Poor's, IBM executives reasoned that they would

EXHIBIT 3

INTERNATIONAL BUSINESS MACHINES CORPORATION AND SUBSIDIARY COMPANIES
Consolidated Statements of Changes in Financial Position
For the Year Ended December 31
(dollars in millions)

	1980	1979	1978
Source of working capital:			
Net earnings.	$ 3,562	$3,011	$ 3,111
Items not requiring the current use of working capital:			
Depreciation	2,362	1,970	1,824
Net book value of rental machines and other property retired			
or sold	1,009	779	562
Other	90	353	287
Total from operations.	7,023	6,113	5,784
Proceeds from stock sold or issued under employee plans. . .	422	416	341
Long-term borrowings	604	1,450	74
	8,049	7,979	6,199
Application of working capital:			
Investment in rental machines	4,334	4,212	2,724
Investment in plant and other property.	2,258	1,779	1,322
	6,592	5,991	4,046
Less: Depreciation of manufacturing facilities capitalized in rental			
machines	397	351	247
	6,195	5,640	3,799
Increase in deferred charges and other assets.	275	338	132
Cash dividends paid or payable.	2,008	1,506	1,763
Reduction of long-term debt.	94	146	45
Treasury stock purchased for employee plan.	484	454	373
Capital stock purchased and canceled	—	—	440
	9,056	8,084	6,552
Decrease in working capital	$(1,007)	$ (105)	$ (353)
Changes in working capital:			
Cash and marketable securities.	$(1,659)	$ (259)	$(1,376)
Notes and accounts receivable	206	537	1,030
Inventories and prepaid expenses	527 ·	252	594
Taxes.	(4)	(261)	(82)
Loans payable.	342	(691)	(69)
Accounts payable and accruals.	(419)	(185)	(372)
Dividend payable	—	502	(78)
Decrease in working capital	(1,007)	(105)	(353)
Working capital at beginning			
of year	4,406	4,511	4,864
Working capital at end of year.	$ 3,399	$4,406	$ 4,511

have to pay bond market investors only slightly more than the current interest rate on long-term government securities (i.e., 9¼ percent).

At the same time that IBM executives had to cope with the question of "where" to obtain additional financing, they faced the related question of "how much." Signs of a recession had begun to appear in 1979 and there was concern that, if the company responded to the current level of sales demand, future sales might turn "soft" and the company would be faced with over-, rather than underproductive capacity. On the other hand, if the firm failed to respond to the current high demand and the market remained strong, the company risked losing business. In the final analysis,

IBM executives decided on a huge expansion of manufacturing capacity. In the past the company had priced new products very competitively—using volume, rather than high margins, as a means of profitability. Following this past and highly successful strategy appeared to be the best option, and hence necessitated a significant infusion of external capital.

INVESTMENT BANKERS

Meetings with investment bankers began in the summer of 1979. Their purpose was to ensure that IBM obtained the best advice possible on how to tap the capital market for a large sum of money for plant expansion and the financing of leased equipment. Initially, the firms of Morgan Stanley and Salomon Brothers were both present. However, when IBM proposed that the two investment houses act as comanagers of the offering, Morgan Stanley declined to participate. IBM executives had reasoned that two brokerage houses could not only provide ample capital to support the offering but that they could also provide quicker and better execution of final sales to the market. Morgan Stanley was soon replaced by Merrill Lynch as comanager of the offering.

While negotiations transpired between IBM and its joint advisory group during the month of September, the economy became increasingly volatile. The prime rate of interest[1] increased five times alone in that month, while simultaneously record-high yields for new offerings were also being set. Recognizing the danger of a highly volatile market, the investment advisers from Merrill Lynch and Salomon Brothers urged IBM to move quickly and to shift the planned offering date from October 15 to the first week of October.

A 225-member underwriting syndicate was quickly organized by the comanagers. The first item of business was to estimate the price that the IBM issues would bring from institutional buyers. The yield on U.S. Treasury issues of comparable maturities provided an initial benchmark. The task of the comanagers then became to price the offering close enough to the Treasury yields to minimize IBM's cost of borrowing, but at the same time to price it high enough to ensure that the huge offering would sell quickly.

PRICING THE OFFERING

On Wednesday, October 3, 1979, a meeting was held at the New York offices of Salomon Brothers. The purpose of the meeting was to arrive at a final price for the IBM securities in anticipation of a public offering shortly thereafter.

At a little after midnight, and after much heated discussion, IBM agreed to a yield on its 7-year notes of 7 basis points[2] above the current Treasury note yield rate and 12 basis points above the current long-term Treasury yield for its 25-year debentures. The resulting effective yields were 9.62 percent (or 4.81 percent semiannually) for the notes and 9.41 percent (or 4.705 percent semiannually) for the debentures.

To achieve these yields, the price to investors for the notes, for example, was set at $994 per $1,000 par value. Of that price, IBM received $987.75, with the remaining $6.25 per note going to the underwriting syndicate. Salomon Brothers and Merrill

---

[1] The prime rate, base rate, or reference rate is that rate of interest charged by banks for loans extended to their best or preferred customers.

[2] A basis point is 1/100 of 1 percent.

Lynch would receive $1.25 per note each for managing the issue, with the actual seller of the note receiving a commission of $3.75.

On Thursday, October 4, the IBM securities were offered for sale in an even more turbulent financial market. The product price index for September 1979 had been released and showed a price increase of over 1.4 percent for the month—the largest monthly increase in over five years. As a consequence, economists began predicting 11 percent inflation for the remainder of 1979 and 1980. The U.S. Treasury had also recently sold $2.5 billion of four-year notes at a record high yield of 9.79 percent. By the close of the capital markets on Thursday, an estimated 25 percent of the IBM offering remained unsold.

On Friday, October 5, Federal Reserve chairman Paul A. Volcker abruptly left the joint International Monetary Fund/World Bank meeting in Belgrade, Yugoslavia, to return to the United States, fueling speculation that the U.S. government would attempt to provide support for the U.S. dollar in international exchange markets. On Saturday, October 6, Mr. Volcker announced several drastic policy changes designed to tighten credit in an effort to control the high level of inflation being experienced in the United States. The actions included: (1) a 1 percent increase in the discount rate,[3] effective Monday, October 8, to a record high of 12 percent; (2) a refocusing of the Federal Reserve monetary policy away from attempting to control interest rates and towards an attempt to control, instead, the supply of money; and (3) the establishment of an 8 percent reserve requirement for certain liabilities of Federal Reserve member banks.

In response to Volcker's announcement, bankers and economists predicted that short-term interest rates would surge in the coming weeks and continue rising for the next several months. The prime rate was expected to climb from its current level of 13½ percent to 15 percent by early 1980.

Market reaction to the Federal Reserve chairman's announcement was swift. On Monday, October 8, and Tuesday, October 9, the Dow Jones Industrial Average dropped over 40 points. Bond prices also dropped record amounts; some "blue-chip" securities fell by as much as 2⅜ basis points (or roughly $23.75 per $1,000 face value). And, as predicted, U.S. Treasury bond yields rose to 9½ percent, forcing a repricing of the IBM offering as investor sales waned (see Exhibit 4).

On Wednesday, October 10, the IBM underwriting syndicate was disbanded and the approximately $400 million of unsold securities were placed on the secondary resale market. An unnamed bond specialist was quoted in *The Wall Street Journal:* "There'll be a much, much greater decline if the huge IBM offering doesn't retail quickly."

The price of the notes quickly fell nearly 5 basis points to a bid of 94⅞, for an effective yield of 10.55 percent. By November, the notes had fallen to 92¼ bid, for a yield of approximately 10.98 percent. As anticipated, the credit tightening actions of the Federal Reserve had resulted in increased interest rates.

QUESTIONS

1. How would IBM account for the proceeds on the sale of the $500 million in seven-year notes? What journal entry would be needed to record the interest expense

---

[3] The "discount rate" is that rate charged to depository institutions on borrowings from Federal Reserve banks.

EXHIBIT 4
The Bad News of Climbing Yields

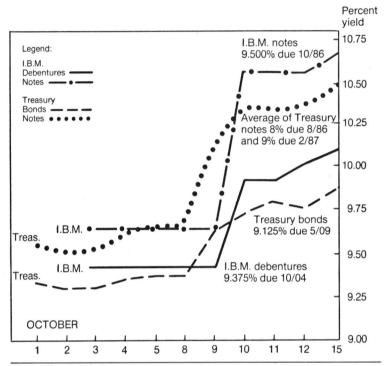

Source: "The Bomb IBM Dropped on Wall Street," *Fortune,* November 19, 1979.

Corporate issues rated triple A, as IBM's notes and debentures were, are usually priced as close as possible to their Treasury and corporate equivalents. A spread of one quarter of 1 percent above Treasuries in yield is a customary standard. The IBM issues, being what Wall Street calls "museum pieces"—meaning unique—were priced at a much narrower spread. When Treasury yields unexpectedly jumped, sales of the IBM obligations virtually stopped until the underwriters set the prices free to fluctuate with the market.

(using the effective interest method) and amortization of note issue costs (using the straight-line method) after the first six months?

2. How would IBM account for the new note market price of 92¼ on November 1? What are the implications of this?

3. Prepare a cash flow statement for IBM for 1979; for 1980.

Three Faces of Early Debt Retirement*

INTRODUCTION

A long-standing principle of accounting asserts that cost savings should never be equated with income generation, if for no other reason than that such cost savings don't produce cash inflows. For example, the funds saved through the self-construction of assets versus their outright purchase are never accounted for as an income flow. The old adage that "a penny saved is a penny earned" doesn't hold in the practice of accounting, at least in most cases.

The accounting treatment of the early retirement of long-term debt, however, provides a notable exception. *APB Opinion No. 26,* "Early Extinguishment of Debt," requires that in the event of an early retirement of long-term debt, the difference between the redemption price of the debt and its net book value be accounted for as a gain or loss in the year of retirement.[1]

Since the adoption of this principle, market interest rates have increased and long-term debt prices, in turn, have declined. As a consequence, many firms have taken advantage of lower bond market prices to retire in whole or in part their outstanding debt issuances through cash repurchase or, in some instances, debt-for-debt swaps. In some cases, these retirements have been mandated by sinking fund requirements, while in others the motivation appears more opportunistic. Regardless of the motivation, these transactions have in *every* case resulted in substantial gains being reported on the earnings statement.

Two additional approaches to financing the early retirement of debt have gained in popularity: debt-for-equity swaps and defeasance. The former was developed and promoted by national brokerage firms, while the latter was so controversial that the Securities and Exchange Commission temporarily banned publicly held companies from using the technique until the Financial Accounting Standards Board could issue a ruling regarding the proper accounting for the event. A recently issued FASB statement (January 1984), "Extinguishment of Debt," provides that such transactions be accounted for as an early retirement.

Early retirements, in general, and the use of defeasance or convertible debt-for-equity "swaps," in particular, raise a number of accounting issues. In particular, is the difference between the redemption price of debt and its net book value really a gain, or is it simply a cost savings? In an era when the financial community and the accounting profession have moved toward the increased utilization and reporting of cash flow and liquidity data, it seems appropriate to reexamine those transactions,

---

* This case was prepared by Kenneth R. Ferris and Connie J. Johnson. Copyright © 1984 by Kenneth R. Ferris. All rights reserved to the authors.

[1] *Financial Accounting Standard No. 4* (1975), "Reporting Gains and Losses from Extinguishment of Debt," requires that such gains or losses be treated as an extraordinary item on the earnings statement.

such as the early retirement of debt, which may actually produce negative cash flows while resulting in a "gain" for income statement purposes.

MARKET CONDITIONS, EARLY RETIREMENT, AND CURRENT ACCOUNTING PRACTICE

Under existing accounting practice, long-term liabilities are recorded at the present value of the future cash flows contractually required to satisfy the obligation. In the case of corporate debentures, this requires the discounting of both the terminal principal amount as well as the periodic interest payments. The appropriate discount rate is assumed to be the market yield on the debentures at the time of the initial sale.

Generally accepted accounting practice does *not*, however, provide for the revaluation of liabilities in the event that subsequent market values differ from book value. Liabilities are placed on the balance sheet at a value reflecting their initial yield rate, which is assumed to remain constant over the life of the debt instrument. In reality, however, the yield rate may actually fluctuate substantially in the marketplace. As a consequence, as long-term interest rates move upward, for example, the fair market value of debt instruments having fixed-coupon rates will decline. On the balance sheet, however, the book value of these instruments will remain unchanged. Thus, the discrepancy between the net book value and market value of debt is actually attributable to changes in the cost of borrowing in the marketplace.[2]

Because current market interest rates are much higher than those existing a decade or more ago, many companies have found themselves facing a situation in which their long-term debt obligations are selling at values well below their recorded book values. Further, most corporate bonds have active sinking funds that mandate the retirement of some predetermined percentage of outstanding bonds each year.[3] Some firms have opted to take advantage of these market conditions and retire or reduce their outstanding debt levels even beyond sinking fund requirements. The extent to which this transaction benefits a company depends, in part, on how the retirement is financed.

A variety of different approaches is available to finance the early retirement of debt transaction: debt-for-cash, debt-for-equity, or defeasance. Each of these techniques produces different tax, reported income, and cash flow consequences. Each alternative is considered in the following series of cases.

I. LOCKHEED CORPORATION: A TRADITIONAL EARLY RETIREMENT

Vincent Marafina's spirits were high as he walked on a deserted California beach in February 1984. As chief financial officer of the Lockheed Corporation, he had

---

[2] A change in a bond's perceived quality (i.e., an agency rating change) will also cause bond prices to change, thus producing a discrepancy between book and market values. However, most bond price fluctuations are attributable to interest rate changes.

[3] Over 80 percent of industrial bonds and nearly one third of public utility bonds have mandatory sinking funds. A typical sinking fund requires the annual retirement of a certain amount of bonds in either of the two following ways: (1) execute a "call" for the needed bonds at face value or a slight premium (the sinking fund call price will be specified in the bond indenture), or (2) purchase the required bonds on the open market.

been instrumental in having "helped pull the company out of a power dive and maneuvered it into a position to cash in on the aerospace bonanza" of the 1980s.

By every measure, 1983 had been the most successful year in the company's history. Sales, net earnings, earnings per share, new sign-ups, and the backlog of orders had all reached record high levels. Shareholders' equity had grown by 97 percent, and long-term debt had been substantially reduced driving the debt-to-equity ratio down from 2.1:1 in 1982 to less than 1:1 for the first time in more than 10 years.

Progress was also continuing on two of Lockheed's three major long-term goals: allocations to research and development in the aerospace business were increasing, and the company had recently won over $40 billion in new government contracts for the construction of military aircraft, communication satellites, and ground management responsibilities for the space shuttle. In spite of these achievements, Lockheed's goal of reducing its debt-to-equity ratio to less than 0.5:1 posed a considerable challenge.

LOCKHEED TAKING FLIGHT

The Lockheed Corporation began operations in 1932 as the Lockheed Aircraft Corporation. From its early focus on the aircraft industry, the company expanded into related industries, and today is engaged primarily in the design, development, and production of missiles, space systems, and military aircraft. The company's recent history, however, had been marred by a number of financial and ethical disasters.

In 1966, Lockheed began production of the giant C-5 transport airplane. Initial testing, however, had shown that the aircraft was either underpowered or too heavy. When the Air Force refused to pay for the development of a bigger engine, Lockheed's only option was to cut the weight of the aircraft—a change that weakened the plane's structure and led to a history of problems with the aircraft's wings. In the end, the contract produced a cost overrun of $1.6 billion—$1.3 billion to rebuild the wings and $0.3 billion in contract penalties (only 81 of the contracted for 115 planes were delivered).

The problems with the C-5 cargo transport plane did not prove to be an isolated incident. In the late 1960s, Lockheed also developed the Cheyenne helicopter for government use in conjunction with the Vietnam War. Operational difficulties, however, caused the government to cancel tentative purchase contracts, subsequently forcing Lockheed to write off over $120 million in 1970 when the program was abandoned.

These financial failures ultimately put in jeopardy Lockheed's efforts to diversify into the civil aircraft industry. In 1971, Lockheed began production of its new, wide-bodied L-1011 TriStar, an aircraft that the company had hoped would make a major impact on the civil aircraft industry. While the TriStar proved to be popular with pilots and passengers, commercial aircraft companies preferred the Boeing 747 and McDonnell Douglas's DC-10. After a long and costly struggle to establish a market for the L-1011, Lockheed finally decided in 1981 to stop producing the aircraft, taking a $466 million write-off, which included $70 million in operating losses.

The TriStar effort had nearly put Lockheed into bankruptcy. In 1972, for example, Rolls Royce, the engine supplier for the TriStar, insisted that the U.S. government guarantee Lockheed's solvency—a guarantee which the company received—as a condition for the continued supply of engines and parts. In the midst of these problems, Lockheed was also implicated in a contract kickback scandal that involved payoffs to Japanese governmental officials in return for favorable contract decisions. Because of material shortages and production delays, the company never attained its projected economies of scale and finally concluded that, unless significant amounts of new capital were obtained to support the TriStar program, the program would never be profitable.

The decision to cancel the TriStar was finally reached in 1981, and it drew considerable support from the financial community. The company's common stock price soared from $40 per share at the beginning of 1981 to a high of $82.50 during fall 1982. Vincent Marafina decided to take advantage of the market's new confidence in Lockheed, and the company issued common stock for the first time in over a decade. With the company's debt-to-equity ratio down to less than 1:1 and a directive to improve the ratio even further, Marafino prepared to consider other debt reducing actions, one of which was the early retirement of Lockheed's 4¼ percent convertible debentures due in 1992.

QUESTIONS

1. Review the "Notice of Redemption" (Exhibit 1) and the excerpts from Lockheed's 1983 financial statements (Exhibits 2 and 3). Why hadn't the debenture holders converted earlier?

2. Assuming that the debentures had been issued in May 1974, what was the total dollar cost of borrowing paid by Lockheed for these funds from 1974 to 1984?

3. How would Lockheed account for the conversion of the debentures? To what extent does generally accepted accounting principles "fairly" reflect the cost of convertible debt? (Note: during the week prior to the "notice of redemption," the Lockheed debentures traded at $147.50.)

EXHIBIT 1
Notice of Redemption

LOCKHEED CORPORATION
4¼ Convertible Subordinated Debentures Due 1992

Notice is hereby given that Lockheed Corporation ("Lockheed") has elected to redeem and will redeem on May 29, 1984 (the "Redemption Date"), all of the outstanding Debentures, with such redemption to be at the redemption price of $1,006.40 for each $1,000 principal amount of Debentures, together with accrued and unpaid interest to the Redemption Date of $10.36 (i.e., a total redemption price of $1,016.76). Payment of the redemption price of the Debentures, including accrued and unpaid interest, will be made on or after the Redemption Date upon presentation and surrender of the Debentures to either Union Bank, the Trustee and Conversion and Redemption Agent, or Bankers Trust Company, the Co-Conversion and Co-Redemption Agent (together the "Agents") at either of the addresses specified below.

All of the outstanding Debentures shall become due and payable on the Redemption Date and after the Redemption Date the Debentures will be deemed to be no longer outstanding. Interest on the Debentures will cease to accrue and the holders thereof will be entitled to no rights as such holders except the right to receive payment on or after the Redemption Date of the redemption price, including accrued and unpaid interest to the Redemption Date.

EXHIBIT 1 *(concluded)*

CONVERSION OF DEBENTURES INTO COMMON STOCK

The Debentures may, at the option of the holder thereof, be converted into Lockheed Common Stock at a conversion price of $21.17 per share or a ratio of approximately 47.24 shares of Common Stock for each $1,000 principal amount of Debentures. Accrued and unpaid interest will not be paid on Debentures which are converted.

The right to convert the Debentures into Common Stock of Lockheed expires at the close of business (5 P.M. local time) on May 29, 1984.

At the close of business on April 12, 1984, the market value of 47.24 shares of Common Stock of Lockheed was $1,700.64 based on the closing price of the Common Stock of $36 per share on the New York Stock Exchange on such date. As long as the price of the Common Stock remains at or above $21⅝ per share, holders of Debentures upon conversion will receive Common Stock (plus cash in lieu of any fractional share) having a market value grater than the amount of cash which would be received upon redemption. Holders of Debentures who elect to convert their Debentures may do so by surrendering such Debentures to one of the Agents prior to the close of business of such Agent (5 P.M. local time) on May 29, 1984, as follows:

Union Bank
P.O. Box 2461, Terminal Annex
Los Angeles, California 90051

Bankers Trust Company
Corporate Trust
P.O. Box 2579
New York, New York 10008

Debentures to be converted must be accompanied by a written notice (or the Letter of Transmittal which is being mailed to each record holder of Debentures) from the holder thereof stating that such holder elects to convert such Debentures and providing the name or names (with addresses) in which the certificate or certificates for Common Stock issuable on such conversion shall be issued.

Failure to surrender Debentures at the office of an Agent for conversion before the close of business on May 29, 1984, will automatically result in such Debentures being redeemed.

Dated: April 16, 1984   LOCKHEED CORPORATION

EXHIBIT 2

LOCKHEED CORPORATION
Consolidated Statement of Earnings

In millions except per-share data	1983	1982	1981
Sales	$6,490.3	$5,613.0	$5,175.8
Costs and expenses	5,962.9	5,156.0	4,715.2
Program profits	527.4	457.0	460.6
Interest expense	(66.2)	(129.8)	(186.2)
Other income (deductions), net	.6	10.4	11.2
Earnings from continuing operations before income taxes	461.8	337.6	285.6
Provision for income taxes	199.0	130.3	130.9
Earnings from continuing operations	262.8	207.3	154.7
Loss from discontinued operations, net of income tax effect			(466.3)
Earnings (loss) before extraordinary item	262.8	207.3	(311.6)
Extraordinary gain on exchange of convertible preferred stock for debentures			22.8
Net earnings (loss)	$ 262.8	$ 207.3	$ (288.8)

Earnings (loss) per share of common stock*		1983	1982	1981
	Primary			
	Continuing operations	$ 4.18	$ 3.65	$ 3.09
	Net earnings (loss)	4.18	3.65	(6.01)
	Fully diluted			
	Continuing operations	4.14	3.59	2.96
	Net earnings (loss)	4.14	3.59	(5.72)

*Adjusted to reflect three-for-one stock split effective August 22, 1983
See accompanying notes.

LOCKHEED CORPORATION
Consolidated Statement of Shareholders' Equity

In millions	$11.25 Convertible Preferred Stock	Common Shareholders' Equity			
		Common stock	Additional capital	Retained earnings	Total
At December 28, 1980		$11.9	$ 91.9	$202.4	$306.2
Stock options and warrants		.2	.8		1.0
Dividends on preferred stock				(8.3)	(8.3)
Provision for $9.50 senior preferred stock redemption				(.8)	(.8)
Issuance of $11.25 convertible preferred stock	$62.6				
Net loss				(288.8)	(288.8)
Quasi-reorganization adjustments as of November 29, 1981					
Restatement of $11.25 convertible preferred stock to par value of $1 per share	(62.0)		62.0		62.0
Restatement of properties held for investment to appraisal values			33.3		33.3
Transfer of retained earnings deficit at November 29, 1981 to additional capital			(116.5)	116.5	
At December 27, 1981	.6	12.1	71.5	21.0	104.6
Net earnings				207.3	207.3
Stock options and warrants		2.1	17.4		19.5
Dividends on preferred stock				(6.4)	(6.4)
Provision for and redemption of $9.50 senior preferred stock			(.2)	(.7)	(.9)
Common stock issued for cash		2.0	90.9		92.9
Conversion of $11.25 convertible preferred stock to common stock	(.6)	1.8	(1.9)		(.1)
Conversion of debentures to common stock			1.5		1.5
At December 26, 1982	—	18.0	179.2	221.2	418.4
Net earnings				262.8	262.8
Stock options		.2	2.8		3.0
Dividends on preferred stock				(2.2)	(2.2)
Provision for $9.50 senior preferred stock redemption				(.4)	(.4)
Common stock issued for cash		3.3	300.4		303.7
Three-for-one stock split		42.0	(42.3)		(.3)
Repurchase of warrants and unregistered shares		(.4)	(9.0)	(156.5)	(165.9)
Conversion of debentures to common stock		.1	7.0		7.1
At December 25, 1983	$ —	$63.2	$438.1	$324.9*	$826.2

*Since November 29, 1981
See accompanying notes.

EXHIBIT 2 *(concluded)*

LOCKHEED CORPORATION
Consolidated Balance Sheet

In millions		1983	1982
Assets			
Current assets	Cash	$ 45.7	$ 35.0
	Accounts receivable	872.9	692.4
	Inventories		
	Continuing operations	713.2	632.2
	Discontinued operations, net	168.7	116.8
	Future tax benefits		131.5
	Prepaid expenses	74.4	64.1
	Total current assets	1,874.9	1,672.0
Property, plant, and equipment, at cost	Land	33.9	22.3
	Buildings, structures, and leasehold improvements	662.2	554.6
	Machinery and equipment	972.6	841.4
		1,668.7	1,418.3
	Less accumulated depreciation and amortization	847.5	754.8
	Net property, plant, and equipment	821.2	663.5
Noncurrent assets	Investment in Lockheed Finance Corporation	66.9	63.9
	Properties held for investment	41.2	46.2
	Other noncurrent assets	25.4	18.8
		$2,829.6	$2,464.4

		1983	1982
Liabilities and Shareholders' Equity			
Current liabilities	Short-term bank borrowings	$ 66.1	$ 25.5
	Accounts payable	464.6	421.0
	Salaries and wages	253.6	229.3
	Income taxes		
	Current	15.2	28.8
	Deferred	58.8	
	Customers' advances in excess of related costs	203.4	129.5
	Retirement plan contribution	65.1	52.4
	Other liabilities	268.7	282.4
	Total current liabilities	1,395.5	1,168.9
Long-term debt		586.8	848.3
Commitments and contingencies			
Redeemable $9.50 senior preferred stock		21.1	28.8
Common shareholders' equity		826.2	418.4
		$2,829.6	$2,464.4

See accompanying notes.

EXHIBIT 3

LOCKHEED CORPORATION
Notes to Financial Statements (excerpts)

Note 9 — Long-Term Debt and Subordinated Debentures

Long-term debt is summarized as follows:

In millions	1983	1982
Notes payable to banks	$500.0	$650.0
Bankers acceptances		34.5
4¼% convertible subordinated debentures (due March 1, 1992)	6.0	13.1
Liabilities to the U.S. government	5.1	16.8
Obligations under long-term capital leases (see Note 8)	29.0	39.7
Notes payable to banks, secured		48.0
Other obligations	64.2	81.8
	604.3	883.9
Less portion due within one year	17.5	35.6
	$586.8	$848.3

Lockheed's credit agreement, as amended, provided for a total commitment of $1 billion through July 31, 1984. In 1983 the company voluntarily reduced the total commitment to $930 million, of which $780 million was represented by an active commitment and $150 million by a reserve commitment. Effective January 20, 1984, the company further reduced the total commitment to $650 million, $500 million of which is represented by the active commitment. On August 1, 1985, the total commitment, including reserve commitment, if any, will be reduced to $500 million. It will be further reduced to $300 million on February 1, 1986. On July 31, 1989 the credit agreement will terminate.

The company's borrowings under the credit agreement are unsecured and bear interest at the bank prime rate or, at the company's option, rates based on the London Interbank Offered Rate (LIBOR) or a "CD Rate" (as defined). The average effective interest rates under the company's bank credit agreements were 11.1 percent in 1983, 17.0 percent in 1982, and 20.5 percent in 1981. At December 25, 1983 the average effective interest rate was 11.9 percent.

Formal compensating balance arrangements under the credit agreement provide for the company to either maintain compensating balances or pay an agreed-upon fee. There are no other formal or informal compensating balance arrangements.

The secured notes payable to banks at the end of 1982 of $48 million represented the balance outstanding under a $67.5 million credit facility to finance the construction of buildings. The notes were paid during 1983.

Other obligations consist primarily of amounts owing to banks and others to finance additions to property and equipment.

The principal amount of 4¼% convertible subordinated debentures outstanding at December 25, 1983 was convertible into 284,412 shares of Lockheed common stock at a conversion price of $21.17 per share (subject to antidilution). These debentures are callable at 100.85 percent during the 12 months ending March 1, 1984, decreasing annually to 100 percent after March 1, 1987.

The company's maturities for the five years following December 25, 1983, excluding those that may be required under the credit agreement, are:

In millions	1984	1985	1986	1987	1988
Obligation to the U.S. government	$ 1.8	$ 1.8	$ 1.5		
Obligation under long-term capital leases	4.3	3.5	3.4	$2.5	$2.5
Other obligations	11.4	5.6	32.0	4.7	2.4
Total	$17.5	$10.9	$36.9	$7.2	$4.9

EXHIBIT 3 *(concluded)*

The credit agreement and the debenture indenture impose certain restrictions with respect to the company's acquisition of shares of Lockheed common stock and impose certain limitations on the payment of dividends on common stock. At December 25, 1983, $115.4 million of retained earnings was available for the payment of common dividends. The credit agreement also contains financial covenants relating to equity, debt, and certain other obligations.

Under bonding agreements with financial institutions and surety companies, Lockheed has established bonding capacity relating primarily to guarantees of contract performance and return of advance payments on certain foreign contracts. At December 25, 1983 the amount of guarantees outstanding totaled approximately $370 million, a substantial majority of which is callable upon determination of a foreign customer that Lockheed is in default under the contract. In such event Lockheed's recourse, if any, would be against the foreign customer.

Note 12 — Preferred Stock

There are 2,500,000 shares of preferred stock, $1 par value, authorized for issuance.

REDEEMABLE $9.50 SENIOR PREFERRED STOCK
At December 25, 1983, 199,980 shares of redeemable $9.50 senior preferred stock were outstanding. Each share has a liquidation preference of $100, a redemption price of $108, and voting rights. Lockheed must redeem 75,000 of the outstanding shares on each December 31st through 1985 at an annual cost of $8.1 million. Lockheed made the required repurchases on December 31st of 1980, 1981, 1982, and 1983. The recorded value of all preferred shares is being increased to redemption value by annual transfers of retained earnings through 1985. The amounts of such transfers were approximately $400,000 in 1983, $700,000 in 1982 and $800,000 in 1981.

Note 13 — Common Stock

On March 30, 1983 the company completed the sale of 3.3 million shares (9.9 million shares as adjusted for the stock split described below) of its common stock. The net proceeds of approximately $304 million were used to reduce outstanding long-term borrowings.

Following approval by its shareholders, the company amended its Articles of Incorporation effective August 22, 1983 to split each share of outstanding common stock into three shares of common stock and to increase the number of authorized shares of common stock to 100,000,000. In connection with the stock split, $42 million was transferred from additional capital to common stock. All references in the consolidated financial statements to the number of shares and per share amounts of common stock have been restated, as applicable, to give effect to the stock split.

At December 25, 1983, 63,170,041 shares of common stock, $1 par value, were issued and outstanding. In addition 284,412 shares were reserved for conversion of debentures (see Note 9) and 2,078,989 shares were reserved for stock options granted.

WARRANTS
Upon the sale of common stock on March 30, 1983, the company signed irrevocable agreements with 23 of its 24 lending banks to acquire all of the outstanding 1,465,000 warrants to purchase common shares and 1,380,000 of the remaining 1,605,000 unregistered shares issued upon previous exercise of warrants. The aggregate purchase price of approximately $166 million for the warrants and unregistered shares was paid on December 15, 1983.

II.   U.S. STEEL CORPORATION: A SWAP

The Pirates and the Steelers had brought several recent world championships to the city of Pittsburgh. Another Pittsburgh team, the "steelers" of U.S. Steel Corporation, had not fared so well.

Yet U.S. Steel had set some records of its own. Over the past 25 years, U.S. Steel's return on shareholders' equity had equaled or exceeded the average return for all U.S. manufacturing companies only twice (in 1974 and 1975); and, during the decade of the 1970s, "Big Steel's" average return was less than half the 14.6 percent return of all manufacturers. In 1979, the company recorded the largest quarterly loss in U.S. business history—a $669 million fourth-quarter loss that produced a $293 million deficit for the year. And in March 1982, U:S. Steel completed the acquisition of Marathon Oil Company for an estimated $6.6 billion ($3.75 billion in cash and $2.87 billion in senior notes). The decline in the steel industry and the massive increase in U.S. Steel's debt stemming from this acquisition would subsequently result in a reduction in the company's debt rating.

Current projections also provided little room for optimism. In spite of the sharp rise expected in 1982 revenues from the recently acquired Marathon oil operations, steel revenues were projected to be substantially lower than 1981 because of decreased demand due to the prevailing economic recession. Profitability would be further constricted by the higher interest costs associated with the increased borrowing and the reduction in interest income from the drawing down of liquid asset reserves to finance the Marathon takeover.

Faced with the prospect of substantially reduced earnings and a multibillion dollar debt, U.S. Steel's Committee on Financial Policy evaluated ways to pare the high debt level, as well as improve current earnings. One proposal concerned the sale of U.S. Steel's Pittsburgh headquarters to the California State Pension Fund for an estimated $260 million, and a pre-tax gain of nearly $150 million. Another proposal called for a debt-for-equity "swap," a new financing ploy developed by the investment banking firm of Salomon Brothers, Inc. A provision in the 1980 tax law appeared to make the gain on such a transaction tax-free.[1]

DEBT-FOR-EQUITY SWAP

In the December 7, 1981, issue of *Forbes* magazine, an article began with the following question: " 'What produces earnings gains, better looking balance sheets, no taxes and enormous fees to investment bankers?' The answer—debt-for-equity swaps—a new Wall Street product developed by the firm of Salomon Brothers, Inc."

During the fiscal year ended August 31, 1982, over 120 swaps were transacted, all resulting in substantial tax-free accounting gains to the debt retiring firm (see Exhibit 1). The debt-for-equity swap works as follows:

A brokerage firm goes into the marketplace and buys substantial quantities of a firm's deep-discounted bonds. The broker then contacts the issuer and proposes to exchange the bonds with the issuer for common stock. Assuming that the issuing

---

[1] In general, any gain on the early retirement of debt is taxable, unless the retiring firm chooses to reduce the cost basis of its depreciable assets by the amount of the gain, or unless the transaction is viewed as a recapitalization (e.g., a debt-for-equity swap or conversion).

EXHIBIT 1
A Sample of 1982 Debt-for-Equity Swaps*

Company	Increase in Earnings Attributed to Swap (in millions)	2nd Quarter Reported Earnings (in millions)	Swap Earnings as a Percent of Reported Earnings
Pfizer, Inc..	$ 5.0	$ 80.6	6.2%
Ohio Edison Co.	20.0	54.0	37.0
Armstrong World Industries	2.1	9.6	21.8
U.S. Home Corp..	2.0	4.1	48.7
California First Bank	6.8	4.3	158.1
Florida Coast Banks	1.3	2.4	54.1
Textron	6.0	24.7	24.2
City Investing	9.9	35.0	28.2
Kroger Co.	1.1	35.8	3.0
Phillips Petroleum Co..	15.0	140.0	10.7
Sherwin-Williams Co.	5.1	18.0	28.2
CPC International	6.0	57.0	10.5
Revlon, Inc..	6.6	39.7	10.6
Houston Natural Gas Corp..	13.9	59.0	23.5

* Source: *Forbes,* August 30, 1982.

company obliges, the broker then sells the stock on the open market, earning commissions at each phase of the transaction (see Exhibit 2).

The debt-for-equity swap has been well received largely because it enables companies to improve the appearance of their balance sheet by paring financial leverage and by increasing their reported earnings, without the attendant problems of increased taxes and significant negative cash flows.[2] It also enables the company to make sinking fund purchases of discounted debt without incurring a tax liability—a problem that now exists with cash-for-debt sinking fund retirements.

Some debt-for-equity swaps may also involve the retirement of convertible debentures. Under existing generally accepted accounting practice, the *conversion* of debt into stock is accounted for at the book value of the debentures and hence no gain is recognized. If, on the other hand, the firm undertakes a convertible debt-for-equity "swap," a gain may be recorded. Although the convertible debt-for-equity swap is economically identical to a debt-for-equity conversion, they may be accounted for differently.

A PENNY SAVED

As the end of the second quarter of operations in 1982 approached, it became clearer to the committee on financial policy that, in spite of the additional Marathon revenues, U.S. Steel would report a substantial loss for the period. An early retirement of debt, however, offered an out.

---

[2] Although the swapping firm does not have to expend cash for the retired bonds, it does experience a cash outflow to accommodate transaction costs. These costs are often meaningful, typically ranging from 4½ to 6 percent of the swap's market value.

EXHIBIT 2
How Debt-for-Equity Swaps Work

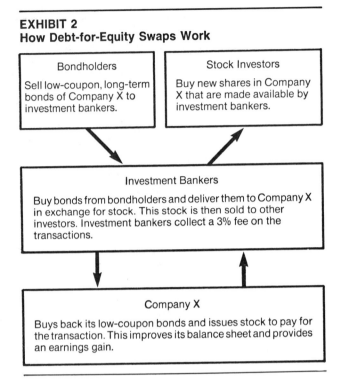

On the morning of June 16, 1982, U.S. Steel announced an agreement with Salomon Brothers, whereby 5 million common shares would be exchanged for certain of its long-term debt owned by Salomon Brothers. The shares were exchanged for an aggregate of $177,940,800 (principal amount) of U.S. Steel's 4⅝ percent subordinated debentures due in 1996, 7¾ percent sinking fund debentures due in 2001, and 5¾ percent convertible subordinated debentures due in 2001. The transaction resulted in a nontaxable gain of $87.3 million in the second quarter.

Later that day, U.S. Steel again made the news. Salomon Brothers announced the trade of the largest block of stock ever on the New York Stock Exchange—5 million shares of U.S. Steel were sold at a price of 18⅛ per share, or nearly $90.625 million.

The reaction of the financial press to the debt-for-equity swap ranged from mere description to concern and ridicule. As one financial writer observed:[3]

> The company's (U.S. Steel) multibillion dollar debt is so huge that reducing it by a mere $178 million is all but meaningless. However, issuing 5 million shares of stock at about $18 a share—the book value at the 1981 year-end (before the Marathon Oil acquisition) was $69 a share—represents a rather meaningful dilution of its equity by increasing the outstanding stock by more than 6 percent. Would you want to buy back a 7 percent mortgage on your home with yet another 15 to 20 years to run, even at a sizable discount, and pay for it by selling shares you own at prices near their lowest price in a decade?

[3] H. H. Biel, "Bad News, Good Opportunity," *Forbes* (August 2, 1982).

I don't think I would, but scores of companies are doing it now. Why? To make a paper profit.

QUESTIONS

1. How did U.S. Steel account for the transaction? Do you agree? If not, what alternative accounting would you suggest?

2. Do you agree with U.S. Steel's presentation (disclosure) of the transaction in its financial statements (Exhibits 3–8)? If not, what alternative presentation would you propose?

3. What effect did the debt-for-equity swap have on U.S. Steel's cash flows? (Assume transaction costs of 3 percent.) Compute U.S. Steel's debt-to-equity ratio both before and after the transaction.

4. Evaluate the quality of reported earnings and assets; prepare a list of items that concern you.

EXHIBIT 3

U.S. STEEL CORPORATION
Consolidated Statement of Income

(Dollars in millions)	1982	1981	1980
Sales *(Note 16)*	**$18,907**	$13,941	$12,492
Operating costs:			
Cost of sales (excludes items shown below) *(Note 3)*	**14,194**	11,095	10,046
Selling, general and administrative expenses	**750**	511	459
Pensions, insurance and other employee benefits *(Note 13)*	**897**	833	764
Depreciation, depletion and amortization	**1,031**	571	524
State, local and miscellaneous taxes *(Note 16)*	**1,328**	227	221
Exploration expenses	**304**	—	—
Total operating costs	**18,504**	13,237	12,014
Operating income (excludes items shown below)	**403**	704	478
Income from affiliates — equity method *(Note 4)*	**59**	57	75
Other income *(Note 18)*	**356**	758	87
Total income from all operations	**818**	1,519	640
Interest and other financial income *(Note 18)*	**291**	410	176
Interest and other financial costs *(Note 18)*	**(911)**	(226)	(209)
Total income before unusual items, taxes on income, minority interest and extraordinary credit	**198**	1,703	607
Unusual Items — *add (deduct):*			
Estimated provision for costs attributable to shutdown of facilities *(Note 20)*	**(123)**	82	—
Adjustment to provision for occupational disease claims *(Note 17)*	**31**	—	—
Revaluation of investments and other assets *(Note 4)*	**(30)**	(42)	—
Total unusual items	**(122)**	40	—
Total income before taxes on income, minority interest and extraordinary credit	**76**	1,743	607
Less:			
Provision for estimated United States and foreign income taxes *(Note 14)*			
Current	**272**	174	59
Deferred	**136**	492	89
Total provision for income taxes	**408**	666	148
Minority interest — Marathon Oil Company *(Note 23)*	**29**	—	—
Total income (loss) before extraordinary credit	**(361)**	1,077	459
Extraordinary credit — tax benefit of net operating loss carryforward	**—**	—	45
Net income (loss)	**$ (361)**	$ 1,077	$ 504

Net income per common share

The accompanying notes are an integral part of these financial statements.

EXHIBIT 4

U.S. STEEL CORPORATION
Consolidated Balance Sheet

(Dollars in millions) December 31	**1982**	1981
Assets		
Current assets:		
Cash *(Note 2)*	**$ 494**	$ 880
Marketable securities, at cost (approximates market)	**42**	1,483
Receivables, less allowance for doubtful accounts of $48 and $20	**1,351**	1,851
Inventories *(Note 3)*	**2,317**	1,198
Other current assets	**43**	—
Total current assets	**4,247**	5,412
Long-term receivables and other investments, less estimated losses of $10 and $9 *(Note 4)*	**1,041**	862
Property, plant and equipment (includes oil lands and leases — successful efforts method), less accumulated depreciation, depletion and amortization of $8,359 and $7,783 *(Note 5)*	**13,774**	6,676
Operating parts and supplies	**107**	111
Costs applicable to future periods	**263**	255
Total assets	**$19,432**	$13,316
Liabilities		
Current liabilities:		
Notes payable *(Note 6)*	**$ 362**	$ 138
Accounts payable	**1,498**	1,034
Payroll and benefits payable	**733**	946
Accrued taxes *(Note 7)*	**356**	562
Accrued interest	**190**	52
Long term debt due within one year *(Note 9)*	**278**	44
Current portion of estimated provision for costs attributable to shutdown of facilities *(Note 20)*	**65**	47
Current portion of redeemable preferred stock of consolidated subsidiary *(Note 12)*	**55**	—
Total current liabilities	**3,537**	2,823
Long-term debt, less unamortized discount *(Note 9)*	**6,843**	2,340
Deferred income taxes	**772**	732
Deferred credits and other liabilities *(Note 24)*	**1,198**	388
Estimated provision for costs attributable to shutdown of facilities *(Note 20)*	**294**	273
Redeemable preferred stock of consolidated subsidiary *(Note 12)*	**320**	500
Total liabilities	**12,964**	7,056
Ownership evidenced by		
Preferred stock *(Note 11)*	**535**	—
Common stock (par value $1 per share, authorized 150,000,000 shares) outstanding — 102,097,852 shares and 90,578,885 shares, stated at $20 per share	**2,042**	1,812
Capital in excess of stated value	**88**	96
Net income reinvested in business	**3,803**	4,352
Total ownership (details on page 29)	**6,468**	6,260
Total liabilities and ownership	**$19,432**	$13,316

The accompanying notes are an integral part of these financial statements

EXHIBIT 5

U.S. STEEL CORPORATION
Statement of Changes in Consolidated Financial Position

(Dollars in millions)	1982	1981	1980
Additions to working capital			
Net income (loss) (before extraordinary tax credit in 1980)	$ (361)	$1,077	$ 459
Add (deduct): Depreciation, depletion and amortization . . . . : .	1,031	571	524
Amortization of discounts	41	—	—
Deferred taxes on income	52	517	97
Unusual items (excludes current portion of $8 in 1982 and $(7) in 1981)	114	(33)	—
Minority interest — Marathon Oil Company	29	—	—
Gain on disposal of assets	(199)	(753)	(83)
Nontaxable gain on exchange of stock for debt . . .	(87)	—	—
Working capital from operations (excludes extraordinary tax credit in 1980)	620	1,379	997
Increase in long-term debt due after one year	4,211	127	247
Increase in preferred and common stock	668	73	29
Exchange of common stock for long-term debt:			
Common stock issued	89	—	—
Long-term debt retired	(176)	—	—
Nontaxable gain and other items	87	—	—
Disposal of assets	596	863	173
Miscellaneous additions (net)	112	26	49
Total additions	6,207	2,468	1,495
Deductions from working capital			
Acquisition of Marathon Oil Company (net of working capital $882) (Note 23)	5,053	—	—
Expended for property, plant and equipment	1,936	843	742
Dividends paid	188	178	140
Decrease in long-term debt due after one year	729	188	154
Decrease in redeemable preferred stock of consolidated subsidiary .	180	—	—
Increase in other long-term receivables and investments	—	—	77
Decrease in estimated long-term shutdown liability . . . . : .	—	—	98
Total deductions	8,086	1,209	1,211
Increase (decrease) in working capital	$(1,879)	$1,259	$ 284

Analysis of increase (decrease) in working capital

	1982	1981	1980
Working capital at beginning of year	$ 2,589	$1,330	$1,046
Cash and marketable securities	(1,827)	1,436	319
Receivables, less allowance for doubtful accounts	(500)	9	243
Inventories	1,119	68	(120)
Other current assets	43	—	—
Notes payable	(224)	(40)	97
Accounts payable	(464)	(24)	(91)
Payroll and benefits payable	213	(158)	(115)
Accrued taxes	206	(93)	(65)
Accrued interest	(138)	(1)	1
Long-term debt due within one year	(234)	(11)	12
Current portion of estimated provision for costs attributable to shutdown of facilities	(18)	73	3
Current portion of redeemable preferred stock of consolidated subsidiary	(55)	—	—
Increase (decrease) in working capital	(1,879)	1,259	284
Working capital at end of year	$ 710	$2,589	$1,330

The accompanying notes are an integral part of these financial statements.

EXHIBIT 6

U.S. STEEL CORPORATION
Consolidated Statement of Income per Common Share

	1982	1981	1980
Primary:			
Weighted average shares (Note 21)	**96,342,160**	89,258,453	87,403,104
Total income (loss) before extraordinary credit and dividends on preferred stock	**$ (3.75)**	$ 12.07	$ 5.25
Extraordinary credit — tax benefit of net operating loss carryforward	**—**	—	.52
Dividends on preferred stock	**(.24)**		
Net income (loss)	**$ (3.99)**	$ 12.07	$ 5.77
Fully diluted:			
Weighted average shares (Note 21)	**96,342,160**	94,892,302	93,031,996
Total income (loss) before extraordinary credit and dividends on preferred stock	**$ (3.75)**	$ 11.47	$ 5.05
Extraordinary credit — tax benefit of net operating loss carryforward	**—**	—	.49
Dividends on preferred stock	**(.24)**	—	—
Net income (loss)	**$ (3.99)**	$ 11.47	$ 5.54

EXHIBIT 7

U.S. STEEL CORPORATION
Consolidated Statement of Ownership

(Dollars in millions)	Preferred Stock		Common Stock		Capital in Excess of Stated Value	Net Income Reinvested in Business
	Shares	Amounts	Shares	Amounts		
Balance, December 31, 1979....	—	—	86,756,062	$1,735	$71	$3,089
1980:						
Common stock issued:						
Dividend Reinvestment Plan			1,404,191	28	1	
Net income						504
Dividends paid ($1.60 per share)						(140)
Balance, December 31, 1980....	—	—	88,160,253	1,763	72	3,453
1981:						
Common stock issued:						
Dividend Reinvestment Plan			1,273,308	26	13	
Employee stock plans(a)			1,145,324	23	11	
Net income						1,077
Dividends paid ($2.00 per share)						(178)
Balance, December 31, 1981....	—	—	90,578,885	1,812	96	4,352
1982:						
Common stock issued:						
Dividend Reinvestment Plan			**1,833,881**	**36**	**1**	
Employee stock plans(a)			**4,685,086**	**94**	**8**	
Exchange for long-term debt			**5,000,000**	**100**	**(11)**	
Preferred stock issued:						
Adjustable rate	**4,000,000**	**$200**			**(6)**	
Convertible	**3,350,000**	**335**				
Net income (loss)						**(361)**
Dividends paid:						
Common ($1.75 per share)						**(166)**
Preferred:						
Adjustable rate ($2.25 per share)						**(9)**
Convertible ($3.72 per share)						**(13)**
Balance, December 31, 1982....	**7,350,000**	**$535**	**102,097,852**	**$2,042**	**$88**	**$3,803**

(a)Includes Stock Option Plan, Savings Fund Plan and additionally, in 1982, Marathon Oil Company Thrift and Employee Stock Ownership Plans.

The accompanying notes are an integral part of these financial statements.

EXHIBIT 8

U.S. STEEL CORPORATION
Notes to Consolidated Financial Statements

1. Summary of Principal Accounting Policies

Principles applied in consolidation — The consolidated financial statements Include the accounts of the Corporation and its majority owned subsidiaries, except for those engaged in leasing and finance activities and subsidiaries not considered to be material, which are carried at the Corporation's equity in their net assets plus advances.

Investments in other entities in which the Corporation has significant influence in the management and control are accounted for using the equity method of accounting. They are carried in the investment account at the Corporation's share of the entity's net worth. The proportionate share of income from equity investments is included in Income from affiliates.

Investments in marketable equity securities are carried at the lower of cost or market and investments in other companies are carried at cost with income recognized when dividends are received.

Income recognition — Sales and related cost of sales are included in income when goods are shipped or services are rendered to the customer, except those related to construction projects which are included in income when the contract is substantially completed.

Property, plant and equipment — Generally, except for oil and gas properties, depreciation is computed on the straight-line method based upon the estimated lives of the assets. For the most part, such depreciation is adjusted within a limited range, based upon the level of production. Depletion of the cost of mineral properties is based on estimated tonnage rates which are expected to amortize the cost over the period during which minerals will be removed.

Depletion and depreciation of oil and gas producing properties are computed at rates applied to the units of production on the basis of oil and gas reserves as determined by the Corporation's geologists and engineers.

When a plant or major facility within a plant is sold or otherwise disposed of by the Corporation, any gain or loss is reflected in income. Proceeds from the sale of other facilities depreciated on a group basis are credited to the depreciation reserve. When facilities depreciated on an individual basis are sold, the difference between the selling price and the remaining undepreciated value is reflected in income.

Inventories — The cost of inventories is determined primarily under the last-in, first-out (LIFO) method which, in the aggregate, is lower than market.

Pensions — Non-contributory pension provisions of the Corporation's plans cover substantially all employees and, in addition, participating salaried employees are covered by contributory pension provisions.

Pension costs under these plans are determined by independent actuaries based upon an acceptable actuarial method and various actuarial factors which, from time to time, are adjusted in light of actual experience. Pension costs reflect current service and amortization of the unfunded accrued liability. The funding policy provides that payments to the pension trusts shall be equal to the minimum funding requirements of ERISA plus such additional amounts as may be approved from time to time.

Insurance — For the most part, the Corporation does not insure for property and casualty losses. Insurance is provided for catastrophic casualty and certain property exposures, as well as those risks required to be insured by law or contract. Costs resulting from non-insured losses are charged against income upon occurrence.

Mineral exploration and development except oil and gas — General prospecting costs are charged to expense as incurred. Exploration expenditures are expensed as incurred, but when projects are determined to be commercially feasible, related exploration expenditures are capitalized. Development expenditures are capitalized as incurred. If a development project is subsequently determined to be commercially unfeasible, related development expenditures are expensed.

Oil and gas exploration and development — The Corporation follows the successful efforts method of accounting.

Deferred income taxes — Deferred income taxes result from recognizing certain items of income and expense in consolidated financial statements in different years than in income tax returns.

Investment tax credit — Investment tax credits are recognized under the flow-through method.

EXHIBIT 8 *(continued)*

2. Cash   The Corporation has a credit agreement, expiring June 30, 1986 if not used, with a number of banks covering $337 million, which involves maintenance of 5% compensating balances on average. In addition, lines of credit exist with other banks aggregating $248 million, with requirements for 5% compensating balances on average. Other lines of credit, which amount to $4.2 billion, are described in Note 9, footnote (c).

3. Inventories

(In millions) December 31	1982	1981
Steel	$ 431	$ 822
Oil and Gas	1,517	—
Chemicals	31	67
Resource Development	21	21
Fabricating and Engineering	189	167
Manufacturing and Other	150	152
Domestic Transportation & Utility Subsidiaries	6	5
Corporate (adjustments and eliminations)	(28)	(36)
Total	$2,317	$1,198

(In millions) December 31	1982	1981
Raw materials	$ 742	$ 337
Semi-finished products	146	292
Finished products	948	271
Supplies and sundry items	453	280
Construction contracts in progress	162	166
Less invoices rendered	(134)	(148)
Total	$2,317	$1,198

Under the LIFO method, current acquisition costs are estimated to exceed the above inventory values at December 31 by approximately $2.120 billion in 1982 and $2.300 billion in 1981.

Cost of sales has been reduced and Total income from all operations increased by $621 million in 1982, $106 million in 1981, and $179 million in 1980 from the liquidations of LIFO inventories.

4. Long-Term Receivables and Other Investments

(In millions) December 31	1982	1981
Receivables due after one year	$ 125	$ 88
Trusteed funds for environmental improvements	214	284
Other trusteed funds and statutory deposits	18	38
Equity method entities:		
Unconsolidated subsidiaries	151	64
Other partially owned companies	370	194
Partnership interests	58	118
Cost method companies	64	26
Other	41	50
Total	$1,041	$ 862

Impairment of Long-term receivables resulted in a charge of $23 million to pretax income as an Unusual item in 1982. Investments in certain partially owned companies were written down to nominal values in 1981, resulting in a $31 million charge to pretax income as an Unusual item.

The following financial information summarizes the Corporation's share in equity method entities and partnership interests (excludes those partnerships from which the Corporation takes production rather than a share of earnings). Geographic areas and industries of principal unconsolidated affiliates are shown on page 42.

(In millions)	Unconsolidated Subsidiaries			50% or Less Owned Entities		
	1982	1981	1980	**1982**	1981	1980
Balance sheet data-December 31:						
Current assets	$ 11	$ —	$ —	$ 254	$246	$233
Noncurrent assets	194	—	—	848	241	242
Leasing and finance assets	529	578	500	—	—	—
Current liabilities	111	—	—	238	141	116
Noncurrent liabilities	19	—	—	425	91	114
Leasing and finance liabilities	457	514	444	—	—	—
Income data-year:						
Net sales/revenues	$ 99	$104	$ 87	$1,086	$382	$414
Gross profit	27	15	14	104	75	79
Net income	7	8	8	52	49	67
Dividends received by the Corporation	$ —	$ —	$ —	$ 26	$ 6	$ 9

EXHIBIT 8 *(continued)*

5. Property, Plant and Equipment

(In millions) December 31	1982	1981
Steel	$ 9,942	$ 9,847
Oil and Gas	7,561	—
Chemicals	731	731
Resource Development	1,773	1,825
Fabricating and Engineering	319	294
Manufacturing and Other	729	741
Domestic Transportation & Utility Subsidiaries	1,113	1,074
Corporate (adjustments and eliminations)	(35)	(53)
Total (at cost)	22,133	14,459
Less accumulated depreciation, depletion and amortization	8,359	7,783
Net	$13,774	$ 6,676

Property, plant and equipment includes gross assets acquired under capital leases of $97 million and $94 million at December 31, 1982 and 1981, respectively; related amounts included in accumulated depreciation, depletion and amortization were $46 million and $41 million at December 31, 1982 and 1981, respectively.

6. Notes Payable

(In millions) December 31	1982	1981	1980
Unconsolidated subsidiary	$ —	$ 18	$ 21
Interest rate	—	*16.8%*	*22.5%*
Banks (principally demand basis)	$362	$120	$ 77
Average interest rate year-end	*9.0%*	*13.0%*	*15.6%*
Total	$362	$138	$ 98
Maximum aggregate amount at any month end	$362	$138	$190
Weighted daily average:			
Borrowing	229	89	151
Interest rate[a]	10.0%	*16.4%*	*13.6%*

[a] Computed by relating interest expense to average daily borrowing.

7. Accrued Taxes

(In millions) December 31	1982	1981
Income taxes — Current	$168	$469
— Deferred	(18)	(76)
Other taxes	206	169
Total	$356	$562

8. Lease Commitments

(In millions) December 31, 1982	Capital Leases	Operating Leases
1983	$ 21	$ 104
1984	18	98
1985	16	86
1986	12	76
1987	10	70
Later years	77	785
Sublease rentals (decrease)	—	(94)
Total minimum lease payments	154	$1,125
Less estimated executory costs	—	
Net minimum lease payments	154	
Less imputed interest costs	66	
Present value of net minimum lease payments included in long-term debt	$ 88	

Operating lease rental expense:

(In millions)	1982	1981	1980
Minimum rental	$ 98	$134	$ 81
Contingent rental	75	36	36
Less sublease	(7)	(6)	(1)
Net rental expense	$166	$164	$116

For 1982, approximately 38% of rentals under operating leases involves land and space, 29% production equipment, 21% vessels, 6% railway equipment and the balance covers a variety of facilities and equipment. Many long-term production equipment, vessel and railway equipment leases include purchase options.

EXHIBIT 8 *(continued)*

9. Long-Term Debt

(In millions)	Interest rates — %	Maturity	December 31 1982	1981
United States Steel Corporation:				
Sinking Fund Debentures (callable)	4	1983	$ 30	$ 35
Sinking Fund Debentures (callable)	4 1/2	1986	44	50
Sinking Fund Debentures (callable)(a)	7 3/4	2001	83	97
Sinking Fund Subordinated Debentures (callable)(a)	4 5/8	1996	245	320
Convertible Subordinated Debentures (callable)(a)(b)	5 3/4	2001	263	353
Obligations relating to Industrial Development and Environmental Improvement Bonds and Notes	4 1/2–8 7/10	1983–2010	895	903
Notes payable to banks(c)	8 1/2–10 1/20	1983–1987	716	—
Notes payable to others(d)	7 3/8–15	1983–1995	304	253
Commercial paper(e)	10 1/5	(e)	1,017	—
Mortgage notes, purchase money obligations and contracts	5 1/2–10 3/5	1983–2002	148	8
Capital lease obligations		1983–2007	43	45
Consolidated subsidiaries:				
Sinking Fund Debentures	4 3/8	1987	4	—
Sinking Fund Debentures	8 1/2	2000	76	—
Sinking Fund Debentures	8 1/2	2006	250	—
Obligations relating to Industrial Development Bonds	5 1/2–7 1/10	1983–1993	80	86
Guaranteed Notes(f)	12 1/2	1994	2,869	—
Notes payable to banks(c)	7 1/4–12 2/5	1983–1991	171	115
Notes payable to others(g)	7 1/2–21	1983–1996	621	77
Mortgage notes, purchase money obligations and contracts	7 1/2–21	1983–2002	37	37
Capital lease obligations		1983–2007	45	14
Total(h)			7,941	2,393
Less unamortized discount(i)			820	9
			7,121	2,384
Less amount due within one year			278	44
Long-term debt due after one year			$6,843	$2,340

(a) On June 23, 1982, in accordance with an Exchange Agreement and Plan of Reorganization, the Corporation issued 5,000,000 shares of common stock at a value of $89 million in exchange for $178 million principal amount of debt securities, comprised of $14 million 7 3/4% Sinking Fund Debentures due 2001, $75 million 4 5/8% Sinking Fund Debentures due 1996 and $89 million of 5 3/4% Convertible Subordinated Debentures due 2001.

(b) Convertible into common stock at $62.75 per share. Sinking fund begins 1987.

(c) In 1982, a Domestic and Eurodollar Revolving Credit agreement which would have permitted total borrowings of $5.0 billion was terminated. The Corporation has lines of credit totaling $4.8 billion at December 31, 1982, with a number of banks. Agreements totaling $3.0 billion were restructured with a consortium of banks to provide for borrowing during a four-year revolving credit period ending June 30, 1986 followed by a three-year repayment period. Principal outstanding at June 30, 1986 will become due in twelve quarterly installments of equal amounts. At December 31, 1982, $700 million was borrowed. Interest shall be paid, at the Corporation's option, based on the prime rate, the London Interbank Offered Rate (LIBOR) or an average CD Rate. During the revolving credit period, the Corporation is obligated to pay a commitment fee of 1/4% on the unused portion. Another credit agreement provides for total borrowings of $800 million in either Domestic or Eurodollar loans with amounts outstanding at September 25, 1985 convertible to term notes payable in eight semi-annual installments beginning March, 1986. Interest rates are based on prime rate or LIBOR. A commitment fee of 3/8% is required for unused credit. In addition to these agreements, two one-year credit agreements aggregating $400 million are with two Canadian banks based on their prime rate or LIBOR and carry a 1/8% commitment fee. The remaining credit of $585 million involves maintenance of compensating balances and is discussed in Note 2. (Also, see Note 23.)

(d) Includes $100 million 8 1/4% note which matures 1986-1995 and $150 million in 7 3/8% notes which mature 1985-1987, all of which were privately placed in 1977 with financial institutions.

(e) At December 31, 1982, the Corporation had outstanding commercial paper in the amount of $1.017 billion, supported by available long-term credit agreements totaling $3.0 billion — see (c) above.

(f) On March 11, 1982, USS Holdings Company, which was later renamed Marathon Oil Company, issued $2.869 billion of 12 1/2% Guaranteed (by the Corporation) Notes. The notes initially traded at 76.125% of the principal amount with a yield to maturity of 17.28%.

(g) Includes the following: $150 million in 7.65% notes maturing in 1983; $200 million in 10 1/4% notes maturing in 1987, $100 million in 8 1/2% notes maturing in 1994, and $96 million in 8 5/8% notes maturing in 1996.

(h) Required payments of long-term debt (excluding commercial paper) for the years 1984-1987 are $82 million, $372 million, $693 million and $490 million.

(i) Unamortized discount at December 31, 1982, consists principally of $670 million on the 12 1/2% Guaranteed Notes and $136 million on acquired Marathon debt, and is being amortized over the lives of the related debt.

EXHIBIT 8 *(continued)*

10. Stock Option Incentive Plan

Under the 1976 Stock Option Incentive Plan, the Compensation Committee of the Board of Directors may grant to key management employees options to purchase, in the aggregate, up to 4,500,000 shares of authorized unissued or reacquired common stock at not less than 100% of market value at date of grant. Options are exercisable after one year, but cannot exceed ten years, from date of grant. The Compensation Committee may authorize the surrender of the right to exercise an option or portion thereof in exchange for an amount of stock and/or cash equal to the excess of the fair market value at the time of surrender over the aggregate option price of such shares. A two-year summary of stock option transactions follows:

	1982		1981	
	Shares	Price	Shares	Price
Options outstanding January 1	**2,987,150**	$19.1875—53.50	2,576,900	$19.1875—53.50
Options granted	**763,800**	23.875	566,250	32.6875
Options cancelled	**(236,600)**	19.1875—53.50	(85,500)	19.1875—53.50
Options exercised	**—**	**—**	(1,000)	19.1875
Options surrendered	**(30,000)**	19.1875—22.3125	(69,500)	19.1875—22.3125
Options outstanding December 31	**3,484,350**	19.1875—53.50	2,987,150	19.1875—53.50
Shares reserved for future grants	**916,150**		1,443,350	

11. Preferred Stock

The Corporation is authorized to issue 20,000,000 shares of preferred stock, without par value. On September 1, 1982, the Corporation issued two series of this stock:

Adjustable Rate Cumulative Preferred Stock — 4,000,000 shares (stated value $50 per share) were sold to the public. The initial dividend rate for the period ended December 31, 1982, was 13.50 percent per annum; subsequent quarterly dividends will vary within a range of 7-1/2 to 15-3/4 percent per annum in accordance with a formula based on various U. S. Treasury security rates. This stock is redeemable, at the sole option of the Corporation, on or after September 30, 1987 and prior to September 30, 1992, at a price of $51.50 per share and thereafter at $50.00 per share.

$12.75 Convertible Cumulative Preference Stock — 3,350,000 shares (stated value $100 per share) were contributed to the Trustee of the Corporation's Pension Plan. Each share of Preference Stock is convertible at its stated value into Corporation common stock at a conversion price of $22.25 per share. Preference Stock is redeemable, at the sole option of the Corporation, on or after September 15, 1985 at a price of $108.93 per share with a declining premium until September 15, 1992 and at $100 per share thereafter.

The Adjustable Rate Cumulative Preferred Stock ranks senior to the $12.75 Convertible Cumulative Preference Stock as to dividends and upon liquidation.

12. Redeemable Preferred Stock of Consolidated Subsidiary

Quebec Cartier Mining Company (QCM) has outstanding 3,750,000 shares of U. S. $100 par, non-voting, floating rate, cumulative, redeemable preferred stock. Shares may be tendered by the holders at specified series installment dates from 1983 through 1985, in the amounts of $208 million, $83 million and $84 million, respectively. If tendered, such shares must be purchased by QCM at par plus accrued dividends. These shares are redeemable at any time by QCM. The Corporation has agreed that upon the happening of certain events, it will, upon tender by any holder, purchase such shares at par plus 200% of accrued and unpaid dividends. In 1982, 1,250,000 shares ($125 million) were tendered and purchased by QCM. Based on current market conditions, tender of $208 million is expected in 1983. QCM has commitments from Canadian banks for long-term debt to finance such redemption, except for $55 million expected to be redeemed with cash.

Quarterly dividends, charged to Interest and other financial costs, were paid based on annual floating rates ranging from 8.37% to 11.19% in 1982, 7.14% to 11.08% in 1981 and 6.37% to 9.91% in 1980.

EXHIBIT 8 *(continued)*

13. Pension Costs

(In millions)	**1982**	1981	1980
Company sponsored plans—domestic(a)	**$307**	$362	$309
Other (including multi-employer plans)	**29**	34	38
Total	**$336**	$396	$347

(a) Years 1982 and 1981 exclude estimated costs attributable to shutdown of facilities. The decrease in 1982 costs versus 1981 resulted from decreased payrolls, partially offset by the effect of an increase in non-contributory pension benefits negotiated in 1980 and the inclusion of Marathon Oil Company.

December 31	**1982**	1981	1980
Estimated actuarial present value of accumulated plan benefits—company sponsored domestic plans(a):			
Vested	**$6,384**	$5,962	$5,457
Non-vested	**415**	391	298
Total	**$6,799**	$6,353	$5,755
Assumed rate of return(b)	**10%**	10%	10%
Net assets available for benefits (current value)	**$7,239**	$6,101	$6,140
Ratio of assets to accumulated plan benefits(b)	**106%**	95%	105%

(a) Estimated value as of December 31 of each year and including benefit improvements through August 1, 1982
(b) Increasing the indicated rate of return by 1% would increase the ratios by about 7.5 percentage points

14. Tax Provision

Provision (credit) for estimated United States and foreign taxes on income:

(In millions)	**1982**		1981		1980	
	Current	**Deferred**	Current	Deferred	Current	Deferred
U. S. Federal	**$(304)**	**$118**	$104	$450	$32	$61
U. S. State and Local	**14**	**3**	60	19	9	13
Foreign	**562**	**15**	10	23	18	15
Total	**$ 272**	**$136**	$174	$492	$59	$89

Components of the deferred tax provision (credit) resulting from timing differences:

(In millions)	**1982**	1981	1980
Depreciation, depletion and amortization	**$332**	$172	$125
Intangible drilling expense	**133**	7	8
Investment and energy credits	**(299)**	284	(122)
Unremitted earnings of foreign consolidated subsidiaries	**(47)**	(5)	11
Estimated provision for shutdown of facilities	**(38)**	74	61
Estimated provision for occupational disease claims	**27**	(1)	(3)
Adjustment of deferred taxes resulting from operating loss	**—**	—	20
Unoperated property	**(28)**	(1)	(1)
Stock options	**17**	(3)	—
Exploration expense	**(25)**	(1)	—
Legal and other contingencies	**24**	(16)	(9)
Discount on debt	**15**	—	—
Installment sales	**31**	3	(1)
Other	**(6)**	(21)	—
Total	**$136**	$492	$ 89

Reconciliation of U. S. Federal statutory tax rate (46%) to total provision (credit):

(In millions)	**1982**	1981	1980
Statutory rate applied to income (loss) before tax	**$ 35**	$802	$279
Investment and energy credits	**(38)**	(50)	(129)
Excess depreciation, depletion and amortization	**(16)**	(23)	(41)
Unremitted earnings of certain foreign subsidiaries	**8**	18	14
Minimum income tax	**(41)**	43	14
State and local income taxes after FIT benefit	**9**	42	12
Foreign income taxes after FIT benefit	**331**	(21)	—
Effect of capital gains rate	**133**	(132)	1
Nontaxable exchange of common stock for long-term debt	**(40)**	—	—
Taxable income on sale of subsidiaries in 1982	**34**	—	—
Other	**(7)**	(13)	(2)
Total	**$408**	$666	$148

Investment tax credits recognized in 1980 included $67 million that were unused in 1979.

Taxes have been provided on unremitted earnings of affiliates included in consolidation to the extent such earnings are planned to be remitted and are not reinvested indefinitely. Undistributed earnings of a subsidiary intended to be reinvested indefinitely amounted to $37 million through 1982.

In 1982, the Corporation settled the audit of the years 1971 and 1972 with the Internal Revenue Service. Marathon's years 1970-1972 and the years 1973-1981 for Marathon and the Corporation are in various stages of audit or administrative review. The Corporation believes it has made adequate provisions for income taxes and interest which may become payable for years not yet settled.

Pretax income includes $394 million, $41 million and $81 million attributable to foreign sources in 1982, 1981 and 1980, respectively.

EXHIBIT 8 *(continued)*

15. Environmental and Safety Matters

Many uncertainties continue to exist concerning the capital requirements of and operating costs associated with various laws relating to the environment and safety. In some instances, regulations still have not been issued, performance standards have not been established and equipment requirements have not been defined. In 1982, the Corporation entered into agreements with agencies which helped resolve many of these uncertainties with respect to air emissions from the facilities covered. As to water discharges, effluent limitation guidelines for the iron and steel industry were not published until May 21, 1982. These guidelines are under litigation and it is anticipated that they will be modified. Although unable to accurately predict water control requirements, the Corporation is attempting to achieve compliance within a reasonable period of time after specific requirements become known.

Predictions beyond 1982 can only be broad-based estimates by the Corporation, in many cases without any detailed engineering or other documentary support. Such estimates indicate probable additional expenditure authorizations for bringing into compliance with the above-mentioned legislative requirements those existing facilities which are currently expected to be economically operational ranging from $570 million to $955 million through 1987 (in 1982 dollars, and includes capitalization of own engineering and interest costs). These estimates assume (a) only minor changes in operating procedures, (b) no process changes and (c) compliance by all Corporation facilities with such environmental and safety laws and regulations as presently enforced. The economics of the required investment may dictate that certain facilities be closed instead of modified to comply with the requirements. The substantial sums required for these non-income generating expenditures will restrict the ability of the Corporation to continue to modernize and expand its facilities. To preclude a negative impact upon the Corporation's earnings in future years, unless there is a substantial increase in productivity, the costs associated with compliance with all these regulations will have to be recovered through cost-covering price increases, market conditions permitting.

The outcome of pending negotiations and potential administrative and judicial proceedings, as well as future legislative and regulatory changes, will be significant factors in determining the specific amount of expenditures required for this purpose and the periods of time for achieving legislatively established goals. Federal laws and regulations provide for the assessment of substantial civil penalties for noncompliance with environmental requirements under specified circumstances. It is not possible at this time to estimate the specific amount of such penalties that might be assessed against the Corporation or the outcome of any pending or future proceeding in which penalties are sought. However, it is not anticipated that the outcome of such proceedings should result in a material adverse effect on the Corporation's consolidated financial position. Settlements of a number of proceedings against the Corporation involving air and water pollution matters have permitted the Corporation to offset penalties assessed against the cost of facilities to be constructed in the future and the Corporation will seek such penalty offsets in any settlements in the future.

16. State, Local and Miscellaneous Taxes

(In millions)	1982	1981	1980
Windfall profit tax	$ 429	$ —	$ —
Consumer excise taxes on petroleum products and merchandise (offset included in Sales)	532	—	—
Other	367	227	221
Total	$1,328	$ 227	$ 221

17. Estimated Provision for Occupational Disease Claims

An estimated accrual of $88 million was provided in 1979 for potential awards to those then retired for pneumoconiosis (black lung) as the result of a dramatic increase in claims following 1978 amendments to the Federal Coal Mine Health and Safety Act of 1969. Commencing in 1979, a provision for future claims is being accrued over the remaining service life of present employees. In 1982, the provision was reduced by $64 million as a result of a triennial valuation of the estimated liability for occupational disease claims. This adjustment resulted in a reduction of $33 million to Cost of sales for present employees, while $31 million was recorded as an Unusual item for pre-1979 retirees.

EXHIBIT 8 *(concluded)*

<table>
<tr><td>18. Other</td><td>(In millions)</td><td>1982</td><td>1981</td><td>1980</td></tr>
<tr><td>Items</td><td colspan="4"></td></tr>
</table>

(In millions)	**1982**	1981	1980
Operating costs include:			
Maintenance & repairs of plant and equipment	**$1,277**	$1,644	$1,475
Research and development	**97**	74	56
Interest and other financial income includes:			
Nontaxable gain on exchange of common stock for debt	**$ 87**	$ —	$ —
Gains resulting from repurchase of debt			
(primarily to satisfy sinking fund requirements)	**2**	43	19
Interest and other financial costs:			
Interest on debt — incurred	**$1,030**	$ 194	$ 179
Less interest capitalized	**(244)**	(17)	(15)
Net interest expense	**786**	177	164
Amortization of discounts	**41**	—	—
Dividend on redeemable preferred stock			
of consolidated subsidiary (Note 12)	**37**	51	42
Other	**47**	(2)	3
Total	**$ 911**	$ 226	$ 209
Other data:			
Aggregate foreign exchange gain (loss)	**$ 4**	$ 24	$ 10
Major items included in Other income:			
Gain on disposal of assets(a)	**199**	753	83
Sale of tax benefits(b)	**115**	—	—

(a) Major 1982 items were: sale of Marathon Oil Company's Canadian subsidiaries — $89 million gain and sale of Pittsburgh head-quarters building for total gain of $164 million, of which $56 million was recognized in 1982. Major items in 1981 include $550 million gain from the sale of certain coal properties to The Standard Oil Co. (Ohio), and $85 million gain from the lease assignment and sale of Manor coal properties. Included in 1980 were $52 million gain from the sale of Universal Atlas Cement and a $23 million gain from the sale of a partnership interest in a New York office building.

(b) In 1982, the Corporation sold tax benefits totaling $115 million. The transactions were structured as leases for tax purposes and did not convey title to the property. Accordingly, the Corporation continued to record book depreciation for financial accounting purposes. The Corporation has provided for deferred taxes on the sale of these benefits.

19. Commitments and Other Contingencies

Contract commitments for capital expenditures for Property, plant and equipment totaled $604 million at December 31, 1982 and $655 million at December 31, 1981.

Guarantees by the Corporation of the liabilities of other companies totaled $870 million at December 31, 1982, and $466 million at December 31, 1981. The 1982 amount includes guarantees of the debt of un-consolidated leasing and finance subsidiaries of $350 million. It also includes the pro rata share of obligations of affiliates secured by throughput and deficiency agreements of $287 million.

The Department of Energy, as a result of continuous audits of Marathon Oil Company's records since 1974, has alleged violations aggregating approximately $370 million, plus interest. The Corporation believes it substantially complied with the Department's regulations. The Corporation is also the subject of, or a party to, a number of pending or threatened legal actions involving a variety of matters. In the opinion of management, any ultimate liability arising from these actions to the extent not otherwise provided for, should not have a material adverse effect on the Corporation's consolidated financial position.

Marathon Oil Company sells certain of its accounts receivable to financial institutions. Those accounts receivable sold are transferred subject to defined recourse provisions. Marathon collects the proceeds from the accounts receivable and collection transfers are made within agreement defined provisions. As defined by the agreements, Marathon is required to calculate on a monthly basis the value of accounts receivable to be conveyed to the institutions. Accounts receivable sold as of December 31, 1982 amounted to $417 million, of which $304 million is subject to recourse.

III. EXXON CORPORATION: DEFEASANCE

Reaction was swift to the headlines in *The Wall Street Journal* (July 7, 1982):

Exxon Corporation Big Debt Restructuring
Raising 2nd Quarter Profit $130 Million

The telephone rang incessantly in the office of C. C. Gavin, Jr., chief executive officer of Exxon, as other debt-strapped corporations sought more information on the company's recent restructuring.

Through a series of transactions, Exxon had "defeased" six long-term debt issues that had been sold between 1967 and 1979. The Exxon bonds had a face value of $515 million; but since interest rates had risen sharply above their coupon rates (5.8 to 6.7 percent), the debt was selling at a deep discount from its original issuance price. For each issue, Exxon had purchased a portfolio of U.S. government securities at an aggregate cost of $313 million. The cash generated by these securities from their higher yield (14 percent) and anticipated maturity would be sufficient to meet the interest and principal payments on each issue.

The portfolio of government securities was placed in a trustee account with Morgan Guaranty Trust Company of New York, with the directive that the cash generated by the securities was to be used only to satisfy the Exxon debt obligations. The difference between the purchase price of the securities and the face value of the bonds enabled Exxon to realize a $132 million gain in the second quarter of 1982.

DEFEASANCE

Defeasance, in legal terms, refers to a "rendering null or void of an existing condition." In the case of corporate debt, defeasance refers to a method of early retirement.

The method involves the creation of a trust fund of low-risk securities, usually U.S. government debt, having a yield great enough to cover the interest and principal repayment of a firm's older lower-yield debt. By offsetting the debt with the trust fund securities, the firm is able to report a gain equal to the difference between the book value of the debt and the current market value of the securities when the trust fund is created. The creation of a trust fund, however, does not end the company's liability to its debtholders but merely ensures the debt repayment.

In August of 1982, shortly after the announcement of the Exxon transaction, the Securities and Exchange commission temporarily banned publicly held companies from using this technique, citing that the transaction might mislead investors about the true amount of a company's liabilities. In the following month, the FASB issued an exposure draft that effectively would prohibit the treatment of defeasance transactions under *APB Opinion No. 26* (i.e., as an early retirement of debt). In January 1984, however, the FASB reversed its prior stand. *FASB Statement No. 76,* "Extinguishment of Debt," stated that if a company irrevocably placed cash or other essentially risk-free monetary assets in a trust solely for the purpose of satisfying a debt, and if the company was virtually assured that it would not be required to make any further payments, the transaction could be accounted for as an early retirement.

Prior to Exxon's massive defeasance, the method had only been used by tax-exempt municipal authorities to prefund outstanding tax-exempt debt.

QUESTIONS

1. How did Exxon account for the debt defeasance? Do you agree with the accounting treatment accorded defeased debt under *FASB No. 76?*

2. What was the impact of the defeasance on Exxon's financial position?

3. Assess the quality of Exxon's reported earnings and assets (Exhibits 1–7); prepare a list of those items that concern you.

EXHIBIT 1

EXXON CORPORATION
Quarterly Income, 1982
(in millions)

	1st	2nd	3rd	4th
Net income	$1,240	$ 885	$1,070	$1,480
Earnings per share	1.43	1.02	1.23	1.71
Percent change from 1981	(22.5)	(51.5)	(0.5)	6.9

+

EXHIBIT 2

EXXON CORPORATION
Consolidated Balance Sheet

Assets	December 31, 1981*	December 31, 1982
Current assets		
Cash, including time deposits of $1,922,987,000 and $1,474,938,000	$ 2,479,367,000	$ 2,216,262,000
Marketable securities	1,404,154,000	1,232,478,000
Notes and accounts receivable, less estimated doubtful amounts of $145,828,000 and $161,222,000	9,664,888,000	8,366,098,000
Inventories		
Crude oil, products and merchandise	5,573,689,000	3,798,532,000
Materials and supplies	1,611,438,000	1,737,689,000
Prepaid taxes and expenses	2,508,712,000	2,441,627,000
Total current assets	23,242,248,000	19,792,686,000
Investments and advances	1,643,229,000	1,714,484,000
Property, plant and equipment, at cost, less accumulated depreciation and depletion of $17,519,872,000 and $19,127,676,000 (Note 1, page 25)	35,285,519,000	38,981,829,000
Other assets, including intangibles	1,403,961,000	1,799,551,000
Total assets	61,574,957,000	62,288,550,000

Liabilities		
Current liabilities		
Notes and loans payable	3,032,343,000	2,747,685,000
Accounts payable and accrued liabilities	12,716,934,000	11,692,366,000
Income taxes payable	1,992,578,000	2,024,689,000
Total current liabilities	17,741,855,000	16,464,740,000
Long-term debt	5,153,444,000	4,555,580,000
Annuity reserves and accrued liabilities	2,041,182,000	2,697,771,000
Deferred income tax credits	7,490,551,000	8,676,170,000
Deferred income	178,694,000	268,170,000
Equity of minority shareholders in affiliated companies	1,226,365,000	1,185,928,000
Total liabilities	33,832,091,000	33,848,359,000

Shareholders' equity		
Capital stock (Note 13, page 31)	1,826,023,000	1,760,554,000
Earnings reinvested	25,629,781,000	27,211,257,000
Cumulative foreign exchange translation adjustments	287,062,000	(531,620,000)
Total shareholders' equity	27,742,866,000	28,440,191,000

Total liabilities and shareholders' equity	$61,574,957,000	$62,288,550,000

*Restated. See Note 2, page 25.
The information on pages 24 through 31 is an integral part of these statements.

EXHIBIT 3

EXXON CORPORATION
Consolidated Statement of Income and Earnings Reinvested

Revenue	1980*	1981*	1982
Sales and other operating revenue, including excise taxes	$108,412,285,000	$113,220,300,000	**$102,058,895,000**
Earnings from equity interests and other revenue	1,778,359,000	1,702,261,000	1,499,650,000
	110,190,644,000	114,922,561,000	**103,558,545,000**

Costs and other deductions

Crude oil and product purchases	60,918,379,000	64,383,105,000	56,083,520,000
Operating expenses	10,878,805,000	11,693,327,000	10,705,840,000
Selling, general and administrative expenses	5,483,257,000	5,232,793,000	5,253,148,000
Depreciation and depletion	2,350,096,000	2,898,920,000	3,333,455,000
Exploration expenses, including dry holes	1,152,588,000	1,650,214,000	1,773,318,000
Income, excise and other taxes	23,186,834,000	23,342,745,000	21,443,070,000
Interest expense	668,624,000	779,688,000	669,595,000
Income applicable to minority interests	201,991,000	115,554,000	110,667,000
	104,840,574,000	110,096,346,000	**99,372,613,000**

Net Income	$ 5,350,070,000	$ 4,826,215,000	**$ 4,185,932,000**
Per share	$6.15**	$5.58	**$4.82**

Earnings reinvested

Balance at beginning of year	$ 20,396,156,000	$ 23,397,835,000	$ 25,629,781,000
Net income	5,350,070,000	4,826,215,000	4,185,932,000
Dividends ($2.70 per share in 1980** and $3.00 in 1981 and 1982)	(2,348,391,000)	(2,594,269,000)	(2,604,456,000)
Balance at end of year	$ 23,397,835,000	$ 25,629,781,000	**$ 27,211,257,000**

*Restated. See Note 2, page 25.
**Reflects May 1981 two-for-one stock split. See Note 13, page 31.

EXHIBIT 4

EXXON CORPORATION
Analysis of Change in Cumulative Foreign Exchange Translation Adjustments

	1980	1981	1982
Balance at beginning of year	$ 1,751,875,000	$ 1,534,582,000	$ 287,062,000
Adjustments for the year	(217,293,000)	(1,247,520,000)	(818,682,000)
Balance at end of year	$ 1,534,582,000	$ 287,062,000	**$ (531,620,000)**

The information on pages 24 through 31 is an integral part of these statements.

EXHIBIT 5
Report of Independent Accountants

To the Shareholders of Exxon Corporation

In our opinion, the consolidated financial statements appearing on pages 21 through 31 present fairly the financial position of Exxon Corporation and its subsidiary companies at December 31, 1981 and 1982 and the results of their operations and the changes in their financial position for each of the three years in the period ended December 31, 1982, in conformity with generally accepted accounting principles applied on a consistent basis after restatement for the change, with which we concur, in the method of accounting for foreign currency translation as described in Note 2 to the financial statements. Our examinations of these statements were made in accordance with generally accepted auditing standards and accordingly included such tests of the accounting records and such other auditing procedures as we considered necessary in the circumstances.

153 East 53rd Street
New York, New York
February 28, 1983

Price Waterhouse

EXHIBIT 6

EXXON CORPORATION
Notes to Financial Statements*

The accompanying financial statements and the supporting and supplemental material are the responsibility of the management of Exxon Corporation.

The corporation's financial reporting is in agreement with the Organization for Economic Cooperation and Development guidelines for multinational enterprises.

1. Summary of accounting policies
Principles of consolidation The consolidated financial statements include the accounts of those significant subsidiaries owned directly or indirectly more than 50 percent.

Amounts representing the corporation's percentage interest in the underlying net assets of less than majority-owned companies in which a significant equity ownership interest is held are included in "Investments and advances." The corporation's share of the net income of these companies is included in the consolidated statement of income caption "Earnings from equity interests and other revenue."

Investments in all other less than majority-owned companies, none of which is significant, are included in "Investments and advances" at cost or less. Dividends from these companies are included in income as received.

Marketable securities Marketable securities are stated at the lower of cost or market.

Inventories Crude oil, products and merchandise inventories are carried at the lower of current market value or cost (generally determined under the last-in, first-out method). Costs include all applicable purchase costs and operating expenses, but not general and administrative expenses or research and development costs. Inventories of materials and supplies are valued at cost or less.

Property, plant and equipment The corporation's exploration and production activities are accounted for under the "successful efforts" method. Under this method, costs

of productive wells and development dry holes, both tangible and intangible, as well as productive acreage are capitalized and amortized on the unit of production method. Costs of that portion of undeveloped acreage likely to be unproductive, based largely on historical experience, are amortized over the period of exploration. Other exploratory expenditures, including geophysical costs, other dry hole costs and annual lease rentals, are expensed as incurred.

Depreciation, depletion and amortization, based on cost less estimated salvage value of the asset, are determined under either the unit of production method or the straight-line method as applied, generally, to groups of assets. Unit of production rates are based on oil, gas and other mineral reserves estimated to be recoverable from existing facilities. The straight-line method of depreciation is based on estimated asset service life taking obsolescence into consideration.

Maintenance and repairs are expensed as incurred. Major renewals and major improvements are capitalized, and the assets replaced are retired.

Upon normal retirement or replacement, the cost of properties, less salvage, is charged to the allowance for depreciation. Gains or losses arising from abnormal retirements or sales are included in operating results currently.

Income taxes Income tax reductions arising from percentage depletion and U.S. investment credits are included in operating results as realized.

2. Accounting change
The method of accounting for foreign currency translation was changed in 1982 by implementation of Financial Accounting Standards Board Standard No. 52—Foreign Currency Translation. The statement was given initial application as of January 1, 1980; all 1980 and 1981 financial data have been restated for comparability.

FAS-52 was implemented by using the local currency of the country of operation as the "functional currency" for translating the accounts of the majority of foreign operations. These operations include essentially all foreign

---

*All data for 1980 and 1981 have been restated, where applicable, for the change in 1982 in the method of accounting for foreign currency translation. See Note 2.

EXHIBIT 6 *(continued)*

petroleum refining and marketing as well as chemical operations, except for those located in highly inflationary economies; also included are exploration and production operations where the production is consumed locally, such as in Australia, Canada, the United Kingdom and continental Europe. For other foreign operations, principally exploration and production operations in Norway, Malaysia and the Middle East, together with operations in highly inflationary economies, the U.S. dollar is used as the functional currency.

FAS-52 provides that asset and liability accounts which are fixed in terms of currencies other than the functional currency be remeasured and stated in the functional currency using the applicable exchange rate at the balance sheet date. Adjustments arising from such remeasurement are included in current net income.

For those operations for which the local currency was adopted as the functional currency, translation of all asset and liability accounts is required to convert the functional currency amounts into U.S. dollars, using exchange rates at the balance sheet date. Adjustments resulting from this translation process are accumulated in a separate component of shareholders' equity entitled "Cumulative foreign exchange translation adjustments," and are not included in determining net income. The initial cumulative adjustment, effective as of January 1, 1980, was an increase in shareholders' equity of $1,752 million.

The effect of implementing these procedures was to decrease net income for 1980, 1981 and 1982 by $300 million ($.34 per share), $741 million ($.86 per share) and $130 million ($.15 per share), respectively. Earnings reinvested at January 1, 1980, December 31, 1980 and December 31, 1981 were reduced from amounts previously reported by $20 million, $320 million and $1,061 million, respectively.

3. Equity company information

The summarized financial information below includes those less than majority-owned companies, except Aramco, for which Exxon's share of net income is included in consolidated net income (see Note 1, page 25). Exxon's earnings from these companies consist in large part of earnings from natural gas production and distribution companies in the Netherlands and West Germany.

These data exclude Aramco, in which the government of Saudi Arabia acquired during 1980 the beneficial interest in substantially all of the assets and operations. Aramco continues to have access to a significant volume of Saudi Arabian crude oil. Exxon's share of earnings of Aramco, after application of adjustments related to crude oil purchased, totaled $205 million, $244 million and $62 million in 1980, 1981 and 1982, respectively.

	1980 Total	1980 Exxon share	1981 Total	1981 Exxon share	1982 Total	1982 Exxon share
			(millions of dollars)			
Total revenues, of which 16%, 15% and 15% in 1980, 1981 and 1982, respectively, were from companies included in the Exxon consolidation	$20,574	$6,395	$24,166	$7,416	$21,999	$6,816
Earnings before income taxes	$ 3,647	$1,634	$ 4,145	$1,825	$ 3,694	$1,660
Less: Related income taxes	(1,706)	(765)	(1,986)	(864)	(1,740)	(777)
Earnings	1,941	869	2,159	961	1,954	883
Less: Interest expense	(408)	(131)	(761)	(238)	(510)	(169)
Related income taxes on interest expense	333	109	367	113	227	74
Net income	$ 1,866	$ 847	$ 1,765	$ 836	$ 1,671	$ 788
Current assets	$ 7,489	$2,561	$ 8,220	$2,752	$ 7,401	$2,476
Property, plant and equipment, less accumulated depreciation	6,111	2,267	5,830	2,213	5,907	2,327
Other long-term assets	424	165	512	209	610	261
Total assets	14,024	4,993	14,562	5,174	13,918	5,064
Short-term debt	3,060	1,001	2,921	951	2,968	964
Other current liabilities	4,735	1,789	5,387	1,983	4,675	1,739
Long-term debt	2,623	844	2,509	807	2,387	832
Other long-term liabilities	807	314	999	409	999	417
Net assets	$ 2,799	$1,045	$ 2,746	$1,024	$ 2,889	$1,112

EXHIBIT 6 *(continued)*

4. Income, excise and other taxes

	1980			1981			1982		
	United States	Foreign	Total	United States	Foreign	Total	United States	Foreign	Total
					(millions of dollars)				
Income taxes									
Federal or foreign–current	$1,231	$ 2,715	$ 3,946	$ 838	$ 2,005	$ 2,843	$ 716	$ 1,204	$ 1,920
–deferred–net	434	742	1,176	604	579	1,183	224	1,322	1,546
U.S. tax on foreign operations	72		72	7		7	26		26
	1,737	3,457	5,194	1,449	2,584	4,033	966	2,526	3,492
State	219		219	204		204	86		86
Total income tax expense	1,956	3,457	5,413	1,653	2,584	4,237	1,052	2,526	3,578
Excise taxes	897	4,409	5,306	784	4,305	5,089	773	4,113	4,886
Other taxes and duties	1,493†	10,975	12,468†	3,318†	10,699	14,017†	2,530†	10,449	12,979†
Total	$4,346	$18,841	$23,187	$5,755	$17,588	$23,343	$4,355	$17,088	$21,443

Memo:

Exxon share of income taxes of equity companies (not included above)	$ 6	$ 3,135	$ 3,141	$ 8	$ 949	$ 957	$ 9	$ 788	$ 797
Effective income tax rate including income taxes of equity companies and state income taxes–percent	48.6	66.6	61.5	44.4	56.2	51.8	35.5	59.2	51.1

Reconciliation between income tax expense and a theoretical U.S. tax computed by applying a rate of 46 percent to earnings before federal income taxes:

Earnings before federal and foreign income taxes	$3,666	$ 6,878	$10,544	$3,514	$ 5,345	$ 8,859	$2,821	$ 4,857	$ 7,678
Theoretical tax	$1,686	$ 3,164	$ 4,850	$1,616	$ 2,459	$ 4,075	$1,298	$ 2,234	$ 3,532
Adjustments for foreign taxes in excess of theoretical U.S. tax		293	293		125	125		292	292
U.S. investment tax credit	(108)		(108)	(199)		(199)	(259)		(259)
U.S. tax on foreign operations	72		72	7		7	26		26
Research credit				(12)		(12)	(26)		(26)
Other	87		87	37		37	(73)		(73)
Federal or foreign income tax expense	$1,737	$ 3,457	$ 5,194	$1,449	$ 2,584	$ 4,033	$ 966	$ 2,526	$ 3,492

Income taxes do not include $59 million, $50 million and $56 million in 1980, 1981 and 1982, respectively, of state franchise taxes which are based on income.

Net deferred income tax expense, above, represents the sum of tax effects related to timing differences, generally between amounts reportable currently for tax purposes and related amounts included in earnings for financial reporting, as follows:

Possible taxes, beyond those provided, on remittances of undistributed earnings of subsidiary companies, after giving consideration to amounts which are reinvested indefinitely, are not expected to be material.

			1982		
Tax effects of timing differences for:	1980	1981	United States	Foreign	Total
			(millions of dollars)		
Depreciation	$1,299	$1,142	$ 332	$ 981	$1,313
Inventories	(547)	(476)	(11)	117	106
Intangible development costs	420	537	356	274	630
Other	4	(20)	(453)	(50)	(503)
Net deferred income taxes	$1,176	$1,183	$ 224	$1,322	$1,546

†Includes U.S. "windfall profit" tax of $595 million, $2,118 million and $1,377 million in 1980, 1981 and 1982, respectively.

EXHIBIT 6 *(continued)*

5. Long-term debt

At December 31, 1982, long-term debt consisted of $3,233 million due in U.S. dollars and $1,323 million representing the U.S. dollar equivalent at year-end exchange rates of amounts payable in foreign currencies. These amounts exclude that portion of long-term debt, totaling $468 million, which matures within one year and is included in current liabilities. Long-term borrowings at year-end 1982 are summarized below, with weighted average interest rates in parentheses.

Exxon Corporation		(millions of dollars)
Floating rate pollution control revenue bonds–due 2012 and 2022	$49	
Other obligations–due 1984-2010	53	**$102**

Exxon Pipeline Company		
8⅞% guaranteed debentures–due 2000	300	
5.50% marine terminal revenue bonds–due 2007	250	
8¼% guaranteed debentures–due 2001	250	
9% guaranteed debentures–due 2004	209	
7½% guaranteed notes–due 1998	131	
Other obligations–due 1987-2008	75	**1,215**

Other consolidated subsidiaries			
Capitalized lease obligations*			
United States dollars	$ 7		
Other currencies	205	212	
United States dollars (11.4%)		1,909	
British pounds (9.6%)		459	
French francs (14.3%)		232	
Canadian dollars (8.8%)		215	
Hong Kong dollars (10.0%)		115	
Norwegian kroner (11.3%)		32	
Finnish markkaa (10.2%)		22	
Italian lire (16.6%)		16	
Other currencies (30.1%)		27	**3,239**
			$4,556

*At an average imputed interest rate of 8.0%.

The amounts of long-term debt maturing, together with sinking fund payments required, in each of the four years after December 31, 1983, in millions of dollars, are: 1984–$371; 1985–$327; 1986–$308; 1987–$604.

During 1982, U.S. government securities costing $313 million were deposited in an irrevocable trust, the principal and interest of which will be sufficient to fund the scheduled principal and interest payments on six debt issues of Exxon Corporation totaling $515 million. The debt issues and government securities were removed from the balance sheet and, after adjustments including a provision of $66 million for income taxes, $132 million was taken into income.

During 1982, an affiliate issued at a discount $771 million of deferred interest debentures due in 2012. There will be no payment of interest on the debentures prior to maturity. At maturity, each holder will be entitled to a payment of interest of $730 in addition to the $270 principal amount of

the debentures. At December 31, 1982, these debentures were included in the United States dollars category of othe consolidated subsidiaries as follows:

	(millions of dollars)
Principal	$771
Less unamortized discount	(659)
Total	$112

6. Miscellaneous financial information

Research and development costs totaled $489 million in 1980, $630 million in 1981 and $707 million in 1982.

Aggregate foreign exchange transaction losses included in determining net income totaled $57 million in 1980, $154 million in 1981, and $107 million in 1982.

Marketable securities at year-end 1981 were carried at their estimated fair market value which was $61 million less than cost. At year-end 1982, marketable securities were carried at cost which was $19 million less than their fair market value.

Interest capitalized in 1980, 1981 and 1982, in conformity with Financial Accounting Standards Board Statement No. 34–Capitalization of Interest Cost, was $58 million, $174 million and $207 million, respectively.

Net income includes $153 million in 1980, $294 million in 1981 and $1,092 million in 1982, attributed to the sale of relatively low-cost crude and products obtained from drawdowns of LIFO inventory quantities.

7. Annuity reserves and accrued liabilities

Annuity reserves amounted to $1,016 million and $1,078 million at December 31, 1981 and 1982, respectively. Employee service and separation payment liabilities amounted to $171 million and $226 million at December 31, 1981 and 1982, respectively. Other liabilities totaling $854 million and $1,394 million at December 31, 1981 and 1982, respectively, covered numerous items, including site restoration.

Under U.S. annuity plans, benefits to former employees and their beneficiaries are paid either directly by the corporation or its affiliates, from amounts previously provided as book reserves, or from funds provided to outside trustees and insurance companies. Such funding by the corporation together with provisions for book reserves corresponds to annuity costs charged against earnings and takes into account actuarial estimates which indicate the amount of assets and reserves which would be needed currently to meet projected benefits from the future income and sales proceeds of those assets. For these estimates, the average assumed future rate of return on assets was 7.8 percent as of year-end 1981 and 7.9 percent as of year-end 1982. On these assumptions, the following table shows the assets which would have been required to equal the estimated present value of future benefits projected as of the end of 1981 and the end of 1982.

EXHIBIT 6 *(continued)*

Domestic annuity plans, as of:	Dec. 31, 1981	Dec. 31, 1982
	(millions of dollars)	
Available for benefits		
Funded assets	$3,571	$4,140
Book reserves	104	105
Total	3,675	4,245
Present value of assets required to provide funds for future payment of:		
Projected benefits payable in the absence of any future employment service by the recipients		
vested	2,835	3,132
nonvested	118	167
Additional benefits from projected future salary increases applied to employment service to date	1,098	1,203
Total	4,051	4,502
Excess of projected benefits	$ 376	$ 257

Under annuity plans outside the U.S., obligations for projected benefits are also determined using actuarial estimates. As under the U.S. plans, benefits are paid either directly by affiliates, representing amounts previously provided as book reserves, or from funds provided to outside trustees and insurance companies. A comparison of assets available for benefits with amounts which would have been required to equal the estimated present value of future benefits projected as of the end of 1981 and the end of 1982 is presented below. The assumed future rate of return on the required assets varies from plan to plan, and ranged from 4 to 15 percent during 1981 and 1982.

Foreign annuity plans, as of:	Dec. 31, 1981	Dec. 31, 1982
	(millions of dollars)	
Available for benefits		
Funded assets	$1,429	$1,558
Book reserves	1,113	1,113
Total	2,542	2,671
Present value of assets required to provide funds for future payment of:		
Projected benefits payable in the absence of any future employment service by the recipients		
vested	1,738	1,843
nonvested	187	184
Additional benefits from projected future salary increases applied to employment service to date	1,082	1,131
Total	3,007	3,158
Excess of projected benefits	$ 465	$ 487

The charges to consolidated income for the domestic and foreign annuity plans were $713 million, $582 million and $557 million for the years 1980, 1981 and 1982, respectively.

8. Litigation

Prior to January 28, 1981, Exxon's United States petroleum operations were subject to Department of Energy (DOE) regulations. The DOE has issued Notices of Probable Violation or filed lawsuits alleging that, in various periods since September 1973, Exxon priced certain crude oil, natural gas liquids, and refined petroleum products in excess of levels permitted by DOE regulations. In its announcements concerning these Notices of Probable Violation and related litigation, the DOE has indicated that the total amount of the alleged overpricing is approximately $1,549 million. Since some of the alleged overpricing relates to activities which continued beyond the periods covered by the allegations, cumulative amounts may be higher than those stated in the allegations. Some of the regulations were vague and ambiguous and in many cases the DOE sought to apply them on a retroactive basis. Exxon has attempted in good faith to comply with these regulations and believes it correctly applied them. The corporation continues to defend its position in these matters.

The Federal Trade Commission's 1979 complaint alleging that the corporation's acquisition of Reliance Electric Company violated federal antitrust laws was dismissed by the FTC on July 30, 1982.

In addition, there are various other lawsuits pending against Exxon and certain of its consolidated subsidiaries in which claims are made in substantial amounts.

The corporation is advised by its general counsel that, in his opinion, the outcome of the matters referred to in this note will not be materially important in relation to the consolidated financial position of the corporation.

EXHIBIT 6 *(continued)*

9. Other contingencies

The corporation and certain of the consolidated subsidiaries were contingently liable at December 31, 1982, for $570 million for guarantees of notes, loans and performance under contracts. This includes $344 million representing guarantees of foreign excise taxes and customs duties of other companies, entered into as a normal business practice, under reciprocal arrangements.

Additionally, the corporation and its affiliates have numerous long-term sales commitments in their various business activities, all of which are expected to be fulfilled with no adverse consequences material to the corporation's consolidated financial position.

The Controller General of Venezuela has filed income tax claims of approximately $275 million for the period January 1, 1970, to March 18, 1971, against the corporation's affiliates operating in Venezuela in that period. The claims relate to alleged retroactive application of tax export values established by the government on March 8, 1971, to be effective from March 18, 1971. The corporation and its affiliates believe that there is no legal foundation for the claims. The affiliates are defending their interest vigorously, utilizing the applicable procedures established under Venezuelan law.

The operations and earnings of the corporation and its affiliates throughout the world have been and may in the future be affected from time to time in varying degree by political developments and laws and regulations, such as forced divestiture of assets; restrictions on production, imports and exports; price controls; tax increases and retroactive tax claims; expropriation of property; cancellation of contract rights; and pollution controls. Both the likelihood of such occurrences and their overall effect upon the corporation vary greatly from country to country and are not predictable.

10. Investment in property, plant and equipment

Petroleum and natural gas	Additions–1982 United States	Foreign	Total	Investment Dec. 31, 1981 Less accumulated depreciation and depletion	Investment Dec. 31, 1982 At cost	Less accumulated depreciation and depletion
			(millions of dollars)			
Exploration and production	$3,130	$2,072	$5,202	$19,377	$30,693	$21,794
Refining and marketing	604	876	1,480	8,026	14,634	8,232
International marine	—	—	56	1,315	2,315	1,157
Total petroleum and natural gas	3,734	2,948	6,738	28,718	47,642	31,183
Other energy	532	498	1,030	2,107	2,891	2,637
Chemicals	320	505	825	2,885	5,182	3,421
Other	273	174	447	1,576	2,395	1,741
Total	$4,859	$4,125	$9,040	$35,286	$58,110	$38,982

11. Stock option plans

The 1978 Incentive Program makes provision for the grant of options on a maximum of 10,000,000 shares of corporation stock over the five-year period ending May 31, 1983. As under earlier plans, options may be granted at prices not less than 100 percent of market value on the date of grant. Options granted under the 1978 plan are exercisable after one year of continuous employment following date of grant.

The 1978 plan also provides for granting stock appreciation rights to holders of options under present and past plans, which permit them to surrender exercisable options in exchange for shares of the corporation's stock having an aggregate market value, at the time of surrender, equal to the difference between the option price and market value of shares covered by surrendered options, or to receive such difference in cash under the conditions provided for in the stock appreciation rights.

Outstanding options for 10,443,521 and 11,955,991 shares at December 31, 1981 and 1982, respectively, had stock appreciation rights attached. In anticipation of settlement of such rights at market value of the shares covered by the options to which attached, $61 million was credited to earnings in 1981 and $8 million was credited to earnings in 1982. The exercise of such rights releases the corporation from the obligation of providing stock under the option at the option price.

Changes that occurred during 1982 in options outstanding are summarized below.

	1968 plan	1973 plan	1978 plan
	number of shares		
Outstanding at December 31, 1981	208,800	2,851,335	7,411,186
Granted at $28.81 per share	—	—	2,154,300
Less: Exercised	42,730	119,340	22,090
Expired	7,000	39,900	86,000
Surrendered	159,070	165,900	12,700
Outstanding at December 31, 1982	None	2,526,195	9,444,696
Available for grant after December 31, 1982	None	None	48,150

The average option price per share of the options outstanding at December 31, 1982, was $30.08 for the 1973 and 1978 plans.

The effect on reported earnings per share from the assumed exercise of stock options outstanding at year-end 1980, 1981 or 1982 would be insignificant.

EXHIBIT 6 *(concluded)*

12. Bonus plan
The 1978 Incentive Program makes provision, in a manner similar to earlier plans, for grants of bonuses in respect of each of the five years beginning with 1978 which are not to exceed 3 percent of the amount by which net income in a given year exceeds 6 percent of capital invested (as defined in the plan). Bonuses may be granted to eligible employees of the corporation and of those affiliates at least 95 percent owned. Under the 1978 plan, bonuses may be granted in cash, shares of the corporation's stock or earnings bonus units, which are rights entitling the grantee to receive on the settlement date, with certain limitations, an amount of cash equal to the corporation's cumulative earnings per share as reflected in its quarterly earnings statements as initially published, commencing with earnings for the first full quarter following the date of grant to and including the last full quarter preceding the date of settlement. Bonuses other than units may be paid in cash or shares of the corporation's stock in full at the time of allotment or retirement or in annual installments. Any unpaid amounts are subject to certain forfeiture provisions contained in the plan.

Grants in cash and shares of the corporation's stock are charged to earnings in the year of grant. Amounts earned under earnings bonus units are accrued as they occur. Total charges to earnings in 1980, 1981 and 1982 were $29,779,000, $28,094,000 and $25,668,000, respectively, reflecting grants substantially less than the maximum permitted under the plan.

13. Capital
On May 15, 1981, the authorized capital stock was increased from 500,000,000 shares without par value to 1,000,000,000 shares without par value and the issued shares were split on a two-for-one basis. All capital stock data and per share amounts presented in this report have been adjusted for the stock split.

At December 31, 1982, there were 906,409,024 shares issued. Of the issued shares, 38,040,815 shares at year-end 1981 and 40,403,333 shares at year-end 1982 were held in treasury at a net cost of $996,231,000 and $1,061,701,000, respectively. During 1981 and 1982, the company acquired for treasury 1,000 shares at a cost of $34,000 and 3,518,000 shares at a cost of $98,351,000, respectively. In 1981 and 1982, 4,208,175 shares and 1,155,482 shares valued at $131,101,000 and $32,882,000, respectively, were utilized in connection with stock options exercised, bonuses and stock appreciation rights under incentive programs, sales to an agent under a dividend reinvestment plan, sales to trustees under employee thrift and stock ownership plans, a corporate acquisition and exchanges for debentures of the corporation.

14. Leased facilities
At December 31, 1982, the corporation and its consolidated subsidiaries held noncancelable operating charters and leases covering tankers, service stations and other properties for which minimum lease commitments were as follows:

	Minimum commitment after reduction for related rental income		Related rental income
	Tankers	Other	
	(millions of dollars)		
1983	$157	$456	$ 38
1984	120	332	41
1985	66	223	39
1986	13	153	35
1987	9	88	30
1988 and beyond	26	392	241

Net rental expense for 1980, 1981 and 1982 totaled $932 million, $1,182 million and $1,245 million, respectively, after being reduced by related rental income of $84 million, $77 million and $72 million, respectively.

15. Investments and advances
Components of investments and advances were as follows:

	1981	1982
	(millions of dollars)	
In less than majority-owned companies		
Carried at equity in underlying assets		
Investments	$1,145	$1,188
Advances	38	36
	1,183	1,224
Carried at cost or less	138	128
	1,321	1,352
Long-term receivables and miscellaneous investments at cost or less	322	362
Total	$1,643	**$1,714**

16. Additional working capital data
Consolidated notes and accounts receivable include:

	1981	1982
	(millions of dollars)	
Trade, less reserves of $132 million and $144 million	$8,389	$7,071
Other, less reserves of $14 million and $17 million	1,276	1,295
	$9,665	$8,366

Notes, loans, accounts payable and accrued liabilities include:

	1981	1982
	(millions of dollars)	
Bank loans	$ 2,157	$ 1,587
Commercial paper	518	596
Trade payables	7,274	6,999
Obligations to equity companies	2,387	1,390
Accrued taxes other than income taxes	1,612	1,481
Other	1,801	2,387
	$15,749	$14,440

Unused lines of credit for short-term financing available at December 31, 1982, totaled approximately $3,748 million.

EXHIBIT 7
Management's Discussion and Analysis*

Net Income

In 1981, net income declined 10 percent to $4,826 million. Following two years of significant growth, the deterioration in earnings occurred in both the petroleum (down 7 percent) and chemical (down 31 percent) segments. The results reflected the effects of a deteriorating industry operating environment characterized by weak product demand and excess production capacity along with higher raw material and operating costs.

Total revenues rose 4 percent in 1981, as higher prices for most products more than offset the revenue effect of lower petroleum product, natural gas and chemicals sales volumes. However, these higher net revenues failed to fully recover escalating raw material and operating costs.

Crude oil supply prices were higher worldwide as a result of OPEC member price actions in late 1980 and early 1981. While these increases led to higher values for Exxon's own production, this benefit was reduced substantially by the imposition of new and increased petroleum production taxes as well as increased costs related to intensified exploration activity.

Despite lower taxable income and reduced volume related excise taxes, total taxes were slightly higher than in 1980 as a result of considerably higher production taxes. The U.S. "windfall profit" tax alone resulted in payments to the Federal government of $2.1 billion (versus $595 million in 1980).

In 1982, the operating environment continued to weaken and net income declined 13 percent to $4,186 million reflecting lower petroleum (down 15 percent) and chemicals (down 61 percent) earnings.

Total revenues were 10 percent lower in 1982 as a result of lower sales volume and prices for petroleum and chemical products. As the excess crude supply situation became more pronounced, increased price competition led to lower crude oil prices for Exxon's own production.

Prices for Exxon's supplies purchased under long-term agreements with foreign governments were, on average, higher in 1982. This situation was further aggravated abroad where the strengthening of the dollar tended to increase the local currency cost of dollar denominated crude imports.

Total operating costs were lower as the effects of lower volumes more than offset increases in exploration costs and inflationary effects.

Some of the steps taken by Exxon to streamline its operations for the future, had an impact on current year earnings. A reduction in inventory resulted in the sale of relatively low cost LIFO inventories which contributed $1,092 million to net income in 1982 (versus $294 million in 1981). A reduction and restructuring of corporate debt generated current year income of $182 million. On the other hand, current year results were reduced by provisions related to the Colony mothballing action, plant closures and staff reductions, and a number of other measures.

The overall decline in income was tempered by considerably lower taxes in 1982. Besides the reductions related to lower taxable income and reduced volume related excise taxes, other taxes and duties were also lower as a result of the decline in oil prices. The U.S. "windfall profit" tax alone was $741 million lower in 1982.

Funds Flow

During 1981, funds provided from operations and other sources, before financing activities, decreased 9 percent to $8.8 billion. Total funds provided of $10.5 billion includes $1.9 billion obtained from financing activities. Total fund requirements were $11.6 billion, primarily for additions to property, plant and equipment (up 39 percent) and cash dividends to shareholders (up 10 percent). The excess of requirements over funds provided resulted in a decrease of $1.0 billion in cash and marketable securities.

Net working capital totaled $5.5 billion at year-end 1981, a decrease of 17 percent from 1980. Total debt compared to shareholders' equity plus debt at year-end 1981 stood at 23 percent. The corporation maintained its strong financial position and flexibility to meet future financial needs.

During 1982, funds provided from operations and other sources, before financing activities, increased 38 percent to $12.1 billion. Funds provided totaled $11.4 billion after a $900 million net reduction of long- and short-term debt. Total fund requirements were $11.8 billion, primarily for additions to property, plant and equipment and cash dividends to shareholders. The excess of requirements over funds provided resulted in a drawdown of $400 million in cash and marketable securities.

Net working capital totaled $3.3 billion at year-end 1982, a decrease of 40 percent from 1981, mainly reflecting inventory reductions. Total debt compared to shareholders' equity plus debt at year-end 1982 stood at 20 percent. Thus, the corporation continues in a strong financial position. Although access to financial markets will be sought from time to time, the corporation continues to rely primarily upon internally generated funds to cover its requirements.

*All data for 1980 and 1981 have been restated, where applicable, for the change in 1982 in the method of accounting for foreign currency translation. See Note 2, page 25.

Worthington Stores, Inc.*

Barry Madigan, newly hired as controller of Worthington Stores, Inc., was concerned. Mr. Madigan had joined Worthington Stores from the cost accounting department of a large manufacturing firm where he worked for five years after receiving his MBA. "Only two days on the job and I face a situation like this," he mused. Mr. Madigan considered the three documents that confronted him: (1) a copy of the board of directors' resolution concerning a deferred compensation contract granted to Thomas Worthington, founder and current president, chairman, and chief executive officer of Worthington Stores; (2) a report from Worthington Stores' actuary on the current status of the firm's pension plan; and (3) a note from the financial statement of Mercantile Stores, Inc., 1982 annual report, which had been given to him that morning by Thomas Worthington.

The ringing of the telephone interrupted his musing. John Jakobski, a partner in the law firm retained by Worthington Stores, confirmed that a deferred compensation contract conforming to the board of directors' resolution had been signed between Worthington Stores and Thomas Worthington subsequent to the resolution. Mr. Jakobski's law firm had represented Worthington Stores in the matter.

After concluding his conversation with John Jakobski, Mr. Madigan was told by his secretary that Worthington Stores' auditors wanted an appointment as soon as possible to discuss certain matters concerning the pension plan.

BACKGROUND

Worthington Stores, Inc. had been founded in 1967 by Thomas Worthington, then 32 years old. Originally, the firm had been a retailer of specialty electrical products serving primarily businesses. There had been some sales to individuals, mostly ham radio operators and similar individuals. Mr. Worthington had recognized the growing personal computer market during the mid-1970s and considerable growth occurred as he expanded Worthington Stores into this area. By 1985, Worthington Stores operated 17 stores selling primarily personal computers and related equipment. A small area in each store continued to carry the specialty electric products, which the company originally sold. Most of the sales were to businesses and professionals, but a growing amount of sales were to individuals.

BOARD OF DIRECTORS' RESOLUTION

The Board of Directors of Worthington Stores, Inc. hereby grants to Thomas Worthington, its Chairman, President, and Chief Executive Officer, a deferred compensation plan on the following terms. Mr. Worthington will receive $100,000 per year upon retirement at age 65 until his death in addition to any retirement due him under other retirement plans for which he qualifies due to his service with Worthington Stores, Inc.

EXCERPTS FROM REPORT OF THE ACTUARY

The Worthington Stores, Inc. retirement plan was evaluated by Holt, Westfall and Company, Inc., as of January 1, 1985, to determine a range of appropriate contributions for the fiscal year ending December 31, 1985. The results were as follows:

Maximum tax-deductible contribution	$625,429
30-year funding policy contributon	544,052
Minimum required contribution	214,986

The contribution levels differ in that it was assumed that the amortization of unfunded past service liabilities would occur over different periods of time: 10 years for the maximum tax-deductible contribution, 30 years for the funding policy contribution, and 30 years for the minimum required contribution. In addition, the minimum required contribution reflects any credit balance in the plan's funding standard account, which is built up over the years by employer contributions in excess of the absolute minimum required by law.

Valuation Results

Present value of future benefits	$ 11,334,482
Plan assets	6,886,552
Unfunded past service liability	1,507,846
Present value of future normal cost payments	2,940,084
Present value of future compensation	121,486,564
Future normal costs as a percentage of future compensation	2.420%
Current year compensation	11,190,451
Normal cost:	
At January 1, 1985	270,809
Interest charge	18,957
Total normal cost	$ 289,766
Amortization of unfunded past service liability based on 30-year period	$ 186,354
Total cost based on 30-year amortization	476,170

Our valuation results are necessarily dependent on the accuracy and completeness of the participant data submitted by the plan sponsor (Worthington Stores, Inc.) and the investment experience information reported by the manager of the plan's assets (Trust Company of Ohio). An actuarial valuation is an attempt to quantify liabilities for obligations which are contingent upon certain circumstances (length of life, duration of employment, etc.). Most of the figures presented in this report are, for this reason, estimates based upon a set of actuarial assumptions. The actuarial soundness of the plan does not depend on the actuarial assumptions being exactly realized.

Actuarial Assumptions

Interest	7% per year.
Mortality	1951 Group Annuity Mortality Table projected to 1985 by Scale C with a five-year setback for females.
Withdrawals	Actuary's Pension Handbook, Scale T-6.
Disability	1956 Railroad Retirement Board Rates.
Salary scale	5% annual increases.

Actuarial Assumptions

Asset valuation	Market value.
Employees recognised in valuation	All plan participants.

Accounting information

Total plan assets	$6,886,552
Actuarial present value:	
Vested benefits	3,139,515
Nonvested benefits.	1,043,365
Total	$4,182,880

MERCANTILE STORES NOTE

The note from the financial statements of Mercantile Stores, Inc. is shown in Exhibit 1.

QUESTIONS

1. How will the granting of the deferred compensation contract affect the financial statements of Worthington Stores, Inc. for 1985? For your information, the following is extracted from a set of relevant mortality tables:

Age	Life Expectancy
48	27
49	25
50	26
51	25
52	24
53	23

2. What action concerning funding should Mr. Madigan recommend concerning the deferred compensation contract?

3. What action concerning funding should Mr. Madigan recommend concerning the pension plan? What factors should Mr. Madigan consider in making this decision concerning his recommendation?

4. What amount will Mr. Madigan record as pension expense for 1985 for Worthington Stores, Inc. 1985 financial statements (assume that the company is publicly held)?

5. Prepare any footnote disclosure that would be required for Worthington Stores, Inc. 1985 financial statements (assuming once again that Worthington Stores is a company whose shares are publicly traded).

6. How would you explain to Thomas Worthington the issues raised in the Mercantile Stores, Inc. financial statement note and how they relate to Worthington Stores, Inc.?

EXHIBIT 1

MERCANTILE STORES, INC.
Excerpt from Financial Statements
For the Period Ending January 31, 1983

6. Pension and Profit-Sharing Plans

The company contributes to a pension plan covering substantially all of its employees who have met certain age and experience requirements.

Statement of Financial Accounting Standards No. 36 requires in essence a *liquidating* comparison of plan net assets to the actuarial value of accumulated plan benefits, assuming that the plan was terminated as of a specific date.

In determining the actuarial present value of accumulated plan benefits, a rate of return, consistent with that realistically achievable, based on the plan's assets and expected investment policy for the periods for which such payment of benefits is to be made, is assumed. In the company's case, the assumed rate of return for both years was 8 percent.

Based on the foregoing, the following latest available data are presented (in thousands):

	January 31	
	1983	1982
Actuarial present value of accumulated plan benefits:		
Vested	$39,656	$35,186
Nonvested	3,797	3,590
Total	43,453	38,776
Net assets available for benefits	$96,055	$71,012

The above disclosure does not recognize the *on going* nature of pension funding. No projections are made for future salary levels, length of service, changing integration levels with Social Security benefits, or similar considerations which are elements of funding for financial statement purposes.

For financial statement presentation, the actuarial assumptions for funding are a 5½ percent investment return, a 6 percent salary increase annually and an average retirement age of 65. The unfunded actuarial liability is being amortized over a 10-year period which began in 1977. Unrealized market value gains and losses are based on a moving three-year average for actuarial purposes. The company funds accrued pension costs currently.

The plan assets, benefits, and the company's unfunded liability under these assumptions for the same two-year period presented for Financial Accounting Standard No. 36 are as follows (in thousands):

	January 31	
	1983	1982
Plan assets:		
Market value	$96,055	$71,012
Actuarial value	85,608	71,859
Plan benefits:		
Actuarial present value of all benefits	163,347	146,670
Less: Actuarial present value of future normal costs	63,797	56,953
	$99,550	$89,717
Unfunded actuarial liability	$13,942	$17,858

During the year, the company also contributed to a savings and profit-sharing plan.

The expenses of the company under both plans for the past three years were as follows (in thousands):

	1983	1982	1981
Pension	$ 8,240	$10,066	$ 9,756
Savings and profit sharing	7,774	6,671	5,578
	$16,014	$16,737	$15,334

Executory Contracts

CASE 4.6

Leases: The Case of the Retail Industry*

Since the early 1960s, leasing has become an important method of acquiring the use of productive assets. There are several reasons why a firm may choose to lease assets, rather than borrow funds to buy them; these include:

- Hedging against obsolescence.
- Avoiding maintenance, service, and administrative problems.
- Maximizing available tax benefits.

Some firms also believe that leasing enables them to utilize more financial leverage than debt financing does. This is because leases can be structured in such a way that they do not have to be reported on the firm's balance sheet.

This case concerns the accounting for leases in the retail industry, and the related question of whether this form of off-balance sheet financing actually increases the debt capacity of such firms.

QUESTIONS

1. Evaluate the financial information in Exhibits 1, 2, and 3.

2. Restate the 1983 financial statements for the Jack Eckerd Corporation, Zale Corporation, and Walgreen Company assuming that all noncancelable lease payments should be treated as actual liabilities in the financial statements.

3. Compare the debt-to-equity and debt-to-total capitalization ratios both before and after restatement (see Exhibit 4).

4. Does leasing increase the debt capacity of the lessee? Explain.

---

* This case was prepared by Kenneth R. Ferris. Copyright © 1984 by Kenneth R. Ferris. All rights reserved to the author.

EXHIBIT 1
Selected Financial Information from the 1983 Annual Report of the Jack Eckerd Corporation

JACK ECKERD CORPORATION AND SUBSIDIARIES
Consolidated Statements of Earnings
Years Ended July 30, 1983; July 31, 1982; and August 1, 1981
(in thousands, except per share amounts)

	1983	1982	1981
Sales and other operating revenue	$2,325,044	2,080,183	1,752,550
Costs and expenses:			
Cost of sales, including store occupancy, warehousing and delivery expense *(note 2)*	1,668,195	1,483,879	1,238,463
Operating and administrative expenses	519,031	464,930	379,445
Interest expense (income), net *(note 1)*	7,634	3,479	(8,302)
Total costs and expenses	2,194,860	1,952,288	1,609,606
Earnings before Federal and state income taxes	130,184	127,895	142,944
Federal and state income taxes *(note 6)*	58,453	57,214	64,434
Net earnings *(note 2)*	$ 71,731	70,681	78,510
Net earnings per common share and common share equivalents *(notes 1 and 2)*	$1.91	1.90	2.19

JACK ECKERD CORPORATION AND SUBSIDIARIES
Consolidated Balance Sheets
July 30, 1983, and July 31, 1982
(in thousands, except per share amounts)

	1983	1982
Assets		
Current assets:		
Cash and short-term investments, at cost plus accrued interest, which approximates market	$ 2,194	5,699
Receivables, less allowance for doubtful receivables of $1,465 in 1983 and $1,039 in 1982	76,024	45,389
Merchandise inventories *(note 2)*	442,878	408,298
Prepaid expenses and other current assets	8,448	4,127
Total current assets	529,544	463,513
Property, plant and equipment, at cost:		
Land	22,206	18,419
Buildings	74,056	68,588
Furniture and equipment	182,976	148,666
Transportation equipment	17,368	16,801
Leasehold improvements	49,256	39,268
Construction in progress	12,349	4,012
	358,211	295,754
Less accumulated depreciation	94,093	77,321
Net property, plant and equipment	264,118	218,433
Excess of cost over net assets of subsidiaries acquired, less applicable amortization	60,597	61,568
Other assets and deferred charges, at cost less applicable amortization	10,626	10,863
	$864,885	754,377

EXHIBIT 1 *(concluded)*

Liabilities and Stockholders' Equity
Current liabilities:

Short-term debt *(note 4)*	71,199	34,826
Current installments of long-term debt *(note 5)*	1,678	1,607
Accounts payable	131,449	111,858
Accrued payroll	15,095	14,224
Other accrued expenses	34,751	31,588
Federal and state income taxes—current *(note 6)*	9,162	4,911
Federal and state income taxes—deferred *(note 6)*	7,959	4,590
Total current liabilities	271,293	203,604
Deferred Federal and state income taxes *(note 6)*	14,167	7,970
Long-term debt, excluding current installments *(note 5)*	11,133	13,061
Stockholders' equity *(notes 2 and 7)*:		
Common stock of $.10 par value. Authorized 100 million shares; issued 37,461,475 in 1983 and 37,325,488 in 1982	3,746	3,733
Capital in excess of par value	108,971	106,666
Retained earnings	455,575	419,343
Total stockholders' equity	568,292	529,742
Commitments and contingency *(notes 8 and 10)*		
	$864,885	754,377

JACK ECKERD CORPORATION AND SUBSIDIARIES
Notes to Consolidated Financial Statements (excerpts)
July 30, 1983; July 31, 1982; and August 1, 1981
(in thousands, except per share amounts)

(4) Short-term Debt

Short term debt at July 30, 1983 and July 31, 1982 consisted of:

	1983	1982
Notes payable to banks	$ 5,000	34,826
Commercial paper	66,199	—
	$ 71,199	34,826

At July 30, 1983 the Company had annual and seasonal lines of credit with various banks aggregating $117,000. These lines of credit support the commercial paper borrowings and permit short-term borrowings at rates of interest negotiated at the time of borrowing. Typically, the lines of credit are reviewed and renewed annually.

Information with respect to both lines of credit and commercial paper borrowings for the three years ended July 30, 1983 are as follows:

	1983	1982	1981
Average amount outstanding	$ 84,278	36,097	2,167
Weighted average interest rate	9.3%	15.4%	15.0%
Maximum amount outstanding during the year	$120,423	71,826	7,000

The average amount outstanding is the average of the weekly balances during the year. The weighted average interest rate is the actual interest costs divided by the average borrowings outstanding. The weighted average interest rate at July 30, 1983 was 9.3%.

(5) Long-term Debt

Long-term debt at July 30, 1983 and July 31, 1982 consisted of:

	1983	1982
9¾% unsecured note payable in annual installments of $162 through December 1, 1984 and $187 thereafter	$ 700	862
Various installment notes secured by fixtures and equipment acquired with acquisition of subsidiary in 1982, payable through 1986	2,806	4,009
6.85-6.95% industrial development bonds, $5,450 due March 1, 2004, annual sinking fund payments of $560 are required commencing March 1, 2005 until maturity March 1, 2009	8,250	8,250
Other	1,055	1,547
	12,811	14,668
Less amounts due within one year	1,678	1,607
Amounts due after one year	$11,133	13,061

The aggregate minimum annual maturities of long-term debt for the five years subsequent to July 30, 1983 are: 1984 $1,678; 1985 $1,411; 1986 $692; 1987 $188; and 1988 $-0-.

(8) Facility Leases

The Company conducts the major portion of its retail operations from leased store premises under leases that will expire within the next 25 years. Such leases generally contain renewal options exercisable at the option of the Company. In addition to minimum rental payments, certain leases provide for payment of taxes, maintenance, and percentage rentals based upon sales in excess of stipulated amounts.

Total rental expense was as follows:

	1983	1982	1981
Minimum rentals	$55,980	47,751	35,632
Percentage rentals	10,735	9,664	8,629
	$66,715	57,415	44,261

At July 30, 1983, minimum rental commitments under noncancellable leases were as follows:

Year	
1984	$ 55,892
1985	54,884
1986	53,434
1987	52,107
1988	50,606
1989-1993	210,166
1994-1998	129,807
1999-2003	54,572
After 2003	4,918
	$666,386

EXHIBIT 2
Selected Financial Information from the 1983 Annual Report of the Zale Corporation
ZALE CORPORATION
Statements of Consolidated Earnings

	Year Ended March 31		
	1983	1982	1981
	(amounts in thousands except per share amounts)		
Net Sales	$939,756	$962,039	$828,709
Costs and Expenses—			
Cost of goods sold (including buying and occupancy expenses)	613,600	603,352	523,172
Selling, general and administrative	300,450	294,774	242,388
Interest	22,706	22,771	22,820
	936,756	920,897	788,380
Gain on Sale of Non-Current Assets	2,782	5,808	10,616
Earnings from Continuing Operations before Income Taxes	5,782	46,950	50,945
Income Taxes—			
Prior years tax assessment (Note 3)	10,600	—	—
Current year provision	1,300	13,698	14,700
Net Earnings (Loss) from Continuing Operations	(6,118)	33,252	36,245
Discontinued Operations—			
Loss, net of income taxes	—	—	(1,584)
Gain on disposition, net of income taxes	—	—	38,071
Net Earnings from Discontinued Operations	—	—	36,487
Net Earnings (Loss) (Note 2)	$ (6,118)	$ 33,252	$ 72,732
Net Earnings (Loss) Per Share—			
Continuing operations	$(.54)	$2.97	$3.08
Discontinued operations	—	—	3.10
Net Earnings (Loss) Per Share	$(.54)	$2.97	$6.18

These Financial Statements should be read in conjunction with the Notes to Consolidated Financial Statements.

EXHIBIT 2 *(continued)*

ZALE CORPORATION
Consolidated Balance Sheets

	March 31	
	1983	**1982**
	(amounts in thousands)	
Assets		
Current Assets—		
Cash	**$ 10,501**	**$ 18,336**
Customer receivables, net of allowance for doubtful accounts of $13.3 million in 1983 and $17.2 million in 1982	196,691	188,907
Income taxes receivable	15,966	10,104
Other receivables	14,645	9,134
Merchandise inventories, net of accumulated LIFO reserve of $165.7 million in 1983 and $170.9 million in 1982	295,816	381,454
Other current assets	6,041	4,323
Total Current Assets	539,660	612,258
Net Property and Equipment, at Cost	162,379	123,635
Investment in Unconsolidated Subsidiaries	21,458	18,477
Other Assets	35,943	46,775
Total Assets	**$759,440**	**$801,145**
Liabilities and Shareholders' Investment		
Current Liabilities—		
Notes payable	**$ 23,229**	**$ 70,845**
Current portion of long-term debt	7,355	6,812
Accounts payable	41,203	42,705
Accrued payroll	15,320	16,010
Other accrued expenses	28,209	23,078
Taxes other than income taxes	12,555	11,782
Dividends payable	2,382	2,316
Income taxes		
Current	2,038	12,714
Deferred	52,370	48,242
Total Current Liabilities	184,661	234,504
Long-Term Debt	149,445	132,777
Deferred Gain from Sale of Corporate Office Building	2,783	5,569
Deferred Income Taxes	13,717	4,012
Commitments and Contingencies (Notes 8 and 9)		
Shareholders' Investment—		
Capital stock—		
Series A Preferred, par value $1 per share (preference on liquidation $4.5 million in 1983); authorized 3 million shares; 150,884 and 168,482 shares issued, respectively	151	168
Common, par value $1 per share; authorized 30 million shares; 10,948,759 and 10,883,927 shares issued, respectively	10,949	10,884
Class B Common, par value $1 per share; authorized 12 million shares; 3,901,689 and 3,745,477 shares issued, respectively	3,901	3,746
Additional paid-in capital	127,682	124,105
Retained earnings	360,480	380,384
Foreign currency translation adjustments (Note 2)	(6,599)	(3,297)
Less Common stock in treasury, at cost; 3,482,460 shares in 1983, 3,639,259 shares in 1982	(87,730)	(91,707)
Total Shareholders' Investment	408,834	424,283
Total Liabilities and Shareholders' Investment	**$759,440**	**$801,145**

These Financial Statements should be read in conjunction with the Notes to Consolidated Financial Statements.

EXHIBIT 2 *(continued)*

ZALE CORPORATION
Notes to Consolidated Financial Statements (excerpts)

(8) LEASES

The Company leases most of its retail space under leases which range from five to fifteen years and which may contain renewal options for consecu- tive one to five year periods. All existing leases are considered to be operating leases. Minimum sublease rentals under noncancelable sub- leases are not material.

Rental expense included in the Statements of Consolidated Earnings is as follows:

	1983	1982	1981
		(amounts in thousands)	
Retail Space—			
Minimum rentals	$ 57,556	$ 48,432	$ 34,183
Rentals based on sales	10,930	11,846	10,941
	68,486	60,278	45,124
Equipment Rentals	5,279	3,496	2,198
	$ 73,765	$ 63,774	$ 47,322

Future minimum rental commitments as of March 31, 1983, for all noncancelable leases are as follows (amounts in thousands):

1984	$ 50,783
1985	44,362
1986	40,787
1987	35,589
1988	32,450
Thereafter	186,425
	$390,396

(10) FINANCING

The Company had a maximum of $244 million (including $90 million in convertible lines as described below) of domestic and foreign short-term lines of credit available during 1983. At March 31, 1983, the Company had $130 million of domestic short-term lines of credit that were available for general cor- porate purposes or to support com- mercial paper borrowings. Of these lines $70 million require mainte- nance of compensating balances ranging from 3¼% to 5% of the lines plus an additional 3¼% to 5% of any portions that are used or commitment fees of ⅛% of the average line plus, in some cases, an additional ¼% of any portions used. The compensating balances are sub- ject to withdrawal by the Company at its option. Total domestic and foreign short-term borrowings and weighted average interest rates are as follows:

	1983	1982	1981
		(amounts in thousands)	
Short-term borrowings at year-end—			
Commercial paper	$ 63,831	$110,986	$ 48,948
Notes payable to banks	24,123	49,859	45,686
Total short-term borrowings	87,954	160,845	94,634
Less short-term borrowings classified as long-term debt	(64,725)	(90,000)	(58,925)
Total borrowings classified as short-term	$ 23,229	$ 70,845	$ 35,709
Average amount of short-term borrowings outstanding for the year	$111,813	$120,646	$180,221
Maximum amount of short-term borrowings outstanding for the year	$159,835	$180,360	$253,735
Average interest rate at year-end	8.9%	13.7%	13.5%
Average interest rate for the year	13.1%	14.3%	13.2%

Short-term borrowings mature within an average of 40 days.

The Company has guaranteed lines of credit totaling approximately $43 million for consolidated subsidiaries, including Keller Christ, of which $22 million was utilized at March 31, 1983. Similar guarantees of approxi- mately $14 million existed for unconsolidated entities of which $6.6 million was utilized at March 31, 1983.

Under the terms of an agreement with a group of banks, the Company can borrow up to $90 million until August 31, 1986, at which time the balance outstanding will be conver- tible into a four-year term loan. Should the Company decide to con- vert to a term loan, one-half of the term loan would be payable in six- teen equal quarterly installments beginning September 30, 1986, with the remainder payable on August 31, 1990. Borrowing costs can be based upon the prime rate, certificate of deposit rate and/or Eurodollar rate, at the Company's option. The Com- pany is required to pay commitment fees throughout the term of the agreement of ¼% of the unused portion of the commitment. In addi- tion the Company is required to maintain compensating balances (or pay equivalent fees) on the average outstanding loan balance of up to 5%, increasing to 8% at August 31, 1986.

EXHIBIT 2 *(concluded)*

The Company intends to refinance up to $65 million of short-term borrowings using the existing $90 million loan agreement or alternate financing. Accordingly, the Company has classified such short-term borrowings as long-term on the accompanying balance sheet.

Among the requirements of the loan agreement are restrictions relative to limitations on debt, minimum working capital levels, guarantees on loans, future purchases of treasury stock, payments of dividends and rental expense ratios. A waiver was obtained for the current year regarding the rental expense ratio limitation. At March 31, 1983, approximately $32.7 million of retained earnings was available for payment of dividends.

In September 1982, the Company issued $50 million of 14% notes due in 1987, the proceeds of which were used primarily to reduce commercial paper borrowing.

Long-term debt consists of the following:

	1983	1982
	(amounts in thousands)	
Short-term borrowings classified as long-term	$ 64,725	$ 90,000
14% notes due in 1987	50,000	—
16½% subordinated promissory note, payable $4.4 million annually	28,788	32,863
8½% promissory note, payable $.6 million annually	588	1,176
13% promissory note, payable $1.4 million annually	8,400	9,800
Foreign bank notes	2,667	3,686
Other	1,632	2,064
	$156,800	$139,589
Less long-term debt due within one year	(7,355)	(6,812)
	$149,445	$132,777

The aggregate amounts of long-term debt maturities, exclusive of short-term borrowings classified as long-term debt, for the years following March 31, 1983, are: 1984—$7.4 million; 1985—$6.0 million; 1986—$5.9 million; 1987—$5.6 million; 1988—$55.6 million; thereafter—$11.6 million.

EXHIBIT 3
Selected Financial Information from the 1983 Annual Report of the Walgreen Company

WALGREEN COMPANY AND SUBSIDIARIES
Consolidated Statements of Earnings and Retained Earnings
For the Years Ended August 31, 1983, 1982, and 1981
(dollars in thousands, except per share data)

Earnings		1983	1982	1981
Net Sales		$2,360,614	$2,039,496	$1,743,471
Costs and Deductions:	Cost of sales	1,637,133	1,416,941	1,231,009
	Selling, occupancy and administration	601,623	534,531	453,131
		2,238,756	1,951,472	1,684,140
Other Income (Expense):	Interest income	3,544	3,836	6,663
	Interest expense	(6,132)	(6,158)	(5,996)
	Gains from sale of assets	1,279	—	1,800
		(1,309)	(2,322)	2,467
Earnings:	Earnings from U.S. operations before income taxes	120,549	85,702	61,798
	Income taxes	53,873	37,209	25,677
	Net earnings from U.S. operations	66,676	48,493	36,121
	Equity in net earnings of Mexican operations	3,113	7,571	6,006
	Net earnings	$ 69,789	$ 56,064	$ 42,127
Net Earnings per Common Share:	Assuming full dilution	$ 2.27	$ 1.83	$ 1.38
	Assuming no dilution	$ 2.28	$ 1.86	$ 1.45

Retained Earnings	1983	1982	1981
Balance, beginning of year	$ 240,164	$ 199,197	$ 169,886
Net earnings	69,789	56,064	42,127
Dividends declared:			
Cash—$.60 per share in 1983, $.50 in 1982 and $.44 in 1981	(18,375)	(15,097)	(12,816)
Stock—100% in 1983	(19,129)	—	—
Balance, end of year	$ 272,449	$ 240,164	$ 199,197

The accompanying statement of major accounting policies and the notes to consolidated financial statements are an integral part of these statements.

EXHIBIT 3 *(continued)*

WALGREEN COMPANY AND SUBSIDIARIES
Consolidated Balance Sheet
At August 31, 1982 and 1982
(dollars in thousands)

	Assets	1983	1982
Current Assets:	Cash	$ 14,767	$ 17,540
	Marketable securities, at cost which approximates market	53,063	23,898
	Accounts receivable, less allowances of $3,687 in 1983 and $3,530 in 1982		
	for doubtful accounts	15,480	16,412
	Inventories	326,816	290,396
	Other current assets	15,937	8,747
	Total Current Assets	426,063	356,993
Non-Current Assets:	Investments in Other Companies—		
	Stated at equity in underlying book values	20,045	18,132
	Stated at cost (market values or equity in underlying book values—$1,856 in 1983		
	and $5,859 in 1982)	1,852	1,942
		21,897	20,074
	Property and Equipment, at cost, less accumulated depreciation and amortization	243,240	213,997
	Leased Properties under Capital Leases, less accumulated amortization	26,822	25,370
		$718,022	$616,434

	Liabilities & Shareholders' Equity		
Current Liabilities:	Trade accounts payable	$144,281	$124,626
	Accrued expenses and other liabilities	108,453	95,142
	Income taxes	13,902	7,750
	Dividends payable	4,599	3,809
	Current maturities of obligations under capital leases	1,045	1,168
	Current maturities of long-term debt	2,251	2,052
	Total Current Liabilities	274,531	234,547
Long-Term Obligations:	Long-Term Debt, less current maturities—		
	General company obligations	9,527	12,257
	Real estate obligations	15,294	15,481
		24,821	27,738
	Deferred Income Taxes	37,823	28,130
	Obligations under Capital Leases, less current maturities	29,142	26,830
Shareholders' Equity:	Common stock, $1.25 par value; authorized 40,000,000 shares; issued and outstanding		
	30,661,734 in 1983 and 30,508,938 in 1982, at stated value	79,256	59,025
	Retained earnings	272,449	240,164
		351,705	299,189
		$718,022	$616,434

The accompanying statement of major accounting policies and the notes to consolidated financial statements
are an integral part of this statement.

EXHIBIT 3 *(continued)*

WALGREEN COMPANY AND SUBSIDIARIES
Notes to Consolidated
Financial Statements (excerpts)

Property and Capital Leases:

Depreciation is provided on a straight-line basis over the estimated useful lives of owned assets. Leasehold improvements and leased properties under capital leases are amortized over the estimated physical life of the property or over the term of the lease, whichever is shorter. Major repairs which extend the useful life of an asset are charged to the Property and Equipment accounts. Routine maintenance and repairs are charged against earnings. The composite method of depreciation is used for equipment; therefore, gains and losses on retirements or other disposition of such assets are included in earnings only when an operating location is closed or completely remodeled. Fully depreciated property and equipment are excluded from the cost and related accumulated depreciation and amortization accounts.

Property and equipment consists of (In Thousands):	1983	1982
Land and land improvements	$ 9,114	$ 10,696
Buildings and building improvements	94,050	83,851
Equipment	225,144	190,324
	328,308	284,871
Less—accumulated depreciation and amortization	85,068	70,874
	$243,240	$213,997

Leased properties under capital leases consists of (In Thousands):	1983	1982
Retail store, warehouse, and office facilities	$ 38,106	$ 34,637
Equipment	69	2,260
	38,175	36,897
Less—accumulated amortization	11,353	11,527
	$ 26,822	$ 25,370

Leases:

The Company generally operates in leased premises. Original non-cancelable lease terms range from ten to twenty years and normally have options that permit renewals for additional periods. In addition to minimum fixed rentals, a number of leases provide for contingent rentals based upon sales. Certain of the Company's leases have been identified as capital leases.

Minimum rental commitments at August 31, 1983, under capital leases, substantially all of which are for leased premises, and operating leases having an initial or remaining non-cancelable term of more than one year are shown below (In Thousands):

Year	Capital Leases	Operating Leases	Total
1984	$ 5,019	$ 53,874	$ 58,893
1985	5,150	53,980	59,130
1986	5,276	51,377	56,653
1987	5,090	49,312	54,402
1988	5,097	46,422	51,519
After 1988	51,344	498,084	549,428
Total minimum lease payments	76,976	$753,049	$830,025
Less: Estimated executory costs	11,994		
Less: Amount representing interest	34,795		
Present value of net minimum capital lease payments	$30,187		

EXHIBIT 3 *(continued)*

In arriving at the present value of net minimum capital lease payments, which are reflected on the accompanying balance sheet as current and non-current obligations under capital leases, estimated executory costs (such as taxes, maintenance and insurance) and interest costs (calculated at the Company's incremental borrowing rate at the inception of the individual leases) which are included in total minimum capital lease payments have been excluded. Total minimum lease payments have not been reduced by minimum sublease rentals of approximately $7,100,000 on operating leases due in the future under non-cancelable subleases.

Rental expense was as follows (In Thousands):

	1983	1982	1981
Capital leases—Contingent rentals	$ 378	$ 288	$ 226
Operating leases—Minimum rentals	59,980	51,095	41,888
—Contingent rentals	14,130	12,450	11,119
Less: Sublease rental income	(2,720)	(2,334)	(1,965)
	$71,768	$61,499	$51,268

Long-Term Debt:

Long-term debt, less current maturities, consists of (In Thousands):

		Principal	
Issue	Interest Rate	1983	1982
General Company Obligations—			
Senior Notes payable to insurance companies,			
due 1984 through 1990	11%	$ 9,000	$10,500
Convertible Subordinated Debentures, due 1991	5½%	527	1,757
		9,527	12,257
Real Estate Obligations—			
Industrial Revenue Bonds	6¼-7.7%	5,035	5,225
Mortgage Obligations:			
Parent company	9.0-9.8%	8,356	7,931
Subsidiary companies	4⅞-5⅛%	1,903	2,325
		15,294	15,481
		$24,821	$27,738

The Senior Notes payable to insurance companies, issued August 15, 1975, require annual principal payments of $1,500,000 from 1984 through 1990. The 5½% Convertible Subordinated Debentures are convertible into common shares at the rate of 124 shares per $1,000 principal amount. At August 31, 1983, 65,348 common shares were reserved for such conversions. The debentures are subordinated to all other borrowings of the Company. At the Company's option, the debentures are redeemable at prices ranging from 102.025% in 1983 to par in 1990.

The Industrial Revenue Bonds are due in annual installments payable from 1984 through 1999. The Mortgage Obligations and Industrial Revenue Bonds are secured by various properties having a net book value of $17,426,000 at August 31, 1983. While Walgreen Co. is not directly obligated for the mortgages of subsidiary companies, these mortgages are secured by lease agreements between Walgreen Co. and its subsidiary companies or by guarantees of Walgreen Co. All mortgages provide for monthly payments of principal and interest and become fully retired between 1984 and 2000.

Under the most restrictive covenants of the Company's debt agreements (a) $184,960,000 of the consolidated retained earnings at August 31, 1983 is available for payment of cash dividends, or for repurchase of the Company's stock, and (b) consolidated net working capital, as defined, must be at least $85,000,000. Consolidated net working capital, as defined, was $214,179,000 at August 31, 1983.

The Company's portion of undistributed earnings of equity subsidiaries was $18,533,000 at August 31, 1983. Restrictions on the payment of dividends by the equity subsidiaries are not considered significant to the Company's operations.

Annual maturities, net of $4,700,000 purchased debentures, due on long-term debt in fiscal 1985 through 1988 are as follows (In Thousands):

1985	1986	1987	1988
$2,226	$2,199	$2,046	$2,087

EXHIBIT 3 *(concluded)*

Short-Term Borrowings:

At August 31, 1983, the Company had approximately $60,000,000 of bank lines of credit. The credit lines are renewable annually at various dates and provide for loans of varying maturities at the prime rate. There are no compensating balance arrangements.

There were no outstanding short-term borrowings at August 31, 1983, 1982 and 1981. No borrowings occurred during fiscal 1981; however during 1983 and 1982, the Company did obtain funds through the placement of commercial paper, as follows (In Thousands):

	1983	1982
Average outstanding during the year	$ 4,700	$ 3,500
Largest month-end balance	25,600	29,000
	(Nov)	(Nov)
Weighted average interest rate during the year	9.0%	13.3%

Interest Expense:

Interest expense includes interest related to capitalized leases of $2,792,000, $2,776,000 and $2,720,000 for the fiscal years ended August 31, 1983, 1982 and 1981. The Company capitalized $344,000, $762,000 and $551,000 of interest expense as part of significant construction projects during fiscal 1983, 1982 and 1981, respectively.

EXHIBIT 4

Debt-to-Total Capitalization Ratios for Sample Companies in the Retail Industry (data based on fiscal year 1981)

	As Reported (in millions)				Adjusted*
	Total Debt	Total Equity	Total Capitalization	Debt ÷ Capitalization	Debt ÷ Capitalization
Allied Stores	$ 868.6	$ 798.6	$ 1,666.6	52.1%	58.4%
Associated Dry Goods.	398.6	718.0	1,116.6	35.7	47.3
Carter Hawley Hale	599.2	647.0	1,246.2	48.1	62.5
Dayton Hudson.	537.7	1,192.7	1,730.4	31.1	38.8
Edison Brothers	51.7	264.5	316.2	16.4	56.7
Federated Department Stores . .	981.5	1,986.1	2,967.6	33.1	35.7
Gordon Jewelry.	95.1	198.1	293.2	32.4	47.2
Jewel Companies	351.7	555.8	907.5	38.8	52.0
K mart	2,399.4	2,455.6	4,855.0	49.4	59.8
Kroger	1,153.9	807.5	1,961.4	58.8	72.7
Lucky Stores	419.7	508.6	928.3	45.2	63.6
Macy's.	231.6	801.3	1,032.9	22.4	25.5
May's Department Stores.	555.3	953.9	1,509.2	36.8	43.5
McDonald's	1,024.7	1,370.7	2,395.4	42.8	51.6
Melville.	144.0	611.8	755.8	19.1	51.7
G. C. Murphy	70.5	126.8	197.3	35.7	63.1
Nordstrom.	123.6	149.1	272.7	45.3	51.2
Pay Less Drug Stores	111.1	91.5	202.6	54.8	64.3
Pay 'N Serve	191.1	146.1	338.0	56.8	63.7
J. C. Penney	1,405.0	2,933.0	4,338.0	32.4	44.5
Revco	69.2	285.1	354.3	19.5	51.7
Rite-Aid	65.3	217.9	283.2	23.1	44.1
Safeway Stores.	1,335.6	1,110.8	2,446.4	54.6	63.9
Sears.	8,557.0	8,268.9	16,825.9	50.9	52.7
Southland	557.0	615.0	1,172.0	47.5	58.1
Super Valu	143.5	277.3	420.8	34.1	40.0
Wal-Mart Stores	324.3	323.9	648.2	50.0	62.3
Woolworth.	891.0	1,372.0	2,263.0	39.4	61.1

* Debt-to-capitalization ratio adjusted for the estimated or actual present value of operating leases.
Source: Goldman, Sachs & Company.

The Case of the Missing Debt*

Consider the following situation:

Mr. Anthony owns a small commercial office building with a net book value of $200,000. The building is located in a highly desirable rental area, and occupancy rates for his and nearby buildings have historically been at 98 percent. Mr. Anthony, however, would like to sell the building for $400,000, a value which he considers to be approximately the fair market value. The building grosses $68,000 per year in rentals and nets about $42,000 per year.

Mr. Barrett, an acquaintance of Mr. Anthony, desires to buy the building but, unfortunately, has only $120,000 in cash.

To help Barrett acquire the property, Anthony proposes a meeting with Mr. Churchill, a business associate of both and a frequent speculator in carved-out oil and gas production contracts. Anthony proposes that Churchill buy a carved-out rental contract on the building. Under the agreement, Churchill would pay Anthony $280,000 and, in return, obtain the right to receive 48.36 percent of the gross rentals each year for the next 20 years (i.e., $32,885 per year for 20 years will yield Churchill a return of approximately 10 percent on his investment).

Since each of the parties had something to gain from the transaction, a deal was made and Anthony sold the building to Barrett for $120,000. Barrett subsequently hired a local real estate firm to manage the property for him.

At the end of the first year of ownership, Barrett decided to have a set of financial statements prepared and consequently employed the accounting firm of Peat, Anderson, Price & Whinney for this purpose. The prepared financial statements appeared as follows:

MR. BARRETT
Balance Sheet
As of December 31, 19XX

Assets		Equities	
Cash	$ 9,115	Owner's equity	$120,000
Building	120,000	Retained earnings	9,115
Total	$129,115	Total	$129,115

---

* This case was prepared by Kenneth R. Ferris and John K. Shank. Copyright © 1984 by Kenneth R. Ferris and John K. Shank. All rights reserved to the authors. The situation is taken from an earlier Harvard College Case, "Sweet Deal No. 847" (9–172–140), written by John K. Shank.

MR. BARRETT
Statement of Earnings
For the Year Ended December
31, 19XX

Rentals	$35,115
Less: Expenses. . . .	26,000
Net earnings	$ 9,115

In reviewing the statements, Barrett mused over the benefits of the transaction: The building was not mortgaged and thus could be used as collateral to help finance the acquisition of other real estate; and since the book value of the property was only $120,000, he would have considerable grounds for obtaining relief from the area's high real estate tax assessment.

QUESTIONS

1. Do you agree with the financial statements as prepared by Mr. Barrett's accountants?

2. What did each party gain from the transaction?

Conoco*

In the early 1960s, the Continental Oil Company (Conoco) made a strategic decision to expand the focus of its primary operations from the exploration, production, and sale of oil and gas to include a broader spectrum of energy production and services. This decision was premised on several facts.

Despite significant increases in the level of exploratory drilling activity, the level of proven U.S. crude oil reserves had continued to decline; and, given that the U.S. reserves represented only 4 percent of the world's total proven reserves (see Exhibit 1), it was clear that domestic oil and gas companies would eventually have to seek out other long-term revenue-producing activities. Further, while the United States ranked only eighth worldwide in oil reserves, it ranked first in both "reasonably assured" coal and uranium reserves. Thus, it was also clear that, if the United States was ever to become energy independent, a greater utilization of both coal and nuclear energy would be required.

Consistent with this decision, Conoco began exploring ways to expand into other energy fields, and on September 15, 1966, purchased all of the coal properties of the Consolidation Coal Company. Conoco subsequently created a wholly owned subsidiary, Consol, to control and manage these new coal properties.

The negotiated purchase price of the properties, which had been carried on the books of Consolidated Coal at a value of approximately $275 million, was 1 million shares of Conoco common stock. At the time of the transaction, the stock had a market value of $78.50 per share. In addition, however, the purchase was made subject to a "reserved production," or "carved-out production," agreement in the principal amount of $460 million. The production contract had been sold by Consolidation Coal to the William Coal Company immediately prior to the Conoco–Consolidation Coal transaction.

Under the terms of reserved production agreement, the William Coal Company was to receive each year for the next 16 years a portion of the gross revenues of Consolidation Coal equal to 87 percent of the pre-tax profit from about 20 percent of the coal properties which Consolidation Coal was actively mining. (The expected life of these properties was 30 years.) In addition, if Consolidation Coal leased any of the specified coal properties to other mining concerns, William Coal Company

---

* This case was prepared by Kenneth R. Ferris and John K. Shank. Copyright © 1984 by Kenneth R. Ferris and John K. Shank. All rights reserved to the authors. The situation is taken from an earlier Harvard College Case, "Consolidation Coal Company" (9–172–141), written by John K. Shank and Jacques Abrams.

EXHIBIT 1
Who Has the Oil? (percentage of world's proved crude oil reserves)

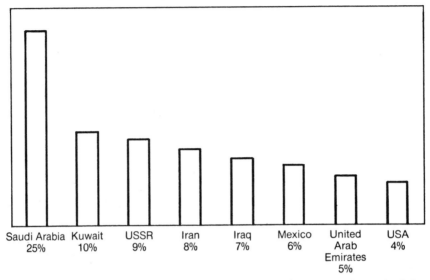

| Saudi Arabia 25% | Kuwait 10% | USSR 9% | Iran 8% | Iraq 7% | Mexico 6% | United Arab Emirates 5% | USA 4% |

America ranks eighth in proven oil reserves. Our reserves have been declining for years, despite a big increase in exploratory drilling.

Source: Energy Information Administration/U.S. Dept. of Energy; Petroleum Information International.

was to receive 100 percent of any royalties from the leased properties until the production payment contract was satisfied.

Assuming production remained constant at 1965 levels, the William Coal Company would receive approximately $44.1 million a year from 1967 through 1982 for a total of about $706 million, or a return of approximately 5¾ percent on its investment. The contract specified that a schedule would be set up, showing the expected unpaid balance of the production payment at the end of each six-month period. If production or profitability levels decreased such that the unpaid balance at the end of any six-month period was higher than the expected balance at that date, the William Coal Company would be entitled to receive the greater of 100 percent of the pre-tax profits from *all* coal mined by Consolidation Coal or $0.90 per ton from coal mined in the properties subject to the production payment. This revised payment plan would then remain in effect until the unpaid balance was reduced to or below the expected level at some succeeding semiannual check point. In the event that production or profitability levels increased above the 1965 levels, the production payments to William Coal Company would increase proportionately and, hence, the production payment would "pay out" in fewer than 16 years.

The William Coal Company was owned by the investment banking firm of Lehman Brothers and certain of its key employees and their families. The company had financed the purchase of the carved-out production payment by borrowing $460 million from a group of institutional lenders headed by the First National City Bank of New

York. The loan was secured by the production payment contract; and in recent months, the prime rate of interest ranged from 5 to 5¾ percent.

FINANCIAL REPORTING

Immediately following the Conoco purchase in September of 1966, the balance sheet of Consol appeared as follows:

(in millions)

Assets		Equities	
Current assets	$ 75.6	Current liabilities	$ 28.9
Investments and other assets	22.7	Reserves and other liabilities.	18.3
Coal properties and equipment (net)	27.4	Shareholder equity.	78.5
Total	$125.7	Total	$125.7

Except for the "coal properties and equipment," the various balance sheet items had been transferred from the books of Consolidation Coal to those of Consol at their book value. The coal properties and equipment were then valued at the difference between the total purchase price and the book value of the other balance sheet items involved.

In Conoco's 1967 annual report, the production payment agreement was summarized as follows:

> Reserved Production Payment—Coal. The coal reserves purchased on September 15, 1966, were subject to a reserved production payment in the primary amount of $460 million. With respect to these reserves, the holder of the production payment receives 100 percent of the royalty income from coal properties leased to others and such percentage of gross revenue as equals 87 percent of net mine revenue from coal production and sales from stipulated mines. Net mine revenue comprises revenue received from the sale of coal less related mining costs, including depreciation and administrative and selling expenses. In 1967, 87 percent of net mine revenue came to about 23 percent of gross revenue from coal production and sales from the stipulated mines. Amounts paid and accrued on the production payment with respect to operations in 1967 totaled $52.3 million, including $24.2 million for interest equivalents and other costs and $28.1 million for reduction of the primary sum. After giving effect to the latter amount, the primary sum had been reduced to $429.6 million.
>
> For financial purposes, Continental is capitalizing the costs of mining coal applicable to the reserved production payment. These costs are being amortized at a rate based on an estimate of the total costs which will be capitalized over the life of the production payment and the quantity of subject coal which will be produced for Continental's account from the stipulated mines over a period of 30 years from inception of the production payment. In 1967, $33.9 million of mining costs were capitalized and $12.6 million were amortized. Because all mining costs are being deducted for income tax purposes as incurred, provision is being made for deferred income taxes. This provision for the year 1967 came to $10.2 million.
>
> Continental's statement of consolidated income for the year 1967 includes revenues of $279.1 million and costs and expenses of $255.3 million from coal and other activities. The revenues exclude royalty income and sales revenues applicable to the production payment. Costs and expenses reflect the capitalization and amortization of mining costs and the related deferred income taxes as previously discussed.

Financial information pertinent to the following questions is in Exhibits 2–7.

QUESTIONS

1. Evaluate the Conoco–Consolidation Coal transaction. What did each party give and receive? Did all parties benefit from the transaction? If so, in what ways?

2. Evaluate the accounting treatment of the acquisition and of the production payment by Conoco (and hence Consol). Do you agree? If not, what alternative accounting would you propose?

3. Restate the financial statements of Consol and Conoco treating the production payment as long-term debt. How does this restatement affect the debt-to-equity ratio, the debt service coverage ratio, and the return-on-assets employed ratio?

EXHIBIT 2

CONOCO
Consolidated Balance Sheet
December 31, 1967, and 1966

Assets	1967	1966
Current assets:		
Cash.	$ 86,805,000	$ 118,645,000
U.S. government and other securities at cost, which approximates market	35,113,000	9,990,000
Accounts and notes receivable	405,489,000	357,263,000
Inventories (Note 2).	213,228,000	213,753,000
Total current assets	740,635,000	699,651,000
Investments, advances, and other assets:		
Investments and advances, at or below cost	97,898,000	93,143,000
Long-term receivables from sales of property.	58,449,000	46,294,000
	156,347,000	139,437,000
Property, plant, and equipment, at cost		
Less: Accumulated depreciation, depletion, and amortization (Note 3)	1,423,182,000	1,198,649,000
Prepaid and deferred charges	34,304,000	32,018,000
	$2,354,468,000	$2,069,755,000

Liabilities and Stockholders' Equity		
Current liabilities:		
Accounts payable	$ 224,614,000	$ 253,060,000
Accrued taxes, including income taxes.	94,649,000	122,263,000
Other accrued liabilities.	30,173,000	28,391,000
Long-term debt due within one year	34,766,000	23,160,000
Total current liabilities	384,202,000	426,874,000
Long-term debt (Note 4)	415,879,000	363,557,000
Deferred credits:		
Sale of leasehold rights (Note 5)	402,280,000	45,446,000
Federal income taxes.	59,885,000	30,553,000
Other	26,103,000	36,147,000
	126,268,000	112,146,000
Minority interest in subsidiaries.	82,135,000	50,012,000
Stockholders' equity (Note 6):		
Preferred stock.	7,150,000	7,447,000
Common stock.	126,458,000	113,390,000
Capital surplus	363,978,000	229,257,000
Retained earnings.	848,398,000	767,072,000
Total stockholders' equity.	1,345,984,000	1,117,166,000
	$2,354,468,000	$2,069,755,000

See notes to consolidated financial statements.

EXHIBIT 3

CONOCO
Statement of Consolidated Income and Retained Earnings
Years Ended December 31, 1967, and 1966

	1967	1966
Revenues:		
Sales and services (including excise taxes—Note 7).....	$2,232,999,000	$1,894,563,000
Dividends, interest, and other income	16,873,000	15,085,000
Gain on sales of mineral rights	4,933,000	4,951,000
	2,254,805,000	1,914,599,000
Costs, expenses, and taxes:		
Costs and operating expenses..................	1,328,198,000	1,111,689,000
Selling, general, and administrative expenses.........	188,306,000	159,412,000
Income and other taxes (Note 7)	430,160,000	376,508,000
Depreciation, depletion, and amortization	110,278,000	98,298,000
Surrendered leases and dry hole costs	29,810,000	26,792,000
Interest and debt expense....................	23,452,000	18,597,000
Minority interest in subsidiaries' net income	8,490,000	7,671,000
	2,118,694,000	1,798,967,000
Income before extraordinary items................	136,111,000	115,632,000
Extraordinary items, net of tax (Note 10).............	12,851,000	41,284,000
Net income (Note 10).......................	148,962,000	156,916,000
Retained earnings:		
Balance at beginning of year	767,072,000	667,996,000
	916,034,000	824,912,000
Dividends paid:		
Common Stock (1967—$2.65 per share; 1966—		
$2.45 per share)......................	63,595,000	53,758,000
Preferred Stock ($2.00 per share)	4,041,000	4,082,000
	67,636,000	57,840,000
Balance at end of year	$ 848,398,000	$ 767,072,000
Per share of Common Stock:*		
Income before extraordinary items	$5.51	$5.08
Extraordinary items, net of tax.................	.53	1.88
Net income	$6.04	$6.96

* Based on weighted average number of Common shares outstanding and after deducting dividends paid on Preferred Stock.

See notes to consolidated financial statements.

EXHIBIT 4

CONOCO
Source and Application of Funds
(in millions of dollars)

	1967	1966	1965	1964	1963
Source:					
Income before extraordinary gains	$136.1	$115.6	$ 96.2	$100.1	$ 87.4
Noncash charges against income:					
Depreciation, depletion, amortization,					
and retirements	110.3	98.3	92.8	86.8	82.7
Surrendered leases and dry hole costs.	29.8	26.8	32.0	29.4	33.5
Other (including minority interest in income) . .	13.0	15.7	5.8	12.5	8.8
Funds derived from operations	289.2	256.4	226.8	228.8	212.4
Common stock issued through rights offered					
to common stockholders	146.1	—	—	—	—
Common stock issued for assets acquired					
from Consolidation Coal company	—	78.5	—	—	—
Preferred stock issued by consolidated					
subsidiary	27.3	—	—	—	—
Extraordinary gains	12.9	41.3	—	—	—
Sales of fixed assets and investments.	18.9	27.2	18.8	25.8	15.6
Increase in long-term debt (net)	52.3	4.3	34.8	32.0	52.4
Repayments of advances previously made					
to other companies	2.6	8.4	3.3	5.4	16.1
Deferred income from oil payments (net)	(9.3)	6.2	(4.4)	(1.5)	(2.8)
Other sources of funds (net)	9.0	1.6	5.4	2.3	10.3
Total funds available	549.0	423.9	284.7	292.8	304.0
Application:					
Capital expenditures—United States	295.5	215.7	146.9	156.3	163.0
—Canada	32.1	29.8	25.0	22.4	47.0
—International (ex-					
cluding Canada)	55.9	36.9	27.9	46.3	39.2
Total	383.5	282.4	199.8	225.0	249.2
Investments in and advances to other com-					
panies	10.2	12.6	13.0	8.6	19.4
Dividends paid on continental common stock . .	63.6	53.8	52.0	45.4	40.7
Dividends paid to preferred stockholders, to					
minority interests, and to stockholders of					
pooled company prior to combination.	8.0	7.2	7.0	6.6	4.5
Increase (decrease) in notes and accounts receiva-					
ble, inventories, less current liabilities.	90.4	(24.5)	3.8	26.9	24.9
Total funds applied	555.7	331.5	275.6	312.5	338.7
Net increase (decrease) in cash and securities					
during the year	$ (6.7)	$ 92.4	$ 9.1	$ (19.7)	$ (34.7)

EXHIBIT 5

ACCOUNTING POLICIES

A summary of Continental's major accounting policies is presented below to assist the reader in evaluating the Company's financial statements and other data contained in this report.

- Consolidated financial statements include the accounts of Continental and majority-owned subsidiaries. Income from affiliates not consolidated is recognized only when dividends are received.

- Inventories of crude oil, refined products, and other merchandise are carried at cost, which is lower than market in the aggregate. Cost has been determined under the last-in, first-out method for approximately 42 percent of the inventories, and the cost of the remainder has been determined under the first-in, first-out and average cost methods. Materials and supplies are carried at or below average cost.

- Depreciation of plant and equipment is provided substantially on a straight-line method at various rates calculated to extinguish the book values of the respective items over their estimated useful lives, although accelerated depreciation rates are used for federal income tax purposes.

- The general policy with respect to accounting for profit and loss on disposal of property, plant, and equipment is to credit or charge such amounts to accumulated depreciation. An exception arises on the disposal of an entire property unit, in which event the profit or loss is credited or charged to income.

- Maintenance and repairs are charged to income. Renewals and replacements of a routine nature are charged to income, while those which improve or extend the life of existing properties are capitalized.

- Intangible development costs applicable to productive oil or gas wells or to the opening of new coal mines are capitalized and amortized on a unit-of-production basis. Costs of additional mine facilities required to maintain production after a mine reaches the production stage, generally referred to as "receding face costs," are charged to expense as incurred; however, costs of additional air shafts and new portals are capitalized and amortized. For federal income tax purposes, all of these costs are deducted as incurred.

- Costs of acquiring undeveloped acreage are capitalized. Costs of such acreage which becomes productive are amortized on a unit-of-production basis. Costs of nonproductive acreage in the United States are carried in the accounts until the properties are surrendered or otherwise disposed of, at which time the full amount is charged against income. The cost of certain foreign concessions and undeveloped leases is being amortized.

- Revenues from sales of carved-out production payments are deferred and are taken into income as production occurs. For federal income tax purposes, such revenues are taxable in the year received.

- Costs of producing oil and gas (lifting costs) applicable to production payments, which are reserved against properties which the Company has purchased, are capitalized and amortized over the Company's estimated net recoverable petroleum reserves. Costs of producing coal (mining costs) applicable to the production payment, which is reserved against properties which the Company has purchased, are capitalized and amortized using per-ton rates designed to write off the capitalized mining costs over the Company's share of the estimated tonnage to be produced in a 30-year period. For income tax purposes, lifting and mining costs are deducted as incurred.

- Exploratory expenses, including geological and geophysical costs and annual delay rentals, and all dry-hole costs are charged to income as incurred.

EXHIBIT 5 *(concluded)*

● The provision for federal taxes on income is charged or credited with the estimated effect on future income taxes resulting from temporary timing differences between financial and taxable income. No such provision is made with respect to differences of a permanent nature, such as statutory depletion and the income tax deduction for intangible development costs. The provision for federal income taxes has been reduced by the amount of investment credit utilized, a procedure sometimes referred to as the "flow-through" method.

EXHIBIT 6
Notes to Consolidated Financial Statements December 31, 1967

Note 1: The inclusion of the operations of Consolidation Coal Company in the consolidated financial statements resulted in an increase in consolidated revenues and income before extraordinary items of $84,196,000 and $8,141,000, respectively, for 1966 and $279,092,000 and $23,806,000, respectively, for 1967. (See Note 3).

Note 2: Inventories at December 31, 1967 and 1966 were as follows:

	1967	1966
Crude oil and refined products ...	$ 93,562,000	$ 94,661,000
Plant foods	43,309,000	47,783,000
Chemicals and plastics	34,617,000	29,385,000
Coal	5,232,000	5,604,000
Other ... .,....................	10,420,000	10,161,000
	187,140,000	187,594,000
Materials and supplies	26,088,000	26,159,000
	$213,228,000	$213,753,000

Inventories, other than materials and supplies, are carried at cost which is lower than market in the aggregate. Cost has been determined under the last-in, first-out method for approximately 42 percent of the inventories and the cost of the remainder has been determined under the first-in, first-out and average cost methods. Materials and supplies are carried at or below average cost.

Note 3: Property, plant and equipment at December 31, 1967 and ,966 is summarized as follows:

	1967	1966
Petroleum production	$1,364,246,000	$1,281,495,000
Refineries and natural gas processing facilities	330,078,000	279,744,000
Petroleum marketing	201,397,000	170,819,000
Petroleum transportation	162,380,000	148,000,000
Plant foods	165,392,000	160,985,000
Chemicals and plastics ....,...	149,330,000	117,023,000
Coal and other (Consol)	145,971,000	54,733,000
Other	35,938,000	33,167,000
	2,554,732,000	2,245,966,000
Less: Accumulated depreciation depletion and amortization	1,131,550,000	1,047,317,000
	$1,423,182,000	$1,198,649,000

Depreciation is provided substantially on a straight-line method at rates calculated to extinguish the book values of the assets over their estimated useful lives. In general, depletion and amortization of producing properties are provided on a unit of production basis over estimated recoverable reserves.

Effective September 15, 1966, the Company acquired the coal properties and related assets of Consolidation Coal Company, subject to a reserved production payment of $460,000,000. For financial statement purposes, certain mining costs attributable to the production payment are being capitalized annually and amortized using per ton rates designed to write off the capitalized mining costs over the Company's share of the estimated tonnage to be produced in a 30-year period. Since these costs are deducted for income tax purposes, as incurred, a provision has been made for deferred income taxes attributable thereto. During 1966 since acquisition and during 1967, revenues of $16,145,000 and $52,294,000, respectively, have been excluded from income and applied against the production payment, including principal and interest and in 1966, closing costs. Capitalized mining costs, net of related income taxes and amortization, amounted to $3,210,000 and $11,055,000, respectively, during the same periods.

Note 4: Long-term debt at December 31, 1967, consisted of:

Continental Oil Company:	
4½% debentures due 1991 (due $3,200,000 annually to 1990)	$ 90,400,000
Thirty-year sinking fund 3% debentures (due $4,000,000 annually to 1984)	64,000,000
5⅞% notes due 1989 (due $5,500,000 annually 1972 through 1988)	100,000,000
Continental Oil International Finance Corporation,*	
6⅜% guaranteed notes due May 1, 1971	20,000,000
Continental Oil (U.K.) Limited:†	
7½% guaranteed unsecured loan stock due 1933 (due $236,400 annually beginning 1972)	15,600,000
Hudson's Bay Oil and Gas Company Limited:‡	
First mortgage sinking fund bonds:	
Series A, 4%, due annually to 1974 and $10,000,000 in 1975	15,858,000
Series B and C, principally 5¾%, due annually to 1977	1,580,000
Series D, 5½%, due annually 1968 through 1982 and $6,937,000 in 1983	26,182,000
Series E, 7%, $462,500 due annually in 1971 and 1972 and $555,000 due annually 1973 through 1987	9,250,000
Term loan, interest at the prime bank rate, payable in quarterly installments to April 1, 1972	12,950,000
Other notes and debentures, principally 4½% to 5%, $11,220,000 due in 1969	36,940,000
Purchase and other obligations, $6,154,000 due in 1969 ,................................	23,119,000
	$415,879,000

Subsequent to December 31, 1967, Continental Oil International Finance Corporation, a wholly owned subsidiary issued its 7 percent guaranteed debentures due 1980 in the amount of $20,000,000.*

Continental may also borrow up to $100,000,000 from a bank under a 4½ percent revolving credit agreement convertible February 1, 1969, into term loans payable 1969–1975.

Note 5: The sales of leasehold rights were made in 1959 and 1961 and the gain thereon was deferred and its being recorded in income, subject to income tax, as payments are received. In 1963 the Federal Power Commission asserted that these were sales of natural gas and hence were subject to the Commission's jurisdiction. During 1965

EXHIBIT 6 *(concluded)*

and 1966 the Courts have upheld the Federal Power Commission's jurisdiction over these sales. Further hearings on this matter are in progress before the Commission the results of which are not presently determinable; however, in the opinion of management, the final outcome will not have a materially adverse effect on the Company.

Note 6: Stockholders' equity at December 31, 1967 and 1966 consisted of:

	1967	1966
$2 cumulative convertible preferred stock, without par value: Authorized: 2,100,000 shares Outstanding: 1967—1,958,914 shares, 1966—2,040,265 shares, after deducting 59,100 shares in treasury	$ 7,150,000	$ 7,447,000
Common stock, par value $5 per share: Authorized: 28,000,000 shares Outstanding: 1967—25,291,685 shares after deducting 142,128 shares in treasury: 1966—22,678,050 shares after deducting 149,069 shares in treasury	126,458,000	113,390,000
Capital surplus	363,978,000	229,257,000
Retained earnings	848,398,000	767,072,000
	$1,345,984,000	$1,117,166,000

Each share of preferred stock is entitled to one vote and is convertible into common stock as follows: Prior to January 1, 1969—.74 of a share; thereafter and prior to January 1, 1974—.70 of a share; and from and after January 1, 1974—.67 of a share. The preferred stock is callable on or after October 21, 1968, at $60 per share plus accrued dividends and has a liquidation value of $60 per share. The value assigned to the preferred stock is $3.65 per share which is equivalent to $5 par value per share on the common stock of the Company which would have been issued if the preferred stock had been converted to common stock at the initial conversion rate. In the opinion of counsel, the excess, approximately $110,500,000, of the liquidation value over the stated value does not restrict retained earnings. During 1967, 60,016 shares of common stock were issued upon conversion of 81,351 shares of preferred stock.

Under Stock Option Plans for Officers and Other Key Employees, options were outstanding at January 1, 1967, for 189,614 shares of the Company's common stock and 77,575 shares were available for the granting of options. During 1967 options for 66,000 shares were granted, options for 4,299 shares were canceled or expired and options for 30,906 shares were exercised at prices ranging from $37 to $63 per share, an aggregate of $1,685,000. At December 31, 1967, options for 220,409 shares at prices ranging from $37 to $74 per share, an aggregate of $14,011,000 were outstanding. At that same date options for 66,844 shares were exercisable and 11,575 shares were available for the granting of future options, generally not to become exercisable until at least two years after date of grant, at prices not less than

market value of the Company's common stock on the date of grant.

At December 31, 1967, 1,777,648 shares of common stock were reserved for issuance including 1,449,596 shares upon conversion of preferred stock; 231,984 shares in connection with stock options; and 96,068 shares upon conversion of outstanding 5 percent convertible debentures.

Capital surplus was increased during 1967 by $1,531,000 resulting from the exercise of stock options and by $133,521,000 representing the excess of the net proceeds from sale over par value of 2,522,713 shares of common stock and was decreased by $324,000 resulting from the issuance of preferred stock by a majority-owned subsidiary and by $7,000 from the conversion of preferred stock.

Note 7: Income and other taxes include the following:

	1967	1966
U.S. federal and state gasoline and oil excise taxes (recovery thereof included in revenues from sales and services)	$150,232,000	$145,443,000
Income taxes:		
U.S.—federal§	30,031,000	24,670,000
U.S.—state	1,118,000	1,130,000
Foreign	61,251,000	63,200,000
	92,400,000	89,000,000
Operating taxes:		
Import duties and excise taxes—foreign	142,749,000	105,127,000
Ad valorem taxes	18,521,000	16,681,000
Production taxes	9,851,000	8,644,000
Unemployment and old age benefits taxes	9,536,000	6,231,000
Other taxes	6,871,000	5,382,000
	187,528,000	142,065,000
	$430,160,000	$376,508,000

Note 8: The Company and certain of its subsidiaries have in effect retirement plans substantially all of which provide for contributions by the employees and the companies. Total pension expense for the year, representing the companies' contributions under the plans, was $5,843,000, of which $581,000 was with respect to prior service costs.

Note 9: The Company and certain of its subsidiaries have long-term leases on certain service stations, office buildings, ocean-going tankers, and other facilities. The aggregate rentals thereon approximated $22,600,000 in 1967 and will approximate $25,500,000 annually to 1972, then $20,600,000 annually to 1977, and in diminishing annual amounts thereafter.

The Company and one of its subsidiaries, under agreements relating to certain companies in which they have substantial stock investments, have guaranteed, directly or indirectly, payments of $32,200,000 of loans to such companies. The company and a subsidiary are also obligated to other companies, in which they have substantial stock investments, to provide specified minimum revenues from product shipments or purchases. No significant loss is anticipated, by reason of such agreements.

Note 10: Extraordinary items consist of gains from sale of coal reserves, net of $9,186,000 income taxes, in 1967 and liquidation of Great Lakes Pipe Line Company, net of $13,736,000 income taxes, in 1966 previously excluded from net income and reported as a special credit.

---

* These borrowings are in the form of Eurodollars borrowed outside of the Unites States.

† Stated in U.S. dollars, payable in pounds sterling.

‡ Stated in U.S. dollars, payable in Canadian dollars.

§ Reduced by $818,000 in 1967 and $6,722,000 in 1966 as a result of the allowable investment tax credit and includes deferred income tax provisions of $19,596,000 in 1967 and $11,451,000 in 1966 due principally to the use of accelerated depreciation for income tax purposes but not for book purposes and the capitalization of mining costs. (See Note 3).

EXHIBIT 7
Report of Certified Public Accountants

ARTHUR YOUNG & COMPANY
1500 First National Building, Tulsa

The Board of Directors and Stockholders,
Continental Oil Company:

We have examined the accompanying consolidated balance sheet of Continental Oil Company and subsidiaries at December 31, 1967 and the related statement of consolidated income and retained earnings for the year then ended. Our examination was made in accordance with generally accepted auditing standards, and accordingly included such tests of the accounting records and such other auditing procedures as we considered necessary in the circumstances. We have received the reports of other public accountants with respect to their examinations of the financial statements of certain subsidiaries.

In our opinion, based upon our examination and the reports of other public accountants referred to above, the statements mentioned above present fairly the consolidated financial position of Continental Oil Company and subsidiaries at December 31, 1967 and the consolidated results of their operations for the year then ended, in conformity with generally accepted accounting principles applied on a basis consistent with that of the preceding year, after restatement to include the extraordinary item in net income for 1966, as explained in Note 10.

February 14, 1968

Arthur Young & Company

Deferred Credits

Heplewhite Manufacturing Company*

Ms. Sheila Davis, assistant to the new president of Heplewhite Manufacturing Corporation, reviewed the notes she had taken in the meeting with the controller or Heplewhite Manufacturing Company. The purpose of the meeting with the controller was some concerns about the 1985 annual financial statements and the 1985 tax return.

NOTES FROM MEETING WITH THE CONTROLLER

	Financial Statement	Tax Return
Income before taxes	$2,500,000	$2,025,000
Provision for taxes.	(900,000)	—
Current income tax liability	—	730,000
Income after taxes	$1,600,000	

Revenues from an investment in tax-free bonds of the Town of Sidney: $100,000.

An investment tax credit for new plant and equipment purchased during the year: $80,000.

Additional tax deduction taken under ACRS (accelerated cost recovery system) above the amount taken as depreciation on the financial statements: $900,000.

Heplewhite Manufacturing Company had recorded $500,000 in goodwill six years ago when it purchased a subsidiary company. This was being amortized over a 10-year period: $50,000.

During 1985, the company had sold a manufacturing plant for $500,000 more than the depreciated cost to an insurance company and leased it back for a 20-year period. The gain

---

* This case was prepared by Ray G. Stephens. Copyright © 1985 by Ray G. Stephens. All rights reserved to the author.

was deferred in accordance with current generally accepted accounting principles and being amortized to the income statement over the life of the lease. The entire gain was counted in taxable income. The amortization of the gain for 1985: $25,000.

CONCERNS OF THE PRESIDENT

Mr. Glynnis, the new president, had sent Ms. Davis to collect the information because of his concern that the company was doing something wrong. "First, I am worried that there is such a large differential between the two statements. Second, everyone knows that the tax rate is 40 percent, yet neither one of these reports shows us with a 40 percent tax rate." Mr. Glynnis, formerly a criminal attorney, had recently assumed the presidency of Heplewhite Manufacturing Company upon the death of his maternal grandfather. He relied on Sheila Davis to explain the business to him on many matters, since all of his previous employment had been with the district attorney's office. Ms. Davis had joined Heplewhite Manufacturing Company after receiving her MBA in the marketing area. She had performed several special projects for John Heplewhite prior to his death and had been selected as assistant to the president by Mr. Glynnis immediately after he assumed the presidency.

QUESTIONS

1. Explain the reasons why the financial statement and tax return don't report the same numbers *and* why a 40 percent tax rate does not appear on either the financial statement or tax return. Your answer should reconcile the income before taxes on the financial statement and the tax return.

2. Evaluate the merits of reporting a "provision for taxes" for financial reporting purposes that differs from a company's actual tax liability?

3. What kind of account (e.g., asset, liability, equity) does the "provision for taxes" represent?

Commitment and Contingencies

Westinghouse Electric Corporation*

July 18, 1975, was not a very good day for the management, customers, and shareholders of Westinghouse Electric Corporation. At a press conference scheduled for the release of second quarter operating results, Westinghouse officials acknowledged for the first time that the company would be unable to fulfill long-term supply commitments to provide uranium to some of its utility customers. The amount of the potential liability was estimated to be as much as $2.5 billion, or about 15 times what net income would be for the year. And although the commitments leading to that liability had been undertaken during a period of seven years, from 1966 to 1973, the financial statements contained no clue as to their existence until 1976, when the litigation which followed the July announcement was duly noted by Westinghouse and its auditors (see financial data in Exhibits 1–4).

BACKGROUND

In 1966, the Westinghouse Electric Company began offering its public utility customers uranium supply agreements as an inducement to purchase nuclear reactors from the company. The agreement called for an average supply price of about $10 per pound. By guaranteeing the uranium supplies at a specific price, Westinghouse was ensuring that the purchaser's investment in nuclear facilities would not become uneconomic as a result of fuel price increases. Between 1966 and 1973, Westinghouse entered into commitments to supply approximately 80 million pounds of uranium to various public utility customers over a 20-year period beginning in 1976.

From the standpoint of the utilities, the commitment represented an option to buy uranium in the future at a stated price. They had no obligation to purchase the 80 million pounds and, presumably, if the price of uranium had fallen below

---

* This case was prepared by Kenneth R. Ferris. Copyright © 1984 by Kenneth R. Ferris. All rights reserved to the author.

$10 a pound, they would have purchased on the open market or renegotiated the price with Westinghouse. The optional nature of the utilities' position protected them from incurring a loss on price movements. Westinghouse, however, had no similar protection against adverse price movements; its commitments represented a firm obligation to deliver uranium at some future date at a price specified prior to delivery.

Despite the fact that these commitments were incurred beginning in 1966, and that according to evidence presented in related court cases, Westinghouse actually reduced its spot holdings of uranium during the early 1970s, Westinghouse's board of directors was apparently not even informed of the exposure until September 1974. As late as March 1975, Westinghouse's public position was to minimize the extent of its difficulties. Appearing before a group of securities analysts, Robert E. Kirby, Westinghouse chairman and chief executive officer, said, "We have some exposure at the present time for the period of 1974 to 1975, but we're working on it quite hard to make sure we aren't overexposed."

Four months later, "some exposure" would evolve to "difficulties" in meeting future commitments. In September 1975, Westinghouse informed its customers that it would be unable to fulfill its contractual obligations calling for the delivery of the 80 million pounds. The company invoked the doctrine of *force majeure,* or overpowering outside events, to void its obligations under the contracts. Westinghouse's holdings of uranium at that time were approximately 15 million pounds, leaving a shortfall of nearly 65 million pounds. The spot price of uranium in September was between $40 and $45 per pound, or about $35 per pound over the contracted price, resulting in a potential liability of $2.275 billion.

The immediate result of the September action was a rash of legal proceedings in which 27 utilities sued Westinghouse for damages relating to the failure to deliver. The company's 1975 annual report noted:

> Until the utility suits are resolved, there will continue to be major uncertainties, as to the financial impact on the Corporation. . . . If the Corporation is not wholly successful and is granted only partial relief from its alleged contractual obligations, the financial impact could be severe. If the Corporation is required to fulfill all the contracts under current market conditions, the financial impact will of course be extremely adverse. In light of the many uncertainties, probable or potential loss cannot reasonably be estimated.

QUESTIONS

1. Comment on the disclosure by Westinghouse of its long-term supply agreements *(a)* in the 1975 annual report and *(b)* in the reports issued prior to 1975. Do you agree that the "probable or potential loss cannot reasonably be estimated"?

2. What disclosures should be required for long-term supply agreements? For long-term purchase agreements?

EXHIBIT 1
Report of Independent Accountants

To the Board of Directors and Stockholders of
Westinghouse Electric Corporation

We have examined the consolidated financial statements of Westinghouse
Electric Corporation and its subsidiaries appearing on pages 22 through 36.
Our examinations of these statements were made in accordance with generally
accepted auditing standards and accordingly included such tests of the
accounting records and such other auditing procedures as we considered
necessary in the circumstances.

Notes 21 and 22 to the consolidated financial statements discuss pending
litigation involving uranium supply contracts with customers, uncertainties
regarding other uranium requirements, other litigation and purported class
actions by shareholders. Because of the uncertainties pertaining to the
foregoing matters, the eventual outcome and potential financial effect cannot
be predicted and, accordingly, no provisions have been recorded in the
consolidated financial statements.

In our opinion, subject to the effect on the financial statements of the ultimate
resolution of the matters discussed in the preceding paragraph, the financial
statements referred to above present fairly the financial position of
Westinghouse Electric Corporation and its subsidiaries at December 31, 1975
and 1974, the results of their operations and the changes in financial position
for the years then ended, in conformity with generally accepted accounting
principles consistently applied.

Price Waterhouse & Co.

600 Grant Street
Pittsburgh, Pennsylvania 15219

February 11, 1976

EXHIBIT 2

WESTINGHOUSE
Consolidated Statements of Income and Retained Earnings

Income Statement	Year Ended December 31 1975	Year Ended December 31 1974
Income:		
Sales	$5,862,747,000	$5,798,513,000
Equity in income (loss) from non-consolidated subsidiaries and affiliated companies (Note 3) .	(4,513,000)	(32,285,000)
Other income	70,374,000	71,890,000
	5,928,608,000	5,838,118,000
Costs and expenses:		
Cost of sales	4,647,161,000	4,669,745,000
Distribution, administration and general	801,283,000	727,426,000
Depreciation	128,828,000	123,518,000
Interest	76,425,000	111,261,000
Income taxes (Note 5)	93,835,000	63,970,000
Minority interest in net income of consolidated subsidiaries	2,452,000	3,261,000
	5,749,984,000	5,699,181,000
Income from continuing operations	178,624,000	138,937,000
Discontinued operations (Note 2):		
Loss from operations of discontinued businesses (net of taxes of $35,274,000)	—	(39,805,000)
Loss on disposal of discontinued businesses (net of taxes of $10,000,000 in 1975 and $42,000,000 in 1974)	(13,400,000)	(71,000,000)
Net income	$ 165,224,000	$ 28,132,000
Earnings per common share:		
Continuing operations	$2.04	$1.57
Discontinued operations:		
Loss from operations	—	(.45)
Loss on disposal	(.15)	(.81)
Net income per common share	$1.89	$ .31

Retained Earnings	Year Ended December 31 1975	Year Ended December 31 1974
Retained earnings at beginning of year	$1,162,556,000	$1,220,914,000
Plus:		
Net income	165,224,000	28,132,000
Less:		
Dividends paid on preferred stock	895,000	1,158,000
Dividends paid on common stock	84,544,000	85,332,000
Retained earnings at end of year	$1,242,341,000	$1,162,556,000

EXHIBIT 3

WESTINGHOUSE
Consolidated Balance Sheet

Assets	At December 31 1975	At December 31 1974*
Current assets:		
Cash and marketable securities (Note 7)	$ 374,584,000	$ 137,806,000
Customer receivables (Note 8)	1,142,267,000	1,247,121,000
Inventories (Note 9)	1,040,571,000	1,072,963,000
Costs of uncompleted contracts in excess of related billings (Note 10)	172,473,000	197,205,000
Prepaid and other current assets	110,729,000	184,417,000
Total current assets	2,840,624,000	2,839,512,000
Investments (Note 11)	289,188,000	226,209,000
Estimated realizable value – discontinued businesses (Note 2)	95,543,000	202,442,000
Plant and equipment, net (Note 12)	1,380,680,000	1,298,576,000
Other assets (Note 13)	260,251,000	246,879,000
Total assets	$4,866,286,000	$4,813,618,000

Liabilities and Stockholders' Equity		
Current liabilities:		
Short-term loans and current portion of long-term debt (Note 14)	$ 131,754,000	$ 236,063,000
Accounts payable – trade	361,310,000	392,835,000
Accrued payrolls and payroll deductions	201,143,000	180,473,000
Income taxes currently payable	50,248,000	47,172,000
Deferred current income taxes	53,597,000	31,146,000
Estimated future costs – discontinued businesses	32,178,000	46,394,000
Billings on uncompleted contracts in excess of related costs (Note 10)	739,480,000	511,814,000
Other current liabilities	453,711,000	382,122,000
Total current liabilities	2,023,421,000	1,828,019,000
Non-current liabilities	43,948,000	62,360,000
Deferred non-current income taxes	117,449,000	97,270,000
Revolving credit notes payable (Note 15)	—	200,000,000
Debentures and other debt (Note 17)	610,242,000	643,123,000
Minority interest	69,534,000	58,775,000
Stockholders' equity (Note 19):		
Cumulative preferred stock	16,593,000	30,482,000
Common stock	277,108,000	277,108,000
Capital in excess of par value	490,697,000	480,896,000
Retained earnings	1,242,341,000	1,162,556,000
Less: Treasury stock, at cost	(25,047,000)	(26,971,000)
Total stockholders' equity	2,001,692,000	1,924,071,000
Total liabilities and stockholders' equity	$4,866,286,000	$4,813,618,000

EXHIBIT 4

WESTINGHOUSE

Notes to Financial Statements (excerpts)

Note 21 – The Corporation is defending 17 lawsuits by 27 public utility customers alleging breach of uranium supply contracts. Two of these lawsuits allege violations of the antitrust laws. Three of the lawsuits are in Sweden, one is in a Pennsylvania state court and the rest have been filed in United States District Court for the Eastern District of Virginia. These suits followed a notification by the Corporation to its customers in September 1975 that performance was excused under the legal doctrine of commercial impracticability.

The alleged contracts call for the delivery of approximately 80 million pounds of uranium over the next 20 years, at an average price of $9.50 per pound, with price escalation based on industrial indices but not keyed to changes in the market price of uranium. The Corporation has approximately 15 million pounds of uranium in inventory or under firm contract, leaving a shortfall of approximately 65 million pounds. Recent market price quotations for uranium have been approximately $40 per pound with substantial down payments required.

Seven of the contracts in litigation are also included in a group of 21 fuel fabrication contracts that require the Corporation to supply, starting in approximately 1982, an additional 3.7 million pounds of uranium for use as diluent in making plutonium fuel. If the plutonium fabrication option in each of those seven contracts should not be exercised for some reason (e.g., government prohibition), the Corporation will be obligated under the seven contracts to supply sufficient uranium to provide equivalent energy, i.e., an estimated 9.2 million pounds. (There would be no such additional requirement under the other 14 contracts.) This would increase the Corporation's uranium shortfall to approximately 74.2 million pounds. Management deems it unlikely that an additional 9.2 million pounds will be needed.

Under an arrangement affirmed by court order on February 4, 1976, in the consolidated action, Westinghouse will deliver approximately 15 million pounds of uranium it has in inventory or on order on the basis of the plaintiffs' claimed rights subject to later final determination of the proper price. The arrangement also provides for the establishment of a utility committee to enter into discussions and negotiations with Westinghouse looking toward a possible amicable resolution of the disputes beyond the 15 million pounds and related financial matters.

Until the utility suits are resolved, there will continue to be major uncertainties as to the financial impact on the Corporation. One possibility is that the lawsuits may be settled under the court-directed negotiating arrangements noted above, in which case the costs of settlement to the Corporation could well be substantial. In the meantime, the Corporation will continue vigorously to assert its defenses under the Uniform Commercial Code. If the Corporation is not wholly successful and is granted only partial relief from its alleged contractual obligations, the financial impact could be severe. If the Corporation is required to fulfill all the contracts under current market conditions, the financial impact will of course be extremely adverse. In light of the many uncertainties, probable or potential loss cannot reasonably be estimated.

The Corporation is also a defendant in a purported class action brought by an individual shareholder alleging securities law violations for the Corporation's failure to make proper disclosures concerning the uranium supply contracts.

Note 22 – At present, there are eight pending cases by utilities seeking damages totaling approximately $270 million in connection with outages of turbine generators sold by the Corporation. Most of the damages sought are consequential or punitive and to date the Corporation's contractual disclaimers of consequential damages have been sustained in all resolved cases.

Manville Corporation*

On August 26, 1982, in a highly unprecedented development, the Manville Corporation filed for petition under Chapter 11 of the federal bankruptcy code. The announcement was surprising because Manville had reported a profit each of the last five years and currently had a net worth equal to $1.1 billion.

Manville filed for Chapter 11 protection after receiving the results of an independent study by Epidemiology Resources, an environmental-health consulting firm. The study concluded that Manville could face over 52,000 asbestos-related lawsuits, involving an estimated $2 billion, or nearly twice its net worth.

Manville had disclosed in its December 31, 1981, financial statements that 9,300 asbestos-health suits had already been filed against the company, with an estimated cost per case of $15,690. The company also disclosed, however, it believed that it had substantial defenses to the legal actions brought against it. Manville's stock price in 1981 had reached a high of $26.50; on August 25, 1982, the day before the Chapter 11 petition announcement, the stock closed at $7.875.

BACKGROUND

The Manville Corporation was founded in 1862, and its principal activities include manufacturing, mining, and forest products. It is the largest manufacturer and distributor of insulation products in the United States, and it is a leading producer of asbestos-cement, polyvinyl chloride plastic pipe, diatomite, and beverage carrier-boards and containers. Until 1982, Manville's common stock was one of the 30 stocks that composed the Dow Jones Industrial Average.

The bankruptcy petition filed by Manville Corporation was just the latest shock for the battered asbestos industry. Problems had plagued asbestos firms since 1964, when a scientific study linked pulmonary disease in insulatory workers to asbestos exposure. As thousands of cases of asbestos-related diseases among asbestos workers and users came to light, U.S. asbestos consumption fell by nearly 50 percent (see Exhibit 1). As a consequence, asbestos manufacturers either tried to get out of the business or dissassociate themselves from the asbestos products.

Some companies even changed their names. The Union Asbestos and Rubber Company became Unarco Industries, Inc., but nevertheless filed for bankruptcy protection in July 1982. The century-old Johns-Manville Corporation became the Manville Corpo-

---

* This case was prepared by Kenneth R. Ferris and David Black. Copyright © 1985 by Kenneth R. Ferris. All rights reserved.

EXHIBIT 1
U.S. Asbestos Consumption: 1976–1981

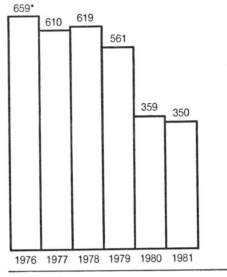

659*   610   619   561   359   350

1976   1977   1978   1979   1980   1981

* Thousands of metric tons.
Source: Interior Department.

ration and underwent an internal reorganization in 1981, which divided the company into five operating subsidiaries; the newly created asbestos subsidiary filed for bankruptcy in August of 1982.

While the change of names was largely cosmetic, the structural change which accompanied Manville's name change was more significant. The newly reorganized parent company assigned its assets to the various subunits under the presumption that the asbestos-related claims could only be paid from the asbestos unit's assets, and not from the parent's assets nor other unrelated subsidiaries. Manville assigned approximately 26 percent of its more than $2 billion in assets to its asbestos subsidiary.

DANGEROUS EFFECTS

The use of asbestos in the United States steadily declined as the dangerous effects of the product became known. According to the U.S. Bureau of Mines, U.S. consumption fell to about 350 metric tons in 1981 from a high of 795 metric tons in 1973.

Asbestos had been used in various applications, primarily because of its excellent insulative properties. A Department of Labor report indicated that between 1940 and 1979 more than 27 million Americans were exposed to asbestos in one form or another. The report estimated that the industry could expect up to 10,000 asbestos-related cancer deaths a year to the end of the century; asbestos-related diseases include mesothelioma, a cancer of the lining of the lungs, and asbestosis, a lung disease similar to emphysema.

MANVILLE'S LITIGATION

By December 31, 1981, Manville had been named as a defendant in 9,300 lawsuits by some 12,800 plantiffs charging exposure to airborne àsbestos fibers, allegedly resulting in health problems. The lawsuits charged, among other things, breach of implied warranty and negligence in failure to warn. In previously settled cases, plaintiffs successfully sued Manville "in strict products liability" for engaging in "outrageous conduct by exhibiting a reckless indifference to the health and well-being" of others. In these cases, the courts upheld punitive damages of up to $500,000 per claimant upon a showing that high-ranking Manville officials became fully aware of the dangers of prolonged exposure to asbestos dust as early as the mid-1940s, yet the company failed to warn those being exposed until 1969.

At the date of bankruptcy petition—August 26, 1982—Manville was a defendant in 11,000 asbestos-related legal actions brought by 15,500 plaintiffs; the average claim was $40,000. Manville commissioned a study, which found that "its potential liability attributable to asbestos litigation would not be less than $2 billion over the next 20 years." The study estimated that 32,000 asbestos-health claims had yet to be asserted, largely because it took up to 15–20 years for asbestosis to manifest itself, and even longer for other diseases linked to inhalation of asbestos dust.

In addition to the asbestos lawsuits, the company was also litigating the extent of its insurance coverage relating to asbestos claims with its primary insurance carriers. These carriers had failed to fund many asbestos-related claims allegedly because primary coverage had been properly exhausted. Thus, Manville filed its petition for reorganization under Chapter 11 of the bankruptcy code due to legal, rather than to operational or purely financial, difficulties. As a result of the filing, Manville froze all claims—such as debt, dividends, and legal claims—while it sought to develop a plan to pay its claimants and creditors.

QUESTIONS

1. Do you agree with Manville's decision to file for protection under Chapter 11 of the bankruptcy code? Explain.

2. Do you agree with the way that Manville accounted for the contingent liabilities as of December 31, 1981? Explain. Would your answer change if the internal consultant's study was available to management prior to the issuance of the 1981 financial report?

3. Do Manville's financial statements (Exhibits 3–6) adequately convey the business risk assumed by the company? Is this business risk correctly reflected in the company's share price (Exhibit 2)?

EXHIBIT 2
Manville Corporation—Share Price Movements:
1976–1982

Price of
share

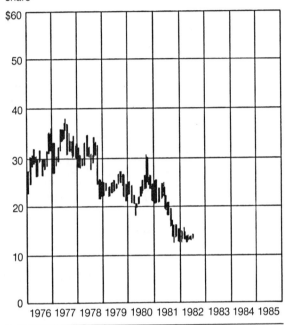

EXHIBIT 3

MANVILLE CORPORATION
Consolidated Balance Sheets
December 31, 1981, and 1980
(thousands of dollars)

Assets	1981	1980
Current Assets		
Cash *(including time deposits of $9,208 in 1981, $12,425 in 1980)*	$ 14,081	$ 19,699
Marketable securities, at cost *(approximates market)*	12,013	12,186
Receivables *(net of allowances of $7,054 in 1981, $7,708 in 1980)*		
Trade	288,702	314,644
Other	37,933	35,492
Inventories *(Notes 1b and 3)*	211,129	216,749
Prepaid expenses *(principally deferred income taxes)*	18,810	20,132
Total Current Assets	582,668	618,902
Property, Plant and Equipment, at cost *(Note 1c)*		
Land and land improvements	119,174	117,671
Buildings	363,308	357,102
Machinery and equipment	1,202,490	1,204,275
	1,684,972	1,679,048
Less, Accumulated depreciation and depletion	524,747	484,397
	1,160,225	1,194,651
Timber and timberlands, less cost of timber harvested	406,205	407,463
Property, plant and equipment, net	1,566,430	1,602,114
Other Assets *(principally investments and long-term receivables)*	148,716	117,143
	$2,297,814	$2,338,159

Liabilities		
Current Liabilities		
Short-term debt *(principally current portion of long-term debt)*	$ 29,437	$ 21,749
Accounts payable	120,295	125,722
Compensation and employee benefits	77,477	80,191
Income taxes	30,335	21,663
Other accrued liabilities	58,031	60,946
Total Current Liabilities	315,575	310,271
Long-Term Debt *(Note 4)*	507,620	519,144
Other Non-Current Liabilities	86,411	75,430
Deferred Income Taxes *(Note 1e)*	184,924	210,997
	1,094,530	1,115,842
Contingencies and Commitments *(Notes 5 and 6)*		

Preferred Stock		
Cumulative Preferred Stock, $1.00 par, authorized 10,000,000 shares:		
Redeemable $5.40 series, at stated value of $65 per share; issued and outstanding:		
1981—4,627,689 shares, 1980—4,621,982 shares *(Note 7)*	300,800	300,429

Common Shareholders' Equity		
Common Stock, $2.50 par, authorized 50,000,000 shares; issued:		
1981—23,640,675 shares, 1980—23,010,433 shares *(Note 8)*	59,102	57,526
Capital in Excess of Par *(Note 8)*	173,950	163,594
Earnings Reinvested	695,362	704,725
Cumulative Currency Translation Adjustments *(Notes 1g and 9)*	(22,443)	
	905,971	925,845
Less, Cost of treasury stock, 1981—114,020 shares, 1980—129,396 shares *(Note 8)*	3,487	3,957
	902,484	921,888
	$2,297,814	$2,338,159

The accompanying notes are an integral part of the consolidated financial statements.

EXHIBIT 4

MANVILLE CORPORATION
Consolidated Statements of Earnings and Earnings Reinvested
For the Years Ended December 31
(thousands of dollars, except per share amounts)

Earnings	1981	1980	1979
Revenues			
Net sales	$2,186,005	$2,266,804	$2,276,429
Other income, net	34,674	25,547	20,933
Total	2,220,679	2,292,351	2,297,362
Costs and Expenses			
Cost of sales	1,730,678	1,771,448	1,747,031
Selling, general and administrative	257,844	263,487	238,964
Research, development and engineering	33,820	34,801	31,100
Total	2,022,342	2,069,736	2,017,095
Income From Operations	198,337	222,615	280,267
Interest Expense	72,661	65,379	62,441
Asbestos Health Costs *(Note 5)*	12,756		
Earnings Before Income Taxes	112,920	157,236	217,826
Income Taxes *(Notes 1e and 11)*			
Current	56,214	46,680	67,261
Deferred	(3,614)	29,920	35,959
Total	52,600	76,600	103,220
Net Earnings *(before preferred dividends)*	60,320	80,636	114,606
Dividends on Preferred Stock	24,987	24,919	23,553
Net Earnings Available for Common Stock	$ 35,333	$ 55,717	$ 91,053

Earnings Reinvested

Earnings Reinvested at Beginning of Year	$ 704,725	$ 692,420	$ 643,317
Net Earnings Available for Common Stock	35,333	55,717	91,053
Dividends on Common Stock	(44,472)	(43,378)	(41,692)
Loss on Dispositions of Treasury Stock *(Note 8)*	(224)	(34)	(258
Earnings Reinvested at End of Year	$ 695,362	$ 704,725	$ 692,420

Net Earnings Per Common Share *(Notes 1f and 8)*	$1.53	$2.47	$4.13

The accompanying notes are an integral part of the consolidated financial statements.

EXHIBIT 5

MANVILLE CORPORATION
Notes to Financial Statements (excerpt)

Note 5—Contingencies

Johns-Manville Corporation and certain of its subsidiaries ("J-M" or "Johns-Manville") is a defendant or co-defendant in a substantial number of lawsuits brought by present or former insulation workers, shipyard workers, factory workers and other persons alleging damage to their health from exposure to dust from asbestos fibers or asbestos-containing products manufactured or sold by J-M and, in most cases, by certain other defendants. The majority of these claims allege J-M and other defendants failed in their duty to warn of the hazards of inhalation of asbestos fiber and dust originating from asbestos-containing products. J-M believes it has substantial defenses to these legal actions, resulting in part from prompt warnings of the possible hazards of exposure to asbestos fiber emitted from asbestos-containing insulation products following the 1964 publication of scientific studies linking pulmonary disease in insulation workers to asbestos exposure.

Also included in these legal actions are a number of cases brought by some employees of J-M and certain of its subsidiaries and by employees of other manufacturing companies which used asbestos fiber in their operations. These suits typically allege that J-M, its subsidiaries, and other defendants failed to warn of the hazards associated with the use of such fiber. J-M believes it has substantial defenses to these legal actions including the fact that, with respect to employees of other manufacturing companies, it had no special knowledge not in the possession of the plaintiffs' employers which would give rise to a special duty on the part of J-M, and, with respect to the employees of J-M subsidiaries, that applicable workers' compensation statutes provide appropriate defenses to many aspects of such claims and there are substantial defenses to other aspects of such claims.

J-M believes that the claims and lawsuits pending and which may arise in the future relate to events and conditions existing in prior years. More specifically, it is J-M's belief, based on the following factors and assumptions, that since at least the beginning of 1978, no significant new potential liabilities have been created for J-M with respect to diseases known to be related to asbestos and arising from asbestos fiber and/or asbestos-containing products manufactured or sold by J-M:

• That since the mid-1970's, J-M has sold asbestos fiber in the United States only in pressure pack, block form or other similar condition and not in a loose form;

• That by 1973, J-M had ceased domestic manufacture of thermal insulation products containing asbestos which are the products principally involved in disease claims made against J-M;

• That the Occupational Safety and Health Administration (OSHA) established a maximum exposure standard for asbestos fiber of five fibers per cubic centimeter in 1972 and lowered that standard to two fibers per cubic centimeter in 1976. It is assumed that compliance with such standards in the work place was achieved within a reasonable time following such promulgation and is continuing to date; and

• With respect to any use not complying with the OSHA asbestos standards, J-M's defensive posture with respect to claims arising out of such environments will be significantly enhanced.

As of December 31, 1981, J-M was a defendant or co-defendant in approximately 9,300 asbestos-health suits brought by approximately 12,800 individual plaintiffs. This represents an increase over the December 31, 1980 level of 5,087 cases (brought by approximately 9,300 plaintiffs) and a substantial increase over the December 31, 1979 level of 2,707 cases (brought by approximately 4,100 plaintiffs) and the December 31, 1978 level of 1,181 cases (brought by approximately 1,500 plaintiffs). During 1979, J-M was named as a defendant in an average of 141 cases per month (brought by an average of 196 plaintiffs) as compared with an average of 65 cases per month (brought by an average of 83 plaintiffs) in 1978. During the first three quarters of 1980, J-M was named as a defendant in an average of 194 cases per month (brought by an average of 382 plaintiffs); this rate increased to an average of 304 cases per month (brought by an average of 403 plaintiffs) in the fourth quarter of 1980 and to an average of 400 cases per month (brought by an average of 525 plaintiffs) during 1981. During 1980, J-M disposed of 401 claims at an average disposition cost of $22,600, and during 1981, a total of 802 claims were disposed of, with J-M's share of disposition costs being an average of $15,430 per claim. All disposition cost references exclude legal expenses, and the verdicts in approximately 20 cases which are presently on appeal (where the average judgment against J-M is approximately $223,360). Substantially all of these disposition costs have been charged to applicable insurance. The 1980 and 1981 level of disposition costs represents a significant growth from the pre-1980 level of approximately $13,000 per claim and results in an increase in the overall disposition cost per plaintiff through December 31, 1981 to approximately $15,640. The growth in these two areas (volume and costs) has significantly increased the uncertainties as to the future number of similar claims which J-M may receive, and the future disposition costs of the pending and future claims. During 1980, to resolve uncertainties as to the correct interpretation of a number of provisions in the various policies of insurance maintained by J-M and applicable to these claims, it was necessary for J-M to bring a declaratory judgment action to have such issues resolved by a court of law. While it continues to be J-M's opinion that its position with respect to these issues is sound and in accord with the weight of judicial precedent, any litigation involves uncertainties to some degree.

Because of the uncertainties associated with the asbestos-health litigation, and in spite of the substantial defenses J-M believes it has with respect to these claims, the eventual outcome of the asbestos-health litigation cannot be predicted at this time and the ultimate liability of J-M after application of available insurance cannot be reasonably determined in accordance with Financial Accounting Standards Board Statement No. 5, "Accounting for Contingencies". No reasonable determination of loss can be made and no liability has been recorded in the financial statements. Liabilities relating to asbestos-health litigation will be recorded in accordance with generally accepted accounting principles when such amounts can be determined. Depending on how and when these uncertainties with respect to J-M are resolved, the cost to J-M and thus to Manville Corporation could be substantial.

Costs associated with asbestos-health claims are presented separately in the 1981 financial statements because of the increased activity related to such claims. The 1980 financial statements, which have not been reclassified to conform to the 1981 presentation, include approximately $8.5 million of similar costs that is reflected in cost of sales and selling, general and administrative expenses. Amounts relating to 1979 were not material.

EXHIBIT 6
Management's Report

The accompanying consolidated financial statements have been prepared by Management in conformity with generally accepted accounting principles appropriate under the circumstances. The representations in the financial statements and the fairness and integrity of such statements are the responsibility of Management. All of the other financial information in the Annual Report to Shareholders is consistent with that in the financial statements.

The financial statements necessarily include some amounts that are based on Management's best estimates and judgments. Management believes that the financial statements reflect in all material respects the substance of transactions which should be included and appropriately account for or disclose all material uncertainties. Uncertainties exist concerning the eventual outcome of Johns-Manville Corporation's asbestos-health litigation. Management is presently unable to predict the ultimate cost to Johns-Manville Corporation and thus to the Company resulting from this litigation. Any liabilities relating to asbestos-health litigation will be recorded in accordance with generally accepted accounting principles when such amounts can be reasonably determined.

The financial statements prepared by Management have been examined in accordance with generally accepted auditing standards by Coopers & Lybrand, Independent Certified Public Accountants, whose report is also presented.

Manville maintains internal accounting control systems to provide reliable financial information for the preparation of financial statements, to safeguard assets against loss or unauthorized use and to ensure proper authorization and accounting for all transactions. Management is responsible for maintenance of these systems, which is accomplished through communication of established written

codes of conduct, systems, policies and procedures; employee training; and appropriate delegation of authority and segregation of responsibilities. To further ensure compliance with established standards and procedures, the Company maintains a substantial program of internal audits.

In establishing and maintaining its internal accounting control systems, Management considers the inherent limitations of the various control procedures and weighs their cost against the benefits derived. Management believes that existing internal accounting control systems are achieving their objectives and that they provide reasonable assurance concerning the accuracy of the financial statements.

Oversight of Management's financial reporting and internal accounting control responsibilities is exercised by the Board of Directors, through an Audit Committee which consists solely of outside directors (see page 22). The Audit Committee meets periodically with financial management, internal auditors and the independent accountants to ensure that each is meeting its responsibilities and to discuss matters concerning auditing, internal accounting control and financial reporting. The independent accountants and the Company's internal audit department have free access to meet with the Audit Committee without Management's presence.

John A. McKinney
Chairman of the Board and
Chief Executive Officer

Leo J. Bartolanzo
Senior Vice President, Finance

EXHIBIT 7
Accountants' Report

To the Shareholders and Directors
of Manville Corporation:

We have examined the consolidated balance sheets of Manville Corporation as of December 31, 1981 and 1980, and the related consolidated statements of earnings and earnings reinvested and changes in financial position for each of the three years in the period ended December 31, 1981. Our examinations were made in accordance with generally accepted auditing standards and, accordingly, included such tests of the accounting records and such other auditing procedures as we considered necessary in the circumstances. The financial statements of Canadian subsidiaries, which reflect total assets and net sales constituting approximately 10% of the related consolidated totals, were examined by other auditors whose report thereon has been furnished to us. Our opinion expressed herein, insofar as it relates to amounts included for Canadian subsidiaries examined by other auditors, is based solely upon their report.

As discussed in Note 5 to the consolidated financial statements, Johns-Manville Corporation (a wholly-owned subsidiary of Manville Corporation) is a defendant in a

substantial number of asbestos-health legal actions. The ultimate liability resulting from these matters cannot presently be reasonably estimated.

In our opinion, based upon our examinations and the report of other auditors, the aforementioned financial statements present fairly the consolidated results of operations and changes in financial position of Manville Corporation for each of the three years in the period ended December 31, 1981 and, subject to the effects of adjustments that might have been required had the outcome of the uncertainties referred to in the preceding paragraph been known, the consolidated financial position of Manville Corporation at December 31, 1981 and 1980, in conformity with generally accepted accounting principles applied on a consistent basis.

Coopers & Lybrand

February 5, 1982
Denver, Colorado

Off-Balance Sheet Debt

CASE 4.12

UFS Corporation*

"Why me?" thought Alan Burke. "My first day on the job at the bank and instead of getting a company with a nice single set of financial statements, I get four separate sets of statements that supposedly fit together."

Alan Burke had just started as a new credit analyst for the First National Bank of Audelia, having just completed an MBA degree with a major in finance at the local university. From the loan officer responsible for this client, Alan learned the following information about each of the three companies associated with UFS Corporation and about the UFS Corporation itself.

UFS CORPORATION

The UFS Corporation was a manufacturing company whose principal products were microwave ovens, refrigerators, and conventional ovens. The company had had a long history (over 50 years) of selling high-quality home appliances; however, recent reductions in the prices of competitor products had forced UFS to consider ways to provide assistance to its customers to help them buy its products. As a consequence, UFS had started its own finance subsidiary, the UFS Acceptance Corporation, to assist customers in the financing of their purchases.

UFS Corporation was also associated with two other companies. It held an 80 percent interest in Scrub-All, a company that made automatic dishwashers. UFS had purchased this interest in Scrub-All because the company's product line complemented its own, and the products were of a quality that UFS would have had difficulty duplicating. Further, to ensure a steady supply of chrome parts for its appliances, UFS had obtained a 10 percent interest in the common stock of Acme Chrome

* This case was prepared by Kirk L. Tennant. Copyright © 1985 by Kirk L. Tennant. All rights reserved to the author.

Company. Well over 50 percent of Acme's sales were attributed to purchases by UFS and Scrub-All.

UFS ACCEPTANCE CORPORATION

Created nearly five years ago, the UFS Acceptance Corporation was a wholly owned subsidiary that purchased consumer notes from its parent, the UFS Corporation. UFS Acceptance also borrowed funds from several banking institutions on a medium and long-term basis, and used the margins between the short-term interest rates on the consumer notes and the rates on its medium and long-term liabilities to cover its overhead costs. The parent company guaranteed all of the borrowings of UFS Acceptance Corporation.

SCRUB-ALL COMPANY

With an ownership interest of 80 percent of the common stock of Scrub-All, UFS Corporation controlled the tactical and strategic policies of the Scrub-All Company through an interlocking board of directors. Scrub-All, like UFS, also sold its consumer notes to UFS Acceptance Corporation. The family that originally started Scrub-All still held a 20 percent ownership interest in the common stock of the company.

ACME CHROME COMPANY

In order to guarantee a steady supply of chrome parts and that a company would work with the engineers of UFS in the design of new parts, UFS had purchased a 10 percent interest in Acme Chrome Company. Over the years, a strong relationship had developed between UFS and Acme. For example, Acme scheduled the production runs of its other customers around the production needs of UFS and Scrub-All.

Mike Hustis, the loan officer responsible for UFS, provided Alan with the financial statements of the four companies (Exhibits 1–4) and asked him to answer some basic credit review questions concerning an expansion loan application that had been received from the parent company. Before Alan could complete the credit review, he identified the following questions that needed to be addressed in order to understand the relationship between the various companies.

QUESTIONS

1. Why are investments in Acme Chrome and UFS Acceptance Corporation shown on the balance sheet, while the investment in Scrub-All is omitted?

2. What is meant by the carrying value "at equity" for the investment in UFS Acceptance Corporation?

3. Why is the investment in Acme Chrome Company shown "at cost"?

4. Explain the "goodwill" account. What other name is sometimes used instead of "goodwill" and to what company is this account related?

5. What is meant by "minority interest" and to what company is this account related? Is this a liability or an equity account?

6. What are UFS Corporation's current ratio, debt-to-equity ratio, and debt-to-asset ratio? Are these ratios at an acceptable level?

7. How would the balance sheet of UFS Corporation appear if UFS Acceptance Corporation were consolidated?

8. How would the ratios calculated in Question 6 above differ after the consolidation of UFS Acceptance Corporation? Can an argument be made for consolidating Acme Chrome Company?

EXHIBIT 1

UFS CORPORATION
Consolidated Statement of Financial Position
December 31, 1985

Assets

Current assets	$ 29,500,000
Investment in stock of UFS Acceptance	
Corporation at equity (100%)	20,400,000 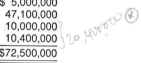
Investment in stock of Acme	
Chrome Company (10%) at cost	5,600,000
Other assets	98,000,000
Goodwill	3,200,000
Total assets	$156,700,000

Liabilities and Stockholders' Equity

Current liabilities	$ 29,500,000
Long-term liabilities	55,000,000
Minority interest	7,500,000
Common stock	15,000,000
Retained earnings	49,700,000
Total liabilities and stockholders' equity	$156,700,000

EXHIBIT 2

UFS ACCEPTANCE CORPORATION
Statement of Financial Position
December 31, 1985

Assets

Current assets	$ 8,000,000
Notes receivable	58,000,000
Other assets	6,500,000
Total assets	$72,500,000

Liabilities and Stockholders' Equity

Current liabilities*	$ 5,000,000
Long-term debt	47,100,000
Common stock ($1 par)	10,000,000
Retained earnings	10,400,000
Total liabilities and equities	$72,500,000

* $3,000,000 of the current liabilities is a promissory note to UFS Corporation. UFS Corporation accounts for this as a long-term receivable in Other Assets.

EXHIBIT 3

SCRUB-ALL COMPANY
Statement of Financial Position
December 31, 1985

Assets

Current assets	$16,400,000
Other assets	52,600,000
Total assets.	$69,000,000

Liabilities and Stockholders' Equity

Current liabilities	$13,350,000
Long-term liabilities	18,150,000
Common stock	12,000,000
Retained earnings	25,500,000
Total liabilities and stockholders' equity.	$69,000,000

EXHIBIT 4

ACME CHROME COMPANY
Statement of Financial Position
December 31, 1985

Assets

Current assets	$14,750,000
Other assets	36,250,000
Total assets.	$51,000,000

Liabilities and Stockholder's Equity

Current liabilities	$ 5,000,000
Long-term liabilities	15,000,000
Capital stock	18,750,000
Retained earnings	12,250,000
Total liabilities and stockholders' equity.	$51,000,000

Carter Hawley Hale Stores, Inc.*

In the past, apparitions and prestidigitations were limited to the seance parlors and magical stages of the world. But today the best mediums and magicians are to be found in the corporate boardrooms of the major companies of America. For in no other place can the medium or prestidigitator perform his or her feats of magic and illusion for such a large audience, the investing public.

The Book of Great Apparitions and Prestidigitations

CARTER HAWLEY UNIT
SETS $125 MILLION NOTES

Los Angeles—Carter Hawley Hale Stores, Inc. said its Carter Hawley Hale Credit Corporation unit registered with the Securities and Exchange Commission to issue $125 million of capital notes.

Unlike most capital notes, the retailer said these will be sold directly to the public through an agent, instead of an underwriter, in multiples of $1,000.

Carter Hawley said the notes will be offered on a continuous basis through Merrill Lynch White Weld Capital Markets Group and will be available with maturities from one to three years from the date issued. The company said net proceeds will be used to reduce short-term borrowings of the credit unit.

Carter Hawley said it hopes the issue will begin next Monday.

The Wall Street Journal,
October 25, 1982

"I have the consolidated balance sheet of Carter Hawley Hale for 1982, but I can't find the capital notes mentioned in the article anywhere in the liability section," said Mike Lowering to his MBA accounting professor, Nancy Wilks. "Maybe Carter Hawley Hale decided not to issue these notes after all."

"I think that is unlikely, Mike, considering the announcement and the apparent needs of the company," said Nancy Wilks. "You'd better read through the annual report and see if the notes are mentioned in the footnotes to the financial statements. Come back in a day or two and tell me what you found."

BACKGROUND

Mike Lowering had chosen Carter Hawley Hale as the company on which he was to do his accounting research report. Being from California, Mike was quite familiar

---

with the fourth largest department and specialty store chain in the United States. While in California, Mike had made many purchases at the Broadway Stores and now, in 1983, having come to Dallas to attend Southern Methodist University, he was making his purchases at Neiman-Marcus. Also, Mike made frequent trips to Carter Hawley Hale's Waldenbooks for purchases of his reading material.

During the 1970s, Carter Hawley Hale had followed an aggressive acquisition strategy. CHH purchased well-known, established department and specialty store chains that were floundering and remodeled and restocked them with high-quality, high-priced goods. Such store chains as Wanamakers in Philadelphia, Bergdorf in New York, and Holt-Renfrew in Toronto were part of this acquisition strategy.

Large amounts of cash were needed by CHH to acquire, remodel, and restock these chain stores. CHH had extensively used short- and long-term borrowings to finance this growth, and quickly became one of the most debt-laden retailers in the industry. Seemingly reaching its debt limit, CHH had created three finance subsidiaries. The finance subsidiaries—Carter Hawley Hale Credit Corporation, Carter Hawley Hale Finance Corporation, and Carter Hawley Hale Overseas Finance—then issued large amounts of their own debt to finance the purchase of trade receivables from CHH at a discount. The collection of purchased trade receivables was performed by employees of the parent company, and the finance subsidiaries were then billed for the service. None of the three finance subsidiaries has, or ever had, any employees.

Exhibits 1–3 present the 1980, 1981, and 1982 financial statements of the parent company and finance subsidiaries.

A LATER CONVERSATION

"Professor Wilks, I finally found the capital notes payable described in a footnote to the company's financial statements; the footnote concerned the company's finance subsidiaries and presented an abbreviated balance sheet for the subsidiaries. I understand how Carter Hawley Hale issued the notes, but doesn't the company have to show them on its financial statements? There were a lot of other liabilities on the finance subsidiaries' balance sheet that were similarly not reported on the consolidated financial statements of Carter Hawley Hale. I just don't understand this accounting! In class, you said that any amount owed to a third party represents a liability to the entity and should be shown in the liability section of the balance sheet."

"You're right, Mike, I said that all amounts owed to third parties should be shown on the balance sheet as a liability; but this is an example of what is called 'off-balance sheet financing.' The authoritative accounting literature doesn't require a finance subsidiary to be consolidated because of the difference in the operating aspects of the two businesses. In the case of Carter Hawley Hale, the main line of business is retailing, while the finance subsidiary was created to purchase the retail receivables of Carter Hawley Hale. The finance subsidiary makes its money by playing the spread on interest rates and not from retailing. It would seem inappropriate to add those businesses together—at least that was the thinking of the individuals responsible for setting reporting standards in accounting."

"But, I would think that, by not adding the companies together, the balance sheet and income statement would be misstated and someone who was going to analyze them might be misled," observed Mike.

"You have the financial statements for the last three years, Mike, why don't you try to estimate the effects of consolidating the finance subsidiaries with the parent

EXHIBIT 1

CARTER HAWLEY HALE STORES, INC.
Statements of Financial Position
For the Years Ended January 29, 1983, January 30, 1982, and January 31, 1981
(in thousands)

	January 29, 1983	January 30, 1982	January 31, 1981
Assets			
Current assets:			
Cash	$ 14,877	$ 17,194	$ 11,269
Accounts receivable (net)	147,288	143,295	216,474
Merchandise inventories.	630,169	554,701	468,893
Other current assets	37,537	29,404	34,576
	829,871	744,594	731,212
Property and equipment (net)	860,188	828,338	772,628
Investment in finance subsidiaries	142,102	126,173	107,903
Other assets	58,681	42,617	39,625
Total assets	$1,890,842	$1,741,722	$1,651,368
Liabilities and Shareholders' Equity			
Current liabilities:			
Current installments on long-term obligations	$ 12,100	$ 14,947	$ 13,299
Accounts payable.	243,712	182,278	140,455
Accrued liabilities	108,042	93,145	87,290
Dividends payable	10,132	9,272	8,488
Current income taxes	4,821	2,936	1,397
Deferred income tax	105,669	100,223	102,731
	484,476	402,801	353,660
Long-term debt	420,516	409,630	408,551
Capital lease obligations	164,376	174,677	181,733
Other liabilities.	128,502	107,575	87,207
Shareholders' equity			
Preferred stock, $5 par value (aggregate liquidation preference $36,535).	4,059	4,510	7,912
Common stock, $5 par value	159,449	144,601	132,704
Other paid-in capital	214,009	192,048	182,221
Accumulated earnings	315,455	305,880	297,380
	692,972	647,039	620,217
Total liabilities and shareholders' equity	$1,890,842	$1,741,722	$1,651,368

company and come back and we'll see if it really makes a difference. Be sure to look at the effects of consolidation on both the balance sheet and the income statement."

QUESTIONS

1. Given the financial statements for 1980 through 1982, prepare the consolidated balance sheets and income statements for Carter Hawley Hale for 1980, 1981, and 1982 as if the finance subsidiaries had been consolidated.

2. Calculate the debt-to-equity ratios of Carter Hawley Hale for the three years before and after the consolidation of the finance subsidiaries?

3. Do you agree with the authoritative literature that finance subsidiaries represent such a different aspect of business that they should not be consolidated?

EXHIBIT 2

CARTER HAWLEY HALE STORES, INC.
Statement of Earnings
For the Years Ended 1982, 1981, 1980
(in thousands, except per share data)

	1982	1981	1980
Sales	$3,054,764	$2,870,735	$2,632,921
Costs and expenses:			
Cost of goods sold.	1,747,470	1,635,733	1,489,126
Selling, operating, and administrative expenses.	926,179	883,564	806,747
Net interest expense and discount.	108,672	101,375	78,578
Taxes other than income taxes.	71,204	66,449	58,981
Rentals of properties.	74,628	65,323	56,151
Depreciation and amortization.	67,442	64,821	57,073
Gains on retirement of debentures	(7,956)	(10,542)	(3,076)
	2,987,639	2,806,723	2,543,580
Earnings before income taxes	67,125	64,012	89,341
Income taxes	18,100	19,250	32,000
Net earnings.	$ 49,025	$ 44,762	$ 57,341
Net earnings per share of common stock:			
Primary.	$1.55	$1.55	$2.08
Fully diluted	$1.53	$1.51	$1.97

EXHIBIT 3
Carter Hawley Hale Stores, Inc., Selected Footnotes for 1982, 1981, and 1980

Carter Hawley Hale Finance Subsidiaries
Statements of Financial Position

The company finances customer accounts receivable through its unconsolidated finance subsidiaries, Credit Corporation, CHH Finance Corporation, and Carter Hawley Hale Overseas Finance N.V. In addition to capital invested by the company and accumulated earnings, the finance subsidiaries finance the purchase of customer accounts receivable through sales of commercial paper, bank borrowings, and debt issuances. The finance subsidiaries purchase the receivables at discounts sufficient to cover their fixed charges, principally interest expense, at least one and one half times. Net earnings of the finance subsidiaries were $15.9 million in 1982, $18.3 million in 1981, and $13.1 million in 1980. The finance subsidiaries combined balance sheet, which reflects the elimination of all intercompany items, is presented below:

	January 29, 1983	January 30, 1982	January 31, 1981
Assets (in millions):			
Customer accounts purchased from Carter Hawley Hale Stores, Inc., less 10 percent withheld pending collection and settlement of discount	$522.3	$478.8	$434.1
Cash and other assets.	1.6	1.3	2.3
Total assets	$523.9	$480.1	$436.4

EXHIBIT 3 *(concluded)*

Liabilities and Investment of
Carter Hawley Hale Stores, Inc.

Notes payable and commercial paper	$ 85.5	$ 97.6	$175.7
Accrued liabilities	3.0	11.3	7.8
7.95 percent notes		50.0	50.0
8.45 percent notes due 1985–1997	35.0	35.0	35.0
9.75 percent notes due 1986	50.0	50.0	50.0
11.75 percent notes due 1986–1988	63.0		
8.75–11.25 percent capital notes due 1983–1986	36.3		
Eurodollar variable rate loan due 1983, subsequently refinanced (9⅜ percent at January 29, 1983)	100.0	100.0	
8.95 percent subordinated notes due 1984–1992	9.0	10.0	10.0
Investment of Carter Hawley Hale Stores, Inc. (including $53.1, $37.2, and $38.9 of accumulated earnings, respectively for 1982 through 1980)	142.1	126.2	107.9
Total liabilities and investment	$523.9	$480.1	$436.4

Interest Expense and Discount

Net interest expense and discount, which includes interest expense attributable to the finance subsidiaries, was $108.7 million in 1982, compared with $101.4 million in 1981 and $78.6 million in 1980.

The increase in net interest expense and discount was due to discount charges on receivables sold to a bank in 1982 partially offset by lower interest rates. Components of net interest expense and discount are shown below (in millions):

	1982	1981	1980
Discount on customer receivables sold to the finance subsidiaries	$ 78.1	$ 87.8	$ 64.4
Earnings and noninterest charges of the finance subsidiaries	(30.8)	(34.6)	(25.0)
Interest expense attributable to the finance subsidiaries	47.3	53.2	39.4
Interest on long-term debt	39.4	40.9	32.8
Imputed interest on capitalized lease obligations	13.9	14.3	14.8
Short-term and other interest, net	5.3	7.7	3.6
Discount on customer receivables sold to a bank	15.0		
Capitalized interest	(12.2)	(14.7)	(12.0)
Net interest expense and discount	$108.7	$101.4	$ 78.6

Accounting for Owners' Equity

Sears, Roebuck & Co.*

Sears Roebuck & Co., once recognized as being one of the largest retail organizations in North America, is today a major conglomerate. Besides the Sears Merchandise Group, which consists of the company's merchandising, credit, and international operations, the company also operates the Allstate Insurance Group (property-liability insurance, life-health insurance, and consumer finance services), the Coldwell Banker Real Estate Group (invests in, develops, manages, and brokers real estate), the Dean Witter Financial Services Group (securities brokerage, mutual fund and money management, investment banking), and the Sears World Trade Group (assists business and governments in the export and import of products and technology).

As of December 31, 1982, the company had over 351 million shares of common stock outstanding and over 350,000 shareholders throughout the world. Selected financial statements and footnotes for the company for the year ended December 31, 1982, are presented in Exhibits 1–5.

QUESTIONS

1. Examine the Consolidated Statement of Shareholders' Equity. Explain how each item was originally created for the period 1980–82. (*Note:* it might be useful to think in terms of journal entries.)

2. Assume that the following events took place during 1983 in the sequence given:

    a. A cash dividend of $0.50 per common share was declared and paid.

    b. A stock dividend of 10 percent was declared and issued. The market price of Sears Roebuck stock was $40 on the date of declaration.

    c. Two million shares of common were repurchased to be held as treasury stock; the cost was $35 per share.

---

* This case was prepared by Kenneth R. Ferris. Copyright © 1984 by Kenneth R. Ferris. All rights reserved to the author.

d. A public offering of 20 million shares was sold out at a price of $41 per share.

e. The stock split 2 for 1.

Determine the number of shares that would be outstanding at the end of 1983 and prepare the shareholders' equity section of the balance sheet to reflect these transacions.

EXHIBIT 1

SEARS ROEBUCK & CO.
Consolidated Statements of Financial Position

millions		December 31
	1982	1981
Assets		
Investments		
Bonds and redeemable preferred stocks, at amortized cost (market $5,862.0 and $4,310.5)	**$ 7,188.1**	$ 6,691.3
Mortgage loans	**3,587.3**	3,311.6
Common and preferred stocks, at market (cost $1,545.7 and $1,344.4)	**1,786.6**	1,412.5
Real estate	**934.8**	813.4
Total investments	**13,496.8**	12,228.8
Receivables		
Retail customers	**7,859.2**	7,552.0
Brokerage clients	**1,767.9**	1,464.0
Insurance premium installments	**724.9**	646.1
Finance installment notes	**481.5**	512.3
Other	**603.2**	570.4
Total receivables	**11,436.7**	10,744.8
Property and equipment, net	**3,396.4**	3,311.6
Merchandise inventories	**3,146.0**	3,103.1
Cash and invested cash (note 8)	**1,307.6**	1,170.7
Securities purchased under agreements to resell	**1,004.7**	832.1
Trading account securities owned, at market	**758.5**	1,274.2
Investments in unconsolidated companies	**434.9**	435.2
Other assets	**1,661.5**	1,408.9
Total assets	**36,643.1**	34,509.4
Liabilities		
Long-term debt (note 9)	**5,816.1**	5,323.6
Reserves for insurance claims and policy benefits	**5,769.6**	5,264.1
Accounts payable and other liabilities	**3,372.8**	3,114.6
Savings accounts and advances from Federal Home Loan Bank	**3,132.8**	2,783.6
Short-term borrowings (note 8)	**2,820.1**	3,233.4
Unearned revenues	**2,695.7**	2,514.8
Deferred income taxes (note 4)	**1,571.8**	1,441.2
Securities sold under repurchase agreements	**1,332.9**	1,564.3
Payables to brokerage clients	**1,318.9**	1,000.9
Total liabilities	**27,830.7**	26,240.5
Commitments and contingent liabilities (notes 1, 6, 10 and 11)		
Shareholders' equity (note 11)		
Common shares ($.75 par value, 351.4 and 347.9 shares outstanding)	**269.4**	268.5
Capital in excess of par value	**1,163.3**	1,143.9
Retained income	**7,426.1**	7,041.2
Treasury stock (at cost)	**(143.5)**	(186.7)
Unrealized net capital gains on marketable equity securities	**171.5**	48.5
Cumulative translation adjustments	**(74.4)**	(46.5)
Total shareholders' equity	**$ 8,812.4**	$ 8,268.9

See accompanying notes which include the summarized Group financial statements.

EXHIBIT 2

SEARS ROEBUCK & CO.
Consolidated Statements of Shareholders' Equity

	Year Ended December 31					
	1982	1981	1980	1982	1981	1980
	millions			shares in thousands		
Preferred shares—$1.00 par value, 50 million shares authorized, none issued						
Common shares—$.75 par value, 500 million shares authorized, issued as follows:						
Balance, beginning of year	$ 268.5	$ 244.0	$ 243.5	357,995.2	325,335.0	324,647.2
Issued for acquired companies (note 7)	—	24.5	—	—	32,619.3	—
Issued under incentive compensation plan	.3	—	—	351.2	27.0	7.7
Dividends reinvested	—	—	.5	—	—	680.1
Stock options exercised and other changes	.6	—	—	884.1	13.9	—
Balance, end of year	269.4	268.5	244.0	359,230.5	357,995.2	325,335.0
Capital in excess of par value						
Balance, beginning of year	1,143.9	640.5	629.5			
Issued for acquired companies	—	508.8	—			
Issued under incentive compensation plan	6.5	.4	.1			
Dividends reinvested	—	—	11.0			
Stock options exercised and other changes	12.9	(5.8)	(.1)			
Balance, end of year	1,163.3	1,143.9	640.5			
Retained income						
Balance, beginning of year	7,041.2	6,820.2	6,639.8			
Net income	861.2	650.1	609.8			
Dividends ($1.36 per share)	(476.3)	(429.1)	(429.4)			
Balance, end of year	7,426.1	7,041.2	6,820.2			
Treasury stock (at cost)						
Balance, beginning of year	(186.7)	(192.4)	(142.9)	(10,107.3)	(10,167.6)	(7,084.6)
Purchased	—	(5.1)	(54.3)	—	(299.8)	(3,331.7)
Exchanged for Sears debt (note 9)	25.3	30.3	—	1,341.4	1,606.0	—
Issued to subsidiary in connection with acquisition	—	(37.8)	—	—	(2,216.4)	—
Reissued under dividend reinvestment plan	17.9	18.3	4.8	945.1	970.5	248.7
Balance, end of year	(143.5)	(186.7)	(192.4)	(7,820.8)	(10,107.3)	(10,167.6)
Unrealized net capital gains on marketable equity securities						
Balance, beginning of year	48.5	152.4	76.0			
Net increase (decrease)	123.0	(103.9)	76.4			
Balance, end of year	171.5	48.5	152.4			
Cumulative translation adjustments						
Balance, beginning of year	(46.5)	—				
Initial application of SFAS No. 52	—	(29.3)				
Net increase in unrealized losses	(36.9)	(17.2)				
Realized on sale of subsidiaries	9.0	—				
Balance, end of year	(74.4)	(46.5)				
Total shareholders' equity and shares outstanding	$8,812.4	$8,268.9	$7,664.7	351,409.7	347,887.9	315,167.4

See accompanying notes which include the summarized Group financial statements.

EXHIBIT 3

SEARS ROEBUCK & CO.
Consolidated Statements of Changes in Financial Position

millions   Year Ended December 31

	1982	1981	1980
Sources of operating funds			
Net income	$ 861.2	$ 650.1	$ 609.8
Reserves for insurance claims and policy benefits	528.8	656.6	345.1
Depreciation	336.5	308.8	273.8
Unearned revenues	186.2	212.1	183.9
Deferred income taxes	97.2	(18.4)	(68.8)
Amortization of debt discount and other non-cash items	103.8	(16.4)	5.2
From operations	2,113.7	1,792.8	1,349.0
Increase in accounts payable and other liabilities	681.0	378.9	137.7
Decrease in trading account securities owned	515.7	—	—
Increase in savings account deposits and advances from Federal Home Loan Bank	349.2	87.5	284.7
Total available operating funds	3,659.6	2,259.2	1,771.4
Uses of operating funds			
Increase in receivables	946.9	336.7	33.4
Net investment additions	863.2	817.7	984.4
Net additions to property and equipment	406.4	347.9	365.7
Increase (decrease) in other assets	274.1	38.1	(11.0)
Net additions to mortgage loans and finance installment notes	244.9	49.7	175.3
Increase in merchandise inventories	161.1	388.6	34.5
Total operating funds used	2,896.6	1,978.7	1,582.3
Net funds generated from operations before dividends, acquisitions and financing transactions	763.0	280.5	189.1
Dividends paid to shareholders, net of reinvested amounts	(458.4)	(410.8)	(413.1)
Cost of acquired companies (note 7)	—	(790.0)	—
Common stock issued for acquired companies	—	495.5	—
Common stock issued for employee stock plans	20.3	(5.4)	—
Proceeds from long-term debt	1,104.0	439.9	—
Repayment of long-term debt	(647.3)	(127.5)	(26.2)
Net increase (decrease) in short-term borrowings	(266.0)	264.8	169.1
Net decrease in securities agreements repurchased and resold	(404.0)	—	—
Treasury stock reissued, net of purchases	25.3	25.2	(54.3)
Dividends, acquisitions and financing transactions	(626.1)	(108.3)	(324.5)
Increase (decrease) in cash and invested cash	$ 136.9	$ 172.2	$ (135.4)

See accompanying notes which include the summarized Group financial statements.

EXHIBIT 4

SEARS ROEBUCK & CO.
Notes to Consolidated Financial Statements

Summary of significant accounting policies

Basis of presentation
The consolidated financial statements include the accounts of Sears, Roebuck and Co. and all domestic and significant international companies in which the company has more than a 50 per cent equity ownership, except those engaged in manufacturing.

Included as an integral part of the consolidated financial statements are, beginning on page 45, separate summarized financial statements and notes for each of the company's business groups as well as the significant accounting policies unique to each group. Unaudited supplemental financial information regarding inflation is presented on pages 60 and 61.

Certain reclassifications have been made in the 1981 and 1980 financial statements to conform to current accounting classifications.

Basis for assignment of debt and related interest expense
Debt and the related interest expense have been assigned to the business groups as incurred by those groups. Corporate debt is legally the responsibility of Sears, Roebuck and Co., Sears Roebuck Acceptance Corp. (SRAC) or Sears Overseas Finance N.V.; the debt financing decisions of these units arise from Corporate decisions. A portion of the pooled Corporate debt is allocated on a consistent basis to credit operations to the extent necessary to finance domestic customer receivables. The remaining portion of Corporate debt has not been allocated to the business groups but has been combined with internally generated funds for various purposes such as dividends, acquisitions, non-portfolio investments and stock repurchases.

Income taxes
The results of operations of the business groups, except life insurance and international operations, are included in the consolidated federal income tax return of Sears, Roebuck and Co. Tax liabilities and benefits are allocated as generated by the respective business groups, whether or not such benefits would be currently available on a separate return basis. U.S. income and foreign withholding taxes are not provided on unremitted earnings of international affiliates which the company considers to be permanent investments. The cumulative amount of unremitted income of $165.5 million at Dec. 31, 1982 would require additional tax payments of $35.2 million, if remitted.

The investment tax credit is reflected as a reduction in current income taxes (flow-through method).

Property and depreciation
Depreciation is provided principally by the straight-line method.

Goodwill
Other assets include goodwill of $349.9 million at Dec. 31, 1982. Goodwill represents the excess of the purchase price over the fair value of the net assets of businesses acquired and is being amortized on a straight-line basis over forty years.

1. Retirement plans
Expenses for retirement benefit plans were as follows:

millions	Year Ended December 31		
	1982	1981	1980
Pension plans	$251.3	$259.0	$263.1
Contribution to The Savings and Profit Sharing Fund of Sears Employees	68.1	37.2	40.6
Retirement incentive	—	—	66.7
Other plans	18.6	19.4	12.2
Total	$338.0	$315.6	$382.6

Pension
Substantially all full-time domestic employees and certain part-time employees are eligible to participate in noncontributory defined benefit pension plans after meeting age and service requirements. Pension benefits are based on length of service, average annual compensation and, in certain plans, Social Security benefits. The company expenses and funds the current costs of its qualified pension plans.

Plan benefits and net assets for the company's domestic defined benefit pension plans, as of Jan. 1, 1982 and 1981, are as follows:

millions	1982	1981
Plan benefits		
Vested	$1,297.7	$1,478.1
Non-vested	120.7	125.5
Total plan benefits	$1,418.4	$1,603.6
Net assets available for plan benefits	$1,440.4	$1,379.4

Vested and non-vested plan benefits represent the actuarially computed present value of pension benefits which employees have earned based upon compensation and length of service, assuming voluntary termination of employment as of Jan. 1, 1982 and 1981 (vested benefits), or have accrued irrespective of vesting provisions of the plan (total plan benefits). The assumed rate of return used in determining the present value of plan benefits was eight per cent in 1982 and six per cent in prior years. The change in this rate caused a decrease in the present value of total plan benefits of approximately $350 million in 1982.

During 1982, the Company reviewed and modified certain demographic, actuarial and financial assumptions used to determine the annual contributions to its pension plans. Changes in the rate of employee withdrawal from the company, the assumed rate of return on the investment portfolio and other actuarial assumptions resulted in a decrease in the 1982 pension cost of approximately $50 million.

EXHIBIT 4 *(continued)*

The company has several non-qualified un-funded pension plans to supplement the primary pension plans. These additional plans ensure that retired employees can be paid their total accrued benefits under the benefit formula.

Profit sharing

Employees of Sears, Roebuck and Co., Allstate and certain domestic subsidiaries are eligible to become members of The Savings and Profit Sharing Fund of Sears Employees. The company contributes six per cent of consolidated income, as defined, before federal income taxes and profit sharing contributions. The company contribution is allocated to the business groups and Corporate based on six per cent of their respective earnings or losses.

Retirement incentive

In September 1980, Sears, Roebuck and Co. offered an early retirement incentive plan to selected management employees in Corporate and the Sears Merchandise Group.

2. Supplementary income statement information

millions	Year Ended December 31		
	1982	1981	1980
Advertising costs (excluding catalog)	$719.7	$680.1	$586.0
Maintenance and repairs	195.3	185.2	187.3
Taxes, other than payroll and income			
Premiums	129.8	118.4	107.5
Property	143.3	120.2	118.5
Other	109.6	106.6	89.7
Provision for uncollectible accounts	121.7	130.2	117.0
Realized foreign currency exchange losses, net of profit sharing and income taxes	(38.4)	(7.4)	(17.3)
Interest capitalized	13.4	17.5	15.9

3. Quarterly results (unaudited)

millions, except per share data

Quarter	Total revenues	Operating income	Realized capital gains and other	Net income	Net income per share
1982 Fourth	$8,872.1	$667.2[1]	$41.8	$459.4	$1.31
Third	7,508.2	238.4	(33.4)	166.7	.48
Second	7,203.4	143.6	30.5	163.7	.47
First	6,436.1	(38.6)	31.8	71.4	.20
1981 Fourth	$8,033.5	$458.0[1]	$13.5	$333.1	$1.05
Third	6,826.3	43.8	69.3	129.7	.42
Second	6,662.2	88.4	35.3	134.5	.42
First	5,835.4	(128.1)	65.5	52.8	.17
1980 Fourth	$7,620.6	$470.8	$14.5	$339.7	$1.07
Third	6,314.1	127.1	12.8	131.4	.42
Second	5,860.3	46.4	8.5	79.2	.25
First	5,366.0	(17.7)	26.0	59.5	.19

[1] Fourth quarter LIFO adjustments were credits of $103.3 million and $32.7 million in 1982 and 1981, respectively, compared to charges of $75.9 million and $127.0 million for the first nine months of the respective years.

4. Income taxes

Income before income taxes, equity in net income of unconsolidated companies and minority interest is as follows:

millions	Year Ended December 31		
	1982	1981	1980
Domestic	$1,080.1	$615.8	$646.2
Foreign	1.2	29.9	42.2
Total	$1,081.3	$645.7	$688.4

Federal, state and foreign income taxes include:

millions	Year Ended December 31		
	1982	1981	1980
Provision			
Current			
Domestic	$142.5	$ 30.3	$176.8
Investment tax credit	(34.6)	(21.0)	(18.3)
Foreign	6.6	16.7	15.6
Total current	114.5	26.0	174.1
Deferred			
Current			
Installment sales	62.0	(44.1)	(68.4)
Pension expense	14.9	12.5	23.9
Maintenance agreement income	(10.0)	(14.5)	(16.5)
Retirement incentive	10.9	8.0	(33.0)
Other	10.5	5.6	10.9
Long-term			
Depreciation	24.1	13.9	8.6
Life insurance reserves	9.5	19.9	5.3
Other	(4.8)	(17.2)	(6.2)
Total deferred	117.1	(15.9)	(75.4)
Financial statement income tax provision	$231.6	$ 10.1	$ 98.7
Classification			
Federal income tax			
Current	$ 81.2	$ (4.9)	$160.2
Deferred	104.8	.5	(66.4)
State income tax			
Current	26.7	14.2	(1.7)
Deferred	8.9	.4	(10.4)
Foreign income tax			
Current	6.6	16.7	15.6
Deferred	3.4	(16.8)	1.4
Financial statement income tax provision	$231.6	$ 10.1	$ 98.7

A reconciliation of the statutory federal income tax rate to the effective income tax rate is as follows:

millions	Year Ended December 31		
	1982	1981	1980
Statutory federal income tax rate	46.0%	46.0%	46.0%
State income taxes, net of federal income taxes	1.8	1.2	(.2)
Tax exempt income	(17.8)	(24.2)	(19.7)
Dividends received exclusion	(5.5)	(9.1)	(6.7)
Investment tax credit	(3.2)	(3.2)	(2.7)
Capital gains deduction	(2.6)	(5.5)	(.2)
Consolidated tax return adjustment	—	(2.7)	—
Other	2.7	(.9)	(2.2)
Effective income tax rate	21.4%	1.6%	14.3%

EXHIBIT 4 *(continued)*

5. Corporate

Corporate operations include revenues and expenses which are of an overall holding company nature, including that portion of administrative costs and interest which is not allocated to the company's business groups. The Corporate statements of income consist of:

millions	Year Ended December 31		
	1982	1981	1980
Revenues	$119.5	$105.1	$ 87.8
Interest expense	272.7	284.6	223.7
Operating expenses	120.1	66.2	58.4
Operating loss	(273.3)	(245.7)	(194.3)
Other (income) expense	(.2)	(22.4)	2.1
Income tax benefit	139.9	119.9	99.9
Net corporate expense	(133.2)	(103.4)	(96.5)
Equity in net income of business groups	994.4	753.5	706.3
Consolidated net income	$861.2	$650.1	$609.8

6. Leases

The company leases certain stores, office facilities, computers and automotive equipment.

Operating and capital lease obligations are based upon contractual minimum rates and, for certain stores, amounts in excess of these minimum rates are payable based upon specified percentages of sales. Certain leases include renewal or purchase options. Operating lease rentals were $332.1, $244.7 and $225.2 million, including contingent rentals of $38.5, $40.1 and $37.0 million, for the years ended Dec. 31, 1982, 1981 and 1980.

Minimum fixed lease obligations, excluding taxes, insurance and other expenses payable directly by the company, for leases in effect as of Dec. 31, 1982 are:

millions	Capital leases	Operating leases
1983	$ 23.1	$ 212.2
1984	16.7	181.0
1985	16.4	137.5
1986	16.0	109.8
1987	15.4	89.4
After 1987	177.9	604.5
Minimum payments	265.5	$1,334.4
Executory costs (principally taxes)	65.2	
Implicit interest	83.8	
Present value of minimum lease payments, principally long-term	$116.5	

7. Acquisitions

Effective Dec. 31, 1981, Sears, Roebuck and Co. acquired Dean Witter Financial Services Inc. and Coldwell, Banker & Company for a total cost, including expenses and $22.0 million expended in prior years, of $610.1 million and $201.9 million, respectively. The acquisitions were accounted for by the purchase method and, accordingly, the operations of the acquired companies are included in the consolidated financial statements since the date of acquisition. The unaudited pro forma combined results of operations, assuming both acquisitions had occurred on Jan. 1, 1980 and after giving effect to the issuance of stock, interest on cash expended, amortization of goodwill, additional depreciation of revalued assets and exclusion of certain nonrecurring acquisition-related expenses, are as follows:

millions, except per share data	Sears as reported	Pro forma combined
1981: Operating revenues	$27,357.4	$28,666.7
Net income	650.1	654.7
Net income per share	2.06	1.88
1980: Operating revenues	25,161.0	26,273.3
Net income	609.8	633.1
Net income per share	1.93	1.82

8. Short-term borrowings consist of:

millions	December 31	
	1982	1981
Commercial paper	$1,842.1	$1,845.5
Agreements with bank trust departments	634.2	701.2
Bank loans	284.7	553.7
Other loans (principally foreign)	59.1	133.0
Total short-term borrowings	$2,820.1	$3,233.4

The company had unused lines of bank credit approximating $6.0 billion and a $2.0 billion dollar revolving credit agreement through SRAC with a group of banks at Dec. 31, 1982. Domestic credit lines are renewable annually at various dates and provide for loans of varying maturities at the prime rate. The company maintains informal compensating balances or pays commitment fees in connection with certain lines of credit. There are no material restrictions on the use of funds constituting compensating balances.

At Dec. 31, 1982, the revolving credit agreement supports $2.0 billion of commercial paper that has been classified as long-term debt. SRAC intends to maintain more than $2.0 billion of commercial paper outstanding during the next twelve months. If needed, SRAC can refinance this debt on a long-term basis using the revolving credit agreement.

EXHIBIT 4 *(continued)*

9. Long-term debt was as follows:

millions		December 31	
Issue		1982	1981
Sears, Roebuck and Co.			
4¾% Sinking Fund Debentures, due 1983	$	70.0	$ 86.0
13½% Note, due 1984		50.0	50.0
7¾% Debentures, due 1985		250.0	250.0
14⅛% Notes, due 1989		250.0	250.0
13¼% Notes, due 1992		250.0	—
6⅜% Sinking Fund Debentures, due 1993		64.3	69.0
8⅝% Sinking Fund Debentures, due 1995		91.8	97.5
6% Debentures, $300 million face value, due 2000, effective rate 14.75%		137.2	—
7% Debentures, $300 million face value, due 2001, effective rate 14.6%		154.9	153.4
8% Sinking Fund Debentures, due 2006		214.5	232.3
7⅞% Sinking Fund Debentures, due 2007		261.4	277.1
Capitalized lease obligations		116.5	123.0
Sears Roebuck Acceptance Corp.			
Commercial paper backed by revolving credit agreement		2,000.0	2,000.0
Variable interest notes 8.79% Notes (13.83% at Dec. 31, 1981), payable 13 months after demand		447.0	675.0
13.73% 400 day demand note		—	25.0
5% Debentures, due 1982		—	50.0
8⅜% Debentures, due 1986		125.0	125.0
9½% to 9¾% Notes, due 1982–1989		107.8	109.4
14⅛% to 14⅝% Notes, due 1984–1989		250.0	—
9⅝% Notes, due 1984–1991		56.5	63.0
Sears Overseas Finance N.V.			
9% Guaranteed Notes, due 1982		—	150.0
6½% Yen Bonds, Series No. 1, due 1984		85.4	91.1
10¼% Dutch Guilder Guaranteed Notes, due 1987		38.0	—
6½% Swiss Franc Guaranteed Notes, due 1988		99.8	—
13½% Notes, due 1990		6.6	—
Zero Coupon Guaranteed Notes, $400 million face value, due 1992, effective rate 15%		111.8	—
Zero Coupon Guaranteed Bonds, $400 million face value, due 1994, effective rate 12.826%		101.2	—
13⅞% Guaranteed Notes, due 1988, with warrants to purchase $193.4 million guaranteed notes due 1990 at 13½%		100.0	—
Allstate Financial Corporation			
9⅝% Senior Notes, due 1986		50.0	50.0
7⅞% Senior Notes, due 1987		75.0	75.0
8⅛% Subordinated Notes, due 1987		25.0	25.0
8½% Subordinated Notes, due 1984–1997		20.0	20.0
Homart Development Co.			
11½% Notes, due 1985–1990		20.1	—
8¼% to 9⅞% Mortgage notes, due 1991 to 2013		132.3	193.1
Dean Witter Reynolds Inc.			
Notes payable to banks		—	14.3
Coldwell, Banker & Company			
6% to 14½% Mortgages, due 1984–2007		12.8	6.4
6% to 20% Notes, due 1984–2001		18.6	23.0
6¾% to 9% Subordinated Convertible Debentures		2.0	2.2
International Subsidiaries			
Notes payable to banks		20.6	37.8
Total long-term debt		$5,816.1	$5,323.6

As of Dec. 31, 1982, long-term debt maturities, excluding $350.0 million of notes payable 13 months or more after demand which have no specified maturities and commercial paper which is classified as long-term debt, are as follows:

Year Ending December 31	millions
1983	$213.0
1984	236.5
1985	464.4
1986	212.3
1987	232.1

During 1982 and 1981 the company exchanged common shares for $36.9 million and $40.6 million principal amounts of long-term debt, resulting in gains of approximately $16.4 and $16.0 million.

10. Pending legal proceedings

Various legal actions and governmental proceedings are pending against Sears, Roebuck and Co. and its subsidiaries, many involving ordinary routine litigation incidental to the businesses engaged in. Other matters contain allegations which are nonroutine and involve compensatory, punitive or antitrust treble damage claims for very large amounts, as well as other types of relief. The consequences of these matters are not presently determinable but, in the opinion of management, the ultimate liability resulting, if any, will not have a material effect on the shareholders' equity of the company.

11. Shareholders' equity

Dividend payments are restricted by several statutory and contractual factors, including:

Certain indentures relating to the long-term debt of Sears, Roebuck and Co., which represent the most restrictive contractual limitation on the payment of dividends, provide that the company cannot take specified actions, including the declaration of cash dividends, which would cause its consolidated unencumbered assets, as defined, to fall below 150 per cent of its consolidated liabilities, as defined. At Dec. 31, 1982 and 1981, $948.9 million and $1.1 billion, respectively, in retained income could be paid in dividends to shareholders under the most restrictive indenture.

The Illinois Insurance Holding Company Systems Act permits Allstate Insurance Company to pay dividends to Sears, Roebuck and Co. during any twelve month period in an amount up to the greater of 10 per cent of surplus (as regards policyholders) or its net investment income (as defined) as of the preceding Dec. 31. Approximately $604.0 million of Allstate's retained income at Dec. 31, 1982 has no restriction relating to distribution during 1983 which would require prior approval of the Illinois Department of Insurance.

EXHIBIT 4 *(concluded)*

The capital of International, Allstate Life Insurance Company and Allstate Savings and Loan Association at Dec. 31, 1982 includes approximately $410.5 million which, if distributed, would be subject to income taxes. It is not contemplated that such amounts will be distributed in a manner which would create additional tax liabilities.

Dean Witter Reynolds Inc. is subject to the Securities and Exchange Commission's Uniform Net Capital Rule and the New York Stock Exchange's Growth and Business Capital Rule. Under these rules the declaration of dividends may be restricted. At Dec. 31, 1982, approximately $93.8 million was available for the declaration of dividends to Sears, Roebuck and Co.

As of Dec. 31, 1982, subsidiary companies can remit to Sears, Roebuck and Co. in the form of dividends approximately $2.3 billion, after payment of all related taxes, without prior approval of regulatory bodies or violation of contractual restrictions.

Employee stock options: The company adopted a new employee stock option plan in 1982 in which six million shares were made available for grant as incentive stock options (which receive special tax treatment) or nonstatutory stock options. Incentive stock options related to approximately 86,700 shares and nonstatutory options related to approximately 151,850 shares were granted during 1982 at $18.44 to $19.00 per share.

Optionees under the 1982 Plan may also be granted the right to surrender all or a portion of their exercisable options in exchange for a cash payment in an amount equal to the excess of the fair market value over the option price. In addition, Sears, Roebuck and Co. or its subsidiaries may pay to the optionee in connection with certain options or rights, an amount generally equal to 46 per cent (or such lower maximum corporate federal income tax rate as is then in effect) of the difference between the option price and the market value of the shares acquired. All of these cash payments are subject to the consent of the Compensation Committee.

Changes in stock options for the three years ended Dec. 31, 1982 are as follows:

thousands of shares	Year Ended December 31		
	1982	1981	1980
Beginning balance	13,826.9	11,345.1	11,850.5
Granted	238.6 (a)	5,180.6	5,240.4
Exercised	(890.3)(b)	(13.9)	—
Cancelled or expired	(603.5)(c)	(2,684.9)	(5,745.8)
Ending balance	12,571.7 (d)	13,826.9	11,345.1
Reserved for future grant	8,577.7 (e)	2,579.3	5,030.3
Exercisable	6,744.0	5,246.8	5,878.5

(a) Consists of 204.2 thousand options granted at $19.00 and 34.4 thousand at $18.44, all under the 1982 Plan.

(b) Consists of 44.4 thousand shares under the 1967 Plan at a price of $26.10, 103.1 thousand shares under the 1972 Plan at a price from $15.94 to $26.10, 241.8 thousand shares under the 1978 Plan at a price from $16.25 to $24.94, 473.0 thousand shares assumed in connection with the acquisition of Coldwell Banker at a price from $4.97 to $7.00 and 28.0 thousand stock appreciation rights exercised under the Coldwell Banker Plan with an option price from $4.97 to $7.00.

(c) The options that expired in 1982 were previously granted a. prices ranging from $4.97 to $33.29.

(d) Consists of 905.9, 7,395.0, 3,929.4, 238.6 and 102.8 thousand shares under the 1967, 1972, 1978, 1982 and Coldwell Banker Plans, respectively. 149.5, 238.6 and 61.8 thousand shares under the 1978, 1982 and Coldwell Banker Plans, respectively, have stock appreciation rights attached.

(e) Shares reserved for future grant total 2,816.2 thousand for the 1978 Plan and 5,761.5 thousand for the 1982 Plan.

The expiration dates of options outstanding at Dec. 31, 1982 ranged from April 21, 1983 to May 1, 1994. The weighted average purchase price per share was $26.10, $21.33, $16.94, $18.92 and $6.30 for outstanding options under the 1967, 1972, 1978, 1982 and Coldwell Banker Plans, respectively. On Dec. 31, 1982, there were 15,600 optionees.

EXHIBIT 5

SEARS ROEBUCK AND CO.
Shareholder Investment Information

Common Stock Market Information
(Unaudited)

	First Quarter		Second Quarter		Third Quarter		Fourth Quarter		Year	
	1982	1981	1982	1981	1982	1981	1982	1981	1982	1981
Market price per share										
High	19⅛	18¾	20¾	20¾	24¼	19⅛	32	18⅛	32	20¾
Low	15¾	14⅞	18½	18⅛	18⅛	15⅝	22⅛	15½	15¾	14⅞
Closing	19	18⅜	19⅜	19¼	22⅜	16⅛	30⅛	16⅛	30⅛	16⅛
Price/earnings ratios (high-low)									13-6	10-7
Dividends per share	.34	.34	.34	.34	.34	.34	.34	.34	1.36	1.36
Dividend payout per cent									55.3	66.0

Stock exchange listings
New York
Midwest, Chicago
Pacific, San Francisco
London, England

Ticker symbol—S
Switzerland:
Basel
Geneva
Lausanne
Zurich

Dividends

The payment of future dividends to shareholders is dependent on business conditions, income, the cash requirements of the company and other factors (see note 11, page 42). The Finance Committee reviews these factors and recommends changes to the Board of Directors. The board determines dividends per share of common stock which are consistent with earnings and the financial condition of the company. Cash dividends have been paid on common shares in every year since 1934. During the past 10 fiscal years, Sears, Roebuck and Co. annual dividend payments have ranged from 36.7 per cent to 70.8 per cent of net income.

Shareholders

Shareholders as of Nov. 19, 1982, record date for the January 1983 dividend, are as follows:

Type of shareholder	Number of share- holders	Number of shares	Average per share- holder	Per cent of total shares
Individuals				
Women	137,914	48,200,667	349	13.7
Men	106,634	45,368,445	425	12.9
Joint tenants	68,905	19,182,914	278	5.5
Bank nominees	2,019	141,948,557	70,306	40.4
Investment organizations	31,668	11,056,023	349	3.1
Brokers	293	12,440,853	42,460	3.5
Corporations and firms	1,253	2,270,282	1,812	.7
Other	1,605	2,393,635	1,491	.7
Employees' Profit Sharing Fund	1	68,266,781		19.5
Total	350,292	351,128,157		100.0

Teledyne, Inc. (B)*

On May 9, 1984, Teledyne, Inc. issued a tender offer to repurchase 5 million shares of its outstanding common stock for $1 billion. If successful, the repurchase would be the largest in New York Stock Exchange history. Prior to the offer, Teledyne's common, which had a par value of $1, had been trading at $155 per share. The market reaction to the offer was both sharp and sudden—the price soared $32.375 on the following day to close at $187.75.

Henry Singleton, Teledyne's chairman and cofounder, declined to give any reason for the tender offer or the large premium (28.4 percent) that was offered. Singleton was also a major stakeholder in Teledyne, owning 1.6 million shares, or 7.9 percent of the shares outstanding.

At the end of the first quarter of 1984, the book value of Teledyne's stock was $131.60 a share. While sales were up 24 percent in this quarter over the previous year, net income was down nearly 50 percent. Losses from Teledyne's casualty insurance subsidiaries were apparently largely responsible for the profit decline.

TENDER OFFER

Under the terms of the tender offer, Teledyne agreed to repurchase up to 5 million of its shares at a price of $200 per share. The company indicated, however, that, if more than 5 million shares were tendered, it may purchase all or any portion of the additional shares tendered. If less than all of the excess shares tendered were purchased, the shares would be acquired on a pro rata basis. The offer expired on May 31, 1984.

Teledyne was not unfamiliar with this type of transaction. Since 1972, the company had made seven different tender or exchange offers for its own shares:

Date	Transaction
1972	● Repurchased 8.9 million shares at $20 per share.
1973	● Repurchased 1.6 million shares at $14 per share.
June 1974	● Accquired 3.8 million shares in exchange for $20 principal amount of 10 percent debentures.

---

* This case was prepared by Kenneth R. Ferris. Copyright © 1985 by Kenneth R. Ferris. All rights reserved to the author.

Date	Transaction
December 1974	● Acquired 1.9 million shares in exchange for $16 principal amount of 10 percent debentures.
1975	● Repurchased 3.6 million shares at $18 per share.
1976	● Repurchased 2.5 million shares at $40 per share.
1980	● Acquired 3.0 million shares (market value of $131 per share) in exchange for $160 principal amount of 10 percent debentures.

In the past, Teledyne had always received more shares than it had sought in its offers, and the company had always purchased or acquired the additional shares.

In its statement filed with the Securities and Exchange Commission on May 14, 1984, Teledyne indicated that it planned to use internally generated funds to finance the stock repurchase, but it reserved the right "to borrow a portion of the funds from banks or other financial institutions." At the end of the first quarter of 1984, the company had cash and marketable securities on hand totaling over $865 million, with other funds available through the cash flow of its insurance subsidiaries and its stock holdings in other public companies, such as Litton Industries, Inc., Curtiss-Wright Corporation, and Kidde, Inc.

EPILOGUE

On May 31, 1984, Teledyne announced that it would purchase and then retire all of the 8.7 million shares that were tendered in response to its May 9 offer. The reported cost was $1.74 billion for the 43 percent of its 20.4 million outstanding shares that were tendered.

On Wall Street analyst predicted that, by reducing its total shares outstanding to 11.7 million, Teledyne would boost its 1985 earnings by approximately $7.75 per share, or to $32 per share.

On June 12, 1984, Moody's Investor Services, Inc. announced that it had lowered the rating on Teledyne's senior debt from Baa-1 to Baa-2 and on its subordinated debt to Baa-3 from Baa-2, as a result of the company's share repurchase. A Moody's representative noted: "This action will reduce Teledyne's equity by 42 percent and increase the leverage ratio."

By mid-September 1984, Teledyne common shares were trading at $302—the highest price stock on the New York Stock Exchange.

QUESTIONS

1. How would you account for the Teledyne share repurchase of May 1984? How would you account for the debt-for-stock exchange of 1980?

2. Why do companies repurchase their own shares? Why do you think Teledyne is repurchasing its stock?

3. Do you agree with the decision by Moody's to lower Teledyne's debt rating?

PART FIVE

Funds Flow and Financial Statement Analysis

Working Capital and Cash Flows

CASE 5.1 _____

Stirling Homex Corporation*

In 1967, the Stirling Homex Corporation was founded by David and William Stirling. The two brothers had pioneered the concept of modular housing, which employed many of the mass-production techniques developed in the automobile industry. Because of the substantial savings in labor cost due to mass production, the company estimated that it could build a modular home, exclusive of land, at a cost of between $16,000 and $25,000.

Because of low construction costs and the ability to erect entire housing projects on site in very short periods of time, the company developed close ties with federal, state, and local housing authorities that were in search of ways to provide housing for low-income groups. In 1968, for example, the company constructed a 275-unit housing project in Rochester, New York, in just 36 hours. Two years later, the company won a U.S. Department of Housing and Urban Development (HUD) contract to construct a 13-story apartment building in Memphis, Tennessee. Shortly thereafter, the company also announced that it had a "tentative understanding" with the Greater Gulfport (Mississippi) Housing Development Corporation to build over $100 million of modular housing for moderate and lower income families.

In February 1970, Stirling Homex went public. The offering prospectus reported earnings of $1 million on sales of $10 million for fiscal year 1969. The public offering opened on the market at $16.50 per share. By mid-March, the stock was selling in excess of $51 per share.

The 1971 annual report provided more good news: Stirling Homex would market its products to a broader consumer spectrum—hotels, motels, colleges and universities, and to private consumers. During that same year the company reported that it had also doubled its manufacturing facilities and created the U.S. Shelter Corporation,

---

* This case was prepared by Kenneth R. Ferris and M. Edgar Barrett. The idea for the case is taken from an earlier case (Stirling Homex 9-173-193) written by Professor Barrett while at the Harvard Business School. Copyright © 1985 by M. Edgar Barrett and Kenneth R. Ferris. All rights reserved to the authors.

a wholly owned subsidiary to provide construction and permanent financing for its customers. As anticipated, record earnings per share ($0.37) were achieved in 1971 (see financial statements, Exhibits 1–5).

On July 10, 1972, however, the Stirling Homex Corporation filed for bankruptcy under Chapter 10 of the Federal Bankruptcy Act. When the company collapsed, some 10,000 modular units were found sealed in plastic and stored in fields around the United States; the value of the units ranged between $35 million and $65 million. Full payment, however, existed for only 900 of those units. The back-log of uninstalled modules had grown from 3,500 as of April 1971, to 6,700 at December 1971, to over 9,000 units as of July 1972. Evidence gathered in the months following the July bankruptcy filing raised questions concerning the firm's method of recognizing revenue.

REVENUE RECOGNITION

Stirling Homex Corporation recognized revenue from the sale of many of its modular units when production was completed. The company did this in those cases where the unit was assigned to a specific contract and if there was an identified site plan and a financially capable purchaser. The company did not, however, require progress payments from its buyers or demand that the housing site itself be approved by the purchaser. Some of these "contracts" were in the form of "leters of intention to buy" from various institutions. These tentative buyers included public housing authorities, whose final decisions were often delayed by such things as the necessity of seeking voter approval through public referenda.

According to corporate insiders, the company's profit margin came primarily from the production of modular units. Revenues from installation operations, on the other hand, were recognized on a percentage of completion basis and were allocated on an estimated break-even point. Neither the February 1970 offering prospectus nor the July 1970 annual report provided a breakdown of revenues and costs between production and installation. The 1970 annual report stated that "contracts generally provided for payment upon completion and receipt of all approvals necessary for occupancy, or for payment upon completion of each respective phase." Because most of its receivables were due from public housing authorities, no provision for doubtful accounts was considered necessary.

EPILOGUE

In July 1975, the Securities and Exchange Commission released the results of its investigation of the Stirling Homex Corporation:

> The consolidated statements of income of Stirling Homex for the seven-month period ended February 28, 1971, included in the registration statement for the preferred stock and the consolidated statements of income of Stirling Homex for the year ended July 31, 1971, contained in the Annual Report to Shareholders and Annual Report on Form 10-K for such fiscal year were false and misleading in that among other things:
>
> ● All modular sales of $12,493,000 for the February 28, 1971, period and $25,292,600 out of total modular sales of $29,482,271 for the July 31, 1971, period were improperly recorded in that the purported sales were not supported by required financing commitments.
> ● Installation sales were overstated by approximately $3,723,000 out of a total reported installation sales of $5,137,000 for the February 28, 1971, period and

EXHIBIT 1

STIRLING HOMEX CORPORATION
Consolidated Balance Sheet July 31, 1971,
With Comparative Figures for 1970

Assets

	1971	1970
Current assets:		
Cash (Note 11)	$ 3,196,457	$ 2,778,077
Preferred stock proceeds receivable (Note 2)	19,000,000	—
Receivables (Notes 1 and 3)	37,845,572	15,486,119
Inventories (Note 5):		
Raw materials, work in process and salable		
merchandise at lower of cost (first-in,		
first-out) or replacement market.	2,614,200	2,167,603
Land held for development or sale, at cost	1,878,343	1,583,621
Prepaid expenses and other current assets	226,530	124,765
Total current assets	64,761,102	22,140,185
Investment in unconsolidated subsidiary (Note 1)	1,134,579	—
Long-term receivables (Note 4)	4,225,349	541,124
Property, plant, and equipment at cost, less		
accumulated depreciation and amortization:		
1971—$733,705; 1970—$230,921 (Notes 6 and 8)	9,426,941	5,245,745
Deferred charges, less accumulated amortization:		
1971—$586,011; 1970—$153,894 (Note 7)	2,558,792	944,109
	$82,106,763	$28,871,163

Liabilities and Stockholders' Equity

	1971	1970
Current liabilities:		
Current portion of long-term debt (Note 8)	$ 295,630	333,036
Notes payable to banks-unsecured (1971—6 to		
6½%; 1970—8 to 8½%) (Note 11).	37,700,000	11,700,000
Accounts payable.	4,025,254	2,480,834
Due to unconsolidated subsidiary (Note 1)	76,894	—
Accrued expenses and other liabilities	577,377	232,819
Current and deferred income taxes (Note 9)	3,528,125	1,387,338
Total current liabilities	46,203,280	16,134,027
Long-term debt (Note 8)	236,588	496,489
Deferred income taxes (Note 9).	2,098,767	587,265
Option deposit on land contract (Note 5)	235,000	—
Stockholders' equity:		
$2.40 cumulative convertible preferred stock		
(Note 2): Authorized 500,000 shares, $1.00		
par value; shares subscribed: 1971—500,000		
(aggregate involuntary liquidation value—		
$20,000,000); 1970—none	500,000	—
Common stock (Notes 2 and 10)		
Authorized 15,000,000 shares, $0.01 par		
value; shares issued: 1971—8,909,200;		
1970—8,897,400.	89,092	88,974
Additional paid-in capital (Note 2)	26,554,453	8,446,738
Retained earnings	6,370,333	3,117,670
	33,513,878	11,653,382
Less treasury stock at cost (60,000 shares)	180,750	—
Total stockholders' equity	33,333,128	11,653,382
Commitments and contingencies (Note 11)		
	$82,106,763	28,871,163

See accompanying Notes to Consolidated Financial Statements.

EXHIBIT 2

STIRLING HOMEX CORPORATION
Consolidated Statement of Income
Year Ended July 31, 1971, with Comparative Figures for 1970

	1971	1970
Revenues:		
Manufacturing division—trade (Note 3)	$29,482,271	$16,492,770
Installation division (Note 3):		
Trade	7,230,878	5,601,357
Affiliate	—	459,941
Equity in undistributed net income of		
subsidiary (Note 1).	134,579	—
Total revenues.	36,847,728	22,554,068
Cost and expenses:		
Cost of sales:		
Manufacturing division.	17,729,078	9,919,327
Installation division.	6,601,413	5,240,388
Administrative and selling expenses.	4,048,113	2,390,604
Interest expense.	1,838,461	648,181
Total costs and expenses.	30,217,065	18,198,500
Income before federal and state income taxes.	6,630,663	4,355,568
Federal and state income taxes (Note 9):		
Current.	368,000	1,965,982
Deferred	3,010,000	354,397
	3,378,000	2,320,379
Net income.	$ 3,252,663	$ 2,035,189
Average common shares outstanding (Note 12)	8,881,938	8,649,483
Earnings per common share (Note 12)	$ 0.37	$ 0.24

See accompanying Notes to Consolidated Financial Statements.

$2,443,000 out of total installation sales of $7,200,000 for the July 31, 1971, period through the inclusion of sales from projects for which there were no commitments of financing and through Stirling Homex's improper reporting of approximately $1,000,000 as of February 26, 1971, and approximately $2,000,000 as of July 31, 1971, of excess installation costs as "cost overruns" reimbursable to the company.

- General, administrative, and other expenses were materially understated by approximately $832,000 as of February 28, 1971, and approximately $1,000,000 as of February 28, 1971, and approximately $1,000,000 as of July 31, 1971, as a result of the improper capitalizing of such expenses. Additionally, certain other expenses and construction costs were improperly capitalized.

On January 29, 1977, David and William Stirling were found guilty on nine counts of fraud; they were sentenced on March 11, 1977.

QUESTIONS

1. Comment on the "fairness' of Stirling Homex's method of recognizing revenue and its allocation of profit between the manufacturing and installations divisions.

2. Comment on Note 7 in Exhibit 5.

3. What other financial reporting issues are present in this case? List and comment briefly.

EXHIBIT 3

STIRLING HOMEX CORPORATION
Consolidated Statement of Changes in Financial Position
Year Ended July 31, 1971, with Comparative Figures for 1970

	1971	1970
Source of working capital:		
Net income.	$ 3,252,663	2,035,189
Expenses not requiring outlay of working capital:		
Depreciation and amortization	529,116	220,227
Amortization of deferred charges.	432,117	133,288
Deferred income taxes (noncurrent)	1,511,502	184,776
Undistributed net income of finance subsidiary	(134,579)	—
Working capital provided from operations	5,590,819	2,573,480
Net proceeds from sales of stock:		
Public offering of common stock.	—	5,985,715
Private sale of common stock	—	516,500
Common stock issued under qualified stock		
option plan	37,200	—
Public offering of preferred stock.	18,570,633	—
Long-term borrowings	51,402	124,677
Decrease in long-term receivables	10,000	43,421
Option deposit received on land contact.	235,000	—
Total source of working capital	24,495,054	9,243,793
Application of working capital:		
Purchase of treasury stock	180,750	—
Additions to property, plant, and equipment.	4,710,312	4,422,506
Additions to deferred charges.	2,046,800	735,093
Reduction in long-term debt.	311,303	3,052,140
Increase in noncurrent portion of long-term		
receivables	3,694,225	—
Investment in unconsolidated subsidiary.	1,000,000	—
Total application of working capital	11,943,390	8,209,739
Increase in working capital.	$12,551,664	1,034,054
Changes in working capital:		
Increase in current assets:		
Cash	$ 418,380	$ 1,357,917
Preferred stock proceeds receivable.	19,000,000	—
Receivables.	22,359,453	12,286,631
Inventories.	741,319	1,236,215
Prepaid expenses and other current assets	101,765	34,973
	42,620,971	14,915,736
Increase in current liabilities:		
Current portion of long-term debt and notes		
payable to banks.	25,962,594	10,721,700
Accounts payable and accrued expenses.	1,888,978	2,155,635
Due to unconsolidated subsidiary	76,894	—
Current and deferred income taxes	2,140,787	1,004,347
	30,069,253	13,881,682
Increase in working capital.	$12,551,664	$1,034,054

During the year ended July 31, 1971, the company assigned $4,650,000 of its accounts receivable, without recourse, to an unconsolidated subsidiary for which that subsidiary paid $4,650,000 to the company. See Note 1.

See accompanying Notes to Consolidated Financial Statements.

EXHIBIT 4

STIRLING HOMEX CORPORATION
Consolidated Statement of Additional Paid-in Capital and Retained Earnings
Year Ended July 31, 1971, with Comparative Figures for 1970

	1971	1970
Additional paid-in capital:		
Balance at beginning of period	$ 8,446,738	$1,949,813
Excess of proceeds over par value of 400,000 shares of common stock issued in public offering (less expenses of $118,285)	—	5,981,715
Excess of proceeds over par value of 129,000 shares of common stock issued in private sales (less applicable expenses)	—	515,210
Excess of proceeds over par value of 500,000 shares of preferred stock issued in public offering (less expenses of $429,367) (Note 2)	18,070,633	—
Excess of proceeds over par value of 11,800 common shares issued under stock options (Note 10)	37,082	—
Balance at end of period	$26,554,453	$8,446,738
Retained earnings:		
Balance at beginning of period	$ 3,117,670	$1,082,481
Net income	3,252,663	2,035,189
Balance at end of period	$ 6,370,333	$3,117,670

See accompanying Notes to Consolidated Financial Statements.

EXHIBIT 5

STIRLING HOMEX CORPORATION
Notes to Consolidated Financial Statements July 31, 1971

1. Principles of Consolidation

The consolidated financial statements included the accounts of the Company and its subsidiaries except for U.S. Shelter Corporation, its financing subsidiary (all of which are wholly owned). The Company carries its investment in all subsidiaries at equity in the underlying net assets. On consolidation, all significant accounts and transactions with consolidated subsidiaries have been eliminated.

The following are condensed financial statements of the unconsolidated financing subsidiary:

Balance Sheet
July 31, 1971
Assets

Cash	$ 5,171
Accounts receivable—unbilled (Note a)	4,950,000
Other assets	24,593
Due from parent company	76,894
	$5,056,658

Liabilities and Stockholders' Equity

Notes payable—bank (7%) (Note b)	$3,750,000
Payables, accruals, and other liabilities	172,079
Stockholders' equity	1,134,579
	$5,056,658

EXHIBIT 5 *(continued)*

**Statement of Income
From Date of Incorporation
(September 25, 1970) to July 31, 1971**

Finance income.	$ 544,946
General and administrative expenses	
(including interest expense of $54,917).	263,367
	281,579
Federal and state income taxes—current.	147,000
Net income	$ 134,579

Notes:

a. Accounts receivable includes $4,650,000 relating to accounts assigned to U.S. Shelter by the Company for which U.S. Shelter remitted cash.

b. The subsidiary has obtained an unsecured $15,000,000 line of credit from a bank. These funds are being used in financing transactions involving customers of the Company. The Company has not guaranteed the line of credit.

2. Preferred Stock Offering

On July 29, 1971, the Company, through its underwriters, offered 500,000 shares of $2.40 cumulative convertible preferred stock to the public at $40 per share. Net proceeds of $19,000,000 after deducting an underwriting discount, were received by the Company on August 5, 1971. Additional paid-in capital has been credited with the net proceeds received less the par value of the stock issued ($500,000) and expenses related to the offering ($429,367).

The preferred stock is nonvoting except for certain defined events which would significantly affect the preferred stockholders' equity interests. The preferred shares are convertible into 1,379,310 common shares subject to adjustment in certain events, including stock split-ups and stock dividends. At its option, the Company may redeem the preferred stock at an initial price of $50 per share, as of August 1, 1971, ranging downward annually to $40 per share as of August 1, 1981 and thereafter.

3. Receivables

The Company enters into various modular housing sales contracts which contain an allocation of the sales price between modules (based on published price lists) and installation work. Sales of modules (Manufacturing Division) are recognized when units are manufactured and assigned to specific contracts. Installation work (Installation Division) is recorded on the percentage of completion method. The contracts generally provide for payment upon completion and receipt of all approvals necessary for occupancy, or for payment upon completion of each respective phase. "Unbilled" receivables represent recorded sales on contracts in process for which billings will be rendered in the future in accordance with the contracts.

Receivables consist of:

	July 31, 1971	July 31, 1970
Contract receivables:		
Billed	$10,382,626	$10,559,145
Unbilled.	24,633,799	4,626,370
Total	35,016,425	15,185,515
Income tax refund receivable (Note 9)	2,498,672	—
Current portion of long-term receivables		
(Note 4).	12,500	17,500
Other receivables	317,975	283,104
	$37,845,572	$15,486,119

Substantially all sales are to local housing authorities and sponsors who qualify for financial assistance from Federal agencies of the U.S. Government or who have made arrangements for long-term financing. In light of this, no provision for doubtful accounts is considered necessary.

EXHIBIT 5 *(continued)*

See the condensed financial statements of U.S. Shelter Corporation in Note 1 for information with respect to receivables assigned by the Company to U.S. Shelter Corporation.

4. Long-Term Receivables

Long-term receivables consist of:

	July 31, 1971	July 31, 1970
Mortgages receivable:		
Mortgage due June 1, 1974—payments of $2,500 due quarterly with interest at the prime commercial rate in effect on the interest payment date	$ 241,624	$256,624
Mortgage due June 30, 1975—payments of $25,000 due June 30, 1973, and June 30, 1974, and the balance due June 30, 1975. Interest payable annually at the prime commercial rate in effect on the interest payment date	302,000	302,000
	543,624	558,624
Less installments due within one year (Note 3).	12,500	17,500
	531,124	541,124
Long-term portion of contract receivables—unbilled	3,694,225	—
	$4,225,349	$541,124

The mortgage notes are secured by mortgages on the property sold.

5. Inventories

Inventories of the Company consist of the following:

	July 31, 1971	July 31, 1970
Raw materials	$1,439,960	$ 963,664
Work in process	1,001,632	139,531
Salable merchandise	172,608	1,064,408
	$2,614,200	$2,167,603

Land held for development or sale is recorded at cost plus real estate taxes, mortgage interest and other related carrying costs. The Company has entered into a contract to sell a parcel of the land with costs of $673,017 for a sale price of $2,100,000. The Company has received nonrefundable payments of $235,000 which have been accounted for as an option deposit.

6. Property, Plant, and Equipment

Property, plant, and equipment consist of the following:

	Useful Life	July 31, 1971	July 31, 1970
Land and land improvements	20 years	$ 1,136,499	$1,002,067
Buildings	10 and 45	4,822,055	1,702,924
Machinery, equipment, and tools	2–10	1,735,396	1,071,515
Furniture, fixtures, and office equipment	5–10	942,131	500,951
Other	1–15	135,952	27,998
Construction in progress		1,388,613	1,171,211
		10,160,646	5,476,666
Less accumulated depreciation and amortization.		733,705	230,921
		$ 9,426,941	$5,245,745

EXHIBIT 5 *(continued)*

The straight-line method of depreciation is used for all depreciable assets. Depreciation expense for the years ended July 31, 1971, and 1970 is $529,116 and $220,227, respectively.

7. Deferred Charges

The unamortized balance of deferred changes consist of:

	Amortization Period	Unamortized Balance	
		July 31, 1971	July 31, 1970
Patents pending and trademarks	Legal life	$ 171,680	$ 88,660
Training and professional development	3 years	491,641	148,636
Research and development. . .	5	671,897	84,496
Project and production start-up costs.	2–5	844,028	503,539
Property acquisition costs.	(a)	379,546	118,778
		$2,558,792	$944,109

---

a. Expenditures in connection with property acquisition will be added to the cost of property subsequently acquired.

In the event of project abandonment or other circumstances causing a loss of value to deferred items, the related unamortized costs are charged to current operations.

8. Long-Term Debt

Long-term debt consists of the following:

	July 31, 1971	July 31, 1970
Mortgages maturing at various dates through December 31, 1976, and bearing interest at rates ranging from 4¾% to 6%	$433,176	$704,615
Installment contracts and lease purchase agreements maturing at various dates through August, 1974.	89,042	124,910
	532,218	829,525
Less payments due within one year	295,630	333,036
	$236,588	$496,489

Land, buildings and equipment with a net book value of $2,223,803 and $2,232,091 as of July 31, 1971 and July 31, 1970, respectively, are encumbered under the above agreements.

9. Income Taxes

Deferred taxes relate principally to manufacturing division and installation division sales, depreciation, deferred costs, and capitalized costs. None of the Company's tax returns have been examined by the Internal Revenue Service. The tax refund included in Note 3 relates to refundable advance tax payments and the planned amendment of the prior year's tax returns.

10. Stock Options

The Company has a qualified stock option plan in effect whereby options to purchase shares of common stock may be granted to officers and key employees at not less than the fair market value on the date of grant. During February 1971, authorized shares under the plan were increased from 400,000 to 900,000 shares. Options expire five years after the date of grant and are exercisable in cumulative installments of 20% after one year. A summary of activity for the year ended July 31, 1971, follows:

EXHIBIT 5 *(concluded)*

	Option Price per Share		
	From	**To**	**Shares**
Options outstanding at July 31, 1970	$ 3.00	$16.50	399,300
New options granted.	15.13	22.00	275,500
Less: Options exercised	3.00	12.00	(11,800)
Cancellations.	3.00	19.25	(61,900)
Options outstanding at July 31, 1971	3.00	22.00	601,000
Options outstanding at July 31, 1971 which are currently exercisable	3.00	16.50	58,360

No entries are recorded with respect to options until exercised at which time the excess of the option price over the par value of common stock issued is credited to additional paid-in capital.

11. Commitments and Contingencies

An action has been brought to enjoin the use of the word *Homex* by the Company. In the opinion of legal counsel, the plaintiff will be unsuccessful in obtaining the relief which it seeks.

A former shareholder of restricted shares of Company common stock has brought an action against the Company and another party, a broker. It is claimed that the Company refused, in concert with the other defendant, to permit the transfer of plaintiff's stock except at a price substantially below its alleged market price. Compensatory damages in the amount of $1,575,000 and treble damages are alleged. In the opinion of management, the suit can be successfully defended in the option of counsel, the claim for treble damages is without merit.

The Company is engaged in other disputes involving claims which, in the aggregate, are insignificant compared to the Company's net worth.

Construction of a manufacturing plant in Mississippi is expected to be commenced in the latter part of 1971 at an approximate cost of $4,900,000. In a contract with the Company, Harrison County (where the plant site is located) has agreed to take the steps necessary to authorize the issuance and sale of tax-exempt industrial revenue bonds in an amount necessary to meet the cost of constructing and equipping the plant. The contract also provides for a 30-year lease to the Company of the completed facility and the related land. Semiannual payments in respect of the bonds will be based on principal and interest requirements; an additional $36,325 is due annually for the land. Options to purchase the plant and the land are provided for during and at the end of the lease term. If the bond offering is not consummated, the Company will arrange to finance the cost of the facility itself.

At July 31, 1971, the Company had leases on various equipment and office facilities with terms ranging from two to six years. Minimum annual rentals under such leases amount to approximately $404,000.

Notes payable consist of 90 day unsecured notes to 11 banks bearing interest at a rate ½% above the respective bank's best rate on the date of issue. The Company is required to maintain average annual compensating cash balances at each of these banks equal to approximately 15% to 20% of the outstanding indebtedness to such bank.

12. Earnings per Share

Earnings per common share are based on the weighted average number of common shares outstanding during the periods presented after giving retroactive effect to the four-for-one stock split effected in February 1970. The preferred stock is not considered a common stock equivalent in accordance with *Opinion 15* of the Accounting Principles Board of the American Institute of Certified Public Accounts. In addition, the effect of the preferred stock offering, for the fiscal year ended July 31, 1971, on a fully diluted earnings per share calculation is insignificant. Stock options outstanding have not been included in these computations since the effect of their inclusion would be insignificant.

EXHIBIT 6
Accountants' Report

The Board of Directors and Stockholders
Stirling Homex Corporation

We have examined the consolidated balance sheet
of Stirling Homex Corporation and consolidated
subsidiaries as of July 31, 1971, and the related
statements of income, additional paid-in capital
and retained earnings, and changes in financial
position for the year ended. Our examination was
made in accordance with generally accepted
auditing standards, and accordingly included such
tests of the accounting records and such other
auditing procedures as we considered necessary in
the circumstances. The financial statements for
the year ended July 31, 1970, included for
comparative purposes, were examined by other
accountants.

In our opinion, such financial statements
present fairly the consolidated financial position
of Stirling Homex Corporation and consolidated
subsidiaries at July 31, 1971, and the results of
their operations and changes in their financial
position for the year then ended, in conformity
with generally accepted accounting principles
applied on a basis consistent with that of the
preceding year.

Rochester, New York
September 15, 1971   PEAT, MARWICK, MITCHELL & COMPANY

Midland Oil & Gas Company*

Midland Oil & Gas Company was founded in 1932 by M. T. McCurdy. The depression of the 1930s had driven McCurdy, formerly a geologist with a major steel company in Pennsylvania, to seek his fortune in "black gold" in the plains of Texas. His first big strike had been in Midland, Texas, for which he named the company.

Over the next 40 years, the company experienced a relatively high rate of growth and by the mid-1970s was regarded as one of the leading domestic companies in the exploration, development, and operation of oil and gas wells. Recently, however, McCurdy had observed that the company was requiring larger and larger quantities of cash just to maintain current reserve and production levels.

McCurdy felt that his company's current cash problems were attributable to several factors. First, the Tax Reform Act of 1975 had eliminated the use of the percentage depletion allowance method for purposes of computing taxable income. This tax change had substantially increased the company's tax bill. Second, the increasing worldwide demand for oil had resulted in a shortage of exploration and extraction equipment. This shortage was accompanied by substantial price increases in the cost of drilling and lifting equipment. And finally, McCurdy noted that the cost of replacing the company's existing reserves through secondary and tertiary extraction methods was considerably greater than the original cost of the reserves.

McCurdy had become quite familiar with the company's recent cash flow situation because, as chairman of the board of directors, he played a central role in the formulation and review of corporate plans. During 1978, he had reviewed a corporate proposal calling for an investment of approximately $200 million during 1979. The funds were to be used to replace worn-out equipment and to obtain new equipment for secondary and tertiary hydrocarbon recovery.

The proposal had assumed that 40 percent of the necessary funds could be internally generated from operations. McCurdy now questioned the validity of that assumption.

McCurdy was also concerned about how the remaining funds could be obtained. He was aware that the company had retired its preferred stock during 1978, but it had also partially replaced this capital with a small public offering of common stock and the sale of $100 million of convertible debentures. McCurdy felt that another public offering of bonds or stock so soon after the previous offerings would not be well received by the market. He was also opposed to the reissuance of the preferred stock for tax reasons.

---

* This case was prepared by Kenneth R. Ferris. Copyright © 1984 by Kenneth R. Ferris. All rights reserved to the author.

As McCurdy looked over the company's recent financial statements, he wondered whether the necessary financing might be arranged through a consortium of banks (Exhibits 1–3).

QUESTIONS

1. Identify the financial strengths and weaknesses of the Midland Oil & Gas Company.

2. How valid is the assumption that 40 percent of the necessary funds can be "internally generated" from operations? (Hint: compute the cash flows from operations.)

3. Would you recommend the extension of credit to Midland Oil & Gas Company?

EXHIBIT 1

MIDLAND OIL & GAS COMPANY
Consolidated Balance Sheet

	December 31, 1978	December 31, 1977
Assets		
Current assets:		
Cash (including certificates of deposit of $8,000,000)	$ 200,133,000	$ 220,500,000
Accounts receivables (net)—trade	138,200,000	106,400,000
Inventories (Note 2)	117,900,000	93,600,000
Prepaid expenses	22,217,000	27,700,000
Total current assets	478,450,000	448,200,000
Investments:		
In affiliated companies (Note 1)	318,000,000	302,000,000
Sinking fund (Note 3)	5,000,000	—
Long-term assets:		
Undeveloped properties (Note 4)	32,700,000	18,800,000
Oil and gas properties, and equipment (Note 5).	670,000,000	675,000,000
Less: Accumulated depreciation and depletion	(227,000,000)	(200,000,000)
Unamortized goodwill	13,500,000	15,000,000
Total assets	$1,290,650,000	$1,259,000,000
Liabilities and Shareholders' Equity		
Current liabilities:		
Accounts payables—trade	$ 10,800,000	$ 23,500,000
Federal income taxes payable	5,500,000	6,500,000
Dividends payable	4,000,000	—
Total current liabilities	20,300,000	30,000,000
Long-term liabilities:		
10% convertible debentures	100,000,000	—
Premium on debentures.	7,014,000	—
Deferred income taxes (Note 1)	92,000,000	80,000,000
Unfunded pension costs.	125,000,000	120,000,000
Total liabilities	344,314,000	230,000,000
Shareholders' equity:		
Common stock, $10 par; authorized shares, 50,000,000 (Note 6)	206,000,000	150,000,000
Preferred stock, $50 par; authorized shares, 1,000,000 (Note 6).	—	25,000,000
Capital in excess of par value:		
Common	315,000,000	300,000,000
Preferred	—	175,000,000
Retained earnings	425,336,000	379,000,000
Total liabilities and shareholders' equity.	$1,290,650,000	$1,259,000,000

EXHIBIT 2

MIDLAND OIL & GAS COMPANY
Consolidated Statement of Income
For the Year Ended December 31, 1978

Revenues:

Oil sales	$630,970,000	
Gas sales	335,300,000	
		$966,270,000

Cost and expenses:

Cost of operations and products sold	741,440,000	
Selling, general and administrative	108,430,000	
Interest	9,514,000	
Amortization of goodwill	1,500,000	
		860,884,000
		105,386,000

Other sources of income:

Income from unconsolidated subsidiaries	73,300,000
Gain on sales of undeveloped properties	2,000,000
Earnings before income taxes	180,686,000
Federal income taxes (Note 1)	88,350,000
Net earnings	$ 92,336,000

EXHIBIT 3

MIDLAND OIL & GAS COMPANY
Notes to Consolidated Financial Statements

1. Summary of Significant Accounting Policies

Principles of Consolidation

The consolidated financial statements include the accounts of Midland Oil & Gas Company and all significant subsidiaries, after elimination of intercompany transactions and balances. Income from subsidiaries in which ownership is 20 percent to 50 percent is recognized on an equity basis. All affiliated companies are engaged in the extraction industry.

Depreciation and Amortization

Depreciation has been provided using the straight-line method, except for depreciation of oil and gas production equipment, which is determined using the unit-of-production method.

Goodwill, obtained in conjunction with the acquisition of Northwest Drilling, Inc., on December 31, 1977, is being amortized on a straight-line basis over a 10-year period.

Exploration and Development Costs

All intangible drilling and development costs are accounted for under the "successful efforts" method of accounting as defined by Financial Accounting Standard (FAS) *No. 19,* entitled "Financial Accounting and Reporting by Oil and Gas Producing Companies." Geological and geophysical expenses are charged against income as incurred.

Income Taxes

The company and its subsidiaries file consolidated federal income tax returns.

Deferred Federal income taxes arise principally from the use of straight-line depreciation for statement purposes and accelerated methods used in computing deductions for current income taxes. The investment tax credit is taken into income currently as a reduction of the provision for income taxes.

EXHIBIT 3 *(concluded)*

2. Inventories

Inventories of crude oil and unrefined products are valued at lower of cost or market, using the first-in, first-out method. The inventory amounts used in the computation of cost of sales were $120,220,000 and $95,300,000 for the years ended December 31, 1978, and 1977, respectively.

3. Sinking Fund

The 10 percent convertible debentures issued on January 1, 1978, are payable December 31, 1987. Under the terms of the bond indenture, a sinking fund was established during 1978. The cash fund will be administered by the First State Bank of Lake Highlands, Texas.

4. Undeveloped Properties

The company follows a policy of both purchasing and leasing undeveloped oil and gas properties. Consistent with *FASB No. 19,* leasehold costs are initially capitalized. Subsequent accounting treatment of these costs depends upon the size and cost of extraction of discovered reserves. All undeveloped properties acquired during 1977 were found to be economically productive.

During 1978, undeveloped oil and gas properties were acquired from a major shareholder in exchange for 1 million shares of the company's common stock. These properties were recorded at the par value of the issued shares.

During 1978, certain undeveloped properties located in Oklahoma were sold to the United Drilling and Exploration Company. The properties were sold for $9 million and had a book value of $7 million.

5. Oil and Gas Properties, and Equipment

Depreciation and depletion taken during 1978 totaled $49,600,000. During 1977, the company began a program of replacing certain outdated extraction equipment. New acquisitions in 1978 amounted to $24,650,000. The company plans to acquire approximately $200 million in new equipment during 1979.

6. Shareholders' Equity

The authorized and issued shares of capital stock at December 31, 1977 and 1978, are summarized as follows:

	Authorized Shares	Issued Shares	
		1977	**1978**
Preferred stock, $50 par . . .	1,000,000	500,000	—
Common stock, $10 par . . .	50,000,000	15,000,000	20,600,000

During the month of January, 1978, 1 million shares of common stock were issued in exchange for undeveloped oil and gas properties (see Note 4). In June 1978, a 25 percent common stock dividend was declared and distributed. A public offering of 600,000 common shares was held in December 1978; the offering was fully subscribed.

As of December 31, 1977, 500,000 shares of $50 par preferred stock was outstanding. The entire amount was redeemed during 1978 for $202 million.

Financial Statement Analysis

W. T. Grant: A Study in Bankruptcy*

Chapter 11 of the National Bankruptcy Act provides opportunities for a business in financial difficulty to seek the protection of the courts while it attempts to recover going-concern status. Various arrangements are possible under Chapter 11 but, in general, management of the debtor company continues to control the assets and operations of the company while a plan for the payment of its debts is developed and implemented. A committee of the company's creditors is normally elected to work with management of the troubled concern.

In contrast, Chapter 10 of the act, when invoked by either the debtor firm or its creditors, generally provides for a court-appointed trustee to assume control of the company's assets and operations. All classes of creditors, as well as shareholders, have a stronger voice and, consequently, more protection as rehabilitation of the company is planned and implemented.

On October 2, 1975, W. T. Grant filed for protection under Chapter 11 of the National Bankruptcy Act. This action followed suspension of trading in Grant's stock on the New York Stock Exchange on Monday, September 30, 1975, and brought to a head the financial problems of Grant which had begun to surface in recent years. For the fiscal year ended January 31, 1975, Grant was the nation's 17th-largest retailer with almost 1,200 stores, a payroll of over 82,000 employees, and sales of $1.7 billion. What happened to Grant, and why, are questions that, with some analysis, can be answered. On the other hand, why the symptoms of Grant's prolonged illness were not diagnosed and treated earlier is difficult to understand.

Using the narrative information and financial data provided in Exhibits 1–7, your

---

* This case was prepared by James A. Largay III, and Clyde P. Stickney, Jr. Copyright © 1979 by James A. Largay III and Clyde P. Stickney, Jr. All rights reserved to the authors. (James A. Largay III is Arthur Andersen & Co. Alumni Professor of Accounting, Lehigh University; Clyde P. Stickney is The Signal Companies Professor of Management, Amos Tuck School of Business Administration, Dartmouth College.)

mission is to apply tools of financial analysis to determine the major causes of Grant's financial problems. If you had been performing this analysis contemporaneously with the release of the publicly reported information, when would you have become skeptical of the ability of Grant to continue as a viable going concern? Why?

GRANT'S LAST DECADE

The Marketing of Grant

During 1963–73, W. T. Grant opened 612 new stores and expanded 91 others. Much of that expansion was concentrated in the 1969–73 period when 369 new stores were opened, 15 on one particularly busy day. Louis C. Lustenberger, president of Grant from 1959–68, started the expansion program, although later, as a director, he became concerned over dimensions of the growth and the problems it generated. After Mr. Lustenberger stepped down, the pace of expansion was stepped up under the leadership of Chairman Edward Staley and President Richard W. Mayer.

Historically, Grant's reputation was built on low-priced softgoods; its clientele tended to be lower-income consumers, with its major competition being growing discount chains like K mart corporation. As the expansion program developed, however, Grant began to alter its marketing strategy to compete also with established private-brand retailers, such as Montgomery Ward and J. C. Penney. Furniture and private-brand major appliances were added to the product line.

To help customers finance purchases of furniture, appliances, and other items, a credit card system was implemented. Each store administered its own credit department and had authority to accept or reject credit applications and establish credit terms. At most stores, customers were allowed 36 months to pay for their purchases; the minimum monthly payment was $1. Consistent with this decentralization of credit administration, inventory and pricing decisions were also made by local store managers. Compensation of store managers included salary plus stated percentages of the store's sales and profits.

Financing the Expansion

Grant leased most of its store space—in 1974–75, Grant was leasing approximately 52 million square feet of space in 1,070 stores around the country. Since Grant was gone by the time the Financial Accounting Standards Board issued *Statement of Financial Accounting Standard No. 13*, its long-term leasing arrangements were not reported on its balance sheet. Plant assets consisted mostly of store fixtures. Grant's recorded long-term debt consisted primarily of two $100 million issues in 1971 and 1973.

Banks entered the picture in a big way in 1974. In the spring of that year, both Moody's and Standard & Poor's eliminated their credit rating for Grant's commercial paper. To provide financing, a group of 143 banks agreed to offer lines of credit totaling $525 million. A short-term loan of $600 million was obtained in September 1974 with three banks—Morgan Guaranty, Chase Manhattan, and First National City—absorbing about $230 million of the total. These same three banks also loaned $50 million out of a total of $100 million provided to Grant's finance subsidiary.

Dividends had been paid consistently from 1906 until August 27, 1974, when they were passed for the first time in the company's history. Treasury stock costing almost $50 million was acquired during 1969–72.

Grant's financial reports were affected by changes in accounting policies. In fiscal year 1970, the company began consolidating its wholly owned finance subsidiary. Through fiscal year 1974, Grant recorded the total finance charge on credit sales as income in the year of the sale. Beginning in fiscal year 1975, finance charges on credit sales were recognized as income over the life of the installment contract.

Advance and Retreat—The Attempt to Save Grant

Support of the banks during the summer of 1974 was accompanied by a top-management change. Messrs. Staley and Mayer had stepped down in the spring and were replaced in August 1974 by James G. Kendrick, brought in from Zeller's Ltd., Grant's subsidiary. As chief executive officer, Mr. Kendrick moved to cut Grant's losses. Payroll was slashed significantly, 126 unprofitable stores were closed, and the big-ticket furniture and appliance lines were phased out. New store space brought on-line in 1975 was 75 percent less than in 1974.

The positive effects of these moves could not overcome the disastrous events of early 1975. In January, Grant defaulted on about $75 million in interest payments, and, in February, results of operations for the year ended January 31, 1975, were released. Grant reported a loss of $177 million, with substantial losses from credit operations accounting for 60 percent of the total.

The banks now assumed a more active role in what was becoming a struggle to save Grant. Robert H. Anderson, a vice president of Sears, was offered a lucrative $2.5 million contract, decided to accept the challenge to turn the company around, and joined Grant as its new president in April 1975. Mr. Kendrick remained as chairman of the board. The banks holding 90 percent of Grant's debt extended their loans from June 2, 1975, to March 31, 1976. The balance of about $56 million was repaid on June 2. A major problem confronting Mr. Anderson was to maintain the continued flow of merchandise into Grant stores. Suppliers had become skeptical of Grant's ability to pay for merchandise and, in August, the banks agreed to subordinate $300 million of debt to the suppliers' claims for merchandise shipped. With the approach of the Christmas shopping season, the need for merchandise had become critical. Despite the banks' subordination of their claims to those of suppliers and the intensive cultivation of suppliers by Mr. Anderson, sufficient quantities of merchandise were not being received in the stores.

During this period, Grant reported a $111.3 million net loss for the six months just ended on July 31, 1975. Sales had declined 15 percent from the comparable period in 1974. Mr. Kendrick observed that a return to profitability before the fourth quarter was unlikely.

On October 2, 1975, the Chapter 11 bankruptcy petition was filed by the company. The rehabilitation effort was formally underway, and the protection provided by Chapter 11 permitted a continuation of the reorganization and rehabilitation activities for the next four months. On February 6, 1976, after store closings and liquidations of inventories had generated $320 million in cash, the creditors committee voted for liquidation and W. T. Grant ceased to exist.

EXHIBIT 1

W. T. GRANT COMPANY
Statements of Income and Retained Earnings
(as originally reported for fiscal years ended January 31, 1966–75)

	1966	1967	1968	1969	1970	1971	1972	1973	1974	1975
Sales	$839,715	$920,797	$979,458	$1,091,658	$1,210,918	$1,254,131	$1,374,811	$1,644,747	$1,849,802	$1,761,952
Concessions	1,614	2,249	2,786	3,425	3,748	4,986	3,439	3,753	3,971	4,238
Equity in earnings	1,186	2,072	2,987	3,537	2,084	2,777	2,383	5,116	4,651	3,086
Other income	999	1,049	2,010	2,205	2,864	2,874	3,102	1,188	3,063	3,376
Total revenues	843,514	926,167	987,241	1,100,825	1,219,614	1,264,768	1,383,735	1,654,804	1,861,487	1,772,652
Cost of goods sold	$478,072	$631,585	$669,560	$739,459	$817,671	$843,192	$931,237	$1,125,261	$1,282,945	$1,303,267
Selling, general, and administration	202,008	228,433	246,653	275,668	306,629	329,768	373,816	444,377	518,280	540,953
Interest[a]	4,846	9,055	11,248	13,146	14,919	18,874	16,452	21,127	51,047	199,238
Taxes: Current	1,413	13,541	17,530	25,600	24,900	21,140	13,487	9,588	(6,021)	(19,439)
Deferred	25,487	11,659	9,120	8,400	13,100	11,660	13,013	16,162	6,807	(98,027)
Other expenses	440	616	567	657	586	557	418	502	—	24,000
Total expenses	812,266	894,889	954,678	1,065,930	1,177,805	1,225,191	1,348,523	1,617,017	1,853,058	1,949,992
Net income	$ 31,248	$ 31,278	$ 32,563	$ 37,895	$ 41,809	$ 39,577	$ 35,212	$ 37,787	$ 8,429	$ (177,340)
Dividends	(10,211)	(14,091)	(14,367)	(17,686)	(19,737)	(20,821)	(21,139)	(21,141)	(21,122)	(4,457)
Change in accounting principles: Consolidation of finance sub.	—	—	—	4,885	(2,932)	—	—	—	—	
Recognition of financing charges	—	—	—	—	—	—	—	—	—	(28,990)
Change in retained earnings	21,037	17,187	18,196	25,094	19,140	18,756	14,073	16,646	(12,693)	(210,787)
Retained earnings—beg. of period	111,025	132,062	149,249	167,445	192,539	211,679	230,435	244,508	261,154	248,461
Retained earnings—end of period	$132,062	$149,249	$167,445	$ 192,539	$ 211,679	$ 230,435	$ 244,508	$ 261,154	$ 248,461	$ 37,674

[a] For fiscal years 1966 to 1973, amounts include only interest expense. The amounts for 1974 and 1975 are composed of:

	1974	1975
Interest expense	$ 78,040	$ 86,079
Estimated Uncollectibles	21,198	155,691
Administration of credit activity	39,803	48,609
Less finance charges on customers' accounts	(87,994)	(91,141)
Total	$ 51,047	$199,238

EXHIBIT 2

W. T. GRANT COMPANY
Comparative Balance Sheets
(as originally reported for fiscal years ended January 31, 1966–75)

Assets	1966	1967	1968	1969	1970[a]	1971	1972	1973	1974	1975[b]
Cash and marketable securities	$ 22,559	$ 37,507	$ 25,047	$ 28,460	$ 32,977	$ 34,009	$ 49,851	$ 30,943	$ 45,951	$ 79,642
Accounts receivable[c]	110,943	110,305	133,406	154,829	368,267	419,731	477,324	542,751	598,799	431,201
Inventories	151,365	174,631	183,721	208,483	222,128	260,492	298,676	399,533	450,637	407,357
Other current assets	—	—	—	—	5,037	5,246	5,378	6,649	7,299	6,581
Total current assets	284,867	322,443	342,174	391,772	628,409	719,478	831,229	979,876	1,102,686	924,781
Investments	38,419	40,800	56,609	62,854	20,694	23,936	32,367	35,581	45,451	49,764
Property, plant, and equipment (net)	40,367	48,071	47,572	49,213	55,311	61,832	77,173	91,420	100,984	101,932
Other assets	5,231	5,704	8,737	6,744	2,381	2,382	3,901	3,821	3,862	5,790
Total assets	$368,884	$417,018	$455,092	$510,583	$706,795	$807,628	$944,670	$1,110,698	$1,252,983	$1,082,267

Equities

	1966	1967	1968	1969	1970	1971	1972	1973	1974	1975
Short-term debt	$ —	$ —	$ 300	$ 180	$182,132	$246,420	$237,741	$ 390,034	$ 453,097	$ 600,695
Accounts payable	64,813	80,802	91,108	109,792	104,144	118,091	124,990	112,896	103,910	147,211
Current deferred taxes	35,038	46,371	52,839	60,848	80,443	94,489	112,846	130,137	133,057	2,000
Total current liabilities	99,851	127,173	144,247	170,820	366,719	459,000	475,577	633,067	690,064	749,906
Long-term debt	70,000	70,000	62,622	43,251	35,402	32,301	128,432	126,672	220,336	216,341
Noncurrent deferred taxes	6,269	7,034	7,551	7,941	8,286	8,518	9,664	11,926	14,649	
Other long-term liabilities	4,784	4,949	4,858	5,519	5,700	5,773	5,252	4,694	4,195	2,183
Total liabilities	180,904	209,156	219,278	227,531	416,107	505,592	618,925	776,359	929,244	968,430
Preferred stock	15,000	15,000	14,750	13,250	11,450	9,600	9,053	8,600	7,465	7,465
Common stock	15,375	15,636	16,191	17,318	17,883	18,180	18,529	18,588	18,599	18,599
Additional paid-in capital	25,543	27,977	37,428	59,945	71,555	78,116	85,195	86,146	85,910	83,914
Retained earnings	132,062	149,249	167,445	192,539	211,679	230,435	244,508	261,154	248,461	37,674
Total	187,980	207,862	235,814	283,052	312,567	336,331	357,285	374,488	360,435	147,652
Less cost of treasury stock	—	—	—	—	(21,879)	(34,295)	(31,540)	(40,149)	(36,696)	(33,815)
Total stockholders' equity	187,980	207,862	235,814	283,052	290,688	302,036	325,745	334,339	323,739	113,837
Total equities	$368,884	$417,018	$455,092	$510,583	$706,795	$807,628	$944,670	$1,110,698	$1,252,983	$1,082,267

[a] In the year ending January 31, 1970, W. T. Grant changed its consolidation policy and commenced consolidating its wholly owned finance subsidiary.

[b] In the year ending January 31, 1975, W. T. Grant changed its method of recognizing finance income on installment sales. In prior years, all finance income was recognized in the year of the sale. Beginning in the 1975 fiscal period, finance income was recognized over the time the installment receivable was outstanding.

[c] Accounts receivable is composed of the following:

	1966	1967	1968	1969	1970	1971	1972	1973	1974	1975
Customer installment receivables	$114,470	$114,928	$140,507	$162,219	$381,757	$433,730	$493,859	$556,091	$602,305	$518,387
Less allowances for uncollectible accounts	(7,065)	(9,383)	(11,307)	(13,074)	(15,270)	(15,527)	(15,750)	(15,770)	(18,067)	(79,510)
Unearned credit insurance	—	—	—	—	(5,774)	(9,553)	(12,413)	(8,768)	(4,923)	(1,386)
Unearned finance income	—	—	—	—	—	—	—	—	—	(37,523)
Net	107,405	105,545	129,200	149,145	360,713	408,650	465,696	531,553	579,315	399,968
Other receivables	3,538	4,760	4,206	5,684	7,554	11,081	11,628	11,198	19,484	31,233
Total receivables	$110,943	$110,305	$133,406	$154,829	$368,267	$419,731	$477,324	$542,751	$598,799	$431,201

EXHIBIT 3

W. T. GRANT COMPANY
Comparative Balance Sheets
(as retroactively reported for changes in accounting principles for fiscal years ended January 31, 1966–75)

Assets	1966	1967	1968	1969	1970[a]	1971	1972	1973	1974	1975[b]
Cash and marketable securities	$ 22,638	$ 39,040	$ 25,141	$ 25,639	$ 32,977	$ 34,009	$ 49,851	$ 30,943	$ 45,951	$ 79,642
Accounts receivable[c]	172,706	230,427	272,450	312,776	368,267	358,428	408,301	468,582	540,802	431,201
Inventories	151,365	174,631	183,722	208,623	222,128	260,492	298,676	399,533	450,637	407,357
Other current assets	3,630	4,079	3,982	4,402	5,037	5,246	5,378	6,649	7,299	6,581
Total current assets	350,339	448,177	485,295	551,440	628,409	658,175	762,206	905,707	1,044,689	924,781
Investments	13,405	14,791	16,754	18,581	20,694	23,936	32,367	35,581	44,251	49,764
Property, plant, and equipment (net)	40,372	48,076	47,578	49,931	55,311	61,832	77,173	91,420	100,984	101,932
Other assets	1,222	1,664	1,980	2,157	2,381	2,678	3,901	3,821	5,063	5,790
Total assets	$405,338	$512,708	$551,607	$622,109	$706,795	$746,621	$875,647	$1,036,529	$1,194,987	$1,082,267

Equities

	1966	1967	1968	1969	1970	1971	1972	1973	1974	1975
Short-term debt	$ 37,314	$ 97,647	$ 99,230	$118,125	$182,132	$246,420	$237,741	$ 390,034	$ 453,097	$ 600,695
Accounts payable	58,252	75,885	79,673	102,080	104,144	118,091	124,990	112,896	104,883	147,211
Current deferred taxes	36,574	44,667	56,545	65,073	80,443	58,536	72,464	87,431	103,078	2,000
Total current liabilities	132,140	218,199	235,448	285,278	366,719	423,047	435,195	590,361	661,058	749,906
Long-term debt	70,000	70,000	62,622	43,251	35,402	32,301	128,432	126,672	220,336	216,341
Noncurrent deferred taxes	6,269	7,034	7,551	7,941	8,286	8,518	9,664	11,926	14,649	—
Other long-term liabilities	4,785	5,159	5,288	5,519	5,700	5,773	5,252	4,694	4,196	2,183
Total liabilities	213,194	300,392	310,909	341,989	416,107	469,639	578,543	733,653	900,239	968,430
Preferred stock	15,000	15,000	14,750	13,250	11,450	9,600	9,053	8,600	7,465	7,465
Common stock	15,375	15,636	16,191	17,318	17,883	18,180	18,529	18,588	18,599	18,599
Additional paid-in capital	25,543	27,977	37,428	59,945	71,555	78,116	85,195	86,146	85,909	83,914
Retained earnings	136,226	153,703	172,329	189,607	211,679	205,381	215,867	229,691	219,471	37,674
Total	192,144	212,316	240,698	280,120	312,567	311,277	328,644	343,025	331,444	147,652
Less cost of treasury stock	—	—	—	—	(21,879)	(34,295)	(31,540)	(40,149)	(36,696)	(33,815)
Total stockholders' equity	192,144	212,316	240,698	280,120	290,688	276,982	297,104	302,876	294,748	113,837
Total equities	$405,338	$512,708	$551,607	$622,109	$706,795	$746,621	$875,647	$1,036,529	$1,194,987	$1,082,267

a See Note a to Exhibit 1.
b See Note b to Exhibit 1.
c Accounts receivable is composed of the following:

	1966	1967	1968	1969	1970	1971	1972	1973	1974	1975
Installment receivables					$381,757	$433,730	$493,859	$556,091	$602,305	$518,387
Less:										
Allowance for uncollectible accounts		*Not disclosed on a fully*			(15,270)	(15,527)	(15,750)	(15,770)	(16,315)	(79,510)
Unearned credit insurance		*consolidated basis*			(5,774)	(9,553)	(12,413)	(8,768)	(4,923)	(1,386)
Unearned finance income		*with finance subsidiary*			—	(61,303)	(69,023)	(74,169)	(59,748)	(37,523)
Net					360,713	347,347	396,673	457,384	521,319	399,968
Other receivables					7,554	11,081	11,628	11,198	19,483	31,233
Total receivables	$172,706	$230,427	$272,450	$312,776	$368,267	$358,428	$408,301	$468,582	$450,802	$431,201

EXHIBIT 4

W. T. GRANT COMPANY
Statements of Changes in Financial Position
(as originally reported for fiscal years ended January 31, 1966–75)

	1966[a]	1967[a]	1968[a]	1969[a]	1970	1971	1972	1973	1974	1975
Sources of working capital:										
Operations:										
Net income	$31,248	$31,278	$32,563	$37,895	$41,809	$39,577	$35,212	$37,787	$8,429	$(177,340)
Plus: Depreciation	6,868	7,524	8,203	8,381	8,972	9,619	10,577	12,004	13,579	14,587
Deferred taxes	1,143	765	517	390	345	233	1,145	2,262	2,723	(14,649)
Other	378	164	130	231	180	74	(520)	(558)	(497)	(2,013)
Less: Equity in earnings	(1,172)	(1,073)	(1,503)	(1,761)	(2,084)	(2,777)	(2,383)	(3,403)	(3,570)	(331)
Total from operations	38,465	38,658	39,910	45,136	49,222	46,726	44,031	48,092	20,664	(179,746)
Sale of Common: To employees	3,431	2,695	4,113	5,432	5,279	5,218	7,715	3,492	2,584	886
On open market	—	—	—	—	—	—	2,229	174	260	—
Issue of long-term debt	35,000	—	—	—	—	—	100,000	—	100,000	—
Other	—	30	59	523	—	—	—	2,228	(601)	—
Total sources	76,896	41,383	44,082	51,091	54,501	51,944	153,975	53,986	122,907	(178,860)
Uses of Working Capital:										
Dividends	10,211	14,091	14,367	17,686	19,737	20,821	21,139	21,141	21,122	4,457
Acquisition of prop., plant, & equip.	8,008	15,257	7,763	10,544	14,352	16,141	25,918	26,250	23,143	15,535
Acquisition of treasury stock	186	441	316	178	22,102	13,224	—	11,466	133	—
Reacquisition of preferred stock	—	—	155	923	1,037	948	308	252	618	—
Retirement of long-term debt	—	—	1,500	1,500	1,687	1,538	5,143	1,760	6,336	3,995
Investment in securities	128	269	418	35	—	436	5,951	2,040	5,700	5,182
Other	548	72	202	735	58	47	46	(79)	41	727
Total uses	19,081	30,130	24,721	31,601	58,973	53,155	58,505	62,830	57,093	29,896
Net change in working capital	$57,815	$11,253	$19,361	$19,490	$(4,472)	$(1,211)	$95,470	$(8,844)	$65,814	$(208,756)
Analysis of Inc. (dec.) in work. cap.:										
Cash and short-term securities	Not disclosed on →	a comparable basis →	with above sources and uses →		$7,338	$1,032	$15,842	$(18,908)	$15,008	$33,691
Accounts receivable					55,491	51,464	57,593	65,427	56,047	(121,351)
Merchandise inventories					13,504	38,365	38,184	100,857	51,104	(43,280)
Prepayments					635	209	428	1,271	651	11,032
Short-term debt					(64,005)	(64,288)	8,680	(152,293)	(63,063)	(147,898)
Accounts payable					(2,064)	(13,947)	(6,900)	12,093	8,987	(42,028)
Deferred taxes (installment sales)					(15,371)	(14,046)	(18,357)	(17,291)	(2,920)	101,078
Net change in working capital	$57,815	$11,253	$19,361	$19,490	$(4,472)	$(1,211)	$95,470	$8,844	$65,814	$(208,756)

[a] Amounts reported each year in the Statement of Changes in Financial Position were based on the assumption that W. T. Grant Financial Corporation, an unconsolidated subsidiary, had been consolidated.

EXHIBIT 5

W. T. GRANT COMPANY
Statements of Income and Retained Earnings
(as retroactively revised for changes in accounting principles for fiscal years ended January 31, 1966–75)

	1966	1967	1968	1969	1970	1971	1972	1973	1974	1975
Sales	$839,715	$920,797	$979,458	$1,096,152	$1,210,918	$1,254,131	$1,374,812	$1,644,747	$1,849,802	$1,761,952
Concessions	1,614	2,250	2,786	2,873	3,748	4,986	3,439	3,753	3,971	4,238
Equity in earnings	1,172	1,073	1,503	1,761	2,084	4,175	3,951	5,116	4,651	3,086
Other income	998	1,314	2,038	2,525	2,864	1,214	1,270	918	2,996	3,376
Total revenues	843,499	925,434	985,785	1,103,311	1,219,614	1,264,506	1,383,472	1,654,534	1,861,420	1,772,652
Cost of goods sold	578,072	631,585	669,560	741,181	817,671	843,192	931,238	1,125,261	1,282,945	1,303,267
Selling, general, and administration	202,011	228,514	246,527	277,366	306,629	363,854	411,225	476,280	540,230	540,953
Interest[a]	4,814	7,319	8,549	9,636	14,919	(11,559)	(16,361)	(7,636)	24,054	199,238
Taxes: Current	1,126	14,463	18,470	27,880	24,900	22,866	13,579	11,256	(6,021)	(19,439)
Deferred	25,487	11,369	9,120	8,400	13,100	9,738	12,166	14,408	9,310	(98,027)
Other expenses	441	616	566	665	586	—				24,000
Total expenses	811,951	893,866	952,792	1,065,128	1,177,805	1,228,091	1,351,847	1,619,569	1,850,518	1,949,992
Net income	31,548	31,568	32,993	38,183	41,809	36,415	31,625	34,965	10,902	(177,340)
Dividends	(10,211)	(14,091)	(14,367)	(17,686)	(19,737)	(20,821)	(21,139)	(21,141)	(21,122)	(4,457)
Changes in accounting principles:										
Consolidation of finance subsidiary	—	—	—	(3,219)	—	—	—	—	—	—
Recognition of financing charges	—	—	—	—	—	(21,820)	—	—	—	—
Changes in retained earnings	21,337	17,477	18,626	17,278	22,072	(6,226)	10,486	13,824	(10,220)	(181,797)
Retained earnings—beginning of period	114,889	136,226	153,703	172,329	189,607	211,607	205,381	215,867	229,691	219,471
Retained earnings—end of period	$136,226	$153,703	$172,329	$ 189,607	$ 211,679	$ 205,381	$ 215,867	$ 229,691	$ 219,471	$ 37,674

[a] For fiscal years 1966 to 1970, amounts include only interest expense. The amounts for fiscal years 1971 to 1975 are composed of the following:

	1971	1972	1973	1974	1975
Interest expense	$ 18,874	$ 16,452	$ 21,127	$ 78,040	$ 86,079
Estimated uncollectibles	257	222	20,049	21,198	155,691
Administration of credit activity				39,803	48,609
Less finance charge on customers' accounts	(30,690)	(33,035)	(48,812)	(114,987)	(91,141)
Total	$(11,559)	$(16,361)	$ (7,636)	$ 24,054	$199,238

EXHIBIT 6

W. T. GRANT COMPANY
Statements of Changes in Financial Position
(as retroactively revised for changes in accounting principles for fiscal years ended January 31, 1966–75)

	1966[a]	1967	1968	1969	1970	1971	1972	1973	1974	1975
Sources of working capital:										
Operations:										
Net income		$ 31,568	$ 32,993	$ 38,183	$ 41,809	$ 36,415	$ 31,625	$ 34,965	$ 10,902	$(177,340)
Plus: Depreciation		7,524	8,203	8,388	8,972	9,619	10,577	12,004	13,579	14,587
Deferred taxes		765	517	390	345	233	1,145	2,262	2,723	(14,649)
Other		374	130	231	180	74	(520)	(558)	(498)	(2,013)
Less: Equity in earnings		(1,073)	(1,503)	(1,761)	(2,084)	(2,777)	(2,383)	(3,403)	(3,570)	(331)
Total from operations		39,158	40,340	45,431	49,222	43,564	40,444	45,270	23,136	(179,746)
Sale of common to employees		2,695	4,113	5,432	5,279	5,218	7,715	3,491	2,584	886
Issue of long-term debt		—	—	—	—	—	100,000	—	100,000	—
Other		30	59	523	—	1,544	2,229	2,484	259	—
Total sources		41,883	44,512	51,386	54,501	50,326	150,388	51,245	125,979	(178,860)
Uses of working capital:										
Dividends		14,091	14,367	17,686	19,737	20,821	21,139	21,141	21,122	4,457
Acquisition of prop., plant, and equip.		15,257	7,763	10,626	14,352	16,141	25,918	26,251	23,143	15,535
Acquisition of treasury stock		—	—	3,665	22,102	13,224	—	11,466	133	—
Reacquisition of preferred stock		—	155	923	1,037	948	308	252	618	3,995
Retirement of long-term debt		—	1,500	1,500	1,687	1,538	1,615	1,584	6,074	5,282
Investment in securities		269	418	35	—	436	5,951	2,216	5,700	627
Other		487	440	636	58	1,960	3,574	—	904	—
Amount due to change in acct. prin.		—	—	—	—	21,820	—	—	—	—
Total uses		30,104	24,643	35,071	58,973	76,888	58,505	62,910	57,694	29,896
Net change in working capital		$ 11,779	$ 19,869	$ 16,315	$ (4,472)	$(26,562)	$ 91,883	$ (11,665)	$ 68,285	$(208,756)
Analysis of inc. (dec.) in working cap.:										
Cash and short-term securities		$ 16,402	$(13,899)	$ 498	$ 7,338	$ 1,032	$ 15,842	$ (18,908)	$ 15,008	$ 33,691
Accounts receivable		57,721	42,023	40,326	55,491	(9,839)	49,873	60,281	72,220	(109,601)
Inventories		23,266	9,091	24,901	13,505	38,364	38,184	100,857	51,104	(43,280)
Prepayments		449	(97)	420	635	209	132	1,271	650	(718)
Short-term debt		(60,333)	(1,583)	(18,895)	(64,007)	(64,288)	8,679	(152,293)	(63,063)	(147,598)
Accounts payable		(17,633)	(3,788)	(22,407)	(2,064)	(13,947)	(6,899)	12,094	8,013	(42,328)
Deferred taxes		(8,093)	(11,878)	(8,528)	(15,370)	21,907	(13,928)	(14,967)	(15,647)	101,078
Net change in working capital		$ 11,779	$ 19,869	$ 16,315	$ (4,472)	$(26,562)	$ 91,883	$ (11,665)	$ 68,285	$(208,756)

[a] Not reported on a retroactively revised basis.

EXHIBIT 7
Other Data

	1965	1966	1967	1968	1969	1970	1971	1972	1973	1974
W. T. Grant Co.:										
Sales (millions of dollars)[a]	$839.7	$920.8	$979.5	$1,096.1	$1,210.9	$1,254.1	$1,374.8	$1,644.7	$1,849.8	$1,762.0
Number of stores	1,088	1,104	1,086	1,092	1,095	1,116	1,168	1,208	1,189	1,152
Store area (thousands of square feet)[a]	◄—— Data not available ——►					38,157	44,718	50,619	53,719	54,770
Dividends per share[a]	$ .80	$ 1.10	$ 1.10	$ 1.30	$ 1.40	$ 1.40	$ 1.50	$ 1.50	$ 1.50	$ .30
Stock price:										
High	$ 31⅛	$ 35⅛	$ 37⅜	45⅛	59	52	70⅝	48¾	44⅜	12
Low	$ 18	$ 20½	$ 20¾	30	39¼	26⅞	41⅞	38¾	$9⅞	1½
Close (12/31)	$ 31⅛	$ 20¾	$ 34⅜	42⅝	47	47⅛	47¾	43⅞	$ 10⅞	1⅞
Variety store industry:										
Sales (millions of dollars)[a]	$5,320	$5,727	$6,078	$6,152	$6,426	$6,959	$6,972	$7,498	$8,212	$8,714
Standard & Poor's Variety Chain Stock Price Index:										
High	31.0	31.2	38.4	53.6	66.1	61.4	92.2	107.4	107.3	73.7
Low	24.3	22.4	22.3	34.7	48.8	40.9	60.2	82.1	60.0	39.0
Close (12/31)	31.0	22.4	37.8	50.5	59.6	60.4	88.0	106.8	66.2	41.9
Aggregate economy:										
Gross national product (billions of dollars)	$684.9	$747.6	$789.7	$ 865.7	$ 932.1	$1,075.3	$1,107.5	$1,171.1	$1,233.4	$1,210.0
Average bank short-term lending rate	4.99%	5.69%	5.99%	6.68%	8.21%	8.48%	6.32%	5.82%	8.30%	11.28%
Standard & Poor's 500 Stock Price Index:										
High	92.6	94.1	97.6	108.4	106.2	93.5	104.8	119.1	120.2	99.8
Low	81.6	73.2	80.4	87.7	89.2	69.3	90.2	101.7	92.2	62.3
Close (12/31)	92.4	80.3	96.5	103.9	92.1	92.2	102.1	118.1	97.6	68.6

[a] These amounts are for the fiscal year ending January 31 of year after the year indicated in the column. For example, sales for W. T. Grant of $839.7 in the 1965 column are for the fiscal year ending January 31, 1966.

PART SIX

Issues in Corporate Financial Reporting

Consolidated Financial Statements

CASE 6.1

CGA Computer Associates, Inc.*

Will the real CGA Computer, Inc. please stand up? Is it the company that earned $3.4 million for the year ended April 30, 1984? Or is it the company that earned $765,000?

Both answers are right. That's because CGA . . . issues an annual report that is bewildering. . . . Because of an unprecedented agreement with the SEC, CGA has issued two sets of earnings statements in its annual report since 1981. Each set is based on a different accounting treatment for a 1981 acquisition.[1]

BACKGROUND

CGA Computer Associates, Inc. is a Delaware corporation that was incorporated in 1973. The company provides a broad range of computer consulting services and markets two proprietary computer software packages, principally to insurance companies, banks, petrochemical, manufacturing, and pharmaceutical companies. On February 21, 1981, CGA acquired all of the assets and assumed substantially all of the liabilities of Allen Services Corporation (ASC). As part of the same transaction, CGA acquired from Arthur Allen and Addison Fischer, the sole stockholders of ASC, all of the computer software program packages that had been marketed by ASC under license from Messrs. Allen and Fischer.

ASC had been engaged in a business substantially similar to that of CGA, although the two companies neither provided services to each other nor had any other intercompany transactions. ASC, like CGA, provided computer consulting services to manufacturing and service companies, primarily in the computer, manufacturing, and oil industries, and marketed five proprietary computer software packages. As a result

---

*This case was prepared by Kenneth R. Ferris and Ann M. Gunn. Copyright © 1985 by Kenneth R. Ferris. All rights reserved to the authors.

[1] "CGA Computer's Baffling Profit Reports Fuel Shareholder Ire Over Buyout Offer," *The Wall Street Journal*, August 9, 1984.

of the combination, CGA substantially increased its product line of software packages and its staff of computer consultants.

In consideration for the assets and business acquired from ASC, the company issued an aggregate of 1,385,356 shares of CGA $0.10 par value common stock to ASC and its principal shareholders. The number of shares issued in the transaction was based on the net earnings of ASC for the year ended December 31, 1980. ASC subsequently distributed its shares to Messrs. Allen and Fischer.

At the time of the combination, CGA's common stock traded over the counter. During the first quarter of 1981, CGA shares traded at a high of $16.50 per share and a low of $9.75. On February 21, 1981, the closing representative bid and asked quotations were $13.50 and $14.50, respectively.

Exhibit 1 presents summary financial data for CGA and for the combined company

---

EXHIBIT 1

CGA COMPUTER ASSOCIATES, INC.
Historical Statement of Income
(000s omitted)

For the Eight Months Ended December 31, 1980

	ASC	CGA	Combined*
Revenue	$3,950	$9,401	$13,351
Income before taxes.	1,327	1,401	2,728
Net income.	691	691	1,382

Selected Balance Sheet Data
(000s omitted)

As of December 31, 1980

	CGA	Combined
Working capital	$6,757	$ 7,497
Total assets	8,214	10,259
Liabilities	1,230	2,232
Long-term debt	—	—
Stockholders' equity.	6,984	8,027

Capitalization
(000s omitted)

As of December 31, 1980

	CGA	Combined*
Stockholders' equity:		
Common stock, $0.10 par value—authorized 5,000,000 shares; issued and outstanding 1,878,997 shares (3,264,353 shares combined).	$ 188	$ 326
Capital in excess of par value	4,031	3,894
Retained earnings	2,765	3,807
Total stockholder's equity	6,984	8,027
Total capitalization	$6,984	$8,027

* Prepared on a pooling-of-interest basis.
Source: Form S-1, Registration Statement, filed by CGA Computer Associates, Inc. with the Securities and Exchange Commission, March 2, 1981.

as of December 31, 1980. Exhibits 2 and 3 present pro forma consolidated financial statements on a pooling-of-interest basis for the years ended April 30, 1979, 1980, and 1981.

PUBLIC OFFERING

On March 2, 1981, CGA filed a registration statement with the Securities and Exchange Commission (SEC) detailing a proposed public offering of 1,050,000 common shares. According to the registration statement, the shares being offered for sale were owned by several existing shareholders and, therefore, did not constitute an offering of new shares. The selling shareholders were:

	Common Shares Owned		Shares to be Sold	Ownership after sale	
	Number	Percent		Number	Percent
Broadview Associates*	16,070	0.5	16,070	–0–	–0–
Arthur Allen	684,643	21.0	516,965	167,678	5.1
Addison Fischer	684,643	21.0	516,965	167,678	5.1

* Broadview Associates acted as a "finder," with respect to the combination of CGA and ASC, and received 16,070 shares of the combined company's common stock as its finder's fee.

The registration statement revealed several relationships between the selling shareholders and CGA:

The company has agreed with Messrs. Allen and Fischer that should they not sell any shares of common stock in a public offering, the company would lend Mr. Fischer up to $1,400,000 and to Mr. Allen up to $600,000, for two years at 12 percent interest per annum to provide for the payment of federal tax liabilities incurred as a consequence of the combination. Such loans would be secured by a portion of the common stock held by such individuals. In addition, the company agreed that under certain conditions the company would, without security, loan up to $1 million to each of such individuals to satisfy certain additional tax liabilities incurred as a consequence of the combination. Such loans would accrue interest at the rate of 6 percent per annum (payable annually) and would be payable as to principal 10 years from the date the loan was made.

Messrs. Allen and Fischer and the two principal executives of the company agreed to vote or cause to be voted their common stock for a one-year period from February 27, 1981, for the perpetuation of the current members of the company's board of directors or their successors as designated by the board.

The company granted to Messrs. Allen and Fischer the right, exercisable once in addition to this offering, to have the company, prior to December 31, 1982, use its best efforts to register for public sale the common stock acquired by them in the combination. Messers. Allen and Fischer are obligated to pay all expenses of such registration except internal expenses of the company. . . . Messrs. Allen and Fischer also have agreed, subject to certain conditions including a minimum price of $8 per share, to sell at least 50 percent of their common stock prior to February 27, 1983.

The public offering was successful and, on April 7, 1981, Messrs. Allen and Fischer sold all but 335,356 shares in CGA.

LEGAL PROCEEDINGS

On July 16, 1981, the SEC instituted a proceeding against CGA pursuant to Section 8(d) of the Securities Act of 1933. The SEC alleged that the company's registration statement (dated April 7, 1981) contained materially false and misleading information

EXHIBIT 2

CGA COMPUTER ASSOCIATES, INC.
Pro Forma Consolidated Statements of Income
(dollars in thousands, except per share amounts)

| | Years Ended April 30 | | |
	1979*	1980*	1981
Revenue.	$15,120	$19,227	$20,358
Operating costs and expenses:			
Direct costs	7,584	9,495	10,091
Selling, general and administrative	4,449	6,299	6,668
	12,033	15,794	16,759
Operating income.	3,087	3,433	3,599
Other income (deductions)			
Interest income	65	175	637
Interest expense.	(3)	(15)	(1)
Gain on sale of subsidiary	53	—	—
Unrealized decline in market value			
of investments.	—	(31)	(29)
Other items, net	1	14	33
	116	143	640
Income before taxes.	3,203	3,576	4,239
Income tax provision:			
Current	731	1,158	944
Deferred	212	41	220
Pro forma, related to distributions			
to stockholders of Allen Services			
Corporation	570	617	900
Total income taxes	1,513	1,816	2,064
Net income before distributions to			
stockholders of Allen Services			
Corporation and after pro forma			
tax provision related thereto	1,690	1,760	2,175
Net income per share of common and			
common equivalent shares.	0.59	0.63	0.70

* Reclassified for comparative purposes.

in that CGA had accounted for its recent combination with ASC on a "pooling of interest" basis, rather than on a "purchase" accounting basis.

The SEC alleged that the treatment of the acquisition transaction as a pooling of interest was inconsistent with generally accepted accounting principles because:

● The agreement with Messrs. Allen and Fischer to sell at least 50 percent of their common stock (subject to certain conditions as to minimum price), and the restrictions on the voting of the common stock acquired by them were inconsistent with pooling of interest criteria.

● CGA's agreement to make substantial loans to Messrs. Allen and Fischer in order to enable them to satisfy tax obligations arising out of the acquisition, part of which loans were to be secured by the common stock obtained in the acquisition, negated the application of the pooling of interests accounting method.

According to CGA's Form 10-K (dated April 30, 1981) filed with the SEC:

EXHIBIT 3

CGA COMPUTER ASSOCIATES, INC.
Pro Forma Consolidated Balance Sheet
(dollars in thousands)

	April 30	
	1980	**1981**
Assets		
Current assets:		
Cash and interest-bearing deposits (including time deposits of $101 and $4,700 at April 30, 1980, and 1981, respectively)	$2,322	$5,522
Short-term investments, at lower of cost or market value	241	205
Receivables:		
Trade.	3,300	4,199
Other.	160	540
Prepaid expenses.	40	68
Total current assets.	6,063	10,534
Equipment and leasehold improvements, at cost:		
Furniture and equipment.	609	657
Leasehold improvement	31	44
	640	701
Less: Accumulated depreciation	192	232
	448	469
Other assets:		
Deferred costs, at cost less accumulated amortization.	35	24
Other assets	48	51
Total assets	$6,594	$11,078
Liabilities and Stockholders' Equity		
Current liabilities:		
Accounts payable.	$ 314	$ 228
Accrued liabilities	1,108	796
Income taxes:		
Current.	959	459
Deferred.	508	728
Total current liabilities.	2,889	2,211
Stockholders' equity:		
Common stock, par value $0.10, authorized 5,000,000 shares; issued and outstanding 949,276 and 3,264,340 shares at April 30, 1980, and 1981, respectively.	95	326
Capital in excess of par value.	351	4,024
	446	4,350
Retained earnings.	3,259	4,517
	3,705	8,867
Commitments and contingent liabilities.	—	—
Total liabilities and stockholders' equity	$6,594	$11,078

If purchase accounting had been used, revenues and net after-tax cash flow for all future fiscal year periods would remain the same. However, the cost of the purchase would have to be charged against the earnings of the company over the estimated useful lives (i.e., approximately five years) of the amortizable assets acquired from the date of acquisition. Accordingly, pro forma fiscal 1981 earnings after taxes would be reduced by $2,200,000 to a loss of $25,000; the impact on future years would be significant as the amortization of the purchase price and related goodwill would amount to a $2,200,000 per year charge to after-tax earnings.

Management Response

Bernard M. Goldsmith, president of CGA, said its method of accounting for the acquisition had been endorsed by both Alexander Grant & Company, its auditor at the time the registration statement was prepared, and Price Waterhouse & Company, CGA's current auditor. CGA officials said the computer consulting company and its auditors "intend to vigorously oppose" any SEC action. Paul Neuwirth, partner in charge of the Philadelphia, office of Alexander Grant & Company, said: "We believe that the accounting treatment is correct. We believe the circumstances are such that a pooling-of-interests treatment is the proper treatment."

If the SEC decides to suspend CGA's registration statement, the move would not affect trading in the securities covered by the registration; however, any SEC finding that the statement was "false and misleading" could lead to private shareholder lawsuits against the company.

EPILOGUE

In July of 1981, CGA and the SEC reached an unprecedented agreement—CGA would issue its annual report in both the pooling-of-interests and purchase formats for the succeeding five years. As a consequence of this decision, investors would be provided with two sets of financial statements and would be required to judge for themselves the financial position and operating performance of the company. Howard Hodges, chief accountant of the SEC's corporate finance division, observed that CGA was the only public company ever permitted this dual financial presentation: "I would never recommend it again."

QUESTIONS

1. How should CGA account for the ASC acquisition?

2. Restate the CGA's financial statements assuming that the purchase method of accounting was utilized.

CASE 6.2 _____

Digilog, Inc.*

The following description of Digilog, Inc. is from its amended filing of Securities and Exchange Commission Form 10-K for the fiscal year ended September 30, 1983.

Digilog, Inc. ("Registrant") develops, manufactures, and sells electronic equipment for the data communications, information processing, and data processing industries in the United States, Canada, and Europe. The Registrant was organized as a Delaware corporation in 1969.

Initially, Registrant produced a line of portable video display terminals for remote access to time-shared computer databases. Beginning in 1973, Digilog's business shifted toward custom-designed and manufactured intelligent data terminals, based on microprocessors. In 1977, when 66 percent of its business consisted of custom products, Registrant determined that it would be prudent to develop several new product areas and to reduce its dependence on custom products manufactured for a small number of customers. Product development efforts were focused on two business areas, small business microcomputers and network test and control equipment. The budgeted research and development costs and the start-up marketing expenditures associated with this transition adversely affected Registrant's result of operations in the last quarter of its 1978 fiscal year and the first three quarters of its 1979 fiscal year. However, beginning with the last quarter of Registrant's 1979 fiscal year, its results of operations reflected the success of this strategy. By 1980, only 24 percent of sales were custom products. During 1980, 64 percent of standard product sales (90 percent of microcomputer sales) was sold to BASF Aktiengesellschaft (BASF) for resale in Europe. During 1980, the Registrant put heavy product development and marketing emphasis on its network testing products, introducing a new data line monitor (DLM III) and several other network testing and control products. At the end of the second quarter of fiscal 1981, Registrant entered into a sales agreement wherein Digilog Business Systems, Inc. ("DBS") agreed to purchase for resale Digilog's new 1000 series small business computers. Registrant provided DBS with working capital in the form of a $450,000 convertible debenture, a $92,000 equipment loan, and bank debt guarantees.

During fiscal 1982, DBS accounted for 18 percent of all revenues (38.2 percent of microcomputer sales) and BASF accounted for 26 percent of total revenues (61.8 percent of microcomputer sales). BASF did not account for any of Registrant's sales in fiscal 1983. DBS accounted for 28 percent of Registrant's total revenue in 1983 and all of its microcomputer sales. Sales of Mailgram terminals to Western Union Electronic Mail,

* This case was prepared by Thomas I. Selling, assistant professor, Amos Tuck School of Business Administration, Dartmouth College. Copyright © 1985 by Thomas I. Selling. All rights reserved to the author.

Inc., which are handled by Digilog's Microcomputer Division, accounted for 3 percent of revenue in 1982 and 4.5 percent of revenue in 1983.

On September 16, 1983, Digilog exercised its conversion rights under the $450,000 convertible note agreement with DBS and received 450 shares of DBS common stock, which was equal to a 90 percent interest in DBS. Subsequent to conversion, Digilog transferred the net assets of its Microcomputer Division to DBS for 50 additional shares. This increased Digilog's ownership in DBS to 91 percent. DBS's name was changed to DBS International, Inc., and all microcomputer operations are generated through DBS International, Inc. The acquisition was accounted for as a purchase and, accordingly, the results of DBS's operations are included in the company's financial statements subsequent to September 16, 1983. As a result of the acquisition, a provision for excess liabilities assumed over assets acquired (goodwill) was charged to expense in 1983.

On November 27, 1984, the SEC, in one of only four administrative proceedings against a "Big Eight" accounting firm since 1978, found the auditors, Coopers & Lybrand, in error for not consolidating Digilog Business Systems (DBS) with those of Digilog since the date of establishment of DBS. The findings are based on Accounting Principles Board *Opinion No. 4* which provides that financial accounting information should emphasize the economic substance of a transaction even though its legal form may suggest different treatment. Although the auditor's interpretation of the transaction which resulted in the issuance of convertible notes by DBS gave Digilog a creditor's interest, the SEC interpreted the transaction to be, in economic substance, a purchase and should have been accounted for as such.

In arriving at their opinion and order, the SEC noted that the loan to DBS was convertible into 90 percent of the outstanding common stock of DBS, and the potential 90 percent share was protected by antidilution covenants. Furthermore, the nature of some of the debenture covenants gave Digilog significant control over many of the business decisions of DBS. For example, (1) the CEO and other key employees served at the pleasure of Digilog, (2) DBS could not merge or sell its assets without Digilog's consent, and (3) DBS's business plan could not be altered without the approval of Digilog. Digilog also had a right of first refusal to purchase any DBS shares the chief executive officer of DBS wished to sell.

Since Coopers & Lybrand chose not to contest the opinion and order (to do so, and to lose, would result in extremely costly sanctions, such as suspension from SEC-related practice), their justification for certification of Digilog's annual report is not available. Possible justifications might have included statements by Digilog that it could not control DBS despite statements to the contrary in the note debenture. The sole shareholder of DBS was a former high-ranking executive in a large, successful microcomputer firm who left a secure position for the psychic advantages of autonomy and who might leave before tolerating interference. Relatedly, Coopers might have been influenced by assurances that Digilog had no plans to exercise its conversion rights until DBS went public. Under such a scenario, Digilog's stock holdings would likely never have been sufficient to constitute a majority share of DBS. Finally, no precedent existed at the time to consolidate any ownership interest, other than majority stock.

Exhibit 1 contains the December 31, 1981, and 1982, balance sheets, income statements for period ending as of the above dates, and selected notes from the 1982 annual report of DBS. Since DBS is not a publicly traded corporation, these statements were not publicly available at the times of their issuance. Exhibit 2 contains the

EXHIBIT 1

DIGILOG BUSINESS SYSTEMS, INC.
Balance Sheets,
December 31, 1982, and 1981

	1982	1981
Assets		
Current:		
Cash	$ 53,289	$ 124,073
Accounts receivable, net of allowance for doubtful accounts of $72,000 and $32,000 in 1982 and 1981, respectively	844,031	386,168
Insurance claim receivable (Note 2)	44,913	44,913
Inventory (Notes 1, 3, and 6)	925,523	405,091
Prepaid expenses.	13,032	8,111
Other current assets	—	2,500
Total current assets	1,880,788	970,856
Equipment, less accumulated depreciation (Notes 1 and 4).	114,152	102,857
Other.	3,472	4,541
Total assets	$ 1,998,412	$1,078,254
Liabilities		
Current:		
Note payable (Note 5)	$ 1,975,000	$ 500,000
Current portion of long-term debt (Note 6)	60,370	1,112
Accounts payable (Note 3)	1,596,997	653,223
Commissions payable:		
Stockholder.	17,000	31,250
Others.	4,480	8,804
Accrued expenses	90,570	61,500
Total current liabilities	3,744,417	1,255,889
Long-term debt (Note 6)	482,345	542,809
Total liabilities	$ 4,226,762	$1,798,698
Stockholders' Deficit (Note 6)		
Common stock—par value $0.01 per share: 2,000 shares authorized and 50 shares issued and outstanding	1	1
Capital in excess of par value.	$ 49,999	$ 49,999
Deficit.	(2,278,350)	(770,444)
Total stockholders' deficit.	(2,228,350)	(720,444)
Total liabilities and stockholders' deficit	$ 1,998,412	$1,078,254

DIGILOG BUSINESS SYSTEMS, INC.
Statements of Operations
(for the year ended December 31, 1982, and
for the period March 20, 1981—date of incorporation—to December 31, 1981)

	1982	1981
Net sales (Note 9)	$ 3,173,444	$1,068,200
Costs and expenses:		
Cost of sales (Note 3)	3,100,383	920,400
Selling expenses.	728,240	399,133
General and administrative expenses.	527,737	444,393
	4,356,360	1,763,926
Loss from operations.	(1,182,916)	(695,726)
Other income (expense):		
Interest expense.	(339,386)	(96,431)
Other income, principally interest	14,396	21,713
	(324,990)	(74,718)
Net loss	$(1,507,906)	$ (770,444)

EXHIBIT 1 *(continued)*

DIGILOG BUSINESS SYSTEMS, INC.
Statements of Stockholder's Deficit
(for the year ended December 31, 1982, and
for the period March 20, 1981—date of incorporation—to December 31, 1981

	Common Stock	Capital in Excess of Par Value	Deficit
Balance, March 20, 1981	—	—	—
Issuance of 50 shares of common stock	$1	$49,999	—
Net loss			$ (770,444)
Balance, December 31, 1981	$1	$49,999	$(770,444)
Net loss	—	—	$ 1,507,906
Balance, December 31, 1982	$1	$49,999	$(2,278,350)

DIGILOG BUSINESS SYSTEMS, INC.
Notes to Financial Statements

3. *Marketing Agreement:*

During 1981, the company entered into a marketing agreement with Digilog, Inc. (Digilog) (see Notes 5,6, and 7), a manufacturer of computer hardware. The marketing agreement extends through 1986 and provides an exclusive distributorship for microcomputers if the company places annual orders for a minimum number of units. The agreement becomes nonexclusive if the specified order levels are not met.

A summary of the transactions with Digilog resulting from the marketing agreement is as follows

	1982	1981
Purchases during 1982	$2,927,000	
Purchases during the period March 20, 1981, to December 31,1981		$1,055,000
Balances at December 31:		
Accounts receivable from Digilog	13,900	—
Accounts payable to Digilog	1,437,000	637,000

In addition, the inventory at December 31, 1982 and 1981, includes $804,000 and $367,000, respectively, of computer equipment purchased from Digilog.

During the fourth quarter of 1982, Digilog and the company modified the foregoing marketing agreement. Under the new terms, Digilog reduced its sales price to the company and the company, in turn, reduced its retail sales prices. As a result of this modification the company reduced the carrying value of the inventory purchased from Digilog by approximately $247,000, which amount was charged to cost of sales in the fourth quarter.

An officer of Digilog serves as a director of the company.

4. *Equipment:*

Equipment at December 31, 1982, and 1981, consists of the following:

	1982	1981
Furniture and equipment	$ 39,820	$ 25,107
Demonstration equipment	131,341	99,361
	171,161	124,468
Less accumulated depreciation and amortization	57,009	21,611
	$114,152	$102,857

5. *Note Payable:*

During 1981, the company entered into an agreement with a bank whereby it has available a $2,500,000 line of credit. Borrowings under the line of credit amounted to $1,975,000 and $500,000 at December 31, 1982 and 1981, respectively. Additional information regarding borrowings under this agreement follows:

EXHIBIT 1 *(concluded)*

	1982	1981
Average interest rate during the year/period	15.20%	19.00%
Interest rate at December 31	12.00%	16.25%
Highest amount outstanding during the year/period	$2,150,000	$500,000
Average daily balance during the year/period	$1,678,000	$272,000

The line of credit has been guaranteed by Digilog (see Notes 3, 6, and 7).

6. *Long-term Debt:*

Long-term debt at December 31, 1982, and 1981, consists of the following:

		1982	1981
15%	convertible notes, interest due quarterly, maturing March 31, 1986 *(a)*	$450,000	$450,000
17.5%	note, interest due quarterly, $20,000 installments, due quarterly commencing June 30, 1983, final installment due June 30, 1984 *(b)*	92,345	92,345
Other		370	1,576
		542,715	543,921
Less amount due within one year		60,370	1,112
		$482,345	$542,809

(a) The 15 percent convertible notes are convertible into shares of the company by Digilog with whom the company has an exclusive marketing arrangement (see Notes 3, 5, and 7). Digilog can convert the principal amount of these notes at any time prior to March 31, 1986. The conversion price for these notes is $1,000 of principal for each share of the company's stock. Maximum conversion would yield 450 shares or 90 percent of the issued shares. These notes are collateralized by the receivables, inventory, and equipment of the company.

(b) The 17.5 percent note arose in connection with the purchase of certain equipment from Digilog (see Notes 3, 5, and 7).

Future maturities of long-term debt are as follows:

Year	
1983	$ 60,370
1984	62,345
1985	—
1986	450,000
	$542,715

7. *Leases:*

The company is party to a noncancelable operating lease for office facilities with Digilog. The lease extends through 1986. Aggregate minimum rental payments at December 31, 1982, are summarized as follows:

Year	
1983	$ 57,367
1984	57,367
1985	57,367
1986	43,025
	$215,126

Rent expense aggregated $68,889 for the year ended December 31, 1982, and $17,599 for the period ended December 31, 1981.

EXHIBIT 2

DIGILOG, INC.
Consolidated Balance Sheets
September 30, 1981 and 1982

	1982	1981
Assets		
Current:		
Cash.	$ 121,623	$ 528,920
Short-term investments (Note 1).	465,225	2,519,882
Accounts receivable less allowance for doubtful accounts of		
$24,000 and $13,000, respectively	3,164,192	774,675
Notes receivable, current (Note 3)	75,000	150,000
Insurance claim receivable (Note 2).	744,100	1,847,100
Inventories (Notes 1 and 4)	3,590,223	1,594,891
Prepaid expenses	91,812	73,137
Other current assets.	139,621	128,504
Total current assets	8,391,796	7,617,109
Notes receivable noncurrent (Note 3)	518,604	585,932
Investment (Note 1)	18,000	20,250
Plant and equipment, less accumulated depreciation and		
amortization (Notes 1 and 5).	2,157,153	744,693
Other.	14,451	5,481
Total assets.	$11,100,004	$8,973,465
Liabilities		
Current:		
Current maturities of long-term debt (Note 7)	$ 96,400	$ 135,000
Accounts payable	1,006,847	1,152,043
Accrued expenses.	196,373	547,747
Accrued commissions.	132,307	34,807
Accrued payroll.	245,103	166,007
Current portion of obligations under capital lease (Note 8)	16,235	13,774
Accrued income taxes payable.	71,589	7,965
Deferred income taxes (Notes 1 and 11).	701,280	83,440
Total current liabilities	2,466,134	2,140,783
Obligations under capital leases (Note 8).	23,733	39,968
Long-term debt (Note 7).	202,100	—
Deferred income taxes (Notes 1 and 11)	28,600	1,900
Total liabilities.	$ 2,720,567	$2,182,651
Commitments and Contingencies (Notes 8, 10, 14, 15, and 17)		
Stockholders' Equity		
Common stock—par value $0.01 per share; 4,000,000 shares		
authorized; 1,570,697 and 1,569,759 shares issued and		
outstanding in 1982 and 1981, respectively (Note 9).	$ 15,707	$ 15,698
Capital in excess of par value	5,964,523	5,957,875
Warrants (Note 10).	150	150
Retained earnings	2,536,276	923,935
	8,516,656	6,897,658
Less:		
Common stock in treasury, at cost	(59,986)	(31,861)
Net unrealized loss on investment (Note 1)	(77,233)	(74,983)
Total stockholders' equity	8,379,437	6,790,814
Total liabilities and stockholders' equity.	$11,100,004	$8,973,465

EXHIBIT 2 *(continued)*

DIGILOG, INC.
Consolidated Statements of Income
Year Ended September 30

	1982	1981	1980
Net sales.	$15,965,291	$7,094,169	$8,365,529
Costs and expenses:			
Cost of sales (Note 2).	9,316,268	3,849,428	5,158,266
Selling expenses.	1,968,481	1,553,444	1,290,636
General and administrative expenses (Note 2).	1,013,330	743,085	543,482
Research and development costs	1,405,051	879,466	611,524
	13,703,130	7,025,423	7,603,908
Income from operations	2,262,161	68,746	761,621
Other income (expense):			
Other income (principally interest).	188,469	468,299	125,291
Litigation (Note 13).	—	(486,323)	—
Interest.	(67,189)	(40,131)	(68,049)
	121,280	(58,155)	57,242
Income before income taxes.	2,383,441	10,501	618,863
Provision (credit) for income taxes (Note 11).	771,100	(21,700)	138,000
Net income	$ 1,612,341	$ 32,291	$ 680,863
Earnings per common share	$1.03	$0.02	$0.50
Weighted average common shares and common stock equivalents outstanding.	1,569,839	1,548,162	1,374,474

September 30, 1981, and 1982, balance sheets and income statements for the years then ended for Digilog. The only references to DBS made in the accompanying notes are to the amounts of long-term receivables and loan guarantees. No mention was made of DBS's financial position or results of operations.

QUESTIONS

1. Recast Digilog's financial statements under the assumption that DBS is accounted for as a consolidated subsidiary since the date of its inception. (For simplicity, assume that both companies' fiscal years end on December 31. Also, assume that sales from Digilog to DBS are priced at twice Digilog's cost.) What effect does this change have on income, and on other key financial statistics?

2. Is consolidation of DBS since the date of its inception consistent with GAAP? Which presentation is most consistent with economic reality? What should be the auditor's role in determining the proper treatment of this and similar transactions?

3. Should GAAP be changed to require consolidation in certain situations where the parent's equity interest is something other than common stock?

Earnings per Share

Anderson Industries, Inc.*

Anderson Industries, Inc. was founded in 1969 by J. R. and Bobby Anderson as an independent producer of oil and gas. The company, which was headquartered in the southwestern United States, grew substantially during the 1970s as it enjoyed the relative boom period of the oil and gas industry which followed the oil embargo of 1973.

The rising profits in the industry, however, brought with it many new competitors, and domestic oil and gas companies frantically scrambled to secure drilling rights on the remaining lands. In response to this, Anderson Industries began to borrow extensively to acquire new leases and to purchase drilling equipment capable of drilling to substantially greater depths. In 1980, for example, the company issued $5 million in preferred stock, followed by a second convertible preferred stock issuance in 1981 for $15 million and two convertible debt offerings totaling $22.5 million in 1982.

However, 1982 marked the beginning of a severe and extended decline in the oil and gas industry. Reduced consumption and excessive production combined to produce a worldwide oil glut which, in turn, drove the price of crude oil down by more than 30 percent. In addition, the company's deep-well exploration program in the Anadarko Basin in Oklahoma had proved to be unsuccessful, thus diminishing the prospect of adding significant quantities of new or replacement reserves in the future.

While the oil and gas industry appeared to be facing an extended period of hard times, the real estate industry in the southwestern United States was experiencing a significant growth period. So aggressive was the market that properties purchased one day would be sold, or "flipped," the next at a substantial gain. In an effort to provide a cushion for its sagging oil and gas operations, Anderson Industries expanded into real estate, acquiring substantial pieces of undeveloped properties, as well as a

---

* This case was prepared by Kenneth R. Ferris and Kirk Lee Tennant. Copyright © 1985 by Kenneth R. Ferris and Kirk Lee Tennant. All rights reserved to the authors.

few developed properties near Dallas and Houston, Texas. In anticipation of quick profits on the deals, the company borrowed extensively from lenders in those cities. In addition, in early 1985 the company borrowed nearly $30 million by issuing $80 million in 10-year convertible zero-coupon bonds.

By late 1985, reports were being published that the real estate markets in both Houston and Dallas had been substantially overbuilt, and that significant quantities of housing and office space in those cities remained unrented. Thus, Anderson Industries found itself faced with the prospect of liquidating its real estate holdings at values well below their original purchase price. Also, since the worldwide oil glut had persisted, the company found that it must consider the prospect of substantially writing down the value of its oil and gas properties.

With the rapid expansion in the real estate market also came a number of unethical businesspersons. In one transaction, Anderson Industries had purchased a complex of condominiums "on the flip." Subsequently, these properties were found to be substantially worthless; and since fraud and deception had been proved on the part of the seller to Anderson Industries, the company took the cost of these properties as an extraordinary loss for 1985.

At the December 1985 board of directors meeting, discussion centered around the options available to the company; they included: file for bankruptcy under Chapter 11 in order to restructure the company's debt position; attempt a public or private placement of stock, the proceeds of which would be used to reduce the level of outstanding debt; or seek out a potential acquiror for the company. The board supported the last option.

In anticipation of merger discussions, preliminary financial statements were prepared for 1985 (see Exhibits 1 and 2). Knowing that earnings per share might be an important discussion point in the valuation of the company, information regarding outstanding securities had also been collected (see Exhibit 3) and the major issues surrounding the calculation of EPS summarized (see Exhibit 4).

QUESTIONS

1. On the basis of the available information, calculate the primary and fully diluted earnings per share (EPS) for Anderson Industries for 1985. Would these figures be disclosed in the audited financial statements? Why or why not?

2. For purposes of valuing the company for possible sale, how valuable is the EPS data? What other information might you want? What EPS figure should the board of directors use in any negotiations?

3. Under what circumstances might an exchange of stock based on the EPS of the acquiring company and the acquired company be appropriate? Are these the circumstances in which Anderson Industries found itself?

4. Did Anderson Industries appropriately account for the loss on the condominium properties?

EXHIBIT 1

ANDERSON INDUSTRIES, INC.
Consolidated Statements of Income
For the Year Ended December 31, 1983 through 1985
(000s omitted)

	1983	1984	Preliminary 1985
Net revenues.	$ 21,123	$ 41,020	$ 81,939
Operating expenses.	(12,299)	(28,271)	(53,178)
Income from continuing operations before provision for taxes	8,824	12,749	28,761
Provision for income taxes.	(3,069)	(3,952)	(10,066)
Income from continuing operations	5,755	8,797	18,695
Income (loss) from discontinued operations (net of tax)	1,740	1,650	(17,000)
Extraordinary loss (net of tax)	—	—	(33,950)
Net income.	$ 7,495	$ 10,447	$(32,255)
Weighted average common shares outstanding	10,000	11,780	21,095

EXHIBIT 2

ANDERSON INDUSTRIES, INC.
Consolidated Balance Sheet
As of December 31, 1984, and 1985
(000s omitted)

	1984	1985
Assets		
Cash	$ 15,702	$ 12,906
Receivables	38,760	68,391
Inventories (at lower of cost or market).	9,690	22,793
Other	2,487	19,345
Total current assets.	66,639	123,435
Oil and gas property and equipment.	131,565	409,380
Less: Accumulated depreciation, depletion, and amortization	(20,910)	(38,418)
Net oil and gas properties.	110,655	370,962
Real estate and other assets (at cost)	44,713	276,455
Total assets	$222,007	$770,852
Equities		
Current liabilities:		
Short-term debt.	$ 7,074	$ 2,865
Current maturities of long-term debt.	2,814	54,825
Trade payables.	46,845	71,457
Advances from venture participants.	—	21,435
Accrued expenses	1,587	19,545
Long-term debt subject to acceleration by lender (net of current maturities)	—	149,855
	58,320	319,982

EXHIBIT 2 *(concluded)*

Convertible debentures (net of discount)	22,675	51,000
Long-term debt (net of current maturities).	30,666	57,759
Deferred income taxes.	8,028	8,048

Shareholders' equity:

Preferred stock, Series A, no par 100,000 shares authorized and issued	5,000	5,000
Preferred stock, Series B, no par 150,000 shares authorized and issued	15,000	15,000
Common stock, $0.10 par value, 40,000,000 shares authorized, 11,780,000 and 24,200,000 issued respectively	1,178	2,240
Capital in excess of par value	59,047	323,510
Retained earnings	22,093	(11,687)
Total equities	$222,007	$770,852

EXHIBIT 3

ANDERSON INDUSTRIES, INC.
Outstanding Securities

a. Common stock, $0.10 par value; 40,000,000 shares authorized
Issued and outstanding:

12/31/84	11,780,000
03/31/85	24,200,000*
12/31/85	24,200,000

*On March 31, 1985, the company successfully completed a public offering of 12,420,000 common shares.

Stock price data (AMEX):

	Close	Average
1984	$18¼	$16½
1985 (year)	10	14¾
First quarter	21½	18½
Second quarter	19½	18¾
Third quarter	14	15⅛
Fourth quarter	10	12

b. Common stock warrants:
Issued June 1976: 500,000 warrants convertible at a rate of 1 common share per warrant, exercise price of $10 per share, expiration date of June 1986.
Issued June 1979: 1.3 million warrants convertible at a rate of 1 common share per warrant, exercise price of $22 per share, expiration date of June 1989.

c. Preferred stock:
Series A, convertible issued January 1980:
Amount: $5,000,000.
Issue price: $50 per share.
Dividend rate: $5.50.
Aa Industrial Bond rate (1/80): 11.50%.
Conversion rate: each share convertible into five common shares.
Series B, convertible, issued January 1981:
Amount: $15,000,000.
Issue price: $100 per share.
Dividend rate: $6.50.
Aa Industrial Bond rate (1/81): 12.30%.
Conversion rate: each share convertible into 7.5 common shares

EXHIBIT 3 *(concluded)*

d. Convertible debentures:
   Issued March 1982:
       Maturity value: $13,000,000.
       Issued price: $980 per $1,000 bond.
       Coupon rate: 9%.
       Aa Industrial Bond rate (3/82): 14%.
       Conversion rate: each bond convertible into 66.67 common shares.
       Interest payments: semiannual, March, and September.
       Maturity Date: March 31, 2002.
   Issued September, 1982:
       Maturity value: $10,000,000.
       Issue price: $976 per $1,000 bond.
       Coupon rate: 8%.
       Aa Industrial Bond rate (9/82): 12.00%.
       Conversion rate: each bond convertible into 62.50 common shares.
       Interest Payments: semiannual, March, and September.
       Maturity Date: September 30, 2002.
   Issued March, 1985:
       Maturity value: $80,000,000.
       Issue price: $375 per $1,000 bond.
       Coupon rate: 0% (yield to maturity—10.25%).
       Aa Industrial Bond rate (3/85): 11.0%.
       Conversion rate: each bond convertible into 55 common shares.
       Interest payment: None.
       Maturity Date: March 1995.

EXHIBIT 4

Earnings per Share

.08   Earnings per share should be computed by reference to common stock and other residual securities. . . . When more than one class of common stock is outstanding, or when an outstanding security has participating dividend rights with the common stock, or when an outstanding security clearly derives a major portion of its value from its conversion rights or its common stock characteristics, such securities should be considered residual securities. . . .

.09   Under certain circumstances, earnings per share may be subject to dilution in the future if existing contingencies permitting the issuance of common shares eventuate. Such circumstances include. . . *(a)* outstanding senior stock or debt which is convertible into common shares, *(b)* outstanding stock options, warrants or similar agreements, and *(c)* agreements for the issuance of common shares for little or no consideration upon satisfaction of certain conditions. . . . If such potential dilution is material, supplementary pro forma computations of earnings per share should be furnished, showing what the earnings would be if the conversion or contingent issuances took place.

.30   Computations of primary earnings per share should not give effect to common stock equivalents or other contingent issuance for any period in which their inclusion would have the effect of increasing the earnings per share amount or decreasing the loss per share amount otherwise computed.* Consequently, while a security once determined to be a common stock equivalent retains that status, it may enter into the computation of primary earnings per share in one period and not in another.

---

* The presence of a common stock equivalent together with extraordinary items may result in diluting income before extraordinary items on a per share basis while increasing net income per share, or vice versa. If an extraordinary item is present and a common stock equivalent results in dilution of either income before extraordinary items or net income on a per share basis, the common stock equivalent should be recognized for all computations even though it has an antidilutive effect on one of the per share amounts.

Source: *AICPA Professional Standards, Volume 3, Current Text.* Copyright by American Institute of Certified Public Accountants, Inc., New York, New York. Reprinted with permission. Copies of the complete document are available from the AICPA.

Nelson Industries, Inc.*

Charles Nelson, president of Nelson Industries, Inc., quietly reflected on the contents of a letter he had sent the day before to his certified public accountant. The letter detailed his board of directors' stance on a significant accounting controversy. Of immediate concern was what strategy he should adopt in reply to the soon expected, but as of yet unknown, auditor's response.

BACKGROUND

Nelson Industries was a manufacturer of tempered steel parts for the heavy machinery industry. The firm had been founded in 1938 by the late Gordon Nelson. In 1964, the company went public with an offering of common stock, and in 1976, the company received listing on the New York Stock Exchange, where it still trades today. In that same year, Charles Nelson replaced his father as president.

From 1964 to 1981, sales and profits had grown each year; 1981 proved to be Nelson Industries best year with profits after tax of just under $4 million. But 1982, however, as well as 1983, heralded a profit downturn. Overall, the 1984 results showed a slight improvement in sales and almost no change in profits after tax (see Exhibit 1).

FINANCING ACTIVITIES

Since 1981, Nelson Industries had twice sought significant external financing to fund the company's investment programs. Exhibit 2 details the company's capital structure and common stock prices for 1983 and 1984.

In September 1981, a common stock issue with warrants added 200,000 common shares to the equity base. The warrants, issued one for each common share acquired, permitted the purchase of one additional share of common stock for $10 cash until September 1996.

In April 1984, the company issued subordinated convertible debentures with a face value of $7.2 million, a 9⅛ percent coupon rate of interest, and a life of 25 years. Each debenture was convertible after March 1986 into Nelson Industries common stock at a conversion price of $20 per share. Thus each $1,000 debenture was equivalent to 50 shares of common stock.

---

* This case was prepared by Dennis P. Frolin and James F. Smith as the basis for class discussion, rather than to illustrate either effective or ineffective handling of an administrative situation. Copyright © 1976, 1985 by the President and Fellows of Harvard College. Reprinted by permission of the Harvard Business School.

EXHIBIT 1

NELSON INDUSTRIES, INC.
Financial

	1983	1984
Net sales (millions)	$102.3	$108.6
Gross margin (millions)	52.4	53.4
Profit after tax (millions).	3.0	3.05
Earnings Per Share:		
Primary	3.00*	3.05†
Fully diluted	3.00	3.05†

* As published in the 1983 annual report.
† Charles Nelson's original computations.

The relatively small size of the debenture issue resulted in somewhat limited distribution of the initial offering, an inability to list the debentures on an exchange, and a very thin, inactive secondary market. Issue terms were finalized on June 22, the debentures were offered and sold out on June 29, and the first trade in the over-the-counter secondary market occurred on July 5 (see Exhibit 3).

1984 ANNUAL REPORT

During the year-end audit examination in preparation for the issuance of the 1984 financial statements, Charles Nelson was informed by his independent auditors, Arthur Marwick & Company, that the 1984 earnings per share computations that he had prepared for the financial statements (Exhibit 4) were not acceptable under Accounting Principles Board *Opinion No. 15,* as amended by *FASB Statement No. 55.* The senior in charge of the audit indicated that Nelson Industries had failed to include as common stock equivalents the convertible debentures issued in 1984 and the outstanding com-

---

EXHIBIT 2

NELSON INDUSTRIES, INC.
Parital Capital Structure and Common Stock Prices

	1983	1984
Common shares outstanding.	1,000,000	1,000,000
Warrants outstanding	200,000	200,000
Exercise price—$10		
Expiration date—September 1996		
Common shares reserved for exercise.	200,000	200,000
Convertible debentures—9⅛%:		
Face value Outstanding	0	$7,200,000
Maturity date—2009		
Conversion price—$20		
Common shares reserved for conversion	0	360,000
Common stock price—NYSE		

	Close	Average	Close	Average
First quarter	6⅝	6¾	12¼	10
Second quarter	7	7⅞	17	15¼
Third quarter.	8⅛	8¾	14½	17⅞
Fourth quarter.	9⅞	8⅝	9¾	12⅛
Year.		8		13¾

EXHIBIT 3

NELSON INDUSTRIES, INC.
9⅛% Convertible Debentures

Date	Event	Price	Average Aa Corporate Bond Yield
June 13.	Issue terms set	99½	13.75%
June 22.	Finalize issue terms	97¾	14.00
June 29.	Issue marketed	96½	14.25
July 5.	First trade secondary market	95	14.50

---

mon stock warrants issued in 1981. The requirement to treat both as common stock equivalents was explained as follows:

1. 9⅛ percent Convertible Debentures: the cash yield, based on its market price, was less than two thirds of the then average Aa corporate bond yield. Thus, the convertible qualifies as a common stock equivalent and must be counted in primary and fully diluted earnings per share on an "as if" converted basis.

2. Common Stock Warrants: the market price of the common stock during the year exceeded the exercise price of the warrant, hence they are dilutive and

---

EXHIBIT 4

NELSON INDUSTRIES, INC.
Auditor's Calculation of Earnings per Share

	Primary	
	1983	1984
Profit after tax (000 omitted).	$3,000	$3,050
Adjustments:		
Add back after-tax interest savings on convertible debentures (tax rate: 46%)	–0–	177
Profits after tax—adjusted	$3,000	$3,227
Common shares outstanding (000 omitted)	1,000	1,000
Adjustments:		
Add conversion of debentures	–0–	180
Add exercise of warrants*.	–0–	47.6
Common shares outstanding—adjusted	1,000	1,227.6
Earnings per share—primary.	$ 3.00	$ 2.63

	Fully Diluted	
Profit after tax—adjusted.	$3,000	$3,227
Common shares outstanding—adjusted	1,000	1,227.6
Add additional shares outstanding upon exercise of warrants based on closing (not average) prices*	–0–	12.6
	1,000	1,240.2
Earnings per share—fully diluted	$ 3.00	$ 2.60

EXHIBIT 4 *(concluded)*

NELSON INDUSTRIES, INC.
***Warrants: Treasury Stock Method**

Primary: Using Average Common Stock Price

1983 — Antidilutive

1984 — Quarter	Exercise	———(000 omitted)——— Purchase	Net Increment
1	200	200	0
2	200	131.1	68.9
3	200	113.5	86.5
4	200	164.9	35.1
	Total		190.5
	Average		47.6

Fully Diluted: using higher of average or
closing quarterly common stock price

1983 — Antidilutive

1984 — Quarter	Exercise	Purchase	Net Increment
1	200	163.3	36.7
2	200	117.6	82.4
3	200	113.5	86.5
4	200	164.9	35.1
	Total:		240.7
	Average:		60.2
Additional shares over primary:			12.6
(60.2 − 47.6)			

---

must be counted as outstanding during the year in primary and fully diluted earnings per share using the "treasury stock" method of calculation.

The audit senior proposed that the following earnings per share figures be published with the financial statements (see Exhibit 4 for calculations):

	1983	1984
Primary	$3.00	$2.63
Fully diluted	$3.00	$2.60

Charles Nelson's reaction to the audit senior's proposal was initially one of bewilderment, soon replaced by one of anger. Not only didn't the rules seem to make sense, the auditors seemingly should have been on top of the situation long before year-end.

Charles Nelson and the controller discussed the matter at length with Katherine Miller, audit partner responsible for the Nelson examination. The result was a stalemate—Miller maintained that her hands were tied by *APB Opinion No. 15* and *FASB Statement No. 55,* and Nelson insisted that the rules were arbitrary and unfair and that he would not abide by them. The meeting ended on strained terms. In the days following, Nelson had several telephone conversations with Ms. Miller and with Mr. Matthew Thomas, the partner-in-charge of the Arthur Marwick & Company Pittsburgh office. Three days later, he received a letter from Mr. Thomas establishing the position that Arthur Marwick & Company intended to maintain in this matter (See Exhibit 5).

On the following day, Charles Nelson met with the company's board of directors.

EXHIBIT 5
Nelson Industries, Inc.

January 20, 1985

Mr. Charles Nelson
President, Nelson Industries
Nelson Building
Pittsburgh, PA 15320

Dear Mr. Nelson:

This letter is written in follow-up to the conversations which you had with Ms. Katherine Miller and me in early January concerning the computation of earnings per common share for the year ended December 31, 1984, for inclusion in the Nelson Industries financial statements as of that same date.

After giving careful consideration to all factors pertinent to the computation of earnings per common share as outlined in APB Opinion No. 15 and FASB Statement No. 55, it is the unanimous opinion of the national accounting and auditing policy committee of our firm that the Nelson Industries convertible debentures and the Nelson Industries warrants must properly be included as common stock equivalents in this computation. The committee also noted that even if the convertible debentures were not counted as common stock equivalents, thereby included in the primary earnings per share calculations, they would always be counted as converted in the fully diluted earnings per share calculations. Thus the decline in earnings per share from 1983 to 1984 would be published on the face of the income statement in any case.

It is our official position that if the earnings per common share included in the financial statements are not computed in accordance with APB Opinion No. 15 and FASB Statement No. 55, we will be unable to issue a "clean," unqualified opinion and must indicate that the computation is not within generally accepted accounting principles.

Sincerely,

Matthew Thomas
Partner, Arthur Marwick & Company

At that time, the board discussed not only the recent letter from Mr. Thomas, but also the implications of the auditor's position for a proposed offering of zero-coupon convertible debentures in the spring of 1985. Since such bonds have no annual interest payments, it appeared that the debentures would automatically be considered common stock equivalents under the cash yield test. Based on the results of the meeting, Charles Nelson drafted a reply to Mr. Thomas (see Exhibit 6).

QUESTIONS

1. Review the auditor's determination of 1984 earnings per share (EPS) for Nelson Industries; do you agree with their results?

2. If you were Charles Nelson, how would you respond to the auditor's position?

3. How would you propose to treat the zero-coupon convertible debentures for EPS purposes?

EXHIBIT 6
Nelson Industries, Inc.

January 22, 1985

Mr. Matthew Thomas
Partner, Arthur Marwick & co.
One Lander Street
Pittsburgh, PA 15320

Dear Mr. Thomas:

I am very disappointed in the position you and your firm seem to have adopted on this earnings per share calculation. We have had a long, satisfying relationship with your firm and I am sure you personally remember that as a then junior staff member one of your first audit assignments was Nelson Industries. I certainly hope this misunderstanding will not harm our future relationship.

It is the position of the Board of Directors of this Company that the rules in question are arbitrary at best and they are unfair to Nelson Industries because they present a distorted picture of the current year's operations. The Board believes that your obligation is to present to our shareholders fair financial statements, not unfair statements that happen to be in accordance with generally accepted accounting principles.

With regard to the convertible debentures, the Board believes that inherent in the argument that these securities should be deemed converted to common shares for earnings per share computations is the assumption that conversion is imminent (or

EXHIBIT 6 *(continued)*

Matthew Thomas
Page Two   January 22, 1985

at least highly probable) in the foreseeable
future. In point of fact, the rational investor
will not convert to common shares until such time
as the market price of the common exceeds the
conversion price of $20 per share. Given the
current market price of 9¼ (down from 9¾ at
December 31, 1984, and over 19 in August 1984) and
its downward trend it would appear that the
probability of conversion in the foreseeable
future is in fact nil. Further, if the Nelson
Industries earnings per share are computed as
prescribed by APB Opinion No. 15 and FASB
Statement No. 55, the resultant decrease in
earnings per share will likely further depress the
market price, thereby even further lessening the
probability of conversion.

It is interesting to note that if the average Aa
corporate bond yield at the date of the debenture
issue had remained unchanged, your position would
reverse. Or if the debenture interest rate had
been a mere 1/4 percent higher, your position
would reverse; or if the initial market price of
the debenture had been 3 percent less, your
position would reverse. Of course, the current
debenture market price would more than meet this
requirement. If you would have bothered to check
the record, you would also see that the average Aa
corporate bond yield for the year would more than
meet the corporate bond yield test.

In a year of short-term interest rate turmoil—a
year in which interest rates changed numerous
times—it hardly seems appropriate for the
accounting treatment for a 25-year debenture to
depend on the average interest rate in effect
during a particular week.

Concerning the warrants, inherent to the argument
that the warrants should be deemed exercised for
earnings per share computations is the assumption
that actual exercise is imminent (or at least
highly probable) in the foreseeable future. In
point of fact, the rational investor will never
exercise a warrant until it expires. Nelson
Industries warrants expire in 1996, more than 10
years hence. The fact that the market price of our
common shares exceeded the warrant exercise price
at various times during 1984 means absolutely
nothing regarding the probability of exercise by
the holder of the warrant; its only effect is to
change the price of the warrant in the
marketplace. We realize the earnings per share
impact of the warrants is relatively insignificant

EXHIBIT 6 *(concluded)*

Matthew Thomas
Page Three   January 22, 1985

this year. Our position now, however, reflects the
stance we expect to adopt in the future as our
share price rises and the EPS impact becomes more
significant.

Based on the <u>realities</u> of the situation, we
cannot abide by the arbitrary and unfair
"guidelines" set forth by <u>APB Opinion No. 15</u> and
<u>FASB Statement No. 55.</u> It is the official position
of the Board of Directors of this Company that our
financial statements will either include an
earnings per common share of $3.05 for the year
ended December 31, 1984, or include <u>no</u> earnings
per share numbers throughout.

Further, the Board requests an explanation of the
failure on the part of your firm to appraise us of
the potential "hazards" in the earnings per share
calculation earlier in the year. You should also
be aware that our interim financial reports which
include an earnings per share calculation did not
reflect either the warrants or debentures as
common stock equivalents.

                    Sincerely,

                    Charles Nelson
                    President, Nelson Industries

Accounting for Inflation

CASE 6.5 _____

NCR Corporation*

In its 1979 annual report, the NCR Corporation (NCR) disclosed unaudited "supplementary financial information adjusted for changing prices" for the first time. As Note 13 in its annual report reveals, NCR disclosed both general price-level adjustments (GPLA) and specific price-level adjustments (SPLA) financial information in 1979. (See Exhibit 1 for NCR's financial statements.) The Financial Accounting Standards Board (FASB) had issued *Statement No. 33,* "Financial Reporting and Changing Prices," in September 1979. This statement required disclosure of the effects of general price-level adjustments (GPLA) in a supplementary financial report accompanying the firm's annual report for fiscal years ending after December 25, 1979. After December 25, 1980, current cost financial data showing the effects of specific price-level adjustments would also be required by *FASB Statement No. 33.* By disclosing this data in its 1979 annual report, NCR provided readers of its report with an early appraisal of the effects of inflation on the company.

Note 13 contains some interesting data. For example, reported net income adjusted for changes in specific prices (current cost), $310.6 million, is greater than reported net income prepared on an historical cost basis, $234.6 million. At the same time, reported net income adjusted for changes in the general price level, $119.8 million, is less than net income reported in the primary historical cost financial statements. The adjustment of income in opposite directions under GPLA and SPLA does not occur frequently for U.S. companies. Hence, the NCR situation merits an explanation in terms of the requirements of *FASB Statement No. 33.*

Statement No. 33 requires large public companies, such as NCR, to report general price-level adjusted income from continuing operations by adjusting the cost of sales

---

* This case was adapted with permission from a case written by Professor Joseph G. San Miguel and Research Assistant Robert A. Maginn, Jr., Harvard Graduate School of Business, with funding from the Touche Ross Foundation. Copyright © 1982 by Joseph G. San Miguel.

and depreciation for the change in the consumer price index for all urban consumers (CPI-U) during the period (see Exhibit 2). The FASB also requires companies to disclose the purchasing power gain or loss caused by holding either net monetary liabilities, accounts payable, or bank indebtedness, for example, or net monetary assets, such as accounts receivable or cash, during the times of inflation or deflation (see Exhibit 3). For comparative purposes, *Statement No. 33* calls for a five-year summary presenting in constant dollars the net sales and other operating revenues, cash dividends declared per common share and the year-end market price per share of common stock. The term *constant dollars* means the number of today's dollars that are equal in general purchasing power (according to the CPI-U) to the dollars reported in a previous year's financial statements (see Exhibit 4).

Some companies have already begun to report specific price (current cost) information. As alluded to earlier, all large public companies will be required to report income from continuing operations adjusted for specific price changes for fiscal years ended after December 25, 1980. Under SPLA, the *current cost* of inventory and property, plant, and equipment is calculated and then the cost of sales and depreciation expense are adjusted accordingly (see Exhibit 2). Finally, *FASB No. 33* requires companies to compute the increase or decrease in specific prices net of inflation, again beginning after December 25, 1980. This computation is accomplished by subtracting the effect of increases in the general price level from the increase or decrease in the specific prices of inventory and property, plant, and equipment (see Exhibit 5).

QUESTIONS

1. Review Exhibits 2–5. Be sure you understand the concepts conveyed by the numerical presentations.

2. Analyze the excerpts from 1979 NCR annual report in Exhibit 1.

    a. How would you explain the difference between the historical, GPLA, and SPLA net income figures?

    b. Discuss the presentation of "inflation accounting" information in Note 13. Be prepared to explain the calculations which underlie the figures presented in this note?

EXHIBIT 1

NCR CORPORATION
Consolidated Financial Position

Assets

	December 31 1979	1978
	(000 omitted)	
Current assets		
Cash and short-term investments	$ 148,253	$ 248,091
Note receivable (including interest).	—	173,505
Accounts receivable		
Current accounts.	753,943	566,943
Installment accounts (including receivables		
due after one year of $146,700 in 1979		
and $60,500 in 1978)	231,600	123,647
	985,543	690,590
Less: Allowance for doubtful accounts	31,268	23,329
	954,275	667,261
Inventories:		
Finished.	509,299	479,261
In-process and raw materials	239,259	163,259
	748,558	642,520
Deferred income taxes	74,976	28,522
Prepaid expenses	20,976	20,922
Total current assets.	1,947,038	1,780,821
Rental equipment and parts.	758,855	676,802
Less: Accumulated depreciation.	505,241	432,005
	253,614	244,797
Property, plant and equipment		
Land.	26,796	25,757
Buildings	336,020	308,973
Machinery and equipment.	464,753	412,851
	827,569	747,581
Less: Accumulated depreciation.	395,064	368,302
	432,505	379,279
Excess of acquisition cost over net assets of		
businesses acquired, net of amortization.	115,144	5,736
Deferred income taxes	40,468	54,573
Other assets.	129,666	130,955
Total assets	$2,918,435	$2,596,161

EXHIBIT 1 *(continued)*

Liabilities and shareholders' equity

	December 31	
	1979	1978
	(000 omitted)	
Current liabilities		
Notes payable	**$ 107,275**	$ 65,465
Current installments on long-term debt	**10,971**	11,613
Accounts payable	**110,354**	93,060
Taxes payable	**190,761**	214,995
Payroll payable	**106,197**	97,673
Other current liabilities	**205,468**	144,707
Customers' deposits and deferred service revenue	**234,341**	187,042
Total current liabilities	**965,367**	814,555
Long-term debt (exclusive of installments due within one year)	**344,568**	347,791
International employees' pension and indemnity liability	**75,605**	81,536
Minority interests	**56,582**	52,694
Shareholders' equity		
Preferred Stock—$5 par value; authorized— 10,000,000 shares; outstanding—$1.25 cumulative convertible — 25,367 shares in 1979 (278,791 in 1978).................	**127**	1,394
Common Stock—$5 par value; authorized— 80,000,000 shares; issued—26,765,809 shares in 1979 (26,455,714 in 1978)	**411,420**	405,594
Retained earnings	**1,102,096**	909,847
	1,513,643	1,316,835
Less: Treasury stock at cost — 551,204 shares of common stock in 1979 (286,489 in 1978)	**37,330**	17,250
Total shareholders' equity	**1,476,313**	1,299,585
Total liabilities and shareholders' equity	**$2,918,435**	$2,596,161

EXHIBIT 1 *(continued)*

NCR CORPORATION
Consolidated Income Statement

	1979	1978
Revenues		
Net sales	$1,840,237	$1,574,776
Rentals and services	1,162,403	1,035,744
	3,002,640	2,610,520
Costs and expenses		
Cost of products sold	845,824	747,328
Cost of rentals and services	639,287	569,211
Selling, general and administrative	930,340	780,999
Research and development	171,122	138,074
Interest expense	39,656	47,780
Other (income) expenses, net	(72,643)	(37,488)
	2,553,586	2,245,904
Income from continuing operations before income taxes	449,054	364,616
Income taxes	211,055	159,000
Income from continuing operations before minority interests	237,999	205,616
Minority interests in net earnings of subsidiaries	3,397	11,885
Income from continuing operations	234,602	193,731
Discontinued operations:		
Income from Appleton Papers Division		
(net of applicable income taxes)	—	13,778
Gain on sale of Appleton Papers Division		
(less applicable income taxes of $78,624)	—	110,495
	—	124,273
Cumulative effect on prior years of		
changes in accounting principles	—	—
Net income	$ 234,602	$ 318,004
Per common share		
Income from continuing operations:		
Primary	$8.78	$ 7.22
Fully diluted	8.78	6.90
Discontinued operations:		
Primary	—	4.63
Fully diluted	—	4.35
Cumulative effect on prior years of		
changes in accounting principles:		
Primary	—	—
Fully diluted	—	—
Net income:		
Primary	8.78	11.85
Fully diluted	8.78	11.25
Cash dividends declared:	1.60	1.00

EXHIBIT 1 *(continued)*

Five-Year Comparison of Selected Supplemental Financial Data Adjusted for Effects of Changing Prices

	(In Average 1979 Dollars)				
	Year Ended December 31				
	1979	1978	1977	1976	1975
		(000 omitted, except per share figures)			
Revenues	$3,002,640	$2,905,773	$2,770,505	$2,724,767	$2,727,412
Historical cost information adjusted for general inflation					
Net income	119,814				
Net income per common share — fully diluted	4.48				
Net assets at December 31	1,819,099				
Historical cost information adjusted for changes in specific prices					
Net income	310,657				
Net income per common share — fully diluted	11.63				
Net assets at December 31	1,814,440				
Loss from decline in purchasing power of net monetary assets	(34,061)				
Cash dividends declared per common share	1.60	1.11	0.96	0.92	0.97
Market price per common share at December 31	69.25	67.34	48.38	47.83	32.04
Average Consumer Price Index (base year 1967 = 100)	217.5	195.4	181.5	170.5	161.2

Note 13 — Supplementary Financial Information Adjusted for Changing Prices (Unaudited).

Background

The information on the following pages was developed in accordance with the requirements of Financial Accounting Standards Board (FASB) Statement No. 33 — Financial Reporting and Changing Prices. The purpose of FAS No. 33 is to provide, on an experimental basis, certain measurements of the effects of changes in prices on a company's operations. It should be noted, however, that the two methods required to be followed by FAS No. 33 in developing the above information involve the use of assumptions, approximations, and estimates, and therefore, the resulting measurements should be viewed in that context and not as precise indicators of the effects of changes in prices.

Methods

The first method adjusts historical financial information for "general inflation" using the Consumer Price Index for all Urban Consumers as the base measure of the general inflation rate.

The second method of measurement adjusts historical financial information for "changes in specific prices," which changes reflect general inflation as well as other factors, such as technological advancements, economies of scale, etc. This method reflects the effects of changes in prices of the particular resources actually used in a company's operations, so that measures of these resources and their consumption reflect the current cost of these resources, rather than the historical cost amounts actually expended to acquire them.

In accordance with FAS No. 33, the adjustments made to NCR's Consolidated Income Statement were only for depreciation expense related to rental equipment and parts and property, plant and equipment, and for inventory reflected in cost of products sold.

The current cost of inventories and rental equipment and parts was estimated based upon NCR's current material, labor and burden rates and adjusted for current cost depreciation expense of manufacturing facilities. The current cost of property, plant and equipment was estimated using engineering estimates, current vendor quotes, external price indexes and current construction cost data.

EXHIBIT 1 *(concluded)*

Review of Information

"Net income adjusted for general inflation" decreased from reported net income as the result of the restatement of cost of products sold and depreciation and amortization expense for the effects of general inflation.

"Net income adjusted for changes in specific prices" increased from reported net income as a result of the restatement of cost of products sold and depreciation and amortization expense under the specific price method. Cost of products sold, exclusive of depreciation expense, decreased under the specific price method because NCR's first-in, first-out method of valuing inventories resulted in a portion of prior year's higher costs to produce being included in this year's cost of products sold for financial statement reporting purposes. Under the specific price method, this year's cost of products sold reflected reduced current year product costs attributable to technological cost savings and economies of scale achieved in the production process over the life of the products. Depreciation expense decreased under this method because the current cost of rental equipment and parts was less than historical cost due again to technological cost savings and economies of scale achieved in the production process over the life of the products. This reduction in rental equipment depreciation expense more than offset increased depreciation expense related to the higher current cost of property, plant and equipment. However, it should not be concluded that lower cost of products sold and lower depreciation expense related to rental equipment and parts under the specific price method are necessarily indicative of additional cost declines in future years as the factors contributing to such cost reductions may not be present.

NCR believes that the specific price method more appropriately reflects the effects of changing prices as related to its business than the general inflation method, which only considers general inflation as a cause of changes in prices. Furthermore, since inflation affects different specific prices in different ways, information about changes in an index of general inflation does not provide sufficient information about the effect of inflation on a specific business enterprise.

"Loss from decline in purchasing power of net monetary assets" under both methods measures the decline in the purchasing power of NCR's net monetary assets (cash, receivables and payables which are fixed in dollar amount) when stated in average 1979 dollars.

The "Decrease in specific prices, net of inflation" of inventories and rental equipment and parts reflected the technological cost savings and economies of scale achieved by NCR in the production process over the life of these products. The "Increase in specific prices, net of inflation" of property, plant and equipment was the result of property costs rising at a higher rate than the rate of general inflation.

The five-year comparison shows the effect of adjusting historical dollar amounts to dollar amounts expressed in average 1979 dollars, as measured by the Consumer Price Index.

Statement of Income Adjusted for Changing Prices
For The Year Ended December 31, 1979

(In Average 1979 Dollars)

	As Reported in Primary Financial Statements	Adjusted for General Inflation	Adjusted for Changes in Specific Prices
	(000 omitted)		
Revenues.................	$3,002,640	$3,002,640	$3,002,640
Costs and expenses:			
Cost of products sold	845,824	912,882	809,710
Cost of rentals and services	639,287	674,860	589,651
Selling, general and administrative	930,340	940,223	938,221
Research and development .	171,122	173,396	172,936
Interest expense	39,656	39,656	39,656
Other (income) expenses, net	(72,643)	(72,643)	(72,643)
	2,553,586	2,668,374	2,477,531
Income from continuing operations before income taxes	449,054	334,266	525,109
Income taxes	211,055	211,055	211,055
Income from continuing operations before minority interests	237,999	123,211	314,054
Minority interests in net earnings of subsidiaries....	3,397	3,397	3,397
Net income...............	$ 234,602	$ 119,814	$ 310,657
Depreciation and amortization expense:			
Rental equipment and parts .	$ 147,651	$ 177,375	$ 93,351
Property, plant and equipment	62,021	89,097	83,613
	$ 209,672	$ 266,472	$ 176,964
Loss from decline in purchasing power of net monetary assets		$ (34,081)	$ (34,081)

	Inventory and Rental Equipment and Parts	Property, Plant and Equipment	Total
Increase (decrease) in specific prices, (current costs) of inventories, rental equipment and parts, and property, plant and equipment held during the year*	$ (96,543)	$ 122,035	$ 25,492
Less effect of increase in general price level	111,872	107,798	219,670
Increase (decrease) in specific prices, net of inflation	$ (208,415)	$ 14,237	$ (194,178)

*At December 31, 1979, current cost of inventory was $725,309,000; current cost of rental equipment and parts, net of accumulated depreciation, was $227,986,000; and current cost of property, plant and equipment, net of accumulated depreciation, was $934,587,000.

EXHIBIT 2
Illustrative Statements

Statement of Income for the Year Ended December 31, 1979
Historical Cost Basis
(in millions)

Sales		$1,000
Cost of sales (exclusive of depreciation expense):		
Beginning inventory (2,700,000 units)	230	
Purchases and production costs	610	
Ending inventory (3,900,000 units).	240	600
Gross margin		400
Depreciation expense		17
Interest expense		33
Selling, general and administrative		
expenses		250
		300
Income from continuing operations before tax . .		100
Income tax.		50
Net income from continuing operations		$ 50

Statement of Income Adjusted for Changing Prices
For the Year Ended December 31, 1979

	Historical Cost	General Price Level (constant dollars)	Specific Price Level (current cost)
Sales.	$1,000.00	$1,000.00	$1,000.00
Cost of sales	600.00	629.00 ✗	534.30 → pg. 3÷3
Depreciation expense	17.00	24.75	25.25
Interest expense	33.00	33.00	33.00
Selling, general, and			
administrative expense	250.00	250.00	250.00
Income from continuing			
operations before tax.	100.00	63.25	157.45
Income tax	50.00	50.00	50.00
Net income	50.00	13.25	107.45
Gain from decline in purchasing power of net monetary			
liabilities		10.00	10.00
(Decrease) in specific prices (current cost) of			
inventories and property, plant, and equipment			(78.45)
Less effect of increase in general price level			34.70
(Decrease) in specific prices—net of inflation			(113.25)

Computation Schedules for Adjustment of Income
For General Price Level Changes

	Historical Cost	Conversion Factor	Average 1979 Dollars (constant dollars)
Beginning inventory . .	$230	$\dfrac{217.4 \text{ average } 1979}{201.9 \text{ 4th qtr. } 1978} = 1.077$	$248
1979 production	610	Assumed-in average 1979 dollars	610
Ending inventory. . . .	240	$\dfrac{217.4 \text{ average } 1979}{227.6 \text{ 4th qtr. } 1979} = .955$	229
Historical cost of sales	$600		
Adjusted cost of sales			$629 ✗

EXHIBIT 2 *(continued)*

Analysis of Selected Accounts and Financial Information
Property, Plant, and Equipment
(in millions)

December 31, 1979:

Account Name	Year Acquired	Cost	Percent Depreciated	Accumulated Depreciation	Annual Average CPI-U
Land	1970	$ 30	NA	NA	116.3
Buildings	1970	100	50%*	50	116.3
Equipment	1970	20	100†	20	116.3
	1975	50	50	25	161.2
	1979	50	10	5	217.4
		250		100	

December 31, 1978:

Account Name	Year Acquired	Cost	Percent Depreciated	Accumulated Depreciation	Annual Average CPI-U
Land	1970	$ 30	NA	NA	116.3
Buildings	1970	100	45%	45	116.3
Equipment	1970	20	90	18	116.3
	1975	50	40	20	161.2
		$200		83	

* Buildings depreciated straight-line over 20 years.
† Equipment depreciated straight-line over 10 years.
Note: NA means not available.

Restatement of Depreciation Expense
For General Price Level Changes
As Measured by the CPI-U, 1979
(in millions)

Account-Year of Acquisitions	Historical Cost	Conversion	Average 1979 Dollars	Annual Depreciation Percentage	Depreciation Expense Constant Dollars
Buildings 1970	$100.0	$\dfrac{217.4 \text{ avg.* } 1979}{116.3 \text{ avg. } 1970} = 1.87$	$187.0	5%	$ 9.30
Equipment 1970	20.0	$\dfrac{217.4 \text{ avg. } 1979}{116.3 \text{ avg. } 1970} = 1.87$	37.0	10	3.70
1975	50.0	$\dfrac{217.4 \text{ avg. } 1979}{161.2 \text{ avg. } 1975} = 1.35$	67.5	10	6.75
1979	50.0	$\dfrac{217.4 \text{ avg. } 1979}{217.4 \text{ avg. } 1979} = 1.00$	50.0	10	5.00
Totals	$220.0		$341.5		$24.75

* Average.

EXHIBIT 2 *(continued)*

Current-Cost (specific price) Financial Information
(in millions)

December 31, 1979:

Account Name	Year Acquired	Current Cost	Percent Depreciation	Accumulated Depreciation	Average Annual CPI-U
Land	1970	$ 55	NA	$ NA	116.3
Buildings	1970	190	50%*	95	116.3
Equipment	1970	40	100†	40	116.3
	1975	75	50	37.5	116.3
	1979	55	10	5.5	161.2
		$415		$178	217.4

December 1, 1978:

Account Name	Year Acquired	Current Cost	Percent Depreciation	Accumulated Depreciation	Average Annual CPI-U
Land	1970	$ 50	NA	NA	116.3
Buildings	1970	180	45%	$ 81	116.3
Equipment	1970	35	90	31.5	116.3
	1975	70	40	40.5	161.3
		$335		$153.0	

* Buildings depreciated straight-line over 20 years.
† Equipment depreciated straight-line over 10 years.
Note: NA means not available.

Current cost per calculator in
  beginning inventory $80
Current cost per calculator
  in ending inventory $50
Average current cost—1979 . . . . $65
Units sold during 1979   8,220,000

Computation Schedules for Adjustment of Income
For Specific Price Level Changes

Calculation of current cost/cost of sales:

Current cost per calculator
  in beginning inventory . . . . $ 80
Current cost per calculator
  in ending inventory . . . . $ 50
                                                          $130
Average current cost per   ÷2
  calculator 1979   65
Units sold in 1979. . . . .   × 8,220,000
Average current cost/cost of sales $534,300,000

EXHIBIT 2 *(concluded)*

Calculation of Current Cost Depreciation Expense
For the Year Ended December 31, 1979
(in millions)

Account	Year	Balance	Annual Depreciation Percentage	Depreciation Expense
Building	1978	$180		
	1979	190		
	Average	185	5%	$ 9.25
Equipment	1978	35		
	1979	40		
	Average	37.5	10	3.75
	1978	70		
	1979	75		
	Average	72.5	10	7.25
	1978	0		
	1979	75		
	Average	50	10	5.00
Total depreciation expense				$25.25

EXHIBIT 3
Illustrative Statements

Calculation of Purchasing Power Gain (Loss) on Net Monetary Liabilities
(Assets) Under Rising General Prices Measured by the CPI-U
(in millions)

	Balance	Conversion Factor	Average 1979 Dollars
Net monetary liability, December 31, 1978	$70	$\dfrac{217.4 \text{ avg. } 1979}{202.9 \text{ December } 1978} = 1.07$	$75
Increase in net monetary liabilities during 1979	20	*	20
			95
Net monetary liabilities, December 31, 1979	90	$\dfrac{217.4 \text{ avg. } 1979}{229.9 \text{ December } 1979} = .946$	85
Purchasing power gain or net monetary liabilities			$10

* Assumed to be in average 1979 dollars.

Monetary Assets and Liabilities

	1979	1978
Cash	$ 15	$ 10
Accounts receivable	275	250
Accounts payable and accrued expenses	(250)	(200)
Current portion of bank indebtedness.	(10)	(10)
Bank indebtedness.	(100)	(110)
Income taxes payable	(20)	(10)
Net monetary items	(90)	(70)

EXHIBIT 4
Illustrative Statements

Five-Year Comparison of Selected Historical Financial Data
Adjusted to Average 1979 Dollars
As Measured by the Consumer Price Index for All Urban Consumers (CPI-U)

	1979	1978	1977	1976	1975
Net sales (in millions)	$1,000	$890.1	$898.3	$828.8	$674.3
Cash dividends per common share	5.00	4.45	4.19	3.82	2.70
Market price per common share at year-end.	75.00	75.66	75.46	63.75	47.20
Average CPI-U	217.4	195.4	181.5	170.5	161.2
Conversion factor	1.00	1.1126	1.1978	1.2751	1.3486

Five-Year Summary

	1979	1978	1977	1976	1975
Net sales (in millions)	$1,000	$800	$750	$650	$500
Cash dividends declared per common shares.	$5.00	$4.00	$3.50	$3.00	$2.00
Market price per common share at year-end	$ 75	$ 68	$ 63	$ 50	$ 35
Average annual CPI-U.	217.4	195.4	181.5	170.5	161.2

EXHIBIT 5
Illustrative Statements

Current Cost Inventory
Adjusted for General Price Level Changes
Using the CPI-U
(in millions)

	Current Cost (nominal dollars)	Conversion Factor	Current Cost (average 1979 dollars)
Inventory: December 31, 1978 (2,700,000 units × $80)	$216	$\frac{217.4 \text{ avg. } 1979}{202.9 \text{ Dec. } 1978} = 1.07$	$231
Production	610	*	610
Current cost/ cost of sales	(534.3)	*	(534.3)
Inventory: December 31, 1979 (3,900,000 units × 50	(195)	$\frac{217.4 \text{ avg. } 1979}{229.9 \text{ Dec. } 1979} = .946$	(185.5)
Decrease in current cost of inventory	(96.7)		(121.2)

Decrease in current cost of inventory	$ (96.7)
Decrease in current cost of inventory adjusted for general price level changes	(121.2)
General price change (inflation) component	(24.5)

* Assumed to be in average 1979 dollars.

EXHIBIT 5 *(concluded)*

**Current-Cost Property, Plant, and Equipment
Adjusted for General Price Level Changes Using the CPI-U**
(in millions)

	Current Cost (nominal dollars)	Conversion Factor	Current Cost (average 1979 dollars)
Property, plant, and equipment net of accumulated depreciation, December 31, 1978	$194.5	$\dfrac{217.4 \text{ avg. } 1979}{202.9 \text{ Dec. } 1978} = 1.07$	$208
Additions	50		50
Current cost depreciation expense	(25.25)		(25.25)
Property, plant, and equipment net of accumulated depreciation, December 31, 1979	(237.5)	$\dfrac{217.4 \text{ avg. } 1979}{202.9 \text{ Dec. } 1978} = .946$	(224.7)
Increase in plant, property, and equipment	18.25		8.05

Increase in plant, property, and equipment	$18.25
Increase in plant, property, and equipment adjusted for general price level changes	8.05
General price change (inflation) component.	$10.20

Increase (decrease) in current cost of inventory and property, plant, and equipment, net of inflation:

Decrease in current cost of inventory (nominal dollars)	$ (96.70)
Increase in current cost of property, plant, and equipment (nominal dollars).	18.25
Net decrease in current cost of inventory and property, plant, and equipment	$ (78.45)
Decrease in current cost of inventory (1979 average dollars)	$(121.20)
Increase in current cost of property, plant, and equipment (average 1979 dollars)	8.05
Net decrease in current cost of inventory and property, plant, and equipment	($113.15)
Inflation component inventory	$ 24.50
Inflation component—property, plant, and equipment.	10.20
Effect of increase in general price level	34.70

Foreign Currency Translation

Data-Chip Technology Corporation*

In late December 1981, Mr. John Hughes, corporate controller of Data-Chip Technology Corporation (DCTC), a U.S.-based multinational firm, was considering adopting *FASB Statement No. 52* for 1981. In the past, the company's financial statements had been prepared in accordance with *FASB Statement No. 8,* reflecting translation gains or losses in the income statement. Mr. Hughes was aware of *FASB 52*'s provision for excluding translation gains or losses from net income which would reduce the volatility in the company's future earnings, but he was uncertain what the impact on DCTC's reported earnings in current and future years might be. He asked Mr. Chris Brown, manager of the international accounting department, to recommend by the afternoon of Tuesday, January 4, 1982, whether or not the company should adopt *FASB 52* for 1981.

BACKGROUND

DCTC was established in the United States in 1970 and was well known in the industry for its electronic innovations. The firm had experienced a growth rate of 25 percent in the first five years of its operations. To maintain this high rate of growth and to capture the vast European market, a wholly owned subsidiary had been established in France in 1975. The French subsidiary catered to the entire European market, and the business was largely carried out in French currency—the franc. The company's product for the European market was primarily produced in France. The volume of intercompany transactions and cash flows had been low, and the subsidiary had little need for long-term debt because of its ability to generate sufficient funds from operations. Most of its expansion since 1975 was internally financed.

---

* This case was prepared by Thomas G. Evans, Martin E. Taylor, and Oscar Holzmann. Copyright © 1985 by MacMillan Publishing Company. Reprinted with permission of MacMillan Publishing Company from *International Accounting* by T. G. Evans, M. E. Taylor, and O. Holzmann.

The subsidiary's financial statements for fiscal year 1981, presented in francs, and the *FASB 8* translation are shown in Exhibits 1 and 2.

The parent company had been quite satisfied with the subsidiary's operating results. For the past six years, as in 1981, the French franc operating profit margin (before translation) was 12.4 percent. The sales volume had grown at an average rate of 30 percent over the last six years. However, the exchange rate movements during the last six years had resulted in reporting increasing or decreasing operating margins and net income.

The average exchange rates for the French franc for the past 10 years are shown in Exhibit 3. The franc started weakening in 1979. It was trading at the rate of 5.748 francs per dollar in 1981, below its previous historical low rate of 5.558 in 1969. The French government made a desperate and vigorous attempt in September 1981 to defend the franc, which caused a serious loss of foreign exchange and forced the government to devalue the franc in October 1981. The government of François Mitterrand was pressing ahead with nationalization plans, and its attempts to stimulate the sluggish French economy produced such a large budget deficit that the government had to impose a price freeze. The consumer price index had risen to 162 in 1981 from 118 in 1978, and the prime interest rate had risen to 15.6 percent.

QUESTIONS

1. What would be the appropriate functional currency for the French subsidiary if *FASB Statement No. 52* were adopted? What translation gains or losses would be reflected in current income under *FASB 52?*

2. What would be the impact on current income if *FASB 52* were adopted? What would be the translation adjustment under *FASB 52,* and how would it be reported? Would the current and future income of the company be completely insulated from changes in the exchange rate of the French franc?

3. What is the nature of accounting exposure in the subsidiary? What would be the result of this exposure on income under increasing and decreasing exchange rates?

4. What appears to be the future outlook for the franc, and how will it affect the subsidiary's position under *FASB 52?*

5. What considerations will be pertinent in making a decision about the adoption of *FASB 52?* Do you recommend that *FASB 52* be adopted for 1981?

EXHIBIT 1

DATA-CHIP TECHNOLOGY CORPORATION OF FRANCE
Income Statement for the Year Ended December 31, 1981
(amounts in thousands)

			FASB 8 Translation		
	Francs		**Exchange Rate**	**Dollars**	
Sales.		29,000	0.190*		$5,510
Cost of goods sold.	14,500		0.200†	$2,900	
Selling and administrative expenses.	6,000		0.190	1,140	
Depreciation expense	2,500		0.222‡	555	
Interest expense	500	23,500	0.190	95	4,690
		5,500			820
Other income principally interest.		500	0.190		95
Earnings before income taxes		6,000			915
Income taxes		2,400	0.190		456
Operating income before translation.		3,600			459
Translation gain					113
Net operating income		3,600			572
Retained earnings	1/1/81	10,100			2,491
Dividends paid		1,200	0.170§		204
Retained earnings	12/31/81	12,500			2,859

* Average exchange rate during 1981.
† Average exchange rate during period when inventory was acquired.
‡ Exchange rate on the date when property was acquired.
§ Exchange rate when dividends were paid.

EXHIBIT 2

DATA-CHIP TECHNOLOGY CORPORATION OF FRANCE
Balance Sheet as of December 31, 1981
(amounts in thousands)

	Francs	FASB 8 Translation Exchange Rate	Dollars
Assets			
Cash assets:			
Cash.	500	.174*	$ 87
Marketable securities	1,500	.174	261
Accounts receivable.	4,000	.174	696
Inventories	2,800	.195†	546
Prepaid expenses	700	.220‡	154
	9,500		$1,744
Plant and other property	30,000	.222§	6,660
Less: Accumulated depreciation	13,000	.222	2,886
		17,000	3,774
Total assets.		26,500	5,518
Liabilities and stockholders' equity			
Current liabilities:			
Accounts payable	1,000	.174	174
Loans payable	500	.174	87
Taxes payable	1,500	.174	261
Obligations under warranties.	400	.174	70
Accrued expenses and liabilities	1,600	.174	278
	5,000		870
Long-term debt.	3,000	.174	522
Deferred income taxes	1,000	.212‖	212
Stockholders' equity	5,000	.211§	1.055
Retained earnings	12,500		2,859
Total liabilities and stockholders' equity.	26,500		5,518

* Exchange rate December 31, 1981.
† Average exchange rate during period when inventory in the December 31, 1981, balance sheet was acquired.
‡ Exchange rate on date when prepaid expenses were incurred.
§ Exchange rates on date property acquired, capital stock issued.
‖ Historical rate applicable to deferred income taxes.

EXHIBIT 3
Average Exchange Rates for Franc

Year	Francs per U.S. Dollar	Percent Variation	Year	Francs per U.S. Dollar	Percent Variation
1972	5.125		1977	4.705	+5.31
1973	4.708	+8.14	1978	4.180	+11.16
1974	4.444	+5.61	1979	4.020	+4.26
1975	4.485	−0.92	1980	4.516	−12.34
1976	4.969	−10.79	1981	5.263	−16.54

JAS Industries*

JAS Industries was founded in 1974 by Jason A. Smith. Smith was a mechanical engineer working in the aerospace industry in 1973 when cutbacks in government funding of the space program caused his layoff. When he was laid off, Smith had been working on quality control problems involving the computer processing of data received from "down range" radar tracking stations. Most of the problems seemed to center on the card-sorting machines that frequently jammed or failed to read the cards property. Smith believed that these problems could be overcome with relatively minor modifications in the machines.

Although Smith was offered jobs in other states and other sectors of the aerospace industry, he did not want to leave his home in Florida. With borrowed money he formed JAS Industries to produce card-sorting machines. The first few machines produced by JAS Industries were actually built in Smith's garage. With Smith's contacts with the major aerospace contractors, he was able to gain access to a large market that could readily appreciate the superior qualities of his product. He was also able to gain access to a large pool of young, eager, and talented engineers who were more than willing to forgo the vicissitudes of the space race to join a rapidly expanding firm that promised them "a piece of the action."

During the 1970s, JAS Industries grew rapidly based on innovations in card sorters, printers, terminals, and other peripheral computer equipment. Also during this period JAS Industries expanded overseas, following a well-established pattern of firms entering international markets. In 1978, some of JAS Industries' products had come to the attention of a major European defense contractor, and by the summer of that year the firm had begun exporting two of its product lines to France. During the same year, the firm entered into a contract with a Japanese firm to supply it with transistors and diodes for computer terminals. Although neither contract represented a large portion of JAS Industries' sales or purchases, it was the firm's first brush with the issues of international finance. It was also this experience that was to set the tone for future financial arrangements involving exchange rate risk.

Rick Fredericks became the treasurer for JAS Industries when the firm moved from Smith's garage to its first manufacturing facility in a rented warehouse. Fredericks was an industrial engineer who excelled in cost accounting. In fact, it was Fredericks's keen attention to detail that had enabled JAS Industries to win several particularly

---

* This case was prepared by Thomas G. Evans, Martin E. Taylor, and Oscar Holzmann. Copyright © 1985 by MacMillan Publishing Company. Reprinted with permission of MacMillan Publishing Company from *International Accounting* by T. G. Evans, M. E. Taylor, and O. Holzmann.

profitable bids from defense contractors. When Fredericks assumed his responsibilities as treasurer for JAS Industries, he enrolled in an evening master of accountancy program at a local college. It was during the course of his studies that he was introduced to and became convinced of the truth of the efficient market hypothesis. If exchange markets were efficient, he reasoned, the cost of hedging was money needlessly spent. In both of the foreign contracts concluded in early 1978, Fredericks acted on his beliefs. Unfortunately, both contracts were unsuccessful from the viewpoint of exchange rate risk.

On large orders, such as that of the French defense contractor, it was customary for JAS Industries to require one third of the contract price (denominated in the foreign currency) to be paid in advance and the balance on delivery. In February 1978, when the contract was signed, the French franc was trading at approximately $1 = Fr 4.2575. By August 1978, when the printers and card sorters had arrived in the port of Le Havre, the spot rate for the French franc was $1 = Fr 4.9570. Needless to say, the anticipated margin of 15 percent was not reached. Likewise, the contract with the Japanese supplier encountered similar problems. In May 1978, JAS Industries agreed to pay Y2,995,750,000 upon delivery of the electronic components it had ordered from its Japanese supplier. In May, the spot rate for the yen was $1 = Y260.50, and by October, when the parts arrived in Jacksonville, Florida, the spot rate was $1 = Y249.25. Jason Smith was not pleased with the results of the company's first venture into the world of floating exchange rates. Following a somewhat heated meeting with Fredericks, he told the treasurer to "do whatever is necessary to see that the company doesn't suffer this kind of loss again."

During the next three years, the company continued to expand and to become more deeply involved in foreign contracts. By 1981, 24 percent of the firm's sales were to European companies, and 9 percent were to Latin American companies. That year the firm's total sales topped the $100 million mark. Imports of Japanese electronic components also increased proportionately. Although Fredericks was uncomfortable with the costs involved, he used forward contracts to hedge all but the smallest transactions, keeping in mind Smith's dictum.

By 1982, JAS Industries was seriously considering opening a final assembly plant in Europe and was actively looking for a plant site. During that same year, Jason Smith's daughter graduated from a well-respected university with a master's degree in international business. Jody Smith joined the firm that summer and was given the responsibility of coordinating the financial planning for the new facility, tentatively sited in Cornwall, England. It was not long before the subject of exchange risk management came up. Jody Smith strongly recommended in a preliminary report that a comprehensive strategy be developed to address JAS Industries' exchange risk management problems. Rick Fredericks (to whom she reported on the project) readily agreed for several reasons: first, he felt that the cost of hedging with forward contracts was becoming burdensome, and second, he recognized that in fiscal year 1983 the company would have to adopt the provisions of *FASB Statement No. 52*. Jason Smith also readily agreed that such a strategy should be developed, but for somewhat different reasons. He hoped that JAS Industries would be in position to make its first public stock offering in 1984. With so much of the firm's business being done overseas, he was concerned with the impact of foreign exchange fluctuations on the future stock price.

Jody Smith was assigned the further responsibility of developing and recommending a foreign exchange risk management strategy for JAS Industries. This task was to be undertaken with the support of the Treasury department, the project team working on the new plant, and the firm's auditors.

QUESTIONS

1. Could JAS Industries have avoided the use of forward contracts and still have projected its exposure to exchange rate risk?

2. Would the use of other techniques (if any) affect the contract prices? How?

3. Is the exposure to exchange rate risk affected by opening the new plant in England? Is this exposure different from the exposure created by the foreign buyers and suppliers?

4. What techniques are available to handle the exposure created by the new plant?

5. Does the existence of a Japanese supplier, who will presumably supply some parts to the plant in England, make available any exposure management techniques that would not exist otherwise?

6. How will the adoption of *FASB 52* affect the exposure to exchange risk? Is hedging as important under *FASB 52*? Would the same hedging techniques be used under *FASB 52* as under *FASB 8*?

7. Do you believe that the way JAS Industries manages its exchange risk could have any effect on its stock price? Why or why not?

8. Based on your answer to Question 7, what objectives do you think JAS Industries should pursue in the area of exchange risk?

International Accounting Issues

Comparative Financial Statements*

One of the special problems created by the diversity in accounting principles from country to country is that it hinders international investment. This is especially true when one attempts to analyze the financial statements of a number of firms from different countries. The differences in accounting principles can be seen in the balance sheet as well as in the income statements of such firms. It is important to recognize the different accounting principles embodied in the financial statements of "foreign" firms. This requires, first, a knowledge of the accounting principles of one's own country, to be used as a benchmark.

This case is an exercise in analyzing the financial statements of firms in foreign nations. Exhibits 1–4 contain examples of the financial statements (balance sheet, income statement, and listing of significant accounting policies) for an American firm, a British firm, a Dutch firm, and a Swedish firm. Study the American financial statements and then analyze the other three sets to determine what the significant differences are in format and underlying accounting principles.

---

* This case was prepared by Thomas G. Evans, Martin E. Taylor, and Oscar Holzmann. Copyright © 1985 by MacMillan Publishing Company. Reprinted with permission of MacMillan Publishing Company from *International Accounting* by T. G. Evans, M. E. Taylor, and O. Holzmann.

EXHIBIT 1
Example of Typical American Financial Statements

I. Consolidated Balance Sheet:

Assets

Current Assets:

Cash	$ 400	
Marketable Securities and Investments	2,900	
Accounts and Notes Receivable	5,000	
Inventories	3,500	
Prepaid Expenses	800	
		$12,600

Long-term Assets:

Plant, Property, and Equipment	20,000
Deferred Charges	2,000
Total Assets	$34,600

Liabilities and Stockholders' Equity

Current Liabilities:

Accounts Payable	$ 1,000	
Loans Payable	600	
Taxes Payable	2,900	
Other Current Liabilities	4,500	
		$ 9,000

Long-term Liabilities:

Long-term Debt		3,000
Stockholders' Equity:		
Capital Stock	$ 5,000	
Retained Earnings	17,600	
		22,600
		$34,600

II. Consolidated Income Statement

Revenue from Sales and Services		$43,000
Operating Expenses:		
Cost of Sales	$ 7,000	
Selling, General, and Administrative	15,000	
Research and Development	3,000	
Interest Expense	400	
		25,400
Operating Income		17,600
Other Income		300
Earnings Before Taxes		17,900
U.S. Federal and State Income Taxes		7,200
Net Earnings		$10,700
Per Share		$ 3.97

III. Significant Accounting Policies

Consolidation: The statements include the parent and its American and foreign subsidiaries.

Marketable Securities and Investments: These are shown at the lower of cost or market.

Accounts and Notes Receivable: These are reduced for estimated uncollectible amounts.

Inventories: These are shown at cost (principally average historical cost) or market, whichever is lower.

Plant, Property, and Equipment: These are shown at the original historical cost, less depreciation.

Depreciation: Computed on original cost, using accelerated methods (principally sum of years digits).

Cost of Sales: Computed on the LIFO (last in, first out) basis.

Research and Development: These costs are expensed as incurred.

Income Taxes: These are computed on the basis of accounting net income; deferred taxes are recorded.

Goodwill: The cost of goodwill is recorded as an intangible asset and is amortized over a forty-year period.

EXHIBIT 2
Example of Typical British Financial Statements

I. Consolidated Balance Sheet

Capital Employed

Preferential Share Capital	£ 68.
Common Shareholders' Equity	2900.
Minority Interest in Subsidiaries	160.
Loan Capital	800.
Deferred Liabilities	900.
Total	£ 4828.

Employment of Capital

Fixed Assets	£ 2400.
Investments in Associated Companies	200.
Working Capital	2228.
Total	£ 4828.

II. Consolidated Income Statement

Sales	£13215.
Costs and Expenses	12500.
Operating Profit	715.
Other Income	58.
Other Expense	40.
Profit Before Taxation	617.
Taxation	300.
Profit After Taxation	317.
Dividends	117.
Profit of the Year Retained	£ 200.

III. Significant Accounting Policies

Consolidation: The subsidiaries included in the consolidated financial statements are those in which the parent holds (directly or indirectly) more than 50 percent of the equity capital.

Goodwill: No value is given to goodwill; it is written off to Retained Earnings in the year of acquisition.

Fixed Assets: These are stated at cost, and depreciation is computed on the straight-line method.

Current Assets: Stocks (inventory) are recorded on the basis of cost or net realizable value, whichever is lower. Cost is based on the average cost method. Debtors (receivables) are shown after deducting provisions for doubtful accounts. Marketable securities are temporary investments and are listed at their market value.

Taxes: These are computed on a deferred basis.

Research and Development: These costs are charged against the revenue in the period in which they are incurred.

EXHIBIT 3
Example of Typical Dutch Financial Statements

I. Consolidated Balance Sheet
Assets

Plant, Property, and Equipment	27,000 G	
Depreciation	13,000	
		14,000
Intangible Assets		1,000
Investments in Nonconsolidated Firms		1,000
Inventories ("stocks")		12,000
Accounts Receivable		10,000
Liquid Assets (cash and marketable securities)		2,000
		40,000

Capital and Liabilities
Shareholders' Equity:

Share Capital	2,000	
Retained Earnings	6,000	
Revaluation Surplus	5,000	
		13,000
Minority Interest		1,000
Provisions		6,000
Long-term Liabilities		5,000
Current Liabilities		13,000
Profit Available for Distribution		2,000
		40,000

II. Income Statement

Sales		38,000 G
Cost of Sales	27,000	
Selling and General Expenses	7,000	34,000
		4,000
Other Income and Expenses		(1,000)
Profit Before Tax		3,000
Tax		1,500
Profit After Tax		1,500
Share in Profit of Nonconsolidated Firms		500
Group Profit		2,000

III. Significant Accounting Policies

Consolidation: The combined statements represent the financial data for the parent firm and all subsidiaries that are over 50 percent owned.

Valuation: The valuation of plant, property, and equipment and stocks (inventories) is based on replacement cost (current costs). Changes in the replacement value of assets are directly credited or charged to the Revaluation Surplus in equity.

Intangible Assets: Except for goodwill, intangible assets are not shown on the balance sheet. Goodwill is amortized over a maximum of five years.

Provisions: These are not related to specific assets; they are created to meet commitments and the risks associated with the normal course of business.

Depreciation: This is based on the replacement cost of the fixed assets.

Cost of Goods Sold: This is based on the replacement cost of the inventory sold.

Research and Development: These costs are expensed in the year incurred.

EXHIBIT 4
Example of Typical Swedish Financial Statements

I. Consolidated Balance Sheet
Assets
  Current Assets:

Cash	1,000 SEK	
Loans and Short-term Notes	6,000	
Accounts Receivable	10,000	
Merchandise Inventory	14,000	
Blocked Account in Bank of Sweden	200	
		31,200
Long-term Assets:		
Long-term Receivables and Notes	900	
Investment in Nonconsolidated Firms		
("shares and participations")	3,000	
Plant, Property, and Equipment	9,000	
		12,900
Total Assets		44,100
Liabilities and Shareholders' Equity		
Current Liabilities:		
Accounts Payable	6,000	
Loans Payable	7,000	
Other Current Liabilities	6,000	
		19,000
Long-term Liabilities:		
Notes and Bonds Payable	8,000	
Pensions	1,000	
Deferred Taxes	1,000	
		10,000
Untaxed Reserves:		
General Inventory Reserve	4,000	
Extra Depreciation	2,000	
Investment Reserves	2,000	
Other Reserves	1,000	
		9,000
Minority Interest		1,000
Shareholders' Equity:		
Share Capital	1,000	
Legal Reserves	2,000	
		3,000
Retained Earnings	900	
Net Income for Year	1,200	
		2,100
Total Liabilities and Shareholders' Equity		44,100

EXHIBIT 4 *(concluded)*

II. Consolidated Income Statement

Sales		75,000 SEK
Cost of Sales and Operating Expenses		70,000
Operating Profit Before Depreciation		5,000
Depreciation		1,000
Operating Profit After Depreciation		4,000
Financial Income and Expenses		(1,000)
Income After Financial Income and Expenses		3,000
Allocations:		
Allocation to General Inventory Reserves	700	
Extra Depreciation	100	
Allocation to Investment Reserves	400	
Allocations to Other Reserves	100	
		(1,300)
Income Before Taxes		1,700
Taxes		500
Income After Taxes		1,200

III. Significant Accounting Policies

Consolidation: The group accounts consist of the parent's financial statements combined with those of firms in which the parent owns more than 50 percent of the voting common stock.

Allocations and Untaxed Reserves: Swedish tax law allows firms to exclude from income certain items, called *allocations*, to strengthen the firm's financial position. Allocations for inventories, investments, and fixed asset replacements are allowed. Firms can also take "extra depreciation" over the straight-line method used for book purposes. Firms can use the reserves to cover future operating losses. A special case is the investment reserve: under tax law, firms can allocate a maximum of 50 percent of their income to this reserve (50 percent of the allocation must be placed in the Swedish central bank). Funds are released and used for investment when allowed by a governmental order to stimulate local construction.

Inventories: Shown at the lower of cost (FIFO) or replacement value.

Deferred Taxes: Refer mainly to the tax portion of the untaxed reserves.

Industry Reporting Issues

Middle South Utilities, Inc.*

In August 1984, *The Wall Street Journal* carried a story with the following headline:

> MIDDLE SOUTH SEEN NEAR FILING FOR CHAPTER 11:
> SEC Aide Terms Possibility "Very Real"

The story detailed that Mr. William Weeden, Securities and Exchange Commission (SEC) assistant director for public utility regulation, had reported to rate-making authorities that on the basis of cash flow projections filed with the agency by Middle South Utilities (MSU), a chapter 11 bankruptcy-law filing by the company was a "very real" possibility. Mr. Weeden stated that without emergency rate relief, MSU's Louisiana Power & Light Company and New Orleans Public Service units faced insolvency within 60 days. Weeden noted that the nation's fifth-largest electric utility holding company "may be as close to Chapter 11 as any major electric utility since the Great Depression."

The comments by the SEC's assistant director came in the wake of two federal court decisions in Louisiana, which failed to force Louisiana public utility commissioners to grant recent MSU rate-hike requests. Mr. Weeden also warned that given the utility's current financial condition, the SEC would almost certainly block any attempt to raise the needed funds through the public securities markets.

BACKGROUND

Middle South Utilities, Inc. is a public holding company for four electric utility companies serving parts of Arkansas, Louisiana, Mississippi, and Missouri—Louisiana Power & Light Company, Mississippi Power & Light Company, New Orleans Public Service, Inc., and Arkansas Power & Light Company. From 1966 to 1983, MSU

---

* This case was prepared by Kenneth R. Ferris and Robert F. Lacroix. Copyright © 1985 by Kenneth R. Ferris. All rights reserved to the author.

enjoyed an average growth rate in net income of 13.8 percent, and it reported record high earnings of $378 million in 1983. Organized in 1949, MSU increased its dividend payments in all but one year since its inception.

MSU, like all electric utilities throughout the United States, is subject to the directives of the Federal Energy Regulatory Commission (FERC), formerly the Federal Power Commission (FPC). This agency is empowered to establish operating and reporting procedures for electric utility companies. Footnote 1, "Summary of Significant Accounting Policies," to MSU's 1983 financial statements states (see attached financial statements and selected footnotes in Exhibits 1–10):

> The accounts of the Company . . . are maintained in accordance with the Public Utility Holding Company Act of 1935, as administered by the Securities and Exchange Commission, which has adopted a system of accounts consistent with the system of accounts prescribed by the Federal Energy Regulatory Commission.

The accounting practices prescribed by the FERC deviate in some cases from generally accepted accounting practice (GAAP) for nonregulated companies.[1] In 1962, the Accounting Principles Board issued an *Addendum* to *APB Opinion No. 2,* which specified that financial statements prepared by a regulated company and intended for public use must be based on existing GAAP, *except* for those accounts specifically required by a regulatory agency. These accounting differences were further institutionalized in 1982 with the issuance of Financial Accounting Standards Board (FASB) *Statement No. 71,* "Accounting for the Effects of Certain Types of Regulation."

FASB Statement No. 71 specifies, among other things, that:

> In the construction or acquisition of plant and equipment, a regulator may require a regulated enterprise to capitalize certain interest as part of the cost of the asset. The capitalized interest usually includes interest costs on borrowing, or interest costs on a designated portion of equity funds, or both. The cost of the asset shall be increased by the amount of capitalized interest; and for regulatory purposes, subsequent depreciation should be based on the total cost of the asset.

Should a conflict exist between *FASB Statement No. 71* and existing GAAP, *Statement No. 71* requires that the provisions of that statement be applied; hence, where conflicts in reporting practice exist, regulated companies must conform to the regulatory accounting requirements specified in *FASB No. 71.*

This case concerns the accounting for the "allowance for funds used during construction" account (AFUDC), and its impact on the financial statements of MSU.

AFUDC

By law, public utilities are required to provide utility services to designated populations; and as the designated population expands, so expands the requirement to provide such service. As a consequence, for most geographical areas in the United States, the level of investment in property, plant, and equipment by public utilities has steadily increased.

To avoid "rate shocks" to utility consumers (i.e., exorbitant rate increases), the

---

[1] In most instances, differences in accounting practice and the system of acounts as required by regulatory agencies versus those specified by GAAP can be traced to the rate-making process. In general, public utilities are allowed to earn a minimum rate of return on invested capital; hence, rate increases are typically approved by public utility authorities when the level of utility net income relative to its investment falls below this minimum rate.

cost of improving existing facilities or of building new facilities are capitalized to the utility's investment base, as opposed to being charged against current earnings. Thus, the cost of new or improved facilities is shared by all future utility customers, instead of being borne solely by the current user base.

Since 1922, regulatory authorities have considered the cost of funds used to construct new facilities (or improve existing ones) to be a capitalizable cost. Until 1976, the cost of borrowed funds, as well as a reasonable rate of return on equity funds used for the construction of assets, were lumped together under the account "allowance for funds used during construction." In 1977, however, the FPC mandated the separation of the common equity component and the borrowed funds component of the AFUDC for financial reporting purposes.

Under the FPC order, the AFUDC for borrowed funds (AFUDC-B) would represent the actual net interest cost for the current period of funds used for asset construction purposes.[2] This account would appear on the income statement under the heading "Interest and Other Charges," and consequently offset the actual construction financing costs deducted as "interest on long-term debt." Thus, the actual borrowing costs would be "transferred" from the income statement (as an expense) to the balance sheet (as an asset).

The FPC order also mandated that an allowance for equity funds used during construction (AFUDC-E) be calculated (see Exhibit 1) and displayed on the income statement under the heading "Other Income." The allowance would be imputed using a weighted average cost of equity funds. Thus, even though no cash was actually dispersed to shareholders in conjunction with the use of the equity funds, an amount would be capitalized representing the implicit cost of using those funds.[3] On the income statement, this implicit cost savings would represent a source of income for shareholders.

Prior to 1960, the ratio of the AFUDC to reported net income averaged only 5 percent in the electric utility industry. With the escalation of inflation, however, this ratio substantially increased, and by 1980, the industry average exceeded 40 percent. Exhibits 2 and 3 present industry-wide data on the relationship of the AFUDC to reported net income and on the components of the AFUDC, respectively. Exhibit 4 presents stock price data for MSU from 1966 through 1983. Exhibit 5 shows the auditor's opinion and Exhibits 5–10 present MSU's financial information useful in answering the following questions.

QUESTIONS

1. Evaluate the practice of capitalizing the AFUDC. Do you agree? Why?

2. Evaluate the financial condition of Middle South Utilities from 1981–83. Do you agree with the stock market's assessment (see Exhibit 4) of MSU's financial strength?

---

[2] The journal entry to provide for capitalization of the interest costs is as follows:

Dr. Construction Work in Progress $XXX
   Cr. Allowance for Borrowed Funds Used
       During Construction $XXX

[3] It can be argued that this method implicitly allows regulated companies to treat at least a portion of their dividend payments as the acquisition of an asset, rather than simply as the distribution of earned capital.

EXHIBIT 1
Middle South Utilities, Inc.

The formula and elements for the computation of the allowance for funds used during construction are as follows:

$$A_t = s\left(\frac{S}{W}\right) + d\left(\frac{D}{D+P+C}\right)\left(1-\frac{S}{W}\right)$$

$$A_e = \left(1-\frac{S}{W}\right)\left[p\left(\frac{P}{D+P+C}\right) + c\left(\frac{P}{D+P+C}\right)\right]$$

where:

A_t = Gross allowance for borrowed funds used during construction.
A_e = Allowance for other funds used during construction.
S = Average short-term debt.
s = Short-term debt interest rate.
D = Long-term debt.
d = Long-term debt interest rate.
P = Preferred stock.
p = Preferred stock cost rate.
C = Common equity.
c = Common equity cost rate.
W = Average balance in construction work in progress plus nuclear fuel in process of refinement, conversion, enrichment, and fabrication.

Source: United States of America, Federal Power Commission—Order No. 561 (issued February 2, 1977).

EXHIBIT 2

MIDDLE SOUTH UTILITIES, INC.
Industry-Wide Data:
Allowance for Funds Used during Construction*
December 31, 1977–81
(thousands of dollars)

Year	Net Income Reported	Net Income after Preferred Stock Dividends	Allowance for Funds Used during Construction	AFUDC as a Percent of Net Income	AFUDC as a Percent of Income Available to Common Stockholders
1977	$ 8,009,549	$ 6,529,620	$2,256,626	28.2%	34.6%
1978	8,716,708	7,091,668	2,746,949	31.5	38.7
1979	9,477,811	7,677,223	3,597,586	38.0	46.9
1980	10,675,977	8,629,620	4,403,289	41.2	51.0
1981	12,729,961	10,475,113	5,254,342	41.3	50.2

EXHIBIT 3

MIDDLE SOUTH UTILITIES, INC.
Industry-Wide Data:
Components of AFUDC*

Year	Total Allowance	Equity Component		Interest Component	
		Amount	Percent	Amount	Percent
1977	$2,256,626	$1,391,708	61.7%	$ 864,918	38.3%
1978	2,746,949	1,643,691	59.8	1,103,258	40.2
1979	3,597,586	2,111,163	58.7	1,486,423	41.3
1980	4,403,289	2,415,815	54.9	1,987,474	45.1
1981	5,254,342	2,820,760	53.7	2,433,582	46.3

* Source: Statistics of Privately Owned Electric Utilities, 1981, Energy Information Administration.

EXHIBIT 4

MIDDLE SOUTH UTILITIES, INC.
Common Stock Price Data

	High	Low
1966	$26.75	$21.00
1968	26.875	20.375
1970	27.625	18.625
1972	28.75	19.375
1974	18.00	9.125
1976	17.375	13.625
1978	17.375	14.25
1979	16.375	12.25
1980	14.25	10.25
1981	13.875	11.00
1982	15.75	12.25
1983	16.75	13.125

EXHIBIT 5
Auditors' Opinion

The Stockholders and the Board of Directors
of Middle South Utilities, Inc.:

We have examined the consolidated balance sheets of Middle South Utilities, Inc. and its subsidiaries as of December 31, 1983 and 1982 and the related consolidated statements of income, retained earnings, paid-in capital, and changes in financial position for each of the three years in the period ended December 31, 1983. Our examinations were made in accordance with generally accepted auditing standards and, accordingly, included such tests of the accounting records and such other auditing procedures as we considered necessary in the circumstances.

In our opinion, the above-mentioned consolidated financial statements present fairly the financial position of the Company and its subsidiaries at December 31, 1983 and 1982 and the results of their operations and the changes in their financial position for each of the three years in the period ended December 31, 1983, in conformity with generally accepted accounting principles applied on a consistent basis.

Deloitte Haskins & Sells

February 20, 1984

EXHIBIT 6

MIDDLE SOUTH UTILITIES, INC., AND SUBSIDIARIES
Statement of Consolidated Income
For the Years Ended December 31, 1983, 1982, and 1981

	1983	1982	1981
		(In Thousands)	
Operating Revenues:			
Electric	$ 2,716,329	$2,673,572	$ 2,582,778
Natural gas	193,328	172,692	139,242
Total	2,909,657	2,846,264	2,722,020
Operating Expenses:			
Operation:			
Fuel for electric generation	942,219	1,066,325	1,083,064
Purchased power	373,712	345,076	263,559
Gas purchased for resale	158,186	138,890	107,768
Deferred fuel and other	363,509	288,283	307,218
Maintenance	149,453	132,031	127,067
Depreciation	183,171	167,725	158,264
Taxes other than income taxes	104,493	101,381	93,058
Income taxes (Notes 3 and 12)	190,589	171,741	175,142
Total	2,465,332	2,411,452	2,315,140
Operating Income	444,325	434,812	406,880
Other Income:			
Allowance for equity funds used during construction (Note 1)	245,640	182,342	143,369
Miscellaneous income and deductions—net (Note 12)	6,799	7,133	24,249
Income taxes—credit (Notes 3 and 12)	157,342	147,186	126,466
Total	409,781	336,661	294,084
Interest and Other Charges:			
Interest on long-term debt	529,597	488,750	441,894
Other interest—net	47,251	74,130	74,507
Allowance for borrowed funds used during construction (Note 1)	(180,858)	(170,438)	(157,511)
Preferred dividend requirements of subsidiaries	80,066	68,436	60,591
Total	476,056	460,878	419,481
Net Income	$ 378,050	$ 310,595	$ 281,483
Earnings Per Common Share	$2.46	$2.33	$2.44
Dividends Declared Per Common Share	$1.71	$1.67	$1.63
Average Number of Common Shares Outstanding	153,383,044	133,193,296	115,175,550

See Notes to Consolidated Financial Statements.

EXHIBIT 7

MIDDLE SOUTH UTILITIES, INC. AND SUBSIDIARIES
Consolidated Balance Sheets
December 31, 1983, and 1982

Assets

	1983	1982
	(In Thousands)	
Utility Plant (Notes 8, 9, and 12):		
Electric	$ 5,688,426	$ 5,158,736
Natural gas	117,848	113,719
Transit	—	15,920
Construction work in progress	5,923,619	5,022,635
Nuclear fuel	212,524	153,178
Total	11,942,417	10,464,188
Less—Accumulated depreciation	1,694,475	1,551,700
Utility plant—net	10,247,942	8,912,488
Other Property and Investments	75,979	83,846
Current Assets:		
Cash (Note 4)	2,843	19,023
Special deposits	12,507	11,198
Temporary investments—at cost, which		
approximates market (Note 11)	9,129	283,142
Notes receivable	2,663	2,584
Accounts receivable:		
Customer (less allowance for doubtful accounts of (in thousands)		
$3,893 in 1983 and $2,602 in 1982)	174,936	147,241
Other	43,025	35,368
Receivable from gas supplier (Note 11)	250,000	250,000
Deferred fuel cost	3,698	24,120
Fuel inventory—at average cost (Note 4)	110,076	146,592
Materials and supplies—at average cost	61,845	63,602
Other	26,177	27,425
Total	696,899	1,010,295
Deferred Debits:		
Receivable from gas supplier (Note 11)	—	250,000
Other	79,847	108,024
Total	79,847	358,024
Total	$11,100,667	$10,364,653

See Notes to Consolidated Financial Statements.

EXHIBIT 7 *(concluded)*

Capitalization and Liabilities

	1983	1982
	(In Thousands)	
Capitalization:		
Common stock, $5 par value, authorized 250,000,000 shares; issued and outstanding 166,082,128 shares in 1983 and 139,333,934 shares in 1982	$ 830,411	$ 696,669
Paid-in capital	1,271,152	994,760
Retained earnings (Note 7)	899,979	790,487
Total common shareholders'equity	3,001,542	2,481,916
Subsidiaries' preferred stock without sinking fund (Note 5)	330,967	330,967
Subsidiaries' preferred stock with sinking fund (Note 5)	429,601	354,957
Long-term debt (Notes 6 and 8)	5,032,175	4,429,447
Total	8,794,285	7,597,287
Current Liabilities:		
Notes payable (Notes 4 and 8):		
Banks	114,573	159,565
Commercial paper	123,000	107,725
Other	50,471	72,885
Currently maturing long-term debt (Note 6)	228,009	73,102
Accounts payable	264,892	316,806
Gas contract settlement—liability to customers (Note 11)	58,884	882,535
Customer deposits	53,285	47,794
Taxes accrued	75,576	67,655
Accumulated deferred income taxes (Note 3)	1,980	12,033
Interest accrued	161,965	104,854
Dividends declared	92,583	77,058
Other	63,720	73,467
Total	1,288,938	1,995,479
Deferred Credits:		
Accumulated deferred income taxes (Note 3)	370,166	331,591
Accumulated deferred investment tax credits (Note 3)	73,849	77,142
Gas contract settlement—liability to customers (Note 11)	475,000	250,000
Other	61,377	79,829
Total	980,392	738,562
Reserves	37,052	33,325
Commitments and Contingencies (Notes 2, 8, and 9)		
Total	$11,100,667	$10,364,653

EXHIBIT 8

MIDDLE SOUTH UTILITIES, INC., AND SUBSIDIARIES
Statements of Changes in Consolidated Financial Position
For the Years Ended December 31, 1983, 1982, and 1981

	1983	1982	1981
Funds Provided By:		*(In Thousands)*	
Operations:			
Net income	$ 378,050	$ 310,595	$ 281,483
Depreciation	183,171	167,725	158,264
Deferred income taxes and investment tax credit adjustments — net	24,787	14,720	37,667
Allowance for funds used during construction (Note 1)	(426,498)	(352,780)	(300,880)
Total funds provided by operations	159,510	140,260	176,534
Other:			
Allowance for funds used during construction (Note 1)	426,498	352,780	300,880
Gas contract settlement (Note 11)	—	1,132,535	—
Funds on hand or due from gas supplier (Note 11)	—	(782,197)	—
Deferred costs relating to SFI's fuel acquisition programs	28,136	2,350	—
Decrease in working capital*	120,945	—	145,207
Miscellaneous — net	—	5,232	24,447
Total funds provided excluding financing transactions	735,089	850,960	647,068
Financing and other transactions:			
Common stock	409,545	211,135	193,314
Preferred stock	85,000	60,000	20,000
First mortgage bonds	320,000	185,000	250,000
Promissory notes and other long-term debt	681,222	515,512	442,315
Book value of utility plant sold	5,151	25,111	—
Short-term securities — net	—	—	139,969
Sale and leaseback transactions	—	—	22,136
Total funds provided by financing and other transactions	1,500,918	996,758	1,067,734
Total funds provided	**$ 2,236,007**	**$ 1,847,718**	**$ 1,714,802**
Funds Applied To:			
Utility plant additions:			
Construction expenditures for utility plant	$ 1,453,662	$ 1,393,399	$ 1,174,944
Nuclear fuel	59,346	51,304	56,132
Other	—	—	3,045
Total gross additions (includes allowance for funds used during construction)	1,513,008	1,444,703	1,234,121
Other:			
Dividends declared on common stock	266,762	224,825	190,175
Increase in working capital*	—	31,628	—
Gas contract settlement (Note 11)	598,651	—	—
Funds on hand or due from gas supplier (Note 11)	(525,128)	—	—
Deferred costs relating to SFI's fuel acquisition programs	—	—	7,934
Refund to retail customers (Note 2)	74,600	—	—
Miscellaneous — net	9,996	—	—
Total other funds applied	424,881	256,453	198,109
Financing transactions:			
Retirement of promissory notes and other long-term debt	127,400	68,320	160,266
Retirement of first mortgage bonds	110,297	48,719	119,363
Redemption of preferred stock	7,175	2,979	2,943
Short-term securities — net	53,246	26,544	—
Total funds applied to financing transactions	298,118	146,562	282,572
Total funds applied	**$ 2,236,007**	**$ 1,847,718**	**$ 1,714,802**

* *Working capital does not include short-term securities, currently maturing long-term debt, the gas contract settlement, MP&L's 1983 refund to retail customers, or deferred taxes included in current liabilities. The 1983 net decrease in working capital is primarily due to decreases in fuel inventory and deferred fuel cost and increases in interest accrued and dividends declared offset by an increase in accounts receivable. The 1982 net increase in working capital is primarily due to increases in deferred fuel cost and customer accounts receivable and a decrease in accounts payable. The 1981 net decrease in working capital is primarily due to an increase in accounts payable and decreases in cash and deferred fuel cost.*

See Notes to Consolidated Financial Statements.

EXHIBIT 9

MIDDLE SOUTH UTILITIES, INC., AND SUBSIDIARIES
Notes to Consolidated Financial Statements

Note 1. Summary of Significant Accounting Policies

A. Principles of Consolidation

The accompanying consolidated financial statements include the accounts of Middle South Utilities, Inc. (the Company or MSU) and its direct and indirect subsidiaries, Arkansas Power & Light Company (AP&L), Louisiana Power & Light Company (LP&L), Mississippi Power & Light Company (MP&L), New Orleans Public Service Inc. (NOPSI), Middle South Services, Inc. (MSS), Middle South Energy, Inc. (MSE), and System Fuels, Inc. (SFI) which are collectively referred to as the System Companies or the Middle South System. All significant intercompany transactions have been eliminated.

B. Systems of Accounts

The accounts of the Company and its service subsidiary, MSS, are maintained in accordance with the Public Utility Holding Company Act of 1935 (Holding Company Act), as administered by the Securities and Exchange Commission (SEC), which has adopted a system of accounts consistent with the system of accounts prescribed by the Federal Energy Regulatory Commission (FERC).

The accounts of the operating subsidiaries, AP&L, LP&L, MP&L, and NOPSI, are maintained in accordance with the systems of accounts prescribed by the applicable regulatory bodies, which systems of accounts substantially conform to those prescribed by the FERC. The accounts of the generating subsidiary, MSE, are maintained in accordance with the system of accounts prescribed by the FERC.

SFI capitalizes all costs related to its exploration activities. These costs are reduced by profits realized on sales to non-affiliated companies and are amortized by the units-of-production method in the period in which revenue is recognized on oil and gas reserves produced and sold.

C. Revenues and Fuel Costs

The operating subsidiaries record electric and gas revenues as billed to their customers on a cycle billing basis. Revenue is not accrued for energy delivered but not billed at the end of the fiscal period. Substantially all of the rate schedules of the operating subsidiaries include adjustment clauses under which the cost of fuel used for generation and gas purchased for resale above or below specified base levels is permitted to be billed or required to be credited to customers.

One operating subsidiary has a fuel adjustment clause which allows current recovery of fuel costs. All the other operating subsidiaries utilize a deferral method of accounting for those fuel costs recoverable under fuel adjustment clauses. Under this method, such costs are deferred until the related revenues are billed.

The fuel adjustment factor for AP&L contains an amount for a nuclear reserve estimated to cover the cost of replacement energy when the nuclear plant is down for scheduled maintenance and refueling. The reserve bears interest and is used to reduce fuel expense for fuel adjustment purposes during the shutdown period.

D. Utility Plant and Depreciation

Utility plant is stated at original cost. The cost of additions to utility plant includes contracted work, direct labor and materials, allocable overheads, and an allowance for the composite cost of funds used during construction. The costs of units of property retired are removed from utility plant and such costs, plus removal costs, less salvage, are charged to accumulated depreciation. Maintenance and repairs of property and replacement of items determined to be less than units of property are charged to operating expenses.

Depreciation is computed on the straight-line basis at rates based on the estimated service lives of the various classes of property. Depreciation rates for AP&L's nuclear station, the System's only operating nuclear station, include a provision for nuclear plant decommissioning costs. Depreciation provisions on average depreciable property approximated 3.3% in 1983 and 1982, and 3.4% in 1981.

Substantially all of the System's utility plant is subject to the liens of the subsidiaries' first mortgage bond indentures.

E. Pension Plans

The Company and its subsidiaries have various defined benefit pension plans covering substantially all of their employees. The policy of the Company and its subsidiaries is to fund pension costs accrued.

EXHIBIT 9 *(continued)*

F. Income Taxes

The Company and its subsidiaries file a consolidated Federal income tax return. Income taxes are allocated to all subsidiaries based on their contributions to the consolidated taxable income. Deferred income taxes are provided for differences between book and taxable income to the extent permitted by the regulatory bodies for ratemaking purposes. Investment tax credits utilized are deferred and amortized based upon the average useful life of the related property.

G. Allowance for Funds Used During Construction

To the extent that the Company's operating subsidiaries are not permitted by their regulatory bodies to recover in current rates the carrying costs of funds used for construction, they capitalize, as an appropriate cost of utility plant, an allowance for funds used during construction (AFDC) that is calculated and recorded as provided by the regulatory systems of accounts. Under this utility industry practice, construction work in progress on the balance sheet is charged and the income statement is credited for the approximate net composite interest cost of borrowed funds and for a reasonable return on the equity funds used for construction. This procedure is intended to remove from the income statement the effect of the cost of financing the construction program and results in treating the AFDC charges in the same manner as construction labor and material costs. As non-cash items, these credits to the income statement have no effect on current cash earnings. After the property is placed in service, the AFDC charged to construction costs is recoverable from customers through depreciation provisions included in rates for utility service.

During 1983, one of the operating subsidiaries used an accrual rate of 3% on $1.3 billion of construction costs in accordance with a May 1981 rate order from its regulatory commission. The effective composite rates of the operating subsidiaries for the balance of AFDC were 9.2%, 9.1%, and 8.8% for 1983, 1982, and 1981, respectively. MSE used an accrual rate for AFDC based on a return on average common equity of 14%, plus actual interest costs net of related income taxes.

The Company's subsidiaries continue to capitalize AFDC on projects during periods of interrupted construction when such interruption is temporary and the continuation can be justified as being reasonable under the circumstances.

H. Reserves

It is the policy of the Company's operating subsidiaries to provide reserves for uninsured property risks and for claims for injuries and damages through charges to operating expenses on an accrual basis. Accruals for these reserves have been allowed for ratemaking purposes.

I. Reclassifications

In 1983, the results of the discontinued transit operations, including the gain on sale, have been accounted for as miscellaneous income. Accordingly, the 1982 and 1981 MSU Consolidated Income Statements have been reclassified to report the results of discontinued transit operations in miscellaneous income. Net income for 1982 and 1981 was not affected by this reclassification. (See Note 12.)

In addition, certain other reclassifications of previously reported amounts have been made to conform with current classifications.

Note 2. Rate Matters

In August 1983, the Arkansas Public Service Commission (APSC) acted on AP&L's November 1982 $93.2 million retail rate request and approved a $39.8 million annual increase in Arkansas retail rates. The increase in rates was effective in August 1983. In appeals still pending before the Circuit Court of Pulaski County, AP&L is asking for a review of the differences between the $101.4 million increase in rates sought in a May 1981 filing and the $29.0 million granted by the APSC in September 1982. AP&L has appealed the APSC's order to refund approximately $19.3 million of revenues collected associated with deferred taxes.

In November 1983, the Louisiana Public Service Commission (LPSC) approved $11.5 million of the $16.9 million annual increase in natural gas rates requested by NOPSI in July 1982. The new rates were implemented in December 1983. In February 1984, the LPSC granted a $69.0 million retail rate increase to LP&L in ruling on a January 1983 filing. The LPSC also approved a $24.0 million annual increase to NOPSI in ruling on its January 1983 filing. The LPSC rejected any allowance in rates at that time to reflect an in-service status for either Unit 1 of MSE's Grand Gulf Steam Electric Generating Station (Grand Gulf) or Unit 3 at LP&L's Waterford Steam Electric Generating Station (Waterford). A major portion of LP&L's proposed rates was designed to cover the revenue requirements associated with the commercial operation of both units, and a major portion of NOPSI's rates would have covered its requirements in connection with the MSE unit.

In January 1983, the Mississippi Public Service Commission (MPSC) granted MP&L $47.5 million of the $93.9 million retail rate increase requested in July 1982. The MPSC, in April 1983, granted MP&L $39.8 million of the $68.8 million retail rate increase requested in May 1980. As a result of this order, revenues collected subject to

EXHIBIT 9 *(concluded)*

refund since July 1980, plus interest accrued thereon, a total of $74.6 million, was refunded to the ratepayers. The refund did not have a material effect on MP&L's net income because MP&L had previously made accruals for the effect of a possible refund.

Note 3. Income Taxes

Income tax expense (credit) consists of the following:

	1983	1982	1981
		(In Thousands)	
Current:			
Federal..	—	—	$ (972)
State..	$ 8,460	$ 9,835	11,981
Total	8,460	9,835	11,009
Deferred — net:			
Liberalized depreciation..	41,766	47,652	31,818
Deferred fuel cost	(10,053)	15,652	(17,986)
Taxes capitalized in the financial statements	8,530	11,783	7,853
Nuclear fuel disposal costs	17,729	(6,074)	(7,491)
Revenues subject to refund..	26,347	(9,567)	(9,224)
Other..	(14,281)	(4,375)	15,277
Restoration (reduction) due to tax loss carryforwards..................	(41,514)	(36,902)	38,190
Total	28,524	18,169	58,437
Investment tax credit adjustments — net	(3,737)	(3,449)	(20,770)
Recorded income tax expense	$ 33,247	$ 24,555	$ 48,676
Charged to operations	$ 190,589	$ 171,741	$ 175,142
Credited to other income..	(157,342)	(147,186)	(126,466)
Recorded income tax expense	33,247	24,555	48,676
Income taxes applied against the debt component of AFDC.............	157,520	145,514	133,896
Total income taxes...	$ 190,767	$ 170,069	$ 182,572

Total income taxes differ from the amounts computed by applying the statutory Federal income tax rate to income before taxes. The reasons for the differences are as follows *(dollars in thousands)*:

	1983		1982		1981	
	Amount	% of Pre-Tax Income	Amount	% of Pre-Tax Income	Amount	% of Pre-Tax Income
Computed at statutory rate....................	$226,027	46.0	$185,650	46.0	$179,745	46.0
Increases (reductions) in tax resulting from:						
Allowance for funds used during construction	(196,242)	(39.9)	(159,912)	(39.6)	(137,099)	(35.1)
State income taxes net of Federal income tax effect	9,964	2.0	8,605	2.1	11,203	2.9
Other — net.................................	(6,502)	(1.3)	(9,788)	(2.4)	(5,173)	(1.3)
Recorded income tax expense	33,247	6.8	24,555	6.1	48,676	12.5
Income taxes applied against the debt component of AFDC.................	157,520	22.6	145,514	24.9	133,896	22.3
Total income taxes.....................	$ 190,767	29.4	$ 170,069	31.0	$ 182,572	34.8

The tax effects of the consolidated 1982 and 1983 Federal tax losses have been recorded as reductions of deferred income taxes. The tax effect of the utilization in 1981 of net operating losses has been recorded as a restoration of deferred income taxes. The remaining Federal tax loss carryforwards at December 31, 1983 amounted to $365.6 million and are available to offset taxable income in future years. If not used, they will expire in 1994 through 1998. Unused investment tax credits at December 31, 1983 amounted to $580.8 million. These credits may be applied against Federal income tax liabilities in future years. If not used, they will expire in 1992 through 1998.

EXHIBIT 10

MIDDLE SOUTH UTILITIES, INC., AND SUBSIDIARIES
1973–1983 Financial Record
(in thousands)

Consolidated Summary of Operations	1983	1982	1981
Operating Revenues:			
Electric	$ 2,716,329	$ 2,673,572	$ 2,582,778
Natural gas	193,328	172,692	139,242
Total	2,909,657	2,846,264	2,722,020
Operating Expenses:			
Operation:			
Fuel for electric generation	942,219	1,066,325	1,083,064
Purchased power	373,712	345,076	263,559
Gas purchased for resale	158,186	138,890	107,768
Deferred fuel and other	363,509	288,283	307,218
Maintenance	149,453	132,031	127,067
Depreciation	183,171	167,725	158,264
Taxes other than income taxes	104,493	101,381	93,058
Income taxes	190,589	171,741	175,142
Total	2,465,332	2,411,452	2,315,140
Operating Income	444,325	434,812	406,880
Other Income:			
Allowance for equity funds used during construction	245,640	182,342	143,369
Miscellaneous income and deductions—net	6,799	7,133	24,249
Income taxes—credit	157,342	147,186	126,466
Total	409,781	336,661	294,084
Interest and Other Charges:			
Interest on long-term debt	529,597	488,750	441,894
Other interest—net	47,251	74,130	74,507
Allowance for borrowed funds used during construction	(180,858)	(170,438)	(157,511)
Preferred dividend requirements of subsidiaries	80,066	68,436	60,591
Total	476,056	460,878	419,481
Net Income	$ 378,050	$ 310,595	$ 281,483
Earnings Per Common Share	$2.46	$2.33	$2.44
Dividends Declared Per Common Share	$1.71	$1.67	$1.63
Average Number of Common Shares Outstanding	153,383,044	133,193,296	115,175,550
Utility Plant and Capitalization: (at December 31)			
Fixed Assets:			
Utility plant	$ 11,942,417	$ 10,464,188	$ 9,080,436
Less—Accumulated depreciation and amortization	1,694,475	1,551,700	1,407,584
Utility plant—net	$ 10,247,942	$ 8,912,488	$ 7,672,852
Capitalization:			
Common equity	$ 3,001,542	$ 2,481,916	$ 2,185,546
Preferred stock (including premium and issuance expense):			
Without sinking fund	330,967	330,967	330,967
With sinking fund	429,601	354,957	300,219
Long-term debt	5,032,175	4,429,447	3,896,370
Total	$ 8,794,285	$ 7,597,287	$ 6,713,102
Capitalization Ratios:			
Common equity	34.1%	32.7%	32.6%
Preferred stock (including premium and issuance expense)	8.7	9.0	9.4
Long-term debt	57.2	58.3	58.0

1980	1979	1978	1977	1976	1975	1974	1973
$ 2,179,232	$ 1,671,491	$ 1,485,901	$ 1,325,264	$ 1,064,116	$ 867,641	$ 768,433	$ 609,082
116,067	117,256	95,284	83,040	63,852	48,928	38,373	38,362
2,295,299	1,788,747	1,581,185	1,408,304	1,127,968	916,569	806,806	647,444
946,145	697,606	623,402	568,990	422,204	294,482	259,435	149,882
281,951	258,377	133,929	86,087	61,439	35,075	43,880	22,458
88,864	88,801	68,657	58,577	37,852	30,994	21,807	19,936
248,601	176,181	171,918	157,791	126,362	121,328	99,116	93,020
104,333	104,340	93,260	67,150	53,863	46,815	42,311	36,908
141,229	118,192	112,108	106,031	100,175	91,761	73,427	67,659
82,584	75,837	68,025	65,388	59,664	54,888	47,433	47,619
104,463	51,395	83,290	96,388	72,873	61,222	38,669	58,456
1,998,170	1,570,729	1,354,589	1,206,402	934,432	736,565	626,078	495,938
297,129	218,018	226,596	201,902	193,536	180,004	180,728	151,506
122,277	124,086	93,573	65,346	62,169	46,064	49,509	31,948
8,272	7,206	7,850	7,719	(1,953)	(6,279)	(10,747)	(7,997)
105,724	77,658	48,947	29,028	22,365	19,837	5,249	4,430
236,273	208,950	150,370	102,093	82,581	59,622	44,011	28,381
327,468	255,242	199,212	153,005	132,719	113,486	105,532	72,464
72,666	43,990	23,161	18,323	15,571	19,177	8,094	3,723
(117,663)	(89,247)	(54,717)	(34,031)	—	—	—	—
55,024	36,264	25,477	23,109	21,780	16,660	15,040	13,181
337,495	246,249	193,133	160,406	170,070	149,323	128,666	89,368
$ 195,907	$ 180,719	$ 183,833	$ 143,589	$ 106,047	$ 90,303	$ 96,073	$ 90,519
$2.01	$2.12	$2.43	$2.16	$1.82	$1.78	$2.17	$2.09
$1.59	$1.535	$1.46	$1.395	$1.335	$1.275	$1.23	$1.15
97,469,169	85,444,691	75,522,179	66,598,876	58,395,628	50,733,782	44,279,481	43,376,255
$ 7,893,636	$ 7,002,052	$ 6,052,023	$ 5,183,284	$ 4,539,891	$ 3,953,814	$ 3,470,598	$ 3,054,867
1,264,525	1,139,164	1,038,256	935,702	831,930	747,612	668,148	608,613
$ 6,629,111	$ 5,862,888	$ 5,013,767	$ 4,247,582	$ 3,707,961	$ 3,206,202	$ 2,802,450	$ 2,446,254
$ 1,901,204	$ 1,659,736	$ 1,412,254	$ 1,196,427	$ 1,010,278	$ 864,035	$ 746,628	$ 705,212
330,967	330,967	280,712	280,712	250,679	240,627	240,627	230,611
283,165	193,507	60,063	60,063	60,063	60,063	—	—
3,392,309	3,017,816	2,629,711	2,175,471	1,965,985	1,751,328	1,529,958	1,341,637
$ 5,907,645	$ 5,202,026	$ 4,382,740	$ 3,712,673	$ 3,287,005	$ 2,916,053	$ 2,517,213	$ 2,277,460
32.2%	31.9%	32.2%	32.2%	30.7%	29.6%	29.7%	31.0%
10.4	10.1	7.8	9.2	9.5	10.3	9.5	10.1
57.4	58.0	60.0	58.6	59.8	60.1	60.8	58.9

PART SEVEN

Overview Cases

Restating Financial Statements

D. F. W. Imports (A)*

In February of 1983, Jerry Pearson began working as an analyst in the credit department of the First National Bank of Dallas, the lead bank of a large southwest bank holding company. He had spent his first few weeks on the job in the bank's orientation and training program and had just received his first real credit analysis assignment.

The assignment concerned D. F. W. Imports, a local company which primarily manufactured electronic components for computers under licensing agreements with several Japanese companies. In addition, however, the company did maintain a small research and development staff which occasionally provided improvements on the foreign-designed products.

Jerry learned that D. F. W. Imports, like many of the companies that he would be asked to analyze, was not publicly held. As a consequence, the financial statements that he had been given to analyze (Exhibits 1 and 2) had not been audited by an independent certified public accountant and, in all likelihood, would not have been prepared in conformity with generally accepted accounting principles.

Concerned about the possibility that the financial statements might have been prepared in a manner that would make the firm look its very best, and possibly even overstate the prior performance of the company, Jerry had been instructed by his supervisor to restate D. F. W.'s balance sheet and income statement in a manner consistent with "conservative generally accepted accounting principles." Because the company's financial statements had no accompanying explanatory footnotes, Jerry proceeded by first contacting by telephone the controller of D. F. W. From this conversation he learned:

1. Inventories were stated on a FIFO basis. If LIFO had been utilized, the value of inventories would have been $889,000 at January 1, 1982, and $1,270,000 at December 31, 1982.

---

* This case was prepared by Kenneth R. Ferris. Copyright © 1984 by Kenneth R. Ferris. All rights reserved to the author.

EXHIBIT 1

D. F. W. IMPORTS
Balance Sheet
As of December 31, 1982

Assets		Equities	
Current assets:		Current liabilities:	
Cash.	$ 436,000	Accounts payable	$ 820,000
Trade receivables		Accrued expenses payable. . .	80,000
(net of allowance		Total current liabilities	900,000
for uncollectible			
accounts).	828,000		
Inventories	1,720,000		
Prepaid expenses	30,000		
Total current assets	3,014,000		
Noncurrent assets:		Noncurrent liabilities:	
Property, plant, and		Notes payable	2,320,000
equipment . . . $3,940,000		Deferred federal	
Less: Accumulated		income taxes	800,000
depreciation . . (1,360,000)		Total Liabilities	4,020,000
. . . .	2,580,000	Owner's equity:	
		Common stock, $1 par	2,000,000
Land	560,000	Retained earnings.	1,284,000
Deferred research &		Total equities	$7,304,000
development cost	1,150,000		
Total assets.	$7,304,000		

EXHIBIT 2

D. F. W. IMPORTS
Income Statement
For the Year Ended December 31, 1982

Sales revenue		$4,950,000
Less: Cost of sales		
Beginning inventory	$1,205,000	
Cost of production.	3,665,000	
Goods available for sale	4,870,000	
Less: Ending inventory	1,720,000	
		(3,150,000)
Gross margin		1,800,000
Less: Research and development		
expenses.	350,000	
Licensing fees	100,000	
Selling and administrative expenses	400,000	
		(850,000)
Net income before taxes		950,000
Less: Income taxes.	475,000	
Investment and research tax credits	(60,000)	
		(415,000)
Net income after taxes		$ 535,000

2. Property, plant, and equipment had been depreciated on a straight-line basis. If an accelerated method had been utilized, the depreciation expense for 1982 would have been $230,000 more, and the balance in the accumulated depreciation account as of December 31, 1982, would have been $450,000 greater.

3. The research and development expense for 1982 represented one half of the actual R&D expenditure for 1982; the remaining balance had been capitalized. The company's policy with respect to capitalized R&D costs was to begin amortization only after a commercially productive asset had been developed; to date, no productive assets had resulted from the research program represented by the currently capitalized R&D costs.

4. During 1982, investment and research tax credits of $60,000 had been earned; no credits had been earned prior to 1982. The tax credits had been accounted for using the flow-through method.

5. The company had no pension plan for its employees, and hence no unfunded pension obligation.

6. For tax purposes, the company had utilized accelerated depreciation, FIFO, and had fully expensed all research and development expenditures.

Jerry realized that, overall, D. F. W. Imports had utilized a relatively liberal set of accounting methods to prepare its financial statements, and that, in at least one instance, the company had not followed generally accepted accounting principles. Accordingly, Jerry decided to restate the financial statements using the following accounting practices:

1. LIFO inventory valuation.
2. Accelerated depreciation.
3. Expensing of R&D as incurred.
4. Deferral of investment and research tax credits.

With respect to the tax credits, Jerry decided to write the credits off over a period of 10 years and to assume that the credits has been earned on June 30, 1982.

QUESTIONS

1. Restate the balance sheet and income statement of D. F. W. Imports using the accounting methods and assumptions selected by Jerry.

2. As part of the credit analysis, compute:

a. The LIFO inventory reserve at January 1, 1982, and December 31, 1982.

b. The current ratio at December 31, 1982, for both the original and revised financial statements.

c. The "Debt to Tangible Net Worth" ratio at December 31, 1982, for both the original and revised financial statements.

3. Compare the creditworthiness of D. F. W. Imports as revealed by the original versus revised financial statements.

D. F. W. Imports (B)*

In January of 1983, D. F. W. Imports had approached the First National Bank of Dallas about the possibility of obtaining a $680,000 loan for the acquisition of new electronic component production equipment. The new equipment was part of a major capital investment program designed to enable the company to manufacture the latest technology in component parts.

On the strength of the company's financial history, and on the condition that the owners of D. F. W. also invest at least $2 million of their own capital in the expansion program, the loan was approved in late March 1983. Because the acquisition and installation of the equipment would take approximately 18 months, and hence would not be generating revenue for some time, the 10-year loan was so structured that only debt service payments were required the first 3 years; thereafter, payments would include both principal and interest.

In February 1985, D. F. W. provided the bank with its 1984 year-end financial statements. The loan agreement required the company to periodically submit its financial reports to the bank to enable the bank to monitor the company's financial condition and determine how adequately the loan covenants were being met. Jerry Pearson, the analyst who had worked on the initial credit investigation in 1983, was given the 1984 statements and instructed to undertake the current loan review (Exhibits 1 and 2).

Jerry immediately observed several major changes in the company's financial statements and disclosure practices. Unlike the initial set of reports he had analyzed, the 1984 statements contained explanatory footnotes and had been audited by an independent certified public accountant. Not only were these latest financial statements prepared on a basis consistent with generally accepted accounting principles, but Jerry soon learned that they had also been prepared using relatively conservative accounting practices. Jerry recalled that, as part of the initial loan review, his supervisor had instructed him to restate the financial statements because the company had utilized such liberal accounting methods in their statement preparation. He also noted that during 1983 the company had adopted a pension plan for its employees and, consistent with existing governmental regulations, had undertaken appropriate funding of the plan.

In developing his strategy for the loan review, Jerry mentally noted that, for compar-

---

EXHIBIT 1

D. F. W. IMPORTS
Income Statement
For the Year Ended December 31, 1984

Sales revenue		$10,588,000
Less: Cost of sales		
Beginning inventory	$ 2,640,000	
Cost of production	8,470,000	
Goods available for sale	11,110,000	
Less: Ending inventory	(3,800,000)	
		(7,310,000)
Gross margin		3,278,000
Less: Research and development expense. . .	514,000	
Licensing fees	200,000	
Selling and administrative expense	1,400,000	
		(2,114,000)
Net income before taxes		1,164,000
Less: Federal income taxes.	582,000	
Investment and research tax		
credits	(20,000)	
		(562,000)
Net income after taxes		$ 602,000

EXHIBIT 2

D. F. W. IMPORTS
Balance Sheet
As of December 31, 1984

Assets			Equities		
Current assets:			Current liabilities:		
Cash	$	872,000	Accounts payable		$ 2,760,000
Trade receivables			Accrued expenses payable . .		160,000
(net of allowance			Total current liabilities		2,920,000
for uncollectible					
accounts)		1,656,000			
Inventories.		3,800,000			
Prepaid expenses		60,000	Noncurrent liabilities:		
Total current assets . . .		6,388,000	Notes payable		2,320,000
			Bank Loan.		680,000
Noncurrent assets:			Total liabilities.		5,920,000
Property, plant, and			Deferred investment and research		
equipment . . $7,880,000			tax credits.		400,000
Less: Accumulated			Owner's equity:		
depreciation. (3,250,000)			Common stock, $1 par		4,000,000
		4,630,000	Retained earnings		1,718,000
Land		1,020,000	Total equities		$12,038,000
Total assets		$12,038,000			

---

ison purposes, it might be useful to restate the 1984 financial statements to an accounting basis consistent with that of the 1982 and 1983 reports. This would provide him with several bases to evaluate the company's performance.

From reading the accompanying footnotes, Jerry learned that the 1984 statements had been prepared using the following accounting methods:

1. Inventories were stated on a LIFO basis.
2. Property, plant, and equipment was depreciated on an accelerated basis.
3. Research and development costs were expensed as incurred.
4. Investment and research tax credits were deferred and written off over the life of the related asset (or a maximum of 10 years).
5. The firm reported no deferred income taxes because its tax return and accounting statements had been prepared on a consistent basis.
6. Pension costs, reported as part of Selling and administrative expenses, included a $200,000 payment into the firm's pension fund to cover $\frac{1}{10}$ of the firm's past service cost liability.

He decided to restate the financial statements as follows:

1. FIFO inventory.
2. Straight-line depreciation.
3. Capitalization of one half of R&D expenditures (effective January 1, 1984).
4. Flow-through of the investment and research tax credits.
5. No funding or accruing of the past service pension cost (effective January 1, 1984).

A conversation with the controller of D. F. W. provided him with the following additional information: (1) the FIFO value of D. F. W.'s inventories was $3,640,000 at January 1, 1984, and $5,200,000 at December 31, 1984, respectively; (2) if straight-line depreciation had been used, the depreciation expense for 1984 would have been $105,000 *less* and accumulated depreciation at December 31, 1984, would have been $950,000 *less;* (3) investment and research tax credits of $100,000 were earned in 1984.

Jerry realized that some of these accounting changes (e.g., the LIFO to FIFO switch) would create real tax effects, and hence decided to assume that any additional tax liabilities for prior years would be immediately paid in cash. In addition, however, he recognized that most of the other changes were only changes for accounting purposes, but nonetheless would have to be accounted for through a deferred income tax account.

QUESTIONS

1. Restate the 1984 D. F. W. Imports balance sheet and income statement using the accounting methods and assumptions selected by Jerry.
2. Calculate:
   a. The LIFO "inventory reserve" at January 1, 1984, and December 31, 1984.
   b. The current ratio at December 31, 1984, for both the original and revised set of financial statements.
   c. The "debt to tangible net worth" ratio at December 31, 1984, for both the original and revised set of financial statements.
3. Compare the creditworthiness of D. F. W. Imports as revealed by the original versus restated financial statements.

Assessing the Quality of Reported Earnings and Assets

Fotomat*

In January 1969, Fotomat Corporation registered a proposed offering of 500,000 shares of common stock with the Securities and Exchange Commission. Proceeds from the sale were to be used to repay debt, finance expansion, and increase working capital. At the time of the SEC filing, Fotomat had 4,573,554 closely held shares outstanding (see prospectus and financial statements, Exhibits 1–6).

On April 30, 1969, Fotomat went public. The offering of shares was quickly oversubscribed at an initial price of $20 per share. Later that day, the shares traded as high as $35 per share.

Fotomat Corporation, through its 200 company-owned and 219 franchised outlets, sold film and photographic equipment and supplies, and provided film processing services on a drive-in, discount basis. According to the company's prospectus, each outlet was operated by a "Fotomate, a specially trained, attractive young lady."

In October 1969, Fotomat released the results of operations for the six months ended July 31. On revenues of $12.2 million, the company had lost over $114,000.

QUESTIONS

1. Evaluate Fotomat's method of recognizing revenue from the sale of franchises. Comment on the company's quality of matching of costs with revenues.

2. Evaluate the transactions described in Footnote 2 to the earnings statement and Footnotes E and H to the balance sheet. Do you approve of the company's treatment of these transactions?

3. Evaluate the quality of reported earnings and assets. Prepare a list of those items that concern you.

---

* This case was prepared by Kenneth R. Ferris from publicly available information. Copyright © 1984 by Kenneth R. Ferris. All rights reserved to the author. The situation is taken from an earlier Harvard College case, "Fotomat Corporation" (8-272-016).

EXHIBIT 1

FOTOMAT CORPORATION
Consolidated Statements of Earnings (Loss)

The following consolidated statements of earnings of Fotomat Corporation for the two years ended January 31, 1969, have been examined by Touche, Ross, Bailey & Smart, independent certified public accountants, as set forth in their report which is subject to the effect of uncertainties resulting from the Eastman Kodak Company litigation referred to in Note L, appearing elsewhere in this Prospectus. Information included in the consolidated statements of earnings (loss) for the two-month periods ended March 31, 1968, and 1969 is unaudited, but includes all adjustments (which comprise only normal recurring accruals) which the Company believes necessary for a fair presentation of the results of operations for such periods. The consolidated statements of earnings (loss) should be read in conjunction with the other financial statements and notes thereto included elsewhere in this Prospectus.

	Year Ended January 31,		Two Months Ended March 31, (unaudited)	
	1968	1969	1968	1969
Revenues (Notes A and E):				
Net sales (including sales at cost to franchisees of $101,438 and $1,916,074, respectively for the years ended January 31, and $67,700 (unaudited) and $694,858 (unaudited), respectively for the two months ended March 31,)(7) . .	$275,767	$ 3,601,362	$118,918	$1,274,933
Initial franchise fees:				
Regular (1)(2)(4)	402,500	5,595,500	253,300	172,000
Limited partnerships (Note B) (1) (4) . .		2,562,000		
Officers and principal stockholders (Note B) (3) (4)		924,000		
Rent and monthly franchise fees.	22,467	489,991	15,281	242,014
Other income	2,413	156,738	1,259	30,043
	703,147	13,329,591	388,758	1,718,990
Costs and expenses (Notes B and M):				
Product and processing costs (Note C) . .	220,054	3,031,060	100,911	1,078,415
Operating	297,420	3,474,985	143,290	1,124,309
Selling, general and administrative(1) . . .	142,753	2,482,693	75,574	429,747
Depreciation and amortization (Note D) . .	8,599	204,080	5,349	109,013
Interest and financing costs.	6,831	94,463	2,521	55,431
	675,657	9,287,281	327,645	2,796,915
Earnings (loss) before taxes on income.	27,490	4,042,310	61,113	(1,077,925)
Taxes on income (Note G).	3,918	2,148,000	33,795	(596,096)
Net earnings (loss)(1)(5)(6)	$ 23,572	$ 1,894,310	$ 27,318	$ (481,829)

Alphabetical notes refer to notes to financial statements appearing elsewhere in this Prospectus.

Notes:
(1) On February 12, 1969, Eastman Kodak Company brought an action against the Company alleging unfair competition and infringement of trademarks and trade dress and requesting injunctive relief. See also Litigation elsewhere in this Prospectus. The existence of this litigation has had and may continue to have an adverse effect on the Company's ability to sell franchises subsequent to February 12, 1969 (see Note L).

Also as a result of the Kodak litigation two franchisees had refused to accept delivery or pay for additional Fotomats provided for in their franchise agreements with the Company. The remaining balance on these receivables at January 31, 1969, was $571,000 which the Company has fully provided for in its allowance for doubtful accounts; however, it is the Company's intention to further pursue the collection of these accounts. It is the opinion of house counsel that the agreements are enforceable.

(2) Initial franchise fees for the year ended January 31, 1969, include $525,000 for sales of franchises which were subsequently repurchased (see Note E).

(3) Substantial sales of franchises were made to principal stockholders and officers in December 1968. These sales, which had a material effect upon net earnings, may not be recurring (see Note B).

(4) The Company allowed sales of franchise units of $1,505,800 to be returned during the year ended January 31, 1969, of which $962,000 were subsequently resold during the year. The franchises returned have been deducted from the regular initial franchise fees and resales have been added to initial franchise fees in the

---

EXHIBIT 1 *(concluded)*

following amounts: regular—$416,600; limited partnerships—$399,000, officers and principal stockholders—$147,000.

(5) Since substantially all of the net earnings have been derived from the sale of franchises, earnings per share have been omitted as such earnings cannot be expected to bear any relationship to future earnings.

(6) No dividends have been declared for years ending January 31, 1968, and 1969.

(7) Net sales for the year ended January 31, 1969 includes sales of $686,709 from Company operated units which had become franchise operated.

The results of operations for the two months ended March 31, 1969, are not necessarily indicative of the results for the full year.

The loss from operations for the two months ended March 31, 1969, is principally attributable to the substantial decline in franchise sales. The Company believes that the initiation of the Eastman Kodak litigation (see Litigation) in February 1969 was a major factor in causing a decline in franchise sales. The Company is not able to measure accurately the future effect of such litigation on the sale of franchises. For a description of franchise sales made subsequent to March 31, 1969, see Business—*Franchise Program* (Recent Developments). Also contributing to the loss was the adverse effect of seasonal sales of photo processing which are typically lower in February and March than in other months whereas increased operating and administrative expenses due to the expanded operations of the Company have continued.

EXHIBIT 2

FOTOMAT CORPORATION
Capitalization

The capitalization of the Company as of April 18, 1969, and as adjusted to give effect to the sale of 500,000 shares of Common Stock offered by the Company and the application of a portion of the proceeds therefrom, is set forth below:

	Outstanding	As Adjusted
Short-term debt (see Note F to Financial Statements):		
5% notes	$ 78,000	$ 78,000
Indebtedness to bank (currently 8%)	1,950,000	—
8% demand notes (payable to stockholders)	3,283,000	—
Long-term debt (including current portion—see Note H to Financial Statements):		
8% notes due 1970	480,000	480,000
8% installment note	396,000	396,000
Common stock, no par value, 10,000,000 shares authorized(1)	4,573,554	5,073,554

(1) 501,430 shares are reserved for options granted or to be granted under the company's Qualified Stock Option Plans (see Management—*Stock Option Plans*).

See Note I to Financial Statements and Business—*Property* for descriptions of obligations under leases.

EXHIBIT 3
Accountants' Report

Board of Directors,
Fotomat Corporation,
San Diego, California.

We have examined the accompanying consolidated
balance sheet of Fotomat Corporation and
consolidated subsidiaries as of January 31, 1969,
and the related statements of earnings and
retained earnings for the two years then ended.
Our examination was made in accordance with
generally accepted auditing standards, and
accordingly included such tests of the accounting
records and such other auditing procedures as we
considered necessary in the circumstances.

On February 12, 1969, Eastman Kodak Company
brought an action against the Company alleging
unfair competition and infringement of trademarks
and trade dress and requesting injunctive relief.
The existence of their litigation has had and may
continue to have an adverse effect on the
Company's ability to sell franchises, see Note L.

In our opinion, subject to the effect on the
financial statements of uncertainties resulting
from the Eastman Kodak Company litigation referred
to above, the statements referred to above present
fairly the consolidated financial position of
Fotomat Corporation and consolidated subsidiaries
at January 31, 1969, and the consolidated results
of their operations for the two years then ended,
in conformity with generally accepted accounting
principles consistently applied.

San Diego, California,   TOUCHE, ROSS, BAILEY
February 24, 1969.   & SMART
(April 17, 1969, as to   Certified Public
  Note L)   Accountants

EXHIBIT 4

FOTOMAT CORPORATION AND CONSOLIDATED SUBSIDIARIES
Consolidated Balance Sheet
January 31, 1969

Assets

Current assets:		
Cash.		$ 1,242,487
Receivables:		
Franchisees, less allowance for doubtful accounts of $595,000		
(Note L) and sales returns of $125,000	$1,507,565	
Other	144,770	1,652,335
Inventories (Note C).		768,403
Other current assets.		116,815
Total current assets		3,780,040
Other assets:		
Advances to related interests (Note B).	74,054	
Deposits and other assets	293,322	367,376
Properties leased to franchisees (Note D)		2,152,196
Property and equipment (Notes D and H).		4,533,311
Intangible assets:		
Franchises (Notes E and H)	602,670	
Cost in excess of net assets of consolidated subsidiaries		
at date of acquisition (Notes A and B).	43,058	645,728
		$11,478,651

Liabilities and Stockholders' Equity

Current liabilities:		
Notes payable, unsecured (Note F).		$ 3,418,565
Accounts payable and accrued liabilities:		
Accounts payable.	$1,255,109	
Payrolls and amounts withheld from employees	246,435	
Other current liabilities	220,708	
Deposits under franchise agreements	302,534	2,024,786
Taxes on income (Note G).		2,054,524
Installments due within one year on long-term liabilities		
(Note H)		89,541
Total current liabilities.		7,587,416
Long-term liabilities, less installments due within one year (Note H) . .		808,317
Other liabilities:		
Deferred taxes on income (Note G).	91,237	
Advance rent and deposits.	61,405	152,642
Commitments and contingent liabilities (Notes B, F, I, and L):		
Stockholders' equity (Note F):		
Common stock, no par value:		
Authorized 10,000,000 shares		
issued and outstanding 4,573,554 shares (Notes J and K). . . .	1,012,394	
Retained earnings.	1,917,882	2,930,276
		$11,478,651

See notes to financial statements.

EXHIBIT 5

FOTOMAT CORPORATION
AND CONSOLIDATED SUBSIDIARIES
Consolidated Statements of Retained Earnings

	Year ended January 31	
	1968	1969
Balance at beginning of year.	—	$ 23,572
Net earnings	23,572	1,894,310
Balance at end of year	$23,572	$1,917,882

See notes to financial statements.

EXHIBIT 6

FOTOMAT CORPORATION AND CONSOLIDATED SUBSIDIARIES
Notes to Consolidated Financial Statements

Note A—Accounting policies and principles of consolidation:

The consolidated financial statements include the accounts of Fotomat Corporation, incorporated in January 1967, under the laws of California, and active subsidiaries, all wholly owned, after elimination of material intercompany accounts and transactions. The subsidiaries are:

Ground and Associates, Inc.	Purchased August 1, 1968
Fotofab Corporation	Organized July 3, 1968
G P 1968-A, Inc.	Organized October 15, 1968
Fotomat Corporation of Florida (Note B)	Purchased December 1, 1968
G P 1968-B, Inc.	Organized December 12, 1968
G P 1969-A, Inc.	Organized January 29, 1969

The following subsidiaries were formed during the year ended January 31, 1969, but had not been activated: Fotomat Corporation of Virginia, Fotomat Corporation of Arizona, Fotomat Corporation of Texas, and Fotomat Corporation (incorporated in Delaware).

The Company's investment in its subsidiaries at January 31, 1969, exceeded its equity in the net assets of its subsidiaries as shown by their books by $43,058. This excess, shown in the accompanying consolidated balance sheet as an intangible asset, is being amortized over a 10-year period.

Initial franchise fees are recorded upon execution of the franchise sales agreement. On multiple sales with the exception of sales to limited partnerships and certain sales to officers and stockholders (Note B), which were for cash, collections after the initial down payment are generally made when the franchise unit is actually delivered, which occurs at a subsequent time.

The Company allowed sales of franchise units of $1,505,800 to be returned during the year ended January 31, 1969, of which $962,600 were subsequently resold during the year. See Business—*Operations* in this Prospectus for a description of the Company's franchise sales return policies.

Note B—Certain transactions and accounts with related interests:
Limited partnerships:

Initial franchise fees of $2,562,000 resulted from sales to limited partnerships in which the general partners are wholly owned subsidiaries of Fotomat Corporation. The

---

EXHIBIT 6 *(continued)*

franchise rights are for 25-years at a sales price for each location which is generally the price applicable to 10-year franchises. The Company will participate, in consideration for management of the franchise operations, in cash income above a certain level. No income had been earned from these partnerships for the periods ended January 31, 1969. The agreements also contain repurchase provisions, at the option of the limited partners, and the requirements that the general partner is to advance any monies required to operate the franchised location not provided by their gross income but does not share any of the franchise acquisition cost. See Business—*Franchise Program* (Limited Partnerships) and Management—*Certain Transactions* in this Prospectus for further discussion of the provisions of the agreements and relationships.

Officers and principal stockholders:

Initial franchise fees of $924,000 resulted from cash sales made in December 1968 to principal stockholders and officers and a company controlled by one of the officers. Fotomat Corporation participates in these franchise operations through a management agreement. Other terms of the management and franchise agreements, including the term of the franchise, repurchase requirements, advance of monies, and participation in cash income by the Company are similar to those outlined in sales to limited partnerships above. See Business—*Franchise Program* (Limited Partnerships) and (Fotomat Managed Franchises) in this Prospectus for a further discussion of the provisions of the agreements and relationships.

Profit on these sales is material in relation to net earnings of the Company, as costs of franchise sales are relatively insignificant. Sales to principal stockholders and officers may not be recurring in the future. The Company and its wholly owned subsidiaries expect to continue sales to limited partnerships in which it will be a general partner.

No income had been earned by the Company for the management of the franchise operations of the limited partnerships or the units sold to principal officers and stockholders. Rent and monthly franchise fees for the period ended January 31, 1969, include approximately $75,000 of fees from these units.

The Company has assigned 21 of its own operating units to franchises purchased by principal stockholders and officers and a minority stockholder and 122 of its units to franchises purchased by limited partnerships in which the Company is a general partner. The units assigned to the limited partnerships include 42 which were assigned in February 1969.

The arrangements for sales of limited partnership interests were made by Hayden, Stone, Inc., a stockholder. A commission in the amount of $18,060 will be paid to that stockholder on sales of $1,806,000.

Costs and expenses include charges for insurance premiums and rent paid to entities in which officers and a principal stockholder have an interest. The charges were approximately $13,300 for the year ended January 31, 1968, and $103,340 for the year ended January 31, 1969.

In December 1968, the Company acquired from two of the officers of the Company, who are principal stockholders, all of the stock of Fotomat Corporation of Florida, which had been sold to these officers in April 1968. The transactions resulted in no profit to either party.

See Management—*Certain Transactions* and Business—*Property* in the Prospectus for other transactions and further discussion.

Note C—Inventories:

Inventories, all of which are finished products, used in determining product and processing costs, were as follows:

EXHIBIT 6 *(continued)*

February 1, 1967 . . . . $—
January 31, 1968   26,132
January 31, 1969   768,403

The inventories were based upon physical determinations and have been stated at the lower of cost (first-in, first-out method) or market.

Note D—Properties leased to franchisees and property and equipment:

	January 31,	
	1968	**1969**
Properties leased to franchisees, at cost:		
Fotomat stores	$ 57,034	$ 890,475
Equipment.	28,683	299,973
Leasehold improvements	31,508	720,982
Leaseholds	5,882	330,682
	$123,107	$2,242,112
Less accumulated depreciation and amortization	3,627	89,916
	$119,480	$2,152,196
Property and equipment, at cost:		
Fotomat stores	$103,831	$ 819,365
Equipment.	60,816	1,232,775
Leasehold improvements	20,867	655,638
Leaseholds	4,578	313,378
Construction in process		1,633,951
	$190,092	$4,655,107
Less accumulated depreciation and amortization.	4,972	121,796
	$185,120	$4,533,311

Included in leaseholds are salaries of leasing personnel, travel expense, and other costs directly attributable to obtaining leases for franchise and Company-operated stores.

Expenditures for maintenance and repairs are charged against earnings. Expenditures for betterments and major renewals are capitalized and are amortized by depreciation charges.

Depreciation and amortization is computed by the straight-line method. Estimated average useful lives for the principal classes of assets are:

Foromat stores . . . .   10 years
Equipment . . . .   4 to 10 years
Leasehold improvements . . . .   1 to 10 years
Leaseholds. . . . .   1 to 10 years

Note E—Franchises:

Franchises of $602,670 represent the cost less amortization of $5,330 on the repurchase of 27 franchise rights during the year ended January 31, 1969. The franchises are being amortized over the remaining lives of the franchises of approximately 9⅔ years.

Initial franchise fee income of $19,600 on two of the repurchased rights was included in the statement of earnings in the year ended January 31, 1968, and initial franchise fee income of $525,000 on the remaining 25 was included in the statement of earnings in the year ended January 31, 1969.

EXHIBIT 6 *(continued)*

Note F—Notes payable:

	January 31, 1969
7½% notes, payable to bank, due June 1969. Interest rate subject to adjustment to ½% above prime rate	$1,600,000
5% note, payable in three 60-day installments of $78,094 beginning February 1969.	234,281
8% notes, payable to stockholders on demand, $500,000 of which is subordinated to the above notes payable to bank in excess of $1,250,000	1,583,211
Other	1,073
	$3,418,565

Notes payable to bank are made under a line of credit agreement which permits the Company to borrow up to $1,750,000 at any time up to June 30, 1969. The agreement also provides that (1) the Company will maintain working capital of $350,000 and a current ratio of 1.25 to 1; (2) maintain a minimum net worth of $1,000,000; and (3) have no outstanding debt with the bank for a 30-day period in each calendar year. The Company has not met the working capital and current ratio provisions of the agreement; however, the bank has waived these provisions through May 15, 1969. The Company plans to retire this debt with a public offering of its Common Stock. See Capitalization in this Prospectus.

Note G—Taxes on income:

Taxes on income have been provided on the basis that the Company and its subsidiaries file consolidated income tax returns.

Certain subsidiaries acquired in 1968 have loss carryovers of approximately $50,000 available as an offset to future taxable income of those subsidiaries only. If these loss carryovers are utilized, the purchase price of the respective subsidiaries may be adjusted.

The provision for consolidated taxes on income comprise the following:

	Year ended January 31,		**Two Months Ended March 31, 1969**
	1968	**1969**	**(unaudited)**
Taxes estimated to be payable:			
Federal	$5,300	$1,381,000	$543,145*
State	3,918	142,000	34,669*
	9,218	1,523,000	577,814*
Deferred tax of which $606,000 is classified as a current liability at January 31, 1969:			
Federal		635,000	6,927*
State		65,000	728*
		700,000	7,655*
	9,218	2,223,000	585,469*
Less investment credit	5,300	75,000	10,627
	$3,918	$2,148,000	$596,096*

* Denotes red figure.

Investment credits are treated as a reduction of federal income tax of the year in which the credit arises.

Deferred taxes result primarily from the reporting of certain franchise sales on the installment basis and depreciating property and equipment on the declining balance method for tax purposes.

EXHIBIT 6 *(continued)*

Note H—Long-term liabilities:

	Current	Long-Term
8% note payable to bank, due 1973	$89,541	$328,317
7½% note payable, due 1970		480,000
	$89,541	$808,317

The note payable to bank includes interest and is payable $7,461 monthly through 1973. Equipment with a net carrying amount of $435,780 is collateral for the note.

The 7½% note payable is collateralized by 25 Fotomat franchises with a net carrying amount of $575,042 (Note E). The note matures in quarterly installments of $120,000 beginning March 31, 1970.

At January 31, 1969, the above notes provide for payments of $89,541 in 1969, $569,541 in 1970, $89,541 in 1971, $89,541 in 1972, and $59,694 in 1973.

Note I—Commitments and contingent liabilities:

The Company leases properties under long-term leases which require aggregate minimum fixed annual rentals as follows:

	Retail Outlets	Office and Warehouse
1970	$1,306,796	$278,451
1971	1,284,146	247,742
1972	1,269,096	176,891
1973	1,248,071	95,455
1974	1,206,336	80,015
1975	1,095,516	22,675
1976	1,094,316	18,000
1977	1,093,266	18,000
1978	1,082,316	13,450
1979	862,729	7,650

Under the terms of most leases for the retail outlets, the Company has at its option both renewal privileges up to an additional 15 years and certain rights of cancellation. Generally, leases also require additional rental payments for a percentage of sales in excess of specified minimum sales.

In October 1968, the Company adopted a noncontributory profit-sharing and retirement plan. (See also Management—*Remuneration* in this Prospectus.) The Board of Directors has authorized a contribution of $60,000 to be made to the plan for the year ended January 31, 1969.

The estimated costs to complete Fotomat stores for which initial franchise fees have been recorded amounted to approximately $900,000 at January 31, 1969.

The Company has a number of claims pending arising from the normal conduct of business which in the opinion of counsel and management are not material. See Note L for subsequent events involving litigation.

Note J—Common stock:

	Shares	Amount
Shares authorized.	10,000,000	
Initially issued, February 1967.	4,281,432	$ 10,000
Sold for cash, June 1968	150,000	1,000,000
Stock options exercised, January 1969	142,143	2,822
Fractional shares retired	(21)	(428)
Balance at January 31, 1969	4,573,554	$1,012,394

The figures above reflect the stock splits of 28,542.88 for 1 in June 1968 and 3 for 2 on January 20, 1969.

EXHIBIT 6 *(continued)*

Note K—Stock options:

At January 31, 1969, 501,430 shares (adjusted for stock splits—see Note J) of no par value common stock were reserved for options under the Company's qualified stock option plans, of which 486,430 had been granted as follows:

		Option Price	
	Number		
Effective Dates of Grant	**of Shares**	**Per Share**	**Total**
February 1, 1968	426,430	$ .020	$ 8,466
January 1, 1969........................	60,000	16.667	1,000,000
Options outstanding, January 31, 1969	486,430		

The option prices were equal to the estimated fair market value at the effective dates of the grants. The stock of the Company is not traded.

The options are exercisable or become exercisable as follows:

Year Ending January 31,	Number of Shares
1970	157,144
1971	157,143
1972	157,143
1973	15,000

In January 1969, options were exercised for 142,143 shares, of which three shares were retired by the Company to eliminate fractional shares. Proceeds of $2,822 from the exercise of these options were credited to common stock.

See Management—*Stock Option Plans* for a description of the Company's two qualified stock option plans.

The stock option plans have been considered not to involve compensation. Therefore, no charges have been made against earnings in accounting for these options.

Note L—Subsequent Events:

On February 18, 1969, Direct Photo Service, Inc, filed suit against the Company claiming unfair competition and requesting the court to declare what design of buildings plaintiff may use in the conduct of its "drive-thru" photo building business, as well as seeking damages against Fotomat. In the opinion of house counsel, the action is without merit.

On February 12, 1969, Eastman Kodak Company brought an action against the Company alleging unfair competition and infringement of trademarks and trade dress and requesting injunctive relief. See also Litigation elsewhere in this prospectus. The existence of this litigation has had and may continue to have an adverse effect on the Company's ability to sell franchises subsequent to February 12, 1969, see Introductory Statement and Consolidated Statements of Earnings in this Prospectus.

Also as a result of the Kodak litigation two franchisees had refused to accept delivery or pay for additional Fotomats provided for in their franchise agreements with the Company. The remaining balance on these receivables at January 31, 1969, was $571,000, which the Company has fully provided for in its allowance for doubtful accounts; however, it is the Company's intention to further pursue the collection of these accounts. It is the opinion of house counsel that the agreements are enforceable.

Through March 31, 1969, the Company had advanced $210,000 (unaudited) to managed franchise operations. See Business—*Franchise Program* (Limited Partnerships) and (Fotomat Managed Franchises).

EXHIBIT 6 *(concluded)*

Note M—Supplementary profit and loss information:

	Charged Directly to Profit and Loss (a)		Charged to Other Accounts (all charged to property, plant, and equipment)	
	Operating Expenses	Other	Amount	Total
Year ended January 31, 1968:				
Maintenance and repairs.	$ 5,150	$ 1,107		$ 6,257
Depreciation and amortization		8,675		8,675
Taxes other than income:				
Federal and state payroll taxes. . .	7,093	2,447	$ 197	9,737
Other taxes	1,247	7		1,254
Management and service fees				—
Rents	30,070	5,609		35,679
Royalties			2,300	2,300
Year ended January 31, 1969:				
Maintenance and repairs.	58,054	24,671	345	83,070
Depreciation and amortization.		204,080	6,438	210,518
Taxes other than income:				
Real and personal property taxes .	418			418
Federal and state payroll taxes. . .	83,073	43,815	90,130	217,018
Management and service fees				—
Rents	480,859	65,148	24,605	570,612
Royalties			39,700	39,700

(a) None of the expenses listed have been charged to product and processing costs.

Questions and Answers about Case Learning*

WHAT IS A CASE?

A case study is a description of a management situation. The analysis of a case study in administration can be thought of as the business equivalent of the medical "second opinion."

In medicine, an individual may seek a physician because of some perceived concern about how the body, or mind, is operating. The physician ordinarily compiles a preliminary problem statement called a *case history*. The case history is a combination of a patient's response to certain queries about his or her symptoms over time ("When did you first get the headaches?"), general history ("Was anyone in your family a diabetic?"), and life circumstances ("About how many hours do you work a week?"). Additionally, other data, both general and problem-related, are collected about the patient's state during the examination. One set, for example, that is routinely taken is called "vital signs," and consists of pulse rate, blood pressure, and respiration rate.

From the sense of this case history, the physician attempts to reach a diagnosis, or statement of the patient's problem in terms suggestive of what might have caused it. Further, a treatment is specified, which is some course of action felt likely to remove or at least ameliorate the problem as diagnosed.

Where the patient's concerns and the physician's diagnosis are in conflict, or when the indicated treatment involves risk, a second opinion may be sought. Here, a new, consulting physician reviews the case history, diagnosis, and treatment plan generated by the first practitioner. The consultant often requires additional data generated by tests in an attempt to rethink the problem and its proposed solution. A course of action (e.g., surgery) or sometimes no course of action is recommended.

When used in the study of an administrative situation, the *case study* offers the student and practitioner a legitimate learning vehicle and the scholar a useful research tool. The "patient" in administration is often the fictional actor called a corporation by the legal system, though a single division, department, or manager in the organization may be the case focus.

The perceived concerns of the individual(s) involved are as varied as those which send a patient to a physician. However, unlike the medical analogy, they also include

---

*This case was prepared by Thomas V. Bonoma as the basis for class discussion, rather than to illustrate either effective or ineffective handling of an administrative situation. Copyright © 1981 by the President and Fellows of Harvard College. Reprinted by permission of the Harvard Business School.

studies of especially excellent administrative health in addition to its more problematical aspects. And, also unlike the medical analogy, the practitioner more often seeks out the company than the company does the casewriter.

HOW IS A CASE WRITTEN?

The construction of the administrative case study is remarkably similar to that of the medical case history. Ordinarily, extensive interviews with management about their behavior and circumstances will be conducted. Also, measures of importance to the issue under investigation often are collected as in the case history. In the administrative world, these often include the "vital signs" of financial, marketing, or productive efficiency measures, depending on the nature of the problem under consideration. General measures of the firm's historical health and status, as well as an examination of its competitive environment, are also constructed or reviewed.

The business counterpart to the physician is the case preparer. He or she often spends 100 or more man-hours collecting information on the corporation and its situation, reducing it to a statement of the essential facts, and presenting it in a manner designed to *(a)* illustrate some rather than other aspects of the situation and *(b)* encourage "second opinions" about the issues facing the firm.

Unlike the general practitioner, who ideally should have no preformed biases or objectives which he or she hopes a patient will satisfy (but like the research physician), the case writer will have a clear set of *objectives* in mind before approaching the company. Is the object of gathering case data to get students to consider the complexities of how a company buys back its distribution after involving numerous others during its growth period? Then a company which has had that experience recently is sought out.

The case study incorporates the writer's developing sense of what the issues of substance are in the situation facing management. In many respects, case preparation in medicine and business is a detective story, where the writer attempts to see and then reconstruct the underlying issues behind the current state of affairs. Thus, neither the case study (medical) nor the case history (administrative) is an inclusive, objective, knowledge-seeking device. It is a subjective, targeted one, often much more valuable for that fact.

WHY DO COMPANIES COOPERATE?

Companies generally perceive several advantages to cooperating with an investigator in the development of a case study. The first is the insight possible from close scrutiny of a current issue with a professional casewriter who has seen other companies and other managers in somewhat similar circumstances. The second is that most managers feel a debt to the management education process which equipped them to deal successfully with their own jobs. They often feel a corresponding desire to give back new materials to improve the educational process. Most importantly, management's opportunity to observe a number of bright and well-prepared students engage in a spirited discussion of their industry, company, and some current issue often provides a rich well of new ideas and perspectives to managers.

WHO GIVES THE "SECOND OPINION"?

The student does, and here lies the power of the case for experiential learning. *Like* a consulting physician, students see a case "worked up" by someone else. They must review the relevant facts, analyze them, reach some conclusion about the problem and its cause (often different from both management's and the case writer's own implicit diagnoses from the identical facts), and recommend some treatment. Also as in medicine, the most powerful and interesting cases are those which permit a multiple analysis of the same evidence to lead to several equally plausible and powerful problem statements, each with different action implications.

Unlike the medical exercise, however, are these important differences:

1. An administrative case is examined not in isolation by one man or woman checking another's work, but in a community of 50–100 other students. Each student has individually invested some two to four hours (or more) making sense of the evidence, diagnosing the problem, and thinking of treatments. Each has probably uncovered some aspect of evidence others have overlooked, and each probably has read identical pieces of information slightly differently. Further, each student has constructed his or her personal action plan, believes in its rightness, and therefore comes prepared to defend it.

2. Because administrative cases are dissected in a community of learners, not only "goodness" of analysis but also persuasiveness of presentation enter the discussion arena as factors with which to be reckoned. Cleverness and even brilliance unpresented or presented poorly will not necessarily dominate mediocrity presented with persuasive genius. Why? Because that is the way the world is, a group interaction in which volume can sometimes dominate veracity. Here is an important lesson in working with, in, and, sometimes, around groups.

3. The individual student placed in such a community of learners is not some static receiver of truth from the mouth of a sage. Rather, he or she is an intimately invested participant (because of preparation and social exposure in a group of prepared peers) who, speak out or not, must dynamically rethink the validity of his or her individual analysis continually as the group discussion unfolds. Thus, different from many learning settings, the student spends much time *thinking* during the case discussion because of investment in his or her own point of view, which is implicitly but constantly challenged by different group construals of the identical facts reviewed during individual preparation. Understanding often becomes a matter of either having to defend one's view publicly, or to abandon it, as the group moves in some direction not supported by the individual's own analysis.

4. A discussion leader is present in this setting, who has a delicate but powerful role. As part of his or her role, the leader must weave individual contributions toward a group discussion product better than, and sometimes different from, the sum of the individual analyses. The Gestalt psychologists understood this phenomenon well when they wrote that the "whole is different from the sum of its parts" in their study of visual illusions.

WHAT DOES THE DISCUSSION LEADER DO?

The discussion leader serves as a recorder and organizer of the group's analysis as it emerges in the fragmented, back-and-fill form so characteristic of verbal interactions. He or she, essentially, can make the product of discussion look as good as the process by organizing and directing its flow. A very important part of this organization comes from the instructor's use of the blackboards to leave a meaningful record of the group's progress and insight in front of all.

The discussion leader also may take a more interventionist role in the classroom, serving to point up critical conflicts in case issues and even playing devil's advocate where no other participant seems inclined to do so. The purposes of challenging individual contributions, whether these challenges come from peers or the discussion leader, are to make the contributor push his or her thinking to its limits, to breed the toughness which comes from successfully coping with challenges, and to force students to grapple with the more subtle issues in the case.

A good discussion leader, more often than not, drives students not only toward diagnosis but toward action. He or she reminds them that analytic brilliance expressed with persuasive efficacy is totally useless unless somebody does something as a result. However, he or she also encourages and wonders with students about what further thought, analysis, and tests might be necessary to inform right action, and is unaccepting of action recommendations unsupported by powerful analysis. Finally, when an action plan is decided upon, what will be looked at to see if the plan succeeded? At what time? No case analysis is complete without measures to monitor the acts being recommended.

WHAT HAPPENS WHEN IT WORKS?

More intense effort, both from students and instructors, is required for case learning than for any other form of instruction I have encountered. Though the instructor may feel uncomfortable about his or her inability to control what contributions may be made in the classroom, the power of case learning is awesome. I am continually amazed at how much men and women change, in the short time of their first year at the Harvard Business School. When they begin, they attack problems with raw, groping, undirected energy which more often than not leads them nowhere. In a short period of constant exposure to cases, they deal with the same ambiguous problem sets in a focused, assured manner which leads to firm and informed action regardless of the problem's fuzziness or the incompleteness of the facts.

The reasons for such sweeping changes from the case method of learning, when other instructors daily make sad little jokes about their students not being able to retain the most elementary of concepts, seem to include these:

1. The student is forced, by exposure to basically insoluble problems with no right answer, to formulate his or her own personally workable approach to problem definition and formulation. Other learning methods teach some set of approved answers, and send students in search of problems to which to apply them. The case method teaches students to learn for themselves what the problems are and how to define the questions.

2. Repetitive exposure to these ambiguous problems has a remarkable confidence-building effect on those who eventually must deal with similar problems in management. What the psychologists call "tolerance for ambiguity" is cultured directly by case learning. The instructor should constantly encourage students to drive toward specific actions in spite of incomplete information, uncertain circumstances, and unclear problems. Though this can sometimes provoke premature action, such a model is much more consistent with the way the "real world" works than is an insistence on complete information or unattainable certainty.

3. The experience of the problem in the case method precedes the structure created to solve it. This is in contradistinction to traditional learning methods, where someone (e.g., a Linnaeus who names all the plants and animals) does the work of providing a useful taxonomy into which students are asked to partition their experiences. That model assumes experience is present, and only wants the addition of clever categorization to produce insight. The case method advocates, at least partially, the notion of throwing students into one end of the forest with a pad and paper to see what they come out with on the other side. Were there a business Linneaus, case method instructors probably would vote not to let students know too much about his ideas before they learned more about administrative problems. *Then,* there would be some "pegs of experience" on which to hang the concepts, not before.

HOW DO I PREPARE A CASE (STUDENT)?

For the student, case preparation is a personal matter of developing a totally individualistic and intimate problem-solving style. Cases are semistructured problems, and problem definition skills the main "product" of repeated exposure to these learning devices. However, even though there can be *no* formula for case preparation, most students seem to travel a general path which includes:

1. Reading the case quickly, almost skimming it for the major issues and sense of its layout provided. One of the most important objectives of this quick reading is to get a sense of who the case protagonist is, and what his or her situation is like. For example, a grand recommendation to fire the vice president of marketing makes little sense if the case actor the student is advising is a junior brand manager.

2. Rereading the case carefully, annotating, highlighting, and distinguishing important information, omissions, and questions raised by the reading.

3. Deciding what the action issues really are. Is this case really about pricing, or is pricing, while an important issue, symptomatic of some deeper management issue needing examination and resolution?

4. Deciding on what analysis questions will inform the issue on what actions need to be taken. Can the data in the case be "worked back" to give contribution figures on each product in the line? Why do selling expenses seem to be so out of line as compared to the competitions' numbers in the case? What is driving that product manager who insists that this little company not only can, but must, compete with the Japanese?

5. Answering these analysis questions as formulated, using the data available from the case, and making clear and well-informed assumptions about necessary but missing information. "If they only had given me the trade margins, I'd *know* what's going on. Well, it says on page 21 that trade margins in related segments were about 23 percent, so maybe . . ."

6. Deciding on a course of action from the analysis, and explicitly considering and rejecting plausible alternative courses because of the analysis.

7. Developing a plan by which the desired action may be achieved or implemented within the company, people, and other constraints encountered in this situation.

8. Testing the plan and the analysis before class against the analyses of others, informally, in a small group. In this way, goodness of analysis and soundness of proposed action can be checked informally, without the social risks a presentation in front of 100 others implies. More importantly, in this way the students can learn from each other's thought patterns and problem definition templates to improve their own thinking.

HOW DO I PREPARE A CASE (INSTRUCTOR)?

For the instructor, all the steps taken in a good student analysis initially must be taken as well. The case method is one way of learning where those who can't do also can't teach: Additionally, there is no need to keep any teaching "plan" secret from the students (as this section's presence shows), because a well-prepared instructor knows that "what comes out" in the discussion is as much under the students' control as his or her own. After making a complete student analysis, however, the real work of case preparation begins:

1. What are the major issues which this case is intended to illustrate?
2. Where in the course (series of cases) does this case come? How can it be related to other cases so far analyzed or yet to come?
3. What are the major "themes" (e.g., the importance of customer and competitive analysis in marketing) with which my course deals? How shall I reinforce those themes with today's case?
4. In what order should the case issues be raised?
5. How should the analytic information from the case be recorded on blackboards? What does my "board plan" look like?
6. What errors, analytic blind alleys, traps, and other "red herrings" does the case encourage from students? What lessons can be learned by students falling into them?
7. Which of my students would learn the most, and from whom would the whole class learn the most, if he or she was allowed the first 10–20 minutes to "open" the case by presenting a detailed analysis? Is such an "opening" the right way to start this discussion?
8. Have I done enough preparation, and do I have the confidence to abandon my plans and do some learning myself as new topics or angles that I have not thought of come up?
9. Are summary comments appropriate at the end of this case? What would they be?

WHO DECIDES WHAT WILL BE LEARNED?

Both the students and the instructor decide what will be learned.

However, my two lists of preparation questions contain a powerful internal contradiction regarding teaching and learning. It is impossible to plan for a discussion controlled by others, to organize the boards, and to bring issues out in a desired order when these matters are at least partially in the students' control as well as in the instructor's. The good case teacher, nonetheless, lives quite nicely with this schizophrenia, never failing to plan the case out thoroughly as he or she might wish it to develop, and never at least partially failing to abandon these plans for the realism and excitement of involved discussion.

The good case learner, on the other hand, analyzes each problem as if he or she *were* the case actor. He or she struggles to find a suitable construal of the problem, and then invests enormous effort in analyzing the quantitative and qualitative data to reach a useful set of action recommendations. But, in spite of all this investment, he or she is continually reminded that problems are ambiguous, and other students' ideas may be as or more worthy than his or her own. In the best sense of the word, he or she remains ready to be an "idea chef," constantly melding the best of his or her own with the best of others' thoughts to reach a better understanding of the problem and its analytic requirements.

WHAT MAKES CASE LEARNING SO EFFECTIVE?

For both the instructor and the student, case learning requires sailing a very narrow channel between the rocks of over control and the shallows of ambiguity. The promise of the case method, for those who successfully thread their course in this careful manner, is *not* that *it* will produce an excellent administrator. Rather, the student, with the discussion leader's aid, will over time *him or herself* produce this transformation and embody the differences rather than being "taught" them. In the case method, birds learn to fly; with other techniques, they are often given an airline pass.